PSYCHOLOGY 90/91

Twentieth Edition

Editor

Michael G. Walraven
Jackson Community College

Michael G. Walraven is Dean of Instruction and a professor of psychology at Jackson Community College. He received a B.A. from the University of Maryland in 1966, an M.A. from Western Michigan University in 1968, and a Ph.D. from Michigan State University in 1974. He is affiliated with the American Psychological Association, the Association for Behavior Analysis, and the Biofeedback Society of Michigan.

Editor

Hiram E. Fitzgerald
Michigan State University

Hiram E. Fitzgerald is a professor and associate chairperson in the Department of Psychology at Michigan State University. He received a B.A. in 1962 from Lebanon Valley College, and an M.A. in 1964 and a Ph.D. in 1967 from the University of Denver. In addition to holding memberships in a variety of scientific associations, he is the executive director of the International Associations for Infant Mental Health, and a regional vice president of the World Association for Infant Psychiatry and Allied Disciplines. He has authored and edited over 140 publications.

Annual Editions
A Library of Information from the Public Press

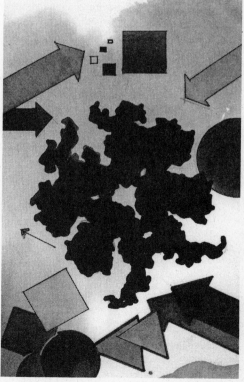

Cover illustration by Mike Eagle

The Dushkin Publishing Group, Inc.
Sluice Dock, Guilford, Connecticut 06437

The Annual Editions Series

Annual Editions is a series of over fifty volumes designed to provide the reader with convenient, low-cost access to a wide range of current, carefully selected articles from some of the most important magazines, newspapers, and journals published today. Annual Editions are updated on an annual basis through a continuous monitoring of over 200 periodical sources. All Annual Editions have a number of features designed to make them particularly useful, including topic guides, annotated tables of contents, unit overviews, and indexes. For the teacher using Annual Editions in the classroom, an Instructor's Resource Guide with test questions is available for each volume.

VOLUMES AVAILABLE

Africa
Aging
American Government
American History, Pre-Civil War
American History, Post-Civil War
Anthropology
Biology
Business and Management
Business Ethics
Canadian Politics
China
Comparative Politics
Computers in Education
Computers in Business
Computers in Society
Criminal Justice
Drugs, Society, and Behavior
Early Childhood Education
Economics
Educating Exceptional Children
Education
Educational Psychology
Environment
Geography
Global Issues
Health
Human Development

Human Resources
Human Sexuality
Latin America
Macroeconomics
Marketing
Marriage and Family
Middle East and the Islamic World
Money and Banking
Nutrition
Personal Growth and Behavior
Psychology
Public Administration
Social Problems
Sociology
Soviet Union and Eastern Europe
State and Local Government
Third World
Urban Society
Violence and Terrorism
Western Civilization,
   Pre-Reformation
Western Civilization,
   Post-Reformation
Western Europe
World History, Pre-Modern
World History, Modern
World Politics

Library of Congress Cataloging in Publication Data
Main entry under title: Annual Editions: Psychology. 1990/91.
   1. Psychology—Addresses, essays, lectures—Periodicals. I. Walraven, Michael G., *comp.*; Fitzgerald, Hiram E., *comp.* II. Title: Psychology.
ISBN 0–87967–853–4   150′.5   79–180263
BF 149.A58

Twentieth Edition

Manufactured by The Banta Company, Harrisonburg, Virginia 22801

Editors/Advisory Board

To the Reader

In publishing ANNUAL EDITIONS we recognize the enormous role played by the magazines, newspapers, and journals of the *public press* in providing current, first-rate educational information in a broad spectrum of interest areas. Within the articles, the best scientists, practitioners, researchers, and commentators draw issues into new perspective as accepted theories and viewpoints are called into account by new events, recent discoveries change old facts, and fresh debate breaks out over important controversies.

Many of the articles resulting from this enormous editorial effort are appropriate for students, researchers, and professionals seeking accurate, current material to help bridge the gap between principles and theories and the real world. These articles, however, become more useful for study when those of lasting value are carefully *collected, organized, indexed,* and *reproduced* in a *low-cost format,* which provides easy and permanent access when the material is needed. That is the role played by *Annual Editions.* Under the direction of each volume's *Editor,* who is an expert in the subject area, and with the guidance of an *Advisory Board,* we seek each year to provide in each *ANNUAL EDITION* a current, well-balanced, carefully selected collection of the best of the public press for your study and enjoyment. We think you'll find this volume useful, and we hope you'll take a moment to let us know what you think.

Psychology means many things to many people. Students select a course in psychology because they want answers to a variety of questions. We want to know how people are motivated, how they think, and how their personalities develop. We are curious about how we learn, how our memories work, what effects certain experiences have on us, how we change as we grow older, why some people respond to life events in maladaptive ways, and how these people can be helped. Psychology attempts to answer all of these questions and more.

But psychology approaches these issues in a specific way: the scientific method. Researchers use carefully defined techniques to discover answers to basic questions, in order that their findings may be combined with the findings of other researchers, to eventually paint a complete picture of that most complex of all living organisms: man himself. These research results are usually published in technical journals written for specialists. It is very difficult for the layperson to keep abreast of new findings; indeed, it is difficult for even the professional psychologist to be current in areas other than her or his specialty.

For these reasons, we find more and more accounts and summaries of psychological research in the popular press. Newspapers and magazines are meeting the need of the average adult to discover and understand the complexities of human behavior. But who can spend the time to search out and sort through the large number of articles? And can the average person accurately distinguish those articles which represent solid findings from those which draw inaccurate or overstated conclusions? *Annual Editions: Psychology 90/91* is designed to meet this requirement, by providing an organized selection of accurate, readable, and current articles drawn from a wide range of sources. Most of these articles are written not by psychologists, but by journalists and science writers who recognize the importance of certain areas of research and match their talents to the needs and interests of their readers. A few of these articles are written by psychologists, researchers who are gifted with the ability to describe their work in clear and uncluttered styles, retaining the excitement of original discovery and sharing it with us.

The particular articles selected for this volume were chosen to be representative of current work in psychology, both theoretical and experimental. They were selected because they are accurate in their reporting, and provide examples of the types of psychological research discussed in most introductory psychology courses and textbooks. As in any science, some of the findings discussed in this collection are startling, while others will confirm what we already suspected. Some will invite speculation about social and personal implications; others will demand careful thought about potential misuse or dangerous applications of research findings. You, as a reader, will be expected to make the investment of effort and critical judgment needed to answer such questions and concerns. For this is a reflection of the field of psychology itself, and we invite you to join in this exploration.

We hope you will find this collection of articles readable and useful. We suggest that you look at the organization of this book, and compare it to the organization of your textbook and course syllabus or outline. By examining the topic guide, you can identify those articles most appropriate to any particular unit of study in your course. Your instructor may provide some help in this effort. As you read the articles, try to connect their contents with the principles you are learning from your text and classroom lectures and discussions. Some of the articles will help you to better understand a specific area of research, while others are designed to help you connect and integrate information from various research efforts. Both of these strategies are important in learning about psychology, or any other science, because it is only through intensive investigation and subsequent integration of the findings of many scientists that we are able to discover and apply new knowledge.

During the course of your reading, please take time to provide us with some feedback to guide the annual revision of this anthology by completing and returning the article rating form in the back of the book. With your help, this collection will be even better next year.

Michael G. Walraven, Ph.D.

Hiram E. Fitzgerald, Ph.D.

Editors

Contents

Unit 1

The Science of Psychology

Two articles examine social evolution, human nature, and the conscious self.

Unit 2

Biological Bases of Behavior

Five selections discuss the biological bases of behavior. Topics include brain functions, the biological clock, the brain's control over the body, and the dynamics of genetics.

The concepts in bold italics are developed in the article. For further expansion please refer to the Topic Guide, the Index, and the Glossary.

Unit 3

Perceptual Processes

Four articles discuss the impact of senses and dreaming on human perceptual processes.

Unit 4

Learning and Memory

Four selections examine how operant conditioning, positive reinforcement, declarative memory, and procedural memory interact during the learning process.

The concepts in bold italics are developed in the article. For further expansion please refer to the Topic Guide, the Index, and the Glossary.

Unit 5

Cognitive Processes

Four articles examine how social skills, common sense, and intelligence affect human cognitive processes.

The concepts in bold italics are developed in the article. For further expansion please refer to the Topic Guide, the Index, and the Glossary.

Unit 6

Motivation and Emotion

Four articles discuss the influences of stress, mental states, motivation, and emotion on the mental and physical health of the individual.

Unit 7

Development

Five articles consider the impact of drugs on early development, the importance of experience, discipline, familial support, and physiological aging during the normal human development process.

The concepts in bold italics are developed in the article. For further expansion please refer to the Topic Guide, the Index, and the Glossary.

Unit 8

Personality Processes

Four selections discuss a few of the processes by which personalities are developed. Topics include sex differences, state of mind, cynicism, and change.

The concepts in bold italics are developed in the article. For further expansion please refer to the Topic Guide, the Index, and the Glossary.

Unit 9

Social Processes

Four selections discuss how the individual's social development is affected by genes, stereotypes, prejudice, and self-help.

Unit 10

Psychological Disorders

Four articles examine several psychological disorders. Topics include Alzheimer's disease, unexpected behavior, and the impact of depression on a person's well-being.

The concepts in bold italics are developed in the article. For further expansion please refer to the Topic Guide, the Index, and the Glossary.

Unit 11

Psychological Treatments

Five selections discuss a few psychological treatments, including psychoanalysis, psychotherapy to alleviate depression, and self-care.

The concepts in bold italics are developed in the article. For further expansion please refer to the Topic Guide, the Index, and the Glossary.

Topic Guide

This topic guide suggests how the selections in this book relate to topics of traditional concern to psychology students and professionals. It can be very useful in locating articles which relate to each other for reading and research. The guide is arranged alphabetically according to topic. Articles may, of course, treat topics that do not appear in the topic guide. In turn, entries in the topic guide do not necessarily constitute a comprehensive listing of all the contents of each selection.

TOPIC AREA	TREATED AS AN ISSUE IN:	TOPIC AREA	TREATED AS AN ISSUE IN:
Addictions	45. Help Yourself	Creativity Training	19. Capturing Your Creativity
Admiration	26. Punishment versus Discipline	Criminal	33. Are Criminals Made or Born?
Adolescence	27. The Myth About Teen-Agers	Cultural Variation	16. Intelligence: New Ways to Measure
Adulthood	32. Erikson, in His Own Old Age	Depression	43. The Good News About Depression
Ageism	28. The Vintage Years	Differentiation	3. Right Brain, Left Brain
Aggression	29. Biology, Destiny, and All That	Discipline	26. Punishment versus Discipline
Alzheimer's Disease	38. The Clouded Mind	Disease	21. Emotions: How They Affect Your Body 22. Thinking Well: The Chemical Links 23. Dangerous Thoughts
Amygdala	14. Our Dual Memory		
Antidepressive	43. The Good News About Depression	Dreams	10. New Light on the Chemistry of Dreams
Anxiety	23. Dangerous Thoughts 40. Anxiety and Panic	Dysthymic Disorder	39. Dysthymic Disorder: The DD's Blues
		Eidetic Imagery	15. Extraordinary People
Attribution	36. Getting Help From Helping	Elderly	28. The Vintage Years
Authoritarianism	34. Marching in Step	Emotional Development	44. Infants in Need of Psychotherapy?
Back-to-Basics	13. How Kids Learn		
Behavior	36. Getting Help From Helping 40. Anxiety and Panic 45. Help Yourself	Emotional Factors	18. New Scales of Intelligence 23. Dangerous Thoughts
		Emotional Problems	45. Help Yourself
Biological Clock	5. Is It One Clock, or Several?	Emotionality	29. Biology, Destiny, and All That
Brain	3. Right Brain, Left Brain 4. How the Brain Really Works 38. The Clouded Mind	Endorphins	7. A Pleasurable Chemistry 23. Dangerous Thoughts
		Family	37. When Mental Illness Hits Home
Cancer	22. Thinking Well: The Chemical Links 31. Health's Character	Forebrain	8. Are We Led by the Nose?
		Gene Therapy	6. The Gene Hunt
Cerebellum	14. Our Dual Memory	Genetic Predisposition	33. Are Criminals Made or Born? 37. When Mental Illness Hits Home
Cerebral Hemispheres	3. Right Brain, Left Brain		
Chemoreceptors	40. Anxiety and Panic	Genome	6. The Gene Hunt
Children	25. Shattered Innocence	Health	30. Do Optimists Live Longer?
Cocaine Addiction	24. Crack in the Cradle	Heart Disease	31. Health's Character
Common Cold	23. Dangerous Thoughts	Hippocampus	14. Our Dual Memory
Common Sense	16. Intelligence: New Ways to Measure	Hormones	5. Is It One Clock, or Several?
Competence	28. The Vintage Years	Hostility	34. Marching in Step
Computer Science	4. How the Brain Really Works	Humility	32. Erikson, in His Own Old Age
Consciousness	1. Consciousness: Science Tackles the Self		

The Science of Psychology

Psychology has been defined as the science of mental activity and behavior. This definition reflects the two parent disciplines from which psychology emerged: philosophy and biology. Historically, philosophy is the elder parent, but current students of psychology are often surprised to discover what a pervasive influence biology and other natural sciences have on the field. Modern psychology traces its heritage as a science to the opening of the first psychological laboratory in Germany, in 1879.

However, compared to fields such as mathematics, physics, or biology, psychology is still very much an infant science.

Some aspects of modern psychology are particularly biological, such as neuroscience, sensation and perception, behavior genetics, development, and consciousness. Other aspects are more philosophical in perspective, such as humanism, phenomenology, and various paradigmatic views of the nature of human nature. However, most of psychology's sub-specialties share a common feature, an emphasis on behavior, particularly human behavior.

In the first article in this anthology, Susan Blackmore examines consciousness, a perplexing phenomenon that has its origins in philosophy but that tends to be studied today with methods used in psychophysiology and neuropsychology. Yet, is there an aspect to consciousness that brain waves and computer simulations cannot reveal? Blackmore suggests that cognitive psychology's answer is yes—consciousness is a mental model, a model of self which provides stability to the organism. It is the mechanism by which I become aware of events, and in so doing become aware of my consciousness. Thus, consciousness is a mental model that is potentially both stable and changing, but is a model of mind, not of substance.

In the second article, Daniel Kriegman and Charles Knight discuss how sociobiological theory aids in the restructuring of psychoanalytic theory. Relational theorists and self theorists challenge classic psychoanalytic assumptions about the nature of human nature. According to the authors, Triver's sociobiological concept of reciprocal altruism merged with Kohut's psychology of the self leads to a rejection of traditional psychoanalytic emphasis on guilt motivation as a motivational force in human behavior.

It is important to recognize that psychologists work in a great variety of specialties and settings. What they all share, however, is a commitment to pursue knowledge in accordance with scientific methodology. Psychologists are often seen as skeptics; they do not readily accept as valid the assumptions or interpretations of others. They are fond of testing their hunches by gathering data to see whether their assumptions and hypotheses are valid.

Any person committed to scientific methodology in the pursuit of knowledge is essentially agreeing to abide by a set of rules which are designed to ensure that findings from one research effort can be replicated by other scientists. The principles of science include the requirement that assumptions be made explicit. These operational definitions enhance communication among scientists, and at the same time keep research on a realistic plane. The experimental method perhaps epitomizes scientific technique. In this procedure, subjects are randomly assigned to conditions, and extraneous variables, which might otherwise influence the data, are controlled. Using this procedure, the scientific investigator can be certain that the conclusions drawn from the data are justified, and can report them with confidence. On the other hand, psychology does not have a single unifying paradigm. Rather, psychologists draw upon a variety of research strategies in their efforts to understand human behavior. Some psychologists use naturalistic methods. Rather than manipulating behavior in the laboratory setting, they are interested in describing behavior as it occurs in nature. Descriptive research is often the first step in the scientific study of a phenomenon. As the comparative psychologist Stanley Ratner often proclaimed, the first step in scientific research is to know your organism.

Many students respond to articles such as these by concluding that psychologists enjoy arguments. We must all recognize that in intellectual conflict lie the seeds of new hypotheses and the curiosity to stimulate the research to test them. Learning more about behavior is the goal all psychologists share, and we invite you to share this goal as you plunge into this collection of contemporary readings.

Looking Ahead: Challenge Questions

What is consciousness? Is it possible to answer this question scientifically, or is the nature of consciousness essentially a philosophical question? Do you believe that consciousness has always been a characteristic of *Homo sapiens*, or do you think that consciousness evolved, perhaps along the lines suggested by Jaynes?

When parents sacrifice themselves to save their child, is it motivated by guilt, or by a desire to preserve their gene pool? Is it possible that neither theory is correct? If so, suggest an alternative explanation for the thesis that cooperative behavior, sharing, and empathy have their origins in reciprocal altruism.

CONSCIOUSNESS: SCIENCE TACKLES THE SELF

We know that we are aware of ourselves. But we don't know how. And we are not even sure why. The answers may lie in the physical processes of consciousness.

Susan Blackmore

Dr. Susan Blackmore is a researcher in the Brain and Perception Laboratory at the University of Bristol.

Why am I aware of anything at all? Wouldn't life be a lot simpler without consciousness? Certainly science would be. But, unfortunately or not, this "experience of being" will not go away. Now, after several decades of trying to ignore it, science is once again tackling the elusive and difficult problem of consciousness. Researchers in the neurosciences may yet produce experimental results that shed light on that long-standing philosophical conundrum, the nature of "self".

One physiological study, by Benjamin Libet at the University of California at San Francisco, has already produced interesting results. His work suggests that it takes time for the brain to produce consciousness—about half a second, in fact. He reached this conclusion by studying patients who had electrodes inserted into the cortex of their brains. By stimulating the electrodes, he could give these people the sensation that their arm had been touched, but only if the electrical stimulation lasted for at least half a second. This finding seems to suggest that it takes half a second of brain activity to produce awareness. We are left with the odd conclusion that we are experiencing everything half a second after it happens. When someone taps me on the shoulder, I react first and become aware of it only later. It is an illusion that I turned round because I felt the heat. Conscious awareness is more like an afterthought.

This process might serve to restrict vast amounts of unnecessary information from entering consciousness. But what is this "consciousness" which information "enters"? Surely it is not a thing or a place. But there must be some difference between whatever is "in consciousness" and the vast mass of processes constantly going on in the brain that are obviously "unconscious". So what is this difference? These questions reveal the depth of our ignorance and confusion over consciousness.

Part of the problem is its reflexive nature. Consciousness cannot be studied in the same way as the things I am conscious of. If I turn my attention to it, it ceases to be consciousness and becomes just another thought or experience.

Another problem is its ever-changing quality. What it means to be conscious is essentially what it is like being me, here and now. And yet as soon as I think that, here and now are already gone: I, and the world around me, have changed. That is why William James, one of the 19th-century pioneers of psychology, used the phrase "the stream of consciousness". It is a stream that is flowing; it feels unbroken but never repeats itself exactly. Science searches for patterns and regularity, so it is hard to know where to start with something whose very nature lies in change.

The best starting place with such problems is always to re-examine the question. Asking "What is consciousness?" is, according to many people, a meaningless question, for consciousness is not a "thing" at all.

A more tractable question is, "Why do we have consciousness?" It might be possible to imagine animals (or even machines) that could carry out all the actions I carry out and yet be blissfully unaware of anything at all. Those in pain, or who enjoy the occasional oblivion of alcohol, might even think this would be preferable. So why did consciousness evolve? Evolution must have had some reason for making us conscious—mustn't it?

John Crook, an ethologist at the University of Bristol, has argued that human consciousness is distinctive

From *New Scientist*, April 1, 1989. Reprinted by permission.

because we are conscious of being conscious; we have a sense of having personal power over our actions and we have self-identity. These together with language, arose, he argues, because our ancestors began using tools. Only an animal that needs to know who owns and uses which tools needs such a strong sense of personal identity.

By contrast the psychologist and writer, Nicholas Humphrey, argues that we evolved self-awareness for social reasons: to hold together a cooperative society, early humans needed to understand their fellows—to become, in Humphrey's words, *Homo psychologicus*. The best way to do that, Humphrey argues, was to use a "privileged picture" of themselves as a model for what it is like to be another person. So, according to Humphrey, we learnt to look into our own mental processes so as to be able to predict (and hence control?) the desires or actions of others.

This connection between consciousness and representing the self is made even more explicit by Richard Dawkins, a zoologist at the University of Oxford. He says: "Perhaps consciousness arises when the brain's simulation of the world becomes so complete that it has to include a model of itself." And yet there is something wrong here. The brain is not really modelling itself. It is not an image of neurons and glial cells that is central to my self-consciousness. Surely people who have never learnt about the structure and function of the brain are just as conscious as neurosurgeons.

WAS HOMER UNAWARE OF HIMSELF?

According to all these theories, self-awareness would have appeared very early in the evolution of humans. By contrast, an American psychologist, Julian Jaynes, proposed the controversial thesis that consciousness appeared only in historical times. The early Greeks and the Hebrews of the early Old Testament period did not, according to Jaynes, experience themselves as thinking beings. Instead of attributing their verbal images to internal processes they attributed them to the voices of the Gods. He cites the *Iliad*, written about 3000 years ago, as having no references to mental concepts such as mind, thoughts, feelings, or even self. People were not to be blamed or held responsible for their actions: they were only instruments of external forces.

This interesting idea puts our views of ourselves in a new light. If the Gods were only a theory invented to account for behaviour, perhaps our present-day concept of self is just another such theory invented to explain ourselves to ourselves. It may be a better theory than the Gods but is it really accurate? Isn't it just another useful illusion?

The problem with all these theories is that none of them directly addresses the question of consciousness itself. Why couldn't a system evolve with a good concept of self, attributing behaviour to internal processes—even with psychological skills modelling other people's (nonconscious) behaviour—without actually feeling like anything? These theories may show how self-identity or the ability to predict behaviour arose, but they say nothing directly about awareness. I can still imagine an animal or machine that does all these things and is completely unaware.

Perhaps, you might say, it is not just passive awareness that distinguishes us from unconscious automata, but the fact that we can consciously control what we do. Recent research, however, reveals that this too may be (partly or wholly) another illusion.

Michael Gazzanioa, a neuroscientist at Cornell University in New York State, has studied "split brain" patients—the left and right sides of their brains have been surgically separated (often as a treatment for severe epilepsy). In most people, the ability to use language is by and large localised in the left brain; but one of his patients had some verbal ability in both halves, although only the left could produce speech. When a written command, such as "laugh", was presented only to the part of the visual field linked to the right brain, he laughed. When asked "Why did you laugh?" he answered, using the left side of the brain, but simply fabricated a reason: "Oh, you guys are really something!" The left hemisphere had apparently observed the laughter and tried to account for it somehow. This may be no quirk of split brains. Most of our reasons for action may be totally unavailable to conscious introspection. Our verbal selves may make up plausible reasons for the actions they observe their body making.

Research on split brains has revealed much more about the nature of consciousness. In some cases, each half brain displays separate desires, intentions and even hopes for the future—and a sense of self. It is easy to think that splitting the brain has split an originally single consciousness, but Gazzanioa believes that the surgery only reveals a general principle: that human minds are multiple entities consisting of many subsystems. It is only the ability to put things into words that creates "a personal sense of conscious reality out of the multiple systems present", he believes.

So is the idea of a single conscious "will" totally false? Here again some recent research provides a clue. Libet turned his attention from conscious sensation to voluntary action and devised an ingenious experiment based on earlier work. Using electrodes fixed to the scalp, other researchers had found that just before someone does something voluntarily the electrical potential of the scalp shifts to the negative, a phenomenon called the readiness potential.

Electrodes pick up readiness potential a second or more before any apparently voluntary movement begins. We might assume, then, that the conscious decision to act must come before the readiness potential, if a conscious decision to act is what starts the train of events. Libet set out to test this. He asked subjects to flex their wrist or fingers at any time they felt the "urge" or desire to do so. To measure the timing of that urge or desire, he asked them also to watch a revolving spot and to report its clock position at the time they felt the urge to move.

CONSCIOUSNESS IS AN AFTERTHOUGHT

His findings were consistent and surprising. The readiness potential came first and the desire to move about 400 milliseconds (nearly half a second) later. The implication seems to be that even in apparently spontaneous voluntary acts, an unconscious brain event happens well before any conscious desire or decision to act. Again, the consciousness seems to be an afterthought.

Libet went on to show that subjects could "veto" the action within a period of between 100 and 200 milliseconds before the action would have started. This, he argues, still leaves some potential role for the "will". Other scientists have argued, however, for more extreme interpretations of his data. The experiments could mean that we do not directly experience an intention to act at all. Rather, we might infer an urge or desire to act after the process has already begun unconsciously. Because this urge precedes the action, we can keep up the illusion that it causes the action—but it is only an illusion. According to this view, consciousness has no active role at all.

This dispute reflects the long philosophical argument over whether mental events, anything from the desire for ice cream to the sensation of pain, can cause physiological events in the brain. Libet maintains they can. He thinks there is still room for the "will", which can intervene to stop physiological processes when required. Other prefer to use his findings as evidence that they cannot. The important question for us is whether science is on the verge of turning a difficult philosophical problem into an empirical one.

Many researchers have argued that consciousness can be modelled by computing systems, and many debates focus on whether consciousness is then associated with the highest level of such a system. Such discussions may help to explain aspects of the working brain. But no such theory can explain why the contents of one part (whichever part it may be) should have the quality of feeling like something while the rest do not.

The American philosopher Thomas Nagel made this crucial point about consciousness in his now famous paper entitled "What is it like to be a bat?", published in his collection of essays *Mortal Questions*. His point was that when we say something is conscious, we essentially mean that there is something it is like to be that thing. Now if humans are complex information-processing systems, why should there be "something it is like to be" some levels of that system but not others? Whichever part of the system you choose, the essential mystery remains untouched.

A radical solution is to sweep this question away and say that all mental models are conscious. Mental models are the internal representations of the world which computers, as well as animals and humans, use to control their behaviour. You could not get around without a good model of your own body and the world around it. I am suggesting that it is not like anything to be the skin, blood or bones of a bat, but it is like something to be the bat's *model* of a bat. This is equivalent to saying that there cannot be such things as not-conscious mental models.

The major objection to this theory is that it does not seem to us as though all the many models our brain constructs are conscious. But the answer all hinges upon who that "us" is. What am "I" who is to be conscious of all that activity? We can suggest an answer. "I" am only one of the models in the system, a model of "self in the world" built largely by language. "I" am a self-image, a body image, a construct of a human being. This makes it perfectly obvious why all the rest of the system appears to be unconscious. It is unconscious to "me" but not to itself.

Before we start thinking of human systems as peopled by infinite conscious models, we should reflect what it would be like to be most of those models. I think the answer is not much. For example, the models in the lower levels of perceptual processing entail no concept of self, action or an external world. Their consciousness would be correspondingly limited. Only the complex model of "self in the world" sustains full reflexive awareness—consciousness of being conscious. It is this which seems to be "me".

Most of us have only one of these (unless you include any "dream selves"). Presumably people with so-called multiple personalities have several models of self, each conscious in its own way and competing for dominance. This situation is abnormal, but now we can see it as only an extreme form of the normal case. Every human brain constructs multiple conscious models, but there is only one "me", my model of self.

This makes sense, too, of the phenomenon of selective attention. When "I" turn my attention to something, that thing seems to come into my awareness. From a computational point of view, we might say that the system has incorporated the model of that thing into the model of self. So "I" become aware of it, and it of "me".

In this view, there need be no top and bottom, no one consciousness controlling the rest. Consciousness is not something that controls. It is not a thing, a place, a substance or a part of the system. Indeed, it has no function. It is only what it is like being a mental model.

This approach transforms the whole evolutionary

question. There is no definite point at which consciousness arises, nor any purpose for it at all. Any organism that constructs representations (as even the most primitive will do) will have correspondingly primitive consciousness. Those that model a self will also be conscious of self. As evolution progresses, the quality of consciousness depends on the kinds of models constructed. So perhaps Jaynes had a point. Once the voices of the Gods were replaced by a concept of an active self, self-consciousness took another step forward.

And what will our next step be? On this view, the mystics' search for higher consciousness or the Buddhists' training for "enlightenment" may be no idle fancy but steps into new mental models.

MIND AND MEDITATION

At the heart of Buddhist training lie the skills of meditation and mindfulness. Pursued far enough, these are supposed to transform consciousness and free the trainee from suffering. Does it help us to understand this transformation to ask how the models of reality are changed?

Most of us, claimed the Buddha, are constantly distracted by sights, sounds and ideas. We live in a whirl of confusion and fantasy: more in the past or future than in the present moment. Struggling to find happiness, we cling desperately to our concept of self and the things we think will make that self happy. But this, paradoxically, is precisely what leads to suffering.

By contrast, mindfulness means living in the present moment, every moment, constantly alert. In meditation, this skill is practised in quiet sitting. Any thoughts that arise are let go again. They may come again and again, but there is no clinging, no leap into the building of fantasies. They just come and go until eventually the mind is still.

These contrasting ways of being can be understood in terms of the mental models that are constructed. In the normal way, attention shifts from one thing to another. Surprising events grab the attention: other chains of thought wait to be finished as soon as there is a gap. So there is never any peace. This is efficient in using all available processing capacity, but what does it feel like to be the models in such a system? I suppose it feels like most of us do feel—pretty confusing. The only thing that gives it any stability is the constant presence of a stable self model. No wonder we cling to it.

On the other hand, being mindful means not following every association; not stacking up ideas to be completed; not rehearsing, planning or even selecting. The models become ever simpler and all processing capacity is not immediately used up.

More and more can be linked into one model because there is less and less being modelled. And what would it be like to be the models in such a system? Obviously very different. Is this why everything seems brighter and more "real" during meditation? Why the quietest sound is clearly heard and the beating of one's heart is constantly present? If so, testable predictions might follow. Long-term practitioners might show greater awareness of normally inaccessible low-level modelling, for example.

In the end, it is not even necessary for the model of self to be constructed at all. Imagine what it would be like to be a system that processes incoming information but builds no further constructions upon it, not even any self to observe. With no modelled distinction between self and other, I imagine the world would all seem one. (This condition might make survival problematic, however.)

People who have this training and experience find it very hard to describe what happens, which is no wonder when "they" (their model of self) have been dissolved. It may, in fact, be impossible to describe using the assumptions of our usual language. But perhaps a new possibility now arises: that science might at least develop the concepts and language needed to understand mystical experiences in terms of information processing.

Buddhism teaches the doctrine of "no-self". There is no thing that is conscious but just consciousness itself. Cognitive psychology reveals that the self is a mental model; if consciousness is just what it is like being a mental model, there is no self being conscious of anything, but just a series of changing models.

So can I now answer my question: "Why am I aware of anything?" The answer seems to be that because I am only a mental model, it could not be otherwise.

Social Evolution, Psychoanalysis, and Human Nature

Daniel Kriegman
and Charles Knight

DANIEL KRIEGMAN is a clinical psychologist in private practice in Cambridge and Newton, Mass., and president of Human Services Cooperative, Inc., an agency structured around the principles of worker ownership. His writing focuses on the application of evolutionary biology to psychoanalysis and group psychology. CHARLES KNIGHT is a senior fellow at the Commonwealth Institute, where he is working on alternatives for U.S. defense policy.

At the very back of a Harvard lecture hall we jealously guarded the last remaining seats for two friends who were working their way through an overflow crowd at the door. The long room was buzzing in the anticipation of hearing a couple of Cambridge intellectual stars. Stephen Jay Gould, the well-known paleontologist, and Richard C. Lewontin, a Harvard biologist, were the featured speakers. Sponsored by the Sociobiology Study Group of Science for the People, the evening was called "Sociobiology, A Retrospective."

Gould has written elegantly and voluminously on the historic misuse of biology to bolster particular world views, especially racism. His books have been widely read, and their images on nineteenth-century scientists measuring cranial capacity with mustard seed seem ridiculous to the modern eye. As a whole, Gould's historical work serves as a powerful reminder of how social and cultural blinders can lead the scientist astray and how such "science" can be misused by political actors with no essential interest in truth.

Lewontin, in his work as a population geneticist, has challenged the very concept of race in the human species. The biological evidence, he says, is of much more genetic variation within the racial populations than between them. The common features of racial identity such as skin, hair, and eye color are best understood as adaptations to indeterminate conditions, perhaps geographical, which simply overlay a basic genetic commonality of the human species. From this perspective, Jensen's work becomes meaningless as it was based on separating IQ test subjects into the conventional racial groupings and comparing scores to arrive at a proof of genetically based difference in racial IQs. Lewontin argues that there is no evidence of consistent genetic difference in the brains of different "races" and, lacking any such evidence, we should assume that differences in IQ arise from the social or physical environment.

So that evening it was not just intellectuals who had gathered at Harvard. This was a political crowd as well. Ever since another Harvard professor, E. O. Wilson, wrote *Sociobiology: The New Synthesis,* sociobiology has been of great interest to competing political ideologues for use in their polemic battles. Those leaning toward the right have used Wilson's ideas to bolster their social Darwinist arguments about the inherent inferiority of the disadvantaged and the inevitability of class differentiation (primate dominance hierarchies); while those on the left use sociobiology as an example of specious "blaming the victim" type of reasoning. Now the left-leaning Science for the People's Sociobiology Study Group had gathered to hear its "heavies" declare the battle won. Sociobiology, it would be shown, was

discredited as science and was, at best, a pseudo-science that served the interests of the right wing.

Although the evening's message was that the Study Group's intellectual work had been completed—they were to declare that "sociobiology is dead"—there was urgency in the air as more work still needed to be done. Ronald Reagan, the great arch-conservative communicator, had formed an unusually effective right-wing coalition that might last well beyond him. Racism waxed as civil rights gains waned. Surely great harm would come if the right's intellectual henchmen were allowed to continue to peddle their dangerously flawed, pseudo-scientific wares unchallenged.

Lewontin rose to the occasion; his voice rang with all the righteousness and contempt of an evangelist proclaiming victory over the devil, as he announced sociobiology's demise. Gould, displaying a better humor, was more even-tempered as he marshalled the facts depicting the misuse of the scientific process by some sociobiologists. The crowd, as evidenced by its enthusiastic response to the oratory, responded with religious fervor. Questions from the floor echoed the sentiments of the speakers as they mockingly dismissed sociobiology as pernicious nonsense. In the back row, the four of us grew ever more uncomfortable. None of us would ever be called conservative in our political beliefs, yet we had each found something attractive in recent advances in evolution theory. Now we found ourselves whispering to each other about "cheap shots" and conclusions "far too sweeping."

Finally one of us spoke up. "Aren't sociobiologists really trying to get at a theory of human nature? Yes, this new science may have been prone to bad

From *Social Policy,* Fall 1988, pp. 49-55. Copyright 1988 by Social Policy Corporation. Reprinted by permission.

method and premature conjecture—which others could use for their political aims. But was that good reason to abandon the study of human nature? Isn't it important to understand human nature; to sort out what it is from what we imagine it to be, or from what we would like it to be? Especially, if ones's goal is the construction of a more just, fair, and humanitarian society, should we not study the nature of the building blocks of such a system?"

Though the crowd was decidedly unfriendly to this challenge, pockets of resistance to the evening's evangelical message began to open up. Those who were cowed by the crowd's fervent and enthusiastic reception of the anti-sociobiology diatribe began to speak up. Their comments did not appear to indicate a right-wing perspective. Rather, there was something in the sociobiological viewpoint that they felt was important and should be respected.

At the time of the Harvard meeting, we had been working on a psychobiological model with an eye toward revision of certain aspects of psychoanalytic theory and progressive political thought. In addition to whatever clinical value this new approach might have, we hoped to develop a better understanding of some of the twentieth-century failures of liberal and radical politics, and to derive guidelines for more effective social change. Hardly a right-wing agenda. In this context, the unrelenting attack from the left on sociobiology was paradoxical, for it was the work of a leading sociobiologist that seemed to us to present the clearest foundation for a human psychology that includes altruism and cooperation as inherent human tendencies. Yet, in Western thought, those who had plumbed the deepest into the human psyche were bringing back the message that humans are basically instinctual, selfish animals.

PSYCHOANALYSIS AND FREUD'S EVOLUTIONARY BIOLOGY

The founder of psychoanalysis had familiarity with Darwinian thought but none with modern genetics. In Freud's model the inherent self-serving drives of sex and aggression were psychological bedrock. Civilization, as he eloquently described in *Civilization and its Discontents*, is a human achievement that stands in opposition to human nature. Humans are inherently unhappy as they are forced to surrender their true instinctual/selfish nature under the oppressive but necessary civilizing forces.

This conceptualization of human nature underlies the most fundamental of dilemmas of twentieth-century liberalism. If "civilizing influences" must be forced upon the reluctant human animal, the prospect of advancing to higher orders of civilization diminish in proportion to the distance we climb from the morass of basic human greed, lust, and aggressiveness. What we have is a law of the diminishing returns of civilization. It is a profoundly pessimistic view of the human situation; one with human nature assumptions that have become closely intertwined with the popular Western perception of the human situation.

Freud's view of human nature is generally consistent with the experience of capitalist competition and its adjunct philosophy at the extreme, social Darwinism. The *inevitable* tendency of human motivation is toward competition. Inevitably struggles ensue and yield a "survival of the fittest" dominance hierarchy. Civilization with its manners, cooperation, sympathy for those suffering, and altruism is a useful achievement, but it is only a "thin sugar coating" over our truer instinctual essential nature. Facing this harsh truth is a cornerstone of both psychoanalytic theory and treatment. Thus, the clinical goal is to enhance the accuracy of the executive agency of the mental apparatus, the ego, in its perception of itself and the world, by overcoming resistance to swallowing this bitter pill and facing the harsh animalistic (instinctual) reality.

Humanists and socialists are simply romantic "nicefiers" who refuse to take their unpleasant but necessary medicine. While Freud was sympathetic to their goals, his psychology was antithetical. As he stated in *Civilization and its Discontents:*

As we already know, the problem before us is how to get rid of the greatest hindrance to civilization—namely, the constitutional inclination of human beings to be aggressive towards one another. . . . I too think it quite certain that a real change in the relations of human beings to possessions would be of more help in this direction than any ethical commands; but the recognition of this fact among socialists has been obscured and made useless for practical purposes by a fresh idealistic misconception of human nature (p. 144).

While Freud's basic notions of human nature still hold for the majority of modern psychoanalytic theorists, they have been modified to include powerful social needs beyond simple discharge of sexual and aggressive drive tensions. Today psychoanalytic thought is in a state of flux between drive-centered theory and viewpoints that place relational or social needs at the core of human psychology. Relational theorists are no longer members of splinter groups that follow the work of Karen Horney, Erich Fromm, or Harry Stack Sullivan. In psychoanalytic writings, these innovators are now given some consideration. Even more influential within modern, mainstream psychoanalysis is the work of the relational theorists such as W. R. D. Fairbairn, D. W. Winnicott, Margaret Mahler, and the influential self psychology of Heinz Kohut; this latter group's writings comprise part of the basic course of study for new psychoanalysts. With the addition of this relational focus, psychoanalysis can no longer be seen as being based upon a theory of an inherently asocial organism reluctantly forced into relatedness.

Despite Freud's influence on our own thinking, our professional experience, clinical and otherwise, was leading us toward human nature assumptions that are consistent with cooperative social models. Yet, doesn't the general observation of ubiquitous human conflict suggest that competition is the central theme? In organizational settings, strife and political tension are so common that we may often wonder how anything gets accomplished at all. At a different level, look at the failure of the Soviet system to create a vibrant and flourishing economy.

Human history includes endless warfare and genocide, with more people killed in this most scientifically informed, civilized century than ever before. And despite promises of arms negotiations, the world, as a whole, continues a suicidal buildup of weaponry. The bottom line for those of us who accept the theory of evolution as the only scientifically credible theory of creation is that competition is inherent, unavoidable, and simply part of the natural order, as natural selection selects the fittest for survival. Evolution theory appears to tip the balance between differing human nature assumptions. Surrender to the conservative view of human nature seems inevitable—and wise.

THE NEXT PARADIGM FOR PSYCHOANALYTIC THEORY

In the psychoanalytic laboratory of practical applications to real people (clinical psychoanalysis) a new perspective has been brewing. This is the psychology of the self as developed by Heinz Kohut. Self psychology is a relational theory that sees interpersonal conflict, regarding selfish drives or instinctual striving, as secondary and not inevitable. From Kohut's viewpoint, Freud's use of drives, "a vague and insipid biological concept," in an attempt to develop psychoanalysis within the domain of biological science, has paradoxically made traditional psychoanalysis mechanistic and out of sync with the natural order. Kohut labels the Freudian vision of the essential nature of the human condition, "Guilty Man":

> ...man as an insufficiently and incompletely tamed animal, reluctant to give up his wish to live by the pleasure principle, unable to relinquish his innate destructiveness.

For Kohut, conflict exists, but rather than being an essential feature of human psychology, it is a "tragedy." It is an unfortunate byproduct of the failure of the human tendency towards empathic relationships that sustain our "selves"—thus, Kohut's concept of "Tragic Man":

> ...healthy man experiences...with deepest joy, the next generation as an extension of his own self. It is the primacy of the support for the succeeding generation, therefore, which is normal and human, and not intergenerational strife and mutual wishes to kill and to destroy—however frequently and perhaps even ubiquitously, we may be able to find traces of those pathological disintegration products...which traditional analysis has made us think [of] is a normal developmental phase.

If healthy self structures are not formed due to parental failure to provide a nutritive psychological and emotional milieu, the result is an enfeebled self that will turn to drive gratifications in an attempt to ward off a more devastating fragmentation of the self. The psychological problem arises from a failure of relatedness, not a failure to learn appropriate control of inner instinctual drives. Without empathic self others to relate to, the individual becomes preoccupied with desires and instinctual demands and struggles in conflict to deal with them.

In traditional psychoanalytic thought, the parents, as society's representatives, are inevitably in conflict with the sexual and aggressive drives of the child. The unavoidable "discontent" begins in childhood as the parents attempt to enculturate their child. They must engage in conflicts with the child, ultimately giving rise to anxiety and guilt, thus internalizing the conflict within the child and removing the need for external control. This solution leaves the child, and later the adult, in the inevitable situation of being torn between instinctual selfish wishes (the id) and socializing internalized guilt (the superego). Discontent is inevitable.

In the self-psychological approach, the essential nature of the parent to the child is as a provider of empathic and soothing mirroring of the child's internal experience and as a provider of opportunities for the child to merge with a calming idealized other. Problems arise not from the essential conflictual nature of the parent/child relationship, but rather from the failure of the parent to provide adequate empathic holding or mirroring and idealized models for the development of the child's self. The parent/child relationship need not be characterized by intense pathology inducing conflict. Pathological conflict only results from the failure—due to their narcissistic defects or other limitations, some of which may be inevitable—of the parents' natural tendency to provide a nutritive, sustaining, and generative milieu for the child's nascent self.

In the applied clinical setting, this relational theory often fits the clinical data much better than Freud's individualistic drive theory. Yet the ubiquitous nature of human conflict along with evolution theory's emphasis on competition and "survival of

the fittest" made Kohut's human nature assumptions appear untenable, even naive. It was an impasse to be traversed using the work of Robert Trivers.

SOCIAL EVOLUTION AND RECIPROCAL ALTRUISM

Trivers is one of the most creative and influential evolutionary theorists on the scene today. His recently published *Social Evolution* is the most authoritative work on the subject. Among his earlier work are three paradigm-defining papers on social evolution: papers that are already considered groundbreaking classics. In one of these, he developed the concept of "reciprocal altruism." This fascinating evolutionary construct undermines the simplistic notions of social Darwinism and provides a basis for reviewing the erroneous thinking underlying the misuse of evolutionary theory in support of reactionary dogma.

The concept of reciprocal altruism suggests that there may be a bio-genetic basis to altruistic behavior. At first glance, altruistic behavior, which in evolutionary terms reduces the altruist's fitness and leads to an increase in the recipient's fitness, appears to be in contradiction to the basic self-serving survival interest of any organism. However, the concept of reciprocal altruism is based on the notion that an altruistic act is often returned to the altruistically behaving organism.

To illustrate the concept of reciprocal altruism, Trivers describes a mutually beneficial relationship between certain host fish and unrelated cleaner fish. The cleaner's diet consists of parasites removed from the host, which can often involve entering the host's mouth. Each fish engages in altruistic behavior towards the other, presumably because of the mutual adaptive advantage of the symbiotic relationship. For example, Trivers describes how a host fish will go through extra movements and delay fleeing when being attacked by a predator in order to allow a cleaner extra time to leave its mouth! One would assume that it would be to the adaptive advantage of the host, at such a moment, to simply swallow the cleaner. Instead, the host delays its departure in order to signal to the cleaner that it is time to get out of its mouth. This type of altruistic behavior seems to reduce the fitness of the host in two ways: it increases the chance that it will be eaten by a predator, and it forgoes a meal of the cleaner.

Yet, Trivers was able to show that there is an adaptive advantage to this altruistic act: being able to have debilitating parasites removed in the future. Because the cleaner fish stays in one spot in the shallow waters along the shore, the host can return to the same cleaner over and over again. In fact, they do and reliable relationships form in which both species benefit. One certainly would not posit guilty self control of selfishness as the motivator of such cooperative, and even altruistic, behavior in the host fish. Nor is it likely to be a calculated action. Most likely this behavior is directly imbedded in the biological responsive structure and motivational system of the fish; a system that yields cooperative altruistic interactions between two unrelated species of fish.

While there may be some intelligent fish, and while one may know some fishy people, it remains dangerous to generalize from fish to humans. What can be demonstrated by the evolutionary analysis are the prerequisites for the evolution of reciprocal altruism: high frequency of association, the reliability of association over time, and the ability of two organisms to behave in ways that benefit the other. If an altruistic act costs the altruist less than the benefit to the recipient then both will benefit from frequent trading of such acts. If this sounds like a perpetual motion machine where the output magically exceeds the input, consider just a few human examples such as a traditional barnraising, the act of helping an unrelated child find its way back to its parents, and many forms of charity. In such situations the cost to the altruist is frequently far less than the recipient's benefit. Those individuals who can trade such acts will have a significant adaptive advantage over non-altruists or those excluded from reciprocal arrangements.

This evolutionary line of thought presents a powerful challenge to the classical Freudian notion that "guilt" is necessary for civilization. Even though Trivers posits an important role for guilt in human social evolution, he points out that evolution theory cannot be used to "predict" guilt as central and necessary for civilization. The prerequisites for the evolution of recip-

rocal altruism are present in our species and have been shown in other species to be capable of shaping extremely cooperative behaviors.

THE COOPERATIVE WINNING STRATEGY

Based on Trivers' model, Robert Axelrod and William Hamilton used game theory to prove that such a strategy is highly effective and can outcompete more selfish strategies. They presented a demonstration that helps explain how the adaptive advantage of cooperative altruistic strategies could have evolved and entered a species repertoire. Axelrod and Hamilton used a modified version of the Prisoner's Dilemma, a game that has been extensively studied by social scientists. They changed it so that it represented opportunities for voluntary cooperation versus a selfish attempt to take advantage of another's willingness to cooperate, or a refusal to cooperate with a non-cooperator. There were various incentives for each of two players to do one of the following: cooperate, punish a non-cooperator (a "cheater") by not cooperating, and attempt to take advantage of a cooperator (to "cheat").

There are a number of rounds of play in which each player makes his or her decision and announces it simultaneously. The "payoff" is defined as follows: cheating a cooperator yields the biggest payoff for the cheater (payoff = 5) and the loss by the cooperator of his/her investment (payoff = 0); when both players are cooperative they are each rewarded (payoff = 3); finally, when both players cheat they protect their investment, but gain nothing (payoff = 1).

Robert Axelrod conducted a computer tournament of different strategies to this game that were submitted by game theorists in economics, sociology, political science, and mathematics. Though some of the strategies were quite intricate, the winning strategy (the highest score averaged against all challengers) was one of the simplest—a basically cooperative strategy called TIT FOR TAT: cooperate on the first move and thereafter do whatever the other player did on the preceding move. Thus, the strategy is to initially "announce" an intention to cooperate and then to let the other player know that cheating will not lead

to a gain. TIT FOR TAT is quick to forgive no matter how many times the other player has cheated—just one indication of a willingness to cooperate from the other player leads TIT FOR TAT to try cooperation again.

What Axelrod and Hamilton were presenting was a theoretical model of how cooperation could evolve. Instead of competitive advantage going to the tough individual oriented toward selfish cheating, it might in fact lie with the wary but open individual oriented toward cooperation. Reality is more complicated than the conventional western view of an "I, I, me, me, mine" human nature. The human world has a *social* dimension as well as an *individual* dimension. Paradoxically, playing the game along *both* dimensions is the strategy most in the *individual's* interest.

One powerful human demonstration of this tendency occurred during the early years of World War I in the trenches. Much to the consternation of the generals, the "disease of cooperation" between the opposing soldiers broke out all along the line. Stationed week after week, and month after month, in the same spot facing the same "enemy," the ideal conditions were present for the generation of reciprocal altruism. Soldiers shot to miss. Troops left the trenches and worked at repairing them in full view and within range of enemy soldiers who passively looked on. Christmas was celebrated together. One striking incident occurred when in one area an artillery burst exploded sending both sides diving for cover. After several moments, a brave German soldier called out to the other side and apologized, saying that his side had nothing to do with it: "It was those damn Prussian artillerymen." Note that artillery is farther from the line, and the mutual trading of beneficial acts (shooting to miss) was not available. Finally, the generals solved this thorny problem by ordering random raids (and shooting those who resisted) that broke down the mutual trust and cooperation that had evolved.

The skeptic could argue that the human examples are anomalies, and, of course, we do not expect humans to behave as fish or relatively simple computer programs. However, human interactions are, in fact, often highly cooperative, and while there may be tension and competitiveness, the destructiveness that supposedly characterizes our species is relatively unseen. Murders are relatively rare within stable living communities and account for very little of human mortality. In fact, it behooves those who would posit that destructiveness and competitive greed lie at the heart of human motivations to explain the enormous amount of cooperation and the relative internal harmony of most human societies. We can conclude that the prerequisites for the evolution of reciprocal altruism—that have been shown in other species to be capable of shaping extremely cooperative behaviors— are present in our species, and are possibly present to a greater degree than in any other species.

THE EVOLUTION OF COOPERATION

What Trivers was able to show is that there are strong adaptive advantages to altruism, and he was able to delineate the necessary prerequisites for the evolution of altruism. Thus, in contrast to Freud's use of primitive evolutionary theorizing, utilizing the modern evolutionary perspective, altruistic behavior can be seen as conferring a powerful adaptive advantage on the altruist. Trivers suggests that this tendency may have been selected for at the same time that the selective pressures were shaping the evolution of human intelligence. This evolutionary scenario is the opposite of the conventional one—used by Freud—in which our animal nature is seen as being forcefully (and only partially) overcome by the pressures of civilization, made possible by increased intelligence and the ability to delay gratification of instincts.

Consider the following evolutionary path that the above suggests. Sympathy for one in pain (the empathic sharing of the experience of pain and the desire to alleviate the sufferer's anguish—a "desire" to act altruistically toward one in need) may have first evolved within the context of kin-directed behavior. In a kin relationship, an altruistic act increases the fitness of the altruist even if the act is not reciprocated. Any act that aids a relative is likely to increase the chance that one's own genes will be replicated because, by definition, a relative is one who carries some of the same genes. Therefore, the evolution of such behavior within kin relation-

ships was not dependent upon there first being a tendency for reciprocation. However, kin altruists who tended to act more altruistically toward relatives that reciprocated were more successful than those who made no such discrimination.

As Axelrod and Hamilton have shown, once a cooperative strategy begins to invade a population it should be able to outcompete the selfish strategies. So, the generalization of altruistic behavior to non-related others became possible as sufficient cognitive abilities were developed so that the altruist could distinguish between those likely to return the altruistic act (reciprocal altruists) and those unlikely to do so (cheaters). The development of large-scale human societies, where participants are only distantly related, is predicated both on emotional tendencies toward reciprocal altruism, and the cognitive ability to distinguish reciprocators from cheaters.

Trivers analyzed some of the subtleties of this ability. He suggested that reciprocal altruism evolved alongside increased cortical capacity and was a major source of selective pressure shaping that development. A moment's reflection will demonstrate that many aspects of human social relations exist within a complex web of kin and reciprocal altruism. In this analysis, rather than being an outcome of conflict brought into being by recent cortical evolution that led to the development of civilization, the tendency to act altruistically is seen as being historically primitive. Recent monkey studies by de Waal suggest that reciprocal altruism existed at a very early stage in primate evolution.

Traditional Freudian psychology clearly sees altruistic behavior as a recent development brought into being *after* increased brain size began to lead to the formation of civilization: civilization, made possible by increased intelligence, leads to pressure to control instinctual behavior. Altruism is understood as being in opposition to our "true" instinctual animal nature: changing an unconscious wish or desire into its opposite in consciousness, due to guilt induced by society. In Trivers' analysis, the adaptive advantage of reciprocal altruism existed at the earliest stages in the development of intelligence, forcing rapid intellectual advancement and the shaping of civiliza-

tion in order to garner the advantages accrued through the successful trading of altruistic acts.

This is consistent with the Kohutian viewpoint and suggests that the traditional psychoanalytic emphasis on guilt does not adequately explain most altruistic behavior. While Trivers discusses a role played by guilt in reciprocal altruism, there is the inescapable self interest that is served by parental altruism towards one's children. This suggests that guilt conflict, which we cannot assume to be a primary factor in other species that also contribute considerable parental care toward their offspring, is unlikely to be the primary or main factor motivating such behavior in humans.

Parental protectiveness and the eager investment in offspring are not adequately explained by traditional psychoanalytic thought using reaction formations, pleasure resulting from the approval of one's super-ego, or de-repressed infantile narcissistic identifications. In focusing on the non-conflictual aspect of human relations (where the individual's and other's needs are in harmony due to the individual's tendency toward altruism), Kohut's self psychology appears to recognize a deep emotional wellspring that gives rise to altruistic behavior and that need not—and Kohut argues can not—be understood within the context of a drive-based, conflict psychology model.

The evolutionary arguments used in analyzing altruistic behavior toward kin and non-kin in many species suggest that there is a basic biological component to this altruistic behavior: that altruistic behavior was not contingent upon the recent increase in the size of the neo-cortex that then allowed for the development of a strong ego and such motivating forces as guilt. Of course, these arguments do not prove that guilt is not a strong motivating factor, and they are consistent with the notion that guilt does, in fact, provide significant motivation for some such behavior.

The arguments do suggest that Kohut's data, as well as his orientation and viewpoint in regard to empathic and altruistic behavior, may have the same biological basis (or rather the same degree of biological foundation in a human motivational system) as we assume that instinctual drives have.

Conflict between our basic selfishness and the needs of others/society may not be at the core of the human psyche as traditional psychoanalytic theory would suggest, but may in fact be, as Kohut views it, a result of the failure of the biological tendency toward altruistic empathic behavior and experience.

EVOLUTION, HUMAN NATURE, AND POLITICS

Modern evolutionary theory beckons us to fresh speculation in regard to many aspects of the human condition. It has certainly proven attractive to social philosophers and political theorists of various persuasions. However, the problems of proving the constructs of sociobiology rival those of proving different aspects of psychoanalytical theory. In his carefully argued study of the sociobiological debate, *Vaulting Ambition,* Philip Kitcher has demonstrated that a careful and difficult path must be traveled from any principal statement of social evolution to any particular statement regarding human nature. Certainly the lesson is to be wary of the grand conclusions of some sociobiologists.

According to Kitcher:

A quick look at actual behavior and at behavior differences among groups has all too frequently served to buttress hypotheses about the fixity of human institutions and the impossibility of eradicating inequalities among races and classes. Plant breeders who inferred the qualities of rival strains from consideration of relative vigor in a single environment, or from casual inspection of a collection of environments, would have a pronounced tendency to go rapidly out of business. By contrast, their imitators in the behavioral sciences usually seem to thrive .

Clearly, the consequences of faulty reasoning in sociobiology go far beyond the success or failure of individual theorists. Bad theory and findings hastily adopted to support social policy can contribute to ongoing and unnecessary social injustice. Such was the effect of Jensen's IQ studies at a time when there was growing political resistance to affirmative action and continuing Head Start programs.

On the other hand, if we look deep enough, in every political philosophy we discover assumptions about human nature. Generally, more conservative political views emphasize the more static and selfish nature of humans. More progressive or change-oriented political views optimistically stress the ability of humans to fashion their existence through social reconstruction without preconceived limits derived from limiting notions in regard to human nature. Yet, the latter assumes humans have a behavioral proclivity to find happiness, satisfaction, and/or meaning through effective or, at least, valued social interaction.

The issue is not whether there is some nature in human behavior, but rather what that nature is and what its effect is. Some answers to these questions would certainly be a useful addition to our thinking about the many institutions that serve to direct and organize human behavior. Sociobiology, despite the claims of its more ambitious practitioners, is still a long way from providing definitive answers, though with recent advances a new conceptual schema is becoming available that may help guide us to a more accurate picture of the human condition. Meanwhile, premature conclusions about human limits have led to a reactionary trend from the left. In this trend, sociobiological attempts to fathom human nature are treated as anathema and are rejected as rightwing racism. Thou shalt not apply the theory of evolution to human nature.

When we strip away the ill-founded and hasty conclusions reached by some sociobiologists, we are left with some very interesting analytical structures and some surprising possibilities for human nature. It has been easy to see why aggression and competition might be favored by evolution. But now we can understand how altruism and cooperation might also be favored. Further sociobiological study will probably show that humans are intrinsically social creatures, and help us to understand the complex design of social creatures who at times also act selfishly to maximize their evolutionary success.

Ironically—given the extremely hostile criticism coming from the left—one definitive political conclusion we can draw from human sociobiology at this stage is a challenging reply to the most pessimistic view of human nature coming from the right. In this pessimistic period of history, this alone may be a significant contribution. The popular view of human nature as simply aggressive, selfish, and competitive is far too narrow. We do not need to pose civilization in opposition to essential human nature, as did Freud. We do not need to deny evolved human behavioral propensities to explain the origin and maintenance of culture. As surprising as it may be, sociobiology appears to provide a scientific basis, however tentative, for an optimistic view of both human psychology and the potential for civilization.

REFERENCES

Axelrod, R., and W.D. Hamilton, "The Evolution of Cooperation," *Science,* 211 (1981), pp. 1390-96.

de Waal, F.B.M., *Chimpanzee Politics: Power and Sex Among Apes* (New York: Harper & Row, 1982).

Freud, S., *Civilization and its Discontents* (Standard Edition), 21 (1930), pp. 59-145.

Kitcher, P., *Vaulting Ambition* (Cambridge: MIT Press, 1985).

Kriegman, D., "Self Psychology from the Perspective of Evolutionary Biology," in A. Goldberg (ed.), *Progress in Self Psychology,* vol. 3 (Hillsdale, N.J.: The Analytic Press, 1988), pp. 253-274.

Trivers, R.L., "The Evolution of Reciprocal Altruism," *Quarterly Review of Biology,* 46 (1971), pp. 35-57.

——.*Social Evolution* (Boston: Addison-Wesley, 1985).

Biological Bases of Behavior

Historically, philosophical questions regarding the nature of human nature and human functions gave way to a scientific methodology promoted by biology. It is to be expected, then, that the biological sciences provide a major source of methodology for psychological inquiry. As psychologists work to uncover the biological correlates of behavior, they also encounter issues of control over behavior. Many of these issues are both scientific and ethical; for example, it is possible to alter the brain to remove aggressive tendencies, but should such procedures be developed for use on humans? On the other hand, if it is discovered that a type of brain disorder can be held responsible for a particular human behavior, should an individual not be punished for that behavior?

Much of what we know about human brain/behavior relationships has been learned from two major sources. Animal studies involving manipulation, stimulation, or destruction of certain parts of the brain, and the observation of the effects of these changes on behavior, have helped us to understand much of the brain's workings. We have also learned much from the observation and testing of humans whose brains were defective at birth, or damaged in accidents or by disease at some time after birth.

The articles in this section were selected to represent the breadth of research efforts and strategies, as well as to represent the state of our knowledge of the biological correlates of human behavior.

The first article enables us to share the excitement of new discoveries about the contribution each hemisphere of the brain makes to the integrated functioning of the human individual. It also teaches us to be conservative in interpreting new evidence. The second article extends our understanding of brain function by proposing a comprehensive theory of brain organization and operation, based on rather complex neural networks.

The presence of biological cycles has been known for many years, and the search for the control circuits or biological "clocks" has been a long one. Now, as the next article shows, we are zeroing in on at least one clock. Are there more? And how do they work? Part of the answer to such questions may come from the National Institutes of Health Human Genome Project, the most ambitious attempt to date to unravel the genetic instructions coded in deoxyribonucleic acid (DNA). Leon Jaroff reviews the scope of the project, focusing on contemporary knowledge of heredity, implications for gene therapy, and elimination of genetic diseases.

The human being begins life with the full set of genetically coded species characteristics that provide the substrate for bio-psycho-social function, including behavior. However, behavior is a function of genotype-environment interaction, an interaction that begins prenatally and includes interaction with the organism's internal biochemical environment. How chemistry affects organization of polygenetic characteristics and/or functional organization is another mystery that awaits unraveling. Nevertheless, studies of hormonal action and brain endorphins have provided intriguing insights about the chemical messengers by which the brain controls the peripheral body, as well as insights about how the brain is influenced by the chemical agents which it secretes. For several years, scientists have sought out the mysterious opiate-like substances which permit severely wounded soldiers and athletes to feel no pain from their injuries. As the last article in this section reflects, we now have detailed evidence about these endorphins and their effects on other bodily functions and systems, including the immune system.

Looking Ahead: Challenge Questions

As we learn more about the special functions of each hemisphere of the brain, how has our approach to research changed? What types of applications should we be focusing on?

Are the unusual abilities of some split-brain patients sufficient evidence to support a theory about how we interpret our own behavior to ourselves? If the theory is correct, does behavior which surprises us also indicate a need we're not satisfying?

How can our theory of the organization of the functioning brain help us to develop new research strategies? What types of questions can this new theory raise? How can we investigate them?

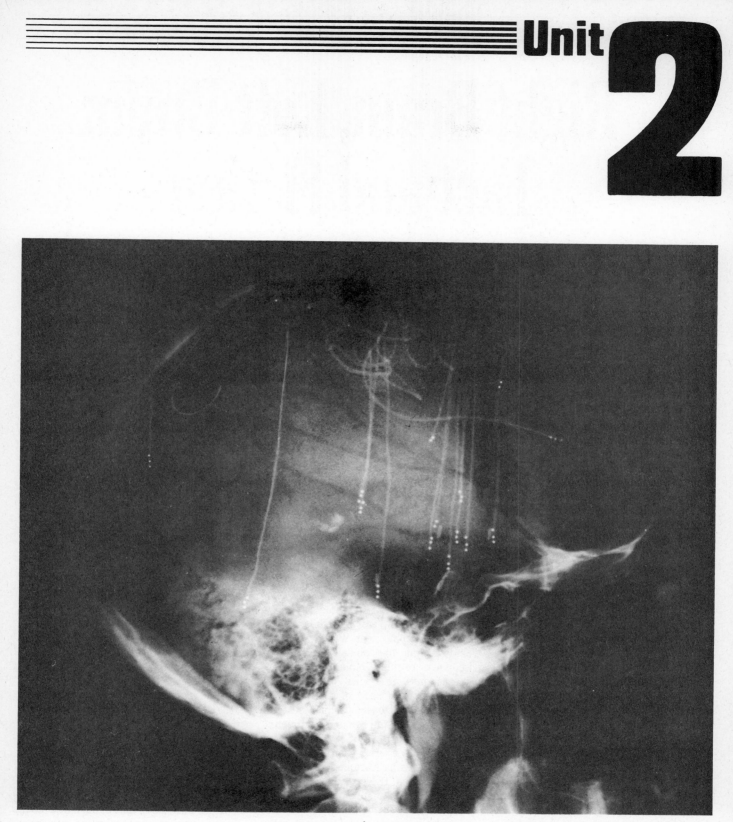

How can we make personal use in our day-to-day lives of knowledge of circadian rhythms and their effects on our moods?

If manipulation of genetic material can lead to prevention of genetic disease, might not similar manipulations be used to genetically engineer intelligence, personality, and social behavior? What individual or societal factors would constrain attempts to explicitly practice selective breeding or attempt genetic manipulation in order to produce "superior" human beings?

If the production of endorphins can accomplish so much in pain relief and support of the immune system, should we teach people how to stimulate endorphin secretion? How could we best do that?

Right Brain, Left Brain: Fact and Fiction

*EACH HEMISPHERE HAS SPECIAL
ABILITIES, BUT, CONTRARY TO POPULAR
MYTH, PEOPLE USE BOTH ALL THE TIME.*

JERRE LEVY

*Jerre Levy is a biopsychologist at the
University of Chicago.*

I guess I'm mostly a right-brain person ... my left side doesn't work long enough for me to figure it out," concludes a character in a *Frank and Ernest* cartoon. "It's tough being a left-brained person ... in a right-brained world," moans a youngster in the cartoon *Wee Pals,* after perusing a tome on the "psychology of consciousness."

The notion that we are "left brained" or "right brained" has become entrenched in the popular culture. And, based on a misinterpretation of the facts, a pop psychology myth has evolved, asserting that the left hemisphere of the brain controls logic and language, while the right controls creativity and intuition. One best-selling book even claimed to teach people how to draw better by training the right brain and bypassing the left. According to the myth, people differ in their styles of thought, depending on which half of the brain is dominant. Unfortunately, this myth is often represented as scientific fact. It is not.

As a researcher who has spent essentially her whole career studying how the two hemispheres relate to one another and to behavior, I feel obliged to set the record straight on what is known scientifically about the roles of the hemispheres. As it turns out, the brain's actual organization is every bit as interesting as the myth and suggests a far more holistic view of humankind.

People's fascination with relating mental function to brain organization goes back at least to Hippocrates. But it was René Descartes, in the 17th century, who came up with the notable and influential notion that the brain must act as a unified whole to yield a unified mental world. His specific mental mapping was wrong (he concluded that the pineal gland—now known to regulate biological rhythms in response to cycles of light and dark—was the seat of the soul, or mind). But his basic premise was on the right track and remained dominant until the latter half of the 19th century, when discoveries then reduced humankind to a half-brained species.

During the 1860s and 1870s, Paul Broca, a French neurologist, and Karl Wernicke, a German neurologist, reported that damage to the left cerebral hemisphere produced severe disorders of language, but that comparable damage to the right hemisphere did not. Neurology was never to be the same.

Despite their generally similar anatomies, the left and right cerebral hemispheres evidently had very different functions. Language appeared to be solely a property of the left side; the right hemisphere, apparently, was mute. The scientific world generalized this to conclude that the left hemisphere was dominant not only for language but for all psychological processes. The right hemisphere was seen as a mere relay station. Since each half of the brain is connected to and receives direct input from the opposite side of the body, the right hemisphere was needed to tell the left hemisphere what was happening on the left side of space and to relay messages to muscles on the body's left side. But the right hemisphere was only an unthinking automaton. From pre-19th century whole-brained creatures, we had become half-brained.

From the beginning, there were serious difficulties with the idea that the left hemisphere was the seat of humanity and that the right hemisphere played no role in thinking. In the 1880s, John Hughlings Jackson, a renowned English neurologist, described a patient with right-hemisphere damage who showed selective losses in certain aspects of visual perception—losses that did not appear with similar damage of the left hemisphere. He suggested that the right hemisphere might be just as specialized for visual perception as the left hemisphere was for language.

 From *Psychology Today*, May 1985, pp. 38-39, 42-44. Copyright © 1985 by PT Partners, L. P. Reprinted by permission.

From the 1930s on, reports began to confirm Hughlings Jackson's findings. Patients with right-side damage had difficulties in drawing, using colored blocks to copy designs, reading and drawing maps, discriminating faces and in a variety of other visual and spatial tasks. These disorders were much less prevalent or serious in patients with left-hemisphere damage.

The investigators, quite aware of the implications of their findings, proposed that although the left hemisphere was specialized for language, the right hemisphere was specialized for many nonlinguistic processes. Nonetheless, these were voices in the wilderness, and their views hardly swayed the general neurological community. Until 1962, the prevalent view was that people had half a thinking brain.

Beginning in the early 1960s, Nobel Prize winner Roger W. Sperry and his colleagues and students demonstrated certain unusual characteristics in patients who, to control intractable epi-

---

A MYTH: THE LEFT HEMISPHERE CONTROLS LOGIC AND LANGUAGE, THE RIGHT CONTROLS CREATIVITY AND INTUITION.

---

leptic seizures, had undergone complete surgical division of the corpus callosum, the connecting bridge between the two sides of the brain. These patients, like split-brain animals that Sperry had studied, couldn't communicate between the cerebral hemispheres. An object placed in the right hand (left hemisphere) could be named readily, but one placed in the left hand (nonverbal right hemisphere) could be neither named nor described. But these same patients could point to a picture of the object the left hand had felt. In other words, the right hemisphere knew what it felt, even if it could not speak.

Outside the laboratory, the split-brain patients were remarkably normal, and within the laboratory, each cerebral hemisphere seemed to be able to perceive, think and govern behavior, even though the two sides were out of contact. In later split-brain studies, a variety of tasks were devised to examine the specialized functions of each hemisphere. These showed that the right hemisphere was superior to the left in spatial tasks but was mute and deficient in verbal tasks such as decoding complex syntax, short-term verbal memory and phonetic analysis. In brief, the split-brain studies fully confirmed the inferences drawn from the earlier investigations of patients with damage to one hemisphere.

These findings were further expanded by psychologist Doreen Kimura and others, who developed behavioral methods to study how functions of the hemispheres differed in normal people. These involved presenting visual stimuli rapidly to either the left or right visual fields (and the opposite hemispheres). Normal right-handers were more accurate or faster in identifying words or nonsense syllables in the right visual field (left hemisphere) and in identifying or recognizing faces, facial expressions of emotion, line slopes or dot locations in the left visual field (right hemisphere).

Another method was "dichotic listening," in which two different sounds were presented simultaneously to the two ears. The right ear (left hemisphere) was better at identifying nonsense syllables, while the left ear (right hemisphere) excelled at identifying certain nonverbal sounds such as piano melodies or dog barks.

By 1970 or soon thereafter, the reign of the left brain was essentially ended. The large majority of researchers concluded that each side of the brain was a highly specialized organ of thought, with the right hemisphere predominant in a set of functions that complemented those of the left. Observations of patients with damage to one side of the brain, of split-brain patients and of normal individuals yielded consistent findings. There could no longer be any reasonable doubt: The right hemisphere, too, was a fully human and highly complex organ of thought.

It was not long before the new discoveries found their way into the popular media and into the educational community. Some mythmakers sought to sell the idea that human beings had neither the whole and unified brain described by Descartes, nor the half brain of Broca and Wernicke, but rather two brains, each devoted to its own tasks and operating essentially independently of the other. The right hemisphere was in control when an artist painted a portrait, but the left hemisphere was in control when the novelist wrote a book. Logic was the property of the left hemisphere, whereas creativity and intuition were properties of the right. Further, these two brains did not really work together in the same person. Instead, some people thought primarily with the right hemisphere, while others thought primarily with the left. Finally, given the presumed absolute differences between hemispheres, it was claimed that special subject matters and teaching strategies had to be developed to educate one hemisphere at a time, and that the standard school curriculums only educated the "logical" left hemisphere.

Notice that the new two-brain myth was based on two quite separate types of scientific findings. First was the fact that split-brain patients showed few obvious symptoms of their surgery in everyday life and far greater integrity of behavior than would be seen if two regions within a hemisphere had been surgically disconnected. Thus, it was assumed that each hemisphere could be considered to be an independent brain.

Second, a great deal of research had demonstrated that each hemisphere had its own functional "expertise," and that the two halves were complementary. Since language was the specialty of the left hemisphere, some people concluded that any verbal activity, such as writing a novel, depended solely on processes of the left hemisphere. Similarly, since visual and spatial functions were the specialties of the right hemisphere, some people inferred that any visuospatial activity, such as painting portraits, must depend solely on processes of that hemisphere. Even if thought and language were no longer synonymous, at least logic and language seemed to be. Since intuitions, by definition, are not accessible to verbal explanation, and since intuition and creativity seemed closely related, they were assigned to the right hemisphere.

Based, then, on the presumed independent functions of the two hemispheres, and on the fact that they dif-

*I*N THE LATE 19TH CENTURY WE WENT FROM BEING WHOLE-BRAINED CREATURES TO HALF-BRAINED.

fered in their specializations, the final leap was that different activities and psychological demands engaged different hemispheres while the opposite side of the brain merely idled along in some unconscious state.

The two-brain myth was founded on an erroneous premise: that since each hemisphere was specialized, each must function as an independent brain. But in fact, just the opposite is true. To the extent that regions are differentiated in the brain, they must integrate their activities. Indeed, it is precisely that integration that gives rise to behavior and mental processes greater than and different from each region's special contribution. Thus, since the central premise of the mythmakers is wrong, so are all the inferences derived from it.

What does the scientific evidence actually say? First, it says that the two hemispheres are so similar that when they are disconnected by split-brain surgery, each can function remarkably well, although quite imperfectly.

Second, it says that superimposed on this similarity are differences in the specialized abilities of each side. These differences are seen in the contrasting contributions each hemisphere makes to all cognitive activities. When a person reads a story, the right hemisphere may play a special role in decoding visual information, maintaining

an integrated story structure, appreciating humor and emotional content, deriving meaning from past associations and understanding metaphor. At the same time, the left hemisphere plays a special role in understanding syntax, translating written words into their phonetic representations and deriving meaning from complex relations among word concepts and syntax. But there is no activity in which only one hemisphere is involved or to which only one hemisphere makes a contribution.

Third, logic is not confined to the left hemisphere. Patients with right-hemisphere damage show more major logical disorders than do patients with left-hemisphere damage. Some whose right hemisphere is damaged will deny that their left arm is their own, even when the physician demonstrates its connection to the rest of the body. Though paralyzed on the left side of the body, such patients will often make grandiose plans that are impossible because of paralysis and will be unable to see their lack of logic.

Fourth, there is no evidence that either creativity or intuition is an exclusive property of the right hemisphere. Indeed, real creativity and intuition, whatever they may entail, almost certainly depend on an intimate collaboration between hemispheres. For example, one major French painter continued to paint with the same style and skill after suffering a left-hemisphere stroke and loss of language. Creativity can remain even after right-hemisphere damage. Another painter, Lovis Corinth, after suffering right-hemisphere damage, continued to paint with a high level of skill, his style more expressive and bolder than before. In the musical realm, researcher Harold Gordon found that in highly talented professional musicians, both hemispheres were equally skilled in discriminating musical chords. Further, when researchers Steven Gaede, Oscar Parsons and James Bertera compared people with high and low musical aptitude for hemispheric asymmetries, high aptitude was associated with equal capacities of the two sides of the brain.

Fifth, since the two hemispheres do not function independently, and since each hemisphere contributes its special capacities to all cognitive activities, it is quite impossible to educate

one hemisphere at a time in a normal brain. The right hemisphere is educated as much as the left in a literature class, and the left hemisphere is educated as much as the right in music and painting classes.

Finally, what of individual differences? There is both psychological and physiological evidence that people vary in the relative balance of activation of the two hemispheres. Further, there is a significant correlation between which hemisphere is more active and the relative degree of verbal or spatial skills. But there is no evidence that people are purely "left brained" or "right brained." Not even those with the most extremely asymmetrical activation between hemispheres think only with the more activated side. Rather, there is a continuum. The left hemisphere is more active in some people, to varying degrees, and verbal functioning is promoted to varying degrees. Similarly, in those with a more active right hemisphere, spatial abilities are favored. While activation patterns and cognitive patterns are correlated, the relationship is very far from perfect. This means that differences in activation of the hemispheres are but one of many factors affecting the way we think.

In sum, the popular myths are misinterpretations and wishes, not the observations of scientists. Normal people have not half a brain nor two brains but one gloriously differentiated

*I*T IS IMPOSSIBLE TO EDUCATE ONE HEMISPHERE AT A TIME IN A NORMAL BRAIN.

brain, with each hemisphere contributing its specialized abilities. Descartes was, essentially, right: We have a single brain that generates a single mental self.

How the brain really works its wonders

A new model of the brain is beginning to explain how it can do things the most powerful computers cannot—recognize faces, recall distant memories, make intuitive leaps. The key: Intricate networks that link together the brain's billions of nerve cells

"Imagine a block of wax. . . ." So wrote the Greek philosopher Plato more than 2,000 years ago to describe memory. Since then, scholars have invoked clocks, telephone switchboards, computers—and even a cow's stomach—in equally futile attempts to explain the mysterious workings of the brain.

But an explosion of recent findings in brain science—aided by new computer programs that can simulate brain cells in action—is now revealing that the brain is far more intricate than any mechanical device imaginable. For the first time, brain researchers are beginning to explain how the brain can call up distant memories from a vast storehouse of recollections and instantly recognize faces, odors and other complex patterns—tasks that even the most powerful electronic computers stumble over.

"For physicists, the most exciting time was during the birth of quantum mechanics earlier this century," says Christof Koch, a brain researcher at the California Institute of Technology. "We are seeing the same excitement now in neuroscience—we are beginning to get an understanding of how the brain really works."

Scientists are now coming to regard the brain as far from some kind of orderly, computerlike machine that methodically plods through calculations step by step. Instead, the new image of our "engine of thought" is more like a beehive or a busy marketplace, a seething swarm of densely interconnected nerve cells—called neurons—that are continually sending electrochemical signals back and forth to each other and altering their lines of communication with every new experience. It is in this vast network of neurons that our thoughts, memories and perceptions are generated in a cellular version of a New England town meeting.

This new view of the brain has burst into every corner of science where researchers think about thinking. Brain scientists are hoping that a comprehensive new theory of how the mind works will lead to ways to control afflictions such as epilepsy and Alzheimer's disease. Computer researchers are looking at how the brain computes in an attempt to give robots eyesight, hearing and memory and to build brainlike machines that can learn by themselves. The new model of the mind even has philosophers dusting off hoary questions about the nature of rationality and consciousness.

A meeting of minds

The revolution in understanding the brain has come about because of a marriage of two widely different fields—neurobiology and computer science—that would have been impossible a decade ago. For years, computer researchers attempting to create machines with humanlike intelligence all but ignored the complex details of the brain's anatomy. Instead, they tried to understand the mind at the more theoretical level of psychology—that is, in terms of the brain's behavior.

Neuroscientists, meanwhile, were focusing on the brain's biology, using microscopic probes to sample electrical pulses from the 100 billion neurons that make up the brain and trying to unravel the chemistry of how those neurons communicate with one another. Many neuroscientists, however, are now beginning to realize that the brain is far more than the sum of its parts. "Suppose you wanted to know how a computer worked," says Koch. "You could sample the signals at all the transistors, and you could crush some up and see what they're made of, but when you were finished you still wouldn't know how the computer operated. For

that, you need an understanding of how all the components work together."

With the recent development of inexpensive, powerful computers and the expansion of knowledge about the details of the brain's anatomy, researchers are finally teaming up with computer scientists to simulate the way neurons might join together in the vast networks that make up our mind. No one is suggesting this new approach will explain, neuron by neuron, how we fall in love or laugh at the Marx Brothers. Nor is it yet clear whether different types of neural networks are responsible for producing all the remarkable things the brain can do. But researchers are beginning to see the outlines of the brain's remarkable organization, which allows it to learn new skills, remember old events, see and hear and adapt itself to new situations.

Laboratory models of the brain—called neural networks—consist of a dozen to several hundred artificial neurons whose actions are simulated on a conventional digital computer, just as modern computers can simulate the way millions of particles of air flow around a fighter jet's wings. Just as a single neuron in the brain is connected to as many as 10,000 other neurons, each artificial neuron in a neural network is connected to many others, so that all the neurons can send signals to each other. Simple rules that mimic how actual neurons alter their communication pathways in the brain are programed into the simulations as well.

The result is a device that shares some properties with the real thing but is far easier for scientists to take apart, examine and run experiments on. "These things aren't toys," says Richard Granger, a brain researcher at the University of California at Irvine who uses neural networks to model how the brain processes smell. "These are from real brain. We put data from the lab into our model, and then we run our model to get predictions that we go back and test in the lab."

Researchers are creating neural networks that show how the brain makes general categories of odors such as cheese or fruit and distinguishes between specific odors such as Swiss or cheddar. Others are modeling the way a casual mention of a particular place or event can evoke a memory of a long-lost friend, how the brain organizes incoming signals from the eyes to give us vision and how neurons rearrange their connections to restore operations after a damaging stroke or in response to a new task.

The models are also giving researchers new insights into the dynamic process by which the brain does all these things. A neuron takes a million times longer to send a signal than a typical computer switch, yet the brain can recognize a familiar face in less than a second—a feat beyond the ability of the most powerful computers. The brain achieves this speed because, unlike the step-by-step computer, its billions of neurons can all attack the problem simultaneously.

This massive collection of neurons acting all at once makes decisions more in the manner of a New England town meeting than of a highly structured bureaucracy. The brain's freewheeling, collective style of processing information may explain why it has trouble doing mathematical computations that are easily done by a $5 calculator. But it may also be what gives the brain its enormous flexibility and the power to match patterns that are similar but not exact, draw scattered bits of visual data into a cohesive picture and make intuitive leaps.

Consider what the brain must do to recognize a smell, for example. It's unlikely that one barbecued-rib dinner will smell exactly like another or that the strength of the odor will be the same each time it is encountered. But a neural network doesn't simply check if the pattern of nerve signals coming from the ribs exactly matches any of the patterns stored in memory: Comparing patterns one by one would take far too long.

Instead, the network goes through a process analogous to a group of people debating evidence. Neurons that are highly activated by the odor signal strongly to other neurons, which in turn activate—or in some cases deactivate—others in the group, and those neurons will influence still others and feed back to the original senders. As the neurons signal back and forth, varying their levels of activity, the group as a whole evolves toward a pattern that most closely matches one in memory, a pattern that reflects

fundamental similarities among the many variations of how barbecued ribs smell.

Completing thoughts

This type of interactive process may be what allows the brain to recognize patterns that are slightly different or incomplete as nonetheless belonging to the same overall group. We are able to recognize all the different kinds of things we sit on as types of chairs, for example, even though we might have a hard time writing down exactly what it is about them that qualifies them as such. Likewise, small bits of a memory can trigger the whole memory, even if some of the incoming information is faulty: If someone asks if you have read the latest issue of *U.S. News & Global Report,* you still know which magazine he is talking about.

This kind of memory is possible because, just as some members of a town meeting outshout others, some neurons in a network have stronger communications pathways to their neighbors. These "rabble-rousing" neurons can have a strong influence on the way other neurons behave, and so even when only a few of them are activated, they can nudge the network in the right direction.

By simulating these processes in the lab, researchers are gaining surprising insights into how neural networks—and thus perhaps the brain itself—can perform these tasks. Granger and his colleague at the University of California at Irvine, neuroscientist Gary Lynch, used data from their lab experiments on neurons in a rat's olfactory system to create a neural-network simulation of smell recognition. The 500-neuron network was presented with groups of simulated odors, each containing variations of a general pattern such as cheese or flowers.

At first, the network responded with a unique pattern of activity for each odor. But as it processed more and more odors that were similar, those neurons that were repeatedly activated became stronger and stronger, eventually dampening the activity of other neurons that were less active. Eventually, these highly activated neurons became representatives of each category of smells: After a half-dozen samplings of the group, says Granger, the artificial brain circuit responded with the same pattern of neurons on the first sniff of any of several smells within one category. On subsequent sniffs, however, the neural network did something totally unexpected. The old pattern disappeared, and new neurons fired, creating a different pattern for each particular smell. "We're thrilled with it," says Granger. "With the first sniff, it recognizes the overall pattern and says: 'It's a cheese.' With the next sniffs, it distinguishes the pattern and says: 'It's Jarlsberg.'"

Studies of actual brain tissue are continually refining the ground rules that scientists program into these models—thus making them more realistic. One recently confirmed rule—that two neurons communicate more strongly if both have been active at the same time—has been incorporated into many neural network simulations. Often, such simple rules are enough to produce the striking result that a network will organize itself to perform a task such as smell recognition when given repeated stimuli.

Biological studies have also given some exciting confirmation that neural network models are on the right track. Recent experiments with neural networks that model vision in monkeys have also shown a surprising match with the actual biology of the brain. They may also explain how the growing brain of a fetus lays down its neural circuitry. Nearly two decades ago, Harvard University brain researchers Torsten Wiesel and David Hubel discovered that a monkey's brain has neurons that respond to very specific types of visual scenes such as spots of light or dark bars set at different angles. Yet these neurons are developed before birth—and before any light signals can influence the way they are organized.

Ralph Linsker, at the IBM Thomas J. Watson Research Center in Yorktown Heights, N.Y., has created a neural-network model of the brain's visual system that shows how the brain might be able to wire itself up spontaneously to do such tasks. Linsker's network consists of several sheets of neurons arranged in layers, with groups of neurons in one sheet connected to various individual neurons in the sheet above it. To make his network evolve, Linsker uses the same neuroscientific rules that govern how synapses in the brain increase their communication strength when the neurons they connect to are active at the same time.

Linsker starts his model off with random connections between neurons and feeds in a random pattern of stimulation to the neurons at the bottom layer. Just as with Granger's smell model, the network's simple reinforcement rules cause the neurons to organize themselves into groups for specific tasks. By the time the input pattern has worked its way up through the network, the neurons in the top layer have formed into specialized clusters that respond the most when bars of light with specific orientations are presented—just like the specialized neurons in the monkey's brain.

The network organizes itself because each neuron in one layer gets information from a committee of neurons in the layer below it. Those neurons that "vote" with the majority get reinforced while lone dissenters lose their influence. "As the

Accounting for emotion

Fear, happiness and love are all part of the mind's machinery

The brain does a lot more than think. At the very moment you're deciding which chess piece to move or whether to invest in stocks or mutual funds, your brain is regulating your body temperature, making sure you're standing upright, telling you if you're hungry or thirsty and reacting to the attractive man or woman in the next room.

And when it comes to fear, anger, love, sadness or any of the complicated mixtures of feeling and physical response we label emotions, a loose network of lower-brain structures and nerve pathways called the limbic system appears to be key. Researchers stimulating various parts of this system with an electrode can produce strong responses of pleasure, pain or aggression. A cat, for example, will hiss, spit and growl when an electrical probe is inserted at a specific spot in the hypothalamus—a part of the limbic system that is also involved in regulating appetite and other bodily functions. An electrode in another region of the hypothalamus triggers pleasure so intense that a rat will press a bar thousands of times to receive it—and die from starvation in the process.

The most recent research, however, indicates that the experience of emotion has less to do with specific locations in the brain and more to do with the complicated circuitry that interconnects them and the patterns of nerve impulses that travel among them. "It's a little like your television set," says neuroscientist Dr. Floyd Bloom of the Scripps Clinic and Research Foundation. "There are individual tubes, and you can say what they do, but if you take even one tube out, the television doesn't work."

A mugger or a cat? Researchers have been able to find out the most about primitive emotions like fear. Seeing a shadow flit across your path in a dimly lit parking lot will trigger a complex series of events. First, sensory receptors in the retina of your eye detect the shadow and instantly translate it into chemical signals that race to your brain. Different parts of the limbic system and higher-brain centers debate the shadow's importance. What is it? Have we encountered something like this before? Is it dangerous? Meanwhile, signals sent by the hypothalamus to the pituitary gland trigger a flood of hormones

alerting various parts of your body to the possibility of danger, and producing the response called "fight or flight": Rapid pulse, rising blood pressure, dilated pupils and other physiological shifts that prepare you for action. Hormone signals are carried through the blood, a much slower route than nerve pathways. So even after the danger is past—when your brain decides that the shadow is a cat's, not a mugger's—it takes a few minutes for everything to return to normal.

Fear is a relatively uncomplicated emotion, however. Sophisticated sentiments—sadness or joy, for example—are much harder to trace. And even primitive feelings such as fear or rage involve complex interactions with the higher parts of the brain—witness our ability to become fearful or angry about an abstract idea. The mechanics of these interactions are still out of reach, but the same computer models scientists are using now to understand thinking may someday shed light on emotions as well.

by Erica E. Goode

---

group develops a consensus," explains Linsker, "the mavericks get kicked out."

New connections

New studies have shown that, even though much of the brain's wiring is laid down in the womb, the connections between neurons can also be rearranged during adulthood. It is likely, in fact, that your brain has made subtle changes in its wiring since you began reading this article. More-substantial rearrangements are believed to occur in stroke victims who lose and then regain control of a limb. Michael Merzenich of the University of California at San Francisco first mapped the specific areas in a monkey's brain that were activated when different fingers on the monkey's hand were touched, then trained the monkey to use one finger predominantly in a task that earned it food. When Merzenich remapped the touch-activated areas of the monkey's brain, he found that the area responding to signals from that finger had expanded by nearly 600 percent. Merzenich found a similar rearrangement of processing areas when he simulated brain damage caused by a stroke.

Researchers Leif Finkel and Gerald M.

Edelman of Rockefeller University were able to duplicate these overall phenomena in a neural network when they applied a simple rule to the behavior of small groups of neurons. Groups of neurons were set up to "compete" for connections to the sensory nerves. The researchers found that when they gave one group an excessive input—analogous to training the monkey to use a particular finger—that patch grew in size. When that input was stopped, the patch grew smaller.

Working in concert

The biggest impact of neural networks may be in helping researchers explore how the brain does sophisticated information processing. Even though scientists can record signals from the individual neurons in the brain that might be involved in such a task as tracking an object with the eyes, they still don't know how the brain puts those millions of signals together to perform the computation. But because a neural network can adapt its connections in response to its experiences, it can be trained to learn sophisticated brainlike tasks—and then researchers can examine the artificial brain in detail to get

clues to how a real brain might be doing it.

In one study, for example, a neural network helped researchers explain how the brain is able to judge the position of an object from signals sent by neurons connected to the eyes. Brain scientists Richard Andersen of the Massachusetts Institute of Technology and David Zipser of the University of California at San Diego trained a neural network to do the task by giving it data recorded from a monkey's neurons as the animal tracked an object moving in front of it. Since the researchers already knew the position of the object that the nerve signals corresponded to, they were able to "train" the network to do the task: They gave the network a series of recorded input signals and let the network adjust itself until it consistently was able to give the right answer. The researchers then examined the network to reveal the complex calculations it uses to forge all the data into the correct answer.

These experiments suggest that some extremely complex feats of perception can, at least in theory, be explained by the interaction of many neurons, each of which performs a seemingly quite simple task. Terrence Sejnowski of Johns Hopkins University, for example, created a neural network that learned to judge how much a spherical object was curved by the way a beam of light cast a shadow on it. Much to his surprise, Sejnowski found that even though the network was trained to compute the object's shape from its shading, individual neurons within the network actually responded with the most activity when he later tested the network not with curved surfaces but with bars of light. In fact, the neurons responded just like the specialized neurons in the monkey's brain discovered years ago by Hubel and Wiesel—neurons that had long been assumed to be involved in helping the brain detect the straight edges of objects, not their curvature. "My network doesn't prove that those cells in the monkey's brain are actually there to compute curvature and not edges," says Sejnowski. "But it does mean that you can't make quick assumptions about what the entire brain is doing simply by sampling what individual neurons are doing. You need to look at the system as a whole." Several neuroscientists, inspired by Sejnowski's study,

plan to investigate whether such curvature-computing cells actually exist in the brain.

The ability of neural networks to learn to simulate these brainlike tasks has also inspired researchers who are interested in creating machines that act more like real brains. While conventional computers can perform powerful feats of number crunching, they are dismal failures at doing more-brainlike operations such as seeing, hearing, and understanding speech—things we usually take for granted but that are extremely complex computationally. "The things that distinguish us from monkeys—playing chess, for example—are easy for computers to do," says Caltech's Koch. "But when it comes to doing things we share with the animal kingdom, computers are awful. In computing vision or movement, for example, no computer comes even close to matching the abilities of a fly." Engineers at the National Aeronautics and Space Administration, the Defense Department and computer companies around the world are all busily scrambling to find

the best ways to implement neural networks on computer chips.

It may be a long time, however, before anybody is able to build a machine that actually works like a brain. After all, nature has had a 7-million-year head start on engineers, and researchers have never encountered anything as complex and ingeniously designed as the 3-pound lump of tissue inside your skull.

Meanwhile, the first steps at understanding how the brain really works have already been taken. Many brain researchers now believe that the bigger mysteries of how we make choices and use language—or why some memories last forever while others fade—will inevitably yield their secrets. Even the nature of the brain's creativity, attention and consciousness may someday be revealed. "Basically, the brain is a neural network —however complicated," says Andersen. "It will take time, but we will solve it."

by William F. Allman

ILLUSTRATIONS FROM JOURNAL OF EXPERIMENTAL PSYCHOLOGY

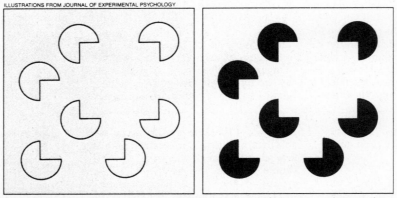

Perceiving depth: Though the two images above have the same shapes, the right one is perceived by the brain as two overlapping squares—evidence that the brain uses multiple visual clues simultaneously to judge depth

Spiral or circle? Try tracing it with your finger. Given conflicting cues, the brain chooses one interpretation over another

Is It One Clock, or Several, that Cycle Us Through Life?

Susan Cunningham

Staff Writer

As regular as the rising and the setting sun, every person's day is marked by cycles of the body. The most obvious, of course, is the inexorable rhythm of sleeping and waking. But there are many other organic functions in humans, as well as in animals, plants and lower organisms, that also follow 24-hour cycles.

Our body temperature is highest at noon, and dips by as much as one degree at its lowest point in the early morning. Blood sugar level, urine excretion, pulse and heart rates, plasma cortisol concentration and secretions of adrenal and most other hormones all follow daily patterns as well.

Hormones are released intermittently in varying amounts into the bloodstream; in the case of cortisol and growth hormone, the levels may vary by as much as 100 percent within a 24-hour period. In some animals, eating, drinking and other activities are regulated by internal clocks and occur at the same time each day.

The rhythms help explain why we are hungry, lively, tired, sleepy or irritable at certain times in the day. They help explain why women often go into labor in the small hours of the morning and why we work more efficiently at certain times of the day.

Greater knowledge about how these rhythms function and interact can help us explain and cope with the discomfiting feelings that accompany jet lag and shift work. They may eventually guide us in choosing the best time of day to administer a drug. If rhythm disorders are at the root of some depressive and manic-depressive illnesses, we may someday be able to treat them with new, even non-chemical, behavioral techniques.

But it has only been within the past 20 years that science has thoroughly discredited the still popularly entrenched idea that the cycles are regulated by light or some other change in the environment outside of the body. Daily rhythms are driven and synchronized by at least one self-sustaining biological clock within each organism. Today, at an accelerating speed, neuroscientists are discovering the nature and function of these internal timing mechanisms in most living things.

Daily rhythms are described as circadian. The word comes from combining the Latin *circa* (about) and *dies* (day). There are shorter and longer cycles which also seem to be governed by internal clocks, but even less is known about their physiological bases. Such rhythms as heart beat and electrical activity in the brain, which follow cycles of less than 24 hours, are called ultradian. Longer cycles, such as menstrual and estrous cycles, hibernation and seasonal gains and losses of weight are described as infradian.

With a series of experiments beginning in the 1950s, Colin Pittendrigh and Jurgen Aschoff demonstrated that external cues didn't control circadian rhythms.

Pittendrigh disproved the theory that circadian rhythms were learned by raising fruit flies in constant environmental conditions. Even when they weren't exposed to a 24-hour light-dark cycle, the flies still exhibited 24-hour rhythms.

Aschoff isolated people from normal temperature, light and sound cues in underground caverns outside Munich for as long as months at a time. He concluded that humans have spontaneous or ''free-running'' periods of activity and rest each day, although the entire cycle doesn't naturally take place over 24 hours. The most common cycle is about 25 hours. So, even though a person freed from environmental cues generally continues to sleep about eight hours, he or she rises an hour later each day.

Environmental changes don't control circadian rhythms, but in normal living, light, darkness, temperature, mealtimes and other environmental and social cues play an integral role in conveying information to which the internal clocks respond. In humans, these external cues reset the "hands" of the clock back an hour each day. Much circadian research today concentrates on the physical and biochemical mechanisms that underlie this resetting and resynchronization, which neuroscientists call entrainment.

Race for the Clock

Launching the race in the 1960s to identify a biological clock, Curt Richter ruled out many parts of the brain as possible pacemakers by a literal process of elimination. He removed, in turn, the adrenals, gonads, pituitary, thyroid and pineal glands of rats. He also gave them shock therapy, induced alcoholic stupors and convulsions and made lesions in various parts of their brains.

Nothing permanently disrupted the circadian rhythmicity of the rats' feeding, drinking and activity until he made lesions in the hypothalamus, the tiny structure deep in the forebrain between brainstem and cerebral hemispheres.

Subsequent research using lesions narrowed the site to the anterior portion of the hypothalamus. In 1972, two groups of researchers made lesions in a cluster of tiny neurons within the anterior hypothalamus of rats and independently discovered that they had destroyed the rats' daily rhythms of water drinking, physical activity and adrenal corticosterone secretion. The results were rapidly duplicated in hamsters, cats, squirrels and, in 1981, in the first nonhuman primates, rhesus monkeys.

The clusters are called the superchiasmatic nuclei (SCN). The nuclei, consisting of thousands of neurons, are each about 5 to 15 microns in diameter and sit on either side of the optic recess of the third ventricle, a fluid-filled space in the midline of the brain. A micron is one-thousandth of a millimeter. The SCN of hamsters, rats, monkeys and humans resemble each other in their general features and, from what little we know, appear to function similarly. From front to back, the SCN in humans are only two to three microns long.

Throughout the 1970s and early 1980s, the number of rhythms that were shown to be regulated by the SCN mounted. Today, we know that the SCN regulate sleeping and waking, heart and pulse rates, and the secretion of thyroid-stimulating hormone, testosterone, prolactin, thyrotropin, growth hormone and pineal N-acetyl-transferase. Pineal A-acetyltransferase is the enzyme controlling production of melatonin, the chief hormone of the pineal gland. Melatonin, in turn, inhibits sex hormone secretions.

Scientists already knew that estrous and menstrual cycles were regulated by biological clocks. But only now are they finding that they are linked to SCN, the daily clock. Newborn rats with SCN lesions fail to develop estrous cycles, and adult female rats with SCN lesions cease ovulating.

Irving Zucker, a psychologist at the University of California in Berkeley and one of the discoverers in 1972 of SCN function, has suggested that the lesions interfere with either the release or the transport of lutenizing hormone-releasing hormone (LHRH) to the pituitary. LHRH, in turn, influences the secretion of other hormones that trigger ovulation.

Most theories about which human functions are regulated by the SCN are extrapolations from data on monkeys. "Some of it is okay. None of it is great. It's reasonable to imagine that it applies to humans," commented Michael Menaker, a University of Oregon neuroscientist.

One rare clinical case offered further validation that the SCN function in humans similar to the way it does in animals.

An autopsy on a woman revealed that she had a tumor in her left ventricle that had virtually destroyed her SCN. Before she died, she had been troubled with excessive sleepiness. However, as is the case with SCN-lesioned animals, she could be easily roused. A tumor in another part of the brain would have caused a much deeper, coma-like sleep.

How Many Clocks?

Early discoveries about the regulatory power of SCN led many people to the conclusion that they were *the* biological clock. The current debate is not over whether SCN are an important clock—indisputably they are—but whether there are others, whether they are subsidiaries of the SCN or autonomous and whether they must be coordinated by the SCN or can take over the regulation of a rhythm when SCN are destroyed.

Tom Wehr, a psychiatrist conducting research on sleep cycles at NIMH, believes that SCN are the master clock in mammals and said "it's not fashionable now" to believe there are multiple clocks. On the other hand, Frank Sulzman, a neuroscientist at the State University of New York in Binghamton, is convinced that SCN are not the single oscillator, "at least not in primates."

As evidence he points to experiments that have shown that, when SCN are destroyed, the rhythms of core body temperature, plasma cortisol, urine potassium excretion and REM (rapid eye movement) sleep are not affected.

Sulzman concedes, however, that most of these experiments are controversial. As is frequently the case in neuroscience, researchers question whether the lesions done in the laboratory were complete. Even having a few SCN cells remain might be sufficient to generate a rhythm.

Another problem is the possibility that entraining agents, such as the light-dark cycle, can mask the effects of a clock. For example, an animal whose SCN has been destroyed often may continue its regular sleeping and activity rhythms. Damage to the clock is revealed only when the entraining agent is removed and the rhythm falls apart.

The strongest evidence for a second oscillator are frequently duplicated experiments showing the persistence of drinking and body temperature rhythms after the destruction of SCN.

In these experiments, SCN does destroy the usual temporal drinking patterns in the sense that drinking gradually becomes spread throughout the day. But the rodents and monkeys still drink the same amount in a 24-hour period as they did before the SCN lesions. One explanation is that there is at least one other, perhaps weaker, secondary oscillator which drives drinking behavior while the SCN coordinates it. In short, SCN may organize the *timing* of drinking behavior.

Numerous experiments have shown that body temperature rhythms likewise persist after the SCN are destroyed. Psychologist Evelyn Satinoff and her colleagues at the University of Illinois in Champaign-Urbana recently completed several years of experiments which showed that lesions in rats' SCN had no effect on the rhythms of body temperature. (The work has led her to believe that rhythms of adrenocorticotropic hormone also are controlled by a separate mechanism.)

Making lesions in the medial preoptic region, another part of the hypothalamus, Satinoff was able to disrupt but not destroy temperature rhythms in rats. Although the medial preoptic area must be intimately involved in regulating body temperature, Satinoff doesn't suggest that it or any other area of the brain is the single regulator for body temperature.

"I don't happen to believe we'll ever find enough data [for a temperature oscillator]. I think it's much more complicated than that . . . [and includes] peripheral blood flow and activity and all those things that make body temperature."

Different areas of the brain may have evolved separately to control the peak, trough, phase, amplitude, period and shape of the waves that measure temperature and other body rhythms, she suggested.

"It's perfectly reasonable to imagine there are other oscillators," said Menaker, "and they could be almost anywhere. There's no reason to exclude any part of the nervous system."

Some amphibians have an autonomous clock in their eyes. In lizards, birds and many vertebrates, although not in mammals, the pineal gland also seems to operate as an independent clock. Removed from animals and cultured, it continues to produce the hormone melatonin in the same rhythm it did within the organism.

"There may be a loop in which the SCN and the pineal are connected by nerves in one direction and hormones in the other, and they may be both oscillating," he speculates.

As scientists zero in on what makes SCN (and the other oscillators in plants and organisms such as fungi) oscillate, they are finding that individual cells oscillate on 24-hour cycles. "Any collection of cells might oscillate," Menaker said.

Satinoff and Menaker agree that the neuroscience of circadian rhythmicity is still in its infancy, that the body of solid research is still very small, and that the mechanisms of the clock are much more complex than anyone anticipated 13 years ago, when the functions of SCN were first discovered. "Everything starts with a nice simple story and then it gets a lot more complicated," commented Satinoff.

Because cycles of light and darkness seem to be such strong entraining agents in most animals, the next great search has been for the pathway or pathways by which light reaches the SCN. Some animals have photoreceptors in several parts of their brains. In adult mammals, however, the only site for light reception is the retina. Information it receives is transmitted neurochemically to the brain via the optic tracts.

Injecting the retina of rats with a radioactive chemical, Robert Y. Moore of the State University of New York at Stony Brook discovered in the early 1970s a bundle of nerve fibers that extended from the optic chiasm and terminated exclusively in the SCN. Neuroscientists thought initially that this pathway, the retinohypothalamic tract (RHT), was the means by which all rhythms were entrained by light.

Now, because of experiments in which other pathways were destroyed, "what's clear is that it is sufficient for entrainment, but it's equally clear that it's not the only pathway involved," explained Benjamin Rusak, a psychology professor at Dalhousie University in Nova Scotia.

Some of the newest research has established the importance of the pathway that runs from the optic chiasm to a thin wedge of cells between the dorsal and ventral geniculates in the hypothalamus. Newly recognized as a distinct structure, it is called the intergeniculate leaflet.

Rusak's colleague, Mary Harrington, and Gary Pickard of the University of Oregon recently have found that destroying the intergeniculate leaflet in rats produces advances and delays in rhythms. Other work has traced neuropeptide-Y (one of the chemical messengers of the nervous system) from the leaflet to the SCN.

At this point, Rusak said, there are many threads of information that have yet to be sewn together.

"The implications are that, when one does intergeniculate leaflet lesions, one could be producing indirect changes in the projections to the SCN." The functioning of the SCN may be damaged, he added, or the impact may be quite the opposite and the SCN may grow and change in response to the RHT being strengthened.

Even harder to trace than the incoming pathways to the SCN are the very fine outgoing fibers which convey temporal information from the SCN to the various parts of the body. But neural connections have been documented to several areas of the hypothalamus and the central nervous system, including the pituitary, pineal and brainstem areas.

Entrainment

Using noninvasive procedures, other kinds of experiments on how SCN interpret light information seems to offer more immediate applications for human health. Both Menaker and Sulzman are studying how pulses of light shift sleeping and other rhythms.

Menaker has found that two brief pulses of light per day, spaced 10 hours apart, will stimulate the growth of gonads in male hamsters otherwise kept totally in the dark. In natural conditions, their gonads begin to grow in the spring just prior to their breeding season. Unlikely as it may seem, the pulses of light seem to mimic the onset of spring. If the pulses are spaced only nine hours apart, mimicking the shorter days of winter, the gonads do not grow.

"It's not the amount of light, it's something about the time between when the light goes on and off," Menaker explained. "So you can represent the whole day just by starting and stopping it. The clock is involved in that measurement, and we're not sure how."

Sulzman is studying how the pulses of light shift circadian rhythms. The lower the species, the stronger the response.

He has found that a 10-minute pulse of light can permanently cause a 12-hour shift in the rhythms of fungi and fruit flies. With rodents, a 15-minute pulse of light can cause all rhythms to advance or be set backward by two hours. Collecting data on monkeys, Sulzman is now painstakingly plotting out which times are most sensitive to light and which set rhythms either forward or backward.

The work could someday help humans with rhythm disorders. A circadian rhythm disorder may be responsible, for example, for chronic insomnia. At the National Institute of Mental Health, Wehr and colleagues have had some success in advancing rhythms with sleep deprivation techniques. NIMH researchers are also treating people who suffer from "winter depression" by exposing them to intense light twice a day.

"The hypothesis is that, during the short days during the winter, the SCN is not getting enough light. So they have an inappropriate phase relationship to the world," Sulzman said.

Manic Depression

Because of the cyclicity of its symptoms, manic-depressive illness is a particularly attractive candidate as a circadian rhythm disorder. One exciting theory, Rusak noted, is that the mechanism that generates the rhythm abnormalities might be identical to the one that generates the abnormal symptoms of behavior and mood.

One reason that lithium is a successful treatment for many manic-depressives, according to Wehr, is that it may slow down the circadian clock by lengthening the phase of a rhythm. But manic-depressives and others with affective disorders may not just have abnormally fast clocks.

The problem might be a lack of synchronization among all their rhythms. It's possible that lithium may lengthen not only the period of an abnormal rhythm, but also lengthen rhythms that were normal. The hope is that drugs could be developed to act only on the abnormal disorders.

People with affective disorders have been reported to have abnormal hormone levels and the drugs with which they are treated can alter them. To Rusak, that treatment points to the importance of obtaining hormone samples many times throughout the day to chart an individual's peaks and troughs.

"The detection of abnormal *rhythms* of endocrine activity is as important a goal as the detection of abnormal levels," according to Rusak. A person that appears to have a low level of cortisol, for example, may in fact have shorter or longer phases—a different rhythm—than a normal control subject. Rusak conceded, however, that there are good reasons why such procedures have not been undertaken on humans: they would be very invasive with no guarantee of a benefit.

Franz Halberg is probably the leading proponent of a circadian approach to treating psychological and medical problems. Director of the chronobiology laboratories at the University of Minnesota, he coined the term "chronobiology" to describe the study of temporal relationships between metabolic, hormonal and neuronal processes. He believes not only that depressed people have clear abnormalities in their rhythms, but "you can also find differences in individuals at high or low risk for depression."

Halberg has also conducted experiments in which he administered chemotherapeutic drugs to cancerous animals. One of the problems with such drugs, of course, is that they may not only kill a tumor but also the patient. As many as 74 percent of rats died when a drug was administered at one time a day, while only 15 percent died at another. The synthesis of DNA in the bone marrow follows circadian cycles, and one theory is that the drug is most toxic to the animals at the beginning of the DNA synthesis phase.

Despite the clear implications in his work for the treatment of cancer patients, Halberg does not know of any drugs being developed with chronobiologic principles in mind. The same indifference has been shown by companies whose employees could benefit from findings that relate to coping with jet lag and shift work.

Scientists who conduct basic research on new fields traditionally face the question of the value of their work in improving the human condition. But those uncovering the physiology of circadian rhythms do not doubt that important applications will someday exist.

"Thirty years ago," noted Menaker, "when the structure of nucleic acid was first understood, it was completely unknown what benefits to mankind would come out of knowing the mechanisms of heredity. Certainly no one thought we could engineer plants with all the amino acids necessary to support animal life."

He recalled what Michael Faraday said when asked about the usefulness of his new invention, the electric motor. Replied Faraday, "What good is a baby?"

The Gene Hunt

Scientists launch a $3 billion project to map the chromosomes and decipher the complete instructions for making a human being

LEON JAROFF

Know then thyself . . . the glory, jest, and riddle of the world.
—Alexander Pope

In an obscure corner of the National Institutes of Health (NIH), molecular biologist Norton Zinder strode to a 30-ft.-long oval conference table, sat down and rapped his gavel for order. A hush settled over the Human Genome Advisory Committee, an unlikely assemblage of computer experts, biologists, ethicists, industry scientists and engineers. "Today we begin," chairman Zinder declared. "We are initiating an unending study of human biology. Whatever it's going to be, it will be an adventure, a priceless endeavor. And when it's done, someone else will sit down and say, 'It's time to begin.'"

With these words, spoken in January, Zinder formally launched a monumental effort that could rival in scope both the Manhattan Project, which created the A-bomb, and the Apollo moon-landing program—and may exceed them in importance. The goal: to map the human genome and spell out for the world the entire message hidden in its chemical code.

Genome? The word evokes a blank stare from most Americans, whose taxes will largely support the project's estimated $3 billion cost. Explains biochemist Robert Sinsheimer of the University of California at Santa Barbara: "The human genome is the complete set of instructions for making a human being." Those instructions are tucked into the nucleus of each of the human body's 100 trillion cells* and written in the language of deoxyribonucleic acid, the fabled DNA molecule.

In the 35 years since James Watson and Francis Crick first discerned the complex structure of DNA, scientists have managed to decipher only a tiny fraction of the human genome. But they have high hopes that with new, automated techniques and a huge coordinated effort, the genome project can reach its goal in 15 years.

The achievement of that goal would launch a new era in medicine. James Wyngaarden, director of the NIH, which will oversee the project, predicts that it will make "major contributions to understanding growth, development and human health, and open new avenues for therapy." Full translation of the genetic message would enable medical researchers to identify the causes of thousands of still mysterious inherited disorders, both physical and behavioral.

With this insight, scientists could more accurately predict an individual's vulnerability to such obviously genetic diseases as cystic fibrosis and could eventually develop new drugs to treat or even prevent them. The same would be true for more common disorders like heart disease and cancer, which at the very least have large genetic components. Better knowledge of the genome could speed development of gene therapy—the actual alteration of instructions in the hu-

*Except red blood cells, which have no nucleus.

man genome to eliminate genetic defects.

The NIH and the Food and Drug Administration have already taken a dramatic step toward gene therapy. In January they gave approval to Dr. W. French Anderson and Dr. Steven Rosenberg, both at the NIH, to transplant a bacterial gene into cancer patients. while this gene is intended only to make it easier for doctors to monitor an experimental cancer treatment and will not benefit the patients, its successful implantation should help pave the way for actual gene therapy.

The very thought of being able to read the entire genetic message, and perhaps alter it, is alarming to those who fear the knowledge could create many moral and ethical problems. Does genetic testing constitute an invasion of privacy, for example, and could it lead to more abortions and to discrimination against the "genetically unfit"? Should someone destined to be stricken with a deadly genetic disease be told about his fate, especially if no cure is yet available? Does it demean humans to have the very essence of their lives reduced to strings of letters in a computer data bank? Should gene therapy be used only for treating disease, or also for "improving" a person's genetic legacy?

Although scientists share many of these concerns, the concept of deciphering the human genome sends most of them into paroxysms of rapture. "It's the Holy Grail of biology," says Harvard biologist and Nobel laureate Walter Gilbert. "This information will usher in the Golden Age of molecular medicine," says Mark Pearson, Du Pont's director of molecular biology. Predicts George Cahill, a vice president at the Howard Hughes Medical Institute: "It's going to tell us everything. Evolution, disease, everything will be based on what's in that magnificent tape called DNA."

That kind of enthusiasm is infectious. In an era of budgetary restraint, Washington has been unblinkingly generous toward the genome project, especially since last April, when an array of scientists testified on the subject at a congressional committee hearing. There, Nobel laureate Watson of DNA fame, since picked by the NIH to head the effort, mesmerized listeners with his plea for support: "I see an extraordinary potential for human betterment ahead of us. We can have at our disposal the ultimate tool for understanding ourselves at the molecular level . . . The time to act is now."

Congress rose to the challenge. It promptly allocated more than $31 million for genome research to the NIH and to the Department of Energy and the National Library of Medicine, which are also involved in the quest. The combined appropriations rose to $53 million for fiscal 1989.

Even more will be needed when the effort is in full swing, involving hundreds of scientists, dozens of Government, university and private laboratories, and several computer and data centers. With contributions from other Government agencies and private organizations like the Hughes institute, the total annual cost of the project will probably rise to $200 million, which over 15 years will account for the $3 billion price tag.

The staggering expense and sheer size of the genome project were what bothered scientists most when the idea was first broached in 1985 by Sinsheimer, then chancellor of the University of California at Santa Cruz. "I thought Bob Sinsheimer was crazy," recalls Leroy Hood, a biologist at the California Institute of Technology. "It seemed to me to be a very big science project with marginal value to the science community."

Nobel laureate David Baltimore, director of M.I.T.'s Whitehead Institute, was one of the many who feared that such a megaproject would have much the same impact on biology that the shuttle had on the U.S. space program: soaking up so much money and talent that smaller but vital projects would dry up. Others stressed that the technology to do the job in a reasonable time was not available. But by 1986 some opponents realized they were fighting a losing battle. "The idea is gaining momentum. I shiver at the thought," said Baltimore then. Now, however, he approves of the way the project has evolved and has thrown his weight behind it.

What really turned the tide was a February 1988 report by the prestigious National Research Council enthusiastically endorsing a project that would first map and interpret important regions of the genome, then—as better technology became available—proceed to reading the entire genetic message. Most of the remaining critics were silenced last fall when the NIH chose the respected Watson as project director. Still, some scientists remain wary of the project. Says David Botstein, a vice president at Genentech and a member of the Human Genome Advisory Committee: "We need to test its progress, regulate its growth and slap it down if it becomes a monster. Jim Watson understands the dangers as well as any of us."

The concern, as well as the cost, reflects the complexity of the human genome and the magnitude of the effort required to understand it. DNA is found in the human-cell nucleus in the form of 46 separate threads, each coiled into a packet called a chromosome. Unraveled and tied together, these threads would form a fragile string more than 5 ft. long but only 50 trillionths of an inch across.

And what a wondrous string it is. As Watson and Crick discovered in 1953, DNA consists of a double helix, resembling a twisted ladder with sidepieces made of sugar and phosphates and closely spaced connecting rungs. Each rung is called a base pair because it consists of a pair of complementary chemicals called nitrogenous bases, attached end to end, either adenine (A) joined to thymine (T) or cytosine © attached to guanine (G).

Fundamental to the genius of DNA is the fact that A and T are mutually attractive, as are C and G. Consequently, when DNA separates during cell division, coming apart at the middle of each rung like a zipper opening, an exposed T half-rung on one side of the ladder will always attract an A floating freely in the cell. The corresponding A half-rung on the other section of the ladder will attract a floating T, and so on, until two double helixes, each identical to the original DNA molecule, are formed.

Even more remarkable, each of the four bases represents a letter in the genetic code. The three-letter "words" they spell, reading in sequence along either side of the ladder, are instructions to the cell on how to assemble amino acids into the proteins essential to the structure and life of its host. Each complete DNA "sentence" is a gene, a discrete segment of the DNA string responsible for ordering the production of a specific protein.

Reading these genetic words and deciphering their meaning is apparently a snap for the clever machinery of a cell. But for mere scientists it is a formidable and time-consuming task. For instance, a snippet of DNA might read ACGGTAGAT, a message that researchers can decipher rather easily. It codes for a sequence of three of the 20 varieties of amino acids that constitute the building blocks of proteins. But the entire genome of even the simplest organism dwarfs that snippet. The genetic blueprint of the lowly E. coli bacterium, for one, is more than 4.5 million base pairs long. For a microscopic yeast plant, the length is 15 million units. And in a human being, the genetic message is some 3 billion letters long.

Like cartographers mapping the ancient world, scientists over the past three decades have been laboriously charting human DNA. Of the estimated 100,000-odd genes that populate the genome, just 4,550 have been identified. And only 1,500 of those have been roughly located on the various chromosomes. The message of the genes has been equally difficult to come by. Most genes consist of between 10,000 and 150,000 code letters, and only a few genes have been completely deciphered. Long segments of the genome, like the vast uncharted regions of early maps, remain terra incognita.

To complicate matters, between the segments of DNA that represent genes are endless stretches of code letters that seem to spell out only genetic gibberish. Geneticists once thought most of the unintelligible stuff was "junk DNA"—useless sequences of code letters that accidentally developed during evolution and were not discarded. That concept has changed. "My feeling is there's a lot of very useful information buried in the sequence," says Nobel laureate Paul Berg of Stanford University. "Some of it we will know how to interpret; some we know is going to be gibberish."

In fact, some of the nongene regions on the genome have already been identified as instructions necessary for DNA to replicate itself during cell division. Their message is obviously detailed and complex. Explains George Bell, head of genome studies at Los Alamos National Laboratory: "It's as if you had a rope that was maybe 2 in. in diameter and 32,000 miles long, all neatly arranged inside a structure the size of a superdome. When the appropriate signal comes, you have to unwind the rope, which consists of two strands, and copy each strand so you end up with two new ropes that again have to fold up. The machinery to do that cannot be trivial."

One of the most formidable tasks faced by geneticists is to learn the nature of that machinery and other genetic instructions buried in the lengthy, still undeciphered base sequences. To do so fully requires achievement of the project's most challenging goal: the "sequencing" of the entire human genome. In other words, the identification and listing in order of all the genome's 3 billion base pairs.

That effort, says Caltech research fellow Richard Wilson, "is analogous to going around and shaking hands with everyone on earth." The resulting string of code letters, according to the 1988 National Research Council report urging adoption of the genome project, would fill a million-page book. Even then, much of the message would be obscure. To decipher it, researchers would need more powerful computer systems to roam the length of the genome, seeking out meaningful patterns and relationships.

It was from the patterns and relationships of pea plants that a concept of heredity first arose in the mind of Gregor Mendel, an Austrian monk. In 1865, after studying the flower colors and other characteristics of many generations of pea plants, Mendel formulated the laws of heredity and suggested the existence of packets of genetic information, which became known as genes. Soon afterward, chromosomes were observed in the nuclei of dividing cells, and scientists later discovered a chromosomal difference between the sexes. One chromosome, which they named Y, was found in human males' cells, together with another, called X. Females' cells, on the other hand, had two copies of X.

ut it was not until 1911 that a gene, only a theoretical entity at the time, was correctly assigned to a particular chromosome. After studying the pedigrees of several large families with many color-blind members (males are primarily affected), Columbia University scientist E.B. Wilson applied Mendelian logic and proved that the trait was carried on the X chromosome. In the same manner over the next few decades, several genes responsible for such gender-linked diseases as hemophilia were assigned to the X chromosome and a few others attributed to the Y.

Scientists remained uncertain about the exact number of human chromosomes until 1956, when improved photomicrographs of dividing cells clearly established that there were 46. This revelation led directly to identification of the cause of Down syndrome (a single extra copy of chromosome 21) and other disorders that result from distinctly visible errors in the number or shape of certain chromosomes.

But greater challenges lay ahead. How could a particular gene be assigned to any of the nonsex chromosomes? Scientists cleverly tackled that problem by fusing human cells with mouse cells, then growing hybrid mouse-human cells in the laboratory. As the hybrid cells divided again and again, they gradually shed their human chromosomes until only one—or simply a fragment of one—was left in the nucleus of each cell.

By identifying the kind of human protein each of these hybrid cells produced, the researchers could deduce that the gene responsible for that protein resided in the surviving chromosome. Using this method, they assigned hundreds of genes to specific chromosomes.

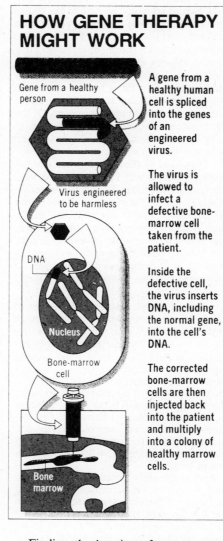

HOW GENE THERAPY MIGHT WORK

Gene from a healthy person

Virus engineered to be harmless

DNA

Nucleus

Bone-marrow cell

Bone marrow

A gene from a healthy human cell is spliced into the genes of an engineered virus.

The virus is allowed to infect a defective bone-marrow cell taken from the patient.

Inside the defective cell, the virus inserts DNA, including the normal gene, into the cell's DNA.

The corrected bone-marrow cells are then injected back into the patient and multiply into a colony of healthy marrow cells.

Finding the location of a gene on a chromosome is even more complicated. But over the past several years, scientists have managed to draw rough maps of all the chromosomes. They determine the approximate site of the genes, including many associated with hereditary diseases, by studying patterns of inheritance in families and chopping up their DNA strands for analysis. With this technique, they have tracked down the gene for cystic fibrosis in the midsection of chromosome 7, the gene for a rare form of colon cancer midway along the long arm of chromosome 5, and the one for familial Alzheimer's disease on the long arm of chromosome 21.

One of the more dramatic hunts for a disease gene was led by Nancy Wexler, a neuropsychologist at Columbia University and president of the Hereditary Disease Foundation. Wexler was highly motivated; her mother died of Huntington's disease, a debilitating and painful disorder that usually strikes adults between the ages of 35 and 45 and is invariably fatal. This meant that Wexler had a 50% chance of inheriting the gene from her mother and contracting the disease.

In a search coordinated by Wexler's foundation, geneticist James Gusella of Massachusetts General Hospital discovered a particular piece of DNA, called a genetic marker, that seemed to be present in people suffering from Huntington's disease. His evidence suggested that the marker must be near the Huntington's disease gene on the same chromosome, but he needed a larger sample to confirm his findings. This was provided by Wexler, who had previously traveled to Venezuela to chart the family tree of a clan of some 5,000 people, all of them descendants of a woman who died of Huntington's disease a century ago. Working with DNA samples from affected family members, Gusella and Wexler in 1983 concluded that they had indeed found a Huntington's marker, which was located near one end of chromosome 4.

That paved the way for a Huntington's gene test, which is now available. The actual gene has not yet been isolated and since there is no cure at present, many people at risk for Huntington's are reluctant to take it. "Before the test," Wexler says, "you can always say, 'Well, it can't happen to me.' After the test, if it is positive, you can't say that anymore." Has Wexler, 43, taken the test? "People need to have some privacy," she answers.

Tracking down the location of a gene requires tedious analysis. But it is sheer adventure when compared with the task of determining the sequence of base pairs in a DNA chain. Small groups of scientists, working literally by hand, have spent years simply trying to sequence a single gene. This hands-on method of sequencing costs as much as a dollar per base pair, and deciphering the entire genome by this method might take centuries.

The solution is automation. "It will improve accuracy," says Stanford's Paul Berg. "It will remove boredom; it will accomplish what we want in the end." The drive for automation has already begun; a machine designed by Caltech biologist Leroy Hood can now sequence 16,000 base pairs a day. But Hood, a member of the Genome Advisory Committee, is hardly satisfied. "Before we can seriously take on the genome initiative," he says, "we will want to do 100,000 to a million a day." The cost, he hopes, will eventually drop to a penny per base pair.

Hood is not alone in his quest for automation. That is also the goal of Columbia University biochemist Charles Cantor, recently appointed by the Energy Department to head one of its two genome centers. "It's largely an engineering project," Cantor explains, intended to produce tools for faster, less expensive sequencing and to develop data bases and computer programs to scan the data. Not to be outdone, Japan has set up a consortium of four high-tech companies to establish an automated assembly line, complete with robots, that researchers hope will be capable of sequencing 100,000 base pairs a day within three years.

Is there a better way? In San Francisco in January, Energy Department scientists displayed a photograph of a DNA strand magnified a million times by a scanning tunneling microscope. It was the first direct image of the molecule. If sharper images can be made, the scientists suggested, it may be possible to read the genetic code directly. But that day seems very far off.

Even before the Human Genome Project was begun by the NIH, others were deeply involved in probing the genome. Building on a long-standing program of research on DNA damage caused by radiation, biologist Charles DeLisi in 1987 persuaded the Energy Department to launch its own genome program. In addition to the sequencer and computer-hardware engineering projects, Energy Department scientists are focusing their attention on mapping seven complete chromosomes.

ictor McKusick, a geneticist at Johns Hopkins University, was much earlier in the game much earlier. He has been cataloging genes since 1959, compiling findings in his regularly updated publication, *Mendelian Inheritance in Man*. In August 1987 he introduced an electronic version that scientists around the world can tap into by computer. At the end of December it contained information on all the 4,550 genes identified to date. Says McKusick: "That's an impressive figure, but we still have a long way to go." Several other libraries of genetic information are already functioning, among them GenBank at the Los Alamos National Laboratory and the Howard Hughes Medical Institute's Human Gene Mapping Library in New Haven, Conn.

McKusick also directs the Human Genome Organization (known informally as "Victor's HuGO"), a group formed last September in Montreux, Switzerland, by 42 scientists representing 17 nations. "The U.N. of gene mapping," as McKusick describes it, plans to open three data-collection and -distribution sites, one each in Japan, North America and Europe.

Geneticist Ray White, formerly at M.I.T., has established a major center for genetic-linkage mapping at the University of Utah in Salt Lake City. In 1980 he began a study of 50 large families, collecting their blood samples, extracting white blood cells, which he multiplies in cell cultures, then preserving them in freezers.

Working with family pedigrees and DNA extracted from the cell bank, White and his group have identified more than 1,000 markers, each about 10 million base pairs apart, on all the chromosomes. They have also been major contributors to the Center for the Study of Human Polymorphisms, set up in Paris by French Nobel laureate Jean Dausset to coordinate an international effort to map the genes. Of the 40 families whose cell lines reside in CEPH's major data banks, 27 have been provided by White's group.

How and if these and other genetic research efforts will be coordinated with the Human Genome Project is a question being pondered by director Watson and his advisory committee. "Right now," says Watson, "the program supports people through individual research grants. We have to build up around ten research centers, each with specific objectives, if we want to do this project in a reasonable period of time."

The effort will also include studies of genes in other organisms, such as mice and fruit flies. "We've got to build a few places that are very strong in mouse genetics," Watson says, "because in order to interpret the human, we need to have a parallel in the mouse." Explains Genentech's Botstein: "Experimentation with lower organisms will illuminate the meaning of the sequence in humans." For example, genes that control growth and development in the fruit fly are virtually identical to oncogenes, which cause cancer in humans.

One of the early benefits of the genome project will be the identification of more and more of the defective genes responsible for the thousands of known inherited diseases and development of tests to detect them. Like those already used to find Huntington's and sickle-cell markers, for example, these tests will allow doctors to predict with near certainty that some patients will fall victim to specific diseases and that others are vulnerable and could be stricken.

University of Utah geneticist Mark Skolnick is convinced that mapping the genome will radically change the way medicine is practiced. "Right now," he says, "we wait for someone to get sick so we can cut them and drug them. It's pretty old stuff. Once you can make a profile of a person's genetic predisposition to disease, medicine will finally become predictive and preventive."

Eventually, says Mark Guyer of the NIH's Human Genome Office, people might have access to a computer readout of their own genome, with an interpretation of their genetic strengths and weaknesses. At the very least, this would enable them to adopt an appropriate life-style, choosing the proper diet, environment and—if necessary—drugs to minimize the effects of genetic disorders.

The ever improving ability to read base-pair sequences of genes will enable researchers to speed the discovery of new proteins, assess their role in the life processes, and use them—as the interferons and interleukins are already used—for fighting disease. It will also help them pinpoint missing proteins, such as insulin, that can correct genetic diseases.

Mapping and sequencing the genes should accelerate progress in another highly touted and controversial discipline: gene therapy. Using this technique, scientists hope someday to cure genetic diseases by actually inserting good genes into their patients' cells. One proposed form of gene therapy would be used to fight beta-thalassemia major, a blood disease characterized by severe anemia and caused by the inability of hemoglobin to function properly. That inability results from the lack of a protein in the hemoglobin, a deficiency that in turn is caused by a defective gene in bone-marrow cells.

To effect a cure, doctors would remove bone-marrow cells from a patient and expose them to a retrovirus* engineered to carry correctly functioning versions of the patient's faulty gene. When the retrovirus invaded a marrow cell, it would insert itself into the cellular DNA, as retroviruses are wont to do, carrying the good gene with it. Reimplanted in the marrow, the altered marrow cells would take hold and multiply, churning out the previously lacking protein and curing the thalassemia patient.

Easier said than done. Scientists have had trouble getting such implanted genes to "turn on" in their new environment, and they worry about unforeseen consequences if the gene is inserted in the wrong place in a chromosome. Should the gene be slipped into the middle of another vital gene, for example, it might disrupt the functioning of that gene, with disastrous consequences. Also, says M.I.T. biologist Richard Mulligan, there are limitations to the viral insertion of genes. "Most genes," he explains, "are too big to fit into a retrovirus."

Undaunted, researchers are refining their techniques in experiments with mice, and Mulligan believes that the first human-gene-therapy experiments could oc-

---

*A virus consisting largely of RNA, a single-stranded chain of bases similar to the DNA double helix.

cur in the next three years. Looking further ahead, other scientists are experimenting with a kind of genetic microsurgery ·that bypasses the retrovirus, mechanically inserting genes directly into the cell nucleus.

Not only those with rare genetic disorders could benefit from the new technology. Says John Brunzell, a University of Washington medicine professor: "Ten years ago, it was thought that only 10% of premature coronary heart disease came from inherited abnormalities. Now that proportion is approaching 80% to 90%.

Harvard geneticist Philip Leder cites many common diseases—hypertension, allergies, diabetes, heart disease, mental illness and some (perhaps all) cancers—that have a genetic component. Unlike Huntington's and Tay-Sachs diseases, which are caused by a single defective gene, many of these disorders have their roots in several errant genes and would require genetic therapy far more sophisticated than any now even being contemplated. Still, says Leder, "in the end, genetic mapping is going to have its greatest impact on these major diseases."

Of all the enthusiasm that the ge-

nome project has generated among scientists and their supporters in Washington, however, none matches that of James Watson as he gears up for the monumental task ahead. "It excites me enormously," he says, and he remains confident that it can be accomplished despite the naysayers both within and outside the scientific community. "How can we not do it?" he demands. "We used to think our fate was in our stars. Now we know, in large measure, our fate is in our genes." —***Reported by J. Madeleine Nash/ San Francisco and Dick Thompson/Washington***

A Pleasurable Chemistry

Endorphins, the body's natural narcotics, aren't something we have to run after.
They're everywhere.

Janet L. Hopson

Janet L. Hopson, who lives in Oakland, California, gets endorphin highs by contributing to Psychology Today.

Welcome aboard the biochemical bandwagon of the 1980s. The magical, morphine-like brain chemicals called endorphins are getting a lot of play. First we heard they were responsible for runner's high and several other cheap thrills. Now we're hearing that they play a role in almost every human experience from birth to death, including much that is pleasurable, painful and lusty along the way.

Consider the following: crying, laughing, thrills from music, acupuncture, placebos, stress, depression, chili peppers, compulsive gambling, aerobics, trauma, masochism, massage, labor and delivery, appetite, immunity, near-death experiences, playing with pets. Each, it is claimed, is somehow involved with endorphins. Serious endorphin researchers pooh-pooh many or most of these claims but, skeptics notwithstanding, the field has clearly sprinted a long way past runner's high.

Endorphin research had its start in the early 1970s with the unexpected discovery of opiate receptors in the brain. If we have these receptors, researchers reasoned, then it is likely that the body produces some sort of opiate- or morphine-like chemicals. And that's exactly what was found, a set of relatively small biochemicals dubbed "opioid peptides" or "endorphins" (short for "endogenous morphines") that plug into the receptors. In other words, these palliative peptides are sloshing around in our brains, spines and bloodstreams, apparently acting just like morphine. In fact, morphine's long list of narcotic effects was used as a treasure map for where scientists might hunt out natural opiates in the body. Morphine slows the pulse and depresses breathing, so they searched in the heart and lungs. Morphine deadens pain, so they looked in the central and peripheral nervous systems. It disturbs digestion and elimination, so they explored the gut. It savages the sex drive, so they probed the reproductive and endocrine systems. It triggers euphoria, so they scrutinized mood.

Nearly everywhere researchers looked, endorphins or their receptors were present. But what were they doing: transmitting nerve impulses, alleviating pain, triggering hormone release, doing several of these things simultaneously or disintegrating at high speed and doing nothing at all? In the past decade, a trickle of scientific papers has become a tidal wave, but still no one seems entirely certain of what, collectively, the endorphins are doing to us or for us at any given time.

Researchers do have modern-day sextants for their search, including drugs such as naloxone and naltrexone. These drugs, known as opiate blockers, pop into the endorphin receptors and block the peptides' normal activity, giving researchers some idea of what their natural roles might be. Whatever endorphins are doing, however, it must be fairly subtle. As one researcher points out, people injected with opiate blockers may feel a little more pain or a little less "high," but no one gasps for breath, suffers a seizure or collapses in a coma.

Subtle or not, endorphins are there, and researchers are beginning to get answers to questions about how they touch our daily lives—pain, exercise, appetite, reproduction and emotions.

•ANSWERS ON ANALGESIA: A man falls off a ladder, takes one look at his right hand—now cantilevered at a sickening angle—and knows he has a broken bone. Surprisingly, he feels little pain or anxiety until hours later, when he's home from the emergency room. This physiological grace period, which closely resembles a sojourn on morphine, is a common survival mechanism in the animal world, and researchers are confident that brain opiates are responsible for such cases of natural pain relief. The question is how do they work and, more to the point, how can we make them work for us?

The answers aren't in, but researchers have located a pain control system in the periaquaductal gray (PAG), a tiny region in the center of the brain, and interestingly, it produces opioid peptides. While no one fully understands how this center operates, physicians can now jolt it with electric current to lessen chronic pain.

One day in 1976, as Navy veteran Dennis Hough was working at a hospital's psychiatric unit, a disturbed patient snapped Hough's back and ruptured three of his vertebral discs. Five years later, after two failed back operations, Hough was bedridden with constant shooting pains in his legs, back and shoulders and was depressed to the point of suicide. Doctors were just then pioneering a technique of implanting platinum electrodes in the PAG, and Hough soon underwent the skull drilling and emplacement. He remembers it as "the most barbaric thing I've ever experienced, including my tour of duty in Vietnam," but the results were worth the ordeal; For the past seven years, Hough has been able to stimulate his brain's own endorphins four times a day by producing a radio signal from a transmitter on his belt. The procedure is delicate—too much current and his eyes flutter, too little and the pain returns in less than six hours. But it works dependably, and Hough not only holds down an office job now but is engaged to be married.

Researchers would obviously like to find an easier way to stimulate the brain's own painkillers, and while they have yet to find it, workers in many labs are actively developing new drugs and treatments. Some physicians have tried direct spinal injections of endorphins to alleviate postoperative pain. And even the most cynical now seem to agree that acupuncture works its magic by somehow triggering the release of endorphins. There may, however, be an even easier path to pain relief: the power of the mind.

Several years ago, neurobiologist Jon Levine, at the University of California, San Francisco, discovered that the placebo effect (relief) based on no known action other than the patient's belief in a treatment) can itself be blocked by naloxone and must therefore be based on endorphins. Just last year Levine was able to quantify the effects: One shot of placebo can equal the relief of 6 to 8 milligrams of morphine, a low but fairly typical dose.

Another line of research suggests that endorphins may be involved in self-inflicted injury—a surprisingly common veterinary and medical complaint and one that, in many cases, can also be prevented with naloxone. Paul Millard Hardy, a behavioral neurologist at Boston's New England Medical Center, believes that animals may boost endorphin levels through self-inflicted pain and then "get caught in a self-reinforcing positive feedback loop." He thinks something similar may occur in compulsive daredevils and in some cases of deliberate self-injury. One young woman he studied had injected pesticide into her own veins by spraying Raid into an intravenous needle. This appalling act, she told Hardy, "made her feel better, calmer and almost high."

Hardy also thinks endorphin release might explain why some autistic children constantly injure themselves by banging their heads. Because exercise is believed to be an alternate route to endorphin release, Hardy and physician Kiyo Kitahara set up a twice-a-day exercise program for a group of autistic children. He qualifies the evidence as "very anecdotal at this point" but calls the results "phenomenal."

•RUNNER'S HIGH, RUNNER'S CALM: For most people, "endorphins" are synonymous with "runner's high," a feeling of well-being that comes after an aerobic workout. Many people claim to have experienced this "high," and remarkable incidents are legion. Take, for example, San Francisco runner Don Paul, who placed 10th in the 1979 San Francisco Marathon and wound up with his ankle in a cast the next day. Paul had run the 26 miles only vaguely aware of what turned out to be a serious stress fracture. Observers on the sidelines had to tell him he was "listing badly to one side for the last six miles." He now runs 90 miles per week in preparation for the U.S. men's Olympic marathon trial and says that when he trains at the level, he feels "constantly great. Wonderful."

Is runner's high a real phenomenon based on endorphins? And can those brain opiates result in "exercise addiction"? Or, as many skeptics hold, are the effects on mood largely psychological? Most studies with humans have found rising levels of endorphins in the blood during exercise.

However, says exercise physiologist Peter Farrell of Pennsylvania State University, "when we look at animal studies, we don't see a concurrent increase in the brain." Most circulating peptides fail to cross into the brain, he explains, so explaining moods like runner's high based on endorphin levels in the blood is questionable. Adds placebo expert Jon Levine, "Looking for mood changes based on the circulating blood is like putting a voltmeter to the outside of a computer and saying 'Now I know how it works.' " Nevertheless, Farrell exercises religiously: "I'm not going to waste my lifetime sitting around getting sclerotic just because something's not proven yet."

Murray Allen, a physician and kinesiologist at Canada's Simon Fraser University, is far more convinced about the endorphin connection. He recently conducted his own study correlating positive moods and exercise—moods that could be blocked by infusing the runner with naloxone. Allen thinks these moods are "Mother Nature's way of rewarding us for staying fit" but insists that aerobic exercisers don't get "high." Opioid peptides "slow down and inhibit excess activity in the brain," he says. "Many researchers have been chasing after psychedelic, excitable responses." The actual effect, he says, is "runner's calm" and extremes leading to exhaustion usually negate it.

In a very similar experiment last year, a research team at Georgia State University found the mood-endorphin link more elusive. Team member and psychologist Wade Silverman of Atlanta explains that only those people who experience "runner's high" on the track also noticed it in the lab. Older people and those who ran fewer, not more, miles per week were also more likely to show a "high" on the test. "People who run a lot—50 miles per week or more—are often drudges, masochists, running junkies," says Silverman. "They don't really enjoy it. It hurts." For optimum benefits. Silverman recommends running no more than three miles per day four times a week.

Silverman and Lewis Maharam, a sports medicine internist at Manhattan's New York Infirmary/Beekman Downtown Hospital, both agree that powerful psychological factors—including heightened sense of self-esteem and self-discipline—contribute to the "high" in those who exercise moderately. Maharam would still like to isolate and quantify the role of endorphins, however, so he could help patients "harness the high." He would like to give people "proper exercise prescriptions," he says, "to stimulate the greatest enjoyment and benefit from exercise. If we could encourage the 'high' early on, maybe we could get people to want to keep exercising from the start."

The questions surrounding exercise, mood and circulating endorphins remain. But even if opioids released into the bloodstream from, say, the adrenal glands don't enter the brain and give a "high" or a "calm," several studies show that endorphins in the blood do bolster the immune system's activity. One way or the other, regular moderate exercise seems destined to make us happy.

•APPETITE CLOCKS AND BLOCKS: Few things in life are more basic to survival and yet more pleasurable than eating good food—and where survival and pleasure intersect, can the endorphins be far behind? To keep from starving, an animal needs to know when, what and how much to eat, and researchers immediately suspected that opioid peptides might help control appetite and satiety. People, after all, have long claimed that specific foods such as chili peppers or sweets give them a "high." And those unmistakably "high" on morphine or heroin experience constipation, cravings and other gastrointestinal glitches.

Indeed, investigators quickly located opiate receptors in the alimentary tract and found a region of the rat's hypothalamus that—when injected with tiny amounts of beta endorphin—will trigger noshing of particular nutrients. Even a satiated rat will dig heartily into fats, proteins or sweets when injected with the peptide. Neurobiologist Sarah Leibowitz and her colleagues at Rockefeller University produced this result and also found that opiate blockers would prevent the snack attack—strong evidence that endorphins help regulate appetite. The opiates "probably enhance the hedonic, pleasurable, rewarding properties" of fats, proteins and sweets—foods that can help satiate an animal far longer than carbohydrates so it can survive extended periods without eating.

Intriguingly, rats crave carbohydrates at the beginning of their 12-hour activity cycles, but they like fats, proteins or sweets before retiring—a hint that endorphins control not just the nature but the timing of appetites. Leibowitz suspects that endorphins also help control cravings in response to stress and starvation, and that disturbed endorphin systems may, in part, underlie obesity and eating disorders. Obese people given opiate blockers, for example, tend to eat less; bulimics often gorge on fat-rich foods; both bulimics and anorexics often have abnormal levels of endorphins; and in anorexics, food deprivation enhances the release of opiates in the brain. This brain opiate reward, some speculate, may reinforce the anorexic's self-starvation much as self-injury seems to be rewarding to an autistic child.

Researchers such as Leibowitz are hoping to learn enough about the chemistry of appetite to fashion a binge-blocking drug as well as more effective behavioral approaches to over- or undereating. In the meantime, people who try boosting their own endorphins through exercise, mirth or music may notice a vexing increase in their taste for fattening treats.

•PUBERTY, PREGNANCY AND PEPTIDES: Evolution has equipped animals with two great appetites—the hunger for food to prevent short-term disintegration and the hunger for sex and reproduction to prevent longer-term genetic oblivion. While some endorphin researchers were studying opioids and food hunger, others began searching for a sex role—and they found it.

Once again, drug addiction pointed the way: Users of morphine and heroin often complain of impotence and frigidity that fade when they kick their habits. Could natural opioids have some biochemical dampening effect on reproduction? Yes, says Theodore Cicero of Washington University Medical School. Endorphins, he says, "play an integral role—probably the dominant role—in regulating reproductive hormone cycles."

This formerly small corner of endorphin research has "exploded into a huge area of neurobiology," Cicero says, and researchers now think the opioid peptides help fine-tune many—perhaps all—of the nervous and hormonal pathways that together keep the body operating normally.

Cicero and his colleagues have tracked the byzantine biochemical loops through which endorphins, the brain, the body's master gland (the pituitary), the master's master (the hypothalamus) and the gonads exchange signals to ensure that an adult animal can reproduce when times are good but not when the environment is hostile. Cicero's work helped show that beta endorphin rules the hypothalamus and thus, indirectly, the pituitary and gonads.

The Washington University group also sees "a perfect parallel" between the brain's ability to produce endorphins and the onset of puberty: As the opioid system matures, so does the body sexually. A juvenile rat with endorphins blocked by naloxone undergoes puberty earlier; a young rat given opiates matures far later than normal and its offspring can have disturbed hormonal systems. Cicero calls the results "frightening" and adds, "there couldn't possibly be a worse time for a person to take drugs than during late childhood or adolescence."

Endorphins play a critical role in a later reproductive phase, as well: pregnancy and labor. Women in their third trimester sometimes notice that the pain and pressure of, say, a blood pressure cuff, is far less pronounced than before or after pregnancy. Alan Gintzler and his colleagues at the State University of New York Health Science Center in Brooklyn found that opioid peptides produced inside the spinal cord probably muffle pain and perhaps elevate mood to help a woman deal with the increasing physical stress of pregnancy. Endorphin activity builds throughout pregnancy and reaches a peak just before and during labor. Some have speculated that the tenfold drop from peak endorphin levels within 24 hours of delivery may greatly contribute to postpartum depression.

•CHILLS, THRILLS, LAUGHTER AND TEARS: Just as the effects of morphine go beyond the physical, claims for the opioid peptides extend to purely esthetic and emotional, with speculation falling on everything from the pleasure of playing with pets and the transcendence of near-death experiences to shivers over sonatas and the feeling of well-being that comes with a rousing laugh or a good cry.

Avram Goldstein of Stanford University, a pioneer in peptide research, recently collected a group of volunteers who get a spine-tingling thrill from their favorite music and gave them either a placebo or an opiate blocker during a listening session. Their shivers declined with the blocker—tantalizing evidence that endorphins mediate rapture, even though the mechanics are anyone's guess.

Former *Saturday Review* editor Norman Cousins may have spawned a different supposition about endorphins and emotion when he literally laughed himself out of the sometimes fatal disease ankylosing spondylitis. He found that 10 minutes of belly laughing before bed gave him two hours of painfree sleep. Before long, someone credited endorphins with the effect, and by now the claim is commonplace. For example, Matt Weinstein, a humor consultant from Berkeley, California, frequently mentions a possible link between endorphins, laughter and health in his lectures on humor in the workplace. His company's motto: If you take yourself too seriously, there's an excellent chance you may end up seriously ill.

Weinstein agrees with laughter researcher William Fry, a psychiatrist at Stanford's medical school, that evidence is currently circumstantial. Fry tried to confirm the laughter-endorphin link experimentally, but the most accurate way to assess it would be to tap the cerebrospinal fluid. That, Fry says, "is not only a difficult procedure but it's not conducive to laughter" and could result in a fountain of spinal fluid gushing out with the first good guffaw. Confirmation clearly awaits a less ghoulish methodology. But in the meantime, Fry is convinced that mirth and playfulness can diminish fear, anger and depression. At the very least, he says, laughter is a good aerobic exercise that ventilates the lungs and leaves the muscles relaxed. Fry advises patients to take their own humor inventory, then amass a library of books, tapes and gags that dependably trigger hilarity.

Another William Frey, this one at the University of Minnesota, studies the role of tears in emotion, stress and health. "The physiology of the brain when we experience a change in emotional state from sad to angry to happy or vice versa is an absolutely unexplored frontier," Frey says. And emotional tears are a fascinating guidepost because "they are unique to human beings and are our natural excretory response to strong emotion." Since all other bodily fluids are involved in removing something, he reasons, logic dictates that tears wash something away, too. Frey correctly predicted that tears would contain the three biochemicals that build up during stress: leucine-enkephalin, an endorphin, and the hormones prolactin and ACTH. These biochemicals are found in both emotional tears and tears from chopping onions, a different sort of stress.

Frey is uncertain whether tears simply carry off excess endorphins that collect in the stressed brain or whether those peptides have some activity in the tear ducts, eyes, nose or throat. Regardless, he cites evidence that people with ulcers and colitis tend to cry less than the average, and he concludes that a person who feels like crying "should go ahead and do it! I can't think of any other physical excretory process that humans alone can do, so why suppress it and its possibly healthful effects?"

All in all, the accumulated evidence suggests that if you want to use your endorphins, you should live the unfettered natural life. Laugh! Cry! Thrill to music! Reach puberty. Get pregnant. Get aerobic. Get hungry, Eat! Lest this sound like a song from *Fiddler on the Roof*, however, remember that stress or injury may be even quicker ways to pump out home-brew opioids. The bottom line is this: Endorphins are so fundamental to normal physiological functioning that we don't have to seek them out at all. We probably surf life's pleasures and pains on a wave of endorphins already.

Test yourself by imagining the following: the sound of chalk squeaking across a blackboard; a pink rose sparkling with dew; embracing your favorite movie star; chocolate-mocha mousse cake; smashing your thumb with a hammer. If any of these thoughts sent the tiniest tingle down your spine, then you have have just proved the point.

Perceptual Processes

The study of sensation and perception is one of the oldest specialty areas in experimental psychology. Much of the work which occurred in Wundt's original psychological laboratory and other labs around the world for several decades had to do with sensation and perception. Indeed, psychology owes much of its early development as a science to the debates which arose over how to define and measure perceptual processes.

For many years it was popular to consider sensation and perception as two distinct processes. Sensation was defined in passive terms as the simple event of some stimulus energy (sound waves, light, atmospheric pressure, etc.) impinging on the body or on a specific sense organ, which then reflexively transmitted appropriate information to the central nervous system. Both passivity and simple reflexes were stressed. Perception, on the other hand, was defined as an integrative and interpretive process which the higher centers of the brain supposedly accomplished based on the sensory information and available memories for similar events. This dichotomy of sensation and perception is no longer widely accepted. The revolution came in the mid-1960s when James Gibson published a then-radical treatise (*The Senses Considered as Perceptual Systems*, Boston: Houghton-Mifflin, 1966). According to this new view, perceptual processes included all the sensory events, which were now seen as directed by a searching central nervous system. This view also provided the thesis that certain perceptual patterns, such as recognition of some types of events and objects, may be species-specific. In other words, all humans, independent of learning histories, should share some perceptual repertoires.

The first article concerns a sensory system only recently receiving significant focused attention: olfaction. Careful behavioral analyses of the conduct of other mammals suggest strong influences of olfactory stimuli, and it appears likely that for humans olfaction is a much more powerful sensory modality than has previously been recognized. But how can we generalize from studies of other animals to humans? And how can we conduct specific olfactory studies with humans when the dependent measures include mate selection?

One of the most puzzling human experiences is sleep, which each of us appears to need, although in varying amounts. James Krueger takes us on a fascinating historical tour of notions about what sleep is and why we need it, and then provides a dynamic review of his own work on the nature of sleep.

The third article in this section deals with dreaming, a perceptual event without a clearly identified sensory source. Dreams have fascinated people, including psychologists, since ancient times. Freud referred to dreams as the "royal road to the unconscious," because he believed that dreams concealed hidden representations of a person's unconscious motives and fears. More recent research, and theories based on this research, refute Freud's arguments and raise new ones. In this way, science goes forward. However, we are left with the question: What is the real purpose of dreaming? Could such an elaborate event have been an accident of nature?

This section ends with an article about hypnosis, considered by many to be a special case of focused perception. Try to read this article without bias; you should find yourself intrigued by the potential this therapeutic tactic offers us.

Looking Ahead: Challenge Questions

If olfactory stimuli can trigger significant behavioral sequences in humans, and if these triggering stimuli can be learned or imprinted very early in life, to what extent are individuals personally responsible for these later behaviors? Should parents be informed about this research, and if so, what recommendations should they consider relative to the olfactory stimulation of their infants?

Aside from providing some rest and respite from work, what purposes could sleep have? How can we differentiate the chemical and the neural benefits of sleep? Can we easily learn to get by with significantly less sleep?

Much dream research is based on EEG patterns. Are we sure that we are measuring dreaming? Is it really possible that dreams don't mean anything? If so, why are they often so troubling?

Since hypnosis appears to be a powerful technique in the alleviation of some human habits and the development of positive behaviors, should its use be restricted? What might be the most appropriate attitude one could take toward hypnosis as a therapeutic agent?

ARE WE LED BY THE NOSE?

TERENCE MONMANEY

Terence Monmaney writes about health for Newsweek.

On a rainy October night in Chicago 11 years ago, 33-year-old mathematician David Griffin* stepped off a curb and into the path of a Dodge van. He was on his usual after-dinner walk, although he was perhaps feeling an unusual need for it—the buffet supper of turkey and potatoes and fixings had not fully agreed with him.

Griffin considered himself something of an epicure, with an ability to taste and smell that was the functional equivalent of perfect pitch. Impressed once, for instance, by the exotic flavor of some broiled fish he had eaten in a restaurant in Pisa, he divined the secret recipe and re-created the dish, down to the basting of lime juice, rosemary, and mustard.

The van was moving about five miles an hour when it hit him. He cracked his skull on the pavement. His recovery

---

*This is not his real name, but all the details of his case are true.

> What a rat smells in the womb is what it seeks in a mate. What mammals smelled 100 million years ago may have led to the human forebrain.

was good, and during the eight days he spent in the hospital he did not have any remarkable symptoms. True, he noticed that the hospital food was terribly bland and yet very salty, but that was clearly just a sign of his good taste. It appeared he would suffer no deep or lasting injury. The day after returning home he poured his father a snifter of pear brandy—sweet, ethereal, redolent of fruit ripening in a sun-washed orchard—and discovered he could smell absolutely nothing. "I was devastated," he says.

The doctors said that if he still couldn't smell anything after six months to a year, he probably never would. The blow, they explained, apparently tore nerves connecting his brain and nose. Griffin's taste buds worked fine, so at least he sensed the salty, bitter, sour, and sweet ingredients in food. Seven years

went by. His condition unchanged, Griffin sued the van's driver and won a modest settlement.

These days—well, he has resigned himself to an odorless existence, rationalizing that it certainly could be worse. Yet he has learned it is a hazardous as well as a hollow way of life.

Shortly after the accident his apartment building caught fire; he awoke to the shouts of neighbors, not to the smell of smoke that might have alerted him sooner. He cannot detect leaking gas. He has been poisoned by spoiled food. But Griffin says he suffers a more profound loss: deprived now of the rush of memory that an odor can let loose, he feels cut off from moments in his own past. "Think about rotting leaves or a campfire or a roast or a Christmas tree—I enjoyed those smells so much. I miss not being able to experience

them again and be reminded of other times. A dimension of my life is missing. I feel empty, in a sort of limbo."

Approximately one out of every 15 victims of head trauma wakes up in a permanently odorless world. Accidents are the leading cause of anosmia (loss of smell) in people Griffin's age. Influenza, brain tumors, allergies, and the uncertain effects of old age are other reasons some 2 million people in the United States can't smell anything. No surveys have charted what these people miss most, but it's safe to say their lives lack spice.

At least three quarters of the flavors in food and drink are not tastes but aromas. The volatile essences of black pepper or blue cheese are breathed into passageways originating at the back of the mouth and delivered to olfactory nerve endings high in the nasal cavities.

Sex without smells is not quite the same either, according to Robert Henkin, former director of the Center for Sensory Disorders, Georgetown University. He says about one in four people with little or no smelling ability loses some

From *Discover,* September 1987, pp. 48–54, 56. Terence Monmaney/© Discover 1987, Family Media, Inc.

Between your eyes, just below the forebrain, some 20 million olfactory nerves hang from the roof of each nasal cavity; their wispy cilia bathed in mucus, swaying in the currents like sea grass.

sex drive. This is hardly the loss suffered by a male golden hamster with such a disability—remove that part of his brain devoted to olfaction and he'll give up mating entirely. But it suggests how our lives are enriched by olfactory signals, however unconsciously we tune them in.

The mysterious way smells refresh memories fascinates novelists as well as neuroscientists. Proust said the aroma of lime-flower tea and madeleines launched his monumental *Remembrances of Things Past*. Kipling, in his poem "Lichtenberg," wrote that the pungence of rain-soaked acacia meant home. That smell should be the most nostalgic sense seems logical. Compared with sights, sounds, and touch, odors are messages that last; the smell of burned gunpowder lingers long after the firecracker has sparkled and popped.

Unlike some other animals, we don't much rely on our noses to get around anymore, although some curious new experiments suggest we could if we were so inclined. Researchers at the Monell Chemical Senses Center in Philadelphia have shown that humans can smell the difference between two mice that are identical except for a small set of genes on one chromosome. People can in fact distinguish the urine of these two mice. If we close our eyes and lower our noses, we might not only find the urine-marked trails mice leave but tell one mouse's route from another's.

ut we don't often track odors— we just keep track of them. The close tie between odors and

memory is more than happy coincidence; without it, odors would be meaningless. You can't identify an odor you've never experienced any more than you can recognize a face you've never seen.

The most primitive and evocative of the senses, smell is also the most intimate. Odors give you away. Everyone knows you can't hide alcohol on the breath. The urine of children with the genetic disease phenylketonuria is mousy. Intimate, too, is the very act of smelling. You have to inhale the stimulus, bring it inside, before you know what to make of it. "Touch seems to reside in the object touched..." Helen Keller wrote, "and odor seems to reside not in the object smelt, but in the organ."

The smelling organ turns out to be a lot more complicated than scientists imagined it would be: Chemicals flowing into some hollow tubes and reacting with a bunch of nerves—what could be simpler? But there are two strange things about olfactory nerves. For one, they constantly replace themselves, the only nerves we have capable of rebirth. One by one they die after a month or so, and new nerves sprout from cells in the nasal lining, growing thin filaments that seek the brain like seedlings pushing toward sunlight.

The reason olfactory nerves probably need to renew themselves is the other strange thing. Protected merely by a film of mucus, they are the only nerve endings out in the open. In the nose, in other words, the brain directly confronts and tries to sort out the world.

Michael Shipley, a neurobiologist at the University

of Cincinnati College of Medicine, is one of the new breed of olfaction researchers trying to get to the brain through the nose. "I've got a hunch if we can come close to understanding how the brain keeps track of odors," he says, "we'll be a long way toward understanding how it processes other kinds of information."

Between your eyes, just below the forebrain, some 20 million olfactory nerves hang from the roof of each nasal cavity, their wispy cilia bathed in mucus, swaying in the currents like sea grass. Just here, where olfactory nerves greet odorants dissolved in mucus, researchers have for decades drawn a blank. What nobody understands is what everybody wants to know: Why do things smell the way they do?

Solving the problem would be easier if all odors could be broken down into a few elements, as visible light can be separated into its spectral colors. The retina can faithfully reproduce a scene, in color, by means of a few sensory cell types, such as those dedicated to picking up red, green, or blue. But there is no odor spectrum. Olfactory nerves must recognize each odorant individually.

Many scientists imagine that olfactory receptors work like other receptors—like, say, the specialized protein on a muscle cell that receives the hormone insulin in the way a lock admits a key, and passes along insulin's message to break down more glucose. One problem with this idea, though, is that it doesn't account for the smell of a new car. While it's conceivable that olfactory nerves have evolved receptors for

natural odorants, surely humans haven't had time to evolve receptors devoted specifically to smelling the vinyl odors in a new car's interior. Around 10,500 chemical compounds are invented or discovered each week, and many are smelly.

Another idea, publicized by physician-essayist Lewis Thomas a decade ago, suggests that the immune and smelling systems, both dedicated to recognizing new, foreign substances, perform that task in much the same way. Recently, researchers at the Johns Hopkins Medical School offered some support for the theory. They discovered a protein in the nasal linings of cows that binds specifically to six different types of smelly chemicals, including pyrazines, which give scent to bell peppers. This pyrazine-binding protein, they say, looks and behaves somewhat like a disease-fighting antibody protein. From this bit of evidence it would appear that our smelling and immune systems literally come to grips with the outside by tailoring a protein to fit new materials encountered.

This theory of made-to-odor receptors represents a promising new approach, but it probably won't tell the whole story even if it holds up. Neurobiologist Robert Gesteland of the University of Cincinnati College of Medicine says, "Since these nerve cells are sitting out there in the fluid, accessible to the world—anything that gets into the fluid in your nose is certainly going to get to those

Boys and girls both start smelling right away. We're generally outfitted to smell days before birth, so it is possible to get a whiff of the world in the womb. Perhaps from spicy amniotic fluid we begin to acquire a taste for garlic.

cells—probably a few different receptor mechanisms have evolved. And no experiment so far favors one mechanism over another."

Seeing, touching, hearing—the neurons controlling these senses are relatively "hard wired," a fact of life the brain seems to have taken advantage of. It keeps track of stimuli by sending them down dedicated circuits. A dot of light on the retina, for instance, sets off an impulse through the optic nerve that activates brain cells corresponding to just that point on the retina.

Gordon Shepherd, a Yale University neuroscientist, believes olfaction works in a manner something like that of the other senses, despite its obvious differences. In his view, an odorant first stimulates particular receptors, which then transmit a signal to neurons dedicated to that odor in the olfactory bulbs, two matchstick-size brain structures above the nasal cavities. Those cells relay the news to brain centers involved, ultimately, in behavior appropriate to that odor. When researchers in Shepherd's lab analyzed the olfactory bulbs of newborn rats, they found that certain odors—especially those associated with the mother rat's nipples—were processed by a particular patch of cells on the bulbs, the makings of a kind of olfactory circuit. One stimulus, one circuit, one response—presented with the odor, the newborn suckles.

Walter Freeman, a neurophysiologist at the University of California, Berkeley, doesn't believe in olfactory circuits. He measures brain waves emanating from the

olfactory bulb of a rabbit while it sniffs an odor. When a rabbit is presented with an odor for the first time, according to Freeman's studies, its olfactory bulbs give off brain waves in fairly disordered fashion. After several exposures to an odor, a pattern emerges, and thereafter that odor prompts that pattern of neuronal activity—the sign of recognition.

The essence of Freeman's view is that olfactory neurons—and perhaps all neurons devoted to the senses—are not hard wired to perform single tasks but are creative; given a stimulus, they improvise a song of brain waves to go with it, and later sing the theme whenever cued. When Freeman speaks of neurons in action, he refers not to circuits but to ensembles.

Freeman's and Shepherd's views of olfactory-signal processing may simply be different versions of the same reality. It is too early to tell. But it's important to know, because the stakes are high: an understanding of the means by which the brain turns stimulus into sensation. Many olfaction researchers believe that even those who study vision and hearing (the so-called higher senses) and touch will have to turn to olfaction for inspiration. Ultimately, sensory biologists are in pursuit of the answer to the same question: How does a particular clump of neurons in the brain generate the awareness of an F-sharp, say, or a 1983 chardonnay?

Richard Doty is in a glistening steel room showing off his olfactometer. Fluorescent lights shine through chrome grids in the ceiling, and the walls and floors are

paneled with stainless steel. The room, in a University of Pennsylvania hospital, is as odorproof as can be.

The olfactometer is a closet-size machine connected by steel piping to a thing on a table that looks like a glass octopus with 11 tentacles. You put your nostril over the tip of a tentacle and the machine serves up a precisely measured wisp of, say, phenylethyl alcohol, an essence of rose. Then you indicate whether or not you detect it. In this way Doty measures smelling thresholds.

From the looks of this room you might get the idea that olfaction research is so advanced that the only task remaining is to add more decimal places to existing data. Yet smelling isn't such a precise experience. Your sensitivity to phenylethyl alcohols depends on your health, your allergies, whether you're tired or rested, whether you smelled it an hour ago, the humidity, the elevation above sea level, your age, and your sex.

So, the exquisite high-tech instruments so impressive to funding agencies won't necessarily solve the mysteries of human smelling. Consider Doty's low-tech success. He recently settled two much-debated questions—does smelling ability decline with age, and are men or women better smellers?—using a $20 scratch-and-sniff test.

It comes in a letter-size envelope and consists of 40 scratch-and-sniff patches: bubble gum, paint thinner, menthol, cherry, leather,

skunk, pizza. Next to each patch are the words, "This odor smells most like," followed by four choices. One is correct. At his lawyer's request, David Griffin, the mathematician struck by a van, took the test twice, and the scores helped convince the judge of Griffin's anosmia. He scored 9 and 8 out of 40. A score of 35 or better is considered normal. By now the researchers have administered the University of Pennsylvania Smell Identification Test to more than 5,000 people—males and females, white and black Americans, Korean-Americans, native Japanese (they had trouble recognizing cherry), some 50 five-year-olds, and many over 90.

Doty and his coworkers discovered that smelling power does fade late in life and that the sense is sharpest around middle age: The average score for 20- to 50-year-olds was 37. The average for 75-year-olds was 30. What's more, a quarter of the people between 65 and 80, and half of those over 80, appear anosmic. As the researchers concluded, "it is not surprising that many elderly persons complain that food lacks flavor and that the elderly account for a disproportionate number of accidental gas poisoning cases each year."

In a study published last May, these investigators showed that patients with Alzheimer's disease are unusually likely to have smelling deficits. Of 25 men and women diagnosed with Alzheimer's, all but 2 scored lower on the test than age-matched control subjects without the degenerative disease. "It's interesting that in a disease like Alzheimer's, where memory loss is a major dysfunction, there is also a problem with olfaction," Doty says. Researchers at Stanford and other universities have also demonstrated that memory and smelling often fade together in Alzheimer's patients. Olfaction may even sometimes disappear before other problems become evident, Doty says. Scratching and sniffing could turn out to be an effective and inexpensive screening tool for the disease.

Digging deeper into the test results, Doty found that at every age, women scored better on the smelling test than men, in all ethnic groups tested so far. At peak performance, by those subjects around middle age, the differences were slight—a point or less, on average. At the extremes it was more dramatic. Five-year-old boys scored an average of 27, while girls of the same age scored 34. At the other end, 65-year-old men averaged 33, compared with the 36 scored by 65-year-old women.

Doty can't explain the sex differences, but he may have ruled out one popular theory. Researchers who previously said women are superior smellers often gave credit to ovarian hormones like estrogen. After all, pregnant women, who are besieged by hormones, are considered especially acute smellers. But, Doty asks, if ovarian hormones are the key, why are five-year-old girls, years shy of puberty, better smellers than five-year-old boys?

Whatever their differences, boys and girls both start smelling right away. We're born with a set of olfactory nerves and bulbs already in working order. We're generally outfitted to smell days before birth, so it is possible we get a whiff of the world in the womb. Researchers have even suggested, and not entirely in jest, that from spicy

ILLUSTRATION BY MICHAEL REINGOLD

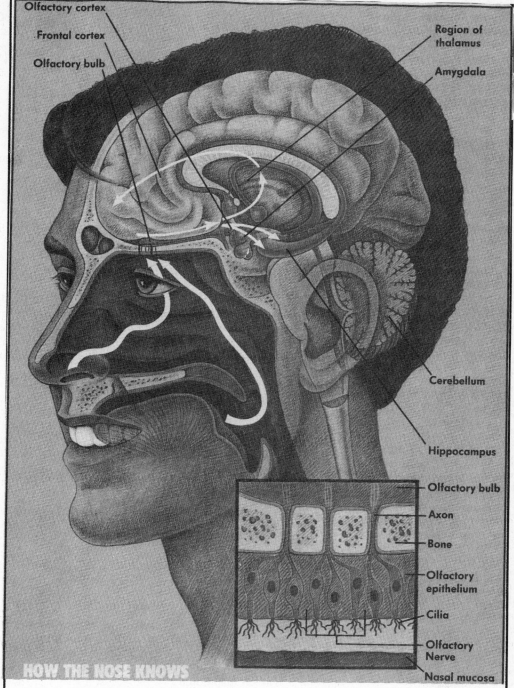

Olfactory cortex
Frontal cortex
Olfactory bulb
Region of thalamus
Amygdala
Cerebellum
Hippocampus

Olfactory bulb
Axon
Bone
Olfactory epithelium
Cilia
Olfactory Nerve
Nasal mucosa

HOW THE NOSE KNOWS

Aromas enter the nasal cavities through the nose and the back of the mouth, swirl around, and flow up to the top, where they encounter the mucus-bathed cilia of millions of tiny olfactory nerve cells. The aromatic molecules react with specific nerve receptors and send signals to the olfactory bulbs. That is where the signal begins to be interpreted; you become aware that you've smelled something, but you still can't identify what it is. The message is then relayed to the olfactory cortex, which puts a label on the odor ("The sea!"). From there it travels down two pathways: to the thalamus and cerebral cortex, where, for example, smell and sight are compared ("I smell the sea, but I'm in the Midwest. Why?"), and to the amygdala and hippocampus, structures that handle emotion and memory. It is there that an experience associated with a smell can be recalled ("The seaside cottage of childhood summers...").

amniotic fluid we might begin to acquire a taste for garlic, or cigarettes.

Rats, anyway, learn a thing or two about their mothers in utero, according to experiments done at Johns Hopkins by psychologists Elliot Blass and Patricia Pedersen, who now works in Shepherd's lab at Yale. A rat pup, born deaf and blind, smells the way to its mother's nipples, homing in on the already familiar odor of amniotic fluid on her underside. They found that if they injected a pregnant rat with citral, a lemon scent, a few days before she gave birth, the pups would prefer citral-rinsed nipples to their own mother's.

Blass and psychologist Thomas Fillion, of Yale, completed further experiments showing how odors shape behavior. Again the experiments were done on rats, and again the researchers can't say what the findings mean for the rest of us. But you have to wonder. They say odors that rats experience while suckling can be a sexual turn-on later in life.

Each experiment began with a litter of pups that were suckled by mothers whose nipples and genitals were painted with citral. After weaning, the male pups were isolated from both citral odors and females until they reached sexual maturity, at about 100 days. Then the rats were introduced to a female in heat—either a normal female or one with citral-scented genitals.

Blass and Fillion found that males exposed to citral while suckling were more eager to mate with citral-scented females and finished mating more quickly—an average of five minutes, or 30 percent, faster than when mating with normal females. "These findings," the researchers concluded, "suggest that, at least for this mammal, the degree to which

a feminine feature is sexually arousing to adult males can be established in the context of suckling."

That's exciting to the male rat, apparently, is not any particular odor—fragrance of lemon furniture polish will do—but the sensation associated with it. "There's a learning process going on," Fillion says. "My intuition is that suckling is such a powerful experience, and the arousal provided by it is so powerful, it's an ideal time and place for any mammal to learn an important sensory cue." Far from coldly objectifying rat sex, Blass and Fillion have revealed its poignance, showing it is in part a rat's pursuit of infantile satisfactions.

No equivalent studies have been done on humans, but research does show that babies experience and recognize maternal odors while suckling. The first such study was done a decade ago at the University of California, San Francisco, by Michael Russell, then a graduate student. A two-day-old infant, he showed, would not respond to a cotton pad worn for three hours in its mother's bra. Yet most six-week-olds tested did begin suckling if they smelled a cotton pad worn by their mothers, although they didn't respond to a pad worn in the bra of an unfamiliar lactating woman. Writing in *Nature,* Russell also noted that most infants were obviously attracted to their mother's scent and often repulsed by a stranger's. Russell concluded: "The existence of olfactory maternal attraction suggests that humans have a pheromonal system and that it operates at a very early age."

A pheromone is a substance that is produced by an organism and that elicits a

specific and unlearned response in another member of the same species. At least that's how researchers defined it in 1959, after collecting several examples of chemicals that insects use to communicate—ant trail markers, queen-bee anointments, and so forth. By the mid-1970s there was an increased interest in human pheromones, and Russell's study was considered by many as support for the substances' existence.

But critics say Russell never ruled out the possibility that the infants were merely recognizing ordinary odors, even traces of their own saliva. What Russell called "olfactory maternal attraction," they said, was simply the infant's recognition, after learning, of their mothers' body odor.

The strongest case for a human pheromone involves menstrual synchrony. Psychologist Martha McClintock wasn't the first to notice that when women live together in close quarters for months at a time, their menstrual cycles begin to coincide. But her 1970 study of women in a college dormitory documented synchrony so thoroughly that the phenomenon is now widely known as the McClintock effect. And she made the crucial observation that many of the dormitory residents adopted the rhythms of a certain few women—perhaps, she said, because they broadcast a chemical signal, a pheromone, that the other women heeded.

Skeptics have said women achieve menstrual synchrony because they eat, study, wash, vacation, talk, and stay up all night together; shared stresses and joys regulate their cycles, not chemical messages. Still, late last year, researchers at the Monell Chemical Senses Center and the University of Penn-

sylvania offered the firmest evidence yet that pheromones mediate the McClintock effect. George Preti and Winnifred Cutler exposed 10 women with normal cycles to underarm sweat from other women. The subjects were daubed under the nose every few days with the female sweat. After three months, the subjects' cycles began to coincide with sweat-donors' cycles—evidence, the researchers say, that a pheromone in sweat mediates menstrual synchrony (other women, controls, were daubed with alcohol and showed no significant change). "Pheromone effects are real in human beings," Preti grandly told the *Washington Post,* "and the anecdotal evidence suggests they even occur here in the United States, where we're all deodorized and perfumized."

Maybe so. But Doty doesn't believe that humans, like moths, have automatic or built-in responses to certain odors or pheromones; instead, he says, we interpret odors much as we do visual or auditory signals: "If I'm walking down the street and see a woman with beautiful blond hair and I get sort of excited—you don't say blond hair is a *visual mone.* Our idea of what is attractive depends on styles we grow up with, what we see on TV, what society values. In some cultures blond hair is unattractive. The same thing occurs in the sense of smell. Smelling is just a way of extracting information from chemicals in the environment. The *meaning* that information may have is affected by locale and learning and memory, by the context of the experience."

That is partly what makes the smell of smoke pleasant at a barbeque, not so welcome in a movie theater. Even a rat can learn that an odor's message depends on

Researchers at the Monell Chemical Senses Center have shown
that humans can smell the difference between two mice that are identical
except for a small set of genes on one chromosome.

the context. Trained to anticipate a rewarding sip of water after smelling the banana odor of amyl acetate, a rat will quickly learn to avoid amyl acetate if the "reward" is changed to an electric shock. A silkworm moth is less flexible. It is difficult to imagine training the moth not to respond to bombykol, a mating pheromone secreted by females that males can detect from miles away.

Psychologist William Cain's experiments at the Pierce Foundation at Yale spell out how important the context is. Cain asked a dozen undergraduates to identify by smell alone 80 familiar things, such as baby powder, burned toast, shoe polish, and popcorn. The samples were kept in opaque jars and the students, eyes closed, sniffed them through cloth. They could identify fewer than half. "They knew the smell was familiar," says Cain. "They just couldn't always name it."

It happens all the time. You've smelled it before, you like it—but what is the spice in that dish, what is it about that perfume? Cain, Shipley, and others believe

odors often leave us dumb because brain centers concerned with language are not richly connected to the olfactory cortex.

For most of us, as Cain's study suggests, smelling is somehow remote from the higher cognitive functions. You cannot really conjure up an odor in the way you can imagine a face or voice. Nor can you manipulate that image as you can rotate an imaginary cube, for example, or put words in someone's mouth. And while odors evoke memories, the opposite is not generally true.

That's because there are different brain structures for detecting and remembering odors, according to Gary Lynch, a neurobiologist at the University of California, Irvine. After the olfactory bulbs receive and sort a signal, they relay it to several places—to the olfactory cortex (to make you aware you smell something), and from there to centers involved in memory (most importantly the hippocampus, which connects to higher visual centers). Although information flows from olfactory bulbs to hippocampus to visual cortex, prompting a memory, visual information can't make it back to odor-sensing areas of the olfactory cortex.

Kipling saw this memory lane as a one-way street in "Lichtenberg." After reaching town and its smell of wattle, or acacia, a cascade of memories—"the picnics and brass-bands"—is let loose, courtesy of hippocampal connection:
"It all came over me in one
  act
Quick as a shot through the
  brain—
With the smell of the wattle
  round Lichtenberg,
Riding in, in the rain."
Lynch believes that the kind of memory we use to store facts began to emerge in some primitive mammal 100 million years ago, as a means of keeping track of odors. It was only a matter of time before a more advanced smeller made a breakthrough, rousing the image corresponding to an odor—"mother," say—without actually smelling her. In this evolutionary view, the collections of neurons originally designed to process olfactory information gave rise to higher forms of memory and cognition; the human forebrain, seat of art making and history writing and joke telling, is basically a souped-up smelling machine.

You can take this as an insult to your intelligence or a

celebration of your nose. But the more neuroscientists learn about smelling, the more it looks right for this sophisticated new role. Olfactory nerves in flux, receptors arising to each smelly occasion, bulbs creating patterns of neuronal activity for each odorant, memory linking the sensation of odor with whatever happens to be around—you'd expect this sort of creativity of the sense that introduced learning and memory into the world.

Brainy snobs, our noses up in the air, we don't follow odor trails anymore. We work in skyscrapers where the windows don't open, drive around in climate-controlled cars, hide behind "five-day deodorant protection," gobble up processed cheese. We are starting to act like birds, too high up and fast-moving to heed earthly chemical signals.

Even as our lives become more rarefied, the orphan sense, as Lynch calls it, is turning into one of the premier problems in biology. "Olfaction has always been in the back shed of neuroscience," Walter Freeman says. "The reason is largely emotional, I think. It has always been thought of as primitive. It's not glamorous. Olfaction is—it's *smells*."

NO SIMPLE SLUMBER

Exploring the Enigma of Sleep

JAMES M. KRUEGER

JAMES M. KRUEGER *is a professor of physiology at the University of Tennessee Medical School, in Memphis.*

DURING THE SECOND ACT of Shakespeare's *Macbeth*, the usurping thane of Cawdor whispers to his wife that he has "done the deed"—that, according to their plan, he has murdered the sleeping King Duncan and thus has cleared his own path to the throne of Scotland. Though the remorseless Lady Macbeth implores her husband to "consider it not so deeply," regicide does not sit well with him. Guilt-ridden, he raves:

> Methought I heard a voice cry "Sleep no more!
> Macbeth does murder sleep"—the innocent sleep,
> Sleep that knits up the ravelled sleave of care,
> The death of each day's life, sore labor's bath,
> Balm of hurt minds, great Nature's second course,
> Chief nourisher in life's feast.

Throughout the play, Shakespeare portrays sleep's contradictory nature—at once soothing and haunting, restorative and tormenting (as in one of the more famous scenes, when Lady Macbeth, at last wracked by guilt, sleepwalks, rubbing her hands together, as if to wash the blood from them, and crying aloud: "Out, damned spot!"). Sleep in *Macbeth* is also a time of death, whether the death "of each day's life" or the murder of a king. Shakespeare was neither the first nor the last to link slumber and mortality; his reference to sleep as "death's counterfeit" echoes both Homer, who, in *The Iliad*, called sleep and death "twin brothers," and Ovid, who wrote, in *The Amores*, "What else is sleep but the image of chill death?" After Shakespeare, the seventeenth-century author and physician Thomas Browne mused, in his *Religio Medici*, that "sleepe . . . is that death by which we may be literally said to die daily." And, not quite two hundred years later, in *Queen Mab*, Shelley remarked, "How wonderful is Death,/Death and his brother Sleep!"

Intimations of mortality notwithstanding, it is common wisdom that sleep is, in fact, the "chief nourisher in life's feast"—the possessor of some essential, recuperative power. And, indeed, a good night's rest has for centuries been a cornerstone of preventive medicine—an observation based largely on the subjective experience that most people feel better when they have slept eight hours than when they have slept substantially less. There have been exceptions, of course. Thomas Edison is said to have resented sleep's hold and to have trained himself to get by on three or four hours of sleep a night—with the help of a midday nap. Similarly, Salvador Dali claimed to have cheated long-term sleep with short-term napping: He liked to doze off holding a spoon above a tin plate. At the moment the spoon slipped from his grasp and struck the plate, the surrealist would awaken, a new man.

But whether we view sleep as benign or malevolent, it draws each of us helplessly into its arms; the average person spends one-third of his existence (which, over the course of a normal life span, amounts to about twenty-five years) asleep. Yet, until recently, science understood surprisingly little about sleep's physiological cause and effects. There has been no shortage of theories—some involving the brain, some the circulation, and others a combination of both—but on the whole, sleep remains largely the same enigma described two hundred years ago by Samuel Johnson (who regularly slept until noon): "No searcher has yet found either the efficient or final cause; or can tell by what power the mind and body are thus chained down in irresistible stupefaction; or what benefits the animal receives from this alternate suspension of its active powers."

Still, a growing body of research is coloring in some of the blank spaces in our picture of sleep. Fittingly, consid-

This article is reprinted by permission of *The Sciences*, May/June 1989, pp. 36-41. Individual subscriptions are $14.50 per year. Write to The Sciences, 2 East 63rd Street, New York, NY 10021 or call 1-800-THE-NYAS.

ering the centuries of mystery that have shrouded it, sleep is no simple matter. Rather, as recent studies indicate, it results from a complicated series of biochemical reactions involving many parts of the brain, various kinds of cells, and the immune system.

SOME twenty-four hundred years ago, Hippocrates advised that a patient "should follow our natural habit and spend the day awake and the night asleep. If this habit be disturbed, it is not so good. . . . It is worst of all when he sleeps neither night nor day." Several times in writings attributed to the Greek physician, sleeplessness (as well as too much sleep) is cited as a sign that something is amiss. Noting the cooling of the limbs experienced by sleepers, Hippocrates concluded that sleep is caused by the retreat of blood and warmth into the body's inner regions. A century or so later, Aristotle proposed another hypothesis, based on humoralism, a medical doctrine that arose in Greece in the late sixth century B.C. and held sway for more than two thousand years.

The Greeks believed that each person's physical and emotional well-being depended upon maintaining a balance between four fluids, called humors, circulating throughout the body: blood, phlegm, black bile, and yellow bile. One of the factors thought to influence this equilibrium was the ingestion of food, a notion Aristotle seized on as an explanation for sleep. Sleep, he suggested, results from "the evaporation attendant upon the process of nutrition. The matter evaporated must be driven onwards to a certain point, then turn back, and change its current to and fro, like a tide-race in a narrow strait." In other words, vapors, emanating from food digesting in the stomach, were transported through the body via the humors, causing sleepiness. This, Aristotle posited, "explains why fits of drowsiness are especially apt to come on after meals."

Scant research was done on the subject during the two millennia after Aristotle, though a sensible routine of bed rest was acknowledged as crucial to a healthy, productive life. Maimonides, the twelfth-century Jewish physician and philosopher, recommended that a person sleep eight hours a night, "not . . . on his face nor on his back but on his side; at the beginning of the night, on the left side and at the end of the night on the right side," and that "he should not go to sleep shortly after eating but should wait approximately three or four hours after a meal." Four hundred years later, in *A Dyetary of Helth*, the English physician Andrew Boorde reflected a concern for psychological, as well as physical, influences on sleep when he offered this exhortation: "To bedwarde be you mery, or have mery company aboute you, so that, to bedwarde, no anger nor hevynes, sorrowe, nor pencyfulnes, do trouble or disquyet you."

During the nineteenth century, humoralism reasserted itself, with some variations (to this day, any theory that attributes sleep to the circulation, or lack thereof, of some substance in blood is referred to as humoral). The circulation of blood, which the ancients considered the most important humor, then lay at the foundation of two popular—albeit diametrically opposed—hypotheses of sleep. According to one, the cardiovascular system brings on sleep by flooding the brain with blood. The second theory suggested that, on the contrary, cerebral anemia—a *lack* of blood in the brain—induces slumber. Proponents of this view believed that, during sleep, blood is rerouted away from the brain, to other organs. The prominence of two such antithetical notions made for quite a dilemma among insomniacs: whereas some physicians prescribed sleeping without pillows, to help draw blood back to the anemic cerebrum, others advised using as many cushions as possible, to divert blood from the congested brain.

Then, in the early twentieth century, René Legendre and Henri Piéron helped fuel a new idea: that during waking hours, the brain produces a variety of substances that combine to cause sleep. The two French physiologists conducted experiments involving pairs of dogs; one of each pair was made to stay awake for as long as two weeks, while the other was allowed to maintain its usual sleeping regimen. When the researchers injected cerebrospinal fluid from the sleep-deprived dogs into those that were well rested, the recipients fell into a deep, unusually long slumber.

Legendre and Piéron concluded that a sleep substance—which they dubbed hypnotoxin—was present in the cerebrospinal fluid and had accumulated in large quantities over the extended period during which the donor dogs had been awake. They were unable to isolate the substance, however, and by the 1920s a new line of inquiry—actually a variety of hypotheses generally classified as neural theories—had gained ascendancy, boosted, in no small measure, by the Russian physiologist Ivan Petrovich Pavlov.

At bottom, all neural theories hold that sleep results not from substances circulating in bodily fluids but from some characteristic change in the patterns of electrical impulses traveling between neurons in the brain. The most popular of these schemes was Pavlov's, according to which sleep originates in the cerebral cortex, the brain's furrowed outer layer. Once each day, Pavlov postulated, cortical neurons, exhausted as a result of overstimulation during wakefulness, become inhibited; then the inhibition spreads to other neurons, and sleep ensues. (Within the past twenty years, Pavlov's theory has been disproved: experiments have shown that laboratory animals sleep even after their cerebral cortices have been removed. Similarly, anencephalic babies, born without cerebral cortices, have sleep–wake cycles.)

Whereas Pavlov concentrated on cortical neurons, other investigators probed beneath the cerebral cortex, in search of an area deep within the brain geared specifically to regulating sleep. Recently, it became clear that there are, in fact, several such areas, including two clusters of neurons (the reticular formation network and the raphe nuclei) located in the brainstem and some parts of the hypothalamus (the small structure, tucked inside the base of the forebrain, that regulates the pituitary gland, along with hunger, thirst, and sexual appetite). It is just as apparent, however, that no one brain site is necessary for at least some sleep to occur: in laboratory animals, sleep continues, albeit impaired, even after any one of these areas is destroyed. Thus, the concept of a single sleep center is gradually being abandoned.

As some scientists groped in vain for clues to the cause of sleep, others made extraordinary progress in different areas of sleep research. Until fifty years ago, it had been assumed that sleep was a homogeneous, unified state, during which the brain is all but inactive. This notion was radically revised upon the development, during the thirties, of the electroencephalograph, the machine that charts the brain's electrical activity by recording rhythmic bursts of voltage oscillations (brain waves). It was then that researchers discovered that sleepers pass through two major stages, as well as a number of transitional phases.

The first stage of sleep was detected in 1935, by the physiologists Alfred L. Loomis, E. Newton Harvey, and Garret Hobart. It is characterized by high-amplitude brain waves of low frequency, during which the sleeper lies still and appears to be in his most restful state, and so came to be called slow-wave sleep. The second stage, discovered in 1952 by Nathaniel Kleitman, a physiologist at the University of Chicago, and his student Eugene Aserinsky, is marked by agitated high-frequency brain waves resembling those experienced during wakefulness; irregular heart rate, respiration, and blood pressure; muscular twitching; and the flurries of frenetic eye movement from which the stage derives its name, REM (rapid eye movement) sleep.

It is now known that sleep begins as a brief light slumber, lasting perhaps ten minutes, during which blood pressure, breathing, and body temperature ease into decline. This phase culminates in the first major sleep stage: deep slow-wave sleep. About an hour and a half later, there is a transition back to light slumber, followed by a shift to REM sleep. Over the course of eight hours, this cycle recurs four or five times; all told, about one-quarter of a night's sleep is spent in REM sleep, and the rest in slow-wave sleep and the transitional phases, all of which scientists group under the umbrella NREM (nonrapid eye movement) sleep.

Although advances in electroencephalopathy illuminated much about how we sleep, they said little about why. Only in the past two decades have scientists renewed the search for the cause—the somnogenic agent, or group of agents, that interacts with sleep centers in the brain to propel us from the structured, goal-directed, often stressful state of wakefulness to the less encumbered repose with which most of us bridge our days.

In the late sixties, John Pappenheimer, a physiologist at the Harvard Medical School, ushered in the modern era of sleep research with a series of studies on goats. Pappenheimer kept the animals awake for one or two days, after which—as did Legendre and Piéron, in their work with dogs—he extracted samples of their cerebrospinal fluid. Within the fluid was a substance that, when injected into rats that had been allowed to sleep normally, proved to be somnogenic.

After several years, Pappenheimer identified the substance as a peptide (a compound containing amino acids, the molecular building blocks of proteins), and in view of its marked sleep-producing ability, he named the compound factor S. Subsequently, other researchers confirmed his work, but because cerebrospinal fluid is available only in limited quantities—as opposed to, say, urine, which is more easily obtained—further characterizing of factor S has moved at a crawl. (We probably never will know whether Pappenheimer's peptide is the same as the mysterious hypnotoxin named by Legendre and Piéron in 1907.)

By 1980, however, Pappenheimer, Manfred Karnovsky, and I had observed that somnogenic substances similar—indeed, very likely identical—to the peptide found in goats are present in the brain tissues of sleep-deprived rabbits and in the urine of humans. These compounds have been further characterized as muramyl peptides, a class of glycopeptides (substances containing sugars as well as amino acids) contained in bacterial cell walls. When injected into laboratory rabbits, the muramyl peptides exert a potent effect: as little as one-billionth of a gram induces deep slow-wave sleep for several hours. Normally, rabbits spend about forty-five percent of their time in slow-wave sleep during daylight hours, but after an injection of muramyl peptides, this percentage jumps to about seventy.

All laboratory animals so far tested have responded to muramyl peptides by increasing the length and number of their sleep episodes. At the same time, their EEG readings have shown slow brain waves of very high amplitude, which are thought to indicate unusually deep slow-wave sleep similar to that which follows prolonged wakefulness. For reasons still unresolved, the effects of muramyl peptides on REM sleep vary from species to species.

Once it became clear that muramyl peptides are somnogenic, the task was to determine exactly how they induce sleep. One particularly intriguing possibility—that there is some link between sleep and the body's immune system—could justify centuries of medical wisdom. In the early seventies, scientists had discovered that muramyl peptides are immune adjuvants: they enhance the production of antibodies in the immune system and, therefore, are potentially valuable components of vaccines. Specifically, muramyl peptides stimulate the manufacture of lymphokines (including interleukin 1, tumor necrosis factor, and interferon)—chemicals involved in immune cell activation and proliferation. (In recent years, several research teams have discovered that one of these substances, interleukin 1, is not only a product of the immune system but also a constituent of the central nervous system.)

The search for a connection between sleep and the body's defenses against disease led us to ask whether lymphokines alter sleep. In fact, all three lymphokines tested—interferon, tumor necrosis factor, and interleukin 1—greatly enhanced slow-wave sleep in rabbits. What's more, the somnogenic effects of these substances were in many ways identical to those of muramyl peptides. But there was a crucial difference: the onset of sleep was much more rapid after the injection of lymphokines than after an injection of muramyl peptides, suggesting that lymphokine release occurs late in the sleep-activation process—that muramyl peptides exert their somnogenic powers only after some intermediate step that involves lymphokine production.

One of the ways in which lymphokines contribute to the immune response is by stimulating the production of prostaglandins—a family of compounds derived from fatty acids, some of which regulate the activities of macrophages, the immune cells that devour bacteria and viruses. Last year, the Japanese biochemist Osamu Hayaishi demonstrated that both muramyl peptides and lymphokines trigger the output of prostaglandin D2—which he had earlier shown to be somnogenic. Hayaishi's findings thus suggest that at least three biochemical events, involving both the immune system and the central nervous system, are associated with sleep: muramyl peptides induce an increase in the manufacture of lymphokines, which, in turn, give rise to prostaglandins.

That such key elements of the immune system as muramyl peptides and lymphokines are somnogenic seems to explain, at least in part, the sleepiness that often overpowers us when we are in the throes of an infectious disease. And because muramyl peptides are key components of bacteria, scientists have begun to suspect that the compounds also play a role in everyday sleep.

Bacteria, of course, are far more than couriers of disease: they contribute in a number of ways to mammalian physiological processes and have established symbiotic relationships with many forms of life. For example, in the rumen, one of the four stomach cavities in cattle and other cud-chewing animals, an ensemble of bacterial strains is essential to the breakdown of complex carbohydrates, which the animals' bodies otherwise would be unable to metabolize. Human skin harbors thriving colonies of the microorganisms, and most of us carry about a kilogram of bacteria in our intestinal tracts, where they help synthesize vitamin K and from which many of them pass through the intestinal wall.

As bacteria enter the body, they are devoured by macrophages, and as a by-product of this processs, muramyl peptides are released. That the macrophages' activity is continuous suggests that muramyl peptides influence not only the excess sleep that often accompanies the body's immune response to infection but also everyday sleep, as a result of the normal metabolism of microbes.

DURING THE PAST SEVERAL YEARS, our understanding of these biochemical relationships has broadened considerably, in large part because of the discovery of close ties between the immune response, the endocrine network (the glands involved in hormone secretion), and the brain. Studies of their elaborate interactions have made it possible to sketch a rudimentary sleep-activation system, incorporating thirty chemicals that interact in various ways, working with—and sometimes against—one another, to both promote and inhibit sleep.

Consider, by way of illustration, some of the metabolic events set in motion when a muramyl peptide stimulates the production of interleukin 1, a key actor in this complex biochemical system of checks and balances. Interleukin 1 triggers an increase in the release of somatotropin —also known as growth hormone. (Exactly how this occurs is uncertain. One theory is that interleukin 1 stimulates the hypothalamus to secrete growth hormone-releasing factor, which regulates somatotropin release.) Somatotropin fosters the development of bone and muscle, aids in protein synthesis and tissue regeneration, and in humans is tightly coupled with sleep: most of the body's supply of the hormone is produced during slow-wave sleep. Moreover, somatotropin both enhances REM sleep, and, in large doses, inhibits NREM sleep. As it accumulates in the bloodstream, the hormone eventually suppresses the very substance that triggers its own synthesis, growth hormone-releasing factor—one of many examples of feedback (inherent self-regulatory "on–off switches") that appear to maintain a balance between the various sleep-inducing and sleep-preventing processes.

Another possible feedback loop underscores the synergism between the brain, the endocrine system, and the immune response that drives the sleep-activation network: Interleukin 1 signals the hypothalamus to secrete corticotropin-releasing factor, which stimulates the pituitary gland to secrete adrenocorticotropin hormone. Adrenocorticotropin, in turn, signals the adrenal gland to produce hormones called glucocorticoids. All the substances produced in this chain reaction—hypothalamic corticotropin–releasing factor, pituitary corticotropin hormone, and adrenal glucocorticoids—inhibit sleep, possibly via a feedback loop that reduces the synthesis of interleukin 1.

Though it is clear that most, if not all, sleep substances are involved in similar biochemical cascades, the timing of these events, and their impact on sleep, remain to be seen. We have yet to learn, for example, why certain of these chemicals promote both NREM and REM sleep in some doses but elicit contradictory results in others. Or why the effects of some substances seem to vary widely from species to species. Or exactly how many as yet unidentified sleep substances are circulating in our bodies. Indeed, at times it seems that for every layer of complexity we strip from sleep countless more lie still concealed. Certainly, to answer Samuel Johnson (and a great many other thinkers), a labyrinth of causes—at once hopelessly tangled yet remarkably synchronized—confine us to the "irresistible stupefaction" without which no mammal has been known to survive.

New Light on the Chemistry of Dreams

Scientists are inducing and delaying dreams to learn why they happen.

Harold M. Schmeck, Jr.

REM sleep, a paradoxical and mysterious state characterized by rapid eye movements, is leading scientists to new insights about the chemistry of the brain.

While the brain registers intense activity during REM sleep, the body enters a temporary state of benign paralysis. It is the stage of sleep in which dreaming occurs, but most dreams elude memory's grasp.

In the new research on REM sleep, scientists are exploring its chemistry, the electrical state of the brain cells and the location and physical characteristics of cells and nerve circuits involved. One objective is to answer a question that has perplexed researchers for generations: Why do people dream? Scientists also want to know whether dreaming is necessary, as well as to understand the mechanics and chemistry of dreaming.

"It's a state in which the hard wiring of the brain doesn't change, but the state of the organism changes more dramatically than in any other situation," said Dr. Robert W. McCarley of Harvard Medical School in Boston and the Veterans Administration Hospital in Brockton, Mass., in a recent interview. "By studying it we can learn what are the mechanisms by which the brain alters its own excitability."

The studies may help doctors better understand the brain in health and disease, he said. He and some other experts view the dreaming phase of sleep as a possible model for the study of bizarre thought processes that occur in mental illness.

Indeed, a hallmark of serious depression is that REM sleep often appears earlier in the sleep cycle. Drug treatment that helps ease severe depression often has the effect of delaying that phase of sleep.

One of the circumstances that brings on the dreaming stage is an abundance of acetylcholine in the brain. This chemical is one of the brain's main neurotransmitters—substances that nerve cells use to signal to their neighbors. While brain cells that use acetylcholine are active, others that use different neurotransmitters are subdued.

Dr. J. Allan Hobson of the Harvard Medical School said he believed the most important development in the last five years was the ability to produce REM sleep experimentally with drugs.

The dreaming state can be brought on abruptly in animals when a substance that acts like acetylcholine is injected directly into certain nerve cells of the pons, a primitive part of the brain. Several studies of this kind, done at Harvard under the leadership of Dr. Hobson and Dr. McCarley showed that drugs similar in action to acetylcholine could produce REM sleep and that other treatment that interfered with the natural breakdown of that nerve signal substance would have the same effect.

In some of the experiments, done on cats by Dr. Helen A. Baghdoyan, now at Pennsylvania State University in Hershey, the responses were dramatic. REM sleep began within two or three minutes after injection, instead of the half hour it would take naturally. The phase of sleep lasted for two to four hours, rather than the usual six minutes.

Dr. J. Christian Gillin's group at the University of California at San Diego has evoked REM sleep in volunteers by giving them drugs that act like acetylcholine in the brain. Related studies have demonstrated that the drug-induced REM sleep produces dreams that are qualitatively no different from those that occur in natural sleep.

In research on REM sleep in animals, Dr. McCarley and colleagues have demonstrated that certain groups of brain cells in the pons become increasingly excitable as the first REM period approaches. That excitability is a chemical and electrical state that brings the cells closer to "firing," or sending signals to other brain cells.

When the same cells of the reticular formation of the pons fire during the waking state, they cause physical movements, particularly the semi-automatic motions that contribute to walking, running and many other physical acts. In the dreaming phase of sleep, eye movements continue but the nerve connections that govern limb movements are shut off.

Almost all of human dreaming occurs during REM sleep, and dreaming has held intense fascination in every civilization and every epoch. The actual stage of sleep and its key characteristics were discovered in the early 1950's. Today this phase of sleep is intriguing to scientists because it may hold clues to the crucial functions of sleep as well as to understanding of the brain.

One theory of REM sleep holds that this combination of signaling within the brain without resultant physical movements is actually the raw material of dreams. The sleeping brain forms images and scenes in trying to make sense of its own internal signaling.

This theory was proposed 10 years ago by Dr. McCarley and Dr. Hobson. In important respects it offered an explanation of dreaming totally different from Freud's theory that the dream was a disguised and censored expression of forbidden ideas.

"We hypothesize that this perceived movement becomes part of the dream plot," said Dr. McCarley and Dr. Edward Hoffman of Harvard in a report that buttressed the theory by analyzing 104 dreams described by people who were awakened at the end of REM sleep episodes. A majority of the dreams involved running, walking and similar behaviors that would be expected from a brain concocting stories to match internal signals.

"The theory challenges the psychoanalytic idea that the many meaningless aspects of dream mentation are the result of an active effort to disguise the meaning of unconscious wishes," said Dr. Hobson in a recent article on dreaming.

But he does not suggest that the

Almost all of human dreaming occurs during the stage called REM sleep.

content of dreams is random. An individual's dreams may contain "unique stylistic psychological features and concerns," he said, "and thus be worthy of scrutiny by the individual to review life strategies."

Dr. McCarley noted that the bizarre features of dreams — including impossible feats such as flying under one's own power and sudden shifts in scene — may be worth study as a temporary and harmless, but possibly enlightening model of mental illness.

The bizarre quality of dreams is probably itself rooted in the neurophysiology of REM sleep, in Dr. Hobson's view. He has argued that the bizarreness of a dream is probably a consequence of changes in properties of the brain and may have no particular psychological significance.

Preserved in Evolution

Specialists say that REM sleep itself must have useful biological functions because it has been preserved throughout mammalian evolution and because it is difficult, perhaps impossible, to eliminate it.

When it is delayed by waking the dreamer every time the rapid eye movements begin, REM returns more insistently in succeeding sleep episodes. Animals have died in experiments in which REM sleep was prevented for long periods.

Dr. Gillin said he and others have eliminated REM sleep for long periods by using drugs of the class of monoamine oxidase inhibitors for treatment of depression. He said some patients have evidently gone without REM sleep for as long as a year and a half. The dream phase rebounds when the drug is discontinued. The depression did not reappear with the renewed dreaming.

In a normal person, each episode of REM sleep is preceded by four earlier stages of sleep, spanning about 90 minutes, in which brain activity and physical activity become progressively more subdued. REM sleep itself is a paradox in that the brain abruptly becomes much more active, while the rest of the body, except the eyes, remains inert.

In many respects the electrical activity of the dreaming brain is like that of the waking brain. But the chemistry is entirely different. In REM sleep the nerve cells that use acetylcholine are active, while those that depend on other neurotransmitters, like norepinephrine and serotonin, are quiet.

Does the Fetus Dream?

REM sleep is experienced by virtually all mammals. The human infant spends 16 hours a day asleep, and half of this time is REM sleep. This stage of sleep actually begins in the fetus at the 23d week of gestation.

Does the fetus dream? If so, of what? No one knows. What is the vital function of REM sleep that has apparently preserved it throughout mammalian evolution? No one knows that, either,.

All of human experience suggests that the nondreaming phases of sleep represent periods of rest and restoration, but this does not seem to fit the characteristics of REM sleep, in which the brain is highly active and uses substantial amounts of energy.

Yet it is a particularly deep stage of sleep. The sleeper's muscles do not respond to signals from the brain, and the brain responds hardly at all to the outside world. But the dreamer's brain waves are more like those of light sleep. The eyes dart back and forth and portions of the brain seem to be intensely active, in some respects as active as in wakefulness.

Dr. Francis Crick of the Salk Institute and Dr. Graeme Mitchison of Cambridge University have proposed a theory that the dreaming phase of sleep helps the brain flush out the day's accumulation of unneeded and unwanted information.

Maintaining Circuits

Another concept assigns REM sleep a more constructive importance. Dr. Hobson summarized this in an article on current theories of sleep published in the new two-volume "Encyclopedia of Neuroscience," edited by George Adelman and published this year by Birkhäuser of Boston.

"In the developing and in the adult animal REM sleep could guarantee maintenance of circuits critical for survival whether or not they were called upon for use during the wake state," he said.

The complex interconnections among nerve cells in the brain seem to be formed through use of the cells, and they need to be used to be maintained. In the fetus, the kind of nerve cell activity that occurs in REM sleep could help establish nerve circuits in the brain that will be necessary after birth.

Furthermore, the fact that use of some neurotransmitters like norepinephrine and serotonin is subdued during REM sleep may be relevant.

REM sleep has been preserved throughout mammmalian evolution.

These neurotransmitters are in continuous use during the waking hours. REM sleep might help replenish the brain's supplies.

Dr. McCarley believes the new research on the chemistry and nerve circuitry of dreaming sleep has exciting implications.

"For physiology, the excitement is in learning how the brain shapes behavior," he said. For psychiatry, meanwhile, the research offers clues to the manner in which different behaviors, normal and abnormal, are controlled by the brain.

THE HEALING TRANCE

After Years of Neglect, Hypnosis Is Winning Respect

DAVID SPIEGEL

DAVID SPIEGEL is an associate professor of psychiatry and director of the adult psychiatric outpatient clinic at the Stanford University Medical Center, in California. He is the author of dozens of articles on hypnosis, associate editor of the AMERICAN JOURNAL OF CLINICAL HYPNOSIS, *and coauthor, with Herbert Spiegel, of* TRANCE AND TREATMENT: CLINICAL USES OF HYPNOSIS, *published by Basic Books in 1978.*

IN THE SMALL New Hampshire town of Bow, during the tumultuous years before the Civil War, a young woman, descended from two venerable New England families, developed a curious malady. The infirmity, which she later described as "spinal weakness," necessitated that she be carried about the house by her father. After many years of invalidism, she sought the help of a popularly acclaimed "mind healer," one Phineas P. Quimby, of Portland, Maine, who succeeded in curing her with "animal magnetism"—a psychological therapy known today as hypnosis. As Freud might have predicted, a strong bond developed between the patient and her therapist, related no doubt to the unconscious oedipal feelings underlying her illness. Shortly after the relationship was brought to an end by Quimby's death, in 1866, the woman suffered a relapse, precipitated by a severe fall on ice. Bedridden, she turned to the New Testament and recovered "miraculously" in a matter of hours, emerging from the experience convinced that she had been cured all along not by hypnosis but by the word of God.

The patient was Mary Baker Eddy, and her revelations began the Christian Science religion, which to this day holds that illness is best combated through a two-pronged spiritual attack involving the affirmation of truth and the denunciation of "malicious animal magnetism." At present, there are approximately three thousand Christian Science churches and societies worldwide but relatively few proponents of hypnosis. Indeed, the failure of hypnosis to gain widespread acceptance is due largely to such accidents of history, which have left not only Christian Scientists but also many psychoanalysts, psychologists, and physicians skeptical of the procedure.

If history has spawned skepticism of hypnosis, so, too, has the modern age of high technology. Most physicians and patients today—enamored as they are of CAT scans and computer-designed drugs, laser surgery and ultrasonic techniques—consider hypnosis as antiquated as the pocket watch once used to elicit it. If a smoker goes to a psychotherapist and, through a brief lesson in self-hypnosis, learns to control his habit, no insurer will reimburse him for the hundred-dollar treatment; but if, instead, the patient incurs thousands of dollars in surgical expenses for treatment of emphysema, his insurance company will readily pay the tab. The reason is that hypnosis is not viewed as a real procedure; it is allied in many minds with faith healing and other nonscientific approaches to disease. Thus has hypnosis been lost in the gap between holism and high technology.

Ironically, evidence is now rapidly accumulating that hypnosis is a far more powerful therapeutic tool than ever suspected. A host of scientifically rigorous studies have demonstrated its usefulness in controlling self-destructive habits, in overcoming fears, and in coping with problems ranging from physical pain to emotional loss. We have rejected hypnosis most soundly at the very time it seems most promising.

ALTHOUGH TRANCELIKE STATES probably were induced as early as ancient Egyptian times, hypnosis was first introduced to modern Western culture by the eighteenth-century Austrian physician Franz Anton Mesmer. Living in an era when the prevailing scientific interests were gravitation and electromagnetism, Mesmer, like many of his colleagues, was intrigued with the notion of influence at a distance by invisible forces. He believed that the physiological equivalent of magnetism was hypnosis, which he dubbed animal magnetism, and held that disease was caused by disruption in the body's flow of "animal magnetic fluid," which could be set back in motion through the use of magnets or of his own body's magnetic fields.

One of Mesmer's methods was to have patients assemble around a magnetized tub with iron rods protruding from its sides. After taking hold of the rods and watching Mesmer make some suggestive gesture, such as passing his hands over their bodies, the ill would fall into convulsive "crises," from which they would emerge healed. Over time, Mesmer's disciples streamlined his therapy, eliminating the tub and, later, the convulsions, to arrive at a procedure much like modern hypnosis, in which the therapist intones a set of simple instructions to bring about in the willing subject a state of relaxed concentration.

Given that bloodletting was a major form of treatment in the eighteenth century, if hypnosis did nothing more than keep Mesmer's patients out of the hands of other physicians, they were bound to fare better than most. This made Mesmer, who developed a lucrative practice in Paris, unpopular with French physicians of the day. In 1784, his methods were investigated by a panel of experts assembled by King Louis XVI, including our own Benja-

This article is reprinted by permission of *The Sciences* and is from the March/April 1987 issue, pp. 35–40. Individual subscriptions are $13.50 per year. Write to The Sciences, 2 East 63rd Street, New York, NY or call 1–800–THE–NYAS.

min Franklin, the renowned chemist Antoine-Laurent Lavoisier, and the notorious doctor Joseph Guillotin. The panel took a rather dim view of animal magnetism, concluding that, although cures were indeed produced, they were due to "nothing but heated imagination."

That was just the first of many flirtations with hypnosis, most followed by public rejection. Nevertheless, when Sigmund Freud began his psychological inquiries in the 1880s, he seized on hypnosis—which he studied under the great French neurologist Jean-Martin Charcot—as a powerful tool for exploring the unconscious. For more than ten years, Freud used hypnosis regularly in therapy and remarked on its "marvellous results" in select cases. But, in 1897, while a neurotic patient was under hypnosis (Freud was coaxing her to recall the childhood origins of her hysteria), she suddenly leapt up and threw her arms around his neck. "The unexpected entrance of a servant," the founder of the "talking cure" later recalled in his *Autobiographical Study*, "relieved us from a painful discussion."

Freud suspected immediately that the patient was responding to him as a father figure and that she might better explore her past by free-associating than through hypnosis. Thus hypnosis was abandoned and the technique now known as psychoanalysis born. From that moment, the psychoanalytic movement has been adamant in its rejection of hypnosis, despite Freud's later comment that the pure gold of psychoanalysis might in fact need to be alloyed with the baser metal of suggestion.

Hypnosis suffered yet another blow during the reign of behaviorism in the 1950s and 1960s. Taken with the scientific aura of behaviorism and its obsession with objectively measurable external actions, psychologists lost interest, ironically, in the mind. Only as it became clear that behaviorists could not deliver the bold therapeutic successes they promised did psychologists in large numbers return to the study of mental processes—particularly within the framework of cognitive psychology (an area of study, arising in the seventies, that employs information-processing models of language, memory, and other higher mental functions). The mind once again became legitimate (indeed, recent research has uncovered direct biochemical links between mental processes and physical well-being), and there ensued a resurgence of interest in hypnosis.

Today, two major journals are devoted to hypnosis, and scientific studies of the phenomenon appear regularly. Although there still are psychologists who doubt that hypnosis is real (social psychologists, in particular, tend to view it as nothing more than compliance in the extreme), their position is becoming increasingly untenable. A landmark study, in 1969, by Thomas McGlashan and several of his colleagues at the University of Pennsylvania, for instance, found that hypnosis can provide far more pain relief than can placebos. (If hypnosis were nothing more than social compliance, patients should have obtained about the same relief from each, since in each case there existed the expectation that they would get well.) This and scores of other recent studies, taken together, lead to two indisputable conclusions: the hypnotic trance is "real"—a distinct state of consciousness, psychologically and physiologically—and it is therapeutically useful.

Rigorous scientific research on hypnosis was facilitated by the discovery that susceptibility to hypnotism is a measurable trait. In 1959, André Weitzenhoffer, of the University of Oklahoma, and Ernest Hilgard, of Stanford University, devised the Stanford Hypnotic Susceptibility Scales, the first widely used measurement. Subjects are hypnotized with relaxation instructions and are then given twelve suggestions designed to gauge different aspects of their hypnotic response. To see, for example, whether a subject will hallucinate at the hypnotist's suggestion, the hypnotist tells him to imagine a mosquito buzzing around himself; to test his motor response to suggestions, the hypnotist asks him to imagine a weight in one hand. In each case, the hypnotist looks for objective evidence of a response: Does the subject shift position to avoid the mosquito? Does the hand holding the imaginary weight begin to droop? The test takes about an hour and the subject is scored from zero (not hypnotizable) to twelve (highly hypnotizable). In 1970, my father, the psychiatrist Herbert Spiegel, of Columbia University's College of Physicians and Surgeons, and I developed an abbreviated hypnotizability test for use in clinical settings. In the Hypnotic Induction Profile, the subject is asked to perform only one activity—to imagine that one of his hands feels like a helium balloon—and different aspects of his response are measured: whether his hand rises; whether he feels that his hand is out of control; and whether he remembers details of the incident upon emerging from the trance.

Ample evidence suggests that such tests are measuring a trait that varies from person to person but is relatively stable in a given individual over time. In a study published in 1974, Hilgard, along with psychologists Arlene Morgan and David Johnson, measured the hypnotizability of eighty-five Stanford undergraduates, then retested the same individuals an average of ten years later. They found a test–retest correlation of 0.6, meaning that hypnotizability is only slightly less stable than IQ. (This finding holds only for adults, however; hypnotizability typically reaches its peak in late childhood and declines through adolescence.)

Another indication that hypnotic susceptibility tests are valid is that high scores on such tests correlate well with measures of personality traits one would expect to find in hypnotizable individuals. Highly hypnotizable people, for instance, also receive high scores in a test, devised by Auke Tellegen and Gilbert Atkinson, at the University of Minnesota, that measures the ability to have intensely absorbing experiences. Thus, people who tend to become so immersed in a good movie or book that they enter an imaginary world and forget about the real one also tend to be highly hypnotizable.

These findings have clinical relevance. Although hypnotic susceptibility was once considered a sign of weak-mindedness (indeed, the turn-of-the-century French psychologist Pierre Janet argued that once a patient was cured of hysterical neurosis, she was no longer hypnotizable), it is now recognized as a sign of relative mental health. As recently as twenty years ago, when I was a medical student at Harvard, hypnosis was demonstrated on nurses because it was considered an insult to presume doctors-in-training might be hypnotizable; today, when I teach the technique, medical students are disappointed if they are not highly hypnotizable. The realization that hypnotic susceptibility is a gift of the healthy mind may help lift a stigma that for years has impeded study and clinical application of the therapy.

WHAT, precisely, is a hypnotic trance? Psychologically, it has been compared to the view through a telephoto lens: one idea is brought into focus, while the field of vision is narrowed and all competing thoughts are omitted. Because the hypnotized individual focuses on only one idea, without considering its consequences or alternatives or making any stressful associations, he is extremely open to suggestion: the trance has been called a state of "resting alertness."

Physiologically, hypnosis is not so well understood. It was once thought that the electroencephalograms of people in a trance might show an unusually high number of alpha waves—periodic electrical activity in the range of eight to thirteen cycles a second—since these brain waves are associated with a mental state of relaxed attention. As it turns out, highly hypnotizable individuals—whether or not they are in a trance—generate only slightly more alpha waves than do people who are less hypnotizable. Interestingly, though, people in a trance generate less alpha activity in the right cerebral hemisphere than in the left, suggesting that the right brain is more involved in hypnosis. Studies of eye movements lead to the same conclusion. People who characteristically look to the left when asked questions favor the use of the right hemisphere, and highly hypnotizable individuals tend to look left. These findings are hardly surprising, since the right brain is more involved in intuitive and imaginative thinking than is the logical, linguistic left brain.

Perhaps the strongest evidence that the hypnotic trance is a distinct state of consciousness, physiologically as well as psychologically, comes from studies showing that subjects in a trance can induce changes in their physiological functions. Recent research at Stanford University, for instance, has demonstrated that a hypnotized subject can suppress his brain's electrical response to a visual stimulus—a response normally considered involuntary—by imagining that a cardboard box is blocking his view of the stimulus. This suppression is significantly greater in the right portion of the visual-association cortex (in the back of the brain) than in the left, suggesting that the internally generated image that dampens processing of the visual stimulus occurs primarily in the right brain. Hypnotized subjects can also raise and lower their skin temperature and control their blood flow. And hypnosis has enabled patients to eliminate warts, asthmatics to improve their bronchodilation, and hemophiliacs to control bleeding. Recent and still-controversial studies at Beth Israel Hospital, in Boston, even suggest that hypnosis may help individuals control their immune response.

HYPNOSIS IS most often valuable, however, not as a treatment but as a facilitator and intensifier of other therapies. Because the hypnotized patient is open to new ideas, the trance can be used to increase his acceptance of more conventional therapies. Hypnosis has been particularly helpful as an aid to a psychotherapeutic technique known as cognitive restructuring, which teaches patients constructive ways of thinking about, and coping with, emotional loss, physical trauma, and destructive habits. In addition, since hypnosis gives individuals "telephoto vision"—enabling them to focus on a single idea, dissociated from any unpleasant emotions—it can help patients control anxiety, phobias, and pain.

An example of the use of hypnosis in this connection is found in the case of a thirty-five-year-old man who was referred to me after he attempted to drive his car off Route 1, near Monterey, into the Pacific Ocean. The patient was a veteran; while in Vietnam, he had adopted a son, whom he loved deeply. During North Vietnam's Tet Offensive, in 1968, he discovered the boy's body, mutilated and dead, in a hospital. Stricken with grief, he went into the jungle to kill Vietcong. Afterward, he had no memory of the rampage but returned to the United States suicidally depressed. By the time he arrived at my office, he had been in and out of psychiatric wards for more than five years.

Under hypnosis, the patient recalled the events that had led to his depression. I asked him to imagine a split screen, filled on one side with images of his son's death and on the other with images of a party he had thrown for the boy. Over time, these symbols were simplified to a grave on one side of the screen and a cake on the other. He began, at first only in the trance state but eventually in his everyday consciousness, to fuse the images—to connect his grief to his love for the boy. This put his loss in a new perspective and made it more bearable. Today the man is living in the community and is no longer depressed.

A similar therapeutic technique has been successful for treating rape victims. Rape is traumatic partly because the victim retains the sense of being completely vulnerable and humiliated. In therapy, the hypnotized patient imagines a split screen with the rape occurring on one side and the memory of something she did to protect herself on the other. As the two images are fused, her feelings of vulnerability become more tolerable, and she can begin to accept the experience.

Cognitive restructuring accompanied by hypnosis can also be used to help patients stop smoking or overeating. Most people who go to a hypnotist to break bad habits expect that they will simply be reprogrammed so that their cravings for cigarettes or midnight snacks will disappear. Such an approach harks back to the nineteenth-century conception of hypnosis and is still employed by some practitioners, though without much success. The problem is that it emphasizes tacit compliance and offers patients little in the way of continued reinforcement unless they are willing to pay for repeated and often tedious visits to the therapist.

A more effective approach involves teaching patients to use their own hypnotic concentration to adopt a new point of view. It is paradoxical to tell oneself, "Don't smoke." It is like saying, "Don't think about purple elephants": the instruction draws attention to the very activity you want to forget. In cognitive restructuring, the smoker learns to think in a new way about quitting—as an affirmative experience that protects the body rather than as an exercise in self-denial. While in a trance, he is given, and later learns to give himself, several subliminal suggestions: "For my body, smoking is a poison." "I need my body to live." "To the extent that I want to live, I owe my body respect and protection." Hypnosis, by heightening the patient's concentration, helps fix these ideas in his mind. The therapy is self-reinforcing, for the patient feels he is doing his body a favor rather than depriving himself of pleasure. Moreover, since most people find the trance state—which they learn to induce themselves—pleasant and relaxing, it becomes a replacement for the cigarette break. Studies show that about one in four people still refrain from smoking six months after an instruction session in self-hypnosis. This is about the same success rate reported of many other smoking-cessation techniques, such as group support, which often take more time and are more expensive than cognitive restructuring with hypnosis.

While under hypnosis, dieters, like cigarette smokers, can learn to view abstinence not as self-deprivation but as a show of respect for the body. In addition, since the experience of being sated occurs in the brain, which processes signals from the stomach, subjects who learn under hypnosis to change their way of thinking during meals—to concentrate more intensely, for example, on their food—can often recognize satiety more easily or even produce it. In one experiment at Stanford, a hypnotized woman increased her secretion of digestive juices while eating an imaginary meal, and after forty-five minutes of mouth-watering imagination announced, "Let's stop. I'm full."

Hypnosis can also aid people in managing anxieties and phobias. Anxiety disorders are the most common psychological affliction in the United States, more prevalent even than depression. (Only alcoholism is comparable in incidence.) Since anxiety is a state both of psychological and physical distress, it makes sense that a treatment that can produce physical relaxation and mental alertness can be particularly helpful in containing it. During the hypnotic state of resting alertness, patients gain practice thinking about stressful situations without becoming anxious. They can also be taught, if they feel an anxiety attack coming on, to imagine themselves engaged in a restful activity, such as floating in a warm bath. This will interrupt the feedback cycle of psychological and somatic anxiety, a snowball effect in which the patient's initial feeling of nervousness triggers a physical response, such as nausea or dizziness, which increases the patient's feelings of distress, causing a further physical reaction, and so forth. Similarly, the patient in a trance can be fed (or, better, can feed himself) suggestions that will give him a sense of control over his phobias. Airplane phobics, for instance, can be told to view the plane as an extension of their bodies rather than seeing themselves as victims trapped inside the machine. In a 1981 study at Columbia and Stanford, we found that of one hundred and seventy-eight aerophobics offered a single training session in self-hypnosis, fifty-two percent were still cured or considerably improved an average of seven years after treatment.

THE POWER OF HYPNOSIS to help people master pain is one of the technique's least controversial claims. Beginning in the nineteenth century, when the Scottish surgeon James Esdaile reported in his book *Mesmerism in India* that hypnosis could effect complete anesthesia in eighty percent of surgical patients—a finding later retracted under the heat of professional scorn and soon overshadowed by the discovery of ether anesthesia—repeated observations have shown that hypnosis can reduce or eliminate intense physical pain. Indeed, hypnosis has been used as general anesthesia for surgery on patients who are unable to withstand inhalation anesthesia. One such patient, during an operation to remove his diseased lung, experienced the scalpel as a pencil being drawn lightly across his chest.

Hypnotic analgesia seems to work by disciplined control of attention. Just as you may be unaware of sensations in, say, your back as you read this article, the hypnotized person can learn to put painful stimuli at the periphery of his awareness, by focusing on a competing sensation in another part of the body, by imagining that the painful area has been made numb with novocaine, or by concentrating on an imagined change of temperature in the painful region. (The effectiveness of the last of these techniques may have something to do with the fact that pain and temperature fibers run separately from all other sensory nerves in the body and spinal cord.) Pain relief can persist indefinitely after the patient emerges from the trance. Thus, hypnosis can even be useful in controlling chronic pain—the pain of cancer, say, or arthritis—freeing the patient from long-term use of narcotic analgesics, with their disabling side effects, including addiction. Children are especially good candidates for this form of pain relief, since they tend to be highly hypnotizable. In 1982, Stanford psychologists Josephine Hilgard and Samuel LeBaron found that leukemic children who underwent bone marrow aspirations were able, with hypnosis, to reduce pain by thirty percent during the procedure.

All these uses of hypnosis, from relieving pain to softening trauma, have one feature in common: they aim to enhance the individual's control over his behavior or emotions—over anxiety attacks, eating binges, episodes of hysteria, or bouts of suffering. Ironically, many patients and physicians still associate hypnosis with a *loss* of control, leading them to reject the trance as something magical—and pseudoscientific. Through much of its history, hypnosis did enable therapists to impose their suggestions on an entirely passive subject (the very word, *hypnos*, is Greek for sleep); today, however, we know that the therapy is most productive when subjects take an active role—learning to induce their own trances and to mobilize their own inner resources toward a therapeutic goal. In an age when increasingly aggressive, high-technology medical interventions have triggered a renewed interest in patient-controlled therapy—when the growing use of drugs for psychiatric therapy, for instance, has been met by an FDA recommendation that mild hypertension be treated when possible by relaxation training, not medication—perhaps the time is finally ripe for hypnosis to take hold of the public's imagination.

Learning and Memory

Over the past hundred years, experimental psychology has enlarged its scope and intensified its efforts to understand the nature of behavior, particularly the behavior of humans. From a simple beginning focused on the subjective correlates of physical sensations, the experimental approach to understanding behavior has grown to the point where today, the technology developed in earlier efforts to control variables now suggests new variables to study. In still other areas, topics and issues formerly the province of philosophy are proving to be gold mines for experimental investigation.

If we attempted to encapsulate the field of experimental psychology today, we would have to describe it as the study of any aspect of behavior by scientific techniques. At the core of this empirical search for the most basic principles of a behavioral science is the study of learning and memory. Historically, learning was equated with conditioning, both respondent and operant. Today we also appreciate the importance of imitation. We are also beginning to appreciate learning as a characteristic ability of all species. Are animals uniquely equipped to learn? Are some animals, perhaps humans, particularly designed to adapt to change, to modify their behavior, and to maintain and transmit (teach) these changes symbolically? In the unit's first article, B. F. Skinner articulates basic principles which seem endemic to humans and some other animals, but he applies them to a distinctly human class of behavior: verbal behavior. This article provides us with an opportunity to learn some direct applications of operant principles in our lives. And the principles, of course, can be as easily applied to other classes of behavior.

The study of basic learning and memory processes is an important venture in its own right. However, application of such knowledge is an equally important research goal. What kind of instructional environment is most beneficial for learning? Understanding the basic processes involved in learning does not necessarily mean that we understand how learners learn best. One approach to instruction, "back-to-basics," emphasizes repetition, drill, and sustained attention in a highly structured classroom setting. Another approach, "open education," emphasizes self-pacing and exploration in an unstructured setting. In the next article, Barbara Kantrowitz and Pat Wingert review evidence suggesting that children learn best when the learning environment is based on the concept of "developmentally appropriate practice." This approach, firmly grounded in the knowledge gained from scientific studies of child development, stresses matching educational programs to the child's developmental level. Implementing "developmentally appropriate practice" in American schools, however, will require extensive retraining of teachers and more parental involvement in the education of children.

If learning has been the prime paradigm of experimental psychology, memory has been the second. Indeed, in human work on learning, memory is often a crucial measure. For many years experimental psychology was characterized by competition in the search for the actual mechanism of memory, which was conceptualized as consisting of real changes in some part of the body, particularly the brain. Joseph Alper extends this basic conceptualization by pointing out that two types of memories may be encoded and stored differently. These distinctions in storage mechanisms and sites should help foster new research discoveries and improve our understanding of memory. This understanding may also be greatly aided by studies of individuals with extraordinary memory abilities. In the final article, Darold Treffert discusses how the study of Savant Syndrome may enhance our knowledge of normal brain function, creativity, the relation between aging and memory, and the link between memory and emotion.

Looking Ahead: Challenge Questions

How is human learning similar to the patterns of learning demonstrated by other animals? If we manipulate consequences of our own behavior, and shape that behavior in the way we want, are we developing or weakening our self-control? What can we learn about ourselves this way?

Is "developmentally appropriate practice" the solution to the crisis in American education, or is it simply the latest fad? Even if it were demonstrated to be the best learning environment for children, what other social and cultural

problems would have to be solved in order to give "developmentally appropriate practice" a fair chance to make a difference in the public school system?

As we discover more of the chemical details of memory storage, what safeguards will be needed to prevent unreasonable attempts to alter (improve or detract) memory chemically?

If facts and skills are encoded differently, what implica-

tions does this have for educational efforts that teach facts but assume students will be able to translate those facts into skills?

How can the study of individuals with unusual talents superimposed on mental illness or intellectual deficiencies aid in our understanding of "normal" behavior and skill acquisition? Are there any examples in the history of psychology where such a strategy has paid off?

HOW TO DISCOVER WHAT YOU HAVE TO SAY— A TALK TO STUDENTS

B. F. Skinner
Harvard University

My title will serve as an outline. It begins with "How to," and this is a "How to" talk. It is about a problem we all face, and the solution I propose is an example about verbal self-management, using my *Verbal Behavior* (1957) as the basis of a technology. At issue is how we can manage our own verbal behavior more effectively. (I may note in passing that psycholinguistics, a very different kind of analysis, largely structural and developmental, has given rise to no comparable technology, in part because it so often devotes itself to the listener rather than the speaker.)

Verbal behavior begins almost always in spoken form. Even when we write, we usually speak first, either overtly or covertly. What goes down on paper is then a kind of self-dictation. I am concerned here only with written behavior and even so with only a special kind, the kind of writing at the heart of a paper, a thesis, or a book in a field such as the analysis of behavior. What such writing is "about" is hard to say—indeed, that is just the problem. Certain complex circumstances call for verbal action. You have a sheet of paper and a pen; what happens next? How do you arrive at the best possible account?

Do I mean how are you to "think" about those circumstances, to "have ideas" about them? Yes, if those terms are properly defined. In the last chapter of *Verbal Behavior,* I argue that thinking is simply behaving, and it may not be too misleading to say that verbal responses do not express ideas but are the ideas themselves. They are what "occur to us" as we consider a set of circumstances. If I have forgotten the key to my house and "it occurs to me" to look under the mat, it is not an idea that has occurred to me but the behavior of looking, and it occurs because under similar circumstances I have found a key under the mat. What

verbal responses "express" are not preverbal ideas but the past history and present circumstances of the speaker. But how are we to arrive at the most effective expression? How can we behave verbally in a way that is most relevant to a problem at hand?

It is hard to give a "how to" talk without posing as an authority. I hasten to say that I know that I could write better than I do, but I also know that I could write worse. Over the years I believe I have analyzed my verbal behavior to my advantage. What distresses me is that I should have done so so late. Possibly some of what I have learned may help you at an earlier age.

The next word in my title is "discover." If it suggests that verbal behavior lurks inside us waiting to be uncovered, it is a bad term. We do not really "search our memory" for forgotten names. Verbal behavior, like all behavior, is not inside the speaker or writer before it appears. True, I have argued that most behavior is *emitted* rather than elicited as in a reflex, but we also say that light is emitted from a hot filament, although it was not *in* the filament in the form of light. Perhaps a better title would have been "How to Succeed in Saying What You Have to Say." ("How to Say It" suggests style-book advice.)

A first step is to put yourself in the best possible condition for behaving verbally. La Mettrie thought he had supporting evidence for his contention that man was a machine in the fact that he could not think clearly when he was ill. (Freud on the other hand said that he could write only when experiencing a certain discomfort.) Certainly many writers have testified to the importance of diet, exercise, and rest. Descartes, one of the heros of psychology, said that he slept ten hours every night and "never employed more than a few hours a year at those thoughts which engage the understanding . . . I

First appeared in *The Behavior Analyst,* 1981, 4, 1-7, No. 1 (Spring), published by the Society for the Advancement of Behavior Analysis.

have consecrated all the rest of my life to relaxation and rest.'' Good physical condition is relevant to all kinds of effective behavior but particularly to that subtle form we call verbal.

Imagine that you are to play a piano concerto tomorrow night with a symphony orchestra. What will you do between now and then? You will get to bed early for a good night's rest. Tomorrow morning you may practice a little but not too much. During the day you will eat lightly, take a nap, and in other ways try to put yourself in the best possible condition for your performance in the evening.

Thinking effectively about a complex set of circumstances is more demanding than playing a piano, yet how often do you prepare yourself to do so in a similar way? Too often you sit down to think after everything else has been done. You are encouraged to do so by the cognitive metaphor of thinking as the expression of ideas. The ideas are there; the writer is simply a reporter.

What about drugs? Alcohol? Tobacco? Marijuana? There are authentic cases of their productive effects in poetry and fiction, but very little in serious thinking. Tactitus said that the Germans made their decisions when drunk but acted upon them when sober, and Herodotus said the same of the Persians. In other words, it may be possible to solve an intellectual problem when drunk or stoned, but only if the solution is reviewed soberly. In spite of much talk of expanded consciousness, good examples of the advantages of drugs are still lacking.

So much for the condition of your body. Equally important are the conditions in which the behavior occurs. A convenient place is important. It should have all the facilities needed for the execution of writing. Pens, typewriters, recorders, files, books, a comfortable desk and chair. It should be a pleasant place and smell good. Your clothing should be comfortable. Since the place is to take control of a particular kind of behavior, you should do nothing else there at any time.

It is helpful to write always at the same time of day. Scheduled obligations often raise problems, but an hour or two can almost always be found in the early morning—when the telephone never rings and no one knocks at the door. And it is important that you write something,

regardless of quantity, every day. As the Romans put it, *Nulla dies sine linea*—No day without a line. (They were speaking of lines drawn by artists, but the rule applies as well to the writer.)

As a result of all this, the setting almost automatically evokes verbal behavior. No warmup is needed. A circadian rhythm develops which is extremely powerful. At a certain time every day, you will be highly disposed to engage in serious verbal behavior. You will find evidence of this when traveling to other time zones, when a strong tendency to engage in serious verbal behavior appears at the usual time, though it is now a different time by the clock.

It may be a mistake to try to do too much at first. Such a situation only slowly acquires control. It is enough to begin with short sessions, perhaps 15 minutes a day. And do not look for instant quality. Stendhal once remarked, ''If when I was young I had been willing to talk about wanting to be a writer, some sensible person might have said to me: 'Write for two hours every day, genius or not.' That would have saved ten years of my life, stupidly wasted in waiting to become a genius.''

How should you spend the rest of the day? Usually you will have little choice, for other demands must be met. But there is usually some leisure time, and a fundamental rule is not to try to do more writing. You may tease out a few more words, but you will pay the price the next morning. The Greeks spoke of eutrapelia—the productive use of leisure. A little experimentation will reveal the kinds of diversion which maximize your subsequent productivity.

There is an exception to the rule against writing elsewhere. Verbal behavior may occur to you at other times of day, and it is important to put it down in lasting form. A notebook or a pocket recorder is a kind of portable study. Something you see, hear, or read sets off something relevant, and you must catch it on the wing. Jotting down a brief reminder to develop the point later is seldom enough, because the conditions under which it occurred to you are the best conditions for writing a further account. A longer note written at the time will often develop into something that would be lost if the writing were postponed. The first thing that occurs to you may not be the most important response with respect to a given situation, and writing a note gives other verbal behavior a chance to emerge.

As notes accumulate they can be classified and rearranged, and they will supply some of the most important materials for your papers or books. One of the most widely reprinted and translated papers of mine, "Freedom and the Control of Men" (Skinner, 1955-56), was first written almost entirely in the form of notes. When I was asked for a paper on that theme, I found that it was practically written. Notes which are left over can of course be published in a notebook, as I have recently found (Skinner, 1980).

The metaphor of discovery redeems itself at this point. When you construct the best possible conditions for the production of verbal behavior and have provided for catching occasional verbal responses on the wing, you are often *surprised* by what turns up. There is no way in which you can see all of your verbal behavior before you emit it.

I am not talking about how to *find* something to say. The easiest way to do that is to collect experiences, as by moving about in the world and by reading and listening to what others say. A college education is largely a process of collecting in that sense. And so, of course, is exploration, research, and a full exposure to daily life. Nor am I talking about the production of ideas through the permutations and combinations of other material. A very different kind of idea is generated, for example, by playing with contradictions or antinomies. The young Marx was addicted: ". . . The world's becoming philosophical is at the same time philosophy's becoming worldly, . . ." "That the rational is real is proved even in the contradiction of irrational reality that is at all points the opposite of what it proclaims, and proclaims the opposite of what it is." "History has long enough been resolved into superstition, but now we can resolve superstition into history." I daresay Marx thought he was discovering something worth saying, and the verbal play suggests profoundity, but it is a dangerous practice.

The next word is "You." Who is the you who has something to say? You are, of course, a member of the human species, absolutely unique genetically unless you have an identical twin. You also have a personal history which is absolutely unique. Your identity depends upon the coherence of that history. More than one history in one lifetime leads to multiple selves, no one of which can be said to be the real you. The writer of fiction profits from the multiplicity of selves in the invention of character.

We also display different selves when we are fresh or fatigued, loving or angry, and so on. But it is still meaningful to ask what *you* have to say about a given topic *as an individual*. The you that you discover is the you that exists over a period of time. By reviewing what you have already written, going over notes, reworking a manuscript, you keep your verbal behavior fresh in (not your mind!) your history, and you are then most likely to say all that you have to say with respect to a given situation or topic.

Obviously, it will not be simply what you have read or heard. It is easy to get books out of the books of other people, but they will not be your books.

The last three words of my title are "Have to Say," and they have at least three meanings.

The first is the verbal behavior I have just identified—the thing we refer to when we ask a person "What do you have to say to that?" We are simply asking "What is your verbal behavior with respect to that?"

A second meaning is what you *have* to say in the sense of *must* say. It is usually easy to distinguish between the things we want to do and those we have to do to avoid the consequences of not doing them, where "have to" refers to aversive control. A familiar example is the pause in conversation which must be filled and which leads, too often, to verbal behavior about trivia—the weather, the latest news, what someone is wearing. It is also the occasion for hasty and ungrammatical speech, or nonsense, or revealing slips. Much the same aversive pressure is felt in completing an hour's lecture when one has prematurely exhausted one's notes, or finishing a paper on time. It is then that we tend to borrow the verbal behavior of others and resort to clichés and phrases or sentences which simply stall for time ("It is interesting to note that . . .," "Let us now turn to . . .").

The results are not always bad. Many famous writers have worked mostly under aversive pressure. Balzac wrote only when he needed money, Dostoevski only in return for advances he had received. Aversive control may keep you at work, but what you write will be traceable to other variables if it is any good. Moreover, it is under such conditions that writers report that writing is hell, and if you write primarily to avoid the consequences of not writing, you may find it hard to resist other forms of escape—stopping to get a cup of coffee, needlessly rereading something already written, sharpening pencils, calling it a day.

There may be an aversive element in maintaining the schedule which builds a circadian rhythm. It is not always easy to get up at five o'clock in the morning and start writing. Even though you make the space in which you work so attractive that it reinforces your behavior in going to it, some aversive control may be needed. But other variables must take over if anything worthwhile is written. Positive reinforcement may be as irresistible as negative, but it is more likely to lead you to say what you have to say effectively.

The great generalized reinforcer, money, is usually poorly contingent upon behavior at your desk. It controls too effectively when a writer begins to write only the kinds of things which have sold well. Prestige and fame are also long deferred consequences inadequately contingent upon the production of sentences, but progress toward the completion of a book which may lead to money or prestige and fame may help if it is made clear. Some kind of record of the number of words or pages you write may act as a reinforcing consequence. For years, an electric clock on my desk ran only when the light was on, and I added a point to a cumulative record whenever the clock completed twelve hours. The slope of the curve showed me how much time I was spending each day (and how damaging it was to go off on a speaking tour!). A simple calculation reinforces that reinforcer. Suppose you are at your desk two hours a day and produce on the average 50 words per hour. That is not much, but it is about 35,000 words a year, and a book every two or three years—which I myself have found reinforcing enough.

Other immediate consequences are more effective in discovering what you have to say. Saying something for the first time that surprises you, clearing up a confusing point, enjoying what you have written as you read it over—these are the things which, in the long run, are most likely to produce verbal behavior which is your own. The best reason for liking what you have written is that it says what *you* have to say.

Your audience as a source of reinforcers is not to be overlooked. As Pascal put it, "There are those who speak well and write badly. The occasion, the audience fires them and draws from them more than they find in themselves without this heat." Writing often suffers when it is not directed toward a particular kind of reader. Just as in writing a letter to a close friend you may find a picture helpful or at least a warm salutation at the head of the letter, so some visible sign of an audience may help. Reading what someone else has said about you sometimes strengthens behavior, since one is seldom at a loss for words in a warm discussion. I once used E. G. Boring's *Physical Dimensions of Consciousness* as an instrument of self-management. I disagreed so violently with the author's position that after reading a page or two I would find my verbal behavior very strong. And one day when I was lecturing to a class but was not speaking well, I noticed that a student had brought his parents. My behavior changed dramatically under the influence of that new audience. Searching for good audiences may be worthwhile.

Just as those who write for money may begin to write things that sell rather than what they have to say as individuals, so an audience may have too strong an effect. I once gave what was supposed to be the same lecture to 15 audiences. I used a good many slides which served as an outline, but I began to abbreviate or drop comments which did not seem to arouse interest and retain everything which brought a clean-cut response or a laugh. Near the end of the series, I had to struggle to say anything worthwhile.

That verbal behavior is sustained by the prevailing contingencies is shown by the fact that writing exhibits many effects of scheduling. Fixed-ratio reinforcement often produces a "snowball effect:" The closer one comes to finishing a piece of work, the easier it is to work on it (where "easy" means that one works without moving to escape or without "forcing oneself" to remain at work). Writing papers, articles, or stories one after the other "for a living" tends to be on a ratio schedule, and the "post-reinforcement pause" takes the form of abulia, or "not being able to get started on something new."

There are many reasons why you may stop writing or "find it difficult" to go on. When something is not going well, when you are not saying anything important, when matters remain as confusing as ever, extinction sets in. You may continue, but only because aversive consequences take over. Punishment in the form of frequent criticism decreases production, a point not recognized by teachers of composition who spend most of their time pointing to the faults in their students' work (Vargas, 1978).

Satiation also weakens behavior. Many novelists never tell a story before they write it. Just as you cannot tell the same story to the same company a second time (or at least with the same effect!), so you are less likely to get a novel written if you have already told the plot. Enforced silence is a useful practice. Satiation also sets in when one writes more or less to the same effect again and again.

There is also a kind of subject-matter fatigue. One starts to write in excellent condition but eventually becomes "sick of the subject." One solution is to work on two subjects at the same time. It is easier to write short sections of two papers during a session than to spend the whole session on one.

A third sense of "have to say" is the heart of the matter. In a paper called "On 'Having' a Poem" (Skinner, 1972), I compared a poet with a mother. Although the mother bears the child and we call it her child, she is not responsible for any of its features. She gave it half its genes, but she got those from her parents. I argued that the same thing could be said of the poet. Critics who trace the origins and influences of a poem seem to agree, at least to the extent that they can account for features of a poem by pointing to the verbal or non-verbal history of the poet. Samuel Butler's comment that "A hen is simply an egg's way of making another egg" holds for the human egg as well and

for the poet. A poet is a literary tradition's way of making more of a literary tradition. (Much the same thing could be said of the scholar. A psychologist is just psychology's way of making more psychology.)

But the mother does make a contribution: She nourishes, protects, and in the end gives birth to the baby, and so does the poet and so does the scholar. There is a process of verbal gestation. Your history as a writer lacks the structure and coherence of the behavior which eventually emerges from it. Sentences and paragraphs are not lurking inside you waiting to be born. You possess some behavior in the form of prefabricated sentences, and may often do little more than utter them as such, possibly with minor changes, but that is not discovering what you have to say.

A new situation may strengthen dozens—possibly hundreds—of verbal responses which have never before been strengthened together at the same time. They may lack organization. Relations among them may be unclear. They will have little effect on the reader who has not had the same history and is not confronted by the same situation. They must therefore be ordered and interrelated in an effective way. That is what you do as you compose sentences, paragraphs, and at last a book. Only then will your verbal behavior lead to successful action by your readers or to a less active but still behavioral "understanding" of what you are saying.

Verbal Behavior (Skinner, 1957) takes up these stages in order. The first half describes the kinds of verbal operants produced by different contingencies of reinforcement. Although these are more than structures because they have probabilities of reinforcement, they are not assertion. The second half describes how they are fashioned into effective verbal discourse as they are asserted, qualified, denied, and so on, in such a way that the reader responds effectively. The writer thus generates sentences as effective sequences of the material emerging upon a given occasion.

I have found the following rules helpful in discovering what one has to say in this sense.

Rule 1. Stay out of prose as long as possible. The verbal behavior evoked by the setting you are writing about does not yet exist in the form of sentences, and if you start by composing sentences, much will be irrelevant to the final product. By composing too early you introduce a certain amount of trash which must later be thrown away. The important parts of what you have to say are more easily manipulated if they have not yet become parts of sentences.

Rule 2. Indicate valid relations among responses by constructing an outline. Very large sheets of paper (say, 22″ by 34″) are helpful. Your final verbal product (sentence, paragraph, chapter, book) must be linear—with a bit of branching—but the variables contributing to your behavior are arranged in many dimensions. Numbering the parts of a composition decimally is helpful in making cross-references and temporary indices and in noting connections among parts. As bits of verbal behavior are moved about, valid arrangements will appear and sentences will begin to emerge. It is then time to "go into prose."

Rule 3. Construct the first prose draft without looking too closely at style. "Full speed ahead, and damn the stylebook." (How hard that will be depends upon the extent to which aversive control has been used in teaching you to write.) When what you have to say about a given state of affairs exists at last in prose, rewrite as you please, removing unnecessary words, articulating sentences with better connectives, making new rearrangements which seem necessary, and so on. At this stage, some advice on style is helpful. I myself read Follett's *Modern American Usage* straight through every two or three years.

There is an old distinction between ecstatic and euplastic composition. There have been times when ecstatic verbal behavior (impulsive, unreasoned) was particularly admired, because it seemed more genuine, less contrived. In poetry and some forms of fiction it may be particularly effective. But in writing about a complex subject matter, it is too much to expect that adequate statements will appear fully formed. Neither phylogenically nor ontogenically has verbal behavior evolved to the point at which a complex combination of personal history and a current situation will give rise to a passage having an appropriate effect upon the reader. Only the most skillful "euplastic" (reasoned) management of verbal behavior will suffice.

Possibly I am confessing some special need for crutches. No doubt other people arrive more quickly at effective statements. They do not need to work so hard to say important things. I myself did not need to work so hard when I was younger. I am simply telling you how I succeed in saying what I have to say. Of course I wish I had more to say and that I had said it better, and I wish I could tell you more clearly what I have learned about saying it. But it would be impossible to tell you all you need to know. No two people are alike; your personal histories will lead you to respond in different ways. You will have to work out your own rules. As in any application of a behavioral analysis, the secret of successful verbal self-management is an understanding of what verbal behavior is all about.

REFERENCES

Follett, Wilson. *Modern American Usage,* New York, 1966.

Skinner, B. F. Freedom and the control of men. *American Scholar,* Winter 1955-56.

Skinner, B. F. *Verbal Behavior.* New York, 1957.

Skinner, B. F. On "having" a poem. *Saturday Review,* July 15, 1972. Reprinted in *Cumulative Record.* New York, 1972.

Skinner, B. F. *Notebooks.* Englewood Cliffs, N. J., 1980.

Vargas, J. S. A behavioral approach to the teaching of composition. *Behavior Analyst,* 1978, *1,* 16-24.

How Kids Learn

BARBARA KANTROWITZ & PAT WINGERT

Ages 5 through 8 are wonder years. That's when children begin learning to study, to reason, to cooperate. We can put them in desks and drill them all day. Or we can keep them moving, touching, exploring. The experts favor a hands-on approach, but changing the way schools teach isn't easy. The stakes are high and parents can help.

With Howard Manly in Atlanta and bureau reports

It's time for number games in Janet Gill's kindergarten class at the Greenbrook School in South Brunswick, N.J. With hardly any prodding from their teacher, 23 five- and six-year-olds pull out geometric puzzles, playing cards and counting equipment from the shelves lining the room. At one round table, a group of youngsters fits together brightly colored wooden shapes. One little girl forms a hexagon out of triangles. The others, obviously impressed, gather round to count up how many parts are needed to make the whole.

After about half an hour, the children get ready for story time. They pack up their counting equipment and settle in a circle around Gill. She holds up a giant book about a zany character called Mrs. Wishy-washy who insists on giving farm animals a bath. The children recite the whimsical lines along with Gill, obviously enjoying one of their favorite tales. (The hallway is lined with drawings depicting the children's own interpretation of the book; they've taken a few literary liberties, like substituting unicorns and dinosaurs for cows and pigs.) After the first reading, Gill asks for volunteers to act out the various parts in the book. Lots of hands shoot up. Gill picks out four children and

they play their parts enthusiastically. There isn't a bored face in the room.

This isn't reading, writing and arithmetic the way most people remember it. Like a growing number of public- and private-school educators, the principals and teachers in South Brunswick believe that children between the ages of 5 and 8 have to be taught differently from older children. They recognize that young children learn best through active, hands-on teaching methods like games and dramatic play. They know that children in this age group develop at varying rates and schools have to allow for these differences. They also believe that youngsters' social growth is as essential as their academic achievement. Says Joan Warren, a teacher consultant in South Brunswick: "Our programs are designed to fit the child instead of making the child fit the school."

Educators call this kind of teaching "developmentally appropriate practice"—a curriculum based on what scientists know about how young children learn. These ideas have been slowly emerging through research conducted over the last century, particularly in the past 30 years. Some of the tenets have appeared

The Lives and Times of Children

Each youngster proceeds at his own pace, but the learning curve of a child is fairly predictable. Their drive to learn is awesome, and careful adults can nourish it. The biggest mistake is pushing a child too hard, too soon.

● Infants and Toddlers

They're born to learn. The first important lesson is trust, and they learn that from their relationships with their parents or other caring adults. Later, babies will begin to explore the world around them and experiment with independence. As they mature, infants slowly develop gross motor (sitting, crawling, walking) and fine motor (picking up tiny objects) skills. Generally, they remain egocentric and are unable to share or wait their turn. New skills are perfected through repetition, such as the babbling that leads to speaking.

■ 18 months to 3 years

Usually toilet training becomes the prime learning activity. Children tend to concentrate on language development and large-muscle control through activities like climbing on jungle gyms. Attention spans lengthen enough to listen to uncomplicated stories and carry on conversations. Vocabulary expands to about 200 words. They enjoy playing with one other child, or a small group, for short periods, and learn that others have feelings too. They continue to look to parents for encouragement and protection, while beginning to accept limits on their behavior.

▲ 3-year-olds

Generally, they're interested in doing things for themselves and trying to keep up with older children. Their ability to quietly listen to stories and music remains limited. They begin telling stories and jokes. Physical growth slows, but large-muscle development continues as children run, jump and ride tricycles. They begin to deal with cause and effect; it's time to plant seeds and watch them grow.

● 4-year-olds

They develop better small motor skills, such as cutting with scissors, painting, working with puzzles and building things.
They can master colors, sizes and shapes. They should be read to and should be encouraged to watch others write; let them scribble on paper but try to keep them away from walls.

■ 5-year-olds

They begin to understand counting as a one-to-one correlation. Improved memories make it easier for them to recognize meaningful words, and with sharper fine motor skills, some children will be able to write their own names.

▲ Both 4s and 5s   *kindergarten*

Both groups learn best by interacting with people and concrete objects and by trying to solve real problems. They can learn from stories and books, but only in ways that relate to their own experience. Socially, these children are increasingly interested in activities outside their immediate family. They can play in groups for longer periods, learning lessons in cooperation and negotiation. Physically, large-muscle development continues, and skills such as balancing emerge.

● 6-year-olds   *Grade one*

Interest in their peers continues to increase, and they become acutely aware of comparisons between themselves and others. It's a taste of adolescence: does the group accept them? Speech is usually well developed, and children are able to joke and tease. They have a strong sense of true and false and are eager for clear rules and definitions. However, they have a difficult time differentiating between minor and major infractions. Generally, children this age are more mature mentally than physically and unable to sit still for long periods. They learn better by firsthand experiences. Learning by doing also encourages children's "disposition" to use the knowledge and skills they're acquiring.

■ 7- to 8-year-olds   *Grade 2*

During this period, children begin developing the ability to think about and solve problems in their heads, but some will continue to rely on fingers and toes to help them find the right answer. Not until they're 11 are most kids capable of thinking purely symbolically; they still use real objects to give the symbols—such as numbers—meaning. At this stage they listen better and engage in give and take. Generally, physical growth continues to slow, while athletic abilities improve—children are able to hit a softball, skip rope or balance on a beam. Sitting for long periods is still more tiring than running and jumping.

under other names—progressivism in the 1920s, open education in the 1970s. But they've never been the norm. Now, educators say that may be about to change. "The entire early-childhood profession has amassed itself in unison behind these principles," says Yale education professor Sharon Lynn Kagan. In the last few years, many of the major education organizations in the country—including the National Association for the Education of Young Children and the National Association of State Boards of Education—have endorsed remarkably similar plans for revamping kindergarten through third grade.

Bolstered by opinions from the experts, individual states are beginning to take action. Both California and New York have appointed task forces to recommend changes for the earliest grades. And scores of individual school districts like South Brunswick, figuring that young minds are a terrible thing to waste, are pushing ahead on their own.

The evidence gathered from research in child development is so compelling that even groups like the Council for Basic Education, for years a major supporter of the traditional format, have revised their thinking. "The idea of putting small children in front of workbooks and asking them to sit at their desks all day is a nightmare vision," says Patte Barth, associate editor of Basic Education, the council's newsletter.

At this point, there's no way of knowing how soon change will come or how widespread it will be. However, there's a growing recognition of the importance of the early grades. For the past few years, most of the public's attention has focused on older children, especially teenagers. "That's a Band-Aid kind of approach," says Anne Dillman, a member of the New Jersey State Board of Education. "When the product doesn't come out right, you try and fix it at the end. But we really have to start at the beginning." Demographics have contributed to the sense of urgency. The baby boomlet has replaced the baby-bust generation of the 1970s. More kids in elementary school means more parents asking if there's a better way to teach. And researchers say there is a better way. "We've made remarkable breakthroughs in understanding the development of children, the development of learning and the climate that enhances that," says Ernest Boyer of The Carnegie Foundation for the Advancement of Teaching. But, he adds, too often, "what we know in theory and what we're doing in the classroom are very different."

The early grades pose special challenges because that's when children's attitudes toward school and learning are shaped, says Tufts University psychologist David Elkind. As youngsters move from home or preschool into the larger, more competitive world of elementary school, they begin to make judgments about their own abilities. If they feel inadequate, they may give up. Intellectually, they're also in transition, moving from the intensely physical exploration habits of infancy and toddlerhood to more abstract reasoning. Children are born wanting to learn. A baby can spend hours studying his hands; a toddler is fascinated by watching sand pour through a sieve. What looks like play to an adult is actually the work of childhood, developing an understanding of the world. Studies show that the most effective way to teach young kids is to capitalize on their natural inclination to learn through play.

But in the 1980s, many schools have tried to do just the opposite, pressure instead of challenge. The "back to basics" movement meant that teaching methods intended for high school students were imposed on first graders. The lesson of the day was more: more homework, more tests, more discipline. Children should be behind their desks, not roaming around the room. Teachers should be at the head of the classrooms, drilling knowledge into their charges. Much of this was a reaction against the trend toward open education in the '70s. Based on the British system, it allowed children to develop at their own pace within a highly structured classroom. But too many teachers and principals who tried open education thought that it meant simply tearing down classroom walls and letting children do whatever they wanted. The results were often disastrous. "Because it was done wrong, there was a backlash against it," says Sue Bredekamp of the National Association for the Education of Young Children.

At the same time, parents, too, were demanding more from their elementary schools. By the mid-1980s, the majority of 3- and 4-year-olds were attending some form of pre-school. And their parents expected these classroom veterans to be reading by the second semester of kindergarten. But the truth is that many 5-year-olds aren't ready for reading—or most of the other academic tasks that come easily to older children—no matter how many years of school they've completed. "We're confusing the numbers of years children have been in school with brain development," says Martha Denckla, a professor of neurology and pediatrics at Johns Hopkins University. "Just because a child goes to day care at age 3 doesn't mean the human brain mutates into an older brain. A 5-year-old's brain is still a 5-year-old's brain."

As part of the return to basics, parents and districts demanded hard evidence that their children were learning. And some communities took extreme measures. In 1985 Georgia became the first state to require 6-year-olds to pass a standardized test before entering first grade. More than two dozen other states proposed similar legislation. In the beginning Georgia's move was hailed as a "pioneering" effort to get kids off to a good start. Instead, concedes state school superintendent Werner Rogers, "We got off on the wrong foot." Five-year-olds who used to spend their days fingerpainting or singing were hunched over ditto sheets, preparing for the big exam. "We would have to spend a month just teaching kids how to take the test," says Beth Hunnings, a kindergarten teacher in suburban Atlanta. This year Georgia altered the tests in favor of a more flexible evaluation; other states have changed their minds as well.

The intense, early pressure has taken an early toll. Kindergartners are struggling with homework. First graders are taking spelling tests before they even understand how to read. Second graders feel like failures. "During this critical period," says David Elkind in his book "Miseducation," "the child's bud-

In Japan, First Grade Isn't a Boot Camp

Japanese students have the highest math and science test scores in the world. More than 90 percent graduate from high school. Illiteracy is virtually nonexistent in Japan. Most Americans attribute this success to a rigid system that sets youngsters on a lock-step march from cradle to college. In fact, the early years of Japanese schooling are anything but a boot camp; the atmosphere is warm and nurturing. From kindergarten through third grade, the goal is not only academic but also social—teaching kids to be part of a group so they can be good citizens as well as good students. "Getting along with others is not just a means for keeping the peace in the classroom but something which is a valued end in itself," says American researcher Merry White, author of "The Japanese Educational Challenge."

Lessons in living and working together grow naturally out of the Japanese culture. Starting in kindergarten, youngsters learn to work in teams, with brighter students often helping slower ones. All children are told they can succeed if they persist and work hard. Japanese teachers are expected to be extremely patient with young children. They go over lessons step by step and repeat instructions as often as necessary. "The key is not to scold [children] for small mistakes," says Yukio Ueda, principal of Mita Elementary School in Tokyo. Instead, he says, teachers concentrate on praising and encouraging their young charges.

As a result, the classrooms are relaxed and cheerful, even when they're filled with rows of desks. On one recent afternoon a class of second graders at Ueda's school was working on an art project. Their assignment was to build a roof with poles made of rolled-up newspapers. The children worked in small groups, occasionally asking their teacher for help. The room was filled with the sound of eager youngsters chatting about how to get the job done. In another second-grade class, the subject was math. Maniko Inoue, the teacher, suggested a number game to practice multiplication. After a few minutes of playing it, one boy stood up and proposed changing the rules just a bit to make it more fun. Inoue listened carefully and then asked if the other students agreed. They cheered, "Yes, yes," and the game continued according to the new rules.

Academics are far from neglected in the early grades. The Education Ministry sets curriculum standards and goals for each school year. For example, third graders by the end of the year are supposed to be able to read and write 508 characters (out of some 2,000 considered essential to basic literacy). Teachers have time for play and lessons: Japanese children attend school for 240 days, compared with about 180 in the United States.

Mothers' role: Not all the teaching goes on in the classroom. Parents, especially mothers, play a key role in education. Although most kindergartens do not teach writing or numbers in any systematic way, more than 80 percent of Japanese children learn to read or write to some extent before they enter school. "It is as if mothers had their own built-in curriculum," says Shigefumi Nagano, a director of the National Institute for Educational Research. "The first game they teach is to count numbers up to 10."

For all their success in the early grades, the Japanese are worried they're not doing well enough. After a recent national curriculum review, officials were alarmed by what Education Minister Takeo Nishioka described as excessive "bullying and misconduct" among children—the result, according to some Japanese, of too much emphasis on material values. So three years from now, first and second graders will no longer be studying social studies and science. Instead, children will spend more time learning how to be good citizens. That's "back to basics"—Japanese style.

BARBARA KANTROWITZ *with* HIDEKO TAKAYAMA *in Tokyo*

ding sense of competence is frequently under attack, not only from inappropriate instructional practices . . . but also from the hundred and one feelings of hurt, frustration and rejection that mark a child's entrance into the world of schooling, competition and peer-group involvement." Adults under similar stress can rationalize setbacks or put them in perspective based on previous experiences; young children have none of these defenses. Schools that demand too much too soon are setting kids off on the road to failure.

It doesn't have to be this way. Most experts on child development and early-childhood education believe that young children learn much more readily if the teaching methods meet their special needs:

Differences in thinking: The most important ingredient of the nontraditional approach is hands-on learning. Research begun by Swiss psychologist Jean Piaget indicates that somewhere between the ages of 6 and 9, children begin to think abstractly instead of concretely. Younger children learn much more by touching and seeing and smelling and tasting than by just listening. In other words, 6-year-olds can easily understand addition and subtraction if they have actual objects to count instead of a series of numbers written on a blackboard. Lectures don't help. Kids learn to reason and communicate by engaging in conversation. Yet most teachers still talk at, not with, their pupils.

Physical activity: When they get to be 10 or 11, children can sit still for sustained periods. But until they are physically ready for long periods of inactivity, they need to be active in the classroom. "A young child has to make a conscious effort to sit still," says Denckla. "A large chunk of children can't do it for very long. It's a very energy-consuming activity for them." Small children actually get more tired if they have to sit still and listen to a teacher talk than if they're allowed to move around in the classroom. The frontal lobe, the part of the brain that applies the brakes to children's natural energy and curiosity, is still immature in 6- to 9-year-olds, Denckla says. As the lobe develops, so does what Denckla describes as "boredom tolerance." Simply put, learning by doing is much less boring to young children.

Language development: In this age group, experts say language development should not be broken down into isolated skills—reading, writing and speaking. Children first learn to reason and to express themselves by talking. They can dictate stories to a teacher before they actually read or write. Later, their first attempts at composition do not need to be letter perfect; the important thing is that they learn to communicate ideas. But in many classrooms, grammar and spelling have become more important than content. While mastering the technical aspects of writing is essential as a child gets older, educators warn against emphasizing form over content in the early grades. Books should also be interesting to kids—not just words strung together solely for the purpose of pedag-

ogy. Psychologist Katherine Nelson of the City University of New York says that her extensive laboratory and observational work indicates that kids can learn language—speaking, writing or reading—only if it is presented in a way that makes sense to them. But many teachers still use texts that are so boring they'd put anybody to sleep.

Socialization: A youngster's social development has a profound effect on his academic progress. Kids who have trouble getting along with their classmates can end up behind academically as well and have a higher incidence of dropping out. In the early grades especially, experts say youngsters should be encouraged to work in groups rather than individually so that teachers can spot children who may be having problems making friends. "When children work on a project," says University of Illinois education professor Lillian Katz, "they learn to work together, to disagree, to speculate,

The early years of a child's education are indeed wonder years. They begin learning to socialize, to study, and to reason. More and more education experts are favoring a hands-on approach to introducing young children to the mysteries of their surroundings.

to take turns and de-escalate tensions. These skills can't be learned through lecture. We all know people who have wonderful technical skills but don't have any social skills. Relationships should be the first 'R'."

Feelings of competence and self-esteem: At this age, children are also learning to judge themselves in relation to others. For most children, school marks the first time that their goals are not set by an internal clock but by the outside world. Just as the 1-year-old struggles to walk, 6-year-olds are struggling to meet adult expectations. Young kids don't know how to distinguish between effort and ability, says Tynette Hills, coordinator of early-childhood education for the state of New Jersey. If they try hard to do something and fail, they may conclude that they will never be able to accomplish a particular task. The effects of obvious methods of comparison, such as posting grades, can be serious. Says Hills: "A child who has had his confidence really damaged needs a rescue operation."

Rates of growth: Between the ages of 5 and 9, there's a wide range of development for children of normal intelligence. "What's appropriate for one child may not be appropriate for another," says Dr. Perry Dyke, a member of the California State Board of Education. "We've got to have the teachers and the staff reach children at whatever level they may be at . . . That takes very sophisticated teaching." A child's pace is almost impossible to predict beforehand. Some kids learn to read on their own by kindergarten; others are still struggling to decode words two or three years later. But by the beginning of the fourth grade, children with very different histories often read on the same level. Sometimes, there's a sudden "spurt" of learning, much like a growth spurt, and a child who has been behind all year will catch up in just a few weeks. Ernest Boyer and others think that multigrade classrooms, where two or three grades are mixed, are a good solution to this problem—and a way to avoid the "tracking" that can hurt a child's self-esteem. In an ungraded classroom, for example, an older child who is having problems in a particular area can practice by tutoring younger kids.

Putting these principles into practice has never been easy. Forty years ago Milwaukee abolished report cards and started sending home ungraded evaluations for kindergarten through third grade. "If anything was developmentally appropriate, those ungraded classes were," says Millie Hoffman, a curriculum specialist with the Milwaukee schools. When the back-to-basics movement geared up nationally in the early 1980s, the city bowed to pressure. Parents started demanding letter grades on report cards. A traditional, direct-teaching approach was introduced into the school system after some students began getting low scores on standardized tests. The school board ordered basal readers with controlled vocabularies and contrived stories. Milwaukee kindergarten teachers were so up-

A Primer for Parents

When visiting a school, trust your eyes. What you see is what your child is going to get.

● Teachers should talk to small groups of children or individual youngsters; they shouldn't just lecture.

■ Children should be working on projects, active experiments and play; they shouldn't be at their desks all day filling in workbooks.

▲ Children should be dictating and writing their own stories or reading real books.

● The classroom layout should have reading and art areas and space for children to work in groups.

■ Children should create freehand artwork, not just color or paste together adult drawings.

▲ Most importantly, watch the children's faces. Are they intellectually engaged, eager and happy? If they look bored or scared, they probably are.

set by these changes that they convinced the board that their students didn't need most of the standardized tests and the workbooks that go along with the readers.

Some schools have been able to keep the progressive format. Olive School in Arlington Heights, Ill., has had a nontraditional curriculum for 22 years. "We've been able to do it because parents are involved, the teachers really care and the children do well," says principal Mary Stitt. "We feel confident that we know what's best for kids." Teachers say they spend a lot of time educating parents about the teaching methods. "Parents always think school should be the way it was for them," says first-grade teacher Cathy Sauer. "As if everything else can change and progress but education is supposed to stay the same. I find that parents want their children to like school, to get along with other children and to be good thinkers. When they see that happening, they become convinced."

Parental involvement is especially important when schools switch from a traditional to a new format. Four years ago, Anne Norford, principal of the Brownsville Elementary School in Albemarle County, Va., began to convert her school. Parents volunteer regularly and that helps. But the transition has not been completely smooth. Several teachers refused to switch over to the more active format. Most of them have since left the school, Norford says. There's no question that some teachers have trouble implementing the developmentally appropriate approach. "Our teachers are not all trained for it," says Yale's Kagan. "It takes a lot of savvy and skill." A successful child-centered classroom seems to function effortlessly as youngsters move from activity to activity. But there's a lot of planning behind it—and that's the responsibility of the individual teacher. "One of the biggest problems," says Norford, "is trying to come up with a program that every teacher can do—not just the cadre of single people who are willing to work 90 hours a week." Teachers also have to participate actively in classroom activities and give up the automatic mantle of authority that comes from standing at the blackboard.

Teachers do better when they're involved in the planning and decision making. When the South Brunswick, N.J., schools decided in the early 1980s to change to a new format, the district spent several years studying a variety of curricula. Teachers participated in that research. A laboratory school was set up in the summer so that teachers could test materials. "We had the support of the teachers because teachers were part of the process," says teacher consultant Joan Warren.

One residue of the back-to-basics movement is the demand for accountability. Children who are taught in nontraditional classrooms can score slightly lower on commonly used standardized tests. That's because most current tests are geared to the old ways. Children are usually quizzed on specific skills, such as vocabulary or addition, not on the concepts behind those skills. "The standardized tests usually call for one-word answers," says Carolyn Topping, principal of Mesa Elementary School in Boulder, Colo. "There may be three words in a row, two of which are misspelled and the child is asked to circle the correctly spelled word. But the tests never ask, 'Does the child know how to write a paragraph?' "

Even if the tests were revised to reflect different kinds of knowledge, there are serious questions about the reliability of tests on young children. The results can vary widely, depending on many factors—a child's mood, his ability to manipulate a pencil (a difficult skill for many kids), his reaction to the person administering the test. "I'm appalled at all the testing we're doing of small children," says Vanderbilt University professor Chester Finn, a former assistant secretary of education under the Reagan administration. He favors regular informal reviews and teacher evaluations to make sure a student understands an idea before moving on to the next level of difficulty.

Tests are the simplest method of judging the effectiveness of a classroom—if not always the most accurate. But there are other ways to tell if children are learning. If youngsters are excited by what they are doing, they're probably laughing and talking to one another and to their teacher. That communication is part of the learning process. "People think that school has to be either free play or all worksheets," says Illinois professor Katz. "The truth is that neither is enough. There has to be a balance between spontaneous play and teacher-directed work." And, she adds, "you have to have the other component. Your class has to have intellectual life."

Katz, author of "Engaging Children's Minds," describes two different elementary-school classes she visited recently. In one, children spent the entire morning making identical pictures of traffic lights. There was no attempt to relate the pictures to anything else the class was doing. In the other class, youngsters were investigating a school bus. They wrote to the district and asked if they could have a bus parked in their lot for a few days. They studied it, figured out what all the parts were for and talked about traffic rules. Then, in the classroom, they built their own bus out of cardboard. They had fun, but they also practiced writing, problem solving, even a little arithmetic. Says Katz: "When the class had their parents' night, the teacher was ready with reports on how each child was doing. But all the parents wanted to see was the bus because their children had been coming home and talking about it for weeks." That's the kind of education kids deserve. Anything less should get an "F."

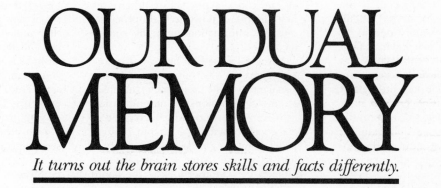

OUR DUAL MEMORY

It turns out the brain stores skills and facts differently.

JOSEPH ALPER

Joseph Alper is a contributing editor of Science 86.

EMEMBER MICKEY MANTLE, the Baseball Hall of Famer? I recently read his autobiography, and it brought back vivid memories of the day I tried out for the Little League. It was April 27, 1963; I was almost nine years old, and my grandpa took me to the trials. I had my Nellie Fox glove that I had gotten for several books of S&H stamps, a Chicago White Sox cap, and some used baseball cleats my dad had bought me the day before.

I registered at a long table, and when they called my name I went over to the diamond, where a fellow with a stopwatch—I remember he had a moustache and wore a Cubs cap—recorded how fast I ran around the bases. Next I played catch with one of the coaches and then

hit a few pitched by another coach. He said I did real well, and I must have, for a few minutes later a woman came over to where my grandpa and I were sitting and handed me my first baseball uniform—a gray wool shirt and pants, blue leggings, and a cap with the Little League emblem on it.

I hadn't thought about that day for probably 20 years, yet as soon as I started reading about Mickey Mantle's earliest baseball experiences in rural Oklahoma, mine in suburban Chicago popped into my mind. If those Little League days were still in my head somewhere after all these years, I wonder what other distant memories are hidden there, wherever "there" might be.

Philosophers and psychologists have long made their livings wondering what memories are and where they are stored. Memory, after all, is the very foundation of our humanity, the basis of our intellect, our ideas, our discoveries. We have the remarkable ability to call up a memory, associate it with other facts or feel-

ings, and use it to create the fantasy world of fiction or explore the invisible world of science.

"We've come to realize that memory is a large word, an umbrella term, for a whole range of processes that the brain uses to translate experience into ability," says Neal Cohen, assistant professor of psychology at Johns Hopkins University in Baltimore.

"This is a golden time in memory and behavior research," says Larry Squire, professor of psychiatry at the University of California at San Diego and research scientist at the Veterans Administration Medical Center, who studies memory deficits in patients with brain injury or disease. "Studies at the molecular level have given us some reasonable ideas about how one nerve can induce permanent, long-lasting changes in another nerve, which tells us about the physical nature of memory.

"At the more global level," Squire says, "we know where certain kinds of sensory information are processed and

4. LEARNING AND MEMORY

"THE OBSERVATION THAT NEURONS CHANGE IN RESPONSE TO STIMULI WAS SIMPLY THE MOST UNUSUAL EVENT I'VE EVER SEEN."

stored to extract different memories. We're starting to make sense of the black box called the brain."

One of the biggest theoretical breakthroughs was the demonstration that there are at least two types of memory, perhaps stored by distinct biochemical mechanisms in different parts of the brain. This idea first surfaced in the 1950s when psychologists started systematically testing the memory deficits of amnesia patients. The first and most famous case was that of a man known as H.M. who had a particularly severe form of epilepsy. Medication had little effect on his seizures, so in 1953, when H.M. was 27, his doctors decided on a drastic treatment—removing a small section of the brain that included most of the hippocampus, the amygdala, and some surrounding cortex.

H.M.'s surgery had the hoped-for result—the epileptic seizures became less severe—but there was one unexpected problem: H.M. could no longer learn new facts, and still cannot to this day. Introduced to his doctors, he forgets their names within minutes regardless of how many times the introductions have been performed before. He can't remember that one of his favorite uncles has died, so he experiences shock and grief each time he hears of the death. He can solve mechanical puzzles—he has even gotten better at solving them—but he never remembers having done so.

H.M.'s form of amnesia demonstrated that there are different forms of memory connected with different parts of the brain. One form, declarative memory, represents memories of facts: names, places, dates, baseball scores. This is the type of memory that can be brought to mind and declared: "I know how to solve this puzzle." It is this type of memory that H.M. is no longer able to acquire.

The other form of memory, which is not affected by damage to the hippocampus and amygdala, is called procedural memory. It is the type of memory acquired by repetitive practice or conditioning and includes skills, such as riding a bicycle. H.M. used procedural memory to solve puzzles. But he didn't know he had learned those skills because he lacked declarative memory.

"H.M. gave us the insight we needed to start a detailed search for those parts of the brain that are important in processing different types of memories," says Mortimer Mishkin, chief of neuropsychology at the National Institute of Mental Health in Bethesda, Maryland. Mishkin himself had already begun the elegant experiments that would give the first glimpse of how the brain processes sensory information into declarative memories.

Mishkin focused on how rhesus monkeys process visual information. To test visual memory, he used a game that takes advantage of a monkey's natural curiosity. Given a board on which a block covers a well containing a peanut or food pellet, a monkey picks up the object to find its reward. After a brief delay, the monkey gets another look at the board with the original block plus a second that differs in size, shape, and color; both objects cover wells but only the new one covers a treat. The monkey quickly learns that it must pick up the new item, thus demonstrating that it can remember what the first one looks like and avoid it.

After the monkeys learned how to play the game, Mishkin carefully removed selected pieces of tissue or severed connections in the brain thought to be involved in the processing and storage of visual information. After a two-week recovery, the animals were tested again to see if their visual memory had been affected. From experiments such as these, Mishkin has developed a detailed map of how visual signals pass through the brain and wind up as memory.

What he has learned is that the most important parts of the visual memory system are the hippocampus and amygdala, which together with other structures make up the limbic system. "One structure is able to pretty much compensate for the other in recognizing things," says Mishkin. On closer examination, he found that each performs a unique function as well. Removing the hippocampus destroys an animal's ability to remember how two objects are related to each other spatially. "If you lost the function of your hippocampus, you could remember what the houses on your block looked like, but you might not remember which houses were next to one another," Mishkin says.

The amygdala, on the other hand, stores information with emotional overtones. Removing the amygdalae did not alter the animals' performance on tests of spatial relationships, but other researchers showed that monkeys could no longer remember their position in the social hierarchy of their colony, nor did they remember socially correct grooming and fear responses. "Without your amygdala you could remember what your hometown looked like," Mishkin says, "but seeing the town might not evoke the fond remembrances connected with living there."

Like others who have pondered the seeming coincidence that the limbic system is a seat of both emotion and memory, Mishkin believes that emotion serves as a gate for what is stored. "We can't store everything, so the brain must discriminate somehow, and if you think about it, your strongest memories are those connected with very emotional events."

Our moods, in fact, appear to exert an extremely powerful influence over what we remember. Psychologist Gordon Bower at Stanford, for example, has reported that a person who learns material in one mood, say a sad one, will recall more of that information later on if he is sad then, too.

It turns out that the amygdala plays a role in other aspects of declarative memory as well. Mishkin and colleague Elizabeth Murray showed monkeys a variety of objects. Then, using a variation of the previous test, they assessed the monkeys' ability to identify the new object by sight alone when they had only felt the first object in the dark. After operating on the animals as before, they found that animals without hippocampi could still make the right visual choice, but the performance of monkeys without amygdalae was only slightly better than chance. Clearly, the amygdala was required for integrating visual and tactile memories.

Other studies have shown, in fact, that each of the five senses has neural connections leading to the amygdala. "We think that when the amygdala is presented with a tactile stimulus, for example, it

PARIETAL LOBE

PRIMARY VISUAL AREA

HIPPOCAMPUS

AMYGDALA

TEMPORAL LOBE

WHERE MEMORIES ARE PROCESSED

Visual information travels from the eye to the primary visual area at the back of the brain. From there, the input simultaneously travels along two separate pathways for processing. As the information travels down toward the temporal lobe, the physical qualities—size, shape, and color—are identified. Spatial qualities—location with respect to other objects—are processed along the second pathway, which leads upward to the parietal lobe. From the temporal and parietal lobes, the information travels through the brain to the hippocampus and amygdala, where scientists think memories may be stored. Without these structures, a scene can be perceived but not remembered.

HOW MEMORIES ARE FORMED

A nerve spine in the hippocampus changes shape after receiving the type of stimulation that occurs during a learning experience. Below left, the first of several bursts of electricity causes a chemical neurotransmitter to be released from a neighboring neuron onto the receptors of the nerve spine shown here. Calcium enters the cell. The calcium activates calpain (orange), an otherwise dormant enzyme, which begins to degrade fodrin, the structural material of the spine. With additional bursts of electricity, the fodrin continues to break down, and more receptors appear, below right. More receptors result in a greater influx of calcium, and therefore more calpain activation and even greater fodrin degradation. With significant loss of structural material, the spine changes shape. A new spine may also begin to extend through the membrane. These permanent changes result in new connections between neurons in the brain, a plausible explanation for memory.

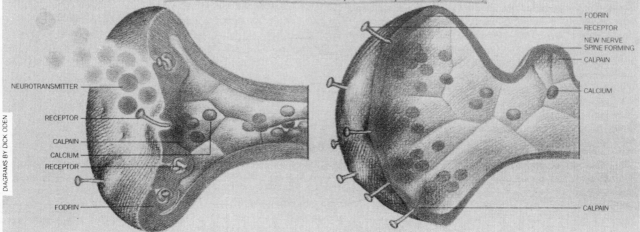

NEUROTRANSMITTER

RECEPTOR

CALPAIN

CALCIUM

RECEPTOR

FODRIN

FODRIN

RECEPTOR

NEW NERVE SPINE FORMING

CALPAIN

CALCIUM

CALPAIN

is able to tickle some area in the cortex that has stored a visual representation of the same object," Mishkin explains. The ability of our memories to make associations of this kind is what gives the human brain its enormous power.

Equally exciting work to determine the site of procedural memory is being done by psychobiologist Richard F. Thompson at Stanford. Working with rabbits, he has determined that procedural memory seems to be stored in a different part of the brain than is declarative memory—in the cerebellum, a structure at the back of the head under the cortex.

Thompson implanted many tiny electrodes in select locations of the brains of laboratory rabbits and recorded the electrical activity as the animals learned to associate a certain tone with an unpleasant stimulus. This type of learning, called classical or Pavlovian conditioning, is considered a prime example of procedural knowledge.

When a tiny puff of air is blown into a rabbit's eye, the animal blinks automatically. On the next trial, a tone sounds just before the rabbit gets a puff. If the tone is paired with the puff enough times, the rabbit comes to associate the two events and will blink its eye at the tone alone. The animal has learned.

Thompson found that a rabbit has much higher electrical activity in several specific areas of its cerebellum when it is learning this procedural task. When he removed those parts of the cerebellum, animals that had learned the task immediately forgot it, although they still blinked their eyes when air was blown into them. But when the animals' hippocampi were removed, their ability to undergo classical conditioning was not impaired in the least. This, according to Thompson, is another demonstration that different types of memory are stored in different parts of the brain.

Studies such as Mishkin's and Thompson's are particularly exciting to neuroscientists because they provide a basis for investigating the physical nature of memory—what changes take place in the brain when a memory is formed. Once researchers know where memories are stored, they can look at neurons in those regions to see if they have been changed in a way that might account for the ability of the brain to make permanent records.

Some of the first evidence that there is a physical memory trace came from researchers like Eric Kandel of Columbia University and Daniel Alkon of the Na-

---

THE MANY FACES OF MEMORY

"Characterizing the nature of memory is probably going to be more difficult than determining where the information contained in a memory is stored in the brain," says Neal Cohen, assistant professor of psychology at Johns Hopkins University in Baltimore. "That's because when we look at even one specific memory we're talking about a whole group of psychological processes that takes place all at once to form what we perceive as a memory."

Some believe, in fact, that it may be impossible to define the borders of a single memory. As an example of how complex the problem is, take the word apple. *How many pieces of information, how many concepts, might the brain extract from this simple word?*

The first time your brain formed the memory apple, *it was probably as a red, crunchy thing that was good to eat. But, more than likely, you store the categories* apple=red, apple=crunchy, *and* apple=food *separately, for if you are asked to list things that are red or things that are crunchy or things to eat, you would be likely to include* apple *in all three groups.*

The idea that each of these concepts is stored as its own memory is supported by studies on patients with language disturbances, or aphasias. One unusual case involves M.D., a 35-year-old man who suffered a stroke in the left side of his brain. At first, M.D. had severe aphasia, but most of his language abilities returned within a month— all except for his ability to identify fruits and vegetables.

When asked to name various objects, either from photographs or when handed the real thing, he could do so easily for toys, tools, animals, body parts, kitchen items, colors, and clothing. But when it came to identifying fruits and vegetables he was at a loss. "Other foods he could name perfectly, but when we gave him an apple or showed him a picture of lettuce he couldn't tell us what they were," says Alfonso Caramazza, professor of psychology at Johns Hopkins.

Caramazza says, however, that M.D.'s memory loss was not a matter of having no knowledge whatsoever about fruits and vegetables. When given a group of objects and asked, "Which one is an apple?" he could point to the apple with no problem. Moreover, M.D. could respond eloquently and correctly when Caramazza asked him to describe an apple. Thus, M.D. still retains the many memories that together represent apple. *It was the general question "What is this?" that he could not answer correctly. His problem must lie in accessing these memories to select the proper name.*

All this suggests that the brain not only stores memories as discrete pieces of information but also somehow organizes this information along a framework that guides its retrieval. Since memory is an active process, this organization must be flexible, as must the framework, for we are continuously exposed to new information, storing some of it as memory and assimilating it into our view of the world.
—J.A.

---

tional Institutes of Health, who found lasting changes in specific neurons of sea snails that had undergone different kinds of learning trials. Other researchers found that a certain pattern of electrical stimulation could make hippocampal neurons more sensitive to further stimulation for weeks at a time; that is, the cells would respond more intensely to a given stimulus. This effect, called long-term potentiation, was the first demonstration of a possible mechanism for long-term memory formation.

Intrigued by this effect, neuroscientist Gary Lynch at the University of California at Irvine performed similar experiments using rat brain tissue. "Sure enough, we got long-term potentiation," says Lynch. Much to his surprise, he also

found structural changes in nerve cells: the number of connections between neurons increased, and certain parts of the neuron actually changed shape, something no scientist had ever seen before. "This was simply the most unusual event I've ever seen. This observation removed the mystery that is memory because it showed that neurons could change in a permanent way in response to physical stimuli," says Lynch.

Lynch and colleague Michel Baudry focused on the hippocampal neurons, and how nerve impulses cross synapses, or gaps, to reach the next neuron. To pass along the electrical impulse, the neuron sending the signal releases a chemical known as a neurotransmitter. Diffusing across the synapse, the neuro-

TAKE THE WORD *APPLE*. HOW MANY PIECES OF INFORMATION, HOW MANY CONCEPTS, MIGHT THE BRAIN EXTRACT FROM THIS SIMPLE WORD?

transmitter binds to receptors on a spine of the next neuron. This activates those receptors, causing charged particles to flow through the membrane of the second, or postsynaptic, neuron, setting off another nerve impulse.

When Lynch and Baudry zapped the hippocampal neurons with electrical pulses to induce long-term potentiation, they discovered an amazing sequence of events. The postsynaptic cells became flooded with unusually large amounts of calcium, which in turn activated a dormant enzyme, called calpain. The primary role of this enzyme seems to be to break down certain proteins.

One of these proteins, named fodrin, is the major structural component of the spines of neurons. When calpain begins to break down fodrin, Lynch believes that extra receptors for the neurotransmitter glutamate are exposed. Since glutamate is the neurotransmitter that hippocampal neurons need to communicate with one another, the uncovering of additional glutamate receptors makes the postsynaptic neuron more responsive to glutamate released by its neighbor.

When this postsynaptic neuron is stimulated again, more calcium enters the cell, causing calpain to break down more fodrin. At that point, says Lynch, "the whole system is free to change its shape because the protein skeleton has been broken down." The shape of the neuron can change, or new nerve connections can form. "This chain of events is a plausible candidate for a memory mechanism," says Lynch, "because it occurs at the synapses in response to a physiological event, changes the responsiveness of the synapse, and is permanent." Further-

more, this mechanism appears to function best in those regions of the brain that are involved in declarative memory.

Long-term potentiation may be a good model for studying what takes place in the hippocampus when declarative memories are processed there. But Lynch felt that until he could show that calpain is involved in forming memories in a live animal, the calcium-calpain-fodrin cascade would be little more than an interesting biochemical process that just happened to take place in hippocampal neurons.

To nail down calpain's role in declarative memory, Lynch used the chemical leupeptin, which inhibits calpain's ability to degrade fodrin. Lynch fitted rats with tiny pumps that released a steady flow of the chemical into all areas of the animals' brains.

None of the rats showed any difference in eating, drinking, or sleeping behavior. However, rats that could remember where to look for rewards in complex mazes could no longer perform the task after getting leupeptin; the same effect is seen in rats whose hippocampi and amygdalae have been removed. "Rats clearly evolved for running mazes, for they normally do so with great enthusiasm and learn quickly," says Lynch, "but the leupeptin-treated animals were real dunces. I think we can infer from this that calpain and the synaptic changes it produces are important for declarative knowledge acquisition."

But what about procedural knowledge? Some investigators have proposed that when this kind of memory forms, neurons must make new proteins. So

Lynch gave one group of rats anisomyocin, which blocks protein synthesis, and gave another group leupeptin. When he tested the rats for their ability to learn shock avoidance, a procedural-type task, the results were reversed—the leupeptin-treated rats did as well as the controls, while those receiving anisomyocin did poorly at this task.

The enzyme calpain seems to play a prominent role in declarative memory, while an undetermined chain of events requiring protein synthesis may be involved in procedural memory. The properties of the two chemical systems fit those of the two behavioral systems. "We think of procedural memory as a kind of memory that takes a lot of time to form, and protein synthesis is a slow process as far as biochemical events are concerned," says Lynch. "On the other hand, declarative memories form much faster, and on a biochemical time scale the calpain-fodrin reaction is pretty fast."

Lynch says that while it is satisfying to have developed a reasonable candidate for the molecular basis of one type of memory, his model does not say much about how we learn and think. "We're witnessing the very beginnings of a concerted, coordinated, intelligent attack on human intellectual thinking," he says. "I really believe that in the next two to three years, theorizing about the nature of memory is going to become the philosophical playground of the Western intellectual world. It will replace evolution as the arena in which anyone interested in philosophy will put their intellectual energies."

Extraordinary People

Understanding the remarkable abilities of the "idiot savant" could help us unlock deep secrets about our own minds.

Darold Treffert, M.D.

Darold Treffert, M.D., a psychiatrist, has been director of several Wisconsin psychiatric hospitals, and has studied savants for the last twenty-six years. He lectures frequently on the subject throughout the country.

LESLIE HAS NEVER HAD any formal musical training. Yet upon hearing Tchaikovsky's Piano Concerto no. 1 for the first time when he was a teenager, he played it back on the piano flawlessly and without hesitation. He can do the same with any other piece of music, no matter how long or complex. Yet he cannot hold a utensil to eat and can only repeat in monotone that which is spoken to him. Leslie is blind, is severely mentally handicapped, and has cerebral palsy.

George and his identical twin brother, Charles, can rattle off all the years in which your birthday fell on a Thursday. They can also tell you, within a span of forty thousand years backward or forward, the day of the week on which any date you choose fell, or will fall. In their spare time George and Charles swap twenty-digit prime numbers for amusement. Yet they cannot add simple figures or even tell you what a formula is, let alone write one out.

Kenneth is thirty-eight years old but has a mental age of eleven. His entire conversational vocabulary consists of fifty-eight words. Yet he can give the population of every city and town in the United States that has a population of over five thousand; the names, number of rooms, and locations of two thousand leading hotels in America; the distance from each city and town to the largest city in its state; statistics concerning three thousand mountains and rivers; and the dates and essential facts of over two thousand leading inventions and discoveries.

All of these people are examples of the fascinating phenomenon called the *idiot savant,* a term coined by J. Langdon Down of London some one hundred years ago, when the word *idiot* did not have the negative, comical implication it now carries. At that time, *idiot* was an accepted medical and psychological term referring to a specific level of intellectual functioning—an IQ level of less than twenty-five. The word *savant* was derived from a French word meaning "to know" or "man of learning." The observation that persons with severe mental handicap displayed advanced levels of learning, albeit in very narrow ranges, led to the once descriptive, still colorful juxtaposition of the two words.

Understandably, some people object to the term *idiot savant* because the word *idiot* now gives the condition a connotation that is neither deserved nor fair. Therefore, the terms *savant* and *Savant Syndrome* will be used hereafter in referring to these remarkable people and the astonishing phenomenon they represent.

Savant syndrome is a condition in which persons with major mental illness or major intellectual handicap have spectacular islands of ability and brilliance that stand in stark, startling contrast to their handicaps. In some savants—those I call *talented savants*—the skills are remarkable simply in contrast to the handicap, but in other, more rare savants— those I call *prodigious*—the abilities and skills would be remarkable even if seen in normal people.

Until now, the scientific articles and media presentations describing the several hundred savants discovered during this past century have been isolated, anecdotal accounts of single individuals and their extraordinary stories. But there is much more to Savant Syndrome than interesting stories. Among these remarkable people, diverse as they may at first appear, is a commonality that deserves study, for in the future it may provide a key to better understanding not only how *they*—handicapped but with uncommon talent—function, but also how *we*— without handicap but with common talent—function as well. Of particular promise is what Savant Syndrome might tell us about memory (and thus conditions such as Alzheimer's disease), the nature of creativity, and the elusive relationship between memory and emotion.

At present, the significance of Savant Syndrome lies in our inability to explain it. The savants stand as a clear reminder of our ignorance about ourselves, for no model of brain function—particularly memory—could be complete unless it included and accounted for this remarkable condition.

When confronted by Savant Syndrome, so many questions leap up: How can extremely handicapped persons possess these islands of genius? What do they have in common? Why, with all the skills in the human repertoire, do the skills of the savant always fall in such narrow ranges and include such rare talents as calendar calculating?

Why is phenomenal memory seen in all the savants, no matter what exceptional individual skills they exhibit? Is the savant's memory qualitatively different from normal memory? Is their genius a direct result of their deficiencies, or do the two factors coexist coincidentally?

What can we learn about this spectacular dysfunction of mind and memory that might provide clues to normal mind and memory? Might the existence of these geniuses among us suggest that some such genius lies within each of us, waiting to be tapped?

The time has come to take the savants out of the "Gee Whiz" category and learn what we can about them, and from them—not just about memory and brain function, but about human potential as well.

I MET MY FIRST SAVANT on July 1, 1959. I was twenty-six years old and had just completed a residency in psychiatry at University Hospital in Madison, Wisconsin.

My first professional assignment was to develop and direct a thirty-bed Children's Unit at Winnebago State Hospital near Oshkosh, Wisconsin. As I walked onto the unit that first day, I noticed David. He stood there with a device he had fashioned out of cardboard and pencils that held a rolled-up paper scroll on which perhaps a hundred names were neatly written. As David turned the pencil on which the scroll had been wound, each name came into view, one at a time, through an opening in the cardboard that had been placed over the scroll. The device looked just like the window on the front of a bus where the destinations are listed and changed as the bus

Some researchers have suggested that such extraordinary talents might be acquired from a shared field of knowledge similar to psychologist Carl Jung's "collective unconscious."

route changes. And that's just what it was. The names on David's homemade scroll were the names of streets—Capitol Drive, State Street, Lincoln Avenue. David had memorized the bus system of Milwaukee. If you gave him the number of a bus and the time of day, he could tell you at which corner the bus was then stopping.

David was a very disturbed boy. His violent temper and his severe behavioral problems necessitated continuous hospitalization. His overall functioning was at a very low level—except for this one peculiar area of exceptional ability. He would have made a great cab dispatcher.

There were other savants on this unit. Billy could make free throws. Could he ever make free throws! He was like a baseball pitching machine, except he used a basketball. He always stood in exactly the same place at the free-throw line, with his feet in exactly the same position and his body in the same stance. For every shot his arm motions were identical, as were the arcs of the ball. He never missed. He showed no emotion, no overcorrection or undercorrection. There was nothing to correct. He was a basketball robot. Unfortunately, he had the same robot-like approach to everything. His mutism and his inability to communicate were evidence of his profound emotional and behavioral disturbance, which required his hospitalization on a long-term basis.

Then there was Tony. Unlike Billy, Tony did use language and, in fact, was a voracious reader. But he, too, had a serious behavioral condition that caused him to make vicious attacks against himself, and sometimes toward others. Tony knew history. He delighted each day in approaching visitors or staff—including new young doctors like me—asking them the significance of that particular date in history. Usually he elicited no answer, or just a few wild guesses, and so Tony would begin spouting off a long list of events that occurred throughout history on that day, much like the radio announcer on the morning show that I listened to on my way to work. Except that the announcer read his information

from an almanac. Tony, it seemed, *was* an almanac.

There were other cases on the unit similar to those of David, Billy, and Tony. I was struck by the islands of intelligence, even genius, that existed in what otherwise was a sea of severe handicap and disability. I soon became fascinated by this paradox of ability and disability, and began my research studying its appearance in patients with Early Infantile Autism, a form of childhood schizophrenia marked by withdrawal. My work eventually put me in touch with researchers throughout the world who were working in related fields. But it also left me with some lingering questions regarding Savant Syndrome—questions that remained unanswered for years.

AFTER TWO YEARS developments in my career forced me to put aside my work with Savant Syndrome until 1979, when I left Winnebago to begin a private practice and run a 150-bed community mental health center in the nearby community of Fond du Lac. Though I had mentally filed away the data on the autistic children I had seen fifteen years earlier on the Children's Unit—and on the savant skills present in some of them—the phenomenon continued to intrigue me.

I didn't see many autistic children in my Fond du Lac practice. What I did see, though, were a number of adult patients on whom I was conducting sodium amytal (truth serum) interviews as a means of enhancing their recall of buried memories and hidden traumas. In those interviews, patients remembered—in extraordinarily minute detail—a whole variety of experiences they thought they had forgotten. It was a demonstration of memory powers that, like Savant Syndrome, seemed to redefine human potential.

In some instances an entire journey down a particular street on a particular night would be recalled with exquisite attention to particulars—changing traffic lights, street signs, and passing cars. Both the patients and I were often startled by the voluminous amount of material that was in storage but unavailable in an everyday waking state. It was as if some sort of tape recorder were running all the time, recording all of our experiences. The memories were there. What was missing was access and recall.

Simultaneously, reports were cropping up in scientific literature about neurosurgical studies of brain mapping, especially concerning the use of tiny electrical probes to determine epileptogenic foci—the seizure trigger—in the exposed cortex of patients who suffered certain kinds of seizures. The brain itself has no pain fibers within it; the pain fibers are in the surrounding capsule of the brain, the dura mater. Once the dura is numbed with a local anesthetic, the patient can remain awake while the surgeon uses a tiny electrical probe to find the site where certain kinds of seizures are triggered. This site then can be surgically removed and some seizure disorders corrected. In the random search for these foci, the probe hits a variety of spots on the cortex, and when it does, memories flood the patient's consciousness.

These memories, long forgotten by our conscious minds, are the kind of "random" recollections we often experience in our dreams: the fifth birthday party, including all the guests present; a day in class twenty years earlier; a walk on a particular path on a particular day, complete with the accompanying aromas and sound. If we were to remember such dream memories upon awakening, we would dismiss them, wondering, Where did that come from? But we know their origin in these instances: The probe had activated a circuit or pathway not ordinarily available to us.

I filed away these accounts, too, along with my observations of the savants I had known, as I continued to be busy with many other things.

Then, in June 1980, I met Leslie Lemke.

THE DEPARTMENT of social services had invited May Lemke and her remarkable foster son, Leslie—then twenty-eight—to give a concert honoring the foster parents of the county. I did not attend, but a short time afterward, in the wake of the publicity that followed, I became intrigued and decided to visit Leslie and his foster parents at their small cottage on Lake Pewaukee.

When I arrived, Leslie was sitting in a chair in his music room, a converted porch. He sat motionless and silent, but he seemed contented and at ease. He echoed my name when May told him who I was. Then he sat motionless and mute once again. May could hardly wait for him to play for me. She was so proud. Despite his blindness he walked unaided,

feeling his way, from the chair to the piano.

Then he played. I don't recall what the song was, but I do recall what I felt—astonishment, fascination, and inspiration. I still have the same reaction, many years and many tunes later, whenever I see and hear Leslie play. Here was someone with a triple handicap—blindness, retardation, and cerebral palsy—playing, for his audience of three, a concert worthy of an audience of a thousand. Though he had had no formal training, piece after piece poured forth: hymns, concertos, arias, popular songs, and imitations of singers. Some pieces he sang; some he just played. Some of the lyrics were in English, some in German, and some in Greek.

Leslie is the most remarkable savant I have ever met, read about, or studied. He was born prematurely in Milwaukee on January 31, 1952, and his mother immediately gave him up for adoption. He spent the first months of his life at Milwaukee County Children's Home. There it was noticed that the baby did not open his eyes, which were swollen and hard and had cloudy corneas. The doctors diagnosed his condition as retrolental fibroplasia, a disorder often seen in premature infants in which the retina proliferates wildly and sometimes, as in this case, blocks drainage in the eye, creating childhood glaucoma or a condition called *buphthalmos*. When Leslie was four months old, his left eye had to be removed. Six weeks later his right eye also was removed because of the glaucoma and because his doctors feared that the eye would burst. That was the source of Leslie's blindness.

Soon thereafter, at age six months, this frail and pathetic baby was given to the care of a remarkable woman. May Lemke was then fifty-two. She had been a nurse/governess and had developed a reputation for the extraordinary skill and love she showed in caring for children, handicapped or well. May received a call from the Social Services Department of Milwaukee County and, without a moment's hesitation, took on the role of foster mother, tutor, therapist, mentor, model, cheerleader, and inspiration to this blind, palsied, and intellectually handicapped little boy.

When Leslie was seven years old, May bought him a piano. She would play and sing for her foster son, running his fingers up and down the keyboard so he could identify the notes. By age eight Leslie could play the piano as well as a number of other instruments, including bongo drums, ukulele, concertina, xylo-

phone, and accordion. By nine Leslie had learned to play the chord organ. Medical notes indicate that, at age ten, Leslie still was not conversant, with the exception of repetition and imitation. He required help in dressing himself. He could not feed himself anything that required the use of utensils.

One evening, when Leslie was about fourteen, he watched a movie on television called *Sincerely Yours*, starring Dorothy Malone and Basil Rathbone. May and her husband, Joe, watched it, too, but then went to bed. At about three o'clock in the morning, May awoke, thinking that Joe had left the television on. She went to the living room to check. There sat Leslie. He had crawled over to the piano and was playing Tchaikovsky's Piano Concerto no. 1—the theme song to *Sincerely Yours*—vigorously and flawlessly. Leslie had heard it one time. That was sufficient. He played it through from beginning to end.

To this day, if you ask Leslie to play that piece, you get not only the song, but the entire television introduction, mimicked exactly as he heard it in true echolalic fashion: "Tonight's movie is *Sincerely Yours*, starring Dorothy Malone and Basil Rathbone. As he falls in love with the beautiful black-haired woman . . . [In the background are heard the beautiful strains of Tchaikovsky's Piano Concerto no. 1.] And now, *The Sunday Night Movie* is proud to present . . ." Usually, there is no stopping Leslie once he begins. He's like a jukebox: You put in your quarter and you hear the whole song. Until recently, the *Sincerely Yours* recitation and lengthy piece were virtually unstoppable. (That was a real hazard during Leslie's live television appearances, where time was so very limited.) Leslie now can be persuaded to stop, or at least to bring the piece to an end more quickly, with a gentle tap on the shoulder from Mary Parker, May's daughter, who acts as Leslie's guardian and caretaker now that May is frail.

Leslie was twenty-two years old when, in 1974, he gave his first public concert, at the Waukesha County Fair, a few miles from his home. He played and sang his hymns and did his Louis Armstrong and Tiny Tim imitations. He was a smash hit. He was "incredible," the newspaper said. As would happen at all of his concerts to follow, the audience members at the Waukesha County Fair shook their heads in astonishment and wiped tears from their eyes as he closed the concert with "Everything Is Beautiful."

Leslie recently completed a tour that included twenty-six cities in Japan. His repertoire now features thousands of pieces and is continually expanding. He is gradually becoming more polished in his presentations, more spontaneous in his conversations, and more sociable in his interaction. He appears to love what he is doing, is remarkably good at it, and seems to enjoy the appreciation and applause of his audiences, whether large or small, prestigious or ordinary, young or old. He has not yet reached his limits.

My personal familiarity with Leslie and his remarkable family made me a popular interview subject whenever the media turned to the topic of savants. These exposures put me in touch with a wide variety of researchers and scientists around the world who shared an interest in this condition. They in turn brought many new cases to my attention, cases I never would have known about were it not for this sudden attention to and curiosity about the puzzling paradox of being backward and brilliant at the same time.

THE OVERRIDING QUESTION for any researcher in this field is all too obvious: How do they do it? How does someone like Leslie Lemke, a person of clear deficiency, achieve such greatness in one limited area? I have found that there are about as many theories attempting to answer this question as there have been investigators. Many of the theories stem from the study of a single case, so-called "undemocratic" research that often provides useful information but also is rather idiosyncratic and limited. Among the recent research, I have found no single finding or theory that could explain all savants. But several theories could explain aspects of the syndrome and are worth exploring.

Eidetic imagery. Some researchers link Savant Syndrome to this fairly rare phenomenon in which a person continues to "see" an object as an afterimage for as long as forty seconds after it has been taken away. The retained image is intensely vivid and absolutely accurate. The term also is used by some to describe what popularly is known as photographic memory (whereby the afterimage can be recalled later and viewed as if it were a photograph). While some studies have found a higher number of "eidekers" among savants than among non-savants, other studies have not documented this difference. At any rate, eidetic imagery is not uniformly present in all savants and thus could not serve as a universal explanation for the condition.

Heredity. Could the savant be the product of two coincidentally inherited genes—one for retardation and the other for special abilities? While some investigators have found higher incidences of special skills in the families of savants, others have not. Thus, like eidetic imagery, heredity cannot serve as the sole explanation.

Sensory deprivation. Other researchers have postulated that Savant Syndrome may be a consequence of social isolation or biologically impaired sensory input. While social isolation does apply to some savants—those in deprived institutional settings, for example—many others come from stimulating environments where they received a great deal of personal attention. There are similar problems with the theory that the syndrome results from some biological form of sensory deprivation such as blindness or deafness. While some sensorily deprived individuals do develop savant skills, most do not.

Impaired ability to think abstractly. Under this theory, organic brain damage reduces the savant's ability to think abstractly, and the savant compensates by developing and refining concrete abilities as well as a vivid memory. While this is an accurate characterization of many savants, it is only a description—not an explanation—of the syndrome.

Compensation for defects and reinforcement from praise. There is no doubt that the praise that savants receive for their unusual skills can compensate for feelings of inferiority and aid in their development of relationships. Yet these same dynamics are factors for many developmentally disabled people, and only a few achieve the performance level of the savant. There must be specific and unique factors that separate the savant from the rest of the mentally handicapped.

Right brain/left brain localization and other organic factors. While not an absolute rule, the left brain hemisphere generally is responsible for skills that require intellect, cognition and logic, such as reading and speaking. The right hemisphere deals with abilities that are more intuitive and nonverbal, such as painting, sculpting, and playing music. In general, skills most often seen in savants are those associated with right hemisphere function, and those lacking tend to be left-hemisphere-related. Could Savant Syndrome result from damage to the left hemisphere of the brain?

One case lending impetus to this last theory involves a normal nine-year-old boy who suffered a gunshot wound very precisely confined to the left side of the brain, leaving him deaf, mute, and paralyzed on the right side. Following that injury, the boy developed a savant-like ability to troubleshoot and repair mechanical devices, presumably resulting from increased function in his undamaged right hemisphere.

Unfortunately, there has been very little research to confirm left brain damage in savants. It is interesting to note, however, that in two of the three reported cases where CAT scans (detailed x-rays of the brain) were performed on savants, there was clear evidence of such left brain damage. The other reported CAT scan—on a very high-functioning autistic savant with mathematical skills—showed an undamaged left brain.

No doubt some savants do have left brain damage as we generally think of it—trauma or injury before, during, or after birth. Yet, in the case of the identical twins George and Charles, both of whom had identical calculating skills, it seems most unlikely that both of them would have incurred such an injury in exactly the same area of the brain to give them their identical abilities. Their case argues for genetic or behavioral factors as well—or perhaps for some other process affecting the left brain.

FURTHER INSIGHT into the damaged-left-brain theory is provided by the 1987 findings of Harvard neurologists Norman Geschwind and Albert Galaburda, who studied right brain/left brain development and cerebral dominance. The doctors note that, from conception onward, the left brain is larger than the right and that it completes its growth and development later than the right brain in utero, leaving it vulnerable for a longer period of time to a variety of prenatal influences and injury. One such influence is the male sex hormone testosterone, which in the male fetus reaches levels that have been shown to impair neural cell development in some instances. This testosterone effect could therefore produce the type of left brain "damage" postulated for the savant.

Such damage—coming before birth at a time when the brain is still developing—would result in right brain cells being recruited for what would ordinarily be left brain circuits. A "pathology of superiority" of the right brain would then develop, along with a preponderance of right-brain-type skills—the kind of skills seen in the savant.

According to Geschwind and Galaburda, testosterone-caused damage would account as well for the correspondingly high male-to-female ratios seen in savants and in other "left brain" disorders such as dyslexia, delayed speech, autism, stuttering, and hyperactivity. It correlates as well with the higher incidence of left-handedness in males.

Further implications can be drawn from the fact that a striking number of savants were born prematurely. The phenomenon of massive brain cell death in humans just before birth is well established and commonly accepted. There are many more brain cells in the fetus than can possibly make connections, and those unconnected neural cells are simply discarded late in the pregnancy.

Geschwind and Galaburda point out that when left brain injury occurs early in pregnancy—as postulated by the testosterone theory—there is still a large reservoir of spare right brain neurons available to accommodate a neuronal shift to the right hemisphere. Indeed, the right brain actually becomes enlarged compared to the left. Could the savant's premature birth prevent the normal brain-cell die-off and provide a large reservoir of right brain cells that, when recruited, produce the extraordinary right brain skills seen in the savant?

Another body of research that could be of importance in understanding the savant is the work of Mortimer Mishkin, M.D., and others at the National Institute of Mental Health. Mishkin outlined two types of memory, each with its own distinct pathways: cognitive or associative memory, in which facts or stimuli first are consciously recognized, then sorted, stored, and later recalled; and habit memory, more a system of conditioned reflexes, such as that used when driving a complex daily route to work while thinking about other things. It is the latter that more accurately characterizes savant memory—the "memory without consciousness" described over and over again in savant literature. Mishkin points to data suggesting two different neurological pathways, or circuits, for these two different kinds of memory. In the savant, it appears that habit memory pathways compensate for damaged cognitive memory circuits.

Clearly, the one quality or trait that all savants have in common, irrespective of their particular skills, is phenomenal memory. It is memory of a specific type: literal, vivid, reflex-like, unconscious, devoid of emotion, tremendously deep but impressively narrow. This is in dramatic contrast to memory in the rest of us, which tends to be much more conscious, highly associative, more abstract,

less literal and precise, emotion-laden, and tremendously wide-ranging in subject matter but conspicuously limited in depth. Savants' unique memory function and circuitry distinguishes them from non-savants and points to the most fruitful area of further study.

Indeed, recent findings from new x-ray studies of the brain and autopsy data suggest that, in addition to the savant's left hemisphere damage, there is corresponding damage in lower brain areas, including those that control memory circuitry. This could explain the characteristic appearance in the savant of both right brain skills and an over developed reliance on habit memory.

Combining the various theories and new research, then, the talented savant emerges as an individual whose left-brain function has been disrupted as a result of some brain injury—perhaps sex-linked—occurring before, during, or after birth that leads to a compensatory increase in right brain function. The left brain damage is coupled with lower brain damage as well, causing a reliance on habit memory circuitry. These two factors somehow combine to produce the savant's characteristic cluster of abilities. Constant repetition and practice then refine these circuits, resulting in conspicuous talent within an exceedingly narrow range.

This scenario would account for the talented savants—those whose skills are remarkable simply in contrast to their obvious mental handicaps. However, in order to explain the prodigious savants, we must take into account some inherited factors as well. The prodigious savant's access to the vast rules of mathematics, art, or music could not be learned by practice alone. Some researchers have suggested that such extraordinary talents might be acquired from a shared field of knowledge similar to psychologist Carl Jung's "collective unconscious," or that these skills could reflect knowledge gained in so-called "past lives." These are explanations that no one can confirm or refute, but they are nevertheless explanations held by some.

Clearly, in both varieties of savant, intense concentration, practice, compensatory drives, and reinforcement play major roles in developing and polishing the skills made possible by this idiosyncratic brain function. But there is another factor as well: the deep care and concern that families or other caregivers have for the savants—not just for what they can do but for who they are; not just for what is missing but for all that remains. By radiating so much love,

encouragement, and praise, they serve to reinforce and motivate in ways that are truly touching and inspirational.

UNTIL RECENTLY, almost all of the technical advances in the study of the brain have allowed us to better and more precisely view brain *structure*: Are all the parts there? Now, for the first time, new technology, such as the positron emission tomography (PET) scan and similar devices, allows researchers to better study brain *function*, the actual way the brain works. Such new technology for studying the brain, coupled with new knowledge about the brain, has far-reaching implications for understanding savants—and thus ourselves.

For starters, the savant's "memory without consciousness"—Leslie's exact mimicry of an overheard German song or a random conversation, for example—can be studied in detail. Surely this distinct memory—so deep but so narrow, so vast but so emotionless—arises from circuitry far different from our ordinary memory, which is shallow and limited but far more flexible, associative, and creative.

By allowing us to better understand memory circuitry, savants may help us counteract the disruption of memory pathways by conditions such as Alzheimer's disease. Such brain repair might take any one of several forms: pharmacologic (with memory-enhancing drugs), neurologic (with brain cells recruited from unaffected areas and rerouted over new pathways), electrical (with brain-pacing devices such as those now used to treat certain types of epilepsy and to pace the electrical system of the heart), or neurosurgical (with brain grafts and neuronal transplants such as those now used in the treatment of Parkinson's disease).

Almost everything we have learned about health we have learned from the study of disease. Thus, from the research on Alzheimer's disease may come applications for expanding and enhancing normal memory. Each of us has tremendous numbers of memories—literally a lifetime's worth—stored in an organ to which we have relatively poor access. In our dreams, under hypnosis, or in sodium amytal interviews, some of this stored data cascades forth. And, as mentioned earlier, when neurosurgeons touch the cortex of a patient's brain with a tiny electrical probe, it also triggers thousands of memories of which the patient is unaware.

It seems "lost" memories have not disappeared; they have simply been misfiled, making them difficult to find. Normal memory enhancement, whether pharmocologic, electrical, or by some other method, promises to someday allow us to tap that tremendous reservoir of data we all possess but cannot now access.

The link between memory and creativity is another area in which studying savants may lead us to better understand ourselves. Their tremendous skills aside, savants almost exclusively echo and mimic—there is little or no creativity involved in what they do. Adding improvisation to existing music—as striking as that is—is still not the same as creating a new musical idea. Alonzo Clemons, a sculpting savant, can recreate fantastically what he sees but cannot do free-form sculpting. This is not to detract from such remarkable skills. It is simply to say that they differ from the creative process, and that difference warrants further study.

Savants, as a group, also demonstrate an unusual emotional flatness. Again, this trade-off is a mixed blessing. While they may miss some of the peaks of normal human emotion, they seem to be spared the valleys. While they may not shout at a ball game or weep at a movie, they also seem to be free of performance jitters or bouts of deep despair or cynicism. They may never feel ecstasy, but neither will they feel despondency. With further study, this emotional detachment may provide clues to the normal interplay of memory and emotion.

Indeed, we can learn a great deal about human potential from the jarring contradiction—the magnificent coexistence of deficiency and superiority—that is Savant Syndrome. We can learn that handicap need not necessarily blur hope and that stereotyping and labeling serve only to obscure—in a pernicious manner—an individual's strengths. We can learn the difference between paucity of emotion and purity of emotion. From the families, teachers, and therapists of the savant, we can learn that in dealing with people who have problems—even severe ones—it is not enough to care *for* those people: We must care *about* them as well. We can learn that there is a difference between sharing the spirit and shaping the spirit. We can learn how to work with a differently shaped soul—to understand, to actualize, and to appreciate it—while still respecting its uniqueness.

In short, a complete understanding of human experience requires that we include and account for Savant Syndrome. Until then, we will be able only to marvel at people such as Leslie Lemke, Alonzo Clemons, or the calendar calculator named George who can compute twenty-digit prime numbers but cannot add two plus two. "It's fantastic I can do that," he says.

For now, it truly is.

Cognitive Processes

Cognitive psychology has grown faster than most other specialties in the past 20 years, responding to new computer technology as well as the growth of psycholinguistics. For contemporary students, these two sources of theoretical and experimental pressure on cognitive psychology have almost totally eclipsed the earlier organismic theories, with the exception of Piaget's theory of cognitive development. Within cognitive psychology we find a growing range of topics. In this section, we will focus on two major areas: intelligence and creativity.

In the area of intelligence, one persistent problem has been the difficulty of defining just what intelligence is. David Wechsler, author of several of the most popular intelligence tests in current clinical use, defines intelligence as the global capacity of the individual to act purposefully, to think rationally, and to deal effectively with the environment. Other psychologists have proposed more complex definitions. But the problem arises when we try to develop tests which validly and reliably measure such concepts. Indeed, Edward Boring once suggested that we define intelligence as whatever it is that intelligence tests measure!

One point that most psychologists now agree on is that intelligence is a concept, not a "thing." Thus, it is more correct to talk about intelligent behaviors than to adhere to the view that intelligence exists as a unitary trait that can be measured. From this point of view, one's ability to score high on an "intelligence test" reflects a form of intelligent behavior, just as one's ability to perform intricate ballet movements reflects a different form of intelligent behavior.

The newer information-processing view holds that first, intelligence must be understood as a series of activities, most of which are covert; then, each activity must be measured individually. Recently, the information-processing perspective has generated more interest and controversy about the possibility of creating a computer program which would simulate human mental operations.

The unit's first two articles reflect and extend these two viewpoints. Kevin McKean reviews traditional attempts to define and measure general intelligence, and demonstrates the advantages offered by newer models which are similar in their empirical bases. The next article further details the work of Sternberg and Gardner. The models they proposed, as well as other models, appeal to a wide professional audience and are regarded as having great promise. The Sternberg and Gardner approaches argue against the idea that there is a single general factor underlying intelligence. In contrast, they emphasize that there are several kinds of intelligence, and individuals who excel in one type of intelligence may not necessarily excel in another. In the next article, Daniel Goleman reviews research that suggests that emotional factors and attitudes also play an important role in regulating intelligent behavior. Just as intelligence is difficult to define, so too is creativity. Indeed, there was a time when psychologists defined the two almost synonymously. There was a circularity to such definitions: highly creative people are so because they have high intelligence. However, in such comparisons intelligence generally was defined by the score one achieved on IQ tests, tests which do not measure one's ability to generate novel ideas, to paint the unusual, to write a book, or to arrive at innovative solutions to complex problems. Can one teach others to be creative? The last article in this unit answers with a resounding yes. Interestingly enough, the impetus for this new interest in creativity has been supplied by the business world.

Looking Ahead: Challenge Questions

Why do all traditional attempts to define and measure intelligence fall short? What benefits do the new models provide for the theorist and for the researcher?

Are Sternberg's triarchic theory and Gardner's seven-facet measure of intelligence simply examples of accommodation to critics who claimed that intelligence did not correlate well with common sense or wisdom? Can all of these components be measured accurately?

If intelligence is not a unitary concept and if it can be affected by one's self-concept and/or attitudes, does it have a place in modern psychology? Why does the academic world continue to use such measures as the ACT, SAT, and GRE as evaluative criteria for admission to college or to graduate school, respectively?

Think of an individual you consider to be high in creativity. Which of that individual's characteristics lead you to your conclusion? Do you agree with the thesis that creativity (your friend's characteristics) can be taught? Why is the business world so interested in enhancing creativity in the work force? Do you think this will succeed?

Unit 5

INTELLIGENCE
NEW WAYS TO MEASURE THE WISDOM OF MAN

KEVIN McKEAN

Mr. McKean is a senior editor of Discover.

On the weekend of July 4th, 1942, when psychologist Seymour Sarason reported for work at the Southbury Training School for the mentally retarded, the place was in an uproar: one of the students had escaped. Southbury was a model new institution set in a lovely Connecticut valley. But the students, who were still more or less prisoners in those days, would occasionally evade supervision long enough to slip into the woods and strike out for home, obliging the school to send out a search party.

Sarason, who had been hired to set up a psychological service, paid little attention to the escapes at first. But as the months wore on, he noticed a curious thing. He was giving the students the Porteus Mazes Test, an IQ exam often used for retarded people since it required no language, simply challenging them to trace their way out of printed mazes. To his astonishment, many of the escapees couldn't work so much as the first and simplest puzzle. "These kids couldn't get from point A to point B on paper, so how did they plan a successful runaway?" says Sarason, now a professor at Yale. "That was when I realized that what these kids could plan on their own was in no way reflected by how they did on tests."

The lesson that there's more to intelligence than IQ is one that most people learn the hard way at one time or another. Everyone has known people with low IQs who get along in the world famously, and others with high IQs who never amount to much. Indeed, the venerable Intelligence Quotient has such an imperfect relationship to intelligence that many psychologists have dropped the term from their lexicon.

FASCINATION WITH IQs

Nevertheless, the subject of intelligence—and how to measure it—continues to engross psychologists and laymen, probably because intelligence is the principal ability that separates man from other creatures. People who readily agree that the results of IQ tests are meaningless shy away from revealing their own scores. Those who did well on such tests during grade or high school tend to recall the results with smug satisfaction. Those who did poorly remember in shame or forget.

A similar division prevails among scientists. Defenders of IQ, like Hans Eysenck of the University of London, points to its eight-decade record of service: "There's an indisputable body of scientific evidence showing that IQ tests do reflect actual cognitive abilities." Says Earl Hunt of the University of Washington, "The intelligence test is probably psychology's biggest technological contribution." Critics counter that IQ's many flaws render it useless. "The assumption that intelligence can be measured as a single number is just a twentieth-century version of craniometry," says biologist and author Stephen Jay Gould, referring to the nineteenth-century "science" that claimed a man's intelligence could be determined by measuring his head. Norman Geschwind, the noted Harvard neurologist, was fond of pointing out that some people with massive frontal-lobe brain damage, whose personality, motivation, and insight had been irreversibly damaged, could still attain near-genius IQ scores—a fact, he said, that showed the bankruptcy of IQ.

IQ fell on hard times through a combination of bad luck and misuse. Its bad luck was to have been invented at the turn of the century, when racial and nationalistic prejudices were more prevalent—or, at least, more apparent—than they are today. Some of the creators of IQ misused it as a justification for repressive measures against foreigners, blacks, and other "undesirables." And scientists are still hotly debating whether the differences in IQ among various races and nationalities mean anything. These controversies leave some researchers doubtful about whether IQ is worth rescuing. "The problem with IQ is that it's been marred

Reprinted from *Current*, Janaury 1986, pp. 15–23. Originally from *Discover*, October 1985, pp. 25–41. Kevin McKean/© Discover 1985, Family Media, Inc.

for decades by the smell of political issues, race, and so on,'' says psychologist Robert Sternberg of Yale. "Intelligence research doesn't have to be that way. There's legitimate scientific inquiry to be pursued."

Sternberg and other young theoreticians are striving to render IQ obsolete by forging new and more realistic definitions of what it means to be intelligent. It would be wrong to characterize this group, which includes, among others, psychologists Howard Gardner at Harvard and Jon Baron at the University of Pennsylvania, as a "school"; their ideas are too diverse. Gardner identifies seven "intelligences," including social grace and athletic skill. Sternberg posits three, one of which, practical intelligence, resembles common sense. Baron stresses the need for rational thinking. Still other theoreticians argue that mental development doesn't cease at adolescence, as many defenders of IQ maintain, but continues throughout life.

What these new theories share is an almost humanistic perspective. Their creators, mindful of the pitfalls of IQ, borrow from cognitive psychology and neuroscience to define smartness as a complex web of abilities; they construct new intelligence exams using realistic problems; they explicitly allow for national and cultural differences in the definition of intelligence; they argue that smartness results from an interaction of genes and environment, making the bitter "nature-nuture" argument pointless; and, contending that much of intelligence consists of learned skills, many of the theorists are devising programs to teach it.

No one expects the new theories to end complaints about intelligence testing, or to settle once and for all what that elusive quality we call intelligence really is. Yet they've already begun to change the scientific establishment's *HUMANISTIC* view of intelligence. Sternberg is devising a *PERSPECTIVE* new exam for the Psychological Corporation, a major test marketer; Gardner is discussing a joint project with the Educational Testing Service, creator of the Scholastic Aptitude Test (SAT). While the direct influence of these researchers may be small, changes in the way such scientists view intelligence have important consequences when they filter into the world at large (as the fact that many people still equate intelligence with IQ shows). To understand what we will mean by intelligence in the next century, we need to understand what psychologists think of intelligence today. So the work of this diverse group of researchers is likely to have far-reaching effects, for better or worse, on our social and public policies, and on our view of ourselves, in the future.

ORIGINS OF THE IQ CONCEPT

The modern conception of intelligence has its roots around the turn of the century, when a number of scientists sought definitions for the term. Sir Francis Galton tried to measure intelligence using simple reaction-time tests. French psychologist Alfred Binet in 1905 published the first modern IQ-like test to help the government identify schoolchildren in need of remedial education.

Binet's test was taken up enthusiastically by American psychologists, chief among them Stanford's Lewis Terman, who, in 1916, produced an expanded version designed for subjects of any age. The Stanford-Binet test, as it was called, consisted of problems that would be familiar to modern IQ test-takers: vocabulary questions, tests of reasoning and logic, questions that involved completing a series of numbers. While Binet's scale had yielded a score expressed in terms of "mental age," Terman called his score an Intelligence Quotient—calculated by dividing a subject's mental age by his physical age and multiplying by 100. (Thus a six-year-old performing at the six-year-old level would have an IQ of 100; if he performed at the nine-year-old level, his IQ would be 150.) And while Binet meant his test simply as an educational tool, Terman had broad ambitions for wide-spread testing of adults. "Intelligence tests," he wrote, "will *STANFORD-* bring tens of thousands of . . . high-grade de- *BINET TEST* fectives under the surveillance and protection of society. This will ultimately result in curtailing the reproduction of feeble-mindedness, and in the elimination of an enormous amount of crime, pauperism, and industrial inefficiency."

Terman's dream of mass testing was quickly realized. A Harvard psychologist named Robert Yerkes persuaded the Army to examine some 1.75 million recruits during World War I. Whether because of poor test conditions— many test halls were so crowded that recruits seated in the back could scarcely hear the instruction—or the soldiers' lack of ability, the average able-bodied white recruit scored a mental age of about 13, a tad smarter than "moron." The test's authors were dismayed by the low scores, but encouraged that the racial and national break-down suited the prejudices of the day. Yerkes' disciple Carl Campbell Brigham calculated that Americans of "Nordic" descent, which meant, more or less, northern Europeans, had an average mental age of 13.28; "Alpines," or middle Europeans, 11.67; "Mediterraneans," or southern Europeans, 11.43; and blacks, 10.41.

With the Army exams as impetus, intelligence testing took off after the war. Brigham and others devised the first SAT; Terman issued a revision of the Stanford-Binet in 1937 (there was third revision in 1960); in the 1940s and '50s, psychologist David Wechsler of Bellevue Psychiatric Hospital in New York devised intelligence tests for adults and children that today rival the Stanford-Binet in popularity.

MODERN IQ TESTS

The modern versions of these tests are fairly straight-forward. The Wechsler Adult Intelligence Scale exam, for example, is given in a personal interview. It consists of eleven subsections that ask examinees to do such things as define words, solve math problems, recall strings of digits in forward or reverse order, and arrange blocks according to a specified design. IQ tests are used to identify children who are slow or speedy learners, to evaluate job candidates, as part of psychological or psychiatric exams, and, when coupled with other tests that assess interests or experience, to help draw a picture of a person's mental strengths and weaknesses.

Gardner well remembers his first exposure to such an IQ test battery. His parents, Jewish refugees from Nazi Germany who had settled in Scranton, Pa., knew they had a bright child and wanted to find out what to do with him. So, in the mid-1950s, when Howard was thirteen, they took him to Hoboken, N.J. for a week of testing. "It cost three hundred dollars—the equivalent of thousands of dollars today," says Gardner, now 42. "At the end of the week they told my parents, 'Your son tests well in everything, but he seems to be best at clerical matters.' Maybe that was when my skepticism about tests got its start."

With true clerical attention to detail, Gardner made sure that nearly every grade he earned at Harvard was an A (he got one B+). Then he headed to England for graduate study in philosophy and sociology. After returning to Harvard in 1966, he worked with gifted children in Project Zero, an innovative task group trying to understand artistic creativity, and also with brain-damaged patients at Boston University and the Boston V.A. Hospital.

This dual exposure, to talented children and grievously ill adults, helped mold Gardner's eclectic view of the mind. He and David Feldman of Tufts were impressed by the tender age at which some children manifest special abilities. Musically inclined pre-schoolers, for example, easily learned to play simple instruments "not only because they found music patterns easy to learn, but because they found them almost impossible to forget!" The observation reminded Gardner of the story of Stravinsky, who, as an adult, could still remember the tuba, drums, and piccolos of the fife-and-drum band that had marched outside his nursery.

At the V.A. hospital, Gardner was struck by the cruel and exquisite selectivity with which disease and injury can damage the mind. Patients with a left-hemisphere lesion might lose the power to speak but still be able to sing the lyrics to songs because the musical right hemisphere was intact. Right-hemisphere patients might read flawlessly but be unable to interpret what they read. (Gardner's findings suggested that the ability to read between the lines—that is, to get the point of something, including a joke—is largely a right-hemisphere function.)

These experiences persuaded Gardner that intelligence, far from being a unitary power of mind, consists of a set of mental abilities that not only manifest themselves independently but probably spring from different areas of the brain. In his book *Frames of Mind* (Basic Books, 1983), he hypothesizes that there are at least seven broad categories of intelligence. Three are conventional: verbal, mathematical, and spacial. But the other four—musical ability, bodily skills, adroitness in dealing with others, and self-knowledge—have sparked controversy because they're far afield of what's usually called intelligence. "If I'd talked about seven talents, nobody would've complained." Gardner explains. "But by calling them intelligences, I hope to shake up the community that wants to reserve this name for the results of a Wechsler exam or the SAT."

In defense of the label "intelligence," Gardner argues that each of the seven abilities can be destroyed by particular brain damage, each shows up in highlighted form in the talents of gifted people or idiots savants, and each involves unique cognitive skills. "Take an athlete like Larry Bird, who has a sixth sense of where to throw a basketball," says Gardner. "He has to know where his teammates and opponents are, judge where they are likely to go, and use analysis, inference, planning, and problem-solving to decide what to do. A number of different intelligences get involved in these decisions. But it's clear that, even in the bodily movements alone, there's a reasoning process."

CATEGORIES OF INTELLIGENCE

Gardner's theory makes room not only for Western definitions of intelligence, but also for other cultures. Intelligence among the Iatmul people of Papua New Guinea, for example, may consist of the ability to remember the names of some 10,000 to 20,000 clans, as adult males of that group do. In the Puluwat culture of the sprawling Caroline Islands, intelligence can be the ability to navigate by the stars.

Because he emphasizes cultural variation, Gardner refuses to define a single IQ-like scale. "When you measure people on only one measure, you cheat them out of recognition for other things," he says. But in a project with Feldman and Janet Stork of Tufts, and Ulla Malkus and Mara Krechevsky of Project Zero, he's seeking ways to characterize the skill patterns of children in a Tufts pre-school. To gauge musical ability, for example, the group may ask a child to listen to a melody and then re-create it on tuned bells. "When they are three or four, we should, without subjecting children to anything intrusive, be able to profile their abilities," Gardner says. "And that's the time when feedback to parents and teachers can make a difference. . . ."

Not content to be a mere taker of tests, Sternberg, the son of a Maplewood, N.J. dressmaker's supply salesman, decided to create his own. At age thirteen he dug up a description of the Stanford-Binet in the library and used it to devise what he called the Sternberg Test of Mental Abilities. He then set about assessing the mental abilities of his classmates until the school psychologist called him in for a scolding. "The psychologist didn't think it was appropriate for seventh graders to be testing each other," Sternberg says.

CULTURAL VARIATION

This early setback didn't prevent Sternberg, now 35, from going on to become one of the foremost figures in the field. He's at once very similar to and strikingly different from Gardner. Both are children of immigrant Jews who fled the Nazis (in Sternberg's case, only his mother came to the U.S. as a refugee—his father had arrived earlier). Both graduated from college summa cum laude, Gardner from Harvard, Sternberg from Yale, and returned to their alma maters to teach. And both aim to broaden the definition of intelligence. . . .

Sternberg's "triarchic theory," laid out in *Beyond IQ* (Cambridge University Press, 1985), breaks intelligence into three parts. The first deals with the mental mechanisms people use to plan and carry out tasks, with special emphasis on what Sternberg calls the "metacomponents" of intelligence—the skills by which people plan and evaluate problem-solving. To Sternberg, planning is often more important than sheer mental speed: good test-takers, for instance, spend more time than poor ones on studying and digesting questions before trying to work them out.

Sternberg's studies also highlight the role of planning in reading comprehension, often a part of standard IQ tests. He and a colleague, Richard Wagner, asked volunteers to read four passages, one for gist only, one for main ideas, one to learn details, and one for analysis. The best readers, as measured by a standard Nelson-Denny reading test, devoted most of their time to the passages that had to be read with the greatest care, whereas poorer readers spent the same amount of time on all four selections. When Sternberg added the results of his time-allocation test to the Nelson-Denny profile, the combined score turned out to be a better predictor of how well people understood the passages than the Nelson-Denny score alone.

The study shows how Sternberg tries to make intelligence tests more realistic. "Think of the reading comprehension tests on the SAT," Sternberg says, "They tell you to read each passage carefully. If you did that in real life, you'd be reading and reading and reading.

You'd never get done."

The triarchic theory's second part deals with the effect of experience: the intelligent person not only solves new problems quickly, Sternberg argues, but also trains himself to solve familiar problems by rote in order to free his mind for other work.

The third part, which focuses on practical intelligence, asserts that common sense depends largely on what Sternberg calls tacit knowledge—which might loosely be defined as all the extremely important things they never teach you in school. He says success in life often depends more on tacit knowledge than on explicit information. "A lot of people in a field don't know it [the tacit knowledge]," says Sternberg. "Or don't know that they know it. Or don't know what it is they know, even if they do know that they know it."

Sternberg is convinced that, if tacit knowledge could be made explicit, it could be taught, and he tries to teach it to his graduate students. "I sit them down and explain the strategy of scientific publishing, how it's better to publish in a journal with a circulation of 40,000 than 4,000, and how to tailor a paper to a journal"—things that many professors don't teach, in the belief that they're "sleazy." Sternberg has also devised a number of tests of practical intelligence. Some pose typical quandaries in business, politics, or science. Others seek the testee's sensitivity to nonverbal cues: one type of question presents a picture of two people and asks which is the boss and which the employee (the boss is usually older and better dressed, of course, but also tends to look directly at the employee, who tends to look away). The aim of such questions is not to train people to spot bigwigs, though that alone might be useful, but to make intelligence tests more realistic. "Standard IQ tests are fairly good for predicting how people will do in school, but they have a very low correlation with job performance," says Sternberg, who has a $750,000 grant from the Army to develop practical intelligence tests for military job placement. "I want to be able to say who's going to be a good officer, a good business executive, or a good scientist." He's also worked up a program for teaching intelligence that is being published as *Intelligence Applied* (Harcourt, Brace, Jovanovich) this winter. . . .

THE NATURE-NURTURE DEBATE

To Arthur Jensen, programs that aim to raise intelligence, like Sternberg's and Baron's, are just wishful thinking. He believes that it's genes, not culture or environment, that do the most to determine intelligence. Specifically, Jensen argues that intelligence is a physical property of the brain; that IQ is a pretty fair measure of that property; that braininess is mostly inherited; that, as a result, there are sharp biological limits set at birth on an individual's intellectual capacity; and that there may also be clear-cut differences in average intellectual potential among races and nationalities.

It's not a position that has won many friends. When Jensen first suggested, in a 1969 article in the *Harvard Educational Review*, that lower intelligence might account for the fact that blacks don't do as well as whites in school, friendly critics called him naïve and hostile ones a racist. Pickets appeared at his University of California at Berkeley office; he had to move classes to a new location each day to avoid demonstrations. Hate mail arrived in such quantities that, for a year, the police bomb squad opened all packages, and campus cops accompanied him to and from work. "It was sort of like having a bear by the tail," recalls Jensen, whose lectures at other campuses are still occasionally disrupted by protests. "I could either run and get out of it, or I could stick to my research and see where it would lead."

As his words imply, Jensen stuck it out. And his research has made him the biggest thorn in the side of people like Gardner and Sternberg who would like to broaden the meaning of intelligence. In intelligence testing Jensen-style, the examinee sits before a control panel featuring an array of buttons. He holds his finger on the center button until one of the eight surrounding buttons lights up. Then he jabs his finger at the lighted button as quickly as he can, turning it off. This procedure is repeated with slight variations about 60 times. Although this apparently mindless exercise doesn't seem to involve much intelligence, performance on a battery of such tasks correlates quite well with performance on standard IQ exams—which implies that Jensen's button-pushing device is nearly as good at measuring IQ as the tests themselves.

THE "g" FORCE

Critics say this only confirms the meaninglessness of IQ, but Jensen, 52, sees more fundamental forces at work—in particular, a force that Charles Spearman called *g*. Spearman observed that there was a high degree of correlation among a wide variety of mental tests, even those that seemed wildly dissimilar. In a classic paper published in 1904, he argued that this correlation reflected a *general* mental ability—hence *g*—involved in all cognitive work, and presented a mathematical method called factor analysis for determining the extent to which *g* was involved in any given task.

Spearman's paper set off a debate that still rages over whether *g* is a real property of the brain (Spearman thought it was a free-floating mental energy, a notion that has since been abandoned). Jensen argues that his button-pushing task measures IQ mainly because the task is highly *g*-loaded, as the jargon goes. And a person's level of *g*, Jensen adds, may be controlled by genes. Identical twins score more nearly alike than fraternal twins on *g*-loaded subsections of the Wechsler exam. Japanese children whose parents are first or second cousins score lower on the *g*-loaded subsections (compared to non-inbred children) than on the portions that are not so *g*-loaded—suggesting that *g* is more vulnerable than other mental abilities to the harmful genetic effects of inbreeding.

In a June article in *Behavioral and Brain Sciences*, Jensen analyzed a number of standard IQ tests and concluded that those showing the largest difference between the average scores of blacks and whites were also the ones with the highest *g*-loading. The gap between the races was small—only about 15 points, less than the average variation between children in a family. Nevertheless, Jensen argues that a small average difference could markedly affect the black-white ratio at the highest and lowest levels. Only 16 percent of test takers score higher than one standard deviation above average (in IQ, one standard deviation—a conventional statistical measure of scatter—equals about 15 points). Fewer than three percent exceed two standard deviations above average. Thus, a group with an average IQ of 115 would have five times as many people over 130 as an equal-sized group with an average IQ 15 points lower—simply because 130 is two standard deviations above the lower group's average but only one standard deviation above the higher group's. "It doesn't take a big shift in average," says Jensen, "to make an enormous difference in the portion of the curve that's above a cut-off like 130."

Jensen thinks this may explain the fact that 39 percent of Asian-American high-school graduates in California meet Berkeley's entrance requirements, versus only 15 percent of other students; his studies of children from San Francisco's Chinatown suggest that Americans of Asian descent may be about 15 IQ points smarter than children of European descent. At the other end of the intelligence distribution, Jensen blames a lower average IQ for the disproportionate numbers of blacks in remedial education. School systems that try to restore racial balance by putting more whites in these programs, he says, only deny help to some who need it while retarding the progress of others who don't.

In Jensen's view, as much as 70 percent of the differences in intelligence—or at least *g*—may be genetic. "There's no doubt that you could breed for intelligence in humans the way you breed for milk in cows or eggs in chickens," he says. Would it be worthwhile?

GENETIC DIFFERENCES Jensen says yes. "If you were to raise the average IQ just one standard deviation, you wouldn't recognize things. Magazines, newspapers, books, and television would have to become more sophisticated. Schools would have to teach differently." Of course, the transition wouldn't be smooth: "You would go from having three percent of the population over IQ 130 to something like 15 percent, meaning that you would have five times as many people wanting to become doctors, lawyers, professors, and so forth. If the change occurred suddenly, you might have to hold lotteries to decide who gets what job."

CULTURAL INFLUENCES

Jensen's critics regard this kind of talk as meaningless. "To say that because black children *don't* do well on IQ tests they *can't* do well is extraordinarily simple-minded," says Sandra Scarr, chairman of the psychology department at the University of Virginia. "Our studies show that blacks reared by whites have an IQ of about 110, the same as white adoptees raised in the same environment." And Berkeley anthropologist John Ogbu, a Nigerian, points to studies showing that Third World schoolchildren who attend Western-style schools score as high as Westerners on IQ tests.

Ogbu and others add that tests designed for one culture are notoriously faulty when applied to another. A classic example is the study by Joseph Glick of Liberia's Kpelle tribesmen. Glick, of the City University of New York, asked the tribesmen to sort a series of objects in a sensible order. To his consternation they insisted on grouping them by function (placing a potato with a hoe, for example) rather than by taxonomy (which would place the potato with other foods). By Western standards, it was an inferior style of sorting. But when Glick demonstrated the "right" answer, one of the tribesmen remarked that only a stupid person would sort things that way. Thereafter, when Glick asked tribesmen to sort the items the way a *stupid* person would, they sorted them taxonomically without difficulty.

Stephen Jay Gould maintains that even if intelligence were 70 percent heritable, which he doubts, it wouldn't prove that racial or cultural differences were genetic. Imagine, he says, a group of malnourished Africans whose average height is a few inches less than that of North Americans. Height is highly heritable—about 95 percent. But that fact gives no assurance that these Africans would stay shorter if they were properly fed. The average height in Japan has gone up several inches since World War II, but no one argues that the Japanese gene pool has changed. As for Spearman's *g*, Gould believes it has no real existence but is simply a mathematical artifact expressing sub-

tle but pervasive advantages of schooling, parental attention, expectations, and motivation. "The chimerical nature of *g* is the rotten core of Jensen's edifice, and of the entire hereditarian school [of IQ]," he wrote in *The Mismeasure of Man* (Norton, 1981).

Critics fear that Jensen's ideas will do psychological damage to the supposedly inferior groups, and could even be used to justify social or political oppression. His defenders counter that this is no excuse for limiting scientific inquiry: "Would you proscribe Charles Darwin because the Social Darwinists used his theory to justify *laissez-faire* capitalism?" asks Bernard Davis, an emeritus bacteriologist and geneticist at Harvard Medical School. To that, critics respond that anyone working in the intelligence field has to be sensitive to the political consequences of his ideas. "If you aren't," says Gardner, "you're just an ostrich."

Moreover, Gardner and the other new theorists believe the whole nature-nurture debate is a red herring. "Suppose we improved our social and educational systems so much that all schools and homes were absolutely equal," says Sternberg. "Then, regardless of how genetically influenced intelligence was, the heritability would go up to 100 percent—since there would be no other differences besides genes. That shows how meaningless heritability is." Utopian visions of a superintelligent future are naïve he thinks, because "some of the brightest people in history have been the biggest bastards."

BIOLOGICAL INFLUENCES ON INTELLIGENCE

Whether or not heritability is meaningless, it's certainly true that intelligence is sometimes biologically influenced, as the work of Julian Stanley and Camilla Benbow dramatically shows. Since 1971, Stanley, of Johns Hopkins University, has collected data on children who, before the age of 13, score 700 or better (of a maximum 800) on the math SAT. These children are culled from annual talent searches like the one Stanley founded at Johns Hopkins, and represents roughly one child out of every 10,000 in that age group nationally.

The startling discovery of Stanley and Benbow, who joined him in 1977, is that among the 292 high scorers on the math test, boys outnumber girls about twelve to one. The effect seems limited to math, since the sex ratio is roughly fifty-fifty among children who score high on the verbal SAT. "We were shocked at first," says Stanley, chief of the Study of Mathematically Precocious Youth, as the program is called. "We knew that by age eighteen, when most kids take the SAT, boys do better than girls. But by that age, boys have usually taken a lot more math. We assumed that at age twelve, when both sexes have taken the same amount of math, there would be little or no difference." And questionnaires aimed at finding a cultural explanation failed: boys and girls in the screening program answered similarly when asked whether they studied math, enjoyed math, or felt math was important to their careers.

Not all scientists have accepted the implication that bright thirteen-year-old boys may be innately better at math than girls. The journal *Science*, in which the report appeared, ran seven letters of rebuttal arguing that Benbow and Stanley had overlooked important social factors—such as the possibility that twelve-year-old girls might not even enter a "talent search" if they thought it would make them brainy or unattractive to boys. But Benbow and Stanley felt some of the criticism was unfair. "People were furious with us for finding what we found, and even more furious that, having found it, we had the ill grace to publish," says Stanley. "We're not saying biology is the cause," adds Benbow. "We're just saying it's premature to rule biology out."

It would be nice to say that the two scientists could at least rule out the stereotype of the bright student squinting through thick glasses and sniveling into a handkerchief. But here, too, their data lend curious support to an old prejudice. The high scorers are about four times as likely as other children the same age to be myopic, and twice as likely to have allergies (or other auto-immune disorders) and to be left-handed. This collection of traits is not as whimsical as it sounds. Geschwind, who died last year, believed that hormonal influences in the womb often caused male fetuses to experience greater development of their brains' right hemispheres at the expense of the left. This, he argued, could account for the fact that males are more likely to be left-handed (the right hemisphere controls the left side of the body), and also for the fact that left-handers are somewhat more prone to auto-immune disorders and reading disabilities.

The fact that the Johns Hopkins kids are anything but reading-disabled doesn't cut them out of this picture. Benbow notes that mathematical reasoning—as opposed to simple calculation—seems associated with the right hemisphere. Thus, if Geschwind's theory is correct, a right-hemisphere hormonal boost may be a double-edged sword, encouraging mathematical genius in some, sending brain development awry in others. Benbow, who moves to Iowa State next year, will pursue this biological puzzle by tracking a number of the children into adult life—a modern variation of Lewis Terman's massive study of high-IQ schoolchildren.

Whatever the cause, it's clear there's a qualitative, not merely a quantitative, difference between prodigies and ordinary bright kids. When these twelve-year-old mathematicians sit down to take the SAT, many of them have never been exposed to the algebra, geometry, and rudimentary calculus that a high school senior might know. Thus, they more or less have to re-invent these disciplines on the spot—deducing things like the Pythagorean theorem, or how to factor algebraic expressions.

What if such a child had been born in classical times? Would he have upstaged Pythagoras? Stanley thinks not. "He would've manifested his ability early and become a great surveyor or engineer," Stanley says. "But remember, if he'd been born in Rome in the year zero, he wouldn't even have had a zero to work with!" It was the decimal system, derived from the Arabs and Hindus, that introduced the mathematically important zero; the citizens of Imperial Rome were hampered by their cumbersome—and zero-less—numeral system.

Stanley's point is that intelligence is meaningless when separated from its cultural roots. That's why Newton, for all his genius, wasn't being unduly modest when he said he stood on the shoulders of giants. Thanks to cultural storage and transmission of knowledge, every person stands on the shoulders of countless giants to whom he owes concepts, like inertia, that are so familiar they seem intuitive, but which were in fact brilliant insights.

QUALITATIVE DIFFERENCES

IS INTELLIGENCE INCREASING WITH TIME?

That fact makes it extremely difficult to say whether intelligence is increasing with time. If one considers cultural advances, the answer is certainly yes: there's little doubt that at least in scientific and technical matters, today's culture is vastly advanced over that of centuries or even decades ago. And a randomly selected sample of modern Americans would easily outscore thirteenth-century Frenchmen in standard IQ. But would the contest be fair?

Gardner adds that different kinds of intelligence have been valued at different times in history. In the pre-literate era, the mark of wisdom was a prodigious verbal memory. Today, that sort of skill is more associated with *idiots savants*. And, while one can only speculate how modern geniuses would fare were they transported to the past, there have been examples of the reverse situation, in which a "primitive" scientist has been thrust into the present. One such case was that of Srinivasa Ramanujan, the renowned Indian mathematician, who was brought up in an isolated village. Ramanujan had an extraordinary talent for seeing the hidden properties of numbers: once, when a friend visited him as he lay ill in England, Ramanujan observed that the number of the visitor's cab—1,729—was the smallest that could be expressed as the sum of two cubes in two different ways. "This was amazingly rapid mathematical insight," says Gardner, "but not [one] that was at a premium, or even especially appreciated, in twentieth-century Britain. Beyond natural gifts, aspiring mathematicians need to be in the right place at the proper time."

Just as each type of intelligence has its time, so does each stage of its development in individuals. This was the insight of the renowned Swiss psychologist Jean Piaget, who charted the intellectual discoveries that make up the mental growth of children. For Piaget, who died in 1980, the last stage of mental development was reached during adolescence with the attainment of what he called "formal operations"—more or less the ability to pose and solve abstract logical problems. But some of Piaget's intellectual descendants think mental development continues in adulthood, and a number of them have devised tests to try to prove it.

Harvard psychologist Michael Lamport Commons, for example, charts three stages of mental development beyond formal operations, each involving the ability to reason abstractly about the achievements of the previous stage. His colleague Lawrence Kohlberg has devised tests of an adult's ethical development. To assess the relationship of such measures to IQ, Commons recently gave a battery of his tests to 150 volunteers from Mensa—the worldwide organization of people with high IQs. The Mensa group didn't score any better than adults of average intelligence. On the contrary, those who claimed to have the highest IQs tended to have lower degrees of ethical judgment on Kohlberg's scale. Says Commons, "The notion that geniuses will solve our problems is a hoax."

Although IQ, by some measures, declines three to four points per decade after age 20, University of Denver psychologist John Horn finds that other aspects of intellectual performance actually increase with time. Horn's chart of mental abilities over a life-time shows most trailing dismally downward with age. But at least two of the lines climb hopefully upward. One represents an ability that Horn and others have called crystallized intelligence, amounting to the sum of a person's knowledge and experience. The other is what Horn calls long-term storage and retrieval, that is, the ability to call

to mind experiences of long ago. Taken together, Horn argues, these two might well be called wisdom. "Their effect shows up on tests like the one in which you ask people to think of all the things they could do with a brick. The older person comes up with more ideas because he has been around longer and had more experiences. And the ideas are good ones, not silly ones."

Perhaps the most troublesome puzzle of intelligence is why some obviously intelligent people make such messes of their lives—as was the sad case with Leonard Ross. A child prodigy who won $164,000 on TV quiz shows in the 1950s, Ross graduated from Yale Law School—where he was editor in chief of the law journal—and seemed destined for a brilliant future. But he drifted from one job to another, never able to settle on a career or find personal happiness. Last May, at age 39, he was found floating in a motel pool in Santa Clara, Calif., apparently a suicide.

Sternberg, who has given this matter much thought, thinks problems like Ross' lie outside the realm of intelligence. He has drawn up a list of factors that undermine intelligence performance—lack of motivation, inability to persevere, uncontrolled impulsiveness, and failure to know one's own limitations. "You have to concentrate on those things you're best at," Sternberg says. "The trick of intelligence is playing to your strengths."

Gardner sees our inability to comprehend why the intelligent often live unintelligently as a consequence of the nature of intelligence testing. Most intelligence tests, even newer ones, last no more than a few hours, and it may simply be impossible to draw a realistic picture of a human being in that time. Gardner contends that testers should dump the short-answer quiz in favor of a system that would assign grades, or even intelligence scores, on the basis of performance on long-term projects. "There are too many people who are brilliant at short-answer quizzes and yet failures at life for that talent to be important," Gardner says. "What was it William F. Buckley said about beating the SAT—that all you had to do was figure out what the guy who made up the test wanted you to say? But creative people look beyond the superficial. It's the ones who don't accept the 'right' answer who come up with the really important ideas."

New research suggests that many people are brainier than you might think

Getting smart about IQ

■ Whatever happened to the good old-fashioned IQ test? These days, the notion that a single number—the "intelligence quotient"—can gauge how smart we are is under fresh attack. A new wave of psychologists and educators are redefining what intelligence really is—and devising ways to improve thinking skills once thought to be fixed for life.

Until recently, much of the controversy over IQ tests had focused on whether the skills and aptitudes measured by traditional intelligence tests are culturally biased against black students. Last year, a federal judge in California issued a sweeping order barring the use of IQ tests with black children for any "special education" purpose, such as assignment to classes for the retarded. On average, blacks score 15 points below whites on the tests—and in California, as elsewhere, those scores resulted in disproportionate assignment of black students to classes for the mildly retarded. Opponents of the tests say that what they really measure is not underlying mental ability but exposure to middle-class experiences.

But today's critics go even further: They attack IQ tests as far too limited in measuring the aptitudes of blacks *and* whites. "They sample only a tiny aspect of the firmament of human abilities, and we're somehow making the IQ score equal to all intelligence," says Harvard psychologist Howard Gardner, whose theory of multiple intelligences undergirds a research program at Harvard and Tufts universities aimed at measuring the different realms of intelligence. Adds Robert Sternberg, a Yale University psychologist: "There are a lot of successful people who didn't do well on IQ tests. The tests put too little emphasis on practical and creative skills."

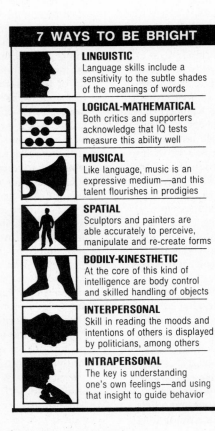

7 WAYS TO BE BRIGHT

LINGUISTIC
Language skills include a sensitivity to the subtle shades of the meanings of words

LOGICAL-MATHEMATICAL
Both critics and supporters acknowledge that IQ tests measure this ability well

MUSICAL
Like language, music is an expressive medium—and this talent flourishes in prodigies

SPATIAL
Sculptors and painters are able accurately to perceive, manipulate and re-create forms

BODILY-KINESTHETIC
At the core of this kind of intelligence are body control and skilled handling of objects

INTERPERSONAL
Skill in reading the moods and intentions of others is displayed by politicians, among others

INTRAPERSONAL
The key is understanding one's own feelings—and using that insight to guide behavior

Downplaying test results

The critics are already having an impact. Outside California, the standard IQ test, with its emphasis on verbal, logical and mathematical abilities, is still widely used to screen children for special-education and gifted classes. But, at the same time, the publicity generated by the California case and the drumbeat of academic criticism have led growing numbers of psychologists and educators to play down the tests' role. At an elementary school in Watertown, Mass., IQ tests are individ-

ually administered to academically troubled children by a psychologist. "We do find them to be one factor in judging a child's ability," says principal Bill Corbett. "But we instruct our people to put it in perspective."

One reason for the wariness about IQ tests is that there is still no widespread agreement even on such basics as a definition of intelligence. But many pyschologists believe there's a general mental ability—called "g"—that encompasses problem-solving, logical, learning and verbal faculties.

It is "g" that most psychologists once thought IQ tests essentially measured. But that idea is being challenged by the cutting-edge work of researchers such as Sternberg and Gardner. Gardner's view of intelligence, for instance, is rooted in biology—particularly in research that shows different parts of the brain to be the sites of different abilities. He also points to extraordinary specific talents in math or music, for instance, in prodigies and idiots savants who are otherwise below average or normal. "The concept of 'smart' and 'stupid' doesn't make sense," he says. "You can be smart in one thing and stupid in something else."

Is Larry Bird a genius?

Gardner, in fact, has identified seven different intelligences. They include not only the standard academic ones of linguistic, logical-mathematical and spatial (the visual skills exhibited by a painter or architect) but also musical, "bodily-kinesthetic" and two "personal" intelligences involving a fine-tuned understanding of oneself and others. "I don't assume what's valued in our culture is all there is to intelligence," he says. An athlete like basketball superstar Larry Bird may not be considered particularly smart in modern America, but in a hunting society, Gardner adds, "Larry Bird would be the smart one."

Gardner's views have real-world applications to U.S. classrooms. The Educational Testing Service in Princeton, N.J., is backing a pilot program in Pittsburgh schools to evaluate artistic abilities. Also, a magnet elementary school in Indianapolis has just been started to offer learning in all seven areas.

In addition, there is Project Spectrum, which Gardner designed with Tufts University psychologist David Feldman. It aims to help parents and teachers identify children's strengths and interests at a young age. On one recent day, a 4-year-old boy in a preschool classroom located on the Tufts campus was tinkering with a food grinder under the watchful eyes of a Spectrum researcher. The goal of the exercise: To evaluate the child's logic and dexterity. Such assessments, says research-staff director Mara Krechevsky, allow children "to capitalize on their strengths in a lot more areas." Just ask Diane Birnbaum, whose daughter was in a Spectrum class last year. Birnbaum says that she was surprised to learn about her daughter's aptitude for math and praises the project for measuring "every part of the kid's intelligence."

Gardner's critics contend that his programs measure abilities that don't qualify as intelligence. While psychologist Sternberg shares Gardner's skepticism about IQ tests, he argues that you don't need musical and athletic abilities to "adapt to the real world."

Sternberg's theory of intelligence starts with the fact that while IQ tests are good predictors of academic success, they are poor indicators of job success. (Indeed, one long-range study found that a third of all the professionals it tracked had below-average childhood IQ's.) So why do some people get ahead? Sternberg looks to three different elements of intelligence: The quality of one's internal mental processes, particularly the planning involved in problem solving; how a person actually functions in his or her environment, and how well people handle novelty and perform the skills they've learned. With the backing of the Psychological Corporation, a leading maker of IQ tests, he is now developing a test to measure those aspects of intelligence.

Boosting scores

Sternberg challenges traditional notions on another front as well: He believes that "intelligence can be raised—within limits." To that end, he has written a how-to book, *Intelligence Applied,* and devised a training program that helps people improve their problem-solving abilities.

Sternberg isn't alone in disputing the view that intelligence is virtually set for

---

Yale psychologist Robert Sternberg is developing tests designed to evaluate thinking skills often overlooked by more traditional IQ tests. Sample questions:

Insight questions

1. Fifteen percent of the people in a certain town have unlisted telephone numbers. You select 200 names at random from the local phone book. How many of these people can be expected to have unlisted telephone numbers?

2. A man who lived in a small town married 20 different women in that same town. All of them are still living, and he never divorced any of them. Yet he broke no laws. How could he do this?

3. According to the U.S. Constitution, if the Vice President of the United States should die, who would be the President?

Novel-thinking questions

Assume that the statement given before the analogy is true, and use that statement to solve the analogy.

4. VILLAINS are lovable. HERO is to ADMIRATION as VILLAIN is to: CONTEMPT / AFFECTION / CRUEL / KIND

5. LEMONS are animals. LIME is to GREEN as LEMON is to: YELLOW / ORANGE / GROW / PICK

6. NEEDLES are dull. THIMBLE is to BLUNT as NEEDLE is to: SHARP / SMOOTH / STAB / BRUISE

7. SPARROWS play hopscotch. TROUT is to SCALY as SPARROW is to: FEATHERY / BUMPY / EAGLE / CANARY

8. COBRAS drink lemonade. ROBIN is to BIRD as COBRA is to: DESERT / LIZARD / SNAKE / JUNGLE

Inference questions

How would you classify the relationships between these words?

9. COVER : BOOK

10. EMPTY SET : NULL SET

11. EARLY : LATE

12. CLUE : HINT

13. NEW : ORLEANS

14. X OR Y : NOT X AND NOT Y

15. HEAVENLY : HELLISH

Answers

1. None. Unlisted numbers do not appear in the telephone book. 2. The man is a minister. The critical word in this problem is "married." The man married the various women, but he did not himself become married to them. 3. The President. The death of the Vice President has no effect upon who is President. 4. AFFECTION 5. YELLOW 6. SMOOTH 7. FEATHERY 8. SNAKE 9. Part to a whole. 10. Equivalent. 11. Antonyms. 12. Synonyms. 13. Completion: New Orleans is a city. 14. Negation. 15. Antonyms.

---

life. For about 20 years, Israeli psychologist Reuven Feuerstein has been diagnosing flaws in basic thinking skills and offering training to low-IQ immigrant children. Feuerstein observes his subjects closely to determine how well they learn, mixing puzzles with coaching and retesting. Then, the children are offered "instrumental enrichment" courses that, through paper-and-pencil exercises and supportive teaching, aim to improve reasoning abilities.

Does such training really work? A recent National Academy of Sciences report raises doubts that it improves actual academic achievement. But studies of slow learners have shown sharp improvements in mental-ability test scores, even years after Feuerstein's training program ended. Carl Haywood, professor of psychology at Vanderbilt University, found IQ rises of up to 15 points when Feuerstein's approach was used in the U.S.

Last year, the Feuerstein method was introduced in special-education classes in Detroit—and has earned enthusiastic applause from teachers and parents. Here,

Feuerstein's "dynamic assessment" approach differs markedly from the high-pressure atmosphere surrounding IQ tests. In one schoolroom, for instance, a 14-year-old boy once classified as retarded was recently trying to remember the placement of pegs on several small boards. A psychologist gently advised him: "Don't jump around. Relax and take your time."

The aim, through repeated testing and coaching, is to pinpoint reasoning and learning problems—in his case, impulsiveness and poor planning. Later, he will be taught thinking skills. His teacher, Linda Roland, has seen eight of 11 students in last year's class for the mildly retarded move into more-advanced classes. Before using the approach, she says, "I felt I was failing my students and they were failing me." Now, she says, "they have a future." Martha Jackson, the mother of a 13-year-old boy diagnosed as retarded at age 3, says, "I've seen so many changes I don't think of him as retarded now."

There are skeptics. "I don't think it

will turn a retarded child into something else," notes Dr. Thomas Koepke, an assistant professor of psychology at Wayne State University School of Medicine. But the school system is conducting a controlled study of the program's impact, and it plans to administer achievement tests in December.

The search for alternatives

Despite all the new ways of evaluating and teaching intelligence, the IQ test, with 80 years of use and extensive research, isn't easily abandoned. After the original 1979 California court decision limiting its use, for instance, administrators continued to give the tests and state education officials continually appealed the decision—until the judge flatly barred the practice last year. Now, school psychologists are reluctantly scrambling to find alternatives to IQ tests for children in need of special help. They're using a bewildering vari-

ety of academic and sensory tests, interviewing parents and even analyzing how students conduct themselves on the playground with friends. "It's more challenging. It's more complex. But you learn a good deal about the youngsters," says Katherine Lindenauer, a psychologist with the Los Angeles Unified School District. But many others agree with Richard Russo, executive director of the California Association of School Psychologists, who says, "I don't think there's anything on the horizon to replace the IQ test"—in large part, he argues, because alternative methods aren't as well validated.

At least one black parent concurs. To the chagrin of the IQ test's critics, Mary Amaya of Rialto, Calif., wants her son Desmond Crawford to be tested—and is planning to go to court to challenge the court order, with the backing of a U.S. civil-rights commissioner and local school officials. Says

Amaya: "I'm not challenging the test; I'm challenging the state because he has no access. They're putting all black people in an intellectual ghetto."

Ironically, that's the same concern shown by the tests' critics. They claim that testing leads to improper placement in special-education classes that stigmatize children without leading to learning improvements. As a result, says Alan Coulter, acting director of special education for the New Orleans School District, "the IQ tests are just labeling people without leading to achievement. They don't tell you how to teach or what to teach." With the new evaluation tools now being developed, advocates hope that educators will be better able to understand young minds—and thus how to teach them.

by Art Levine with bureau reports

New Scales of Intelligence Rank Talent for Living

Tests measure useful habits of mind or ability to learn unspoken rules.

DANIEL GOLEMAN

In an effort to make up for some of the glaring limitations of I.Q. tests, researchers have begun to develop new ways to measure the kinds of emotional factors and psychological attitudes that lead to success in everyday life.

While I.Q. tests remain excellent predictors of how well one will do in school, they have little or nothing to do with who will earn the most money or prestige, or have the most satisfying social life or relationships. The new tests are intended to assess the more practical intelligence that underlies these accomplishments.

The new approach goes beyond purely mental skills to assess emotional factors and psychological attitudes that can either interfere with or facilitate the use of those skills.

The recent research has fostered new theories of what it means to be smart. The old theories focused on academic skills, such as verbal or mathematical quickness. But the new theories describe a spectrum of practical talents, such as the ability to pick up the unspoken rules that govern success in a corporate or professional career, or the habits of mind that foster productivity.

"I.Q. and success in living have little to do with each other," said Seymour Epstein, a psychologist at the University of Massachusetts. "Being intellectually gifted does not predict you will earn the most money or achieve the most recognition, even among college professors."

One factor emerging as crucial for life success is what might be called emotional intelligence.

"How well people manage their emotions determines how effectively they can use their intellectual ability," Dr. Epstein said. "For example, if someone is facile at solving problems in the quiet of her office, but

falls apart in a group, then she will be ineffective in a great many situations."

Dr. Epstein has developed a test that measures "constructive thinking," the ability to respond effectively to life. The test measures how well a person manages his emotions and challenging situations, as well as habitual responses to problems such as setbacks and failures. It differs from earlier alternatives to the I.Q. scale that attempted to measure such factors as creativity.

Most of the constructive attitudes the test measures have the ring of common sense. People who think constructively, for instance, tend not to take things personally and not to fret about what others think of them. Rather than complaining about a situation, they take action.

Dr. Epstein has found that many academically bright people have self-destructive habits of mind, such as holding back from new challenges because they fear the worst possible outcome for themselves. Among these non-constructive ways of thinking were holding to private superstitions, such as that talking about a potential success would keep it from happening; a naïve, unrealistic optimism—for instance, that people can do absolutely anything if they have enough willpower—and a generally negative, pessimistic outlook.

"Typical of destructive ways of thinking is one student I recall who played a beautiful solo with a band," Dr. Epstein said. "He had been dreading it, convinced he would do terribly. When people praised him, he discounted it, saying that even if he did well that once, he'd certainly do terribly the next time."

How well people score on the test of constructive thinking, Dr. Epstein has found, predicts a great range of

life success, from salaries and promotions, to happiness with friendships, families and romantic relationships, to physical and emotional health. Among people bright enough to attend college he found that I.Q., was related to none of these sorts of success; it was simply irrelevant.

"In a sense, there are two minds," Dr. Epstein said. "One, the experiential mind, has to do with how you react to the world emotionally; it makes instantaneous decisions and calls the shots day to day. It has nothing to do with I.Q. The other, the rational mind, has to do with how we explain what we do, and how well we understand a novel or know math. It has little to do with success in living."

Certain childhood experiences seem to shape constructive thinking, for better or worse. Those who scored higher on the test of constructive thinking, Dr. Epstein found, reported having parents who did not overprotect them, but rather trained them in independence. The sense of having been loved or rejected by one's parents, however, did not relate to scores on the test.

"Constructive thinking depends to a large extent on having parents who teach you to be strong in the world, to learn to handle things on your own," Dr. Epstein said. "Love is not enough; it takes training in doing things yourself."

Still, many practical talents that lead to success in life are rarely taught explicitly. Rather, those who excel seem able to absorb this knowledge tacitly.

In one recent study, psychologists at Yale developed a test that measures the knack of selling. The psychologists see the art of persuasion as essential to success in much of life.

"The ability to sell is a kind of persuasion everyone needs," said Robert

Sternberg, the psychologist at Yale who is doing much of the new work. "You sell yourself when you meet someone, you sell your ideas or point of view, you sell when you negotiate a deal. Sales is a skill that demands a specific kind of practical intelligence."

Factors in Talent for Sales

In research with Richard Wagner and Carol Rashotte at Florida State University, Dr. Sternberg found that the talent for sales included such things as knowing that when someone stalls in making a decision, the best approach is not to press him but rather to ask him why he's not prepared to make a decision at that moment. Another persuasion tactic used by those with sales talent was not to argue with the person one is selling to, but rather to acknowledge the validity of his position and then make one's own point.

While such rules of thumb may sometimes be taught as sales strategies, more often successful sales people seem to grasp them intuitively.

When the test was given to people who sell insurance, high scores were correlated with the number of years they had been in sales, the number of sales they made and awards they had received.

Practical Intelligence

In another study with Dr. Wagner, included in "Practical Intelligence," published by Cambridge University Press, Dr. Sternberg studied the kinds of tacit knowledge typical of successful business managers. The test assessed three kinds of practical intelligence. One was how well a per-

Some psychologists see the art of persuasion as essential.

son managed himself, dealt with procrastination, for instance. Another was the ability to manage others, such as knowing how to assign and tailor tasks to take maximum advantage of another person's abilities. The third was knowing how to manage one's career: how to enhance one's reputation, for example.

A typical question asks what should be the basis for selecting new projects to tackle; often there are more than a dozen choices, including that the project should be "fun," that it enable one to demonstrate one's talents, or that it require working di-

rectly with more senior executives. The people that are most successful tend to choose the same top priorities. Those executives who did best on the test tended to have more years of management experience and to have higher salaries than those who did less well, Dr. Wagner and Dr. Sternberg found.

One of the first techniques for assessing practical intelligence was developed by David McClelland, a psychologist at Boston University, and George O. Klemp, Jr, a consulting psychologist at Charles River Associates in Cambridge, Mass. By careful comparisons of outstanding performers in a given field with mediocre ones, they were able to uncover many of the specific competencies that set the two groups apart.

In a study of managers, for instance, the problem-solving skills of the best managers included the tendency to push for concrete information when faced with ambiguity; another was the ability to seek information from as wide a range of sources as possible. They also displayed a curious knack for finding unusual analogies to explain the essence of a situation.

The best managers were adept, too, at influencing people. They consistently anticipated the impact of their actions on others in the company and did not hesitate to confront people directly when there were problems. They also were adept at building a sense of collaboration by, for instance, involving subordinates in making decisions that would affect them, particularly controversial decisions, according to results obtained by Drs. Klemp and McClelland.

The new line of research was triggered by an influential critique of I.Q. tests Dr. McClelland published in in 1973 when he was at Harvard, and by a series of equally skeptical articles written about the same time by Ulric Neisser, a cognitive psychologist then at Cornell. They were among the first prominent psychologists to argue that academic intelligence had little or nothing to do with success in life. Until then, it was widely assumed that a central core of intelligence, which was measured by I.Q. tests, could be applied by bright people to find success in almost any field.

But as Dr. Neisser pointed out, the questions on I.Q. tests are nothing like the challenges one meets in life. I.Q. questions tend to be formulated by other people, to offer all the information one needs to answer them, and to have nothing to do with people's own experience or interests. They are also well defined, Dr. Sternberg observes, with only one correct solution, and usually just one way to arrive at the right answer. But none of that is usually true of the problems people face in their daily lives, such as how to find a mate or a better apartment, handle

personal finances or get ahead in one's career.

7 Kinds of Intelligence

Dr. Sternberg has proposed a theory of intelligence that includes such traits as how well a person plans strategies for problem-solving or handles novel situations. And a theory put forth by Howard Gardner of Harvard describes seven kinds of intelligence, including the body control displayed by athletes and dancers, musical talent, interpersonal skills such as being able to read another's feelings, as well as more academic abilities like mathematical and logical reasoning.

Much of the new work examines attitudes that allow people to make best use of whatever mental skills they may have. One such outlook is what psychologists call "self-efficacy," the belief that one has mastery over the events of one's life and can meet a given challenge.

"People's beliefs about their abilities have a profound effect on those abilities," said Albert Bandura, a psychologist at Stanford University, who has done the major research on self-efficacy. "Ability is not a fixed property; there is huge variablitiy in how you perform. People who have a sense of self-efficacy bounce back from failure; they approach things in terms of how to handle them rather than worrying about what can go wrong."

In the study of exceptional managers by Drs. McClelland and Klemp, for instance, the best ones displayed a strong self-confidence, seeing themselves as the most capable person for their job and as being stimulated by crisis. Along similar lines, Dr. Martin Seligman, a psychologist at the University of Pennsylvania, has shown that people who are more optimistic do better than pessimists in a wide variety of endeavors, from selling insurance to achievement in school.

Self-efficacy varies from one part of a person's life to another. A self-confident manager, for instance, may feel ineffective as a father. Dr. Bandura and other researchers have found that self-efficacy acts as a powerful force in people's choices of what they will try in life and what they avoid. Many women, they have found, have a low level of self-efficacy with regard to computers or math, and so tend to shy away from careers that depend heavily on those skills.

Some of the psychologists believe that although the practical intelligence seems to come naturally to certain people, other people can be trained to be smarter in this way, to some extent. Dr. Sternberg and Dr. McClelland, for example, have worked on developing training techniques to enhance different aspects of practical intelligence.

Capturing Your Creativity

Steve Kaplan

Steve Kaplan is a free-lance writer living in St. Paul, Minnesota, and a contributing editor of St. Paul Magazine.

Many creative people approach their own creativity much as the Supreme Court approaches pornography: They cannot define it, but they can recognize it when they see it. However, the last few decades have witnessed the rise of a group of creative people who believe that creativity is a skill that can be learned, exercised, and developed by people of all ages and occupations.

This concept has been warmly welcomed by people who would like to think more creatively. But nowhere has the teaching of creativity been more openly embraced and supported than in the business world. The creative edge can often mean the difference between a failed product and a resounding success. Take, for example, the case of the forgotten adhesive and the creative chorister.

Art Fry, a researcher for 3M, sings every Sunday in his choir at North Presbyterian Church in St. Paul, Minnesota. Fry marked the pages of his hymnal in the time-honored way—with scraps of paper. Often, though, the paper would fall out of place without his noticing. He'd get up to sing only to find the marker gone, leaving him scrambling to find his place.

"I don't know if it was a dull sermon or divine inspiration," says Fry, "but one morning during services my mind began to wander and suddenly I thought of an adhesive that had been discovered several years earlier by another 3M scientist." That scientist had been attempting to find a strong adhesive product but instead had discovered an unusually weak one: It was strong enough to hold but could be easily removed. The product was considered a failure and was relegated to descriptions in the back pages of dusty files. In a burst of creativity, Fry realized that the failed adhesive would be ideal as a "temporary, permanent" bookmark.

By the time he took the idea to work with him the next morning, he had already made the mental leap to using the adhesive for notepaper. In a moment of inspiration Fry had created Post-its, the most successful new product 3M has had in the past decade.

With stakes so high, it's little wonder that business and education have taken a serious interest in the matter of creativity training.

In the early 1970s, studies began to suggest that creativity was not some special and mysterious force but a faculty inherent in all human beings. That great gift, though, begins to fade as children become socialized and learn to see the world as everyone around them does. Tests have shown that a child's creativity plummets 90 percent between the ages of five and seven. By the time they're forty, most adults are about 2 percent as creative as they were at five.

But some of what has been lost can be recovered. In 1975 psychologists began experimenting with creativity training, with overwhelmingly positive results. Since that time, creativity training has become a growing business in the United States. Much of this training is aimed at the business community, which has both the will to use it and the money to seek it out. The techniques taught by creativity trainers, though, work as well for homemakers and salesmen as they do for researchers and chief executive officers.

Creativity training comes in all shapes and packages. There are creativity purveyors who specialize in group process, in individual training, in product positioning and naming, and a hundred other specialized areas. Below, three successful creativity trainers share some of the methods they use to jog their clients' imaginative faculties. What works for their clients is bound to work for you.

Al Fahden: Pumping irony

"Creating is quite easy," says Al Fahden, creativity teacher, "if we can just get our clinging minds out of the way." The mind, Fahden says, wants to cling to order, to things as they have been in the past. We program our minds, like a computer, to do a particular task; thereafter, the mind looks for a replicable pattern to use. "But when we decide to go another way," he says, "the mind clings, it fights back, it doesn't want to change. It's been said that the mind is a much better slave than it is a master. But if that is so, we're going to be stuck doing the same things again and again."

To find a way out of this dilemma, Fahden has developed a relatively simple three-point system that he believes can turn everyone into a creative person. "The theory itself is very simple," Fahden says.

"I'll say it the way that Niels Bohr, the Danish physicist, said it, and that is that the opposite of truth is not necessarily a falsehood, but often an even greater truth. And this is what I have observed as well. That there is some kind of unity in opposites in every great idea. Using this, I've tried to find a structure for creativity. I've read just about everything you can read about creativity, and they give you everything but a structure, the basic tool. I offer the tool."

Fahden's tool is a three-part process that involves discovering a paradigm and its opposite, then creating a new truth that comes from resolving the first two steps.

"The paradigm," he says, "is reality, or the fact. The important thing here is that facts should be more properly understood, as widely held beliefs. Generally, the reason that we're not creative is that we're stuck in our paradigms. So the first thing I try to do is get people to become aware of their paradigms. We often use selling refrigerators to Eskimos as an example of this process. Most people assume that Eskimos have no use for a refrigerator. But that's because of their assumptions about Eskimos. They're working with Eskimo paradigms of north, igloos, blubber, and parkas, and refrigerator paradigms of cold, insulated, white, and food, among others.

"The second part of the process is to take a paradigm's opposite and put it into a concept statement that creates a contradiction. For example, some opposites of the Eskimo paradigms might be south, condos, pizza, and T-shirts. Some refrigerator opposites would be hot, open, black, and nonfood. Making contradiction statements from these, we would get such things as Eskimos live in the south and refrigerators keep things hot."

The third step of the process is resolving the contradiction, or finding a group of people for whom the statement is true or a way in which the statement is true. In this example, it could be that an Eskimo couple decides to move to Phoenix and live in a condo. Then they might want a refrigerator. Or a refrigerator shipped to the northern wilderness could be used for its insulating properties to keep your food from freezing.

"The irony," says Fahden, "is that there is no right answer, only the most elegant solution. Using this system will help to reach the contradiction, and from there the mind will take over and resolve it, thus getting an abundance of ideas with no anxiety."

Fahden says his three-part process can be used to approach virtually any problem in a creative fashion. He began thinking about creativity after he took charge of a large advertising agency. He tried to recruit all the creative hotshots he knew around town, but none of them would join his agency. He was left with an agency to run and no great creative talent to run it. "All I had working there were beginners," Fahden says, "so I realized I'd better come up with a way to train them or I was in big trouble."

It was that challenge that led Fahden into the creativity theory he now teaches at seminars across the country under the name of "Pumping Irony." Fahden has written a book about his creativity theories, tentatively titled *Aha*, which he expects to publish within the next year.

Paul Maccabee: Make bagels, not war

Anyone can solve a problem by throwing money at it, but it takes a special kind of person to solve his problem using bagels; ten thousand bagels, to be precise. That's the solution that Paul Maccabee, a madman-with-a-method at Mona, Meyer & McGrath Public Relations agency, came up with when commissioned by the owner of a small delicatessen in St. Paul, Minnesota, to solve a parking problem.

It seems that when the property upon which the delicatessen sat was bought by a Texan, he abolished all the barriers that had traditionally delineated parking reserved for deli customers only. Parkers from nearby office buildings cut into customer parking for the restaurant, and the store owner's business began to decline. Instead of suing him, Maccabee designed a program to heighten the landlord's awareness of the problem by blitzing him with free bagels.

Thousands of the deli's customers signed a petition, and the owner was encouraged by Maccabee to send the petition plus ten thousand bagels to the property owner. Not only did the "bagel blitz" campaign save the deli's parking, and possibly the restaurant itself, but because of Maccabee's calls to major newspapers, it earned press attention across the country (including bits in the *Wall Street Journal* and *U.S.A. Today*). Maccabee even had the nerve to write a song rhyming "bagel" with "Hegel" ("Danny's no philosopher, / He's no Nietzsche, Kant, or Hegel, / He's just a little guy with chutzpah, / Who wants to bake a better bagel").

Paul Maccabee is obviously a creative guy, and he owes that, he says, to what he calls the Pasteur theory of creativity.

"I base it," he says, "on Louis Pasteur's comment 'Chance favors the prepared mind.' That means when I begin a campaign, I try to pack my mind with all the possible information about my subject. Then I have to rely on the images that are in my head and everything I've learned about culture and society in the past. That's why the education of a creative person is so important.

"One very famous copywriter goes to see abstract art to jog his creativity . . . then his mind interacts with the abstract forms and he can reach into his subconscious and get what he needs. But to make that method work, you have to have something in your subconscious when you finally do get there."

Maccabee lectures on creativity in advertising and offers the following guidelines:

1. There are no rules for creativity.

2. Avoid any formal education in advertising or public relations. If you must go to school, try studying magic, juggling, improvisational theater, or whatever. Read about the lives of creative people. Reading about Harry Houdini has helped me much more than reading Lee Iacocca could.

3. Creativity is not pretty. You

have to go through a lot of failure before you come to your success. A truly creative person doesn't care if he comes up with a hundred names that are stupid and silly before he finds the right one. Even dare to come up with ideas that are dangerous.

4. Know what to discard as well as what to create. You have to know when to let go of an idea but also when to hold onto it in the face of disagreement. *Casablanca* was originally titled *Everybody Goes to Rick's.* On the other hand, the executives at the movie studio that produced the movie we know as *Star Wars* urged George Lucas to change the title. But Lucas held his ground.

5. Get excited and obsessed. I find that when creative people are excited about a problem, they don't sleep, they eat lousy food, they're totally obsessed with the creative process and the problem they're working on at the moment. As an example, architect Eero Saarinen was assigned to redesign the TWA terminal at JFK Airport in New York. He studied the problem completely but was stumped for a solution. Then one morning he began staring at the grapefruit in front of him at breakfast. He flipped the fruit over and carved into it the revolutionary shape that was to shake the design world.

6. Be curious. Nothing escapes the view of creative people. Louis Pasteur used to drive his friends crazy because when he'd eat dinner, he'd examine their hands and the tablecloth, and if there was a crumb of bread, he'd study it to see its shape.

7. Pay attention. Over and over you'll hear creative people say "I see things other people can see but I think things other people don't think." Consider Bob Chesebrough, a traveling inventor who noticed how Texas oilmen would wipe the gooey "rod wax" off their oil pumps into wounds as salve. This rod wax was a throwaway by-product of the oil. Chesebrough packaged the odorless substance, and now it's sold across the world as Vaseline.

8. Go to sleep. Sleep has creative properties. Thomas Edison would literally doze off for hours at a time

Serendipity, the Mother of Invention

James Schlatter, a chemist with G.D. Searle & Company, was heating a combination of amino acids when he accidentally spilled some on his fingers. A few moments later, trying to pick up a piece of paper, Schlatter licked his fingers and noticed a very sweet taste. The chemist wasn't looking for an artificial sweetener, but good luck—and his own clear observations—dropped the discovery into his lap. He eventually traced the sweet taste back to his mixture of amino acids, which resulted in the discovery of aspartame, an artificial sweetener that Searle has marketed since 1982 under the names "NutraSweet" and "Equal." The company, which wasn't even in the food business at the time, now makes almost a billion dollars a year from aspartame.

Other creative ideas that were born from haphazard observations include:

● *The circular saw.* Sister Tabatha Babbett, a Shaker, was sitting at her spinning wheel early in the nineteenth century, watching two men sawing a board. She wondered why the men couldn't put the blades of a saw on a wheel such as the one she was working on, thus making their work a lot easier. The men listened to her idea, and the circular saw was born.

● *Teflon.* Chemist Roy J. Plunkett was experimenting with gases in 1938 while looking for alternate refrigerant materials when he noticed that one of the gases he had stored had turned into a waxy, white solid. He tested the strange solid and found it to be extremely slippery, unaffected by extreme temperatures, and resistant to most chemicals. Today Teflon is used not only for kitchenware, but in space suits, automobiles, fabrics, and even to insulate subway cables.

● *Slinkys.* Lots of sailors saw the torsion springs of boats during World War I, but naval engineer Richard James saw the springs fall off a table and bounce and thought they would make a good children's toy. He obtained a patent on the device and began producing the toys with his wife. Toy stores were not interested in buying the strange item, so the Jameses demonstrated them directly to children at Gimbel's Philadelphia store in 1945. Their entire stock of four hundred was sold out in an hour and a half. Since that day, tens of millions of Slinkys have been sold across the world.

● *Scotchgard.* After a 3M laboratory assistant spilled a fluid being developed for aircraft use on her sneaker in 1956, she noticed that the spotted area remained cleaner than the rest of the shoe. She brought her observation to the attention of 3M chemists Patsy Sherman and Samuel Smith, who immediately recognized the potential in such a product. Smith and Sherman eventually developed Scotchgard out of that observation. Today, Scotchgard protects carpets, furniture, clothing and, in other formulations, has more than twenty-five additional applications in home and industry.

while inventing. Elias Howe, the inventor of the sewing machine, was trying to solve the problem of how the machine could be threaded properly. He thought and thought about it and, exhausted, finally fell asleep. While asleep he began to have a nightmare. He was being chased by cannibals who had spears shaped like sewing needles. He tripped and fell; the cannibals were upon him. They lifted their spears and were about to plunge them into him when he looked up and noticed

that there, at the tip of the spear, was the exact kind of eye necessary for his sewing machine. He woke up, grabbed a pen and sketched it out, and his problem was solved.

9. Stop trying so hard. King Gillette was a frustrated inventor who obsessively went through the alphabet looking to jog his mind to find a product he could produce to make him rich. When he finally gave up and went to his bathroom to shave, he thought of the idea of the disposable safety razor.

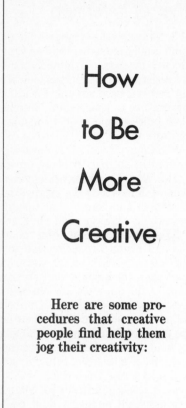

How to Be More Creative

Here are some procedures that creative people find help them jog their creativity:

- *Communicate.* People talking in halls are not necessarily wasting their time; often quite the opposite. Chatting in an informal place is a good way to share ideas and can lead to effective brainstorming.
- *Cross-fertilize.* Encourage meetings among people from diverse backgrounds. A company working on problems with construction equipment asked an entomologist to sit in on a brainstorming session. He provided an analysis of strength-to-weight ratios in ants that contributed to the development of a new earth mover.
- *Take the negative out of failure.* Errors and mistakes can be great opportunities for learning. Edison considered each of his mistakes a brick in the path to success.
- *Don't close your mind.* No matter how unlikely the idea, pay attention.
- *Have fun.* Many people believe that fun and creativity are closely allied.
- *Think positively.* In a group, don't look for the unworkable in an idea, but rather its possibilities.
- *Allow for individuality.* Different people stimulate their creative minds in different ways. Don't demand that a pattern be followed, and don't assume that the man out jogging is merely shirking work.
- *Use humor.* Humor has been shown to be a stimulant to problem solving and productivity. Some research suggests that putting people in a good mood by telling them jokes makes them think through problems more broadly and with more ingenuity.
- *Relax.* Stress is the surest depressor of the creative spark.
- *Don't be afraid to ask dumb questions.*
- *Have outside interests.*
- *Be observant.* A third grader, noticing her parents were trying to cut back on the use of sodium, suggested that they dye their salt red to be better able to judge how much they were using.
- *Keep careful track of your ideas.* Carry a notebook and jot ideas down the moment you think of them; they can quickly sink into the subconscious.

Fred Meyer: Mine your subconscious

"What creativity is all about," says Fred Meyer, "is delving into the data banks we all have in our heads. In your head is your life experience, your career, your education, but also the time somebody beat up on you when you were in fourth grade, and so on. It's all there and available to tap into, if you can find it. Being able to touch the subconscious data bank is a big part of what creativity is all about."

Meyer runs a business that helps corporate executives reach their subconscious data banks. Executives who come to him may spend anywhere from a few hours to an entire weekend brainstorming new product ideas, product names, manufacturing improvements, or whatever is important to the client. The rules at such sessions are minimal: no ties, shoes off, and no negativity. Out of such sessions have come scores of new products, including Dial's Pure & Natural Soap and General Mills' Brownie Sundaes. A one-day session of General Mills ex-

ecutives responsible for Granola bar production resulted in ideas that reduced production costs by almost a million dollars a year.

Meyer believes that how people get along with each other is vital to the creative process. He calls himself a "process consultant" and is as concerned with the way a group interacts as he is with fostering creativity inside that group. Negativity and fear of speaking up are, to his mind, among the great destroyers of creativity.

"A business that has a problem to discuss," he says, "will call a business meeting, with three levels of management sitting around the table. Imagine that you're a junior there. Everyone is wearing a suit and tie and looking very stiff. You don't dare open your mouth unless you've got a very carefully thought-out position that you know is going to make you look sensible and smart. Here, though, we offer an entirely different situation. We're trying to tap into intuition and hunches and strange new ways of thinking about things and so we encourage people to speculate. About

the only thing not allowed in this room is negative criticism."

Meyer has discovered a number of methods to tap into the subconscious data banks of his clients and release their creativity. Among the methods he uses are:

THE EXCURSION. "We may be examining a problem," Meyer explains, "and this is where we say 'Let's forget about this right now and go off and do something else.' If we're working at how to make better flashlights, we'll take the conversation way out to, say, the sex life of clams, or something like that. After we've talked about that for a while we'll say 'O.K., this is what we know about clams, now how does that relate back to making a better flashlight?' I promise you this is going to result in some new ways of thinking about flashlights. You've tapped into some data to bring to the problem that you wouldn't logically bring to it. This process is forcing an incubation artificially."

ATTRIBUTE TWISTING. The first step in this process is to take the attributes of the item in question and list them. If you were dealing with a flashlight, its attributes might be that it has a length, batteries inside, and a switch; it furnishes light; it wears down, and anything else you can think of about a flashlight that is true. Meyer then has his participants match each attribute with an arbitrary choice of two long lists of words that he has labeled "MAKE IT" and "CHANGE." Under the former list are words such as the following: flexible, flicker, zigzag, vacillate, portable, copy, and self-destruct. Meyer says it doesn't actually matter which words are chosen for which list, as the intent is to force new ideas. Participants attempt to make the arbitrary match of word and attribute somehow make sense. Matching, for example, the attribute "batteries inside" with the CHANGE IT word "portable" could lead to imagining a flashlight that could be telescoped from large to small when the batteries were removed.

ROLE-PLAYING. Meyer has some participants enter method acting role-playing games. He may assign such roles as a bag lady in New York, a kid who lives on a ranch in North Dakota, and an over-the-road truck driver. He'll then ask the players to get themselves into the feelings and value systems of their roles, what those lives are like, what kinds of problems those people have and, as much as possible, to step into their shoes. When the players have the role down completely, he'll ask them for ways they can help think about the product or problem in question—for example, the ways in which flashlights might be helpful in their (assumed) lives.

FREE ASSOCIATION. Pure Freudian-type word associations are used to jog the mind into illogical connections.

FANTASY TRIP. After putting participants through relaxation exercises, Meyer may take them on an imagination-provoking fantasy. For instance, "We'll walk them across a field," he says, "and up a hill, and on top of the hill is a big old white house. The doors of the house are open, and we'll walk in the door and turn to the room at the left." Then the participants are encouraged to relate what their experience of the imaginative journey has been."

What all of these exercises are designed to do is move into what Meyer calls "approximate thought," which, he explains, lies somewhere near metaphorical thinking and between rational thought, and the other extreme —hypnotism, meditation, and hallucination. "If we use the same kind of analytical thinking that most of us have been trained to do," Meyer says, "we're not apt to get any ideas that are very new. But if we get up into metaphorical and associative thinking, strange new ways of thinking about problems, we've got a better chance of finding an original approach and answer."

Creativity Teachers, Seminars, and Books

There are scores of good creativity courses available. The most famous include:

Bienstock & Associates, Eric Bienstock, 205 E. 78th St., New York, NY 10021

Center for the Study of Thinking and the Cognitive Research Trust, Edward de Bono, M.D., Cambridge University, Cambridge, England

Center for Studies in Creativity, SUNY at Buffalo, Chase Hall, Room 218, 1300 Elmwood Ave., Buffalo, NY 14222

Creative Thinking, Roger von Oech, P.O. Box 7354, Menlo Park, CA 94026

Creativity in Business, Michael Ray and Rochelle Meyers, Stanford University Graduate School of Business, Palo Alto, CA 94305

Princeton Creative Research, Inc., Eugene Raudsepp, P.O. Box 122, Princeton, NJ 08542

Synectics Inc., 17 Dunster Street, Cambridge, MA 02138

Whole Brain Corporation, William Edward Herrmann, 105 Laurel Drive, Lake Lure, NC 28746

Some recommended books on the subject:

A Whack on the Side of the Head, by Roger von Oech (Warner Books)

Creating Excellence, by Craig R. Hickman and Michael A. Silva (New American Library)

Creativity in Business, by Michael Ray and Rochelle Meyers (Doubleday)

How Creative Are You? by Eugene Raudsepp (Putnam)

How to Tap into Your own Genius, by Thomas Cowan (Fireside Books)

The Art of Creative Thinking, by Gerald Nierenberg (Cornerstone Library)

And any works by Dylan Thomas, Gerard Manley Hopkins, or any great poet or novelist.

Motivation and Emotion

Some of the earliest work in animal research examined the role of motivation in determining behavior patterns. This work led to the general view that motivation resulted from the deprivation of some desired or needed stimulus event. For example, rats being trained to lever-press under a variety of circumstances were first deprived of food for 23 hours and then reinforced with small food pellets to reward lever-pressing. Unfortunately, such deprivation patterns heavily influenced theories of personality development such as Freud's. Maslow's approach to motivation changed our way of thinking about not only motivation but also personality in general. Applications of his work in education, business, and politics have generally brought about a deeper appreciation of his insightful theory.

One very important part of motivation is emotion; people often report making decisions or taking action based on their feelings. Moreover, the experience of emotion is often very powerful; some people report emotional arousal at levels above their ability to manage. Another way to express this is to argue that high levels of emotional arousal are stressful. Since the mechanisms of emotional response and arousal are well known in their physiology, it is reasonable to wonder whether such high levels of arousal cause changes in the body which may be damaging.

Gina Maranto's article details the impact of emotions on the body; the resulting weakening of defenses against disease is an important part of the picture. More crucial, however, is the question of whether we can be adapted to such an experience. Can we be protected against such dangers?

The next two articles focus and extend Maranto's beginning. In "Thinking Well," Nicholas Hall and Allan Goldstein connect the sensitivity and vigor of the immune system to experiences. In fact, animals (including humans) can be conditioned (taught) to alter their immune responses. We can learn to be less or more healthy! In "Dangerous Thoughts," Bernard Dixon extends the level of analysis to the molecular, focusing on neuropeptides. At the same time, he provides an evolutionary basis for understanding the rise in incidence of certain diseases and disorders over generations: increasing levels of stress have systematically weakened natural defenses.

Looking Ahead: Challenge Questions

What types of political and social assertions reflect the influence of Maslow in our everyday lives? To what extent is it reasonable for individuals to use operant conditioning to modify their own behavior? Are there circumstances in which this would not be desirable?

What types of experiences should young children have to inoculate them against the stresses of elementary school? What types of inoculating experiences would help college students deal with the stresses they face?

If diseases such as cancer may be linked to attitudes, what attitudes will foster the most healthy and vigorous immune responses? Can these attitudes exist comfortably in a social setting without increasing the risk of aggression toward others?

What assurance do we have that the links between chemical agents in the body and susceptibility to disease are in fact cause and effect? To be healthy, must we change our life-styles?

Abraham Maslow and the New Self

To him, man was not a mass of neuroses but a wealth of potential by George Leonard

With the coming of this relatively little-known scientist, a uniquely American school of psychology blossomed. Before Maslow—who, like his colleagues, had been trained in the precepts of Freud and Jung—the emphasis in psychiatry was on neurotic behavior, psychosis, the disorders of the mind. Maslow, in contrast, accentuated the positive, stressing self-help and human potential. In its basic optimism, Maslow's thinking was as American as cherry pie— and a lot more healthy.

Humanistic Psychology

He wrote with none of the dark grandeur of a Freud or the learned grace of an Erik Erikson or the elegant precision of a B.F. Skinner. He was not a brilliant speaker; in his early years he was so shy he could hardly bring himself to mount the podium. He traveled little; Brooklyn was his home for nearly half his life. The branch of psychology he founded has not achieved a dominant position in the colleges and universities. He died in 1970, but a full-scale biography remains to be written.

And yet, Abraham Maslow has done more to change our view of human nature and human possibilities than has any other American psychologist of the past fifty years. His influence, both direct and indirect, continues to grow, especially in the fields of health, education, and management theory, and in the personal and social lives of millions of Americans.

Maslow confronts us with paradoxes. He started out as a behaviorist, a skilled experimenter, and then went on to demonstrate the crippling limitations of just that kind of psychology in the study of human affairs. He coauthored a textbook on abnormal psychology, a classic in its field, and then went on to investigate, not the pathological, but the exceptionally healthy person. Considering himself a Freudian, he went on to take Freudian psychology out of the basement of warring drives and inevitable frustration, up into the spacious, previously unexplored upper stories of the human personality, where entirely different, non-Freudian rules seemed to prevail.

Working ten to twelve hours a day in the shadow of a heart condition that was to kill him at sixty-two, Maslow produced a rich and varied body of work, one that has altered our way of thinking about human needs and motivations, neurosis and health, experience and values. Some of his theories are still controversial, especially in their particulars, but no one can deny that this dogged and daring explorer has radically revised our picture of the human species and has created a vastly expanded map of human possibilities.

Abraham H. Maslow was born on April 1, 1908, in

a Jewish slum in Brooklyn, the first of seven children. His father, a cooper by trade, had come to America from Kiev, then had sent for a hometown cousin to join him as his wife. Young Maslow's childhood was generally miserable. He was alienated from his mother ("a pretty woman, but not a nice one," he later told English writer Colin Wilson) and afraid of his father ("a very vigorous man, who loved whiskey and women and fighting"). His father's business succeeded, and when Abe was nine the family moved out of the slums and into the first of a series of lower-middle-class houses, each slightly more comfortable than the one preceding it. But these moves took the family into Italian and Irish neighborhoods and made Abe the victim of terrifying anti-Semitism. He was not only Jewish but also, by his own account, a peculiar-looking child, so underweight that the family doctor feared he might get tuberculosis. "Have you ever seen anyone uglier than Abe?" his father mused aloud at a family gathering.

Reading was his escape, the library his magic kingdom. And when he chose to go to Brooklyn Borough High School, an hour-and-a-half's journey from his home, Abe got his first taste of success. He became a member of the chess team and of the honor society Arista. He edited the Latin magazine and the physics magazine, for which, in 1923, at the age of fifteen, he wrote an article predicting atom-powered ships and submarines. In terms of sheer, raw intelligence, Maslow was a true prodigy. Tested years later by the psychologist Edward L. Thorndike, he registered an IQ of 195, the second highest Thorndike ever encountered.

At eighteen, Maslow enrolled in New York's City College. It was free and his father wanted Abe to study law. But Maslow found the school impersonal and the required courses dull. He skipped classes, made poor grades, and was put on probation for the second semester.

No matter. Maslow was intoxicated with the rich artistic and intellectual life of New York City in the vintage year of 1927. He discovered the music of Beethoven and the plays of Eugene O'Neill. He went to two concerts a week at Carnegie Hall and sold peanuts to get into the theater. He at-

HE LOVED THE LIFE OF THE MIND.

PHOTOGRAPH · HENRY GROSSMAN

tended lectures by Will Durant and Bertrand Russell and Reinhold Niebuhr. Like most young American intellectuals of that period, he became a socialist and an atheist.

But if Maslow was in love with the life of the mind, he was even more in love— blissfully, hopefully—with his cousin Bertha. And it was during the year he was nineteen that he experienced two of the great moments of his life, the kinds of moments he was later to call "peak experi-

ences." The first came when he read William Graham Sumner's *Folkways*, a book that introduced him to the idea of cultural evolution, forever disabused him of the assumption that his own society was the "fixed truth from which everything else was a foolish falling away," and triggered a lifelong interest in anthropology. By his own account, he was never again the same.

The second peak experience of that year came when he kissed Bertha. Previously, he had never dared to touch her. His frustration was indeed so painful that it drove him to leave New York City for a semester at Cornell. When he returned, Bertha's sister Anna took matters into her own hands by literally pushing him into Bertha's arms. "I kissed her," Maslow later told Colin Wilson, "and nothing terrible happened—the heavens didn't fall, and Bertha accepted it, and that was the beginning of a new life.... I was accepted by a female. I was just deliriously happy with

IT WAS DURING THE YEAR HE WAS NINETEEN THAT HE EXPERIENCED TWO OF THE GREAT MOMENTS OF HIS LIFE, THE KINDS HE WOULD LATER CALL "PEAK EXPERIENCES."

her. It was a tremendous and profound and total love affair."

By now it was clear that Maslow would not become a lawyer, and he went away to the University of Wisconsin to study psychology in earnest. A few lonely, frustrated months later, Abe wired Bertha that they were going to get married. The wedding took place in New York during the December holidays of 1928. Bertha returned to Wisconsin with him and enrolled as a student.

Thus began Abraham Maslow's life as a psychologist. It was a life that would be graced with an extraordinary succession of mentors, distinguished scholars who were somehow drawn to this shy, brilliant young man and wanted him to work with them; they invited him to meals, drove him to meetings, helped get him jobs. One might say that these mentors served an emotional function as surrogate mothers and fathers, but if the Fates had conspired to choose ideal professional influences, they could not have done a better job.

As an undergraduate, Maslow became a lab assistant to William H. Sheldon, who later was to achieve fame with his theory of constitutional types (endomorph, mesomorph, ectomorph). Sheldon and other professors provided a solid grounding in classical laboratory research. Professor Harry Harlow, the noted primate researcher, eventually became Maslow's chief mentor at Wisconsin. In 1932 Harlow shared authorship of a paper on the intelligence of primates with Maslow, and the twenty-four-year-old undergraduate was so inspired by seeing his name in print in the *Journal of Comparative Psychology* that he spent all of his next summer vacation, helped by Bertha, repeating the experiment with every primate in the Bronx Park Zoo.

As a graduate student at Wisconsin, Maslow came up with a truly original line of research. He discovered that the incessant mounting behavior of primates, which involved males mounting males, females mounting females, and females mounting males, as well as the "conventional" mounting of females by males, had more to do with dominance than with sexuality. This activity was, in fact, a means of sorting out the hierarchy of the primate horde. What's more, he learned that the ferocity involved in dominance behavior tends to fade away as one goes up the primate intelligence scale: the monkey uses its dominance position to tyrannize; the chimpanzee, to protect.

Maslow moved from Wisconsin to Columbia University as the eminent behaviorist Edward Thorndike's research associate. And he continued his work on dominance and sexuality, going from simple dominance in animals to dominance-

HE FOUND HIMSELF INCREASINGLY ALONE OUT ON THE FRONTIERS OF HUMAN KNOWLEDGE..."A DANIEL BOONE," ONE WHO ENJOYS BEING THE "FIRST IN THE WILDERNESS."

feeling in humans to the relationship between self-esteem and sexuality. In 1936, while still at Columbia, he began doing Kinsey-type interviews with female college students, possibly inspiring Kinsey's own work, which began some two years later. Maslow's interviews showed that highly dominant women, regardless of their sex drives, are more likely to be sexually active and experimental than are less dominant women. But he also found—and this is important in terms of his later work—that "any discussion of dominance must be a discussion of insecure people, that is, of slightly sick people.... Study of carefully selected psychologically secure individuals indicates clearly that their sexual lives are little determined by dominance-feeling." Here was a hint, a seed: there seems to exist a state of psychological health that transcends at least one lower drive.

During this period of inspired excitement and feverish work, Maslow continued to collect mentors. One of them was Alfred Adler, an early disciple of Freud who eventually broke with his master.

Maslow also sat at the feet of such eminent psychologists and anthropologists as Erich Fromm, Kurt Goldstein, Karen Horney, and Margaret Mead—some of them refugees from the Nazi terror. It was the late Thirties and New York was both an exciting and a sobering place for a Jewish intellectual.

Of all his mentors, Ruth Benedict, the anthropologist, and Max Wertheimer, the founder of the European Gestalt school of psychology, had the greatest influence on Maslow's life. Both became good friends and often came to dinner with him and Bertha at their modest Brooklyn home. Maslow admired Benedict and Wertheimer inordinately. Not only were they giants in their fields, but they were also, to put it simply, wonderful human beings. He began making notes on these exceptional people. Nothing he had learned in psychology equipped him to understand them. How could they be what they so clearly were in a world of savage, repressed Freudian drives and Nazi horrors? Who was the real human species-type, Hitler or Benedict and Wertheimer?

These questions helped set the stage

for the major turning point in Maslow's life, one that was to change psychology and our view of the human personality for all time. The year, as best as it can be reconstructed, was 1942; the place, New York City. By now, though not a great lecturer, Maslow was a beloved teacher, so popular that the college newspaper characterized him as the Frank Sinatra of Brooklyn College. He was working very hard, sometimes teaching nights as well as days for the extra income. He adored his daughters, who were now two and four; their innocence and potential in a darkening world sometimes moved him to tears. And the war was always in the back of his mind. He was too old to be drafted for military service but he wanted to make his contribution in the fight against Hitler. He wanted somehow to enlist himself in the larger enterprise of helping create a world in which there would be no Hitlers, in which "good people" would prevail.

It was in that emotional climate that he happened upon a parade of young American servicemen on their way to combat duty. And he was overcome by the evils of war, the needless suffering and death, the tragic waste of human potential. He began weeping openly. Against the backdrop of those times, the conventional, step-by-step psychology he had been doing was entirely inadequate. He knew he would have to change his life and career. It would have been easy enough to stay on his present course. His research credentials were firmly established. His recently published *Principles of Abnormal Psychology,* co-authored with Bela Mittelmann, was being well received. Maslow was undoubtedly on his way to a successful career in mainstream psychology. But now, tears streaming down his cheeks, he determined to take a more difficult, more uncertain course.

The direction of his exploration was set by a flash of insight that came to him while he was musing over his notes on Ruth Benedict and Max Wertheimer, trying to puzzle out the pattern that made these two people so very different from the neurotic, driven people who are usually the subject of psychological study. As he wrote years later, "I realized in one wonderful moment that their two patterns could be gener-

20. Abraham Maslow and the New Self

SELF-ACTUALIZING PEOPLE, MASLOW DISCOVERED, ARE MORE LIKELY TO HAVE PEAK EXPERIENCES—THAT IS, EPISODES OF DELIGHT, HEIGHT-ENED CLARITY, EVEN REVELATION.

alized. I was talking about a kind of person, not about two noncomparable individuals. There was a wonderful excitement in that. I tried to see whether this pattern could be found elsewhere, and I did find it elsewhere, in one person after another."

Like many historic breakthroughs, this one, in retrospect, seems obvious, so simple a child might have hit upon it: Up until that time, the field of psychology had by and large concentrated on mental illness, neglecting or entirely ignoring psychological *health*. Symptoms had been relentlessly pursued, abnormalities endlessly analyzed. But the normal personality continued to be viewed primarily as a vague, gray area of little interest or concern. And *positive* psychological health was terra incognita.

From the moment of the turning point at the parade in New York City, Maslow would devote his life and his thought to the exploration of this unknown land, of what he called in his last book "the farther reaches of human nature." In this exploration, he would find it necessary to leave his mentors behind. Though he would go on to form his own network of colleagues and supporters, he would find himself increasingly alone out on the frontiers of human knowledge. He was to become, in his words, "a reconnaissance man, a Daniel Boone," one who enjoys being "first in the wilderness."

Maslow stayed at Brooklyn College until 1951, then went to Brandeis University, in Waltham, Massachusetts, where he became chairman of the psychology department. In 1969 he moved to Menlo Park, California. A special fellowship set up by an industrialist would give him unlimited time for writing. But time was short; he died a year later. Still, in the twenty-seven years after the turning point in his career, he published close to a hundred articles and books that add up to a great synthesis, a bold and original psychological theory.

Maslow's theory is built upon his finding that human needs can be arranged in a hierarchy, beginning with the physiological needs for oxygen, water, food, and the like, then moving up through the needs for safety, belongingness, love, and esteem. Each lower need is, in Maslow's term, "prepotent" to the one above it. A very hungry person, for example, will quickly

forget hunger if deprived of oxygen. Generally, each of the lower needs must be met before the one above it emerges. Taken this far, his "hierarchy of needs" is a useful but not particularly shattering formulation. For one thing, it avoids the twists and turns in the Freudian notion that all so-called higher feelings and actions are merely disguised versions of the primary drives of sex and ego-need; tenderness, for example, is seen by Freud as nothing more than "aim-inhibited sexuality." But Maslow goes even further: After all of the "deficiency-needs" listed above are fairly well satisfied, then a need for "self-actualization" emerges. This "being-need" is just as real, just as much a part of human nature as are the deficiency-needs.

The concept of self-actualization crystallized during Maslow's moment of insight about Ruth Benedict and Max Wertheimer, but it evolved and developed through years of studying exceptionally healthy and successful individuals. Self-actualization is, in short, the tendency of every human being—once the basic deficiency-needs are adequately fulfilled—to *make real* his or her full potential, to become everything he or she can be. The self-actualizing person is the true human species-type; a Max Wertheimer is a more accurate representation of the human species than is a Hitler. For Maslow, the self-actualizing person is not a normal person with something added, but a normal person with nothing taken away. In a "synergic" society—the term is Benedict's—what is good for the development and well-being of the individual is also good for the development and well-being of the society. Our type of society is obviously not synergic, which accounts for the rarity of self-actualizing people. Though the physiological needs of most of our citizens are fulfilled, the safety needs are hardly to be taken for granted, what with the prevalence of dog-eat-dog competition and crime. And many lives are lacking in an adequate supply of belongingness, love, and esteem. Maslow sees these lacks, these "holes" in the development of a person, as a prime cause of mental illness. Indeed, for Maslow, neurosis can be viewed largely as a deficiency disease. Thus, the Maslovian thesis cries out

against the injustice that deprives so many people of their most basic needs and suggests major reforms in our ways of relating, especially in the family.

For those people who somehow transcend the deficiency-needs, self-actualization becomes a growth process, an unfolding of human nature as it potentially could be. Maslow defines this "true" human nature in terms of the characteristics of self-actualizing people, using not just personal interviews but also the study of such historical figures as Thomas Jefferson, Albert Einstein, Eleanor Roosevelt, Albert Schweitzer, and Jane Addams.

One of the most striking characteristics of these people is that they are strongly focused on problems *outside* of themselves. They generally have a mission in life; they delight in bringing about justice, stopping cruelty and exploitation, fighting lies and untruth. They have a clear perception of reality, along with a keen sense of the false, the phony. They are spontaneous and creative, sometimes displaying what might be called a mature childlikeness, a "second naiveté." They are autonomous, not bound tightly to the customs and assumptions of their particular culture. Their character structure is highly democratic, so that their friendships tend to cut across the dividing lines of class, education, politics, and ethnic background. At the same time, they are marked by a certain detachment and a need for privacy; they generally limit themselves to a relatively small circle of close friends. Significantly, they do not lump people or ideas in the usual categories but rather tend to see straight through "the man-made mass of concepts, abstractions, expectations, beliefs and stereotypes that most people confuse with the world."

Self-actualizing people, Maslow discovered, are far more likely than others to have peak experiences—that is, episodes of delight and heightened clarity and even revelation, during which all things seem to flow in perfect harmony. Through numerous interviews and questionnaires, he found that even ordinary people take on self-actualizing qualities during peak experiences. He also comes very close to saying that such experiences provide a glimpse into the realm of Being, into ultimate reality itself.

Here is another paradox: Maslow the self-proclaimed atheist insisting upon the importance of a class of human experience that includes the experiences of the greatest religious figures back through the ages. But he himself was always filled to the brim with a religious wonder, with a profound sense of what Rudolf Otto calls *das Heilige*, "the holy"; and he never shrank from presenting the transcendent realm of Being forcefully, even if he did so in a secular, psychological context. At the turn of the century William James had written eloquently about the mystic experience, but most psychologists ignored this entire aspect of human life or dismissed it as some kind of compensation mechanism. For Freud, who confessed he had never had such an experience, the "oceanic feeling" is mere infantile regression. Maslow's courage in bringing the peak experience out of the closet has since been validated by several studies and polls showing its universality and value.

When people reach the stage of self-actualization, according to Maslow, many of the assumptions of conventional psychology are overturned. For example, human motivation prior to Maslow was generally treated in terms of tension reduction, and impulses were considered to be dangerous. But Maslow points out that this is true only in the realm of the lower needs. The "growth-needs" of the self-actualizing person ware not mere itches to be relieved by scratching. The higher tensions (problems to be solved, human relations to be deepened) can be pleasurable. Creative impulses, then, are to be welcomed and trusted.

By opening up the previously hidden area of psychological health, Maslow provides a new kind of guidance for the human journey. Self-actualizing people, he argues, are good choosers. When given an opportunity, they gravitate toward what is good for them and, in his view, good for the human race. "So far as human value theory is concerned," Maslow writes in his 1962 book, *Toward a Psychology of Being*, "no theory will be adequate that rests simply on the statistical description of the choices of unselected human beings. To average the choices of good and bad choosers, of healthy and sick people, is useless. Only the choices and tastes and judgment of healthy human beings will tell us much about what is good for the human species in the long run."

In the 1950s Maslow began to see his work as part of a Third Force in psychology, representing a decisive, positive move beyond standard Freudian psychology, with its sickness-oriented view of humankind, and beyond behaviorism, which tends to treat the individual as a mere point between stimulus and response. With his generous, inclusive spirit, Maslow viewed Third Force psychology as large enough to hold Adlerians, Rankians, Jungians, Rogerians, neo-Freudians, Talmudic psychologists, Gestaltists, and many others. In 1961 his mailing list, which had long been used to circulate papers and ideas, became the basis for the *Journal of Humanistic Psy-*

MASLOW'S THEORY, EVEN IF IT IS INCOMPLETE, NEVER FAILS TO CHALLENGE US WITH A SPINE-TINGLING VISION OF INDIVIDUAL POTENTIAL, HEALTH, AND A SYNERGIC SOCIETY.

chology. A year later Maslow was a guiding force in starting the Association for Humanistic Psychology, whose founding members included Charlotte Bühler, Kurt Goldstein, David Riesman, Henry Murray, and Lewis Mumford, Two of the most influential founders were Rollow May, who was instrumental in introducing European existential psychology to the U.S., and Carl Rogers, whose humanistic, client-centered approach to psychotherapy and counseling has since spread throughout the world.

The summer of 1962 was to see two events that would play a major role in Maslow's influence on the culture. The first involved his appointment as a visiting fellow to Non-Linear Systems, a high-tech plant in Del Mar, California. Here, Maslow first realized that his theories could be applied to management. He discovered that there were just as many self-actualizing people in industry—perhaps more—than in the universities, and he got the idea that a humane, enlightened management policy devoted to the development of human potential could also be the most effective. He called this concept "eupsychian management," which became the title of his 1965 book on the subject. As it turned out, Maslow's ideas foreshadowed those that are now associated with the best of Japanese management, and it is hard to find a book on management theory today that does not give a prominent place to Abraham Maslow.

The second event of that summer was synchronistic—to use a word coined by Jung to describe coincidences that are more than just that. Abe and Bertha were driving down California's Highway 1 for a holiday, and their progress was slower than anticipated on that spectacular and tortuous coast road. Looking for a place to spend the night, they saw a light and drove off the road down a steep driveway toward what they took to be a motel. They were astonished to find that almost everybody there was reading the recently published *Toward a Psychology of Being* and enthusiastically discussing Maslovian ideas.

The Maslows had stumbled upon what was to become Esalen Institute on the eve of its opening to the public. The institute's cofounder, Michael Murphy, had just bought a dozen copies of the book and

given them to the members of his staff. Later, Maslow and Murphy became close friends and Maslow became a major influence on Esalen and on the entire counterculture of the 1960s.

This association was to raise some eyebrows among Maslow's conservative colleagues. The first press reports on the newly minted human-potential movement were, to be as charitable as possible, sensationalized and uninformed, and a less courageous man might have pulled back. But Maslow was not one to flinch under fire. "Esalen's an experiment," he told Bertha. "I'm glad they're trying it." And later, in public symposia, Maslow called Esalen "potentially the most important educational institution in the world."

Maslow's influence on America, transmitted through this lineage, can hardly be overstated. What has happened is that the counterculture of the 1960s has become a major and influential segment of the mainstream culture of the 1980s. This development has been largely ignored by the established journals of opinion but is clearly seen in the surveys of Louis Harris and Daniel Yankelovich, in the sophisticated Trend Reports of John Naisbitt, and in Naisbitt's recent best seller, *Megatrends*.

It is also becoming clear that while the quest for self-actualization might lead some people to a narrow preoccupation with the self, the number who go to this extreme is small, and the "me first" stage is generally temporary, a way station on the journey to social consciousness. This is seen in the Values and Lifestyles (VALS) Program of SRI International, a California-based research and consulting organization, which has adapted Maslow's hierarchy of needs to an analysis of the U.S. population and which numbers some of the nation's most successful corporations among its subscribers. The VALS study shows that the "Inner-Directeds," those who might be said to be on the path toward self-actualization, now make up 21 percent of all Americans and represent the fastest-growing segment of the population. Of this 21 percent, only 3 percent are in the self-centered, narcissistic "I-amme" category. The Inner-Directeds, for the most part, tend to move inexorably toward social consciousness, service to

At Brooklyn College in 1943, Maslow was a much-loved teacher, so popular that the school newspaper characterized him as the Frank Sinatra of Brooklyn College.

PHOTOGRAPH · COURTESY OF MRS. BERTHA MASLOW

Dossier

Abraham Maslow

was born on April 1, 1908, in Brooklyn. The eldest of seven children, he remembered "clinging" to his father. "I have no memory," he wrote, "of expecting anything from my mother." He later called his mother a "schizophrenogenic...one who makes crazy people....I was awfully curious to find out why I didn't go insane."

In elementary school he met anti-Semitism and a teacher he later described as a "horrible bitch." Challenging his reputation as the class's best speller, the teacher made Maslow stand up and spell one word after another. When he finally missed one—*parallel*—the teacher publicly concluded, "I knew you were a fake."

Throughout his adolescence he was intensely shy and, he recalled, "terribly unhappy, lonely, isolated, self-rejecting." A loving uncle, his mother's brother, looked after him. "He may have saved my life, psychically," Maslow said.

He left New York for Cornell University partly because of his strong passion for his cousin Bertha: "I had not yet touched Bertha....And this was getting kind of rough on me—sexually, because I was very powerfully sexed...."

At the University of Wisconsin his professors accepted him as a colleague. Still, he was amazed when, one day in a

men's room, a professor stepped up to the urinal next to his. "How did I think that professors urinated?" he later marveled. "Didn't I know they had kidneys?"

At Columbia University he found the initial research he conducted for psychologist E. L. Thorndike boring. He wrote Thorndike a note saying so—even though he stood to lose his job during the Depression. Far from firing Maslow, Thorndike respected his opinion.

For all his popularity with students, Maslow was terrified of public speaking until he was over fifty. In 1925 a paper he wrote never got published because he fled a conference rather than read it. In 1959 he delivered a talk, then for days afterward stayed in bed recovering from it.

He suffered his first heart attack in 1945 and never again was completely healthy. He had an arthritic hip, and though he was always tired, he had trouble sleeping. Only in the year before his death did a doctor discover that Maslow's chronic fatigue was a form of hypoglycemia. For years the ailment had made him crabby, inhibited his work, and stifled his sex life.

Until the age of thirty he considered himself a socialist—"Fabian rather than Marxist." He said he dropped socialism after Franklin Roosevelt put "our whole socialist

programme...into law" and he didn't see "any great miracles occur."

After his bar mitzvah, at thirteen, he became "a fighting atheist." Yet later in life, when offers came to teach at other universities, he would not leave his teaching job at Brandeis. "Why?" he asked himself. "Partly it's the Jewish business. I have been so proud of the great Jewish university—I didn't realize how much—and I feel like a rat deserting the sinking ship...just the way I did when I left Brooklyn and abandoned the poor Jewish students whom nobody loved but me. The guilt of upward mobility."

In 1954 he wrote, "Human nature is not nearly as bad as it has been thought to be.... In fact it can be said that the possibilities of human nature have customarily been sold short...."

He enjoyed art museums, shopping, and reading science fiction. He admired J. D. Salinger. ("...read *Fanny and Zooey*....He says in his way what I've been trying to say. The novelist can be *so* much more effective.") He also liked Betty Friedan's *The Feminine Mystique*, which discusses his views on sex and dominance. ("A passionate book—I was swept along unintentionally.")

In 1969 the White House invited him to join a committee to define national goals, but he was too sick to attend. He was

miffed by the popular press's indifference to his work: "A new image of man...a new image of nature, a new philosophy of science, a new economics, a new everything, and they just don't notice it."

Still, at fifty-six he wrote: "With my troubles about insomnia and bad back and conflict over my role in psychology and...in a certain sense, *needing* psychoanalysis, if anyone were to ask me 'Are you a happy man?' I'd say 'yes, yes!' Am I lucky?...The darling of fortune? Sitting as high up as a human being ever has? Yes!"

Five years later, on June 8, 1970, he died of a heart attack. *The New York Times* published no obituary.

> "[Maslow's is] a voice that has not been heard before ... it is hard to do justice to ... the challenge of Maslow's amazingly fertile mind; his combining of teacher, seer, ...physician, visionary, social planner, critic; his ambition in tying together all varieties of apparently unrelated phenomena; his unstoppable optimism."
> —JOYCE CAROL OATES

others, and personal integration—which should come as no surprise to anyone who has given Maslow more than a cursory reading.

Critics argue that Maslow did not adequately deal with the problem of evil, with humanity's darker side, and there is something to this criticism. But Maslow himself was aware that he had much more work to do, "at least two hundred years' worth," he told Bertha shortly before his death. True, Maslow's theory might not be complete, but it never fails to challenge us with a spine-tingling vision of individual potential and health and of a synergic society.

Despair is often comfortable, in some circles even fashionable, and it is easy enough to dismiss or even ridicule Maslow's challenge. After all, nothing is more difficult or painful than to look clearly at your own wasted potential, then start doing something about it. But ever-increasing numbers of Americans are taking the challenge. For example, the fastest-growing movement in health management today involves the field of holistic, health-oriented approaches to the physical that Maslow applied to the psychological. If

anything can solve the crisis of medical depersonalization and rising costs, it is this classically Maslovian shift: more and more people working against a pathogenic environment and society while taking personal responsibility for their own positive good health.

In spite of his unorthodox views, Maslow was elected to the presidency of the American Psychological Association in 1967, and now, more than twelve years after his death, his voice is still being heard, even if indirectly, even if by people who barely know his name. Warren Bennis, professor of management at USC, recalls it as "that incredibly soft, shy, tentative, and gentle voice making the most outrageous remarks." Bennis also remembers Maslow for "a childlike spirit of innocence and wonder—always wearing his eyebrows (as Thomas Mann said about Freud) continually raised in a constant expression of awe."

Still, it takes another characteristic to join the shyness, the outrageousness, and the awe into a complete human being, and that is courage, which is the essence of

Abraham Maslow's story. Psychologist James F.T. Bugental, who served as the first president of the Association for Humanistic Psychology, lived near Maslow during the last year of his life. "Abe used to go for his walks," Bugental recalls, "and he'd come by our house. We had this myth that one of the cans of beer in the refrigerator was his, and he'd always say, 'Is my beer cold?'

"And he'd drink his beer and get a little sentimental and sometimes show us pictures of his granddaughter and weep because she was so beautiful and innocent and would have to lose her innocence. And sometimes he would talk about the time in his childhood when he'd have to go through a tough Irish neighborhood to get to the library, and about how he would plan his route and sometimes get chased and sometimes get beat up. But he never let that stop him. He went to the library even though he might have to get beat up.

"That's the way I see his life. He never stopped doing what he thought he had to do, even though he might get beat up. He had courage, just plain courage."

EMOTIONS: HOW THEY AFFECT YOUR BODY

GINA MARANTO
Gina Maranto is a staff writer for Discover.

Be cheerful while you are alive.
—Ptahhotep

Authors of maxims over the millennia have suggested, as did this 24th-century B.C. Egyptian vizier, that life is borne more easily with a smile—even a wan half-smile—than a grimace. That philosophy has survived to the 20th century, which has seen countless practices, both plausible and bizarre, from psychosomatic medicine to biofeedback to hypnosis, proclaiming the relationship between emotions and health, and touting the power of the mind to thwart disease. But only in the past few years have researchers confirmed experimentally that the psyche can actually affect the body.

DEPRESSION AND THE PHYSICAL STATE

Even before solid evidence was in hand, long-range studies of people revealed a tantalizing connection between such psychological states as depression, pessimism, loneliness, and anxiety on the one hand with cancer, heart disease, and other wasting or potentially fatal ailments. The link is now fairly well established. For instance, a National Academy of Sciences panel announced in September that grief over the death of a family member may substantially raise the risk, especially among men, of contracting an infectious disease or of dying of a heart attack or stroke. And although experiments with human subjects are still far from conclusive, a variety of experiments with animals have now proved that higher functions of the brain can influence the physical state. These discoveries suggest that what a person feels, and how he perceives himself and his place in the world, are critical to his physical well-being.

Many researchers—including immunologists, physiologists, psychiatrists, psychologists, and neurobiologists—who have explored the murky boundary between mind and body now suspect that certain negative psychological states, brought on by adversity or a chemical imbalance, actually cause the immune system to falter. Says John Liebeskind, a UCLA psychologist, "I'm fascinated by the possibility that the brain can exert control over the immune system, that our welfare might be determined by our training." Some biologists go so far as to claim that psychological therapy that teaches people how to feel in control of their lives might in some measure "inoculate" against disease and act as a valuable supplement to conventional medical care.

Because evidence buttressing such claims has been hard to come by, most researchers warn against overenthusiastic interpretations of the findings. Nonetheless, they view the new field—whether it goes by the name of psychoneuroimmunology or simply behavioral medicine—as the hottest and most promising area of medical research today. Says Carl Eisdorfer, president of Montefiore Hospital in New York, "One of the great and terribly exciting mysteries is how cognition, or mental activities, relates to physiology."

Detailing that relationship will take years. No one yet knows, for instance, whether each individual emotion sparks a distinct bodily response, or even precisely what emotions are. But, says Paul Ekman, a psychologist at the University of California at San Francisco, "there are now the first glimmerings of hope that researchers can define the role that all the universal emotions—fear, happiness, anger, disgust—play in health."

Reprinted from *Current*, February 1985, pp. 3–5. Originally appeared in *Discover*, November 1984, pp. 35–38. Gina Maranto/© Discover 1984, Family Media, Inc.

EARLY RESEARCH   The course of the investigation thus far has been a twisted one. Having only primitive knowledge of the workings of the brain and the complex mechanisms the body uses to maintain its equilibrium, early researchers into psychosomatics (from the Greek for mind and body) studied not specific emotions but the effects of the broad group of phenomena that they defined as stressful. These included any stimulus that seemed extreme enough to provoke a physiological response—for example electric shock, loud noise, cold, starvation, surgery, or fear.

MODERN EXPERIMENTS

Early in this century, the American physiologist Walter Cannon sketched the broad outlines of the body's response to this kind of stress. In a series of experiments he showed that several organs and glands were involved in the response, including the hypothalamus in the brain, the pituitary gland directly beneath, and the adrenal glands atop the kidneys. During the 1930s, the Austrian-born doctor Hans Selye proved that under stress this interconnected system and the sympathetic nervous system primed the heart and muscles for action, for fighting or fleeing; hence the name fight-or-flight response.

These findings soon filtered into the popular press, where they appeared in slightly modified form as the maxims "Stress is bad for you," and "Stress causes disease." But no scientific data then, or now, have actually ever supported either contention. "Stress does not actually cause disease," Eisdorfer says. "What it may do is predispose you to illness or promote a latent disease."

Getting the hard data to support this view required that scientists perform an arduous series of distinctly unglamorous experiments. In the mid-1960s Martin Seligman and Steven Maier at the University of Pennsylvania found that rats given electrical shocks they could not escape became passive. They called the phenomenon "learned helplessness." Then, in the late 1970s, Seligman and colleagues determined that learned helplessness increased a rat's susceptibility to disease. When rats were injected with tumor-causing cells and subjected to inescapable shock, a high percentage of them developed tumors. Rats that could escape the shock by moving to another part of their cage, as well as those given no shock, tended to reject the tumor cells. Recently, Mark Laudenslager, a psychologist at the University of Denver, confirmed that inescapable shock dulls the response of T-lymphocytes—key cells in recognizing bodily invaders—to chemicals that normally cause them to divide rapidly.

Other teams of researchers, working both independently and in concert, helped prove that stress directly interfered with the body's defenses by crippling lymphocytes and other white blood cells, leaving the way open for disease. Then a team of investigators in John Liebeskind's psychology lab at UCLA showed in 1982 that two different kinds of shock triggered two different reactions in a rat's brain. Intermittent shocks of a certain intensity caused it to release endorphins and enkaphalins, the powerful, opiate-like chemicals normally involved in dampening pain. Continuous shock of the same intensity did not prompt this reaction. Following up on this work, Yehuda Shavit, then a graduate student in the lab, showed conclusively that the opiate shock harmed the body.

Shavit suspects that opiates wreak havoc with the immune system by latching on to white blood cells called natural killer cells, which hunt out and kill certain tumor cells. Laden with opiates, the killer calls may falter and be less successful in their vigil against cancers. Or the opiates may boost the release of some hormones that, in the test tube at least, slow the activity of killer cells.

Why should the brain's reaction to terrifying or inescapable situations harm the immune system? Some researchers suggest that the difference may be one of degree: only stresses extreme enough to provoke the release of opiates may lower resistance. Says Laudenslager, "I don't think we would be here today if every time we had a minor pain our immune system went down." In fact, other scientists think that small periodic doses of stress may actually have some benefit: they may help an animal learn how to deal with its environment more rapidly than it otherwise would.

Still other investigators believe that the brain and the immune system may sometimes be at odds, that, ordinarily, merely adopting a positive attitude toward problems or difficulties may prevent the tilt in body chemistry that harms immunity. "One of the things we now know," says Carl Eisdorfer, "is that if you create a way of dealing with the event mentally, it decreases your chance of being negatively affected."

THE SIGNIFICANCE OF PERCEPTIONS

Several recent studies support that contention. September's National Academy report notes that a sizable fraction of Americans whose spouses die (800,000 annually) sink into depression for as long as three years. This mental agony has a bodily counterpart: depressed activity of the immune system's lymphocytes. For men in poor health, especially those with few friends or relatives, the NAS panel concluded, the result can be a fatal illness. A report released by the Health Insurance Plan of Greater New

York in August showed that of more than 2,000 men who had suffered one heart attack, those who were loners and under a great deal of stress on the job or at home had four times the risk of having a second, fatal attack than men who were sociable and under little stress. (In addition, the study contradicted the theory that hard-driving, so-called type A people are most likely to succumb to heart attacks, because few of the victims fitted that profile.) The researchers hypothesize that hormones released during stress may have made the hearts of the high-risk men vulnerable to fibrillation.

The fact that individuals show such a varied degree to resilience to disease has suggested that dumping all seemingly negative events under the category "stress" is sloppy and unscientific. "Using the overarching term stress smears all results," Seligman says. He recommends that events be categorized according to a person's perception of them: good or bad, controllable or uncontrollable, predictable or unpredictable, intense or mild. Laudenslager offers an example: the death of a spouse will be viewed differently, depending on the context. "If the police come to your house in the middle of the night to tell you your husband is dead, that's a totally unpredictable, uncontrollable event. That's going to hit you very differently from watching your spouse dying of a painful form of cancer. Then, you might actually prefer to see him taken out of his misery."

Ekman thinks researchers also need to define more precisely just what qualifies as an emotion. In a provocative report last year, he and his colleague Robert Levenson concluded that simply moving the facial muscles to create the masks of anger, fear, or other emotions, or re-creating the feeling mentally, can have profound physiological effects: increasing the heartbeat, raising body temperature, and producing other distinct shifts in the autonomic nervous system, the network of nerves that carries signals directly from the brain to the heart muscle, smooth muscles, and glands.

These findings, Ekman contends, offer strong evidence that each emotion wreaks its own unique changes on the autonomic nervous system. Yet, he says, because normal emotions are fleeting, they are unlikely to provoke health problems. The villains, he suggests, are psychological states of longer duration—emotions that have run amuck. He breaks these states into four categories: emotions, moods, emotional traits, and emotional disorders, each lasting for a longer period than the one before. Sadness, for example, is an emotion; feeling blue is a mood; melancholy is a trait; and depression is the disorder. Only traits and disorders, Ekman thinks, can have long-term health consequences. "Emotions have evolved because they are useful to the species," he says, "and it's possible that moods have as well. But when a whole personality is organized with anger as its salient emotion, it may cause health problems."

IMMUNE SYSTEM

Before behavioral medicine investigators can track the way in which the mind can harm or help the body, they may need to devise new and better procedures for assessing the strength of the immune system. In addition, they need to have a better understanding of how the entire immune system works. Doing more experiments will require more financing, which could be a problem; government and private agencies are reluctant to provide money for research that crosses scientific disciplines. But the researchers remain hopeful. "We always work by half measures in science," says Eisdorfer. "At least people from various disciplines are talking about the issues now."

"We're beginning to discover the anatomical connections between the brain and the body," says Yehuda Shavit. "Now we just have to show how the whole thing works." Indeed, Jonas Salk, developer of the first polio vaccine, thinks that the time may be right for a major clinical study of the effects of emotional states on the body. The study would take years, might cost millions, and would involve an enormous cast: dozens of scientists from various disciplines and as many as 4,000 children would would be monitored over a period of years. But if the project could show that children who consciously attempted to view themselves as creatures in control of their lives thrived and stayed healthier than their peers, it would be worth the investment. "The people who do such a study," says Salk, "will be the poets of biology."

THINKING WELL

The Chemical Links Between Emotions and Health

Nicholas R. Hall and

Allan L. Goldstein

Nicholas R. Hall, with training in psychology, neuroendocrinology, and immunology, is associate professor, and Allan L. Goldstein is professor and chairman, in the department of biochemistry at the George Washington University School of Medicine, in Washington, D.C.

In 1977, a twenty-eight-year-old Philippine-American woman, feeling weak and complaining of pain in her joints, visited a clinic in Longview, Washington. A physician there ordered blood and urine tests and, based on their results, concluded that the woman was suffering from systemic lupus erythematosus, a disease in which the body's immune system attacks healthy organs with all the ferocity it usually reserves for life-threatening intruders. After various drugs failed to restore her health, the woman sought the advice of another physician, who examined samples of her kidney tissue, confirmed the original diagnosis, and recommended that she follow an aggressive therapeutic regimen using drugs that would dampen the immune system's misguided assault. Instead, the patient decided to return to her native village, in a remote part of the Philippines, where she was treated according to local custom: a witch doctor removed the curse that had been placed on her by a former suitor. Three weeks later, back in the United States, she showed none of the symptoms she had earlier displayed, and two years afterward she gave birth to a healthy girl.

Had this case been reported in one of the nation's tabloids (indeed, it bears all the earmarks of such a sensational story), it might have escaped serious attention. But it was published in *The Journal of the American Medical Association*, in 1981. Significantly, neither the author—Richard Kirkpatrick, of Saint John's Hospital, in Longview—nor, by implication, the journal disputed the basic facts: a serious form of autoimmune disease had been swiftly and, by all indications, permanently reversed. Rather than attempt to explain the transformation, Kirkpatrick concluded his report with a question: By what means did an Asian medicine man cure the woman and, moreover, prevent the medical complications that invariably accompany a precipitous withdrawal from the sort of drug treatment she had been receiving?

The idea that mental states—the target, presumably, of the witch doctor's treatment—influence the body's susceptibility to and recovery from disease has a long and hallowed history. As early as the second century A.D., the Greek physician Galen asserted that cancer struck more frequently in melancholy than in sanguine women. And the belief that disease is a consequence of psychic or spiritual imbalance governed the practice of medicine in both Asia and Europe until the rise, after the seventeenth century, of modern science and its mechanistic view of physiology. But from that point onward, the role of behavior in human disease became a concern proper to none but the superstitious; attempts to empirically investigate the relationship were almost unheard of. Only within the past thirty years, and in particular during the past ten, has the systematic study of this ancient concept been broadly regarded as a legitimate aim of serious medical research.

Scientists have known since the 1950s that the immune systems of laboratory animals can be influenced by behavior. One of the modern pioneers in the field, Robert Ader, of the University of Rochester School of Medicine and Dentistry, has shown that, using the methods of classical conditioning—in this case, by associating the taste of a sweetener with the effects of an immunosuppressive drug—rats can be taught to suppress their own immune responses. And numerous other investigators have demonstrated that when rats and mice are subjected to acute stress—for example, by being confined for short periods of time in crowded living quarters—they become increasingly susceptible to disease.

But in recent years, Marvin Stein and his colleagues, of the Mount Sinai School of Medicine, in New York City, have documented a similar impairment in humans, particularly among men whose wives had recently died. Stein found that during the first few months of bereavement the ability of the widowers' lymphocytes (small white blood cells that spearhead the immune response) to react to intruders sharply diminished. He has also discovered a hampered immune response in people hospitalized for severe depression. In a study done in 1984, Stein documented in such patients not only an ebbing of lymphocyte activity but also a decline in the number of certain kinds of lymphocytes circulating in their bloodstreams.

Less established are the effects on the immune system of positive mental states. Indeed, until quite recently, the data have been largely anecdotal. When, in 1976, Norman Cousins, then editor of *Saturday Review*, described how he

This article reprinted by permission of *The Sciences* and is from the March/April 1986 issue, pp. 34-40. Individual subscriptions are $13.50 per year. Write to The Sciences, 2 East 63rd Street, New York, NY 10021 or call 1-800-THE-NYAS.

overcame ankylosing spondylitis, a chronic, progressive disease of the spine, through the use of vitamin C and laughter (and the buoyant, affirmative frame of mind it produced), there existed no empirical evidence beyond the sheer fact of his restored health to support his claims. As many critics were quick to note, information about the influence of behavior on health was scant and equivocal and, besides, spontaneous remissions of ankylosing spondylitis, inexplicable as they may be, were known to occur.

Since Cousins's recovery, however, a number of rigorously controlled studies have provided evidence of a strong link between behavioral therapy and patient prognosis. In one of the most notable, conducted from 1974 to 1984 at King's College Hospital Medical School, in London, a strong correlation was found between the mental attitudes of women with breast cancer and life expectancy. Of the women who displayed aggressive determination to conquer their disease, seventy percent were still alive ten years after their mastectomies; but among those who had felt fatalistic or hopeless, only twenty-five percent survived. And in our own two-year-long investigation, with Stephen Hersh, Lucy Waletzky, and Barry Gruber, we evaluated the effects of a behavioral approach to disease by measuring certain physiological dimensions of immune responsiveness in cancer patients. Among other things, the therapy consisted of relaxation techniques and guided exercises in which patients imagined that feeble cancer cells were crushed by stalwarts of the immune system. The preliminary results of this investigation show that behavioral therapy amplified the immune system's response to disease; in physiological terms, it accelerated the rate at which lymphocytes mobilized to attack foreign bodies and possibly increased their own numbers. This pilot study, if its results are confirmed by further research, will have provided the first thoroughly empirical confirmation of a correlation between mental states and immunity that as recently as five years ago the medical community viewed as a mixture of pseudoscientific hocus-pocus, self-delusion, and dumb luck.

But for all its novelty and importance, documenting a correspondence between behavioral events and the body's response to disease no more constitutes a satisfactory understanding of immune processes than an observed association between eating and tissue growth constitutes an understanding of digestion and absorption. By what means does stress disturb the functions of lymphocytes? Or, to return to the woman with systemic lupus erythematosus, which physiological systems did the witch doctor engage to relieve her of autoimmune disease? If, as a growing body of evidence suggests, mental states can both retard and enhance the body's ability to fight illness, there must exist a functional pathway that links the organ most closely associated with emotions and ideas—the brain—to the organs and tissues that collectively make up the immune system. In fact, two such pathways—one biochemical, the other anatomical—have been discovered.

THE FIRST LINE OF DEFENSE against viruses and bacteria that invade the body is the phagocyte, or cell-eater. When the skin is breached, by means of a wound or a lesion, swarms of these scavenging white blood cells descend upon the scene and devour the trans-gressors one by one until the phagocytes literally eat themselves to death.

Though indispensable, phagocytes make up only the most elementary part of the immune response. In humans, as well as in other mammals, a second type of defense also comes into play, one whose chief distinctions are its abilities to recognize particular invaders (phagocytes are indiscriminate in their appetites) and to tailor highly specific chemical counterattacks. The basic functional units of this immunity are the lymphocytes, so named because of the clear fluid in which they are stored and conveyed.

Like all white blood cells, lymphocytes derive from bone marrow; but whereas some remain in the marrow until they reach full maturity, and are therefore designated B cells, others, early in their development, migrate to the thymus—the master gland of the immune system—and for that reason are called T cells. Both types of lymphocytes circulate through the bloodstream before lodging in such lymphoid tissues as the spleen, the tonsils, and the adenoids, where they remain inactive until confronted with any of thousands of antigens, or foreign substances—organic waste, toxins, viruses, and bacteria.

In the presence of a particular antigen, B cells synthesize and release proteins, called antibodies, that are designed specifically to destroy that antigen. T cells also respond to individual antigens, though not by producing antibodies but by performing a variety of special immunological support tasks. Some, called helper T cells, release lymphokines, chemicals that assist B cells in producing antibodies. Others, killer T cells, attack antigens directly, with lethal substances of their own manufacture. Still others, known as suppressor T cells, help protect the body's tissues from being ravaged by its own immune response, by preventing B cells from making antibodies when they are no longer needed (a breakdown of this function is implicated in such autoimmune diseases as systemic lupus erythematosus).

Other chemical mediators of the immune response that are released by T cells and macrophages (a type of phagocyte) include histamine, which dilates blood vessels in preparation for the arrival of legions of lymphocytes; complement proteins, which, by inflaming the afflicted area, create an inhospitable thermal environment for foreign tissues; and prostaglandins and leukotrienes, substances that help start and stop the activities of macrophages and T cells. This complex arrangement lends to the immune system the flexibility it requires to strategically orchestrate its responses to countless new and varied microorganisms that invade the microenvironment of the body.

IN THE 1960s, investigators discovered that in test tubes certain immune functions of lymphocytes transpired spontaneously, suggesting that the immune system, for the most part, functions independently of the rest of the body; that the behavior of lymphocytes is governed solely by the number and kinds of antigens encountered—a system of self-contained biochemical reflexes. But subsequent research, much of it done in the past few years, has disclosed that not only is the immune system heavily influenced by other bodily processes—in particular, by those of the central nervous system, via the endocrine network (the glands that secrete hormones into the bloodstream), and the autonomic nervous system—but it is also impossible to separate the day-to-day functions of the immune system from those processes.

The best-documented influence occurs along a biochemical pathway that links the part of the brain located beneath the cerebral hemispheres—the hypothalamus—with the thymus gland, where the T cells mature, by means of two endocrine organs—the pituitary and adrenal glands. Outlining the cascade of biochemical exchanges that occur along this hypothalamic-pituitary-adrenal axis illuminates well the subtle but infrangible ways in which the brain and the immune system are knit together. In stressful conditions, the hypothalamus produces a chemical called corticotropin-releasing factor, which induces the pituitary to secrete adrenocorticotropic hormone. This hormone, in turn, stimulates the adrenal glands to release steroid hormones (glucocorticoids) into the bloodstream. It happens that T cells are acutely sensitive to glucocorticoids. This is especially true of nascent T cells, which represent about ninety percent of all T cells present in the thymus at any time. Abnormally elevated glucocorticoid levels will either damage or destroy these cells or prematurely induce their migration from the thymus to other immune tissues. The resultant shrinkage of the thymus is so pronounced that the gland has been called a barometer of stress and its weight used as an indirect way to assay the release of adrenal glucocorticoids. Left on their own, the adrenal glands secrete glucocorticoids in a daily tidal rhythm, and the point at which lymphocytes respond most aggressively to antigens has been correlated with the interval during which the level of circulating glucocorticoids falls to its lowest point.

In short, the biochemistry of the hypothalamic-pituitary-adrenal axis is far more complex than anyone ever dreamed. Not only are the participating hormones diverse, including even such agents as those that regulate reproduction and growth, but they produce different effects from one circumstance to another as well. Glucocorticoids, for instance, are biphasic: in high concentrations they mute the immune response, whereas in small amounts they have been shown to activate it. Complicating the issue further is the disparity between the consequences of acute and chronic stress. Whereas acute stress causes immunosuppression, chronic stress sometimes enhances the immune response. Thus, stress-induced modulation of the immune system involves a matrix of factors, any or all of which may be at work in the response of a single lymphocyte.

A T THE TOP of the hypothalamic-pituitary-adrenal axis, shuttling electrical impulses across the gaps that separate nerve cells in the brain, are the neurotransmitters. These compounds—in particular, serotonin, acetylcholine, and norepinephrine—regulate the secretion of corticotropin-releasing factor from the hypothalamus, thereby triggering the serpentine chain of events that arouse or pacify the immune response. The same neurotransmitters are now being implicated in the control of the immune system via a second, anatomical pathway—the autonomic nervous system.

The autonomic nervous system is to the central nervous system what an automatic pilot is to a pilot; in some sense the autonomic system can be overridden, but it typically operates on its own, regulating the involuntary actions of the heart, the stomach, the lungs, and other organs through a pervasive network of nerve fibers. Only in the past two years have we learned that branches of this network, chiefly the norepinephrine and acetylcholine circuits, are rooted deep within the body's lymphatic tissues as well. In ground-breaking work at the State University of New York at Stony Brook, Karen Bulloch demonstrated that signature patterns of autonomic nerve fibers radiate into the thymic tissues of reptiles, birds, and mammals, including humans, and that the acetylcholine portions of these circuits appear to originate within the brain stem and the spinal cord. No less striking is the discovery, by David Felten, of the University of Rochester, of a similarly unique mesh of nerves in the spleen, bone marrow, and lymph nodes, as well as in the thymus. These neural fibers follow blood vessels into the glands and radiate into fields profuse with T cells, where they likely manipulate lymphocyte processes. All the biological equipment required for such direct intervention is at hand: adrenaline, norepinephrine, and acetylcholine receptors have been identified on the surfaces of lymphocytes.

The discovery that autonomic nerves interlace lymph tissues has recast our view of the immune system. As a whole, it now seems to resemble an endocrine gland, and, like all endocrine tissue, possesses a direct anatomical link to the brain. Though it remains to be seen whether messages carried by that anatomical link flow in both directions—as they do with the endocrine glands—there now is ample reason to believe that such two-way communication takes place by means of the hypothalamic-pituitary-adrenal axis. Since the substances that exert this influence—adrenocorticotropic hormone and beta-endorphin, an internally manufactured opiate; lymphokines and cytokines, the chemical products of macrophages; and the hormonelike thymosins, which are synthesized in the thymus—originate within the immune system itself, they might be called immunotransmitters.

Unknown until recently, immunotransmitters are now turning up everywhere in the body. Here is a partial list of the disparate phenomena under review: Eric Smith and J. Edwin Blalock, of the University of Texas Medical Branch at Galveston, have reported that adrenocorticotropic hormone and beta-endorphin, once thought to have been released only by the pituitary and the brain, are also secreted by lymphocytes. This suggests that many cells of the immune system act as separate, minuscule glands, dispensing agents that modulate the immune response as they migrate throughout the body. According to a 1984 study by James Krueger and his colleagues, of the University of Health Sciences-Chicago Medical School, the cytokine interleukin-1 (also called T-cell activating factor) induces deep sleep and hyperthermia. Both effects accelerate disease recovery and can thus be regarded as elements of the body's sequence of defensive tactics. And in still another confirmation of the action of immunotransmitters, Hugo Besedovsky, of the Swiss Research Institute, has shown that the firing rates of neurons in the brain can be altered by lymphokines similar to those that assist in the fight against viruses.

But it is the family of substances that originate in the thymus—the thymosins—that best demonstrate how the immune system may influence the central nervous system. When injected into the cavities of the brain, thymosin beta four stimulates the pituitary, via the hypothalamus, to release luteinizing hormone, which helps regulate other endocrine glands. Further, adrenocorticotropic hormone and beta endorphin are released by isolated pituitary cells when cultured in the presence of another group of thymic hormones—thymosin fraction five. But most important, it has been shown that immunotransmitters can exercise a direct influence on a neurotransmitter. Hugo Besedovsky has found that the amount of norepinephrine, the neurotransmitter that suppresses the secretion of corticotropin-releasing factor by the hypothalamus, in the brains of rats drops significantly after administration of a preparation that contains thymosin and lymphokines. If the same holds true for humans, it may be that the thymosins can themselves stimulate the hypothalamus by way of a neurotransmitter and thereby set in motion the chain of chemical reactions associated with the hypothalamic-pituitary-adrenal axis.

The precise function of thymosins and other immunotransmitters in the body's defense against viruses and bacteria has yet to be explained, but they most likely modulate the immune response and therefore constitute the final stage of a feedback loop between the central nervous system and the immune system's lymphatic tissues. The concept of a self-correcting functional circuit that ties the brain to the pituitary, adrenal, and thymus glands has been proposed by many investigators. But missing from this hypothetical circuit has been evidence of chemically defined molecular signals between the thymus and the pituitary, by which the brain adjusts immune responses and the immune system alters nerve cell activity. That link is now known to include such immunotransmitters as thymosin.

CLINICAL PRACTICE cannot long remain unaffected by this research. The discovery of pathways that bind the brain and the immune system rescues the behavioral approach to disease from the shadowy practices of witch doctors and places it squarely within the rational tradition of Western medicine. Aware now of the complex physiological basis for behavioral modification of the immune response, physicians can spend less time fielding criticism and more time exploring which types of therapy are of the greatest benefit. We are witnessing the birth of a new integrative science, psychoneuroimmunology, which *begins* with the premise that neither the brain nor the immune system can be excluded from any scheme that proposes to account for the onset and course of human disease.

Regrettably, much of the present debate is preoccupied with the results of behavioral approaches to the treatment of the most intractable, least understood diseases. Consider the argument that unfolded in the pages of *The New England Journal of Medicine* during 1985. In the journal's June 13 issue, Barrie R. Cassileth and her colleagues, of the University of Pennsylvania Cancer Center, reported that in a study of three hundred fifty-nine cancer patients no correlation could be found between behavioral factors and progression of the illness. The same issue included an editorial in which Marcia Angell, a physician and deputy editor of the journal, cited Cassileth's findings to support the view that the contribution of mental states to the cause and cure of disease is insignificant.

If they accomplished nothing else, the responses, to both the study and the editorial, published in the journal's November 21 issue, called attention to the difficulties facing anyone attempting to unravel the relationship between illness and what one writer called the "dynamic richness and variety of human experience." Most of the correspondents had found (or, at least, acknowledged) evidence for the contribution of mental states to human health, but none could agree as to how such states might affect the myriad immunological factors that come into play during the course of a malignant disease.

Unquestionably, much more research regarding the behavioral approach to illnesses such as cancer has to be done. But in the meantime, the most immediately realizable applications of behavioral medicine lie elsewhere. The first, and, in the long run, the most valuable, clinical spinoffs of psychoneuroimmunology will be in disease prevention—initially, in the development of ways to manage stress. As we study further the relationship between behavior and the biochemistry of immunity, the aim should not be to replace the witch doctor with a Western equivalent so much as to reduce the need for both.

DANGEROUS THOUGHTS

How we think and feel can make us sick.

BERNARD DIXON

Bernard Dixon is a contributing editor of
Science 86.

UNTIL RECENTLY, Ellen hadn't seen a physician in years. When other people got a bug, she was the one who invariably stayed healthy. But then her luck seemed to change. First she caught a bad cold in January, then had a bout of flu in February, followed by a nasty cough that still lingers. What an infuriating coincidence that these ailments hit as her career was faltering—months of unemployment following companywide layoffs.

But is it a coincidence? Intuition may suggest that we have fewer colds when we are content with our lives, more when we are under stress. That the mind can influence the body's vulnerability to infection in an insidious but potent way is a perennial theme of folklore and literature. Now even scientists are beginning to take that idea seriously. An alliance of psychiatrists, immunologists, neuroscientists, and microbiologists, specialists who rarely look beyond their own disciplines, are beginning to work together in a field so new that it goes under a variety of names, including behavioral immunology, psychoimmunology, and neuroimmunomodulation. Behind these polysyllables lies the challenge of understanding the chemical and anatomical connections between mind and body and eventually,

perhaps, even preventing psychosomatic illness.

Just 10 years ago, most specialists in communicable disease would have scoffed at any suggestion that the mind can influence the body in this way. Textbooks portrayed infection as the simple, predictable outcome whenever a disease causing microbe encountered a susceptible host. Various factors such as old age, malnutrition, and overwork could make a disease more severe. But there was no place for the fanciful notion that elation, depression, contentment, or stress could affect the course of disease.

Today, that once-conventional wisdom is being revised by scientists around the world. Playing a major role in these investigations are researchers at England's Medical Research Council Common Cold Unit near Salisbury. Their work shows that even this relatively trivial infection is affected by the psyche. And the lessons learned may apply to more serious diseases, including cancer.

For nearly four decades now, volunteers at the Common Cold Unit have helped test the efficacy of new antiviral drugs and have proven that colds are caused by rhinoviruses and a few related viruses. In 1975 psychologist Richard

Totman at Nuffield College, Oxford, and Wallace Craig and Sylvia Reed of the Common Cold Unit conducted the first psychological experiments. The scientists infected 48 healthy volunteers by dribbling down their nostrils drops containing two common cold viruses. The researchers then offered 23 of their subjects the chance to take a new "drug," actually a placebo, that would presumably prevent colds. The investigators warned these subjects that if they accepted this treatment, they would have to have their gastric juices sampled with a stomach tube. The scientists had no intention of doing this; the warning was simply a ruse to put the volunteers under stress. The other half of the group was neither offered the drug nor cautioned about the stomach tube. Totman and his colleagues theorized that the 23 offered the placebo would experience either mild anxiety or regret, depending on the decision they made. This might cause them to allay their state of mind by justifying to themselves their decision—as a theory called cognitive dissonance predicts—which would result in greater bodily resistance and milder colds.

The experts were wrong. When an independent physician assessed the volun-

IT'S JUST AN OLD WIVES' TALE

For some researchers, the idea that an individual's attitude can cause or cure disease is nothing more than an old wives' tale. Doctors have been treating the body and mind as separate entities for decades, and many see no reason for change.

In a highly controversial editorial in the prestigious *New England Journal of Medicine*, senior deputy editor and pathologist Marcia Angell said that the media have sold the public a bill of goods on the connection between mental state and disease. She notes that popular literature is full of "heal thyself" incantations, such as Norman Cousins's laughter-and-vitamin-C remedy for disease and Carl and Stephanie Simonton's program, which teaches cancer patients to imagine their healthy white blood cells gobbling up tumors. Angell fears that regimens like these may instill enormous guilt in patients who succumb to illness despite all their attempts to maintain positive attitudes.

She also fears that many studies done under the banner of psychoimmunology suffer from serious flaws in design, analysis, or interpretation. "We have let our standards slip a bit," she says, "because we are too ready to accept our mental state as a major and direct cause or cure of disease." In a notable study of recently widowed spouses published in 1959, for example, Arthur Kraus of the Maryland Department of Health and Abraham Lilienfeld of Johns Hopkins University found a high death rate among the survivors. Angell says, "Although the authors were cautious in their interpretation, others have been quick to ascribe the findings to grief rather than to, say, a change in diet or other habits." She cautions both researchers and the public not to jump to conclusions from meager experimental findings.

Suggesting that there is little evidence for linking stress and disease, Angell writes, "The known physiologic effects of stress on the adrenal glands are often overinterpreted so that it is a short leap to a view of stress as a cause of one disease or another."

Supporting Angell's views is James Melby, chief endocrinologist at Boston University. Melby suggests that researchers sometimes put the cart before the horse—a lymphocyte disorder might cause a debilitating depression, rather than the other way around, for instance—but he notes that such ideas have not yet been tested experimentally.

Not all psychoimmunology research shows a correlation between mental state and illness. In a study published in 1985, Barrie R. Cassileth and her colleagues at the University of Pennsylvania determined that neither positive attitudes nor feelings of depression or hopelessness had significant effects on the survival rate of 359 patients with advanced cancers. Cassileth concedes, however, that a good outlook may improve the quality of a patient's life.

In another study, published in March 1985, Robert B. Case, a cardiologist at St. Luke's-Roosevelt Hospital Center in New York, found no relation between the much-publicized type A behavior and heart disease.

Despite these studies and Angell's persuasive editorial, most researchers in the field of psychoimmunology remain firm believers in the mind-body connection. But they agree they have little in the way of proof. "A lot of the mechanisms for mind-and-body interaction are just being put into place. It is very difficult to do a totally conclusive experiment," says Michael Ruff of the National Institutes of Health in Bethesda, Maryland. But Ruff believes that "emotions and feelings are fundamentally biochemical in nature" and thus could affect the immune system both directly and indirectly.

Neurobiologist Novera Herbert Spector at NIH agrees with Angell on one point only—that patients should not be made to feel guilty about their illnesses. But, he says, popular conceptions that the mind influences the body are not necessarily inaccurate: "The public is sometimes ahead of the medical community." Laughter and a cheerful spirit, he says, are useful in creating a relaxed environment in the body for the immune system to function better.

Angell is not convinced. "Laughter is a worthy end in itself, not as a means or a medicine toward curing disease. That is not science." —*Beth Py*

teers' symptoms, he found that the 23 offered the choice had cold symptoms that were significantly more severe than those given no option. Apparently anxiety generated by contemplating something unpleasant or refusing to help a worthy cause had a tangible influence on the course of the illness.

Totman's group also made some intriguing observations about the way stress affects people outside the laboratory. Volunteers were interviewed by a psychologist, received rhinoviruses, caught colds, and were monitored. Individuals who during the previous six months had experienced a stressful event, such as death of a loved one, divorce, or a layoff, developed worse colds than the others, and introverts had more severe colds than extroverts. Not only were the introverts' symptoms worse than those of their peers, their nasal secretions contained more rhinovirus, confirming that their illnesses were worse.

The Common Cold Unit is now trying to find out how stress affects people with

In one landmark study, 15 men showed depressed immunity after their wives died of breast cancer.

strong social networks compared with their more introverted colleagues.

But how could an individual's mental state encourage or thwart the development of a cold? Research at several centers in the United States supports the most plausible explanation—that psychological stress impairs the effectiveness of the immune system, which has the dual role of recognizing and eliminating microbes from outside the body as well as cancer cells originating within.

The first line of defense of the immune system is the white blood cells called lymphocytes. These include B cells, which manufacture antibodies against microbes; helper T cells, which aid the B cells in making the right kind of antibodies; and killer T cells, which wipe out invading organisms if they have been exposed to them before. Another kind of lymphocyte, the natural killer cell, has received a lot of attention lately for its ability to detect and destroy harmful cells, including malignant ones, even if it hasn't encountered the invaders previously. Together with scavenging white blood cells that gobble up dead cells and debris, the various types of lymphocytes work in complex, coordinated ways to police the body's tissues.

Researchers can measure the efficiency of the immune system by measuring how well a patient's lymphocytes respond to foreign substances. For instance, they can grow the patient's lymphocytes in glassware and expose them to substances called mitogens, which mimic the behavior of microorganisms by stimulating the white cells to divide. Since a rapid increase in the number of white cells is a crucial early stage in the defense against invasion, patients whose white cells don't proliferate may have malfunctioning immune systems.

But most researchers are cautious

about generalizing from the results obtained from a single technique of this sort, since the immune system has complicated backups to keep us healthy even when our lymphocytes aren't proliferating. Nevertheless, reports of stress reducing the efficiency of the immune system have been accumulating on such a scale—and with such variety—that it is becoming difficult to resist the conclusion that anxiety increases our vulnerability to disease.

In one landmark study, for example, Steven Schleifer and his colleagues at Mt. Sinai School of Medicine in New York sought help from spouses of women with advanced breast cancer. They persuaded 15 men to give blood samples every six to eight weeks during their wives' illnesses and for up to 14 months after the women died. While none of the men showed depressed lymphoctye response while their wives were ill, their white cell response was significantly lowered as early as two weeks after their wives died and for up to 14 months later. Schleifer believes he has shown, contrary to earlier studies, that it was bereavement, not the experience of the spouses' illness, that lowered immunity.

Prompted by his observations of the bereaved widowers, Schleifer wondered if serious, debilitating depression would also show up as weakened immunity. When he took blood samples from 18 depressed patients at Mt. Sinai and the Bronx Veterans Administration Hospital, he found their lymphocytes were significantly less responsive to mitogens than those of healthy individuals from the general population matched for age, sex, and race.

We sometimes think humans are uniquely vulnerable to anxiety, but stress seems to affect the immune defenses of lower animals too. In one experiment, for example, behavioral immunologist Mark Laudenslager and colleagues at the University of Denver gave mild electric shocks to 24 rats. Half the animals could switch off the current by turning a wheel in their enclosure, while the other half could not. The rats in the two groups were paired so that each time one rat turned the wheel it protected both itself and its helpless partner from the shock. Laudenslager found that the immune response was depressed below normal in the helpless rats but not in those that could turn off the electricity. What he has demonstrated, he believes, is that lack of control over an event, not the

Scavenging white cells may serve as free-floating nerve cells able to communicate with the brain.

experience itself, is what weakens the immune system.

Other researchers agree. Jay Weiss, a psychologist at Duke University School of Medicine, has shown that animals who are allowed to control unpleasant stimuli don't develop sleep disturbances, ulcers, or changes in brain chemistry typical of stressed rats. But if the animals are confronted with situations they have no control over, they later behave passively when faced with experiences they can control. Such findings reinforce psychiatrists' suspicions that the experience or perception of helplessness is one of the most harmful factors in depression.

One of the most startling examples of how the mind can alter the immune response was discovered by chance. In 1975 psychologist Robert Ader at the University of Rochester School of Medicine and Dentistry conditioned mice to avoid saccharin by simultaneously feeding them the sweetener and injecting them with a drug that while suppressing their immune systems caused stomach upsets. Associating the saccharin with the stomach pains, the mice quickly learned to avoid the sweetener. In order to extinguish the taste aversion, Ader reexposed the animals to saccharin, this time without the drug, and was astonished to find that those rodents that had received the highest amounts of sweetener during their earlier conditioning died. He could only speculate that he had so successfully conditioned the rats that saccharin alone now served to weaken their immune systems enough to kill them.

If you can depress the immune system by conditioning, it stands to reason you can boost it in the same way. Novera Herbert Spector at the National Institute of Neurological and Communicative Disorders and Stroke in Bethesda, Maryland, recently directed a team at the University of Alabama, Birmingham, which confirmed that hypothesis. The researchers injected mice with a chemical that enhances natural killer cell activity while simultaneously exposing the rodents to the odor of camphor, which has no detectable effect on the immune system. After nine sessions, mice exposed to the camphor alone showed a large increase in natural killer cell activity.

What mechanism could account for these connections between the psyche and the immune system? One well-known link is the adrenal glands, which the brain alerts to produce adrenaline and other hormones that prepare the body to cope with danger or stress. But adrenal hormones cannot be the only link between mind and body. Research by a group under Neal Miller, professor emeritus of psychology at the Rockefeller University in New York City, has shown that even rats whose adrenal glands have been removed suffer depressed immunity after being exposed to electric shocks.

Anxiety, it seems, can trigger the release of many other hormones, including testosterone, insulin, and possibly even growth hormone. In addition, stress stimulates secretion of chemicals called neuropeptides, which influence mood and emotions. One class of neuropeptides known as endorphins kills pain and causes euphoria. Endorphins have another interesting characteristic: they fit snugly into receptors on lymphocytes, suggesting a direct route through which the mind could influence immunity.

This idea is borne out in the lab, where one of the natural pain-killers, beta-endorphin, can impair the response of lymphocytes in test tubes. Evidence from cancer studies shows that chemicals blocking the normal functions of endorphins can slow the growth of tumors. And other work suggests that tumor cells may be attracted to certain neuropeptides, providing a route for cancer to spread all over the body.

Neuropeptides are turning out to be extraordinarily versatile in their interaction with the immune system. At the National Institutes of Health in Bethesda, Maryland, Michael Ruff has found neuropeptides that attract scavenging white cells called macrophages to the site of injured or damaged tissue. There the macrophages regulate and activate other immune cells as well as gobble up bacteria and debris. What is even more surprising, however, is that the macrophages themselves actually release neuropeptides. This has led Ruff to speculate that these scavenging white cells may also serve as free-floating nerve cells able to communicate with the brain.

But why should that two-way communication sometimes have the effect of allowing stress to upset the body's defenses? One answer may lie in evolution. When early man was attacked by a saber-toothed tiger, for example, it may have been more important from a survival standpoint for his immune system to turn off briefly. In its zeal to get rid of foreign matter and damaged tissue, a revved-up immune system can also attack healthy tissue. Shutting down the immune system for a short time would avert any damage to the body's healthy tissues and would cause no harm, since it takes a while for infection to set in. As soon as the danger had passed, the immune system was able to rebound—perhaps stronger than before—and go about its main business of fighting invading organisms. But the kind of stress we modern humans suffer is of a different kind: it is rarely life threatening and often lasts a long time, weakening our immune defenses for long periods and making us vulnerable to infections and cancer.

The immune system is extraordinarily complex, and the mind is even more so. As Nicholas Hall of George Washington University School of Medicine says, "We're putting together two kinds of black boxes and trying to make sense of what happens."

In the process, researchers are wrestling with three issues of scientific and social import. First, what can be done to protect people at vulnerable times in their lives from a potentially catastrophic failure of their immune defenses? Second, should counseling and psychological support become as important as traditional therapeutic measures in the treatment of disease? And finally, what are the corresponding benefits to health of the positive emotions of hope, affection, love, mirth, and joy?

Development

Philosophical principles that give definition to developmental psychology have their roots in the evolutionary biology of Darwin, Wallace, and Spencer, and in the embryology of Preyer. Both James Mark Baldwin and G. Stanley Hall, the two most influential developmental psychologists of the early twentieth century, were influenced by questions about phylogeny (species' adaptation) and ontogeny (individual adaptation or fittingness). Baldwin challenged the assertion that species changes (phylogeny) precede individual organism changes (ontogeny). Instead, he argued that ontogeny precedes phylogeny. Thus, from the outset, developmental psychology has focused on the forces that guide and direct development. Early theorists like Arnold Gesell stressed maturation as the guiding force in development. Other theorists argued that the guiding forces of development were to be found in the environment. Contemporary developmentalists generally accept some version of the epigenetic principle which asserts that development is an emergent process of active, dynamic, reciprocal, and systemic change. This systems perspective forces one to think about the historical, social, cultural, interpersonal, and intrapersonal forces that shape the developmental process, and it explicitly endorses heredity-environment interactionism.

Today, American society faces a social problem—substance abuse—that has profound implications for development. Andrew Revkin details the devastating consequences of cocaine addiction for the fetus and newborn, consequences that significantly increase chances for morbidity or mortality for an estimated 200,000 infants annually.

In the past few years we have all been made aware that the sexual abuse of children is more common than was previously known. Alfie Kohn's article not only details some of the serious consequences of this abuse, but also suggests some appropriate interventions.

One of the oldest and most vigorous arguments among developmental psychologists deals with the effectiveness of punishment in the development of appropriate behavior in children. Bruno Bettelheim clearly distinguishes punishment from discipline, and identifies the major consequences of each. We can choose techniques which foster the type of development we want for our children and for each other.

Some researchers argue that much of the storm and stress attributed to adolescence is a myth, created from an overemphasis on adolescent fads and rebelliousness and an underemphasis on obedience, conformity, and cooperation. Focusing on the negative aspects of adolescent behavior may create a set of expectations which the adolescent then strives to achieve. Moreover, for some adolescents the transition to adulthood is marked by despair, loneliness, and interpersonal conflict. The pressures of peer group, school, and family may produce conformity, or may lead to rebellion toward or withdrawal from friends, parents, or society at large. These pressures may peak as the adolescent prepares to separate from the family and assume the independence and responsibilities of adulthood. However, as Richard Flaste points out in the next article, many adolescents describe their relationships with peers and parents in essentially positive terms.

Old age has long been considered either a problem in itself, or at best, a time in which many problems arise. As the number of elderly Americans rises rapidly, descriptions of them as a group are also changing. Jack Horn and Jeff Meer suggest strongly that these trends are progressive; what will aging be like in another 100 years?

Looking Ahead: Challenge Questions

Recently, a woman addicted to cocaine during pregnancy was charged with the murder of her stillborn infant. Infants exposed to excessive alcohol prenatally often display signs of fetal alcohol syndrome. Should women who ingest harmful substances be held legally responsible for the consequences of such drugs on their fetuses? What about cigarette smoking? While we wait for the development of an effective child abuse prevention strategy, what should we do to ensure minimal damage to an abused child's development, particularly in terms of self-esteem? Are there some direct ways to break the intergenerational cycle of abuse?

What are some of the benefits and limitations of punishment and discipline? Are they ever the same? Which techniques or procedures are most likely to result in a happy, well-behaved child? Which techniques or procedures will, in the long run, produce a happy, well-adjusted adult?

What historical factors created the myth that adolescence was a time of storm and stress? Is it actually a myth? Cultism, suicide, substance abuse, antisocial behavior and violence, and mental illness are hardly descriptors that suggest peace and harmony in the teen years. What parenting strategies might effectively prevent such Sturm und Drang in adolescence?

If Horn and Meer are correct in their observations about successful aging, what advice would you give a 20-year-old to help prepare him or her to be 70? To what extent are these strategies for successful aging dependent on the personality of the individual applying them?

CRACK IN THE CRADLE

Hundreds of thousands of babies are being attacked by cocaine while still in their mothers' womb. Some will die. The others will have their development dangerously impaired.

ANDREW C. REVKIN

Call him Timothy. He's a robust baby boy, about to have his first birthday. Lying in a stainless steel crib, he giggles and reaches for a blue plastic hose dangling nearby. He puts it to his mouth and sucks some of the misty gases coming from the end. "Good boy, you're taking your inhaler yourself," says Kathryn Crowley, a neonatologist at New York's Harlem Hospital. Timothy has lived the first year of his life in the sunny west wing of the hospital's fourth floor, the neonatal intensive care unit. On one side is a room full of extremely sick premature infants, encased in clear plastic incubators; on the other is a room full of not-so-sick babies—intermediate care, they call it.

Timothy doesn't need to be in the hospital. Although his lungs were underdeveloped at the time of his premature birth—after only 29 weeks of gestation—he has now caught up to the point where he could easily be cared for at home. He spends much of his time like any healthy one-year-old, suspended in a walker, feet just touching the floor, scooting across the linoleum. "Everybody here loves him," Crowley says. "Everybody wants to take him home." Everybody except Timothy's mother.

No one seems to know where she is. She was too busy for prenatal care. The first time she saw a doctor was when she entered the delivery room. She was high on cocaine throughout the pregnancy, she had cocaine in her system when she walked into the hospital in labor, and when last seen she was spending all her time trying to score another five-dollar rock of the pure, crystallized, fast-food form of cocaine called crack.

It's almost certain that Timothy was born prematurely because cocaine caused his mother's uterus to contract spasmodically; the connection is understood even on the streets, where the word is that a crack binge is a surefire way to give yourself a no-fuss abortion. It's almost certain too that when Timothy was a fetus, cocaine stanched the flow of nutrients and oxygen to his developing body and brain. And it's almost certain that cocaine has denied Timothy any chance he might have had for a normal family life.

Cocaine is having a devastating impact on the lives of a booming generation of babies born to addicted women. The effects include strokes while the baby is still in the womb, physical malformations, and an increased risk of death during infancy. And the number of cocaine-exposed babies is growing explosively, doubling each year in many major cities; estimates put the number in the United States as high as 200,000. And the problem, although at its worst in crack-infested inner-city neighborhoods, cuts across lines of race and class and the borders of geography to infest not just the cities but the suburbs and rural towns.

Cocaine is not only destroying individual lives but overburdening obstetric and pediatric wards around the country and adding to the ever-mounting cost of health care. If cocaine use during pregnancy were a disease, its impact on infants would be considered a national health-care crisis. And the effect will ripple onward as these children grow up and enter the school system.

One can get a quick reading of the scope of the problem by walking around the corridors at Harlem Hospital. On this day there are ten preemies in the intensive care nursery. Four were born steeped in cocaine. One of them, over in the corner, is noticed only because there's a slight movement beneath a nest of tubes and wires as his leg, just a little bigger than a man's index finger, gives a kick. This baby is six days old and shouldn't have been born for another three and a half months.

In intensive care a newborn's weight is measured in grams. This infant tips the scale at 890 grams—just under two pounds. He's kept warm by bright lights similar to the heat lamps that keep burgers warm in a take-out restaurant. A tube that runs beneath a bandage on his chest drains air that's leaking from a tear in his fluid-clogged lungs. Two of the other cocaine babies are "thousand-gramers" who lie in incubators across the room. The fourth, just down the row, is now a solid 1,500 grams, but he was born just above the line technology draws between life and death—500 grams.

According to David Bateman, the hospital's chief of neonatology, in a typical week 50 to 70 percent of the babies in the unit had cocaine in their urine when they were born. These high numbers are most likely the result of cocaine's tendency to trigger uterine contractions and raise blood pressure. The latter effect often leads to a condition called abruptio placentae, in which the capillary-rich placenta rips away from the lining of the uterus, causing bleeding and early labor. Big-city hospitals report that in recent years the number of abruptions has increased dramatically. The number of emergency calls for which ambulance teams find a mother deep in sudden labor has also risen sharply. The preemies that result tend to be extreme preemies—24, 25, 26 weeks—and very small infants require a vastly greater amount of care and cost far more to treat.

Just down the hall there's a room designated convalescent care. Most of the ten babies in this room are being treated for syphilis they contracted from their mothers. And most also had cocaine in their bodies at birth. "Five years ago we never really saw syphilis," Crowley says. The rampant trade in sex for crack has apparently contributed to the sudden resurgence of this disease.

Crowley walks toward the floor's other wing, where the "boarder babies" live. In New York and a handful of other states, when it has been determined that a newborn infant has drugs in its system, the case must be investigated. At hospitals in places like New York City, Los Angeles, and Washington, D.C., babies are piling up by the dozen as case workers arrange home inspections and decide which babies must go to foster homes or grandparents and which stay with the mother. (A nurse at Howard University Hospital in the nation's capital says, "We've got storage rooms that can't be used for storage anymore because they're storing babies.")

Crowley peeks into three boarder nurseries. There are ten steel carts to a room, each with a plastic bassinet on top. Each bassinet holds a baby. The typical stay for the boarder babies at Harlem Hospital is one to two months, and a stay of three or four months is far from uncommon.

> **If cocaine use during pregnancy were a disease, its impact on infants would be considered a national health-care crisis.**

Only in some of the communities where the crack problem originated are neonatologists seeing a leveling off of the flood of cocaine babies—and not for any encouraging reason. "It's reached a saturation point," says Bateman. "There's a certain group of people who are going to be susceptible to this, and that group has been used up." What he's seeing more frequently now are repeats: mothers who year after year come in to deliver babies—and who still have cocaine in their systems. "They almost always look much worse each time," he says. "We've got some mothers coming in now on their third try."

Hospitals in Dallas, San Francisco, and Gainesville, Florida, have found that about 10 percent of all births show signs of cocaine. A study conducted last year confirmed that such numbers do not vary significantly nationwide. And because the urine tests can only detect cocaine use by the mother within the last 24 to 48 hours, physicians say that this is just the tip of the iceberg. Undoubtedly, many more women used the drug during pregnancy.

A basic understanding of how cocaine affects the adult brain and body has begun to develop only over the past decade, as the level of urgency has risen along with the drug's popularity. Even now little is known about the mechanism by which cocaine exerts its addictive pull—a pull so powerful that monkeys in laboratories have been known to inject themselves with the drug for days, until they convulse and die. There is even less understanding of how the drug affects a fetus. As recently as 1982 there were still textbooks on high-risk obstetrics stating that cocaine had no harmful effects on a fetus.

Cocaine is derived from the leaves of the coca plant of Central and South America, in which it occurs naturally in an alkaloid form. At the wholesale level, the drug is almost always bought and sold as a hydrochloride salt that has been "cut," or diluted, by mixing it with inert substances. As a salt, it's water-soluble and can thus readily cross the mucous membranes in the nose. By that route, it takes about three minutes for the drug to reach the brain. With crack, that trip can take as little as eight seconds.

Crack is manufactured by "cooking" cocaine hydrochloride in boiling water and baking soda, a process that converts the salt back into the alkaloid, which can then precipitate out of the solution as pure cocaine crystals. Crack is no different than what used to be called freebase cocaine. Unlike the salt, the alkaloid form doesn't degrade when heated, and so it can be smoked. It also dissolves in fat and thus instantly passes across fatty cell membranes, speeding the passage from the lungs to the blood and from the blood to the brain.

Once they enter the body, both forms of cocaine act the same way. In the brain, cocaine stimulates certain neurons to release their loads of neurotransmitters, the chemicals that carry messages across the gap between one neuron and the next. Most affected are the compounds that cause much of the "fight or flight" reflex—the rush of accelerated heart rate, raised blood pressure, and lowered digestive activity with which the body prepares itself for action.

Normally, after these neurotransmitters are released, they are quickly sopped up again to be rereleased when the next bit of neural activity occurs. But cocaine also blocks the recycling of neurotransmitters. The result is a brief period of intense stimulation—cocaine users talk of euphoria and mental clarity—that is followed by a tumultuous crash as the nervous system finds itself fresh out of the chemicals it needs to do normal things like thinking and feeling. Frequent users of the drug fall into a cycle in which the aftermath of the high—intense depression, paranoia, loss of appetite, sexual impotence, and profound irritability—leads right back to the need for more cocaine.

Just how addictive is crack? Alicia is 25 years old and pregnant. She lives in the Bushwick section of Brooklyn, in a forgotten wasteland of poverty across the East River from the sparkle of Manhattan. Alicia started shooting heroin after dropping out of high school at age 17. She switched to crack two years ago and wasn't able to stop until she was brought to an emergency room last September naked and comatose. She doesn't remember how she got there.

The pull of crack far exceeds the pull of heroin, she says. "When I was shooting, I'd like do two or three bags and I was all right. Crack is much worse. The high isn't good at all. When you inhale it, you feel it, but as soon as you exhale it, it's gone. You go out and do things you never felt you'd do for just a few dollars."

Only her coma pulled her out of crack's grip; until then, she ignored the starkest warnings: "A friend just passed away about a year and a half ago," Alicia recalls. "They found him in his house. His brains were beat open. But that didn't stop me from getting high. You know, my brother, they beat him up with an ax and busted his mouth. That didn't stop me. I've been in jail. That didn't stop me."

Alicia now attends a clinic for addicts at Kings County Hospital in Brooklyn. She often catches herself thinking about the fetus growing in her womb. "I worry a lot. I've got this feeling that something's going to happen because of the things I used to do. They're going to backfire on me."

A fetus is particularly vulnerable to cocaine for several reasons. First, although the placenta does shield the womb from many large, complex molecules—particularly those that can't diffuse across fatty cell membranes—it is an open door to cocaine. Because the cocaine molecule "likes" fatty compounds, the drug readily crosses the placental barrier. Once cocaine enters the fetus's blood and tissues, it lingers there much longer than in adults: the liver has not yet developed into the powerful detoxifying agent it will become, and cocaine is broken down much more slowly.

The fetus is not only exposed to the direct effects of cocaine but also subjected to abuses brought on by the drug's effect on the mother-to-be. When a woman on crack gets pregnant, the last thing she is thinking about is the care of the developing fetus, let alone care of herself. The result is an explosion in the number of pregnancies taking place with absolutely no health care. Eighteen percent of all mothers who gave birth at Harlem Hospital last year had no prenatal care. That number was double what it had been in 1987. Almost all of that rise is because of crack.

The hospital estimates that between 40 and 50 percent of these so-called unregistered pregnant women have been exposed to the AIDS virus. Neonatologist Leonard Glass of the Children's Medical Center of Brooklyn says, "We have reason to believe that as much AIDS or more AIDS is being transmitted in the crack houses of 1989 as in the bathhouses of 1980." Between 30 and 50 percent of the babies born to these infected women will themselves develop AIDS. Asked how the situation is in his intensive care nursery, Glass says, "We may be a little slow today. We're down to one hundred percent occupancy."

No one has more single-mindedly absorbed himself in the direct consequences of fetal exposure to cocaine than pediatrician Ira Chasnoff of Northwestern Memorial Hospital in Chicago. He has published more than a dozen frequently cited studies of the effects of cocaine on some 200 pregnant women who have sought drug treatment or prenatal care at Northwestern Memorial over the past four years. Many of the studies have traced the progress of individual babies for two years or more.

Chasnoff is rarely at his home base these days. He is on the road constantly, lecturing on fetal problems caused by drug use. "Two years ago," he says, "I was giving maybe one or two lectures a month on this. Now I'm up to fifteen or more." On this day Chasnoff finds himself at Howard University Hospital, in the middle of one of Washington's crack zones. He's there to speak at a conference called "Perinatal Substance Abuse—the Cry of the City," which has attracted about 200 nurses, doctors, and social workers from as far away as California.

He quickly paints a portrait of the consequences of cocaine exposure in the womb, based on his most recent study. His research team compared the outcomes of pregnancies in three groups: women who used cocaine throughout pregnancy, women who stopped using cocaine after the first three months of pregnancy, and a control group who never used drugs.

The numbers tell the story. Ten pregnancies out of the 75 in the cocaine-exposed groups ended in abruptions; there were none in the control group. The average reduction of head circumference in the babies exposed to cocaine throughout pregnancy was about three-quarters of an inch. The reduction in birth weight was about 21 ounces. These differences are significant: obviously many small babies or babies with small heads live perfectly normal lives; statistically, however, these characteristics have been clearly linked to later learning problems and an increased risk of infant mortality. The prevailing theory is that this group of relatively subtle effects have a common cause—the tendency of cocaine to restrict the flow of blood to the uterus and placenta.

Chasnoff and others have also often noted a period of extremely disturbed behavior in cocaine-exposed babies that lasts eight to ten weeks after delivery. In some cases it may continue for as long as four months. The tragedy of this, Chasnoff says, is "that's exactly when the newborn infant begins to interact with its mother, begins to bond, to have a relationship with its environment." During this time cocaine babies are often hypersensitive. Just picking up the baby can unleash a torrent of tremors and crying.

"Cocaine-exposed infants spend all their time either crying and irritable or in deep sleep," Chasnoff tells his audience. "They don't go in between." On top of that, the babies tend to shun intimate contact, even the stare of a mother simply trying to catch her child's eye. "If you try to make eye contact with a cocaine-exposed infant," Chasnoff says, "you see a specific behavior called gaze aversion. If you do make eye contact with the infant, you overpower him. He gets so overloaded that he shuts down; he closes his eyes."

It is this kind of behavioral profile that has sociologists and pediatricians convinced that cocaine is contributing to a recent sharp rise in child abuse in cities around the United States. One of the researchers looking into this is neonatologist Loretta Finnegan, who for 19 years has run a drug-treatment program for pregnant addicts at Jefferson Medical College in Philadelphia. An explosive situation is bound to develop when a difficult baby is placed in the care of a woman on cocaine. "It's not too good to have a child in front of you," she says, "when you're irritable or depressed and you have a drive for cocaine. What are you going to do with that baby? Certainly not what you're supposed to do."

In the recent study at Northwestern Memorial, Chasnoff and several psychologists assessed the behavioral development of the cocaine-exposed babies and controls. The findings were startling: "At one month, the cocaine-exposed babies still have not reached the functional level of a two-day-old drug-free infant," Chasnoff says. There are indications that in a good environment cocaine-exposed babies can catch up developmentally. But these babies are rarely in a good environment.

Chasnoff goes on to tell his audience about rarer but much more dramatic effects of fetal exposure to cocaine. He unreels a case study he often uses to illustrate one of the most devastating effects of cocaine (and to remind everyone that cocaine babies aren't restricted to poor, black communities). He describes a 32-year-old white housewife from a prosperous suburb of Chicago. She was near the end of her pregnancy and, although she'd used cocaine quite a bit in the past, had held off during most of the nine months.

On their wedding anniversary, her husband, who worked at the Chicago Board of Trade, forgot until the last minute to get a present. So he bought five grams of cocaine on the trading floor and brought it home. Chasnoff continues in a sing-songy, story-telling style: "Her husband said, 'Dear, I wanted to give you something special.' The woman snorted most of the cocaine over the next three days and noticed that her baby began to get extremely active." The next day, the woman began to have contractions. "During the thirty-minute drive to the hospital, she used the last gram." Sixteen hours after delivery, the baby boy stopped breathing and turned blue several times. His right arm, shoulder, and hip became limp. He had several seizures and his heart stopped.

The baby was resuscitated. A CT scan of his skull showed the problem. Chasnoff flicks on a slide. There is a white ovoid ring, the skull, surrounding a gray lacy area, denoting brain tissue. Pointing to the image, Chasnoff says, "If you look right here, you can see an area where this baby had an acute cerebral

infarction, a stroke, in utero." The region he indicates is a dark blotch, shaped like South America. He flicks to the next slide—a CT scan taken three months later. The infarcted area has coalesced into a kidney-shaped cyst of functionless tissue. Chasnoff's voice hardens. "It's been three years now and this boy is microcephalic"—he has a small head for his size, a condition leading almost invariably to some degree of developmental disability.

Such strokes may be caused by high blood pressure brought on by cocaine's tendency to raise levels of the vessel-constricting neurotransmitter norepinephrine. "We've now collected cases from all over the country of babies having strokes," Chasnoff says. "They're usually referred to us by lawyers in cases where an obstetrician is being sued for malpractice. It turns out that the stroke was not caused by forceps, but by cocaine."

"I worry a lot about my baby. I've got this feeling that something's going to happen because of the things I used to do. They're going to backfire on me."

Chasnoff reviews some other cases of damage wrought by cocaine used during pregnancy. The common feature to all of them is that they seem to have resulted from a reduction in the flow of blood to some particular organ or tissue. In his last study, 15 of the cocaine-exposed babies developed malformed or malfunctioning kidneys or genitals. He and other researchers have found numerous cases in cocaine-exposed babies of a condition called ileal atresia, or dead bowel—in which part of the intestine fails to develop for lack of blood. An infant must quickly undergo surgery to make the digestive tract intact. In several instances, Chasnoff notes, cocaine babies have been born without the two middle fingers of a hand. This is probably caused not by some genetic

defect, but rather by the loss of blood flow into those digits.

These cases might be considered statistical flukes, but strong supporting evidence for cocaine's role in such disruptions comes from the laboratory of Australian researcher Bill Webster, some of whose slides Chasnoff now shows on the screen. An image appears of a nearly full-term rat embryo, from a mother that was exposed to cocaine. Lighted from behind, the embryo glows milky white. Chasnoff points to red blotches on one paw where the digits are forming. "This is cocaine's work," he says. "You can see there are hemorrhages in some of the digits here. If this animal had been born, the digits wouldn't be there."

Other new work with animal models is disclosing that there may be lifelong damage to learning ability and other cognitive processes. At the State University of New York at Binghamton, psychologist Linda Spear has been testing nervous-system development in the offspring of female rats that were exposed to cocaine through the last half of pregnancy. The good news is that the offspring developed normal reflexes and their motor development seemed unimpaired. But there is no shortage of bad news. "The cocaine-exposed rats showed deficits in their ability to learn a variety of tasks," Spear says. While normal rats readily learn to associate a particular odor with the reward of a drink of milk, the cocaine group was unable to make the connection. It's still too soon to see if cocaine-exposed children are tending to show signs of such behavioral problems.

Spear is also focusing her attention on benzoylecgonine, a substance produced as cocaine is broken down in the body, and one that has physiological effects of its own. Tests in rats show that when benzoylecgonine is injected directly into the brain, it vacuums up calcium. "Virtually everything with respect to brain development is calcium regulated," says Spear. "If you go into the brain with a substance that has a tendency to muck up calcium levels, that will have consequences." In adults benzoylecgonine doesn't present much of a problem because it doesn't cross the blood-brain barrier, a figurative term for a physical and chemical sieve that prevents large molecules, some disease-producing organisms, and many toxins from reaching the brain. What concerns Spear and others is that in the fetus the blood-brain barrier has not fully formed.

Recent laboratory research also hints that the threat to infants from cocaine may not end at birth. Cocaine users who breast-feed may pass along a strong hit of the drug to the suckling infant. Neuroscientist Richard Wiggins of West Virginia University Medical School has fed radioactively labeled cocaine to lactating female rats, then measured levels of the drug in the rats' blood and milk. "The bottom line," says Wiggins, "was that the concentration of cocaine was eight times higher in their milk than in their blood."

In the long run, he says—although the strokes and missing bowels and the like are terrible—it may be the subtlest aspects of the epidemic of cocaine babies that create the biggest problems for society. Even a 5 percent drop in scores of learning ability, for instance, is important. "A child doesn't have to be in a wheelchair to have a birth defect," says Wiggins. "Whenever you limit a child's full potential, even by a small amount, that's going to have an effect on society—particularly when you multiply that by the thousands of women who are addicted to cocaine."

He and many other researchers studying the problem predict that the most dramatic impact won't really be registered until today's cocaine babies grow up to become tomorrow's school-age children. Judy Howard, a pediatrician at the UCLA School of Medicine, agrees. "What I'm concerned about is, these children are going to hit school age and the teachers aren't going to know what to do with them," she says. Efforts are under way to follow the progress of children who were exposed to cocaine in the womb as they enter the Los Angeles school system. Preliminary findings show that there may indeed be lasting effects of drug exposure, says Howard. "They're socially not real initiators. They need a lot of direction. They have short attention spans, exhibit short-term memory loss, and are uncomfortable in new situations."

There are a few bright notes in this otherwise grim scenario. Chasnoff's group has classes for mothers to teach them how to swaddle and hold the difficult babies to minimize their crying and foster a mother-child bond. In several cities, progress has been made in reaching out to cocaine-using women before they become pregnant, or at least early in pregnancy. The Commission of Public Health in Washington has a "Mom Van" cruising the district's most desolate neighborhoods, driven by a zealous outreach worker named Tawana Fortune. When Fortune hears of a woman in a crack neighborhood who is pregnant, she will go up to the house and knock on windows until she gets someone's attention. She has successfully gotten dozens of women into treatment.

At Harlem Hospital, perinatologist Janet Mitchell runs a clinic for pregnant addicts that has such high ratings from patients that several have volunteered to go out and recruit other young crack-using mothers. "Our goal is not only to keep them off drugs but to keep them in care," says Mitchell. "They know that they can come in with dirty urines. We'll talk about it. They can bring in the father. We let him listen to the baby's heartbeat."

In St. Petersburg, Florida, Shirley Coletti, president of a program called Operation Parental Awareness and Responsibility, was recently given 16 houses that the county had removed from their foundations to make way for a highway. The houses will provide shelter for pregnant addicts, away from the drugs in their neighborhoods.

The problem remains that these outreach programs are treating only dozens of women in a nation where Florida alone conservatively estimates that its hospitals delivered 10,000 cocaine babies last year. Also, the others are extremely difficult to work with. In some cases the only way to get them to participate is to threaten to place their other children in foster care, on the grounds that an addicted mother poses a threat to her children. Most of these outreach programs have drop-out rates of 50 percent or more. Says Coletti, "We've worked with women with alcohol and heroin problems. Often the maternal instinct of those women has overpowered the drug. They've stayed clean through pregnancy. But with crack, they're unable to do that. It's the nature of the drug; it's so potent and powerfully addictive. Crack always wins."

The most discouraging fact of life for those attempting to solve the problems posed by crack-using mothers is that, ultimately, the only solution to the cocaine-baby problem would be to eliminate the conditions that lead a young woman, in the prime of life, to use cocaine. That is a daunting challenge.

No one adequately describes the environment that is causing America's epidemic of crack use better than Alicia, the young addict who narrowly escaped crack's hold once, sought help at Kings County Hospital last fall, and is expecting her baby this month. She reflects on the situation that nearly killed her and that she and her child will go home to: "My brother is on drugs. I've got three cousins, they're on crack. One is nine months pregnant. She's got three other kids. She stays out like three or four days at a time. I used to do the same thing. Didn't care about nothing or nobody. That's just the way it is when you're on crack. You just don't care about nothing. It's got you stuck in a place that you don't want to be, like a black hole, you know. Basically, I didn't really want to get high. I just wanted something better for myself. And then they all came knocking on my door with the crack and saying this is the cure."

Shattered Innocence

CHILDHOOD SEXUAL ABUSE IS YIELDING ITS DARK SECRETS TO THE COLD LIGHT OF RESEARCH.

Alfie Kohn

Alfie Kohn's book, No Contest: The Case Against Competition, *has just been published by Houghton Mifflin.*

No one would claim today that child sexual abuse happens in only one family in a million. Yet that preposterous estimate, based on statistics from 1930, was published in a psychiatric textbook as recently as 1975. Sensational newspaper headlines about day-care center scandals seem to appear almost daily and, together with feminist protests against sexist exploitation, these reports have greatly increased public awareness of what we now know is a widespread problem.

Even so, the most recent scientific findings about child sexual abuse—how often it happens and how it affects victims in the short and long term—have received comparatively little attention. These findings suggest that as many as 40 million people, about one in six Americans, may have been sexually victimized as children. As many as a quarter of these people may be suffering from a variety of psychological problems, ranging from guilt and poor self-esteem to sexual difficulties and a tendency to raise children who are themselves abused.

The startling figure of 40 million is derived from several studies indicating that 25 to 35 percent of all women and 10 to 16 percent of all men in this country experienced some form of abuse as children, ranging from sexual fondling to intercourse. In August 1985, *The Los Angeles Times* published the results of a national telephone poll of 2,627 randomly selected adults. Overall, 22 percent of respondents (27 percent of the women and 16 percent of the men) confided that they had experienced as children what they now identify as sexual abuse.

Some victims of abuse may be reluctant to tell a stranger on the telephone about something as traumatic and embarrassing as sexual abuse, which suggests that even the *Times* poll may have understated the problem. When sociologist Diana Russell of Mills College sent trained interviewers around San Francisco to interview 930 randomly selected women face-to-face, she found that 357, or 38 percent, reported at least one instance of having been sexually abused in childhood. When the definition of abuse was widened to include sexual advances that never reached the stage of physical contact, more than half of those interviewed said they had had such an experience before the age of 18.

Confirming the *Times* and Russell studies is a carefully designed Gallup Poll of more than 2,000 men and women from 210 Canadian communities. The results, published in 1984, show that 22 percent of the respondents were sexually abused as children. As with Russell's study, that number increases dramatically, to 39 percent, when noncontact abuse is included.

John Briere, a postdoctoral fellow at Harbor-University of California, Los Angeles Medical Center, has reviewed dozens of studies of child abuse in addition to conducting several of his own. "It is probable," he says, "that at least a quarter to a third of adult women and perhaps half as many men have been sexually victimized as children."

One reason these numbers are so surprising, and the reason estimates of one family in a million could be taken seriously for so long, is that many children who are sexually abused understandably keep this painful experience to themselves. In the *Times* poll, one-third of those who said they had been victimized also reported that they had never before told anyone. Many therapists still do not bother to ask their clients whether abuse has taken place, even when there is good reason to suspect that it has.

Studies demonstrate that most child sexual abuse happens to those between the ages of 9 and 12 (although abuse of 2- and 3-year-olds is by no means unusual), that the abuser is almost always a man and that he is typically known to the child—often a relative. In many cases, the abuse is not limited to a single episode, nor does the abuser usually use force. No race, ethnic group or economic class is immune.

All children do not react identically to sexual abuse. But most therapists would agree that certain kinds of behavior and feelings occur regularly among victims. The immediate effects of sexual abuse include sleeping and eating disturbances, anger, withdrawal and guilt. The children typically appear to be either afraid or anxious.

Two additional signs show up so frequently that experts rely upon them as indicators of possible abuse when they occur together. The first is sexual

abuse, it is far more difficult to draw a definitive connection between such abuse and later psychological problems. "We can't say every child who is abused has this or that consequence, and we are nowhere near producing a validated profile of a child-abuse victim," says Maria Sauzier, a psychiatrist who used to direct the Family Crisis Program for Sexually Abused Children at the New England Medical Center in Boston. In fact, some experts emphasize that many sexual abuse victims emerge relatively unscathed as adults. Indeed, David

der," people whose relationships, emotions and sense of self are all unstable and who often become inappropriately angry or injure themselves. "Not all borderlines have been sexually abused, but many have been," Briere says.

Briere, working with graduate student Marsha Runtz, has also noticed that some female abuse victims "space out" or feel as if they are outside of their own bodies at times. And he has observed that these women sometimes have physical complaints without any apparent medical cause. Briere points out that these two tendencies, known as "dissociation" and "somatization," add up to something very much like hysteria, as Freud used the term.

Other therapists believe the label Post-Traumatic Stress Disorder (PTSD), which has most often been applied to veterans of combat, may also be an appropriate diagnosis for some of those who have been abused. Symptoms of the disorder include flashbacks to the traumatic events, recurrent dreams about them, a feeling of estrangement from others and a general sense of numbness. "It feels to me like the fit is very direct to what we see with [victims of] child sexual abuse," says Christine Courtois, a psychologist from Washington, D.C. "Many victims ... experience the symptoms of acute PTSD." She describes an 18-year-old client, abused by her father for nine years, who carved the words "help me" in her arm. In the course of dealing with what had happened, she would sometimes pass out, an occasional response to extreme trauma.

---

*A*T LEAST 25 PERCENT OF ALL WOMEN AND
10 PERCENT OF ALL MEN IN THIS COUNTRY
EXPERIENCED SOME ABUSE AS CHILDREN,
RANGING FROM SEXUAL FONDLING TO INTERCOURSE.

---

preoccupation: excessive or public masturbation and an unusual interest in sexual organs, sex play and nudity. According to William Friedrich, associate professor of psychology at the Mayo Medical School in Rochester, Minnesota, "What seems to happen is the socialization process toward propriety goes awry in these kids."

The second sign consists of a host of physical complaints or problems, such as rashes, vomiting and headaches, all without medical explanation. Once it is discovered that children have been abused, a check of their medical records often reveals years of such mysterious ailments, says psychologist Pamela Langelier, director of the Vermont Family Forensic Institute in South Burlington, Vermont. Langelier emphasizes that children who have been sexually abused should be reassessed every few years because they may develop new problems each time they reach a different developmental stage. "Sometimes it looks like the kids have recovered," she says, "and then at puberty the issues come back again."

While there are clear patterns in the immediate effects of child sexual

Finkelhor, associate director of the Family Violence Research Program at the University of New Hampshire, has warned his colleagues against "exaggerating the degree and inevitability of the long-term negative effects of sexual abuse." For example, Finkelhor and others point out that studies of disturbed, atypical groups, such as prostitutes, runaways and drug addicts, often find that they show higher rates of childhood sexual abuse than in the general population. Yet according to the estimate of Chris Bagley, a professor of social welfare at the University of Calgary, "At least 50 percent of women who were abused do not suffer long-term ill effects."

If 50 percent survive abuse without problems, of course it follows that 50 percent do not. And Bagley, in fact, has conducted a study indicating that a quarter of all women who are sexually abused develop serious psychological problems as a result. Given the epidemic proportions of sexual abuse, that means that millions are suffering.

Briere, for example, has found a significant degree of overlap between abuse victims and those who suffer from "borderline personality disor-

Even when no such serious psychological problems develop, those who were sexually abused often display a pattern of personal and social problems. Abused individuals in psychotherapy have more difficulties with sexuality and relationships than do others in psychotherapy, for instance. And women who have been victimized often have difficulty becoming sexually aroused. Ironically, others engage in sex compulsively.

Abused women often feel isolated, remain distrustful of men and see themselves as unattractive. "Some [victims] become phobic about intimacy. They can't be touched," says Gail Ericson, a social worker at the Branford Counseling Center in Connecticut. "These women feel rotten about themselves—especially their bodies." As a group, adults who were sexually abused as children consistently have lower self-esteem than others. Other studies have found abuse victims to be more anxious, depressed and guilt-ridden.

Might there be a connection between the high incidence of child sexual abuse among girls and the fact that women tend, in general, to score lower on measures of self-esteem than men? Bagley believes that this disparity may simply reflect the fact that in our society, more women are abused: Seven of ten victims are girls, so any random sampling of men and women will pick up more abused women than men,

those in Russell's survey who had been abused as children reported that they were later victims of rape or attempted rape. Abuse victims "don't know how to take care of themselves," Courtois says. "They're easy targets for somebody, waiting for victimization to happen." This may be due to poor self-image, lack of assertiveness or the feeling that they deserve to be punished.

Women, of course, are not to blame for being victims. "In a society that raises males to behave in a predatory fashion toward females, undermining a young girl's defenses is likely to be exceedingly perilous for her," Russell says, since childhood abuse "could

that the prognosis is particularly bad for those who have been abused by more than one person. Counselor Claire Walsh, director of the Sexual Assault Recovery Service at the University of Florida, has paid special attention to this subgroup. She studied 30 women who were in psychotherapy and who had been abused by their fathers, 18 of whom had also been abused by at least one other person. Walsh found a different psychological profile for those who had been molested by more than one person, which included more anxiety, fear and flashbacks. She also believes that PTSD may show up more often when there is more than one abuser.

Another important variable is the age of the abuser. Russell found that victims are most traumatized if their abuser was between the ages of 26 and 50.

Victims seem to experience more serious problems if force is used during the abuse and if the abuser is a close relative, but evidence for these claims is not conclusive.

Obviously, large gaps remain in the research on the long-term effects of child sexual abuse. This is not very surprising given how new the field is. Most of the studies reported here have been conducted since 1980, and the five scholarly journals devoted to the subject have all been launched within the last two years. Only in 1986 was the groundwork finally laid for an American professional society dealing with sexual child abuse.

There is no question that the field already has produced striking findings. "We now clearly know that sexual abuse is a major risk factor for a lot of later mental-health problems," Finkelhor says. "What we don't yet know is who is most susceptible to these problems, how other experiences interact with abuse or what can be done."

Finkelhor adds that research on child sexual abuse "should teach all social scientists and mental-health practitioners some humility. Despite several generations of clinical expertise and knowledge of childhood development, it was only very recently that we came to see how incredibly widespread this childhood trauma is.

"It may make us realize that there are other things about childhood that we don't have a clear perspective on as well," he says.

---

*S**INCE GIRLS IN OUR SOCIETY ARE ABUSED MORE COMMONLY THAN BOYS, PERHAPS IT'S UNDERSTANDABLE THAT WOMEN, AS A GROUP, HAVE LOWER SELF-ESTEEM THAN MEN.***

---

perhaps enough of a difference to account for the gender gap in self-esteem.

In one study, Bagley discovered that half of all women with psychological problems had been abused. "The reason for the higher rate [of psychopathology] for women is the higher rate of sexual abuse in women," he says. Other researchers might not support so sweeping a conclusion, but Bagley points to a study of his that showed that nonabused men and women have comparable self-esteem.

One of the most disturbing findings about child abuse is its strong intergenerational pattern: Boys who are abused are far more likely to turn into offenders, molesting the next generation of children; girls are more likely to produce children who are abused. Two of five abused children in a study conducted by Sauzier, psychologist Beverly Gomes-Schwartz and psychiatrist Jonathan Horowitz had mothers who were themselves abused.

In addition, victimization can lead to revictimization. Nearly two-thirds of

have stripped away some of [her] potential ability to protect" herself.

Men who were abused, meanwhile, are likely to be confused about their sexual identity, deeply ashamed, unwilling to report the experience and apt to respond aggressively. Says Jack Rusinoff, a counselor in Minneapolis who works with male victims, "I have one 5-year-old boy who's already on the road to being an abuser." This boy, like many others, has displayed sexual aggression, even at this age. Langelier, who has seen more than 200 victims over the last three years, notes that her young male clients are sometimes caught reaching for others' genitals or "making demands for sexual stimulation."

Is there any indication, given this variation in psychological outcome, why one case of childhood sexual abuse leads to serious adult problems while another does not? So far, only two characteristics of abuse have consistently been linked with major difficulties later on. For one, studies by Bagley, Briere and others have shown

*A child can be expected to behave well
only if his parents live by the values they teach*

PUNISHMENT
VERSUS
DISCIPLINE

BRUNO BETTELHEIM

MANY PARENTS WONDER WHAT IS THE BEST WAY TO teach their children discipline. But the majority of those who have asked my opinions on discipline have spoken of it as something that parents impose on children, rather than something that parents instill in them. What they really seem to have in mind is punishment—in particular, physical punishment.

Unfortunately, punishment teaches a child that those who have power can force others to do their will. And when the child is old enough and able, he will try to use such force himself—for instance, punishing his parents by acting in ways most distressing to them. Thus parents would be well advised to keep in mind Shakespeare's words: "They that have power to hurt and will do none. . . . They rightly do inherit heaven's graces." Among those graces is being loved and emulated by one's children.

Any punishment sets us against the person who inflicts it on us. We must remember that injured feelings can be much more lastingly hurtful than physical pain.

A once common example of both physical and emotional punishment is washing out a child's mouth with soap because the child has used bad language. While the procedure is only uncomfortable, rather than painful, the degradation the child experiences is great. Without consciously knowing it the child responds not only to the obvious message that he said something bad but also to the implicit message that the parent views his insides as dirty and bad—that the child himself is vile. In the end the parent's goal—to eliminate bad language from the child's vocabulary—is rarely achieved. Instead, the punishment serves to convince the child that although the parent is very much concerned with overt behavior, he is completely uninterested in whatever annoyance compelled the child to use bad language. It convinces him that the parent is interested only in what he wants, and not in what the child wants. If this is so, the child in his inner being reasons, then why shouldn't he too be interested only in what he wants, and ignore the wishes of his parent?

I have known children who, upon having their mouths washed out with soap, stopped saying bad words out loud but continually repeated the words to themselves, responding to even the slightest frustration with streams of silent vituperation. Their anger made them unable to form any good relationships, which made them angrier still, which made them think up worse swear words.

Even if a child feels he has done wrong, he senses that there must be some better way to correct him than by inflicting physical or emotional pain. When we experience painful or degrading punishment, most of us learn to avoid situations that lead to it; in this respect punishment is effective. However, punishment teaches foremost the desirability of not getting caught, so the child who before punishment was open in his actions now learns to hide them and becomes devious. The more hurtful the punishment, the more devious the child will become.

Like the criminal who tries to get a more lenient sentence by asserting that he knows he has done wrong, our children learn to express remorse when we expect them to. Usually they are sorry only that they have been found out and may be punished. Thus we should not be fooled when they tell us that they know they did wrong, and we certainly should not extract such an admission from them, since it is essentially worthless—made to pacify us or to get the reckoning over with.

It is much better to tell a child that we are sure that if he had known he was doing wrong he would not have done so. This is nearly always the case. The child may have thought, "If my father finds out, he will be angry," but this is very different from believing that what one is doing is wrong. At any moment a child believes that whatever he is doing is fully justified. If he takes a forbidden cookie, to his mind the intensity of his desire justifies the act. Later, parental criticism or punishment may convince him that the price he has to pay for his act is too high. But this is a realization after the event.

When we tell a child that we disapprove of what he has done but are convinced that his intentions were good, our positive approach will make it relatively easy for him to listen to us and not close his mind in defense against what we have to say. And while he still might not like our objecting, he will covet our good opinion of him enough to want to retain it, even if that entails a sacrifice.

Although we may be annoyed when our children do wrong, we ought to remember Freud's observation that the voice of reason, though soft, is insistent. Shouting will not help us. It may shock a child into doing our will, but he knows and we know that it is not the voice of reason. Our task is to create situations in which reason can be heard. If we become emotional, as we are apt to do when we are upset about our child's undisciplined behavior and anxious about what it may foretell about his future, then we are not likely to speak with this soft voice of reason. And when the child is upset by fear of our displeasure, not to mention when he is anxious about what we may do to him, then he is in no position to listen well, if at all, to this soft voice.

Even the kindest and most well-intentioned parent will sometimes become exasperated. The difference between the good and the not-so-good parent in such situations is that the good parent will realize that his exasperation probably has more to do with himself than with what the child did, and that showing his exasperation will not be to anyone's advantage. The good parent makes an effort to let his passions cool. The not-so-good parent, in contrast, believes that his exasperation was caused only by his child and that therefore he has every right to act on it.

The fundamental issue is not punishment at all but the development of morality—that is, the creation of conditions that not only allow but strongly induce a child to wish to be a moral, disciplined person. If we succeed in attaining this goal, then there will be no occasion to think of punishment. But even setting aside the goal of inspiring ethical behavior, punishing one's child is, I believe, undesirable in every respect but one: it allows the discharge of parental anger and aggression.

There is little question that when a child has seriously misbehaved, a reasonable punishment may clear the air. By acting on his annoyance and anxiety, the parent finds relief; freed of these upsetting emotions, he may feel some-

what bad about having punished the child, maybe even a bit guilty about having done so, but much more positive about his child. The child, for his part, no longer feels guilty about what he has done. In the eyes of the parent he has paid the penalty; in his own eyes, usually, he has more than paid it.

In this manner parent and child, freed of emotions that bothered them and stood between them, can feel that peace has been restored to each of them and between them. But is this the best way to attain the long-range goal: to help the child become a person who acts ethically? Does the experience of having a parent who acts self-righteously or violently produce in the child the wish to act ethically on his own? Does that experience increase the child's respect for and trust in his parent? Would it not have been better, from the standpoint of deterrence and moral growth, if the child had had to struggle longer with his guilt? Isn't guilt—the pangs of conscience—a much better and more lasting deterrent than the fear of punishment? Acting in line with the urgings of one's conscience surely makes for a more responsible and sturdy personality than acting out of fear.

Punishment is a traumatic experience not only in itself but also because it disappoints the child's wish to believe in the benevolence of the parent, on which his sense of security rests. Therefore, as is true for many traumatic experiences, punishment can be subject to repression.

A good case can be made that adults who remember childhood punishments as positive experiences do so because the negative aspects were so severe that they had to be completely repressed or denied. When the punished child reaches adulthood, he remembers only the relief that came with the re-establishment of positive feelings—with the reconciliation that followed the punishment. But this does not mean that at the time the punishment was inflicted it was not detrimental. As far as I know, no child claims right after being punished that it did him a lot of good.

PROBABLY NONE OF THE COMMON TRANSGRESSIONS OF childhood upsets parents more than stealing. What disturbs them most is usually not the thefts themselves—bad as they are. It is the idea that their children may grow up to be thieves. But a child has no intention of becoming a criminal when he takes some small item, and he can be deeply hurt when his parents react as if he might become one. The child nearly always knows that he has done wrong, and if his parents are dissatisfied with him, he understands, but if they are anxious about him, his self-esteem is shaken. We ought not to view what the child has done as a crime. According to law, a child cannot commit a crime. So why should we be more severe with our child than the law would be?

I am not saying that parents should disregard what their child does. The reactions of a child's parents strongly influence the formation of that child's personality. Any transgression that parents consider serious requires an appropriate response, so that the child can learn. If a child's error remains unrecognized, or is made light of, he is likely to feel encouraged to repeat what he has done, maybe even on a larger scale. (This is why it is important for parents to be aware of what their child is doing—what he's been up to when, say, he acquires a new possession of unknown origin.) But though parents should take seriously what their child does, they should not make more of it than the child can comprehend as justified.

Clearly, a child must not be permitted to enjoy ill-gotten goods. He must immediately restore what he has taken to its rightful owner, with the appropriate apologies. If some damage has been done, the owner must be adequately compensated. Every child can understand the necessity of this, even though he might be afraid to approach the owner.

Having the child see the owner all by himself is usually not the best idea. When we supervise, we can be sure of the manner in which he returns what he has taken. More important, the child can observe directly how embarrassed we are by what he has done. One of the worst experiences a child can have is to realize that he has embarrassed his parents in front of a stranger. If we punish the child in addition to putting him through such an experience, we may considerably weaken the impression we have made. The child's sense of guilt usually centers more on the pain he has caused us than on the misdeed itself. For this reason punishment is a weak deterrent: it makes the offender so angry at those who inflict it that his sense of guilt is diminished.

It may make little difference to parents who fear for their child's future whether the child has stolen from them or from others. Parents tend to lump those two actions together in their minds. But for the child, taking things from a member of the family and taking things from a stranger are entirely different matters. We do him an injustice if we do not discriminate between these two situations. We also hamper our efforts to set things straight in the present and to prevent repetitions in the future.

Most children are occasionally tempted to take some small change from their parents. The reasons are manifold. The child wishes to buy something he longs for; he wishes to find out how observant his parents are, with respect both to their own possessions and to those the child acquires; he wishes to make his parents aware of how desperately he wants something. He may wish to keep up with his friends, or to buy their friendship. He may wish to punish the person from whom he takes something.

Parents ought to be careful not to be satisfied with the idea that their child took something, such as money, simply to indulge himself. In my experience, whenever a child—especially a middle-class child, whose needs are well taken care of—takes something from a relative, the attitude of the child toward that relative is always an important factor. For example, the child may take from a sibling because he thinks that this sibling receives more from his parents than he does. Or perhaps the child thinks that his parents have deprived him unnecessarily, or that they have shortchanged him in some way. In such cases the child thinks that he is merely correcting an unfair situation. Simply asking why the child took from one family member rather than from another may be instructive—revealing, for example, that he was angry at this person, or

that the person's negligence tempted him. But parents can elicit such important information only if they remain calm. A child is not likely to be able to discover or reveal his motives when pressed to do so by people who are very angry with him or who think they know what he is going to say.

The deepest concern of most parents is their child and his future development, not their loss, which in most cases is relatively small. But a child has a hard time realizing this unless his parents go out of their way to make it clear, by trying to understand what motivated his action. Only the child's conviction that his parents care a great deal for him—not for his future, but for him right now—will strongly motivate him to preserve their good opinion of him, by striving to do nothing that is wrong in their eyes.

Children tend not to view family possessions the way their parents do. So much that is around the house is free to be used by all family members that children may have a hard time drawing the line. Moreover, if parents play loose with their child's possessions, they ought to expect that the child might be at least tempted to do the same with their possessions.

Because of his dependence on the family, the child often has a keener sense of family—on an intuitive, subconscious level—than do his parents. Being a more primitive person, he experiences things in much more primitive and direct ways. It is *his* family; it must be *his* for him to feel secure and to be able to grow up well. If so, is not then everything that is the family's property also his? If he belongs to his parents, and they belong to him, then don't silly objects—silly by comparison with the importance of persons—such as money or other valuables that belong to his parents also belong to him? When all family possessions were really that—possessions of the family, not the private property of individual family members—perhaps the sense of family was stronger and gave each family member more security than people now experience.

We can instill in our children a much deeper feeling of family cohesiveness if we make it clear that—within reason—family property is for everyone's use. This includes relatively small amounts of money or minor valuables, the expenditure or loss of which cannot jeopardize the family's future.

THE ORIGINAL DEFINITION OF THE WORD *DISCIPLINE* refers to an instruction to be imparted to disciples. When one thinks about this definition, it becomes clear that one cannot impart anything, whether discipline or knowledge, that one does not possess oneself. Also it is obvious that acquiring discipline and being a disciple are intimately related.

Most of us when hearing or using the word *disciple* are likely to be reminded of the biblical Apostles. Their deepest wish was to emulate Christ. They made him their guide not just because they believed in his teachings but because of their love for him and his love for them. Without such mutual love the Master's teaching and example, convincing though they were, would never have persuaded the disciples to change their lives and beliefs as radically as they did.

The story of Christ's disciples suggests that love and admiration are powerful motives for adopting a person's values and ideas. By the same token, the combination of teaching, example, and mutual love is most potent in preventing one from going against what this admired individual stands for, even when one is tempted to do so. Thus the most reliable method of instilling desirable values and a discipline based on these values into the minds of our children should be obvious.

Probably the only way for an undisciplined person to acquire discipline is through admiring and emulating someone who *is* disciplined. This process is greatly helped if the disciple believes that even if he is not *the* favorite of the master, at least he is one of the favorites. Such a belief further motivates the disciple to form himself in the image of the master—to identify with him.

Fortunately, the younger the child, the more he wishes to admire his parents. In fact, he cannot do other than admire them, because he needs to believe in their perfection in order to be able to feel safe himself. And in whose image can the young child form himself but in that of one or both of the parents, or whoever functions in their place? Nobody else is as close and as important to him as they are; nobody else loves him as much or takes such good care of him. It is for these reasons, too, that the child wishes to believe that he is his parents' favorite. Sibling rivalry is caused by the fear that he might not be the favorite, and that one of his siblings is. How acutely a child suffers from sibling rivalry is a clear indication of how great his wish is to be the parents' favorite, and how consuming his fear is that he is not.

It is natural and probably unavoidable for parents sometimes to prefer one of their children to others. Parents sometimes fool themselves into believing that they love all their children equally, but this is rarely the case. At best, a parent will like each of his children very much—most parents do—but he will like each child in different ways, and for different reasons. Most parents love one child more at one time and another more at another time, which is only natural, because children behave differently at various moments in their lives and thus evoke different emotional reactions in their parents. But if a child has reason to feel that he is the favorite some of the time, he is likely to believe that he is the favorite most of the time. In this situation, as in so many others, the wish is father to the thought. All of this works, of course, only if the child is not too often and too severely disappointed by the attitudes of his parents.

As the child grows older, he will cease to admire his parents so single-mindedly. By comparison with the wider circle of people he gets to know as he grows up, his parents will seem deficient in some respects. However, while the child may admire his parents less and question aspects of their behavior, his need to admire them unconditionally is so deeply rooted that it will be powerfully present in his

unconscious for a long time—at least until he reaches maturity, if not longer. Thus, fortunately, in most families there is a solid basis for the child's wish to be his parents' disciple—to be able to love and admire them, and to emulate them, if not in all then certainly in some very important respects, and if not in his conscious then certainly in his unconscious mind.

We all know families in which this is not the case—in which the parents do not like their child very much, are disappointed in him, or do not behave so that the child can love and admire them. When a child neither admires his parents nor wishes to emulate them, he will not become disciplined under their influence. How can he, when they are not suitable models?

Such a child often finds some other person to admire, whose favorite he wishes to be, and whom he therefore comes to emulate, acquiring discipline in order to find favor in this person's eyes. The trouble is that the child is likely to seek and find an undisciplined master. An example of this syndrome is the member of a delinquent gang who is so impressed by its delinquent or otherwise asocial leader that he admires and emulates him, with disastrous consequences for the youngster and for society. On some level the youngster may know that he has not chosen well, but his need to attach himself to someone whom he can admire, and who seems to offer acceptance and security in return, is so great that it drowns out the voice of reason. It is on their child's need for such an attachment that parents can and must build in order to promote not just disciplined behavior of the child around particular issues—this is not all that difficult to obtain—but a lasting inner commitment to be, or at least to become, a disciplined person.

It is by no means easy for a child to become disciplined. Often part of the reason is that his parents are not very well disciplined themselves and thus do not provide clear models for their child to follow. Another difficulty is that parents try to teach self-discipline to their child in ways that arouse his resistance rather than his interest. And still another difficulty is that a child responds to his parents most readily—both positively and negatively—when he sees that their emotional involvement is strong. When parents act with little self-discipline, they show their emotions. When they get their emotions under control, they are nearly always again able to act in line with their normal standards of discipline. Rare as it may be for a parent to lose control, those are the times that impress a child most. Disciplined behavior, while pleasing and reassuring to the child and likely to make life good for him in the long run, does not make such a strong impression on him.

For these and many other reasons teaching discipline requires great patience on the part of the teacher. The acquisition of true inner discipline, which will be an important characteristic of one's personality and behavior, requires many years of apprenticeship. The process is so slow that in retrospect it seems unremarkable—as if it were natural and easy. And yet if parents could only remember how undisciplined they themselves once were and how hard a time they had as children in disciplining themselves—if they could remember how put upon, if not abused, they felt when their parents forced them to behave well against their will—then they and their children would be much better off. One of the world's greatest teachers, Goethe, wrote an epigram that turns on this very point: "Tell me how bear you so comfortably/The arrogant conduct of maddening youth?/Had I too not once behaved unbearably,/They would be unbearable in truth." Goethe could write these lines and enjoy their humor because he had achieved great inner security, which made it possible for him to understand with amusement the otherwise "unbearable" behavior of the young. The same feeling of security allowed him to remember how difficult—unbearable, even—he himself had been in his younger years, which many of us are tempted to forget, if our self-love does not compel us to repress or deny it.

Despite all the obstacles that parents encounter in trying to impart discipline to their children, they are the logical persons to do so, because the learning has to start so early and continue for so long. But while most parents are ready to teach their children discipline and know that they are the ones to do so, they are less ready to accept the idea that they can teach only by example. Unfortunately, the maxim "Do as I say, not as I do" won't work with children. Whether they obey our orders or not, deep down they are influenced less by what we tell them than they are by who we are and what we do. Our children form themselves in reaction to us: the more they love us, the more they emulate us, and the more they respond positively to our consciously held values and to those of which we are not conscious but which also influence our actions. The less they like and admire us, the more negatively they respond to us in forming their personalities.

A study conducted in Sweden demonstrates how persuasive the example set by the parents can be to a child. Some years ago the Swedish government became concerned because undisciplined behavior among Swedish teenagers—as indicated by alcoholism, vandalism, delinquency, drug use, and criminal behavior—had become prevalent. To find out why some children become troublesome and others did not, researchers compared the homes of law-abiding teenagers with those of delinquents. They found that neither material assets nor social class exercised a statistically significant influence on the behavior of these young people. Instead, what was decisive was the emotional atmosphere of the home.

Teenagers who behaved well tended to have parents who were themselves responsible, upright, and self-disciplined—who lived in accord with the values they professed and encouraged their children to follow suit. When the good teenagers were exposed, as part of the investigation, to problem teenagers, their behavior was not permanently affected. They had far too securely internalized their parents' values. While some, out of curiosity, joined the activities of the delinquent or drug-using group, such experimentation was always tentative and shortlived. By the same token, when problem teenagers were forced to associate solely with "square" peers, they showed no significant improvement. Indeed, they did not even temporarily adopt nondelinquent ways of living.

The Swedish researchers found that undisciplined, asocial, problem teenagers did not necessarily come from what one would consider undisciplined or disorganized homes, nor did they have visibly asocial parents. But the parents of the asocial youngsters did tend to have conflicting values or to be inconsistent in putting their values into practice. And they tended to try to hold their children to values that they themselves did not live by. As a result the children had not been able to internalize those values. Expected by their parents to be more disciplined than the examples set, most of the children turned out to be much less so.

Further study of the family backgrounds of these youngsters revealed that it hardly mattered what specific values the parents embraced—whether the parents were conservative or progressive in the views they held, strict or permissive in the ways in which they brought up their children. What made the difference was how closely the parents lived by the values that they tried to teach their children.

A parent who respects himself will feel no need to demand or command respect from his child, since he feels no need for the child's respect to buttress his security as a parent or as a person. Secure in himself, he will not feel his authority threatened and will accept it when his child sometimes shows a lack of respect for him, as young children, in particular, are apt to do. The parent's self-respect tells him that such displays arise from immaturity of judgment, which time and experience will eventually correct.

Demanding or commanding respect reveals to the child an insecure parent who lacks the conviction that his way of life will, all by itself, over time, gain him the child's respect. Not trusting that respect will come naturally, this parent has to insist on it right now. Who would wish to form himself in the image of an insecure person, even if that person is his parent? Unfortunately, the child of insecure parents often becomes an insecure person himself, because insecure parents cannot inculcate security in their children or create an environment in which the children can develop a sense of security on their own.

To be disciplined requires self-control. To be controlled by others and to accept living by their rules or orders makes it superfluous to control oneself. When the more important aspects of a child's actions and behavior are controlled by, say, his parents or teachers, he will see no need to learn to control himself; others do it for him.

How parents in other cultures try to inculcate self-control in their children can be instructive. Consider, for example, a study designed to find out why young Japanese do much better academically than Americans. When the researchers studied maternal behavior they saw clear differences between the Japanese and the Americans. Typically, when young American children ran around in supermarkets, their mothers—often annoyed—told them, "Stop that!" or "I told you not to act this way!" Japanese mothers typically refrained entirely from telling their children what to do. Instead they asked them questions, such as "How do you think it makes the storekeeper feel when you run around like this in his store?" or "How do you think it makes me feel when my child runs around as you do?'' Similarly, the American mother, wanting her child to eat what he was supposed to eat, would order the child to do so or tell him that he ought to eat it because it was good for him. The Japanese mother would ask her child a question, such as ''How do you think it makes the man who grew these vegetables for you to eat feel when you reject them?'' or ''How do you think it makes these carrots that grew so that you could eat them feel when you do not eat them?'' Thus from a very early age the American child is told what to do, while the Japanese child is encouraged not only to consider other persons' feelings but to control himself on the basis of his own deliberations.

The reason for the higher academic achievement of Japanese youngsters may well be that the Japanese child in situations important to his mother is invited to think things out on his own, a habit that stands him in good stead when he has to master academic material. The American child, in contrast, is expected to conform his decisions and actions to what he is told to do. This expectation certainly does not encourage him to do his own thinking.

The Japanese mother does not just expect her child to be able to arrive at good decisions. She also makes an appeal to her child not to embarrass her. In the traditional Japanese culture losing face is among the worst things that can happen to a person. When a mother asks, "How do you think it makes me—or the storekeeper—feel when you act this way?" she implies that by mending his ways the child does her, or the storekeeper, a very great favor. To be asked to do one's own thinking and to act accordingly, as well as to be told that one is able to do someone a favor, enhances one's self-respect, while to be ordered to do the opposite of what one wants is destructive of it.

WHAT IS A PARENT TO DO IN THE SHORT RUN TO prevent a child from misbehaving, as children are apt to do from time to time? Ideally, letting a child know of our disappointment should be effective and should lead the child to abstain from repeating the wrongdoing in the future. Realistically, even if a child has great love and respect for us, his parents, simply telling him of our disappointment, or showing him how great it is, will not always suffice to remedy the situation.

When our words are not enough, when telling our child to mend his ways is ineffective, then the threat of the withdrawal of our love and affection is the only sound method to impress on him that he had better conform to our request. Subconsciously recognizing how powerful a threat this is, some parents, with the best of intentions, destroy its effectiveness by assuring their children that they love them no matter what. This might well be true, but it does not sound convincing to a child, who knows that he does not love his parents no matter what, such as when they are angry at him; so how can he believe them when he can tell that they are dissatisfied, and maybe even angry at him? Most of us do not really love un-

conditionally. Therefore any effort to make ourselves look better, to pretend to be more loving than we are, will have the opposite effect from the one we desire. True, our love for our child can be so deep, so firmly anchored in us, that it will withstand even very severe blows. But at the moment when we are seriously disappointed in the child, our love may be at a low point, and if we want the child to change his ways, he might as well know it.

The action to take is to banish the child from our presence. We may send him out of the room or we ourselves may withdraw. Whatever, the parent is clearly indicating, "I am so disappointed in you that I do not wish, or feel unable, to maintain physical closeness with you." Here physical distance stands for emotional distance, and it is a symbol that speaks to the child's conscious and unconscious at the same time. This is why the action is so effective.

Sending the child out of sight permits both parent and child to gain distance from what has happened, to cool off, to reconsider. And that does help. But it is the threat of desertion, as likely as not, that permanently impresses the child. Separation anxiety is probably the earliest and most basic anxiety of man. The infant experiences it when his prime caretaker absents herself from him, an absence that, should it become permanent and the caretaker not be replaced, would indeed lead to the infant's death. Anything that rekindles this anxiety is experienced as a terrible threat. Hence, as long as a child believes, however vaguely, that his very existence is in danger if his prime caretaker deserts him, he will respond to this real, implied, or imagined threat with deep feelings of anxiety. Even when he is old enough to know that his life is not in real danger, he will respond to separation from a parent with severe feelings of dejection, because to some degree he will feel as if he were endangered. The difference is that at an older age the fear is not of physical but of emotional starvation.

If we should have any doubt that physical separation can be an effective expression of our disgust with a child's behavior, we can look to our children themselves to set us straight. The worst that a child can think of when he is disgusted with his parents is that he will run away. He makes such a threat because he is convinced that it is so terrible that it will compel us to mend our ways. Clearly, a child understands very well that when we threaten to distance ourselves from him physically we are threatening to distance ourselves from him emotionally. That threat makes a very deep impression.

We must be honest about our strong emotional reactions to our children's behavior, showing our children how deeply we love them, on the one hand, and, on the other, letting them know when we are disappointed in them, provided we do not become critical or punitive. This is all just part of being ourselves. We need not make any claim to be perfect. But if we strive as best we can to live good lives ourselves, our children, impressed by the merits of living good lives, will one day wish to do the same.

The Myth About Teen-Agers

Richard Flaste

Richard Flaste is Science and Health Editor of The New York Times.

A FATHER I KNOW TELLS of one unsettling moment when he was sure he would never understand the teen-age mind. The mind in question was that of his own teen-ager, a 15-year-old blonde possessed of considerable charm and an aggressive reticence. The pivotal moment was this effort at conversation:

"So, how was your day at school?"

"Good."

"Was it more than just good? I mean, did anything actually happen that was interesting?"

"No, it was just good."

"What about the bio test? Didn't you have a test?"

(The answer this time came with a gleam of irritation in her eyes.) "I told you, everything was *good.*"

He backed away, feeling foolish, sorry he had tried, sorry he'd stirred her pique. What could possibly be going on in her mind? And he wondered about himself, too, as he slipped away into a friendlier room. Was he actually afraid of her?

Later, having thought about that scene many times, he concluded that he had in fact been frightened, but not so much of her — after all, they had their good times, and she did seem to love and respect him at least every now and then. Rather it was the condition of adolescence that scared him. On occasions like that abortive effort at conversation he wasn't just confronting a teen-ager who might or might not be in the mood to talk to him but also everything he had ever heard about adolescence, the Sturm, the Drang and the plain old orneriness of it. That flash of annoyance in her eyes was all that was necessary to evoke an image of those infamous raging hormones boiling inside a pubescent caldron.

The burden was a heavy one to take into a small inquiry about a person's day. It was an unnecessary burden, too. For, although most of us aren't aware of it, the concept of adolescence as a period of angry, dark turmoil has largely been overthrown, and along with it the idea that kids need to be tormented and perverse to make the storm-tossed transition to adulthood. That concept is being replaced by a new psychology of adolescence, a growing body of work that reflects a vigorous attempt to find out what life is genuinely like for normal teen-agers, and which reveals that delight plays as large a role among most adolescents as misery does.

A substantial number of psychotherapists and personality theorists still believe that adolescence is a trial by fire, as do many writers of juvenile fiction. But what is now the mainstream of psychological research dismisses this emphasis on turmoil as balderdash. It is a misguided emphasis, many researchers say, which grew out of the overwrought imaginations of romanticists ranging from the Freuds (mostly Anna) to Goethe (particularly, "The Sorrows of Young Werther").

In the 1970's, I wrote regularly about child-development issues for this newspaper, and I accepted the idea that any teen-ager was necessarily a little mad. To a large extent this notion was promoted by the psychoanalytic literature, but it was embraced by many of us as a handy way to explain hard times with our teen-agers. We could say that noxious behavior such as naked aggression was normal, and so we didn't have to worry. We reassured ourselves constantly, usually with a knowing laugh about the craziness of teen-agers. But I did not believe it completely. Why should only this age group carry the label of madness? Coming back to the question now, I am struck by how different the mood among many psychologists and psychiatrists is. By and large, they are more determined to draw an empirical and detailed picture of the varied and complex adolescent experience.

Some researchers have surveyed thousands of teen-agers to learn what they believe about themselves and their families. Others have given youngsters beepers to carry around, so that when they are signaled they will report their moods at that moment. And still others have worked with families, asking parents, teen-agers and their siblings to take batteries of tests.

Among the most influential of this cadre of researchers is Dr. Daniel Offer of the University of Chicago, a psychiatrist who believes that the widespread idea that the teen years are unavoidably insane has mischaracterized the lives of millions of people. Moreover, he contends that the emphasis on turmoil has created the expectation of Sturm and Drang for every teen-ager, thereby masking the serious emotional difficulties of a significant minority of adolescents who need professional help. Dr. Offer was moved to declare a "Defense of Adolescents" in The Journal of the American Medical Association, and he made a presentation along the same lines to the convention of the American Psychiatric Association last May.

Dr. Offer's team was among the earliest to plumb the day-to-day feelings of large numbers of teen-agers. Their first explorations, in the 1960's, began to reveal that, incredible as it might have seemed, most teen-agers were happy most of the time. After years of confirmatory work, he confidently told the psychiatrists' convention that "the vast majority of adolescents are well-adjusted, get along well with their peers and their parents, adjust well to the mores and values of their social environment and cope well with their internal and external worlds." Dr. Offer recalled in a recent interview that this message disturbed some of his colleagues, because they didn't believe that teen-agers' responses to questions could be trusted.

The work of Dr. Offer and his team has provided a starting point for many of the nation's researchers. By no means do they make adolescence out to be an easy time, any more than life as a whole is easy. Adolescence is a period of rapid and profound change in the body and mind. It is a time to find out who you are and

Adolescence is a time when you begin to find out who you are.

to begin to move toward what you will become. Family bickering is bound to escalate during this period, but it usually centers on what one psychologist calls the "good-citizen topics," such as chores, dress and schoolwork. Most researchers feel that this conflict is useful, because it allows a teen-ager to assert his or her individuality over relatively minor issues.

There are several explanations for this rise in family quarreling. A widely cited cognitive explanation comes from the work of the Swiss psychologist Jean Piaget, who showed that children do not have the capacity for the abstract, analytical thinking he called "formal operations" until the teen years. The arrival of that tool is what enables them, in the view of some experts, to question their parents' thinking.

Research by Judith G. Smetana, an associate professor of education, psychology and pediatrics at the University of Rochester, has recently aroused much interest among psychologists. She contends that concentrating on the development of a child's ability to think logically isn't useful in elucidating family relationships. Instead, she focuses on the way parents and children conceptualize their experiences. According to her research, there are two fundamentally different world views at the core of family conflict: adolescents tend to see much of their behavior as a "personal" matter, affecting no one but themselves and therefore up to them entirely, while their parents tend to hold to what she calls "conventional thinking," which sees society's rules and expectations as primary. The dichotomy provides for commonplace clashes:

"Clean up your room. This family does not live in a hovel."

"It's my room and I like hovels."

In a recent paper Smetana charts the typical evolution from personal to conventional thinking in a teen-ager. A child of 12 or 13 generally has no use for conventions when it comes to family issues. Between 14 and 16 the teen-ager comes to recognize conventions as the way society regulates itself. Then comes a brief period in which conventions are rejected again, but more thoughtfully. Between 18 and 25 conventions are seen as playing an important and admirable role in facilitating the business of society.

As the teen-ager moves in fits and starts in the direction of his or her parents, the parents generally stick to their guns. Nevertheless, the adolescent has begun to reason like them, and so, by the age of 15 or 16, the quarreling usually subsides, at least for a while.

It is replaced by a period in which members of the family are able to negotiate more successfully than in the past. The teen-ager learns how to "work on mom and dad" to achieve goals like staying out late at night or using the family car.

Indeed, "negotiation" has emerged as one of the key words in the new psychology of adolescence. Instead of talking about rebellion and a painful separation from the family, many psychologists now see adolescence as a time in which parents and children negotiate new relationships with one another. The teen-ager must gain more authority over his or her own life; the parents must come to see their child as more nearly an equal, with a right to differing opinions.

Parents often mistake normal self-assertion for rebellion and defiance.

Another way of looking at this period of negotiation has been formulated by psychologists Harold D. Grotevant at the University of Texas at Austin and Catherine R. Cooper at the University of California, Santa Cruz. They believe that typically there is an elaborate interplay between a teen-ager's striving to be an individual who is separate from the family and his attempts to maintain a close, caring relationship with his parents. In a recent study they found that teen-agers who had the strongest sense of themselves as individuals were raised in families where the parents offered guidance and comfort but also permitted their children to develop their own points of view.

For some families, this can be a terrible period. Parents who try to exert too much control over their children and find it impossible to yield in a conflict can be driven into a frenzy by the efforts of their teen-agers to establish their own identities. But most parents are more pliable, and find ways to compromise.

A neighbor of mine, unlucky enough to have a son who became a teen-ager when punk was hot, remembers how uncontrollably rattled she would get when she saw him dressed for school in the morning. "He would throw on any rag, this way and that," she recalls. She couldn't contain her exasperation and her fear that this monstrous style of dressing would somehow reflect on her. She imagined that others might pity her for her misfortune. After repeated failed confrontations, she decided not to come downstairs until her son was gone. It seems to her now that he dressed a little more sensibly if he knew she wouldn't be there to see it.

The influence of peers in everything from dress to sexual mores is undeniably strong during the teen-age years, although some experts downplay it because, like turmoil, it's been given more press than they think it's worth, and because they believe the emphasis on peers underestimates the importance of continuing attachments to the family. Parents may find it comforting to realize that this growing influence of friends is not the first assault on their authority. Throughout most of a child's life—not just in adolescence—parents share control with others: teachers, friends, siblings. After the earliest years parents are no longer in a position to know about whole segments of their children's lives, because so much takes place outside the home. Gerald R. Adams, a psychologist at Utah State University, making this point in a recent conversation, said, "If I interviewed your family, you'd be shocked at how little you know about the life of your child—school life, social life. Most parents don't really know the world of their children."

There are many things that children don't tell us because they know we won't approve, even if we are trying very hard to give them a measure of greater freedom. Who among us really wants to know everything about a child's sexual experimentation or moments of embarrassment?

But that isn't the only reason for reticence. Sometimes, teen-agers, like the rest of us, just don't feel like talking. The notorious moodiness of teen-agers is one of the most interesting areas of the latest psychological investigations. Dr. Offer says that he has found little tendency among normal teen-agers to plummet into deep and dark despair. (He points out that, although teen-age suicide is a deeply troubling phenomenon, the suicide rate for adolescents is lower than it is for people in their 20's and far lower than it is for people in their 70's.)

Reed Larson, a psychologist at the University of Illinois, has found a middle ground between coloring all of adolescence with dark moods or dismissing moodiness altogether. In studies carried out by giving kids beepers that signaled them when to report their feelings, he found that mood swings are a fact of teen-age life. On average, adolescents feel more delight and more sadness at any given moment than adults and move from one mood to another more rapidly. For teen-agers, emotional states generally last no more than 15 minutes. Even the strongest feelings tend not to last more than a half-hour, while the same kinds of feelings may last for two hours or longer among adults. But Larson and his colleagues concluded that these mood swings are healthy and natural, a reasonable response to a time of life filled with fast-paced events. "The typical adolescent may be moody," they wrote in a recent paper, "but not in turmoil."

As word of the new insights into teen-age life gets out, parents are bound to benefit. They will learn to expect a certain amount of bickering in early adolescence, and they'll realize that it has a normal course to run. Parents might find it helpful to abandon the old vocabulary of rebellion and defiance. The words have been so widely misapplied that they are even used to characterize things like the piercing of ears against mother's wishes or staying out late. When self-assertion and self-indulgence are overdramatized by parents and viewed as rebellion or defiance, they take on the aura of criminal acts instead of being part of the fascinating interplay between parent and child in which the child eventually becomes an adult and the parent eventually accepts that.

In the case of the teen-ager who resists parental efforts at conversation, parents should realize that kids are sometimes out of sorts, or they may be too bewildered by the hectic events of their lives to find the words to describe them. Some teen-agers are more apt to engage in friendly conversation at dinner time, or just before they go to bed, than at times when the stresses of the day are still fresh. (Of course, when a teen-ager senses that his or her parents' attempts at conversation are prompted by their need to be in control, conversation will often be resisted on that ground alone.)

While a momentary rebuff or a bit of surliness should not be reason for deep concern, parents ought to worry about those moods that don't change. Teen-agers who are depressed for long periods of time, relentlessly combative, friendless, reclusive or miserable in other ways are not going through a normal adolescence; they and their families need help, perhaps professional.

Implicit in much of the new work on adolescence is the belief that parents must take a strong grip on their own sense of themselves, their own worth, so that they are not so easily shaken by every normal challenge to their control, and so that they can hold on to their children while confidently letting out some line.

Parents should find life a little easier, in any event, if the bogeyman of necessary insanity in adolescence is finally vanquished. For many parents that will mean they no longer need to fear their children's adolescence but can relax and maybe even enjoy it.

The Vintage Years

THE GROWING NUMBER OF HEALTHY, VIGOROUS OLDER PEOPLE HAS HELPED OVERCOME SOME STEREOTYPES ABOUT AGING. FOR MANY, THE BEST IS YET TO COME.

Jack C. Horn and Jeff Meer

Jack C. Horn is a senior editor and Jeff Meer is an assistant editor at the magazine.

Our society is getting older, but the old are getting younger. As Sylvia Herz told an American Psychological Association (APA) symposium on aging last year, the activities and attitudes of a 70-year-old today "are equivalent to those of a 50-year-old's a decade or two ago."

Our notions of what it means to be old are beginning to catch up with this reality. During the past several decades, three major changes have altered the way we view the years after 65:

• The financial, physical and mental health of older people has improved, making the prospect of a long life something to treasure, not fear.

• The population of older people has grown dramatically, rising from 18 million in 1965 to 28 million today. People older than 65 compose 12 percent of the population, a percentage that is expected to rise to more than 20 percent by the year 2030.

• Researchers have gained a much better understanding of aging and the lives of older people, helping to sort out the inevitable results of biological aging from the effects of illness or social and environmental problems. No one has yet found the fountain of youth, or of immortality. But research has revealed that aging itself is not the thief we once thought it was; healthy older people can maintain and enjoy most of their physical and mental abilities, and even improve in some areas.

Because of better medical care, improved diet and increasing interest in physical fitness, more people are reaching the ages of 65, 75 and older in excellent health. Their functional age—a combination of physical, psychological and social factors that affect their attitudes toward life and the roles they play in the world—is much younger than their chronological age.

Their economic health is better, too, by almost every measure. Over the last three decades, for example, the number of men and women 65 and older who live below the poverty line has dropped steadily from 35 percent in 1959 to 12 percent in 1984, the last year for which figures are available.

On the upper end of the economic scale, many of our biggest companies are headed by what once would have been called senior citizens, and many more of them serve as directors of leading companies. Even on a more modest economic level, a good portion of the United States' retired older people form a new leisure class, one with money to spend and the time to enjoy it. Obviously not all of America's older people share this prosperity. Economic hardship is particularly prevalent among minorities. But as a group, our older people are doing better than ever.

In two other areas of power, politics and the law, people in their 60s and 70s have always played important roles. A higher percentage of people from 65 to 74 register and vote than in any other group. With today's increasing vigor and numbers, their power is likely to increase still further. It is perhaps no coincidence that our current President is the oldest ever.

Changing attitudes, personal and social, are a major reason for the increasing importance of older people in our society. As psychologist

From *Psychology Today,* May 1987, pp. 76-77, 80-84, 88-90. Copyright © 1987 by PT Partners L. P. Reprinted by permission.

Bernice Neugarten points out, there is no longer a particular age at which someone starts to work or attends school, marries and has children, retires or starts a business. Increasing numbers of older men and women are enrolled in colleges, universities and other institutions of learning. According to the Center for Education Statistics, for example, the number of people 65 and older enrolled in adult education of all kinds increased from 765,000 to 866,000 from 1981 to 1984. Gerontologist Barbara Ober says that this growing interest in education is much more than a way to pass the time. ''Older people make excellent students, maybe even better students than the majority of 19- and 20-year-olds. One advantage is that they have settled a lot of the social and sexual issues that preoccupy their younger classmates.''

Older people today are not only healthier and more active; they are also increasingly more numerous. ''Squaring the pyramid'' is how some demographers describe this change in our population structure. It has always been thought of as a pyramid, a broad base of newborns supporting successively smaller tiers of older people as they died from disease, accidents, poor nutrition, war and other causes.

Today, the population structure is becoming more rectangular, as fewer people die during the earlier stages of life. The Census Bureau predicts that by 2030 the structure will be an almost perfect rectangle up to the age of 70.

The aging of America has been going on at least since 1800, when half the people in the country were younger than 16 years old, but two factors have accelerated the trend tremendously. First, the number of old people has increased rapidly. Since 1950 the number of Americans 65 and older has more than doubled to some 28 million—more than the entire current population of Canada. Within the same period, the number of individuals older than 85 has quadrupled to about 2.6 million (see ''The Oldest Old,'' this article).

Second, the boom in old people has been paired with a bust in the proportion of youngsters due to a declining birth rate. Today, fewer than one American in four is younger than 16. This drop-off has been steady, with the single exception of the post-World War II baby boom, which added 76 million children to the country between 1945 and 1964. As these baby boomers reach the age of 65, starting in 2010, they are expected to increase the proportion of the population 65 and older from its current 12 percent to 21 percent by 2030.

The growing presence of healthy, vigorous older people has helped overcome some of the stereotypes about aging and the elderly. Research has also played a major part by replacing myths with facts. While there were some studies of aging before World War II, scientific

*B*Y THE YEAR 2030 MORE THAN 20 PERCENT OF THE POPULATION IS EXPECTED TO BE 65 OR OLDER.

interest increased dramatically during the 1950s and kept growing.

Important early studies of aging included three started in the mid or late 1950s: the Human Aging Study, conducted by the National Institute of Mental Health (NIMH); the Duke Longitudinal Studies, done by the Center for the Study of Aging and Human Development at Duke University; and the Baltimore Longitudinal Study of Aging, conducted by the Gerontological Institute in Baltimore, now part of the National Institute on Aging (NIA). All three took a multidisciplinary approach to the study of normal aging: what changes take place, how people adapt to them, how biological, genetic, social, psychological and environmental characteristics relate to longevity and what can be done to promote successful aging.

These pioneering studies and hundreds of later ones have benefited from growing federal support. White House Conferences on Aging in 1961 and 1971 helped focus attention on the subject. By 1965 Congress had enacted Medicare and the Older Americans Act. During the 1970s Congress authorized the establishment of the NIA as part of the National Institutes of Health and NIMH created a special center to support research on the mental health of older people.

All these efforts have produced a tremendous growth in our knowledge of aging. In the first (1971) edition of the *Handbook of the Psychology of Aging*, it was estimated that as much had been published on the subject in the previous 15 years as in all the years before then. In the second edition, published in 1985, psychologists James Birren and Walter Cunningham wrote that the "period for this rate of doubling has now decreased to 10 years...the volume of published research has increased to the almost unmanageable total of over a thousand articles a year."

Psychologist Clifford Swenson of Purdue

University explained some of the powerful incentives for this tremendous increase: "I study the topic partly to discover more effective ways of helping old people cope with their problems, but also to load my own armamentarium against that inevitable day. For that is one aspect of aging and its problems that makes it different from the other problems psychologists study: We may not all be schizophrenic or neurotic or overweight, but there is only one alternative to old age and most of us try to avoid that alternative."

One popular misconception disputed by recent research is the idea that aging means inevitable physical and sexual failure. Some changes occur, of course. Reflexes slow, hearing and eyesight dim, stamina decreases. This *primary aging* is a gradual process that begins early in life and affects all body systems.

But many of the problems we associate with old age are *secondary aging*—the results not of age but of disease, abuse and disuse—factors often under our own control. More and more older people are healthy, vigorous men and women who lead enjoyable, active lives. National surveys by the Institute for Social Research and others show that life generally seems less troublesome and freer to older people than it does to younger adults.

In a review of what researchers have learned about subjective well-being—happiness, life satisfaction, positive emotions—University of Illinois psychologist Ed Diener reported that "Most results show a slow rise in satisfaction with age. . .young persons appear to experience higher levels of joy but older persons tend to judge their lives in more positive ways."

Money is often mentioned as the key to a happy retirement, but psychologist Daniel Ogilvie of Rutgers University has found another, much more important, factor. Once we have a certain minimum amount of money, his research shows, life satisfaction depends mainly on how much time we spend doing things we find meaningful. Ogilvie believes retirement-planning workshops and seminars should spend more time helping people decide how to use their skills and interests after they retire.

A thought that comes through clearly when researchers talk about physical and mental fitness is "use it or lose it." People rust out faster from disuse than they wear out from overuse. This advice applies equally to sexual activity. While every study from the time of Kinsey to the present shows that sexual interest and activity diminish with age, the drop varies greatly among individuals. Psychologist Marion Perlmutter and writer Elizabeth Hall have reported that one of the best predictors of continued sexual intercourse "is early sexual activity and past sexual enjoyment and frequency. People who have never had much pleasure from sexu-

WHILE THE OLD AND THE YOUNG MAY BE EQUALLY COMPETENT, THEY ARE DIFFERENTLY COMPETENT.

ality may regard their age as a good excuse for giving up sex."

They also point out that changing times affect sexual activity. As today's younger adults bring their more liberal sexual attitudes with them into old age, the level of sexual activity among older men and women may rise.

The idea that mental abilities decline steadily with age has also been challenged by many recent and not-so-recent findings (see "The Reason of Age," *Psychology Today,* June 1986). In brief, age doesn't damage abilities as much as was once believed, and in some areas we actually gain; we learn to compensate through experience for much of what we do lose; and we can restore some losses through training.

For years, older people didn't do as well as younger people on most tests used to measure mental ability. But psychologist Leonard Poon of the University of Georgia believes that researchers are now taking a new, more appropriate approach to measurement. "Instead of looking at older people's ability to do abstract tasks that have little or no relationship to what they do every day, today's researchers are examining real-life issues."

Psychologist Gisela Labouvie-Vief of Wayne State University has been measuring how people approach everyday problems in logic. She notes that older adults have usually done poorly on such tests, mostly because they fail to think logically all the time. But Labouvie-Vief argues that this is not because they have forgotten how to think logically but because they use a more complex approach unknown to younger thinkers. "The [older] thinker operates within a kind of double reality which is both formal and informal, both logical and psychological," she says.

In other studies, Labouvie-Vief has found that when older people were asked to give concise summaries of fables they read, they did so. But when they were simply asked to recall as much of the fable as possible, they concentrat-

THE OLDEST OLD: THE YEARS AFTER 85

Every man desires to live long, but no man would be old," or so Jonathan Swift believed. Some people get their wish to live long and become what are termed the "oldest old," those 85 and older. During the past 22 years, this group has increased by 165 percent to 2.5 million and now represents more than 1 percent of the population.

Who are these people and what are their lives like? One of the first to study them intensively is gerontologist Charles Longino of the University of Miami, who uses 1980 census data to examine their lives for the American Association of Retired People.

He found, not surprisingly, that nearly 70 percent are women. Of these, 82 percent are widowed, compared with 44 percent of the men. Because of the conditions that existed when they were growing up, the oldest old are poorly educated compared with young people today, most of whom finish high school. The average person now 85 years and older only completed the eighth grade.

Only one-quarter of these older citizens are in hospitals or institutions such as nursing homes, and more than half live in their own homes. Just 30 percent live by themselves. More than a third live with a spouse or with their children. There are certainly those who aren't doing well—one in six have incomes below the poverty level—but many more are relatively well-off. The mean household income for the group, Longino says, was more than $20,000 in 1985.

What of the quality of life? "In studying this group, we have to be aware of youth creep," he says. "The old are getting younger all the time." This feeling is confirmed by a report released late last year by the National Institute on Aging. The NIA report included three studies of people older than 65 conducted in two counties in Iowa, in East Boston, Massachusetts, and in New Haven, Connecticut. There are large regional differences between the groups, of course, and

they aren't a cross-section of older people in the nation as a whole. But in all three places, most of those older than 85 seem to be leading fulfilling lives.

Most socialize in a variety of ways. In Iowa, more than half say they go to religious services at least once a week and the same percentage say they belong to some type of professional, social, church-related or recreational group. More than three-quarters see at least one or two children once a month and almost that many see other close relatives that often.

As you would expect, many of the oldest old suffer from disabilities and serious health problems. At least a quarter of those who responded have been in a hospital overnight in the past year and at least 8 percent have had heart attacks or have diabetes. In Iowa and New Haven, more than 13 percent of the oldest old had cancer, while in East Boston the rate was lower (between 7 percent and 8 percent). Significant numbers of the oldest old have suffered serious injury from falls. Other common health problems for this group are high blood pressure and urinary incontinence. However, epidemiologist Adrian Ostfeld, who directed the survey in New Haven, notes that "most of the disability was temporary."

Longino has found that almost 10 percent of the oldest old live alone with a disability that prevents them from using public transportation. This means that they are "isolated from the daily hands-on care of others," he says. "Even so, there are a surprising number of the oldest old who don't need much in the way of medical care. They're the survivors.

"I think we have to agree that the oldest old is, as a group, remarkably diverse," Longino says. "Just as it is unfair to say that those older than 85 are all miserable, it's not fair to say that they all lead wonderful lives, either."
—Jeff Meer

ed on the metaphorical, moral or social meaning of the text. They didn't try to duplicate the fable's exact words, the way younger people did. As psychologists Nancy Datan, Dean Rodeheaver and Fergus Hughes of the University of Wisconsin have described their findings, "while [some people assume] that old and young are equally competent, we might better assume that they are differently competent."

John Horn, director of the Adult Development and Aging program at the University of

Southern California, suggests that studies of Alzheimer's disease, a devastating progressive mental deterioration experienced by an estimated 5 percent to 15 percent of those older than 65, may eventually help explain some of the differences in thinking abilities of older people. "Alzheimer's, in some ways, may represent the normal process of aging, only speeded up," he says. (To see how your ideas about Alzheimer's square with the facts, see "Alzheimer's Quiz" and "Alzheimer's Answers," this article.)

Generalities are always suspect, but one generalization about old age seems solid: It is a different experience for men and women. Longevity is one important reason. Women in the United States live seven to eight years longer, on the average, than do men. This simple fact has many ramifications, as sociologist Gunhild Hagestad explained in *Our Aging Society.*

For one thing, since the world of the very old is disproportionately a world of women, men and women spend their later years differently. "Most older women are widows living alone; most older men live with their wives. . .among individuals over the age of 75, two-thirds of the men are living with a spouse, while less than one-fifth of the women are."

The difference in longevity also means that among older people, remarriage is a male prerogative. After 65, for example, men remarry at a rate eight times that of women. This is partly a matter of the scarcity of men and partly a matter of culture—even late in life, men tend to marry younger women. It is also a matter of education and finances, which, Hagestad explains, "operate quite differently in shaping remarriage probabilities among men and women. The more resources the woman has available (measured in education and income), the less likely she is to remarry. For men, the trend is reversed."

The economic situations of elderly men and women also differ considerably. Lou Glasse, president of the Older Women's League in Washington, D.C., points out that most of these women were housewives who worked at paid jobs sporadically, if at all. "That means their Social Security benefits are lower than men's, they are not likely to have pensions and they are less likely to have been able to save the kind of money that would protect them from poverty during their older years."

Although we often think of elderly men and women as living in nursing homes or retirement communities, the facts are quite different. Only about 5 percent are in nursing homes and perhaps an equal number live in some kind of age-segregated housing. Most people older than 65 live in their own houses or apartments.

We also think of older people as living alone. According to the Census Bureau, this is true of 15 percent of the men and 41 percent of the women. Earlier this year, a survey done by Louis Harris & Associates revealed that 28 percent of elderly people living alone have annual incomes below $5,100, the federal poverty line. Despite this, they were four times as likely to give financial help to their children as to receive it from them.

In addition, fewer than 1 percent of the old people said they would prefer living with their children. Psychiatrist Robert N. Butler, chairman of the Commonwealth Fund's Commission

AMONG OLDER PEOPLE TODAY, REMARRIAGE IS STILL LARGELY A MALE PREROGATIVE, DUE TO THE SEX DIFFERENCE IN LONGEVITY.

on Elderly People Living Alone, which sponsored the report, noted that these findings dispute the "popular portrait of an elderly, dependent parent financially draining their middle-aged children."

There is often another kind of drain, however, one of time and effort. The Travelers Insurance Company recently surveyed more than 700 of its employees on this issue. Of those at least 30 years old, 28 percent said they directly care for an older relative in some way—taking that person to the doctor, making telephone calls, handling finances or running errands—for an average of 10 hours a week. Women, who are more often caregivers, spent an average of 16 hours, and men five hours, per week. One group, 8 percent of the sample, spent a heroic 35 hours per week, the equivalent of a second job, providing such care. "That adds up to an awful lot of time away from other things," psychologist Beal Lowe says, "and the stresses these people face are enormous."

Lowe, working with Sherman-Lank Communications in Kensington, Maryland, has formed "Caring for Caregivers," a group of professionals devoted to providing services, information and support to those who care for older relatives. "It can be a great shock to some people who have planned the perfect retirement," he says, "only to realize that your chronically ill mother suddenly needs daily attention."

Researchers who have studied the housing needs of older people predictably disagree on many things, but most agree on two points: We need a variety of individual and group living arrangements to meet the varying interests, income and abilities of people older than 65; and the arrangements should be flexible enough that the elderly can stay in the same locale as their needs and abilities change. Many studies have documented the fact that moving itself can be stressful and even fatal to old people, particularly if they have little or no influence over when and where they move.

This matter of control is important, but more complicated than it seemed at first. Psychologist Judith Rodin and others have demonstrated that people in nursing homes are happier, more alert and live longer if they are allowed to take responsibility for their lives in some way, even in something as simple as choosing a plant for their room, taking care of a bird feeder, selecting the night to attend a movie.

Rodin warns that while control is generally beneficial, the effect depends on the individuals involved. For some, personal control brings with it demands in the form of time, effort and the risk of failure. They may blame themselves if they get sick or something else goes wrong. The challenge, Rodin wrote, is to "provide but not impose opportunities. . . . The need for self-determination, it must be remembered, also calls for the opportunity to choose not to exercise control. . . ."

An ancient Greek myth tells how the Goddess of Dawn fell in love with a mortal and convinced Jupiter to grant him immortality. Unfortunately, she forgot to have youth included in the deal, so he gradually grew older and older. "At length," the story concludes, "he lost the power of using his limbs, and then she shut him up in his chamber, whence his feeble voice might at times be heard. Finally she turned him into a grasshopper."

The fears and misunderstandings of age expressed in this 3,000-year-old myth persist today, despite all the positive things we have learned in recent years about life after 65. We don't turn older people into grasshoppers or shut them out of sight, but too often we move them firmly out of the mainstream of life.

In a speech at the celebration of Harvard

If I had known when I was 21 that I should be as happy as I am now, I should have been sincerely shocked. They promised me wormwood and the funeral raven.

—Christopher Isherwood, letter at age 70.

University's 350th anniversary last September, political scientist Robert Binstock decried what he called The Spectre of the Aging Society: "the economic burdens of population aging; moral dilemmas posed by the allocation of health resources on the basis of age; labor market competition between older and younger workers within the contexts of age discrimination laws; seniority practices, rapid technologi-

---

ALZHEIMER'S QUIZ

Alzheimer's disease, named for German neurologist Alois Alzheimer, is much in the news these days. But how much do you really know about the disorder? Political scientist Neal B. Cutler of the Andrus Gerontology Center gave the following questions to a 1,500-person cross section of people older than 45 in the United States in November 1985. To compare your answers with theirs and with the correct answers, turn to the next page.

	True	False	Don't know
1. Alzheimer's disease can be contagious.		✓	
2. A person will almost certainly get Alzheimer's if they just live long enough.		✓	
3. Alzheimer's disease is a form of insanity.	✓	✓	
4. Alzheimer's disease is a normal part of getting older, like gray hair or wrinkles.		✓	
5. There is no cure for Alzheimer's disease at present.	✓		
6. A person who has Alzheimer's disease will experience both mental and physical decline.	✓	✓	
7. The primary symptom of Alzheimer's disease is memory loss.	✓		
8. Among persons older than age 75, forgetfulness most likely indicates the beginning of Alzheimer's disease.		✓	
9. When the husband or wife of an older person dies, the surviving spouse may suffer from a kind of depression that looks like Alzheimer's disease.			✓
10. Stuttering is an inevitable part of Alzheimer's disease.			✓
11. An older man is more likely to develop Alzheimer's disease than an older woman.			✓
12. Alzheimer's disease is usually fatal.		✓	
13. The vast majority of persons suffering from Alzheimer's disease live in nursing homes.	✓		
14. Aluminum has been identified as a significant cause of Alzheimer's disease.	✓		
15. Alzheimer's disease can be diagnosed by a blood test.		✓	
16. Nursing-home expenses for Alzheimer's disease patients are covered by Medicare.	✓		
17. Medicine taken for high blood pressure can cause symptoms that look like Alzheimer's disease.			✓

Alzheimer's Answers — National Sample

	True	False	Don't know
1. False. There is no evidence that Alzheimer's is contagious, but given the concern and confusion about AIDS, it is encouraging that nearly everyone knows this fact about Alzheimer's.	3%	83%	14%
2. False. Alzheimer's is associated with old age, but it is a disease and not the inevitable consequence of aging.	9	80	11
3. False. Alzheimer's is a disease of the brain, but it is not a form of insanity. The fact that most people understand the distinction contrasts with the results of public-opinion studies concerning epilepsy that were done 35 years ago. At that time, almost half of the public thought that epilepsy, another disease of the brain, was a form of insanity.	7	78	15
4. False. Again, most of the public knows that Alzheimer's is not an inevitable part of aging.	10	77	13
5. True. Despite announcements of "breakthroughs," biomedical research is in the early laboratory and experimental stages and there is no known cure for the disease.	75	8	17
6. True. Memory and cognitive decline are characteristic of the earlier stages of Alzheimer's disease, but physical decline follows in the later stages.	74	10	16
7. True. Most people know that this is the earliest sign of Alzheimer's disease.	62	19	19
8. False. Most people also know that while Alzheimer's produces memory loss, memory loss may have some other cause.	16	61	23
9. True. This question, like number 8, measures how well people recognize that other problems can mirror Alzheimer's symptoms. This is crucial because many of these other problems are treatable. In particular, depression can cause disorientation that looks like Alzheimer's.	49	20	30
10. False. Stuttering has never been linked to Alzheimer's. The question was designed to measure how willing people were to attribute virtually anything to a devastating disease.	12	46	42
11. False. Apart from age, research has not uncovered any reliable demographic or ethnic patterns. While there are more older women than men, both sexes are equally likely to get Alzheimer's.	15	45	40
12. True. Alzheimer's produces mental and physical decline that is eventually fatal, although the progression varies greatly among individuals.	40	33	27
13. False. The early and middle stages of the disease usually do not require institutional care. Only a small percentage of those with the disease live in nursing homes.	37	40	23
14. False. There is no evidence that using aluminum cooking utensils, pots or foil causes Alzheimer's, although aluminum compounds have been found in the brain tissue of many Alzheimer's patients. They may simply be side effects of the disease.	8	25	66
15. False. At present there is no definitive blood test that can determine with certainty that a patient has Alzheimer's disease. Accurate diagnosis is possible only upon autopsy. Recent studies suggest that genetic or blood testing may be able to identify Alzheimer's, but more research with humans is needed.	12	24	64
16. False. Medicare generally pays only for short-term nursing-home care subsequent to hospitalization and not for long-term care. Medicaid can pay for long-term nursing-home care, but since it is a state-directed program for the medically indigent, coverage for Alzheimer's patients depends upon state regulations and on the income of the patient and family.	16	23	61
17. True. As mentioned earlier, many medical problems have Alzheimer's-like symptoms and most of these other causes are treatable. Considering how much medicine older people take, it is unfortunate that so few people know that medications such as those used to treat high blood pressure can cause these symptoms.	20	19	61

cal change; and a politics of conflict between age groups."

Binstock, a professor at Case Western Reserve School of Medicine, pointed out that these inaccurate perceptions express an underlying ageism, "the attribution of these same characteristics and status to an artificially homogenized group labeled 'the aged.'"

Ironically, much ageism is based on compassion rather than ill will. To protect older workers from layoffs, for example, unions fought hard for job security based on seniority. To win it, they accepted mandatory retirement, a limitation that now penalizes older workers and deprives our society of their experience.

A few companies have taken special steps to utilize this valuable pool of older workers. The Travelers companies, for example, set up a job

GREAT EXPECTATIONS

SOURCE: U.S. NATIONAL CENTER FOR HEALTH STATISTICS

If you were born in 1920 and are a . . .

	. . .white man	*. .white woman*
your life expectancy was . . .		
at birth	*54.4 years*	*55.6 years*
at age 40	*71.7*	*77.1*
at age 62	*78.5*	*83.2*

If you were born in 1940 and are a . . .

	. . .white man	*. . .white woman*
your life expectancy was . . .		
at birth	*62.1 years*	*66.6 years*
at age 20	*70.3*	*76.3*
at age 42	*74.7*	*80.7*

If you were born in 1960 and are a . . .

	. . .white man	*. . .white woman*
your life expectancy was . . .		
at birth	*67.4 years*	*74.1 years*
at age 22	*73.2*	*80.0*

bank that is open to its own retired employees as well as those of other companies. According to Howard E. Johnson, a senior vice president, the company employs about 175 formerly retired men and women a week. He estimates that the program is saving Travelers $1 million a year in temporary-hire fees alone.

While mandatory retirement is only one example of ageism, it is particularly important because we usually think of contributions to society in economic terms. Malcolm H. Morrison, an authority on retirement and age discrimination in employment for the Social Security Administration, points out that once the idea of retirement at a certain fixed age was accepted, "the old became defined as a dependent group in society, a group whose members could not and should not work, and who needed economic and social assistance that the younger working population was obligated to provide."

We need to replace this stereotype with the more realistic understanding that older people are and should be productive members of society, capable of assuming greater responsibility for themselves and others. What researchers have learned about the strengths and abilities of older people should help us turn this ideal of an active, useful life after 65 into a working reality.

Personality Processes

The psychological study of personality has included two major thrusts. The first thrust has focused on the search for the commonalities of human life and development. Its major question would be: How are humans affected by specific events or activities? Personality theories are based on the assumption that given events, if they are important, will affect almost all people in similar ways, or that the processes by which events affect people are common across events and people. Most psychological research into personality variables has also made this assumption. Failures to replicate a research project are often the first clues that differences in individual responses require further investigation.

While some psychologists have focused on personality-related effects which are presumed to be universal among humans, others have devoted their efforts to discovering the bases on which individuals differ in their responses to environmental events. In the beginning, this specialty was called genetic psychology, since most people assumed that individual differences resulted from differences in genetic inheritance. By the 1950s, the term genetic psychology had given way to the more current term: the psychology of individual differences.

Does this mean that genetic variables are no longer the key to understanding individual differences? Not at all. For a time, psychologists took up the philosophical debate over whether genetic or environmental factors were more important in determining behaviors. Even today, behavior geneticists compute the heritability coefficients for a number of personality and behavioral traits, including intelligence. This is an expression of the degree to which differences in a given trait can be attributed to differences in inherited capacity or ability. Most psychologists, however, accept the principle that both genetic and environmental determinants are important in any area of behavior. These researchers are devoting more of their efforts to discovering how the two sources of influence interact to produce the unique individual.

Some of the most intriguing individual differences are those attributed to sex. That males and females differ biologically is hardly argued. Females generally have higher survival rates at all ages, and outlive males by about seven years. They seem more resistant to mild infections, able to withstand greater variability in temperature, and have, pound for pound, superior musculature. They also suffer less frequently from serious emotional and mental problems. But how do we know that these differences are the result of genetic or genital sex, and not the result of the way the sexes are treated? For example, we know that mothers talk more than twice as much to baby girls as they do to baby boys, and baby boys are held more tightly, jostled more vigorously, and moved through space more rapidly than baby girls. Could these early differences in handling account for later behavioral differences?

Another area of contention about sex differences is their statistical versus pragmatic significance. Suppose we find that there is a difference between males and females, and the difference is statistically significant—that is, reliable. How will we know whether the difference is due to genetic or social factors, and how will we be able to discern whether the difference has interpersonal implications? The first article in this section, "Biology, Destiny, and All That," begins to answer some of these questions. If you read this article critically, however, you will find that it raises as many questions as it answers. This is truly the nature of research into individual differences.

Perhaps the most devastating experience one can have is the feeling of helplessness. Seligman, who developed the best current paradigm of learned helplessness (the basis for human depression) has turned his attention to a more positive viewpoint. As Nan Silver tells us, optimism may cause us to live longer.

It has become almost a truism that certain personality traits are associated with increased likelihood of certain diseases. In the third article in this section, the highly regarded researcher Hans Eysenck explains how he has been conducting experiments to determine whether those traits can be changed, and if so, whether the change is for the better.

One of the foremost personality theories of all time is that of Erik Erikson, who initially sought to simply extend Freudian theory into adulthood. Now in late adulthood himself, Erikson and his wife have formulated a conceptual framework for understanding human wisdom and the humility which often accompanies wisdom in older individuals.

Looking Ahead: Challenge Questions

How can evidence of sex differences be used to reduce discrimination on the basis of sex or gender? Could the same evidence be used by others to increase discrimination? Who would be the most likely target? Which sex really deserves to be the target of discrimination?

Is optimism really related to health and longevity? If it is desirable, how can optimism be developed?

If a person exhibits personality traits associated with fatal illnesses, what can be done to change both the traits and the likelihood of becoming ill?

What benefits can be derived and applied from Erikson's latest ideas about wisdom and humility? How should we prepare ourselves for these experiences?

BIOLOGY, DESTINY, AND ALL THAT

Grabbing hold of a tar baby
of research findings, our writer
tries to pull apart truth from myth
in ideas about the differences
between the sexes.

Paul Chance

Paul Chance is a psychologist, writer, and contributing editor of *Psychology Today*.

In the 1880s, scholars warned against the hazards of educating women. Some experts of the day believed that too much schooling could endanger a woman's health, interfere with her reproductive ability, and cause her brain to deteriorate. In the 1980s we laugh at such absurd ideas, but have we (men and women alike) really given up the ancient idea that a woman is fundamentally an inferior sort of man? It seems not.

It's hard to find evidence these days of gross discrimination against women as a company policy. Successful lawsuits have made that sort of prejudice expensive. Yet evidence of more subtle forms of bias abound. The sociologist Beth Ghiloni conducted a study while she was a student at the University of California, Santa Cruz, that shows that some corporations are meeting the demands of affirmative action by putting women into public relations posts. Public relations is important but distant from the activities that generate revenue, so PR assignments effectively keep women out of jobs that include any real corporate power. Thus, women increasingly complain of facing a "glass ceiling" through which they can see, but cannot reach, high level corporate positions.

It seems likely that such discrimination reflects some very old ideas about what men and women are like. Men, the stereotype has it, are aggressive and self-confident. They think analytically, and are cool under fire. They enjoy jobs that offer responsibility and challenge. They are, in other words, ideally suited for important,

high-level positions. Put them on the track that may one day lead to corporate vice president.

Women, the thinking goes, are passive and filled with self-doubt. They think intuitively, and are inclined to become emotionally distraught under pressure. They therefore enjoy jobs that involve working with people. Give them the lower-rung jobs in the personnel department, or send them to public affairs.

Figuring out how truth and myth intertwine in these stereotypes is difficult. The research literature on sex differences is a tar baby made of numbers, case studies, and anecdotal impressions. To paraphrase one researcher, "If you like ambiguity, you're gonna love sex-difference research." Nevertheless, let us be brave and take the stereotypes apart piece by piece.

Aggression

On this there is no argument: Everyone agrees that men are more aggressive than women. In a classic review of the literature, the psychologists Eleanor Maccoby of Stanford University and Carol Jacklin of the University of Southern California found that boys are more aggressive than girls both physically and verbally, and the difference begins to show up by the age of 3. Boys are more inclined to rough-and-tumble play; girls have tea parties and play with dolls.

The difference in aggressiveness is most clearly seen in criminal activity. There are far more delinquent boys than girls, and prisons are built primarily to contain men. The most aggressive crimes, such as murder and assault, are especially dominated by men.

It seems hardly likely that male aggressiveness, as it is documented by the research, would win favor among personnel directors and corporate headhunters. Yet aggressiveness is considered not only a virtue but an essential trait for many jobs. Vice President George Bush learned the value of aggressiveness when he managed to put aside his wimp image by verbally attacking the CBS news anchorman Dan Rather on national television. The assumption seems to be that the same underlying trait that makes for murderers, rapists, and strong-arm bandits also, in more moderate degree or under proper guidance, makes people more competitive and motivated to achieve great things.

But the research suggests that women may be just as aggressive in this more civilized sense as men. For instance, most studies of competitiveness find no differences between the sexes, according to the psychologists Veronica Nieva and Barbara Gutek, co-authors of *Women and Work*. And many studies of achievement motivation suggest that women are just as eager to get things done as men.

Self-confidence

Men are supposed to be self-confident, women full of self-doubt. Again there is some evidence for the stereotype, but it isn't particularly complimentary to males. Various studies show that males overestimate their abilities, while females underestimate theirs. Researchers have found, for instance, that given the option of choosing tasks varying in difficulty, boys erred by choosing those that were too difficult for them, while girls tended to select tasks that were too easy.

Other research shows that women are not only less confident of their ability to do a job, when they succeed at it they don't give themselves credit. Ask them why they did well and they'll tell you it was an easy task or that they got lucky. Ask men the same thing and they'll tell you they did well because of their ability and hard work.

It is perhaps this difference in self-confidence that makes women better risks for auto insurance, and it may have something to do with the fact that almost from the day they can walk, males are more likely to be involved in pedestrian accidents.

Rational Thinking

A great many studies have found that men do better than women on tests of mathematical reasoning. Julian Stanley, a psychologist at Johns Hopkins University, has been using the mathematics portion of the Scholastic Aptitude Test to identify mathematically gifted youths. He and his colleagues have consistently found that a majority of the high scoring students are boys. Stanley reports that "mathematically gifted boys outnumber gifted girls by a ratio of about 13 to 1." Moreover, the very best scores almost inevitably come from boys.

But while some findings show that men are better at mathematical reasoning, there is no evidence that they are more analytical or logical in general. In fact, the superiority of men at mathematical problem solving seems not to reflect superior analytical thinking but a special talent men have for visualizing objects in space. Women are every bit the match of men at other kinds of problems such as drawing logical conclusions from written text. Indeed, girls have an advantage over boys in verbal skills until at least adolescence.

As for the idea that women are more intuitive, forget it. Numerous studies have shown that women are better at reading body language, and it is probably this skill (born, perhaps, of the need to avoid enraging the more aggressive sex) that gives rise to the myth of women's intuition. In reality, women and men think alike.

Emotionality

In Victorian England, to judge by the novels of the day, a woman was no woman at all if she didn't feel faint or burst into tears at least once a week. The idea that women are more emotional than men, that they feel things more deeply and react accordingly, persists. Is it true?

No. Carol Tavris and Carole Wade, psychologists and co-authors of *The Longest War: Sex Differences in Perspective*, write that the sexes are equally likely to feel anxious in new situations, to get angry when insulted, to be hurt when a loved one leaves them, and to feel embarrassed when they make mistakes in public.

The sexes are equally emotional, but there are important differences in how willing men and women are to express emotions, which emotions they choose to express, and the ways in which they express them. If you ask men and women in an emotional situation what they are feeling, women are likely to admit that they are affected, while men are likely to deny it. Yet studies show that when you look at the psychological correlates of emotion—heartbeat, blood pressure, and the like—you find that those strong silent men are churning inside every bit as much as the women.

Men are particularly eager to conceal feelings such as fear, sorrow, and loneliness, according to Tavris and Wade. Men often bottle these "feminine" feelings even with those they hold most dear.

Another difference comes in how emotions are expressed. Women behave differently depending upon what they feel. They may cry if sad, curse if angry, pout if their pride is hurt. Men tend to respond to such situations in a more or less uniform way. Whether they have been jilted, frightened, or snubbed, they become aggressive. (Men, you will recall, are very good at aggression.) As for the notion that keeping one's head is characteristic of men, well, don't get sore fellows, but it ain't necessarily so.

Job Interests

If you ask men and women what they like about their work, you will get different answers. In 1957, Frederick Herzberg published a study of what made work enjoyable to employees. Men, he concluded, enjoyed work that offered responsibility and challenge. For women, on the other hand, the environment was the thing. They wanted an attractive work area, and some pleasant people to talk to while they did whatever needed to be done. Give your secretary an office with some nice wallpaper, put a flower on her desk once in a while, and she'll be happy.

Experts now agree, however, that such differences probably reflect differences in the jobs held by the people studied. You may get such findings, suggest *Women and Work* co-authors Nieva and Gutek, if you compare female file clerks and male engineers—but not if you compare female and male engineers. In a study of workers in various jobs, Daphne Bugental, a psychologist at the University of California, Santa Barbara, and the late Richard Centers found no consistent differences in the way men and women ranked "intrinsic" job characteristics such as responsibility and challenge and "extrinsic" characteristics such as pleasant surroundings and friendly co-workers. In other words, the dif-

ferences in what men and women find interesting about work reflect differences in the kinds of work men and women characteristically do. People in relatively high level jobs enjoy the responsibility and challenge it offers; people in low level jobs that offer little responsibility and challenge look elsewhere for satisfaction.

Where Do the Differences Come From?

So, what differences separate the boys from the girls? Men are reported to be more aggressive than women in a combative sense, but they are not necessarily more competitive. Men are more confident, perhaps recklessly so, and women may be too cautious. Men are not more likely to be cool under fire, but they are more likely to become aggressive regardless of what upsets them. Men are not more analytic in their thinking, nor women more intuitive, but men are better at solving mathematical problems, probably because they are better at spatial relationships. Finally, women are less interested in the responsibility and challenge of work, but only because they usually have jobs that offer little responsibility and challenge.

While this seems to be the gist of the matter, it leaves open the question of whether the differences are due to biology or to environment. Are

THE DEVELOPMENT OF THE "WEAKER SEX"
(AND THE DEMORALIZATION OF THE DUDE).

VASSAR GRADUATE.—"These are the dumb-bells I used last term in our gymnasium; won't one of you gentleman just put them up? It's awfully easy."

men more aggressive because they are born that way or because of lessons that begin in the cradle? Are women less confident than men because different hormones course through their blood, or because for years people have told them that they can't expect much from themselves?

The research on the nature-nurture question is a candy store in which people of varying biases can quickly find something to their liking. Beryl Lieff Benderly, an anthropologist and journalist, critiqued the physiological research for her new book, *The Myth of Two Minds*. The title tells the story. She even challenges the notion that men are stronger than women. "The plain fact is that we have no idea whether men are 'naturally' stronger than women," she writes. Short of conducting an experiment along the lines of *Lord of the Flies*, we are unlikely to unravel the influences of nature and nurture to everyone's satisfaction. Nevertheless, research does offer hints about the ways that biology and environment affect stereotypical behavior. Take the case of aggression. There are any number of studies linking aggression to biological factors. Testosterone, a hormone found in much higher levels in men than in women, has been found in even larger quantities in criminally aggressive males. Castration, which decreases the level of testosterone, has been used for centuries to produce docile men and animals. And girls who have had prenatal exposure to high levels of testosterone are more tomboyish than other girls.

Yet biology is not quite destiny. In her famous *Six Cultures* study, the anthropologist Beatrice Whiting and her colleagues at Harvard University found that in each of the societies studied, boys were more aggressive than girls. But the researchers also found such wide cultural differences that the girls in a highly aggressive society were often more aggressive than the boys in another, less aggressive society.

The same mix of forces applies wherever we look. Biology may bend the twig in one direction, but the environment may bend it in another. But whether biology or environment ultimately wins the hearts and minds of researchers is less important than how the differences, wherever they come from, affect behavior in the workplace. If someone explodes in anger (or breaks down in tears) in the midst of delicate contract negotiations, it matters little to the stockholders whether the lost business can, in the end, be blamed on testosterone or bad toilet training. The more important question is, what are the implications of sex difference research for business?

What Difference Do the Differences Make?

The research on sex differences suggest three points that people in business can usefully consider. First, the differences between the sexes are small. Researchers look for "statistically significant" differences. But statistically significant differences are not necessarily practically significant. There is a great deal of overlap between the sexes on most characteristics and especially on the characteristics we have been considering. Men are, on average, better at solving mathematical problems, but there are many women who are far above the average man in this area. Women are, on average, less confident than men. But there are many men who doubt themselves far more than the average woman. A study of aggressiveness is illustrative. The psychologist D. Anthony Butterfield and the management expert Gary N. Powell had college students rate the ideal U.S. President on various characteristics, including aggressiveness. Then they had them rate people who were running for President and Vice President at the time: Ronald Reagan, Walter Mondale, George Bush, and Geraldine Ferraro. Researchers found that the ideal president was, among other things, aggressive. They also found that Geraldine Ferraro was judged more aggressive than the male candidates. The point is that it is impossible to predict individual qualities from group differences.

Indeed, Carol Jacklin suggests that differences in averages may give a quite distorted view of both sexes. She notes that while, on average, boys play more aggressively than girls, her research shows that the difference is due to a small number of very aggressive boys. Most of the boys are, in fact, very much like the girls. "I'd be willing to bet," Jacklin says, "that much of the difference in aggressiveness between men and women is due to a small number of extremely aggressive men—many of whom are in prison—and that the remaining men are no more aggressive than most women."

Second, different doesn't necessarily mean inferior. It is quite possible that feminine traits (in men or women) are assets in certain situations, while masculine traits may be advantageous in other situations. The psychologist Carol Gilligan, author of *In a Different Voice*, says that women are more comfortable with human relationships than men are, and this may sometimes give them an edge. For instance, Roderick Gilkey and Leonard Greenhalgh, psychologists at Dartmouth University, had business students simulate negotiations over the purchase of a used car and television advertising time. The women appeared better suited to the task than the men. They were more flexible, more willing to compromise, and less deceptive. "Women can usually come to an agreement on friendly terms," says Greenhalgh. "They're better at avoiding impasses."

In another study, the psychologist Wendy Wood of Texas A&M University asked college students to work on problems in groups of three.

Some groups consisted only of men, others of women. The groups tried to solve problems such as identifying the features to consider in buying a house. The men, it turns out, came up with more ideas, while the women zeroed in on one good idea and developed it. Wood concluded that all-male groups might be better for brainstorming, while all-female groups might be better for finding the best solution to a problem.

Third, sometimes people lack the characteristics needed for a job until they are in the job. Jobs that offer responsibility and challenge, for example, tend to create a desire for more responsibility and challenge. While there are research studies to support this statement, an anecdote from the sociologist Rosabeth Moss Kanter is more telling. Linda, a secretary for 17 years in a large corporation, had no interest in being anything but a secretary, and when she was offered a promotion through an affirmative action program, she hesitated. Her boss persuaded her to take the job and she became a successful manager and loved the additional responsibility and challenge. She even set her sights on a vice president position. As a secretary, Linda would no doubt have scored near the female stereotype. But when she became a manager, she became more like the stereotypical male.

Kanter told that story a dozen years ago, but we are still struggling to learn its lesson. A discrimination case against Sears, Roebuck and Company recently made news. The Equal Employment Opportunity Commission (EEOC) argued that Sears discriminated against women because nearly all of the employees in the company who sell on commission are men. Sears presented evidence that women expressed little interest in commission-sales work, preferring the less risky jobs in salaried sales. In the original decision favoring Sears, the U.S. District Court had found that "noncommission saleswomen were generally happier with their present jobs at Sears, and were much less likely than their male counterparts to be interested in other positions, such as commission sales. . . ." But in the U.S. Court of Appeals, Appellate Judge Cudahy, who dissented in part from the majority, wrote that this reasoning is "of a piece with the proposition that women are by nature happier cooking, doing the laundry, and chauffeuring the children to softball games than arguing appeals or selling stocks."

The point is not that employees must be made to accept more responsible positions for their own good, even if it is against their will. The point is that business should abandon the stereotypes that lock men and women into different, and often unequal, kinds of work. If it finally does, it will discover the necessity—and value—of finding ways of enticing men and women into jobs for which, according to the stereotypes, they are not suited. If business doesn't do that, it may discover that differences between men and women really do separate the sexes.

Mind Over Illness

Do Optimists Live Longer?

To stay healthy, think positive—don't let tough situations weigh you down.

Nan Silver

Nan Silver, *a Senior Editor of* American Health, *is converting to optimism.*

"Giving orders was sometimes very hard, if not impossible, because I always had this problem of dealing with men under me, even later in the war and when I had the appropriate rank."—Frank

"During the war I was occasionally bored, because anyone who's ever been aboard ship is bored to tears."—Joe

Frank and Joe are pseudonyms for Harvard University graduates from the early '40s. Both survived World War II. And both were young and healthy veterans when they wrote these lines about their wartime troubles in a 1946 survey. They had similar backgrounds, similar experiences, and neither had glowing memories of the war. Yet their fates would be dramatically different. In the years since, Joe has lived a healthy, robust life, and Frank has been chronically ill.

What's the key reason? Most of us would probably shrug and say luck, or perhaps genetics. But not University of Pennsylvania psychologist Martin E.P. Seligman. At the recent annual meeting of the American Psychological Association (APA) in Washington, DC, he offered a far more surprising—

and controversial—theory, based on research done with psychologist Christopher Peterson of the University of Michigan and Dartmouth College psychiatrist George Vaillant.

After analyzing the words of 99 such Harvard vets, the researchers believe the men's future may have been there, waiting to be discovered, in the very words they used 40 years ago to describe their war experiences. Based on complex analytic measures, Seligman and his colleagues have pegged Frank as a pessimist and Joe as an optimist. That difference may be crucial to mental and physical health, says Seligman. The latest studies even suggest that people like Joe may be more resilient in the face of cancer.

The Harvard study is a recent addition to a growing body of research that suggests a rosy way of thinking and speaking may help protect body and mind from harm. It may also do wonders for your career (see "Stress or Success?"). These studies are adding scientific credence to the old sayings about the power of positive thinking. By changing the way we think about the bad things that happen to us, says Seligman, we may be able to boost our moods—and our physical vitality.

What's Wrong With Frank?

Although both Frank and Joe have

negative memories of military life, Seligman's analysis reveals they differ tremendously in what he calls *explanatory* or *attributional* style. The term refers to how people explain the events in their lives—anything from winning at poker to being bored on ship.

Through explanatory style, Frank and other pessimists (as Seligman defines the term) are identified by three elements in their speech. First (and, Seligman believes, most disastrously), pessimists assume the problem is never-ending, or *stable*. Says Frank: "I always had this problem. . . ." Next, they believe the cause of their problem is *global* rather than specific—it will ruin every aspect of their lives. Frank does a little better here. He's not completely global, because he relates his difficulty with giving orders only to the war. Finally, pessimists blame themselves when trouble arises. Seligman calls this being *internal*. Frank assumes *he's* the cause of his problem, not the sullen privates who refuse to listen.

In general, then, Frank's a far cry from his buddy Joe, whom Seligman considers an optimist. Joe is bored only "occasionally." He thinks his hardship is temporary (unstable), and entirely specific (only on the ship) rather than global. And, for Joe, problems are caused by *external* circumstances. His boredom isn't his fault;

anyone aboard ship feels that way. (To test *your* explanatory style, see "How Optimistic Are You?")

The evidence is mounting that people tend to stick to one explanatory style throughout their lives. At the APA meeting, Seligman reported on a study by University of Pennsylvania psychologist Melanie Burns. She compared the teenage diaries of 30 people now in their 70s with current writing samples. Their styles had remained the same.

And in their study of Harvard vets, Seligman and colleagues found that the statements Joe, Frank and the others had made when young and fit told much about their futures. Seligman's theory: "If you always go around thinking, 'It's my fault, it's going to last forever, and it's going to undermine everything I do,' then when you do run into further bad events, you become at risk for poor health."

More evidence comes from a study by Christopher Peterson. While at Virginia Polytechnic Institute and State University in Blacksburg, he measured the way 172 college students reacted to bad events. He also checked their health and moods. One month later he found that, whatever the initial health status, pessimists had become ill more often. "And," he adds, "a year later, they had made significantly more visits to the doctor."

Most research suggests that pessimism is much more dangerous in the face of bad events than when the going's good, says Seligman. But in one study, he did find that consistently pooh-poohing success *can* do long-term damage—at least to famous baseball players.

A pessimistic response to *good* news is unstable, specific and external—"It won't last, it won't change my life, I was just lucky." So far, Seligman's research team has analyzed the sports-page quotes of 34 Baseball Hall of Famers who played between 1900 and 1950. Result: Pessimists, who said their ballpark victories were short-lived and due to "luck," lived significantly shorter lives than extreme optimists like Rube Marquard (who died at age 90).

The Talking Blues

Baseball players, war veterans, students. In every case, chronic negative thinking has been linked to poorer health. What makes doom and gloom so dangerous? Years of research by Seligman and other psychologists into *depression* offers an explanation.

How Optimistic Are You?

The scene: Your mate has just walked out on you. Which of the eight reasons below do you think best represents the way you'd honestly react?

It's good news if you chose an unstable reason (Nos. 5 through 8)—you don't tend to think bad times last forever. The healthiest choice: No. 8; it's also external (your mate's problem caused the breakup) and specific (not all men or women are moody). If you chose a stable reason (Nos. 1 through 4), you may want to work on being more optimistic. No. 1's the least healthy: It's self-blaming and all-encompassing.

		Global	Specific
STABLE	**Internal**	1. I'm completely unlovable.	3. I'm unlovable because I'm so moody (picky, boring, unattractive).
	External	2. My mate and *all* men (women) are jerks.	4. My mate is a jerk.
UNSTABLE	**Internal**	5. Sometimes I just get so moody.	7. Sometimes I get so moody toward my mate.
	External	6. Sometimes, my mate and *all* men (women) get into terrible moods.	8. Sometimes my mate gets into terrible moods.

Stress or Success?

Optimism doesn't just help keep you healthy and in high spirits—it's also linked to greater activity and risk-taking. The reason: Quitting often stems from helplessness, says psychologist Martin E.P. Seligman. And your explanatory style may determine how active or helpless you are.

One of Seligman's favorite examples: Lyndon Baines Johnson. Normally he had "an average explanatory style for an American man," says Seligman. But before making certain crucial and controversial decisions as President—such as doubling the troop commitment in Vietnam—his words (measured from transcripts of press conferences) suddenly became wildly optimistic. And, right before his decision not to run for re-election, his style swung the other way—a cue that he would soon make a passive decision.

LBJ, of course, was overly optimistic and took risks that harmed others. But for many people, an optimistic style is linked to *true* success.

In fact, explanatory style may be better than more standard measures at predicting achievement in certain situations.

In one of Seligman's studies, a "special force" of 100 insurance salesmen who failed Metropolitan Life's traditional entrance exam—but scored as high optimists on Seligman's explanatory-style questionnaire—is outselling Met's regular recruits by 20% to 25%.

Studies of students have brought similar results. At the University of Pennsylvania, psychologist Leslie Kamen found that optimistic freshmen did better in their first-semester grades than the admissions committee had predicted from high-school scores and averages. Pessimists did worse.

These "cognitive" psychologists have long believed our thoughts—written, spoken or silent—may play a determining role in behavior and health. But at first their work focused not on physical health but on the link between low moods and feelings of helplessness. A key to their theories: studies by Seligman and others showing that animals faced with unavoidable electric shocks eventually stop trying to escape. They become helpless—and depressed—and may continue to behave passively ever after. In extreme cases they succumb to what Seligman calls "submissive death."

Many psychologists believe that in humans, too, helplessness can lead to low mood. But Seligman, for one, doesn't think it's helpless *situations* that cause the problem, but *thoughts* of helplessness—the negative explanatory style—that those situations may generate.

Why? Thoughts triggered by a specific event—say a failure at work—can build a power all their own, Seligman believes: "If you consistently respond to such events pessimistically, that negative style can actually *amplify* your feelings of helplessness and spread to other areas of your life."

Psychologists have already studied the explanatory style of all types of people—children, students, the elderly, even prisoners—and found evidence that a pessimistic style may indeed cause depression.

In one series of studies, psychologists Susan Nolen-Hoeksema (now at Stanford University) and Joan Girgus of Princeton University repeatedly tested the mood and explanatory style of 168 third, fourth and fifth-graders. Those who had an optimistic style, but were depressed for some reason in the first month, tended to feel upbeat three months later. And those who started out momentarily happy, but spoke like pessimists, later became blue.

The Dangerous Difference

How does pessimism lead to poor *health*? For one thing, people who develop an "I surrender" attitude are less likely to take good care of themselves, eat right, see doctors or seek support from family and friends, says Seligman.

But the latest research also suggests a far more direct route to harm: Pessimistic thinking may actually hamper your immune system. When laboratory rats were made helpless, their immune systems were often slower and less successful in battling implanted tumor cells, according to research by Hymie Anisman of Carleton University in Ottawa and Steven Maier of the University of Colorado in Boulder. More of these rats died than others who hadn't been made helpless but were fighting the same cancer (see "The Hope Factor," *AH*, July/August, '83).

Now psychologists are finding similar results in people faced with illness. In a pilot study of 13 cancer patients with advanced melanoma, Sandra Levy at the University of Rochester reports that an optimistic style was the *number one* psychological predictor of who would live longest. The study was so small that Levy believes the results are only "suggestive." Yet at the recent APA meeting, she announced the latest results of a study of recurring breast cancer. Again, a connection: Optimism was linked to a longer cancer-free period before the disease returned.

On the basis of these findings, Levy believes that "joy," as opposed to helplessness, may help cancer patients by giving them more stamina to withstand the disease's onslaught. Levy is now collaborating with Seligman on further studies of breast cancer patients.

As part of yet another continuing research project, University of Pennsylvania psychologist Leslie Kamen, along with Seligman and psychologist Judith Rodin of Yale, is studying the explanatory style of 58 healthy people ages 60 to 90. No matter how healthy they seemed, those elderly people who began the study with a pessimistic style had lower levels of certain immune system cells than the optimists.

Psychologists are still debating whether pessimism has to be long-lasting and pervasive in order to harm. Seligman believes it does. Others think it can cause trouble even if it crops up in just one situation—say, when you're battling cancer.

In either case, the latest research offers compelling evidence of the rich rewards positive thinking can bring—and the damage negative thoughts can cause. Says Seligman: "It's not reality itself that's producing this risk factor, but what you do with reality and the way you think about it."

Detoxing Your Thoughts

Whatever causes pessimistic thinking, it *can* be changed, says psychologist Martin E.P. Seligman. The tool: cognitive therapy, in which the therapist helps the patient examine—and alter—erroneous and pessimistic thinking patterns. Studies have shown that cognitive therapy is as successful as drug therapy in alleviating depression. And research by psychologist Robert DeRubeis of the University of Pennsylvania and Mark Evans of the University of Minnesota suggests it may work by changing your explanatory style.

Now psychologists are studying whether cognitive therapy can do for the immune system what it seems to do for mood. In a joint project, psychologists Seligman, Judith Rodin and Sandra Levy are giving 12 weeks of cognitive therapy to cancer patients.

Will this treatment help battle the disease? "I think it's kind of a long shot," Seligman admits. "If, for example, it's a small tumor load, then I think what goes on in our heads can make a difference—maybe even a life-saving one. But if a crane falls on you, it doesn't much matter whether you're an optimist."

In the future, Seligman hopes that short-term cognitive therapy will be used as prevention—before illness or depression strikes. If you want to try the treatment, look for a therapist specifically trained in *cognitive* techniques, as developed by University of Pennsylvania psychiatrist Aaron T. Beck or New York psychologist Albert Ellis (his brand is called Rational Emotive Therapy). Also check for membership in professional organizations, such as the APA.

Dr. Beck's group, the Center for Cognitive Therapy (133 S. 36th St., Suite 602, Philadelphia, PA 19104, 215-898-4100), offers a nationwide referral service that can match you with a therapist in your area.

HEALTH'S CHARACTER

Hans J. Eysenck

Hans J. Eysenck, Ph.D., D.Sc., is one of the world's most cited psychologists. He is a professor at the Institute of Psychiatry of the University of London, where he started the discipline of clinical psychology in Great Britian. He is a pioneer in the use of behavior therapy as well as research in personality theory and measurements.

Imagine this: A simple, six-question test predicts whether you are likely to get cancer or heart disease or to stay healthy. These predictions would not be based on traditional medical risks such as smoking or obesity but on your personality.

If the test indicates that you have a disease-prone personality, there would be some short-term behavior therapies (no radiation treatments, no surgery, no drugs) that protect you against cancer or a heart attack or help you live longer if you are already sick.

It sounds too good to be true, but it just might be. Dramatic results from studies completed in Europe over the past several years point to a very strong connection between certain personalities and specific illnesses. If the research I am about to describe holds up under ongoing scrutiny, we will be entering a new era of health care and disease prevention.

Theories about disease-prone personalities usually draw loud protests from the medical community, but such ideas are hardly new. The notion that people with certain personality characteristics are likely to develop coronary heart disease dates back more than 2,000 years to Hippocrates. The idea that people of a different personality type are more likely to develop cancer has also been around for a long time. These ideas are based on centuries of observations made by keen-

The world's most-quoted psychologist contends that a Yugoslav's controversial experiments prove that certain personalities are prone to cancer, others to heart disease. But you can learn to be prone to health.

eyed physicians; they should not be rejected simply because they were made without modern methodological and statistical expertise.

The type of personality often ascribed to the cancer-prone individual combines two major features. One is an inability to express emotions such as anger, fear and anxiety; the other is an inability to cope with stress and a tendency to develop feelings of hopelessness, helplessness and

finally depression. In the late 1950s, a Scottish oncologist, David Kissen, and I tried to test some of these ideas. We administered psychological questionnaires to patients coming to Kissen's lung cancer clinic before they were diagnosed as having cancer. We wanted to find out how readily these people expressed their emotions. We then compared those with a diagnosis of lung cancer to those with a non-malignant diagnosis. People who found it easier to express their emotions seemed to be protected from cancer, while those who could not suffered from cancer much more than chance would have predicted.

These results have been replicated by other researchers studying lung cancer in men and breast cancer in women. In general, the more recent studies characterized the cancer-prone person as un-assertive, over-patient, avoiding conflict and failing to express negative emotions. However, many of these studies were small and had some technical problems with methodology, and other studies found no association between cancer and personality traits (see "Fighting Cancerous Feelings," *Psychology Today*, May 1988).

Coronary heart disease has also been linked to certain personality types, most often to the so-called "Type A" personality or behavior pattern, which was summarized by its discoverers in the late 1950s as "excessive and competitive drive, and an enhanced sense of time urgency". Later research in the '70s and '80s has shown that Type A behavior is actually composed of several different components and that many of them do not in fact predict coronary heart disease. The only components that seem to stand up to the test are tendencies towards anger, hostility and aggression.

But many studies of heart disease and behavior focused on people who were already ill, and it is possible that the disease caused the personality pattern, rather than the other way around. And several studies of healthy people using the Type A behavior scales and interviewing methods found a very weak link to heart disease or no link at all (see "Type A On Trial," *Psychology Today*, February 1987).

So the whole question of personality and disease has been shrouded in uncertainty, due to the absence of large-scale studies in which personality traits are determined first and the people under investigation are then observed for many years to see who dies and of what disease.

Three such studies have recently been completed and published, all of them carried out by Ronald Grossarth-Maticek, a Yugoslav psychologist who carried out his original research in the 1960s in his home country and then went to West Germany to work in Heidelberg. He took large random samples of people, measured their personality traits, smoking and drinking habits, physical health and other characteristics. He then checked on them for periods of 10 or more years to learn whether aspects of personality could be linked to death from cancer or heart disease or to a long and healthy life. Several American and British psychologists, including myself, have collaborated with him in recent years.

Grossarth-Maticek measured personality in two ways. He used a series of short questionnaires to look at various aspects of the cancer-prone personality and the heart disease-prone personality, as he conceptualized them. The most important questions measured tendencies toward hopelessness and helplessness, rational and anti-emotional behavior and a lack of angry responses to traumatic life events (it is a testament to Grossarth-Maticek's astuteness that his ideas in the early 1960s agree almost perfectly with the most recent results of American and British research in this field).

An alternative method of ascertaining personality involved lengthy interviews in which the subjects were allocated to one of four types: Type 1, cancer-prone; Type 2, coronary heart disease-prone; Types 3 and

4, relatively healthy people who could deal with stress in a non-self-destructive fashion. Grossarth-Maticek has also developed a short questionnaire that distinguishes these four personality types (see "The Health Personality Test"). You can take it and score yourself to find out your health personality.

Based on these personality types, Grossarth-Maticek was able to predict death from cancer among these people with an accuracy of 50 percent, which is six times higher than a prediction from cigarette smoking. Of the Type 1 people who died, almost half died from cancer, while fewer than one-tenth died from heart disease. About one-third of the Type 2 people died of heart disease, but only about one-fifth died from cancer. Type 3 and Type 4 showed relatively few deaths.

In the Yugoslav study, the people were

Until recently, no large studies have determined personality first, then followed people for years to see who dies of what disease. A few years ago, Grossarth-Maticek completed three such studies.

for the most part the oldest inhabitant in every second house in a small town; however, Grossarth-Maticek also included a number of people who were suggested as being in a state of high stress. It is unscientific to throw together two different populations in one study, and adding stressed individuals to the study has been criticized, since it might have artificially strengthened the connection between the death rates and the disease-prone personality groups. But a recent reanalysis has shown that the connection is actually stronger without the stressed people.

Later, in Heidelberg, Grossarth-Maticek studied a random group of men and women between 40 and 60 years of age (see "Mind-Body Connections"). The overall number of deaths in this study was much smaller than it was in the Yugoslav study because the people in Heidelberg were much younger on average. However, as before, Type 1 people tended to die of cancer and Type 2 people tended to die of heart disease.

In Heidelberg, Grossarth-Maticek also examined a second group, closely resembling the first in age, sex and smoking habits. However, this second group of

people was nominated as people suffering from severe stress. If stress plays an important part in causing death from cancer and heart disease, far more people in this group should have died of these illnesses. This was indeed so: Approximately 40 percent more people in the stressed group died of these diseases. These data are for a 10-year follow-up, and there was little change when a 13-year follow-up was completed.

These dramatic results, indicating a powerful role for personality and behavior in cancer and heart disease, lead to an all-important question: Can we prevent these deaths by changing people's personalities?

Grossarth-Maticek and I tried to use behavior therapy to teach cancer- and heart disease-prone people to express their emotions more readily, to cope with stress, to wean them of their emotional dependencies and to make them more self-reliant. In other words, we taught them to behave more like the healthier personality types. We used relaxation, desentisization, modeling, suggestion and hypnosis and other standard behavioral techniques (see "Steps To A Healthier Self"). The results were astonishing.

100 people with cancer-prone personalities were divided into two groups: 50 who received no therapy and 50 who did receive it. Far more people died of cancer (and of other causes) in the no-therapy group than in the therapy group. After 13 years, 45 people who got therapy were still alive. Only 19 were alive in the no-therapy group.

We tried a similar experiment with 92 heart disease-prone people, divided into therapy and no-therapy groups. Here too there were marked differences 13 years later, with 37 people surviving with therapy and 17 surviving without it.

These results were encouraging, to say the least; however, the therapy in these studies consisted of about 30 hours of individual treatment, which is fairly lengthy and expensive. We decided to look for ways to reduce the treatment time and expense.

We tried using group therapy, in which groups of some 20 people met for about six hours in all, on two or three occasions. Here too we found a marked difference in the number of people who died of cancer and coronary heart disease, again favoring the therapy group. In a third study, we tried short-term therapy on an individual basis, again with favorable results.

There is also evidence that similar treatment can prolong life in people who

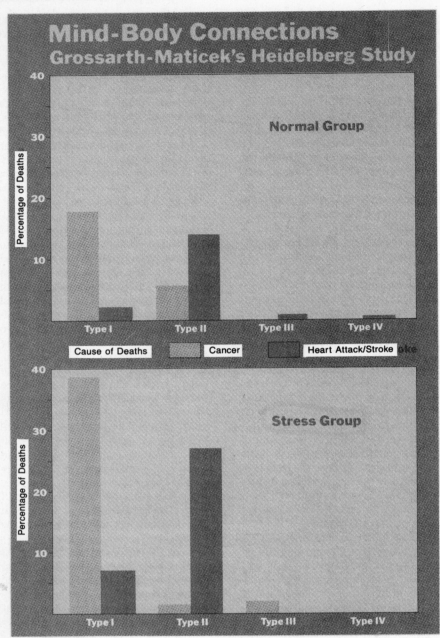

Mind-Body Connections
Grossarth-Maticek's Heidelberg Study

Normal Group

Percentage of Deaths

Type I   Type II   Type III   Type IV

Cause of Deaths   Cancer   Heart Attack/Stroke

Stress Group

Percentage of Deaths

Type I   Type II   Type III   Type IV

Top: More of the Type 1 (cancer-prone personality) people who died during a 10-year period in Heidelberg, West Germany, succumbed to cancer than died of heart disease. More of the Type 2 (heart disease-prone personality) people died of heart-related problems. These two diseases claimed only a small percentage of Types 3 and 4 (healthy personalities). **Bottom:** This mind-body pattern showed up to a much greater degree among people living under a lot of stress, indicating that stress can exacerbate these illnesses.

already have cancer. Grossarth-Maticek formed 24 pairs of cancer patients, each pair equal in age, sex, social background, type and extent of cancer and medical treatment. One person in each pair was allocated by chance to behavior therapy, one to a no-therapy group. Survival on the average was about five years for the

therapy group and only three years for the other group.

In another study, we compared the effectiveness of behavior therapy as an adjunct to chemotherapy. Of 100 woman, all with terminal breast cancer, 50 elected to have chemotherapy and 50 rejected it.

Half of each group also received behavior therapy. Survival rates were 11 months for those who received no type of therapy, 14 months for those who received only chemotherapy, 15 months for those who received only behavior therapy and 22 months for those who received both. The combined effect of both types of therapy is stronger than simply adding the individual effects of chemotherapy and behavior therapy.

The names and addresses of all participants in the preventive therapy studies were given to two independent research organizations, which were responsible for ascertaining death and cause of death. Thus there was reasonable control over the procedures.

Similar results, although using somewhat different methods and populations, have been obtained independently in the United States. In one study, psychiatrist David Spiegel and his colleagues at the Stanford University School of Medicine have reported on the effects of a psychotherapy group treatment for breast cancer patients. The average survival rate during the study was 35 months for the group in therapy, as opposed to just 19 months for the group that was not — a difference even greater than that reported by Grossarth-Maticek.

Psychologist Judith Rodin at Yale University Medical School has also found that a similar type of therapy can lower the cortisol levels of elderly women in a nursing home and prolong their lives. This is very important: Cortisol may be the link between personality and stress, on the one hand, and cancer on the other. Cortisol has often been linked with depression and feelings of hopelessness and helplessness; also, cortisol weakens the immune system, thus rendering it less capable of dealing with menaces such as cancer cells. This may be one way in which personality, stress and disease interact.

These results are impressive and suggest a revolution in medical practice. The type of therapy I've described would go a long way toward preventing early deaths from cancer and coronary heart disease. It would also significantly decrease the enormous health budget which has to pay for diagnosis and treatment, hospital care and operations, and so much else entailed by high rates of cancer and heart disease. Equally important, life prolonged through behavior therapy might not entail the very severe side effects of chemotherapy and other types of medical intervention.

I am not suggesting that we should completely reorganize modern medicine

Steps to a Healthier Self

KATARINA KOLB loved her married boyfriend, but he seemed to be much more concerned about his wife than he was about her. Katarina, a 38-year-old German woman, also felt rejected by her father but could not speak to him about it. And she had breast cancer.

Katarina — not her real name — felt depressed and hopeless. According to psychologists Ronald Grossarth-Maticek and Hans Eysenck, she had the classic personality traits of a person vulnerable to cancer. She repressed her anger and anxiety, and felt helpless to find ways to solve her problems.

To change this disease-prone behavior, Katarina took a course of treatment that Grossarth-Maticek and Eysenck call "autonomy training." During either individual or group sessions, therapists explain the difference between the healthy and disease-prone personalities and use relaxation methods, coping techniques and desensitization to help patients move toward the healthy personality style. Grossarth-Maticek and Eysenck use this approach with both cancer-prone and heart-disease-prone people. Individuals susceptible to heart disease learn to abandon the tendencies toward hostility and aggression that the researchers say put them at risk. The key change for cancer-prone people is to stop being overly passive.

Cancer-prone personality types often believe that they are incapable of meeting their needs on their own and depend on another person, job or institution to enhance their sense of self. Katarina, for example, could not get the support she longed for from her married boyfriend but felt she couldn't get along without him. Her feelings of helplessness and anxiety led to passive acceptance of the situation.

When the therapist asked Katarina to explain her behavior, she gained a sense of perspective on herself for the first time. "I've never really thought about this, but it's very destructive, really. Every time I get rejected I get depressed." At her therapist's suggestion, she began to write down ways to get rid of self-defeating behavior.

Her first step was to avoid confrontations with her father in which she knew she would end up feeling rejected. "I won't make demands on him, because when I do, I usually lose and I find that difficult to bear." The therapist helped her use mental imagery to picture several situations involving her father in which she had no expectations and did not need to make any demands.

Katarina reported success at her next session and said she was beginning to like and value herself. She was becoming less dependent on her father and boyfriend and wanted to find new, interesting activities to take her mind off her illness. "I will call up my girlfriend and ask her to go for a walk with me every day, and I will ask my old tennis partner whether he would like to come and have a game with me," she decided.

By the next session, Katarina had gone for several walks and had found three new tennis partners. She told her therapist that she wanted to be more relaxed; she wanted "a state in which inner inhibitions and fears are reduced, in which I believe in myself, trust myself and think I am doing the right thing." The therapist put her into a state of deep hypnosis and repeated some suggestions, created by Katarina herself: "I become more relaxed, happier and happier, and find myself in a wonderful landscape near the sea. I am at one with nature and free of all inhibitions. At the same time I can believe in myself and the success of all my wishes."

Eventually, Katarina sought ways to change her relationship with her boyfriend. He usually visited her once a day, promising to stay for a long visit but always left after only a short time. "Such behavior I will not tolerate any more!" she decided. Again, she used mental imagery, picturing unfulfilling moments in the relationship, and soon she had little desire to see her boyfriend again.

Mental imagery is also used to help other cancer patients combat their disease. Patients visualize white blood cells conquering a malignancy, and by doing so begin to feel some mastery over the illness, while also learning to release anger and resentment.

Autonomy training emphasizes avoiding behavior that leads to short-term solutions, such as escaping a personal rejection, but has long-term negative effects, such as an overall sense of helplessness. And Katarina had clearly reached a new level of autonomy. By ending her relationship with her boyfriend she chose long-term independence over the short-term goal of having some of her boyfriend's attention.

Grossarth-Maticek and Eysenck have found that the patients who succeed in changing their behavior in this way become more self-reliant, less demanding and less rigid than those who don't learn to make these changes. And for those who make the changes, Grossarth-Maticek and Eysenck's research shows that chances of getting cancer are greatly reduced. If they already have the disease, their lives should be prolonged by several years. While Katarina still had some self-doubts at the end of her therapy, she also had learned coping skills to deal with her problems. "I have experienced the negative consequences from putting one's self second," she said. "I shall always keep these consequences in my thoughts, act accordingly and feel good about myself."

— MIA ADESSA

on the basis of these results; obviously as in all such studies, there are faults and possible errors which make it imperative that an independent replication be carried out. No study is perfect, and science demands replication, particularly where life-and-death consequences are so strongly involved.

We obviously are only at the beginning of understanding the apparent interaction between body and mind, but as the Indian sage, Mahābhārata, said 4,000 years ago, "There are two classes of disease — bodily and mental. Each arises from the other, and neither exists without the other. Mental disorders arise from physical ones, and likewise physical disorders arise from mental ones." As the physicist has given up contrasting time and space and now deals with a space-time continuum, so we should stop talking about body and mind as separate entities and rather speak of a body-mind continuum. The study of this continuum will have vital consequences for our understanding of the human condition and may revolutionize our conception of disease, prevention and cure.

The Health Personality Test

THIS IS a short scale for rating yourself according to the four health personality types. This test is intended to illustrate the differences among the personality types. Indicate how closely the description in each question fits you by circling a number from **1** to **10** that best describes you or your situation. **1** means "Not at all" and **10** means "Very much."

1) Have you been repeatedly hopeless and helpless during the last 10 years of your life, either because of the withdrawal of persons who were very important to you and/or your failure to achieve particularly important aims in life? This hopelessness and depression was caused because these events made it impossible for you to satisfy your most important emotional needs, such as those for love, nearness, understanding and recognition. The cause might be the death of or separation from some particularly important person, causing disappointment and difficulties. How closely does this description fit your own case?

Not at all 1 2 3 4 5 6 7 8 9 10 Very much

2) Have you been repeatedly excited, annoyed and resigned in the last 10 years because people disturbed you and interfered with your plans? This excitement and annoyance was caused by your failure, in spite of constant effort to change the situation, allowing some person or persons to prevent the satisfaction of your all-important needs or the achievement of an all-important goal, such as happiness with a sexual partner or advancement at work. How closely does this description fit your own case?

Not at all 1 2 3 4 5 6 7 8 9 10 Very much

3) Considering the past 10 years, particularly your relations with people who were particularly important to you from an emotional point of view (either positively or negatively), which of the four reactions described below would be most descriptive of you and to what extent?

A) I seek and long for closeness and emotional contact with a person or persons who are at the moment too distant from me because of a death, a separation, lack of understanding on the part of my partner, or some shocking or too-demanding events. I would be willing to do anything to diminish this distance, but I do not succeed in reaching the wished-for intimacy. How closely does this description fit your own case?

Not at all 1 2 3 4 5 6 7 8 9 10 Very much

B) I seek distance or separation from one person or persons whose closeness to me (as a partner, in a work or other situation) I experience as crushing. In spite of my efforts I fail to achieve this distancing or separation, largely because of fear of the consequences, such as fear of financial difficulties. How closely does this description fit your own case?

Not at all 1 2 3 4 5 6 7 8 9 10 Very much

C) I alternate between great emotional closeness to a person who is important to me and great emotional distancing and separation. My actions only achieve a regular alteration of too-great closeness and too-great distance interspersed with moments in which distance and nearness are optimal. How closely does this description fit your own case?

Not at all 1 2 3 4 5 6 7 8 9 10 Very much

D) My relations with people who are important to me are neither crushingly close nor too-distant emotionally. Near-ness and distance are for the most part optimal and regulated appropriately. I increase the distance from people who annoy me and decrease the distance to people with whom I interact positively. How closely does this description fit your own case?

Not at all 1 2 3 4 5 6 7 8 9 10 Very much

4) During the past 10 years, have you always been in a position to enjoy relaxation in various bodily activities, such as sports, work and sex, using these activities as a pleasant alternative to mental relaxation and activity? Yes/No
If the answer is No, were you prevented from doing so:
A) By the sudden or gradual change due to persons distancing themselves from you or by the loss of a position in a work situation?
B) Because of people or conditions disturbing or annoying you without your having the power to change them according to your desires, or to leave them?
C) Through people who alternated and made emotionally unacceptable demands on you while at other times distancing themselves from you.

5) In the past 10 years, have you repeatedly acted in such a way that emotionally negative (undesirable) consequences occurred? Were you unable to find ways of acting that led to more positive and desirable consequences, such as better interaction between you and emotionally important persons? How closely does this description fit your own case?

Not at all 1 2 3 4 5 6 7 8 9 10 Very much

6) Do you have frequent feelings of fear and anxiety (a general state of anxiety, a syndrome of anxiety, periods during which you suffer from anxiety, fears of being threatened or persecuted, fear of not being able to cope with life and its problems, fear of specific situations)? These fears should be relatively unrealistic, in the sense that you are in the position to avoid them if need be. How strong is this anxiety?

Not at all 1 2 3 4 5 6 7 8 9 10 Very much

HOW TO SCORE THE TEST. You get four scores on this test, not just one; each score corresponds to a health personality type. Type 1 is cancer-prone, Type 2 is heart-disease-prone, Type 3 is healthy with a tendency to act unconventionally and Type 4 is also healthy. You compare your four scores with one another, not to the scores of other people. The highest of your scores indicates your health personality.

Type 1 Add the ratings for question 1 and question 3A. If the answer to question 4 is "No" and the reason is A, add 10 more points. Add on the ratings for question 5 and question 6. Sum up the total.

Type 2 Add the ratings for question 2 and question 3B. If the answer to question 4 is "No" and the reason is B, add 10 more points. Add on the ratings for question 5 and question 6. Sum up the total.

Type 3 Add the rating on any part of question 3 to the rating on question 3C. If the answer to question 4 is "no" and the reason is C, add 10 more points. Add on the ratings for question 5 and question 6. Sum up the total.

Type 4 If your total score on questions 1, 2 and 3 was less than 15, give yourself 10 points. Add the rating on question 3D. If the answer to question 4 is "Yes," add 10 more points. If your rating on either question 5 or question 6 was less than 5 points, give yourself 10 points for that question. Sum up the total.

Erikson, In His Own Old Age, Expands His View of Life

In partnership with his wife, the psychoanalyst describes how wisdom of the elderly is born.

Daniel Goleman

In his ninth decade of life, Erik H. Erikson has expanded the psychological model of the life cycle that he put forward with his wife, Joan, almost 40 years ago.

Their original work profoundly changed psychology's view of human development. Now, breaking new ground, they have spelled out the way the lessons of each major stage of life can ripen into wisdom in old age. They depict an old age in which one has enough conviction in one's own completeness to ward off the despair that gradual physical disintegration can too easily bring.

"You've got to learn to accept the law of life, and face the fact that we disintegrate slowly," Mr. Erikson said.

On a recent afternoon, in a rare interview, they sat in their favorite nook in a bay window of Mrs. Erikson's study on the second floor of their Victorian house near Harvard Square in Cambridge, Mass. "The light is good here and it's cozy at night," Mrs. Erikson told a visitor.

Although Mr. Erikson has a comfortable study downstairs, and Mrs. Erikson, an artist and author in her own right, has a separate workroom, they prefer to spend their time together in this quiet corner, in the spirit of their lifelong collaboration.

Mr. Erikson, who never earned an academic degree (he is usually called Professor Erikson), deeply affected the study of psychology. Many believe that his widely read books made Freud pertinent to the struggles of adult life and shaped the way people today think about their own emotional growth. He gave psychology the term "identity crisis."

When Mr. Erikson came to this country in 1933 from Vienna, he spoke little English. Mrs. Erikson, a Canadian, has always lent her editorial hand to those writings of her husband on which she did not act as co-author.

As Mr. Erikson approaches 87 years of age and Mrs. Erikson 86, old age is one topic very much on their minds.

Their original chart of the life cycle was prepared in 1950 for a White House conference on childhood and youth. In it, each stage of life, from infancy and early childhood on, is associated with a specific psychological struggle that contributes to a major aspect of personality.

In infancy, for instance, the tension is between trust and mistrust; if an infant feels trusting, the result is a sense of hope.

In old age, according to the new addition to the stages, the struggle is between a sense of one's own integrity and a feeling of defeat, of despair about one's life in the phase of normal physical disintegration. The fruit of that struggle is wisdom.

"When we looked at the life cycle in our 40's, we looked to old people for wisdom," Mrs. Erikson said. "At 80, though, we look at other 80-year-olds to see who got wise and who not. Lots of old people don't get wise, but you don't get wise unless you age."

Originally, the Eriksons defined wisdom in the elderly as a more objective concern with life itself in the face of death. Now that they are at that stage of life, they have been developing a more detailed description of just what the lessons of each part of life lend to wisdom in old age. For each earlier stage of development they see a parallel development toward the end of life's journey.

For instance, the sense of trust that begins to develop from the infant's experience of a loving and supportive environment becomes, in old age, an appreciation of human interdependence, according to the Eriksons.

"Life doesn't make any sense without interdependence," Mrs. Erikson said. "We need each other and the sooner we learn that the better for us all."

The second stage of life, which begins in early childhood with learning control over one's own body, builds the sense of will on the one hand, or shame and doubt on the other. In old age, one's experience is almost a mirror image of what it was earlier as the body deteriorates and one needs to learn to accept it.

In "play age" or preschool children, what is being learned is a sense of initiative and purpose in life, as well as a sense of playfulness and creativity, the theory holds.

Two lessons for old age from that stage of life are empathy and resilience, as the Eriksons see it.

"The more you know yourself, the more patience you have for what you see in others," Mrs. Erikson said. "You don't have to accept what people do, but understand what leads them to do it. The stance this leads to is to forgive even though you still oppose."

The child's playfulness becomes, too, a sense of humor about life. "I can't imagine a wise old person who can't laugh," said Mr. Erikson. "The world is full of ridiculous dichotomies."

At school age, the Erikson's next stage, the child strives to become effective and industrious, and so develops a sense of competence; if he or she does not, the outcome is feelings of inferiority.

HUMILITY IN OLD AGE

In old age, as one's physical and sensory abilities wane, a lifelong sense of effectiveness is a critical resource. Reflections in old age on the course one's life has taken—especially comparing one's early hopes and dreams with the life one actually lived—foster humility. Thus, humility in old age is a realistic appreciation of one's limits and competencies.

The adolescent's struggle to overcome confusion and find a lifelong identity results in the capacity for commitment and fidelity, the Eriksons hold. Reflections in old age on the complexity of living go hand in hand with a new way of perceiving, one that merges sensory, logical and esthetic perception, they say. Too often, they say, people overemphasize logic and ignore other modes of knowing.

"If you leave out what your senses tell you, your thinking is not so good," Mrs. Erikson said.

In young adulthood, the conflict is between finding a balance between lasting intimacy and the need for isolation. At the last stage of life, this takes the form of coming to terms with love expressed and unexpressed during one's entire life; the understanding of the complexity of relationships is a facet of wisdom.

"You have to live intimacy out over many years, with all the complications of a long-range relationship, really to

The Completed Life Cycle

In the Eriksons' view, each stage of life is associated with a specific psychological conflict and a specific resolution. In a new amplification, lessons from each of the earlier stages mature into the many facets of wisdom in old age, shown in column at right.

Conflict and resolution	Culmination in old age
Old Age Integrity vs. despair: wisdom	Existential identity; a sense of integrity strong enough to withstand physical disintegration.
Adulthood Generativity vs. stagnation: care	Caritas, caring for others, and agape, empathy and concern.
Early Adulthood Intimacy vs. isolation: love	Sense of complexity of relationships; value of tenderness and loving freely.
Adolescence Identity vs. confusion: fidelity	Sense of complexity of life; merger of sensory, logical and aesthetic perception.
School Age Industry vs. inferiority: competence	Humility; acceptance of the course of one's life and unfulfilled hopes.
Play Age Initiative vs. guilt: purpose	Humor; empathy; resilience.
Early Childhood Autonomy vs. shame: will	Acceptance of the cycle of life, from integration to disintegration.
Infancy Basic trust vs. mistrust: hope	Appreciation of interdependence and relatedness.

understand it," Mrs. Erikson said. "Anyone can flirt around with many relationships, but commitment is crucial to intimacy. Loving better is what comes from understanding the complications of a long-term intimate bond."

She added: "You put such a stress on passion when you're young. You learn about the value of tenderness when you grow old. You also learn in late life not to hold, to give without hanging on; to love freely, in the sense of wanting nothing in return."

In the adult years, the psychological tension is between what the Eriksons call generativity and caring on the one hand and self-absorption and stagnation on the other. Generativity expresses itself, as Mrs. Erikson put it, in "taking care to pass on to the next generation what you've contributed to life."

Mr. Erikson sees a widespread failing

in modern life.

"The only thing that can save us as a species is seeing how we're not thinking about future generations in the way we live," he said. "What's lacking is generativity, a generativity that will promote positive values in the lives of the next generation. Unfortunately, we set the example of greed, wanting a bigger and better everything, with no thought of what will make it a better world for our great-grandchildren. That's why we go on depleting the earth: we're not thinking of the next generations."

UNDERSTANDING GENERATIVITY

As an attribute of wisdom in old age, generativity has two faces. One is "caritas," a Latin word for charity, which the Eriksons take in the broad sense of caring for others. The other is "agape," a Greek word for love, which they define as a kind of empathy.

The final phase of life, in which integrity battles despair, culminates in a full wisdom to the degree each earlier phase of life has had a positive resolution, the Eriksons believe. If everything has gone well, one achieves a sense of integrity, a sense of completeness, of personal wholeness that is strong enough to offset the downward psychological pull of the inevitable physical disintegration.

Despair seems quite far from the Eriksons in their own lives. Both continue to exemplify what they described in the title of a 1986 book, "Vital Involvement in Old Age." Mr. Erikson is writing about, among other things, the sayings of Jesus. Mrs. Erikson's most recent book, "Wisdom and the Senses," sets out evidence that the liveliness of the senses throughout life, and the creativity and playfulness that this brings, is the keystone of wisdom in old age.

"The importance of the senses came to us in old age," said Mr. Erikson, who now wears a hearing aid and walks with a slow, measured dignity.

In her book, Mrs. Erikson argues that modern life allows too little time for the pleasures of the senses. She says: "We start to lose touch with the senses in school: we call play, which stimulates the senses and makes them acute, a waste of time or laziness. The schools relegate play to sports. We call that play, but it isn't; it's competitive, not in the spirit of a game."

The Eriksons contend that wisdom has little to do with formal learning. "What is real wisdom?" Mrs. Erikson asked. "It comes from life experience, well digested. It's not what comes from reading great books. When it comes to

understanding life, experiential learning is the only worthwhile kind; everything else is hearsay."

Mr. Erikson has been continuing a line of thought he set out in a Yale Review article in 1981 on the sayings of Jesus and their implications for the sense of "I," an argument that takes on the concept of the "ego" in Freudian thought.

"The trouble with the word 'ego' is its

The Eriksons contend that wisdom has little to do with formal learning.

---

technical connotations," Mr. Erikson said. "It has bothered me that 'ego' was used as the translation of the German word 'Ich.' That's wrong. Freud was referring to the simple sense of "I."

Another continuing concern for the Eriksons has been the ethics of survival, and what they see as the urgent need to overcome the human tendency to define other groups as an enemy, an outgrowth of the line of thinking Mr. Erikson began in his biography of Gandhi.

Mr. Erikson was trained in psychoanalysis in Vienna while Freud was still there, and worked closely with Freud's daughter Anna in exploring ways to apply psychoanalytic methods to children. That expertise made him welcome at

Harvard, where he had his first academic post.

There he began the expansion of Freud's thinking that was to make him world famous. By describing in his books "Childhood and Society" and "Identity and the Life Cycle" how psychological growth is shaped throughout life, not just during the formative early years that Freud focused on, Mr. Erikson made a quantium leap in Freudian thought.

Over the years since first coming to Harvard, Mr. Erikson has spent time at other universities and hospitals, including Yale in the late 1930's, the University of California at Berkeley in the 40's, the Austen Riggs Center in Stockbridge, Mass., in the 50's, and again at Harvard through the 60's. Until last year, the Eriksons lived in Marin County near San Francisco, but it is to Cambridge that they returned.

One lure was grandchildren nearby. Their son Kai, with two children, is a professor of sociology at Yale, and their daughter Sue, with one child, also lives nearby.

Informally, Mr. Erikson still continues to supervise therapists. "The students tell me it's the most powerful clinical supervision they've ever had," said Margaret Brenman-Gibson, a professor of psychology in the psychiatry department at Cambridge City Hospital, a part of Harvard Medical School.

In Cambridge, the Eriksons share a rambling three-story Victorian with three other people: a graduate student, a professor of comparative religion and a psychologist. The housemates often take meals together.

"Living communally," said Mrs. Erikson, "is an adventure at our age."

Social Processes

Most psychologists focus their work on the level of the individual person. However, people do not live in social vacuums, but rather interact frequently. If you ask someone to list some of the important aspects of her or his life, you will probably hear several having to do with relationships. The study of how individuals behave in interpersonal relationships has been largely the province of social psychology, although clinical psychology certainly has much to offer as well.

One of the primary focuses of social psychological research has been aggression. As the number of prisoners continues to rise and new prisons are required, the questions about the causes of aggression become more common and urgent. Richard Herrnstein and James Wilson examine the traditional wisdom about criminal behavior running in families, and look specifically at the heritability component.

A very specific and worrisome form of criminal aggression is terrorism, which seems to require and spring from an authoritarian outlook on life. As Bob Altemeyer tells us, prejudice may be dangerous in more ways than we realize.

Social psychology has long been interested in the study of social interaction, but has only recently delved into that most intimate language: touch. Clearly, we touch for a variety of reasons, in varying contexts, and in many different patterns and styles. What forces determine the nature and meaning of touching, and are touches easily discriminated and correctly interpreted? Stephen Thayer's article will fascinate you with the answers to these questions.

One social phenomenon growing rapidly in the United States is the self-help group. Whether aimed at personal growth, the learning of new skills, or the conquering of an addiction, self-help groups are widely claimed to be effective and affordable alternatives or adjuncts to traditional therapy. How do they work? When do they work? Do they sometimes not work at all?

Looking Ahead: Challenge Questions

How convincing is the evidence for a genetic component in criminal behavior? In the best interests of a non-criminal majority, should the reproduction of criminals be prevented?

What should authoritarian leaders, parents, and supervisors expect from the people they interact with? What clues do we get from studies on authoritarianism that might help us to deal with international terrorists?

What factors determine the frequency, intimacy, and meaning of a human touch? Do men and women interpret touch differently?

Under what circumstances should a person be encouraged to participate in a self-help group? Are there any circumstances when you might suggest to a friend that she or he not participate?

ARE CRIMINALS MADE OR BORN?

Evidence indicates that both biological and sociological factors play roles.

Richard J. Herrnstein and James Q. Wilson

Richard J. Herrnstein is a professor of psychology and James Q. Wilson a professor of government at Harvard.

A revolution in our understanding of crime is quietly overthrowing some established doctrines. Until recently, criminologists looked for the causes of crime almost entirely in the offenders' social circumstances. There seemed to be no shortage of circumstances to blame: weakened, chaotic or broken families, ineffective schools, antisocial gangs, racism, poverty, unemployment. Criminologists took seriously, more so than many other students of social behavior, the famous dictum of the French sociologist Emile Durkheim: Social facts must have social explanations. The sociological theory of crime had the unquestioned support of prominent editorialists, commentators, politicians and most thoughtful people.

Today, many learned journals and scholarly works draw a different picture. Sociological factors have not been abandoned, but increasingly it is becoming clear to many scholars that crime is the outcome of an interaction between social factors and certain biological factors, particularly for the offenders who, by repeated crimes, have made public places dangerous. The idea is still controversial, but increasingly, to the old question "Are criminals born or made?" the answer seems to be: both. The causes of crime lie in a combination of predisposing biological traits channeled by social circumstance into criminal behavior. The traits alone do not inevitably lead to crime; the circumstances do not make criminals of everyone; but together they create a population responsible for a large fraction of America's problem of crime in the streets.

Evidence that criminal behavior has deeper roots than social circumstances has always been right at hand, but social science has, until recent years, overlooked its implications. As far as the records show, crime everywhere and throughout history is disproportionately a young man's pursuit. Whether men are 20 or more times as likely to be arrested as women, as is the case in Malawi or Brunei, or only four to six times as likely, as in the United States or France, the sex difference in crime statistics is universal. Similarly, 18-year-olds may sometimes be four times as likely to be criminal as 40-year-olds, while at other times only twice as likely. In the United States, more than half of all arrests for serious property crimes are of 20-year-olds or younger. Nowhere have older persons been as criminal as younger ones.

It is easy to imagine purely social explanations for the effects of age and sex on crime. Boys in many societies are trained by their parents and the society itself to play more roughly and aggressively than girls. Boys are expected to fight back, not to cry,

Intelligence and temperament have heritable bases and influence behavior.

and to play to win. Likewise, boys in many cultures are denied adult responsibilities, kept in a state of prolonged dependence and confined too long in schools that many of them find unrewarding. For a long time, these factors were thought to be the whole story.

Ultimately, however, the very universality of the age and sex differences in crime have alerted some social scientists to the implausibility of a theory that does not look beyond the accidents of particular societies. If cultures as different as Japan's and Sweden's, England's and Mexico's, have sex and age differences in crime, then perhaps we should have suspected from the start that there was something more fundamental going on than parents happening to decide to raise their boys and girls differently. What is it about boys, girls and their parents, in societies of all sorts, that leads them to emphasize, rather than overcome, sex differences? Moreover, even if we believed that every society has arbitrarily decided to inculcate aggressiveness in males, there would still be the greater criminality among *young* males to explain. After all, in some cultures, young boys are not denied adult responsibilities but are kept out of school, put to work tilling the land and made to accept obligations to the society.

But it is no longer necessary to approach questions about the sources of criminal behavior merely with argument and supposition. There is evidence. Much crime, it is agreed, has an aggressive component, and Eleanor Emmons Maccoby, a professor of psychology at Stanford University, and Carol Nagy Jacklin, a psychologist now at the University of Southern California, after reviewing the evidence on sex differences in aggression, concluded that it has a foundation that is at least in part biological. Only that conclusion can be drawn, they said, from data that show that the average man is more aggressive than the average woman in all known

societies, that the sex difference is present in infancy well before evidence of sex-role socialization by adults, that similar sex differences turn up in many of our biological relatives—monkeys and apes. Human aggression has been directly tied to sex hormones, particularly male sex hormones, in experiments on athletes engaging in competitive sports and on prisoners known for violent or domineering behavior. No single line of evidence is decisive and each can be challenged, but all together they convinced Drs. Maccoby and Jacklin, as well as most specialists on the biology of sex differences, that the sexual conventions that assign males the aggressive roles have biological roots.

That is also the conclusion of most researchers about the developmental forces that make adolescence and young adulthood a time of risk for criminal and other nonconventional behavior. This is when powerful new drives awaken, leading to frustrations that foster behavior unchecked by the internalized prohibitions of adulthood. The result is usually just youthful rowdiness, but, in a minority of cases, it passes over the line into crime.

The most compelling evidence of biological factors for criminality comes from two studies—one of twins, the other of adopted boys. Since the 1920's it has been understood that twins may develop from a single fertilized egg, resulting in identical genetic endowments—identical twins—or from a pair of separately fertilized eggs that have about half their genes in common—fraternal twins. A standard procedure for estimating how important genes are to a trait is to compare the similarity between identical twins with that between fraternal twins. When identical twins are clearly more similar in a trait than fraternal twins, the trait probably has high heritability.

There have been about a dozen studies of criminality using twins. More than 1,500 pairs of twins have been studied in the

United States, the Scandinavian countries, Japan, West Germany, Britain and elsewhere, and the result is qualitatively the same everywhere. Identical twins are more likely to have similar criminal records than fraternal twins. For example, the late Karl O. Christiansen, a Danish criminologist, using the Danish Twin Register, searched police, court and prison records for entries regarding twins born in a certain region of Denmark between 1881 and 1910. When an identical twin had a criminal record, Christiansen found, his or her co-twin was more than twice as likely to have one also than when a fraternal twin had a criminal record.

In the United States, a similar result has recently been reported by David Rowe, a psychologist at the University of Oklahoma, using questionnaires instead of official records to measure criminality. Twins in high school in almost all the school districts of Ohio received questionnaires by mail, with a promise of confidentiality as well as a small payment if the questionnaires were filled out and returned. The twins were asked about their activities, including their delinquent behavior, about their friends and about their co-twins. The identical twins were more similar in delinquency than the fraternal twins. In addition, the twins who shared more activities with each other were no more likely to be similar in delinquency than those who shared fewer activities.

No single method of inquiry should be regarded as conclusive. But essentially the same results are found in studies of adopted children. The idea behind such studies is to find a sample of children adopted early in life, cases in which the criminal histories of both adopting and biological parents are known. Then, as the children grow up, researchers can discover how predictive of their criminality are the family histories of their adopting and biological parents. Recent studies show that the biological family his-

tory contributes substantially to the adoptees' likelihood of breaking the law.

For example, Sarnoff Mednick, a psychologist at the University of Southern California, and his associates in the United States and Denmark have followed a sample of several thousand boys adopted in Denmark between 1927 and 1947. Boys with criminal biological parents and noncriminal adopting parents were more likely to have criminal records than those with noncriminal biological and criminal adopting parents. The more criminal convictions a boy's natural parents had, the greater the risk of criminality for boys being raised by adopting parents who had no records. The risk was unrelated to whether the boy or his adopting parents knew about the natural parents' criminal records, whether the natural parents committed their crimes before or after the boy was given up for adoption, or whether the boy was adopted immediately after birth or a year or two later. The results of this study have been confirmed in Swedish and American samples of adopted children.

Because of studies like these, many sociologists and criminologists now accept the existence of genetic factors contributing to criminality. When there is disagreement, it is about how large the genetic contribution to crime is and about how the criminality of biological parents is transmitted to their children.

Both the twin and adoption studies show that genetic contributions are not alone responsible for crime — there is, for example, some increase in criminality among boys if their adopted fathers are criminal even when their biological parents are not, and not every co-twin of a criminal identical twin becomes criminal himself. Although it appears, on average, to be substantial, the

precise size of the genetic contribution to crime is probably unknowable, particularly since the measures of criminality itself are now so crude.

We have a bit more to go on with respect to the link that transmits a predisposition toward crime from parents to children. No one believes there are "crime genes," but there are two major attributes that have, to some degree, a heritable base and that appear to influence criminal behavior. These are intelligence and temperament. Hundreds of studies have found that the more genes people share, the more likely they are to resemble each other intellectually and temperamentally.

Starting with studies in the 1930's, the average offender in broad samples has consistently scored 91 to 93 on I.Q. tests for which the general population's average is 100. The typical offender does worse on the verbal items of intelligence tests than on the nonverbal items but is usually below average on both.

Criminologists have long known about the correlation between criminal behavior and I.Q., but many of them have discounted it for various reasons. Some have suggested that the correlation can be explained away by the association between low socioeconomic status and crime, on the one hand, and that between low I.Q. and low socioeconomic status, on the other. These criminologists say it is low socioeconomic status, rather than low I.Q., that fosters crime. Others have questioned whether I.Q. tests really measure intelligence for the populations that are at greater risk for breaking the law. The low scores of offenders, the argument goes, betray a culturally deprived background or alienation from our society's values rather than low intelligence. Finally, it is often noted that the offenders in some studies have been caught for their crimes. Perhaps the ones who got away have higher I.Q.s.

But these objections have proved to be less telling than they once seemed to be. There are, for example, many poor law-abiding people living in deprived environments, and one of their more salient characteristics is that they have higher I.Q. scores than those in the same environment who break the law.

Then, too, it is a common misconception that I.Q. tests are invalid for people from disadvantaged backgrounds. If what is implied by this criticism is that scores predict academic potential or job performance differently for different groups, then the criticism is wrong. A comprehensive recent survey sponsored by the National Academy of Sciences concluded that "tests predict about as well for one group as for another." And that some highly intelligent criminals may well be good at eluding capture is fully consistent with the belief that offenders, in general, have lower scores than nonoffenders.

If I.Q. and criminality are linked, what may explain the link? There are several possibilities. One is that low scores on I.Q. tests signify greater difficulty in grasping the likely consequences of action or in learning the meaning and significance of moral codes. Another is that low scores, especially on the verbal component of the tests, mean trouble in school, which leads to frustration, thence to resentment, anger and delinquency. Still another is that persons who are not as skillful as others in expressing themselves verbally may find it more rewarding to express themselves in ways in which they will do better, such as physical threat or force.

For some repeat offenders, the predisposition to criminality may be more a matter of temperament than intelligence. Impulsiveness, insensitivity to social mores, a lack of deep and enduring emotional attachments to others and an appetite for danger are among the temperamental characteristics of high-rate offenders. Temperament is, to a degree, heritable, though not as much so as intelligence. All parents know that their children, shortly after birth, begin to exhibit certain characteristic ways of behaving — they are placid or fussy, shy or bold. Some of the traits endure, among them aggressiveness and hyperactivity, although they change in form as the child develops. As the child grows up, these traits, among others, may gradually unfold into a disposition toward unconventional, defiant or antisocial behavior.

Lee Robins, a sociologist at Washington University School of Medicine in St. Louis, reconstructed 30 years of the lives of more than 500 children who were patients in the 1920's at a child guidance clinic in St. Louis. She was interested in the early precursors of chronic sociopathy, a condition of antisocial personality that often includes criminal behavior as one of its symptoms. Adult sociopaths in her sample who did not suffer from psychosis, mental retardation or addiction, were, without exception, antisocial before they were 18. More than half of the male sociopaths had serious symptoms before they were 11. The main childhood precursors were truancy, poor school performance, theft, running away, recklessness, slovenliness, impulsiveness and guiltlessness. The more symptoms in childhood, the greater the risk of sociopathy in adulthood.

Other studies confirm and extend Dr. Robins's conclusions. For example, two psychologists, John J. Conger of the University of Colorado and Wilbur Miller of Drake University in Des Moines, searching back over the histories of a sample of delinquent boys in Denver, found that "by the end of the third grade, future delinquents were already seen by their teachers as more poorly adapted than their classmates. They appeared to have less regard for the rights and feelings of their peers; less awareness of the need to accept responsibility for their obligations, both as individuals and as members of a group, and poorer attitudes toward authority."

Traits that foreshadow serious, recurrent criminal behavior have been traced all the way back to behavior patterns such as hyperactivity and unusual fussiness, and neurological signs such as atypical brain waves or reflexes. In at least a minority of cases, these are detectable in the first few years of life. Some of the characteristics are sex-linked. There is evidence that newborn females are more likely than newborn males to smile, to cling to their mothers, to be receptive to touching and talking, to be sensitive to certain stimuli, such as being touched by a cloth, and to have less upper-body strength. Mothers certainly treat girls and boys differently, but the differences are not simply a matter of the mother's choice — female babies are more responsive than male babies to precisely the kind of treatment that is regarded as "feminine." When adults are asked to play with infants, they play with them in ways they think are appropriate to the infants' sexes. But there is also some evidence that when the sex of the infant is concealed, the behavior of the adults is influenced by the conduct of the child.

Premature infants or those born with low birth weights have a special problem. These children are vulnerable to any adverse circumstances in their environment — including child abuse — that may foster crime. Although nurturing parents can compensate for adversity, cold or inconsistent parents may exacerbate it. Prematurity and low birth weight may result from poor prenatal care, a bad diet or excessive use of alcohol or drugs. Whether the bad care is due to poverty, ignorance or anything else, here we see criminality arising from biological, though not necessarily genetic, factors. It is now known that these babies are more likely than normal babies to be the victims of child abuse.

We do not mean to blame child abuse on the victim by saying that premature and low-birth-weight infants are more difficult to care for and thus place a great strain on the parents. But unless parents are emotionally prepared for the task of caring for such children, they may vent their frustration at the infant's unresponsiveness by hitting or neglecting it. Whatever it is in parent and child that leads to prematurity or low birth weight is compounded by the subsequent interaction between them. Similarly, children with low I.Q.s may have difficulty in understanding rules, but if their parents also have poor verbal skills, they may have difficulty in communicating rules, and so each party to the conflict exacerbates the defects of the other.

THE STATEMENT that biology plays a role in explaining human behavior, especially criminal behavior, sometimes elicits a powerful political or ideological reaction. Fearful that what is being proposed is a crude biological determinism, some critics deny the evidence while others wish the evidence to be confined to scientific journals. Scientists who have merely proposed studying the possible effects of chromosomal abnormalities on behavior have been ruthlessly attacked by other scientists, as have those who have made public the voluminous data showing the heritability of intelligence and temperament.

Some people worry that any claim that biological factors influence criminality is tantamount to saying that the higher crime rate of black compared to white Americans has a genetic basis. But no responsible work in the field leads to any such conclusion. The data show that of all the reasons people vary in their crime rates, race is far less important than age, sex, intelligence and the other individual factors that vary within races. Any study of the causes of crime must therefore first consider the individual factors. Differences among races may have many explanations, most of them having nothing to do with biology.

The intense reaction to the study of biological factors in crime, we believe, is utterly misguided. In fact, these discoveries, far from implying that "criminals are born" and should be locked up forever, suggest new and imaginative ways of reducing criminality by benign treatment. The opportunity we have is precisely analogous to that which we had when the biological bases of other disorders were established. Mental as well as physical illness — alcoholism, learning disabilities of various sorts, and perhaps even susceptibilities to drug addiction — now seem to have genetic components. In each case, new understanding energized the search for treatment and gave it new direction. Now we know that many forms of depression can be successfully treated with drugs; in time we may learn the same of Alzheimer's disease. Alcoholics are helped when they understand that some persons, because of their predisposition toward addiction to alcohol, should probably never consume it at all. A chemical treatment of the predisposition is a realistic possibility. Certain types of slow learners can already be helped by spe-

cial programs. In time, others will be also.

Crime, admittedly, may be a more difficult program. So many different acts are criminal that it is only with considerable poetic license that we can speak of "criminality" at all. The bank teller who embezzles $500 to pay off a gambling debt is not engaging in the same behavior as a person who takes $500 from a liquor store at the point of a gun or one who causes $500 worth of damage by drunkenly driving his car into a parked vehicle. Moreover, crime, unlike alcoholism or dyslexia, exposes a person to the formal condemnation of society and the possibility of imprisonment. We naturally and rightly worry about treating all "criminals" alike, or stigmatizing persons whom we think might become criminal by placing them in special programs designed to prevent criminality.

But these problems are not insurmountable barriers to better ways of thinking about crime prevention. Though criminals are of all sorts, we know that a very small fraction of all young males commit so large a fraction of serious street crime that we can properly blame these chronic offenders for most such crime. We also know that chronic offenders typically begin their misconduct at an early age. Early family and preschool programs may be far better repositories for the crime-prevention dollar than rehabilitation programs aimed — usually futilely — at the 19- or 20-year-old veteran offender. Prevention programs risk stigmatizing children, but this may be less of a risk than is neglect. If stigma were a problem to be avoided at all costs, we would have to dismantle most special-needs education programs.

Having said all this, we must acknowledge that there is at present little hard evidence that we know how to inhibit the development of delinquent tendencies in children. There are some leads, such as family training programs of the sort pioneered at the Oregon Social Learning Center, where parents are taught how to use small rewards and penalties to alter the behavior of misbehaving children. There is also evidence from David Weikart and Lawrence Schweinhart of the High/Scope Educational Research Foundation at Ypsilanti, Mich., that preschool education programs akin to Project Head Start may reduce later deliquency. There is nothing yet to build a national policy on, but there are ideas worth exploring by carefully repeating and refining these pioneering experimental efforts.

Above all, there is a case for redirecting research into the causes of crime in ways that take into account the interaction of biological and social factors. Some scholars, such as the criminologist Marvin E. Wolfgang and his colleagues at the University of Pennsylvania, are already exploring these issues by analyzing social and biological information from large groups as they age from infancy to adulthood and linking the data to criminal behavior. But much more needs to be done.

It took years of patiently following the life histories of many men and women to establish the linkages between smoking or diet and disease; it will also take years to unravel the complex and subtle ways in which intelligence, temperament, hormonal levels and other traits combine with family circumstances and later experiences in school and elsewhere to produce human character.

MARCHING IN STEP

A Psychological Explanation of State Terror

BOB ALTEMEYER

BOB ALTEMEYER, *an associate professor of psychology at the University of Manitoba, in Winnipeg, is the author of* RIGHT-WING AUTHORITARIANISM, *published in 1981, and of the forthcoming* UNDERSTANDING RIGHT-WING AUTHORITARIANISM, *to be published by Jossey-Bass. The research described in this article was awarded the American Association for the Advancement of Science's Prize for Behavioral Science Research in 1986.*

DURING THE SECOND WORLD WAR, as the persecution of European Jews was reaching its terrible, final savagery, a team of social scientists at the University of California at Berkeley embarked on a research project of rare urgency: they set out to uncover the psychological roots of anti-Semitism—a prejudice that had proved virulent enough not only to place innocent people on trains to Auschwitz and Buchenwald but to turn millions of their neighbors into indifferent spectators. In a series of attitude surveys, conducted with American subjects, the Berkeley researchers found that people who were hostile toward Jews often expressed similar feelings toward other minorities as well, including blacks, Hispanics, and Filipinos. In addition, these highly prejudiced people seemed to share a great reverence for their own ingroup (a sentiment reminiscent of the Nazis' belief in Aryan supremacy) and an extreme willingness to prostrate themselves before established authorities. All of this led the researchers to conclude that anti-Semitism was not a self-contained phenomenon but a symptom of what they dubbed the prefascist, or authoritarian, personality. Drawing on psychoanalytic theory to describe this odd combination of hostility and submissiveness, they defined the authoritarian as a person whose conscious, rational ego had been overpowered by an overzealous superego and by a seething id.

Starting from the Freudian assumption that the way a person responds to the world is determined largely by early experiences within the family, the Berkeley researchers speculated that authoritarianism is a disguised and delayed expression of the anger felt by children toward cold, harsh, punitive parents. In a 1950 book entitled *The Authoritarian Personality,* the group theorized that, to avoid retaliation, the enraged child learns to conceal these hostile feelings both from his parents and from himself and to direct them instead at society's traditional scapegoats. By belittling and brutalizing social outcasts, the authoritarian could vent his fury at his parents and other dominating authorities without ever appearing defiant. Such behavior would meet the demands of the superego (to be an obedient child or citizen) while at once satisfying the id's urge to attack someone.

From this general idea, the Berkeley group eventually developed a more detailed model, which defined the authoritarian personality in terms of nine distinctive char-acter traits, and designed a test—the F, or Fascism, scale—to measure those traits in people. The F scale consisted of statements, such as "No weakness or difficulty can hold us back if we have enough will power" and "Someday it will probably be shown that astrology can explain a lot of things," with which subjects could agree or disagree to varying extents. A person's response to any given statement was considered a sign of his predisposition toward one of the nine telltale traits: submissiveness; conventionalism; aggressiveness; a concern with power and toughness; a reliance on superstitions and stereotypes; a preoccupation with sex; a projection of one's own undesirable qualities onto others; a lack of introspection; or destructiveness and cynicism. Since people who scored high on the F scale tended also to be extremely prejudiced, the theory appeared valid, and it eventually permeated the culture at large. Anyone who has heard that Hitler's hatred of Jews was rooted in repressed hostility toward his stern father has encountered the popular version of the Berkeley theory.

But there were doubts from the outset about the scientists' methods and conclusions. For one thing, the research was not based on a representative sample of Americans; indeed, forty percent of the highly prejudiced men interviewed for one key study were inmates at the San Quentin penitentiary. Nor had the interviews been conducted by "blind" interrogators (people ignorant of the hypothesis being tested), to guard against biased results. But the loudest criticisms were directed at the F scale itself. Responses to the items in the survey simply did not indicate that highly prejudiced people share all nine character traits. Many respondents who seemed highly superstitious, for example, showed little concern with power and toughness. Similarly, subjects might appear preoccupied with sex but not seem destructive or cynical. And even when relationships were apparent between people's responses to particular survey items, one could not be sure there were similar relationships between the traits supposedly measured by those items. Because the authoritarian response was always to *agree* with a particular statement, it was possible that subjects who seemed to exhibit all nine traits were just engaged in yea-saying—the tendency of test subjects to respond affirmatively to survey items when they have no real opinion.

Because the F scale, for all its shortcomings, served as a general predictor of prejudice, studies based on the test continued for some time to appear in the journals. In the long run, though, these findings showed an uncanny ability to contradict one another, and by the end of the sixties the literature on authoritarianism was such a tangled web that researchers turned to more promising endeavors. The quest to understand the authoritarian

This article is reprinted by permission of *The Sciences*, March/April 1988, pp. 30-38. Individual subscriptions are $14.50 per year. Write to The Sciences, 2 East 63rd Street, New York, NY 10021 or call 1-800-THE-NYAS.

personality, instead of being successfully concluded, was merely abandoned.

There was, however, an underlying pattern in the web. During the late 1960s, I noticed that although F-scale studies had not produced a rigorous definition, much less a convincing explanation, of the authoritarian personality, three of the scale's nine target traits had turned up more regularly than the others. Specifically, the data suggested that people who are highly submissive to established authority (readier than others to accept its judgments and trust its words) tend also to be conventional (clinging to orthodox notions of proper behavior) and to become highly aggressive when they think established authorities will approve.

To test this interpretation, I spent several years analyzing people's responses to hundreds of survey statements taken from the F scale and various other attitude tests. My objective was to determine which traits, of all those that had been deemed relevant to authoritarianism, actually ran together. Consistently, the data suggested that submissiveness, conventionalism, and aggressiveness did but that other traits, including superstition and dogmatism, did not. So, to get a clearer view of the relevant traits, I developed an alternative to the F scale, an attitude survey called the Right-Wing Authoritarianism (RWA) scale. Unlike the old test, the RWA scale has demonstrated consistent statistical links between the traits it measures and has thus provided a reliable overall index of people's authoritarian leanings. And it is now beginning to *explain* particular aspects of the authoritarian's personality, including his propensity to behave so aggressively.

It has been evident, ever since the psychologist Stanley Milgram conducted his famous electric shock experiments during the 1960s, that ordinary people can easily be induced to hurt an innocent victim if commanded by someone (even a scientist in a lab coat) who is perceived as a legitimate authority. But some people seem far readier than others to attack on command. The question of what motivates such behavior in the name of higher authorities is hardly an idle curiosity; some of the most horrifying events of our time—from the Holocaust to the My Lai massacre; from the persecution of dissidents in Chile to the deaths by torture in South African prisons—have been acts of authoritarian aggression. Such atrocities are not unique to any political or economic system; Communist and anti-Communist dictatorships seem equally capable of violent repression. But to the degree that such violence is committed in behalf of a society's established traditions and authorities, it can be called right-wing. In this sense, the mistreatment of Soviet dissidents is no less right-wing than is Guatemalan repression. Understanding the causes and dynamics of such behavior could be a first step toward stopping it—and stopping it surely ranks among the world's more urgent political tasks.

Because people are not necessarily aware of their authoritarian tendencies, let alone prepared to admit them to others, the RWA test does not ask subjects to assess themselves directly. It is presented as a public opinion poll, with each of its thirty statements designed to gauge the respondent's submissiveness ("It is always better to trust the judgment of the proper authorities in government and religion") or conventionalism ("It may be considered old-fashioned by some, but having a decent, respectable appearance is still the mark of a gentleman and, especially, a lady") or aggressiveness ("Once our government leaders and the authorities condemn the dangerous elements in our society, it will be the duty of every patriotic citizen to help stomp out the rot that is poisoning our country from within"). There are nine possible responses to each statement, ranging from "very strongly disagree" (-4) to "very strongly agree" ($+4$), and half the items are worded in such a way that the authoritarian response is to disagree, as with "It is important to protect fully the rights of radicals and deviants." Taken together, a subject's responses provide a numerical measure of his authoritarian leanings.

Since the RWA scale was developed, in 1973, it has been administered to groups throughout North America and in other parts of the world, and those who have scored high on it have been found to share a wide range of attitudes and behavioral patterns. For example, high scorers are more tolerant than others of abuses by government officials (Americans with high RWA scores supported Richard Nixon the longest during the Watergate crisis); they tend, in hypothetical situations, to impose harsher sentences on most lawbreakers; and they are more likely than others to express contempt for various minorities, including Jews, blacks, Asians, Africans, Native Americans, homosexuals, and people with "strange" religions.

Perhaps the most chilling finding of all came from an attitude survey devised in 1982 to see how far people with high RWA scores would go toward supporting state-sanctioned persecution of some group. The survey, known as Posse, was administered to roughly six hundred Canadian college students and several hundred of their parents. It began with this scenario:

Suppose the Canadian government, sometime in the future, passed a law outlawing the Communist Party in Canada. Government officials then stated that the law would be effective only if it were vigorously enforced at the local level, and appealed to every Canadian to aid in the fight against Communism.

This was followed by six statements, and the subjects were asked to indicate on a scale of -4 to $+4$ how well each statement applied to them. Would they tell their friends it was a good law? Identify any Communists they happened to know? Help the police hunt them down? Participate in an attack on the Communist headquarters if it were organized by "the proper authorities"? Endorse the use of "physical force" to make captured Communists reveal the identities of others? Support the execution of Communist leaders?

Most of the subjects said they were unlikely to do these things. But whereas people with low RWA scores considered themselves extremely unlikely to participate, those with high scores said they were only moderately unlikely. These people would presumably be the first to change their minds if the government launched a campaign of propaganda or pressure, as the Nazis did against Jews in Germany. And one could, of course, assemble a fair-sized posse from the respondents who were ready to saddle up **today if the authorities would only give the word.**

Similar studies have shown that high scorers are more likely than others not only to hunt down and kill Communists but to help persecute others, as well. One might expect low scorers to be more aggressive than highs toward, say, the Ku Klux Klan; yet when the Klan was hypothetically outlawed, high scorers remained the least reluctant of five hundred and twenty-six respondents to accept and act on the edict. The same pattern held when Canada's Progressive Conservative Party—a party for which high scorers had, in other surveys, voiced strong support—was banned. Though reluctant to persecute such a respectable group, people with high RWA scores were once again more likely than others to accept the "necessity" of destroying the party. It seems, in short, that they would be the first to attack almost *any* target—left-wing or right-wing, respectable or unsavory—as long as their behavior was sanctioned by some established authority. They themselves surely would feel more hostile toward Communists than toward Progressive Conservatives, but, as these tests make clear, it is not just an authoritarian's hostility that sets him apart. It is his submissiveness—his readiness to substitute an authority's judgment, however depraved, for his own.

WHAT MIGHT ACCOUNT for the authoritarian's hostile tendencies? Of the three classic models of aggression—those defining it broadly as a product of repressed instinctual drives, of frustration, and of social learning—two seem to have little bearing on the authoritarian syndrome.

The repressed-drive explanation advanced by the Berkeley theorists in 1950 has proved difficult to test. When authoritarians are asked to describe their childhoods, or their parents are asked to talk about how they raised their children, there is little evidence of a cold, harsh upbringing. In a sense, this is exactly what the theory predicts—that the authoritarian will conceal his resentment against his parents, even from himself. But, regardless of how well the authoritarian has succeeded at repressing such feelings, they should, according to psychoanalytic theory, be discernible in his dreams, fantasies, and slips of the tongue. Yet when students, identified only by their RWA scores, are encouraged to record their daydreams and fantasies, their journal entries and those of nonauthoritarians are largely indistinguishable. Thus, there is still no sign that authoritarians are motivated by the repressed destructive drives postulated by psychoanalytic theory.

The second classic theory—which says aggression is usually the result of some frustration in life—was first advanced by John Dollard and Neal E. Miller, both of Yale University, in 1939. To support this idea, Dollard and Miller cited, among other things, an inverse relationship between the annual per-acre value of cotton and the number of blacks lynched in fourteen southern states each year. (Low prices, presumably, increased economic frustration among whites, prompting aggression against the scapegoat minority.)

The frustration–aggression hypothesis was taken a step further in 1962 by Leonard Berkowitz, of the University of Wisconsin at Madison, who argued that angry people are especially likely to attack someone if there are cues in their environment that carry violent connotations. In Berkowitz's most celebrated study, students participating in a bogus behavioral experiment were insulted by a confederate whom Berkowitz had instructed to pose as a fellow volunteer. Shortly thereafter, the subjects got a chance to administer what they thought were electric shocks to the confederate—but whereas some of the angry subjects did their shocking at a table strewn with badminton equipment ("for another experiment"), others administered shocks in a room where there were guns on the table. As Berkowitz had predicted, the frustration elicited more aggression from angry subjects with guns in their midst than from those eyeing implements of backyard leisure. Since the two environments were identical in every other respect, the guns seemed to be decisive.

If the frustration model were applicable to *authoritarian* aggression, authoritarians would typically be highly frustrated people—sexually frustrated, perhaps, or financially disappointed, or angry about a lack of social esteem. The reason criminals, minorities, and social outcasts would so easily elicit the authoritarian's hostility is that they are often associated, either as perpetrators or as victims, with violence. The problem is that authoritarians do not seem, as a group, to be any more frustrated than the rest of us. When subjects are surveyed, anonymously, on whether they get as much sex as they want or expect, males typically voice more frustration than females, but this is true regardless of whether the men score high or low on the RWA scale. Nor does frustration over money, social standing, or self-esteem seem to vary in proportion to RWA scores. Such discontent is the fate of authoritarians and nonauthoritarians alike.

THE THIRD CLASSIC THEORY of aggression is somewhat more useful for our purposes. As formulated by the Stanford University psychologist Albert Bandura, during the 1960s and 1970s, it stresses the social-learning experiences of the individual—in particular, his capacity for learning aggression from such models as parents and television personalities. Once learned, aggression is said to be triggered by various "instigators"—including not only frustration but also anxiety, threats and insults, physical pain, and the anticipation of rewards. Bandura does not assume that instigation leads automatically to aggressive responses, however. At the same time that children are learning aggressive responses from parents and others, he believes, they are being taught that it is not acceptable to act aggressively. These learned inhibitions against attacking must, according to Bandura, be breached before people will strike out at others.

A social-learning theorist might propose that the authoritarian's tendencies have been copied from hostile, bigoted parents. As it turns out, though, there is no strong correlation between the prejudices of university students and those of their folks. Authoritarian aggression seems to have deeper roots; it is not simply grafted by one generation onto the next.

Another possibility consistent with Bandura's model is that the authoritarian's hostility is rooted in the guilt he feels at falling short of the demands made by parents and other authorities. People with high RWA scores tend to come from highly religious backgrounds and often recall being expected to live up to a stricter moral code than others. Such circumstances create rich opportunities for feeling sinful, and, as Bandura has pointed out, "there is no more devastating punishment than self-contempt." It follows that, just as threats or physical pain may instigate attacks on others, so might feelings of guilt.

Still another possibility consistent with the social-learning model is that the authoritarian is motivated by the envy he feels toward those who are not so burdened by restrictive moral conventions. Indeed, college students with high RWA scores are more likely than their peers to report that they missed out on "fun times" during high school by adhering to a strict code of conduct. Feeling thus deprived, might they not take consolation in seeing sinners punished for their transgressions? Apparently so. For the same students are the most likely, when asked how they feel about schoolmates who got into trouble by way of sex, drugs, or alcohol, to agree that it "serves them right."

Fear is another aversive stimulus that could have special relevance to authoritarian aggression. It may be that people who are especially submissive to authorities, and who cling to conventional notions of proper behavior, are especially fearful of social change and disorder. When questioned about their upbringings, people with high RWA scores typically recall receiving relatively stern warnings during childhood about kidnappers, molesters, tramps, winos, and other potentially dangerous people. The world, in short, was presented to them as a dangerous place. So it is not surprising to find that, as adults, authoritarians are more anxious than others about terrorist attacks and highway accidents, and more likely to worry about catching AIDS from drinking fountains, nor that they tend to agree with such statements as "It seems that every year there are fewer and fewer truly respectable people" and "Any day now, chaos and anarchy could erupt around us."

Any of these aversive stimuli—guilt or envy or fear— might, by the logic of Bandura's theory, instigate aggressive impulses. But if those impulses are normally kept in check by learned inhibitions, what might serve to unleash them? One strong candidate would be a sense of self-righteousness. There is compelling evidence that authoritarians consider themselves morally superior. They are not unique in this regard; almost anyone will, if asked, report that he is more moral than other people, not to mention a better driver, lover, friend, or worker. But this self-serving bias is especially pronounced in authoritarians. They may not actually conduct themselves any more virtuously than other people—studies have shown that students with high RWA scores are no more willing than others to donate blood during a campus drive, and no less likely to cheat on exams—but they perceive themselves as being far more virtuous. When high scorers are asked to evaluate a fictitious person whose responses to the statements on the RWA test are opposite their own, they are more likely than low scorers to agree that the person has not "thought carefully" about the issues, that he is not particularly "good or moral," and that his ideas may be "dangerous to our society."

It seems clear, then, that authoritarians are more prone than others both to feelings that might produce aggressive impulses and to a sense of self-righteousness, which might weaken their inhibitions against attacking others. The question is: In what measure do these qualities contribute to authoritarian aggression?

I T STANDS TO REASON THAT, if any one of these factors—guilt, envy, fear, or self-righteousness— helps make authoritarians aggressive, then eliminating that factor should make them less so. We cannot work such magic on real people, unfortunately, but we *can* do something mathematically akin to it—by testing subjects for authoritarianism and for aggressiveness, then determining how each measurement correlates with a measure of one of the contributing factors under investigation. To the extent that any third factor correlates with both of the first two, it can be said to account for part of the relationship between them. In other words, if people who score high on tests that measure authoritarianism and aggressiveness also score high on a test that measures, say, their fear of a dangerous world, then fear can be said to account, statistically, for part of the correlation. Exactly how great a part can be determined through a technique known as partial correlation analysis.

The correlation between two sets of numbers (a statistic that can range in absolute value from 0.00 to 1.00) is the square root of another value known as the index of codetermination. That is to say, it reveals, when multiplied by itself, just how much of the variation within one set can be attributed to variation within the other. If we compare the adult heights of several hundred parents and several hundred offspring, the statistical correlation is usually about 0.50, indicating (when squared) that parents' heights account for 0.25, or a quarter, of the variation in the adult heights of their children. The remaining seventy-five percent presumably reflects other factors.

Because human behavior is shaped by so many variables, a measure of just one personality trait rarely accounts for more than about ten percent of the variation in a particular form of behavior. But the RWA scale often correlates 0.50 or more with measures of authoritarian aggression, which is to say, RWA scores typically explain about twenty-five percent of the variation in certain forms of hostility. It is this statistical relationship between authoritarianism and hostility that we are trying to explain in terms of possible instigators and disinhibitors.

The relationship is particularly well captured by a tool called the Attitudes Toward Homosexuals (ATH) scale, a survey, scored in the same manner as the RWA scale, that consists of such statements as "Homosexuals should be locked up to protect society" and "In many ways, the AIDS disease currently killing homosexuals is just what they deserve." An experiment conducted at the University of Manitoba found a correlation of 0.54 between subjects' RWA scores and their ATH scores. Authoritarianism, then, accounted for fully twenty-nine percent of the variation in the subjects' aggressiveness toward homosexuals.

The question is: What makes authoritarians so hostile toward gays? To find out, I asked the same subjects who had been given the RWA and ATH tests to complete sixteen other measures, as well. These assessed not only the hypotheses about guilt, fear, envy, and self-righteousness but also a number of other possible contributors, including the influence of parents, teachers, peers, religious authorities, the media, even the subjects' own experiences with homosexuals. The answers to the vast majority of these tests failed to correlate strongly with the RWA and ATH scores, suggesting that most of the factors had little to do with the authoritarians' aggressiveness. But there were two notable exceptions: fear and self-righteousness. When the students completed a Fear of a Dangerous World survey (composed of such statements as "The world is full of dangerous people who will attack you for no reason at all"), the scores correlated appreciably with both the RWA results and the ATH responses. And when the subjects were given a test designed to measure self-righteousness (the one that invited them to pass judgment on people whose RWA responses were opposite their own), the correlations were even stronger.

If authoritarians are aggressive partly because they associate their targets (homosexuals, in this case) with a disintegrating, threatening world, then mathematically eliminating the part of the RWA–ATH relationship that consists of the correlation of those two scores with fear of a dangerous world should make a noticeable difference. And it does. When the fear factor is "partialed out," the 0.54 correlation between RWA and ATH scores drops to 0.46, and the amount of ATH variation that can be predicted on the basis of RWA scores drops from twenty-nine percent (0.54 squared) to just twenty-one (0.46 squared), or about seventy-two percent of its original value. Self-righteousness seems to be an even more important factor; mathematically eliminating it reduces the authoritarianism–aggressiveness relationship to just sixty-two percent of its original value.

None of this would be very impressive if fear and self-righteousness were two competing explanations for the authoritarian's aggressiveness, for neither one accounts for the majority of it. But the two factors are highly compatible, with fear of a dangerous world serving as the instigator that arouses the authoritarian's hostility and self-righteousness serving as the disinhibitor that unleashes it. If we partial out their *combined* effect, the RWA–aggressiveness correlation drops from 0.54 to 0.35, and the original twenty-nine-percent overlap between the two shrinks to a mere twelve percent, or about forty-one percent of its original value. In short, most of the relationship disappears. With just two variables, more than half the authoritarian's aggressiveness has been explained. Fear's fingerprints seem to be all over the trigger of the weapon, and those of self-righteousness all over the unlocked safety.

HOSTILITY TOWARD HOMOSEXUALS is not the only form of authoritarian aggression that fear and self-righteousness seem to account for; similar experiments, involving other authoritarian tendencies, have produced similar results. When, for example, fear and self-righteousness are partialed out of the correlation between RWA scores and scores on a test in which subjects impose prison sentences on hypothetical criminals, they account for nearly three-quarters of the RWA–harshness correlation. No other variable tested explains as much, alone or in combination with anything else. In another experiment, subjects were asked to complete a booklet containing the RWA test and five indexes of aggressiveness: the ATH scale, a criminal-sentencing scale, a general prejudice scale, and two posse scales (one in which the government bans Communism and one in which it outlaws "weird" religions). In every case, fear and self-righteousness, when partialed out in tandem, accounted for most of the relationship between RWA scores and aggressiveness. The pattern held whether the subjects were college students or their parents.

Together, these results suggest an answer to the question that posed itself so grotesquely in Nazi-occupied Europe, an answer more compatible with Bandura's social-learning theory than with Berkowitz's frustration hypothesis or the psychoanalytic explanation ventured by the Berkeley theorists. It seems that highly submissive, conventional people easily come to feel gravely threatened by social change or disorder. This fear seems to originate with their parents' warnings that the world is a dangerous and hostile place, though it may be reinforced by the mass media's emphasis on crime and violence in our society. Other emotions, such as envy, may feed the authoritarian's hostility, but not to nearly as great an extent.

Fear will not produce aggression if one's learned inhibitions are strong; people with low RWA scores may want to lash out at times and yet not feel entitled to do so. But authoritarians, because they identify so strongly with established authorities (including, in many cases, God), perceive themselves as morally superior, and this moral certainty impels them toward brutality.

This research, for reasons that should be obvious, is conducted at one remove from reality. No one has taken a group of subjects, made them fearful and self-righteous, and then handed them a whip and a scapegoat to see how they behave. Instead, we have examined relationships between the attitudes that people express on questionnaires. This sort of analysis never actually proves the hypotheses it supports; it is not known, empirically, that fear and self-righteousness *cause* authoritarian aggression, only that particular forms of authoritarian aggression vary in proportion to certain measurable attitudes. But that in itself could be powerful knowledge. If authoritarian aggression is often accompanied by fear and self-righteousness, then finding ways of freeing authoritarians from that explosive combination of feelings may not only improve their lives but help shelter their neighbors from their wrath.

CLOSE ENCOUNTERS

Silent but powerful, a touch can comfort, greet, persuade, inflame.
Small wonder societies keep our contacts under tight control.

STEPHEN THAYER

*Stephen Thayer, Ph.D., is a professor of psychology at City College
and the Graduate Center of the City University of New York.*

IN MAY 1985, Brigitte Gerney was trapped beneath a 35-ton collapsed construction crane in New York City for six hours. Throughout her ordeal, she held the hand of rescue officer Paul Ragonese, who stayed by her side as heavy machinery moved the tons of twisted steel from her crushed legs. A stranger's touch gave her hope and the will to live.

Other means of communication can take place at a distance, but touch is the language of physical intimacy. And because it is, touch is the most powerful of all the communication channels— and the most carefully guarded and regulated.

From a mother's cradling embrace to a friend's comforting hug, or a lover's caress, touch has the special power to send messages of union and communion. Among strangers, that power is ordinarily held in check. Whether offering a handshake or a guiding arm, the toucher is careful to stay within the culture's narrowly prescribed limits lest the touch be misinterpreted. Touching between people with more personal relationships is also governed by silent cultural rules and restraints.

The rules of touch may be unspoken, but they're visible to anyone who takes the trouble to watch. Psychologist Richard Heslin at Purdue University, for instance, has proposed five categories of touch based on people's roles and relationships. Each category includes a special range of touches, best described by the quality of touch, the body areas touched and whether the touch is reciprocated.

FUNCTIONAL-PROFESSIONAL touches are performed while the toucher fulfills a special role, such as that of doctor, barber or tailor. For people in these occupations, touch must be devoid of personal messages.

SOCIAL-POLITE touches are formal, limited to greeting and separating and to expressing appreciation among business associates and among strangers and acquaintances. The typical handshake reflects cordiality more than intimacy.

FRIENDSHIP-WARMTH touches occur in the context of personal concern and caring, such as the relationships between extended-family members, friendly neighbors and close work mates. This category straddles the line between warmth and deep affection, a line where friendly touches move over into love touches.

LOVE-INTIMACY touches occur between close family members and friends in relationships where there is affection and caring.

SEXUAL-AROUSAL touches occur in erotic-sexual contexts.

These categories are not hard and fast, since in various cultures and subcultures the rules differ about who can touch whom, in what contexts and what forms the touch may take. In the Northern European "noncontact cultures," overall touch rates are usually quite low. People from these cultures can seem very cold, especially to people from "contact cultures" such as those in the Mediterranean area, where there are much higher rates of touching, even between strangers.

In the United States, a particularly low-touch culture, we rarely see people touch one another in public. Other than in sports and children's play, the most we see of it is when people hold hands in the street, fondle babies or say hello and goodbye. Even on television shows, with the odd exceptions of hitting and kissing, there is little touching.

The cultural differences in contact can be quite dramatic, as researcher Sidney Jourard found in the 1960s when he studied touch between pairs of people in coffee shops around the world. There was more touch in certain cities (180 times an hour between couples in San Juan, Puerto Rico, and 110 times an hour in Paris, France) than in others (2 times an hour between couples in Gainesville, Florida, and 0 times an hour in London, England).

Those cultural contact patterns are embedded early, through child-rearing practices. Psychologist Janice Gibson and her colleagues at the University of Pittsburgh took to the playgrounds and beaches of Greece, the Soviet Union and the United States and compared the frequency and nature of touch between caregivers and children 2 to 5 years old. When it came to retrieving or punishing the children, touching rates were similar in all three countries. But on touches for soothing, holding and play, American children had significantly less contact than those from the other cultures. (Is that why we need bumper stickers to remind us: "Have you hugged your child today?")

Greek and Soviet kids
are held, soothed and touched playfully much more than American kids.

Men greet people
with fewer lip kisses, embraces and kinds of touch than women do.

Generalizations about different national or ethnic groups can be tricky, however. For example, despite widespread beliefs that Latin Americans are highly contact-oriented, when researcher Robert Shuter at Marquette University compared public contact between couples in Costa Rica, Colombia and Panama, he found that the Costa Ricans both touched and held their partners noticeably more than the couples did in the other two countries.

Within most cultures the rules and meanings of touch are different for men and women, as one recent study in the United States illustrates. Imagine yourself in a hospital bed, about to have major surgery. The nurse comes in to tell you what your operation and after-care will be like. She touches you briefly twice, once on the hand for a few seconds after she introduces herself and again on the arm for a full minute during the instruction period. As she leaves she shakes your hand.

Does this kind of brief reassuring touch add anything to her talk? Does it have any kind of impact on your nervousness or how you respond to the operation? Your reaction is likely to depend upon your gender.

Psychologist Sheryle Whitcher, while working as a graduate student with psychologist Jeffrey Fisher of the University of Connecticut, arranged for a group of surgery patients to be touched in the way described above during their preoperative information session, while other patients got only the information. Women had strikingly positive reactions to being touched; it lowered their blood pressure and anxiety both before surgery and for more than an hour afterwards. But men found the experience upsetting; both their blood pressure and their anxiety rose and stayed elevated in response to being touched.

Why did touch produce such strikingly different responses? Part of the answer may lie in the fact that men in the United States often find it harder to acknowledge dependency and fear than women do; thus, for men, a well-intentioned touch may be a threatening reminder of their vulnerability.

These gender differences are fostered by early experiences, particularly in handling and caretaking. Differences in parents' use of touch with their infant children help to shape and model "male" and "female" touch patterns: Fathers use touch more for play, while mothers use it more for soothing and grooming. The children's gender also affects the kinds of touches they receive. In the United States, for example, girls receive more affectionate touches (kissing, cuddling, holding) than boys do.

By puberty, tactile experiences with parents and peers have already programmed differences in boys' and girls' touching behavior and their use of personal space (see "Body Mapping," this article). Some results of this training are evident when men and women greet people. In one study, psychologists Paul Greenbaum and Howard Rosenfeld of the University of Kansas watched how travelers at the Kansas City International Airport touched people who greeted them. Women greeted women and men more physically, with mutual lip kisses, embraces and more kinds of touch and holding for longer periods of time. In contrast, when men greeted men, most just shook hands and left it at that.

How do you feel about touching and being touched? Are you relaxed and comfortable, or does such contact make you feel awkward and tense? Your comfort with touch may be linked to your personality. Psychologist Knud Larsen and student Jeff LeRoux at Oregon State University looked at how people's personality traits are related to their attitudes toward touching between people of the same sex. The researchers measured touch attitudes through questions such as, "I enjoy persons of my sex who are comfortable with touching," "I sometimes enjoy hugging friends of the same sex" and "Physical expression of affection between persons of the same sex is healthy." Even though men were generally less comfortable about same-sex touching than women were, the more authoritarian and rigid people of both sexes were the least comfortable.

A related study by researchers John Deethardt and Debbie Hines at Texas Tech University in Lubbock, Texas, examined personality and attitudes toward being touched by opposite-sex friends and lovers and by same-sex friends. Touch attitudes were tapped with such questions as, "When I am with my girl/-boyfriend I really like to touch that person to show affection," "When I tell a same-sex intimate friend that I have just gotten a divorce, I want that person to touch me" and "I enjoy an opposite-sex acquaintance touching me when we greet each other." Regardless of gender, people who were comfortable with touching were also more talkative, cheerful, socially dominant and nonconforming; those discomforted by touch tended to be more emotionally unstable and socially withdrawn.

A recent survey of nearly 4,000 undergraduates by researchers Janis Andersen, Peter Andersen and Myron Lustig of San Diego State University revealed that, regardless of gender, people who were less comfortable about touching were also more apprehensive about communicating and had lower self-esteem. Several other studies have shown that people who are more comfortable with touch are less afraid and suspicious of other people's motives and intentions and have less anxiety and tension in their everyday lives. Not surprisingly, another study showed they are also likely to be more satisfied with their bodies and physical appearance.

These different personality factors play themselves out most revealingly in the intimacy of love relationships. Couples stay together and break apart for many reasons, including the way each partner expresses and reacts to affection and intimacy. For some, feelings and words are enough; for others, touch and physical intimacy are more critical.

In the film *Annie Hall*, Woody Allen and Diane Keaton are shown split-screen as each talks to an analyst about their sexual relationship. When the analyst asks how often they have sex, he answers, "Hardly ever, maybe three times a week," while she describes it as "constantly, three times a week."

How important is physical intimacy in close relationships? What role does touch play in marital satisfaction? Psychologists Betsy Tolstedt and Joseph Stokes of the University of Illinois at Chicago tried to find out by interviewing and observing couples. They used three measures of intimacy: emotional intimacy (feelings of closeness, support, tolerance); verbal intimacy (disclosure of emotions, feelings, opinions); and physical intimacy (satisfaction with "companionate" and sexual touch). The

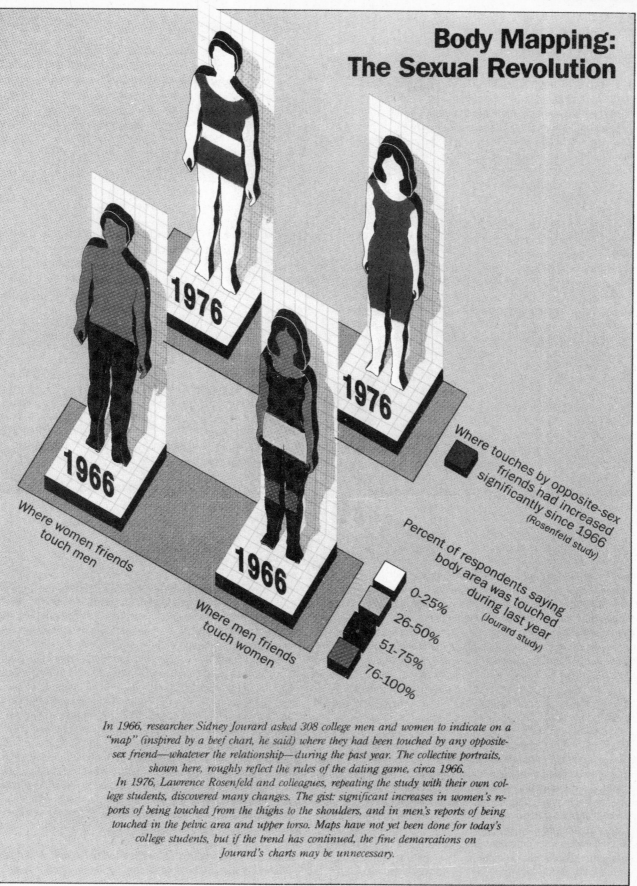

Body Mapping: The Sexual Revolution

Where women friends touch men

Where men friends touch women

Where touches by opposite-sex friends had increased significantly since 1966
(Rosenfeld study)

Percent of respondents saying body area was touched during last year
(Jourard study)

0-25%

26-50%

51-75%

76-100%

In 1966, researcher Sidney Jourard asked 308 college men and women to indicate on a "map" (inspired by a beef chart, he said) where they had been touched by any opposite-sex friend—whatever the relationship—during the past year. The collective portraits, shown here, roughly reflect the rules of the dating game, circa 1966.

In 1976, Lawrence Rosenfeld and colleagues, repeating the study with their own college students, discovered many changes. The gist: significant increases in women's reports of being touched from the thighs to the shoulders, and in men's reports of being touched in the pelvic area and upper torso. Maps have not yet been done for today's college students, but if the trend has continued, the fine demarcations on Jourard's charts may be unnecessary.

researchers also measured marital satisfaction and happiness, along with conflicts and actual separations and legal actions.

They found that each form of intimacy made its own contribution to marital satisfaction, but—perhaps surprisingly to some—physical intimacy mattered the least of the three. Conflict and divorce potential were most connected to dissatisfaction with emotional and verbal intimacy.

Touch intimacy may not usually have the power to make or break marriages, but it can sway strangers and even people close to you, often without their knowledge. The expressions "to put the touch on someone" and "that person is an easy touch" refer to the persuasive power of touch. Indeed, research shows that it is harder to say no to someone who makes a request when it is accompanied by a touch.

Politicians know this well. Ignoring security concerns, political candidates plunge into the crowd to kiss babies and "press the flesh." Even a quick handshake leaves a lasting impression—a personal touch—that can pay off later at election time.

A momentary and seemingly incidental touch can establish a positive, temporary bond between strangers, making them more helpful, compliant, generous and positive. In one experiment in a library, a slight hand brush in the course of returning library cards to patrons was enough to influence patrons' positive attitudes toward the library and its staff. In another study, conducted in restaurants, a fleeting touch paid off in hard cash. Waitresses who touched their customers on the hand or shoulder as they returned change received a larger percentage of the bill as their tip. Even though they risked crossing role boundaries by touching customers in such familiar ways, their ingratiating service demeanor offset any threat.

In certain situations, touch can be discomforting because it signals power. Psychologist Nancy Henley of the University of California, Los Angeles, after observing the touch behavior of people as they went about their daily lives, has suggested that higher-status individuals enjoy more touch liberties with their lower-status associates. To Henley, who has noted how touch signals one's place in the status-dominance hierarchy, there is even a sexist "politics of touch." She has found that women generally rank lower than men in the touch hierarchy, very much like the secretary-boss, student-teacher and worker-foreman relationships. In all of these, it is considered unseemly for lower-status individuals to put their hands on superiors. Rank does have its touching privileges.

The rules of the status hierarchy are so powerful that people can infer status differences from watching other people's touch behavior. In one experiment by psychologists Brenda Major and Richard Heslin of Purdue University, observers could see only the silhouettes of pairs of people facing each other, with one touching the other on the shoulder. They judged the toucher to be more assertive and of a higher status than the person touched. Had the touch been reciprocal, status differences would have disappeared.

Psychologist Alvin G. Goldstein and student Judy Jeffords at the University of Missouri have sharpened our understanding of touch and status through their field study of touch among legislators during a Missouri state legislative session. Observers positioned themselves in the gallery and systematically recorded who initiated touch during the many floor conversations. Based on a status formula that included committee leadership and membership, they discovered that among these male peers, the lower-status men were the ones most likely to initiate touch.

When roles are clearly different, so that one individual has

TOUCHY ISSUES

TOUCH IS A GESTURE of warmth and concern, but it can also be seen as intrusive, demeaning or seductive. Because of these ambiguous meanings, touch can sometimes be problematic for therapists, who must be careful to monitor their touch behavior with clients. Because difficult legal and ethical issues surround possible misinterpretation of touch, many therapists avoid physical contact of any sort with their clients, except for a formal handshake at the first and last sessions. But in a number of body-oriented psychotherapies, such as Wilhelm Reich's character analysis and Alexander Lowen's bioenergetic therapy, touch is used deliberately as part of the treatment process; it is meant to stir emotions and memories through the body and not just the mind.

Imagine meeting your therapist for the first time. You are greeted in the waiting room and guided into the consultation room. You have the therapist's full attention as you speak about what brings you to therapy. Twice during the session the therapist briefly touches you on the arm. Before you leave, you make an appointment to meet again.

How are you likely to evaluate your first session? Do you think the therapist's touch might affect your reactions to therapy or to the therapist? Could it affect the process of therapy?

Sessions like the one just described have been studied by psychologist Mark A. Hubble of Harding Hospital in Worthington, Ohio, and colleagues, using therapists specially trained to touch their clients in consistent ways during their first counseling session. Results show that, compared with clients who were not touched, those who were touched judged the therapist as more expert. In an earlier, similar study by researcher Joyce Pattison, trained judges rated clients who had been touched as deeper in their self-exploration.

Although there are clearly some risks, perhaps more therapists should consider "getting in touch" with their clients by adding such small tactile gestures to their therapeutic repertoire.

control or power over the other, such as a boss and a secretary, then touch usually reflects major dominance or status differences in the relationship. But when roles are more diffuse and overlapping, so that people are almost equal in power—as the legislators were—then lower-status people may try to establish more intimate connections with their more powerful and higher-status colleagues by making physical contact with them.

Touching has a subtle and often ambivalent role in most settings. But there is one special circumstance in which touch is permitted and universally positive: In sports, teammates encourage, applaud and console each other generously through touch. In Western cultures, for men especially, hugs and slaps on the behind are permitted among athletes, even though they are very rarely seen between heterosexual men outside the sports arena. The intense enthusiasm legitimizes tactile expressions of emotion that would otherwise be seen as homosexually threatening.

Graduate student Charles Anderton and psychologist Robert Heckel of the University of South Carolina studied touch in the competitive context of all-male or all-female championship swim meets by recording each instance of touch after success and failure. Regardless of sex, winners were touched similarly, on aver-

At swim meets, winners were touched six times more than losers were.

age six times more than losers, with most of the touches to the hand and some to the back or shoulders; only a small percent were to the head or buttocks.

This swimming study only looked at touch between same-sex teammates, since swim meets have separate races for men and women. Would touch patterns be the same for mixed-gender teams, or would men and women be inhibited about initiating and receiving touches, as they are in settings outside of sports? Psychologists David Smith, Frank Willis and Joseph Gier at the University of Missouri studied touching behavior of men and women in bowling alleys in Kansas City, Missouri, during mixed-league competition. They found almost no differences between men and women in initiating or receiving touches.

Without the social vocabulary of touch, life would be cold, mechanical, distant, rational, verbal. We are created in the intimate union of two bodies and stay connected to the body of one until the cord is cut. Even after birth, we need touch for survival. Healthy human infants deprived of touch and handling for long periods develop a kind of infant depression that leads to withdrawal and apathy and, in extreme cases, wasting away to death.

As people develop, touch assumes symbolic meaning as the primary system for expressing and experiencing affection, inclusion and control. Deprived of those gestures and their meanings, the world might be more egalitarian, but it would also be far more frightening, hostile and chilly. And who would understand why a stranger's touch meant life to Brigitte Gerney?

GETTING HELP FROM HELPING

As self-help groups proliferate, psychologists and other professionals are trying to figure out what they are and just how they work.

DAN HURLEY

Dan Hurley, a New York writer, is a frequent contributor to Psychology Today.

It's the Tuesday night meeting of the Staten Island chapter of Recovery Inc. Mac, speaking in the West Indies accent of his native St. Vincent, tells the 17 men and women seated around a table in a local church how he handles the severe anxiety that once kept him from working as a construction foreman. Frank, a New Jersey electrician in his 50s, explains how he keeps himself from relapsing into the paranoid schizophrenia that less than three years ago had him growing a long beard, wearing a rope belt and rusty knife and believing that he was the greatest saint of all time. Finally, Bettyann, a gray-haired housekeeper and mother of four, tells of the 24 years she spent inside her home, a hostage of agoraphobia.

"I couldn't go out to the garbage can at the curb," Bettyann says. "I couldn't go to church. Then, six months after I started coming to Recovery, I was able to drive all the way down to Florida with my husband. I'm not saying I don't have the anxiety anymore, but I am able to overcome it. Recovery made me feel like I'm not singled out. Somebody else is in the same boat."

An estimated 12 million people now help themselves and their neighbors by participating in roughly 500,000 self-help groups. These groups range from such nationally established organizations as Recovery Inc., founded 50 years ago by psychiatrist Abraham A. Low to help people with debilitating psychological problems, to Mistresses Anonymous, Bald-Headed Men of America and Fundamentalists Anonymous (see "Leaving the Fold," this article).

"Self-help gives you control of your own life," says Frank Riessman, a psychologist at the City University of New York and founding director of the National Self-Help Clearinghouse. "It's being accepted far more than it used to be. It's very populist, very participatory."

Fifteen years ago, not one clearinghouse existed to provide information on self-help groups or encourage the development of new ones. The creation of more than 40 clearinghouses since then "is an important social phenomenon," says Fran Dory, executive director of the New York City Self-Help Clearinghouse. In 1985, Riessman and Dory led the first national meeting of local clearinghouses; the International Network for Mutual Help Centers was formed that year. And in September 1987, Surgeon General C. Everett Koop sponsored a workshop to create a national agenda of policies, programs and activities to promote self-help.

Although people have joined together to find strength in groups for thousands of years, the modern self-help group composed of people facing a single problem can be traced back to June 10, 1935, when two men known to the public as Bill W. and Doctor Bob first met to help each other stay sober. They eventually founded Alcoholics Anonymous (AA). By 1986, AA membership totaled an estimated 804,000 in the United States and Canada, with 41,000 registered groups meeting regularly. Worldwide membership is estimated at 1.5 million, making AA by far the largest self-help group in the world. In the 1970s, it spawned similar groups for people closely involved with alcoholics (Al-Anon), teenage children living with alcoholic parents (Alateen), Gamblers Anonymous and Overeaters Anonymous. Today, at least 14 organizations follow the AA format.

As self-help, or, more accurately, mutual-help groups proliferate, psychologists and other professionals are trying to define exactly what a self-help group is. The California Self-Help Center, located at the psychology department at the University of California, Los Angeles, has created 198 categories to cover the state's 3,300 groups and broken them into

From *Psychology Today*, January 1988, pp. 63-64, 66-67. Copyright © 1988 by PT Partners, L. P. Reprinted by permission.

four broad types: those for physical and mental illness, those for reforming addictive behavior, those for coping with a crisis of transition and those for friends and relatives of the person with the problem.

Uniting all types of self-help groups is what Riessman calls the "self-help ethos. It's the spirit of the movement: getting help from helping. It's very democratic and destigmatizing. Any type of behavior or condition can be accepted. You don't have to hide that you're a drug abuser or that you have cancer. You share it with other people and help each other."

Yet within the common philosophy, "you get a million and one formats," says psychologist Morton A. Lieberman, of the University of California, San Francisco. Recovery Inc., for example, follows a rigid format beginning with a reading from *Mental Health Through Will-Training,* written by the group's founder. Then, five or six members give examples of upsetting events and how they dealt with them in light of the group's teachings. Other groups that try to change members' behavior usually use a similarly rigid format. Groups that focus on facing a painful situation, such as bereavement, tend to have a more loosely structured "care and share" style.

Some groups do not even hold meetings. Mended Hearts, for heart-disease patients and their families, visits hospital patients to offer reassurance. Eight years ago, Sam Fixman was visited just after his open-heart surgery, and today he is president of the Brooklyn chapter of Mended Hearts. Each week a local hospital provides him with the names of new patients, and he and other group members make the rounds.

"About a month ago I had the most incredible emotional experience of my life," says Fixman, a 55-year-old account executive at a subscription agency. He visited a man who had just come out of surgery and was still under anesthesia, with tubes attached to his chest and in his mouth. "Listen, I've been through this before," Fixman told him. "You're coming off the anesthesia now." The man grabbed Fixman's arm tightly and began to cry. Barely fighting off tears himself—"I needed to be strong for him"—Fixman promised to return that night and again the next day. "And I did. He just wanted someone to reassure him that he was going to be OK. I got help and I made it, and I've got to see that someone else gets the same help. For me it's a must thing to do."

Other groups actively reach out to people not likely to form self-help groups on their own. Roger Williams, of the health and human issues outreach department at the University of Wisconsin-Madison, for example, has helped form many of the 30 self-help groups for Wisconsin farm families in the past two years. The Sisterhood of Black Single Mothers, founded 14 years ago by Daphne Busby in Brooklyn's devastated Bedford-Stuyvesant neighborhood, offers more than support groups to its nearly 1,000 members. "It has to be more than just sitting around talking," Busby says. "We provide courses in basic literacy and life management, we do peer counseling and

we're preparing to offer housing. Our job is to empower women, to connect them to a network."

Perhaps the newest type of self-help group is one held via computer networks. "One member is in Oregon, another is in Minnesota, another is in Florida, but they're all together," says Edward Madara, who as director of New Jersey's Self-Help Clearinghouse has helped form four computer-linked groups so far.

What makes self-help groups work is still a puzzle to psychologists, but they have a few clues. One key process that psychologist Stephen B. Fawcett sees at work in self-help groups is that members learn about common aspects of their problem. Fawcett and his colleagues at the University of Kansas have audiotaped several groups' meetings "to get a sense of the anatomy of self-help groups," he says. "To our surprise, the predominant activity seems to be information-giving; especially important are personal disclosures. We find relatively few statements of support and sympathy."

A second factor is that members often come to accept an ideology that allows them to reattribute the cause of their problem and thereby change their behavior. Alcoholics are told in AA that they are not in control of their drinking and must turn their lives over to a Higher Power; parents of schizophrenic children are told in the National Alliance for the Mentally Ill that biochemistry, not their child rearing, is the primary culprit. Some psychologists may dispute these claims, but few would deny the improvements in behavior they permit. To researcher Paul Antze, such ideologies offer a "cognitive antidote" to the problem.

Strong group acceptance and shared understanding of what was previously a hidden problem are other keys to making self-help groups effective. "Homogeneity among the members seems to be one of the critical and distinguishing factors in what makes many self-help groups powerful," says Marion Jacobs, codirector of the California Self-Help Center and adjunct professor of psychology at UCLA.

The power of meeting with other alcoholics through AA changed the life of Ellen M. After starting with glue-sniffing in sixth grade, Ellen reached the point three years ago, at the age of 27, where she was shooting heroin, drinking daily, having repeated blackouts and at times working as a prostitute. She credits an intensive treatment program with helping her quit drugs and alcohol. "But quitting is easy," she says. "I quit a thousand times. AA has taught me constant abstinence. What did it for me at the beginning was that I was not alone, that there was a roomful of people working toward what I was working toward. Normies [the term she uses for nonaddicts] don't understand. AA showed me that I wasn't so different. I had always thought I was dropped here by aliens. Until AA, nobody understood how I felt at 3 a.m. sitting by myself with a bottle."

The sense of normalization that grows from being with people who share a problem leads to development of a social support network. An important ingredient in AA's success, for instance, is the use of spon-

fundamentalist?

LEAVING THE FOLD

In April of 1985, Wall Street lawyer Richard Yao and banker James Luce placed a two-line classified ad in the *Village Voice* to announce the formation of a new group, Fundamentalists Anonymous (FA). The pair hoped to get a few encouraging responses. Instead, they received 500 calls from around the country and within three weeks found themselves on the *Phil Donahue Show*. Less than three years later, they have 46 chapters, 40,000 members and a national office in New York City, for which Yao has left his legal career to become executive director.

"There's obviously an incredible need out there," says Yao, whose only training in psychology was a few courses while attending Yale Divinity School. The need, he says, comes from the "fundamentalist mindset," a tendency to be authoritarian, intolerant and compulsive about control. Yao claims that this mindset often causes intense fear and guilt, inability to talk about the fundamentalist experience, depression, loneliness, low self-esteem, aversion to authority and anger over the time lost while in the fold. The cure, as he sees it, is support from other former fundamentalists. FA also makes referrals to licensed psychologists for any member who needs one, and psychologists likewise have referred many clients to FA.

Psychologist Marlene Winell of Fort Collins, Colorado, has treated about 40 former fundamentalists in her private practice, and she finds great support for Yao's claims. "I was a zealous fundamentalist myself," says Winell, who was reared by missionary parents in Taiwan and spent much of her youth proselytizing door-to-door. "If you stay inside the fundamentalist system, you're fine. But if you try to get away from it, it's like having the ground pulled out from beneath your feet. You have to restructure your entire world."

Other psychologists agree that while fundamentalism itself does not seem pathological, the experience of leaving it behind can cause a transition crisis similar to divorce or the death of a loved one. "FA helped me go back and look at my resentment," says Gary W. Hartz, a psychologist with the Veterans Administration in Los Angeles. "I felt bitter about the time I lost," he says, "and ashamed about some of the things I did, like evangelizing students at Daytona Beach during spring break to give up two of the Five S's—sex and suds—and stick to the sun, surf and sand."

Another person who seems to have gone through many of the typical problems of erstwhile fundamentalists is former presidential candidate Gary Hart, who was reared in the Church of the Nazarene. "He did not get a chance to party or date or drink like a normal teenager," Yao says. "In my opinion he's trying to make up for lost time."

Despite Yao's claims and the popular reception FA has received, "There are not enough data to support the idea that fundamentalism in general is bad for people, based exclusively on the claims of former fundamentalists," says Lee A. Kirkpatrick, a doctoral candidate in psychology at the University of Denver. "Saying that personality characteristics associated with fundamentalism are 'pathological' is merely a value judgment." In fact, studies by psychiatrist Marc Galanter have found that while 36 percent of Unification Church dropouts had "serious emotional problems," most new members showed a dramatic decrease in neurotic distress. Noting that all of Yao's members are fundamentalist dropouts, Kirkpatrick says psychologists should find out if Yao's claims are valid for current fundamentalists. Yao admits, "I'm not an academic. All I know is it works."

sors, members who are already sober and who serve as guides to new members. In Ellen's case, her sponsor would come to her house in the middle of the night when Ellen was drunk and violent. "She could talk to me heart-to-heart, not down to me like some nurse in an addiction ward," Ellen says. "We're human beings. We have to be connected, to have a social core. AA is my social core." Today, Ellen has been sober for more than two years, lives with her husband again and works as a service coordinator at a community alcoholism program in Los Angeles.

Not all the results of the self-help process are positive. To psychologist Stanton Peele, author of *The Meaning of Addiction,* AA's cognitive antidote is "essentially a religious conversion experience. There's a very heavy group socialization process that goes on,

a kind of brainwashing. You're not allowed to say you used alcohol socially and under control. You have to say you've lost total control. In fact the research shows that people go through cycles in which they manage it, and then go off the deep end."

The social support that a newcomer gets from a sponsor can also be dangerous, says psychologist Linda W. Scheffler, author of *Help Thy Neighbor.* In her experience with members of Overeaters Anonymous, "I've seen at least one person who has been damaged in a relationship with a sponsor. There is a real danger in the intimate pairing and counseling that goes on. I found it a malevolent influence in some patients' lives." Counseling is hard for professionals, she says, but harder still for untrained group members.

At best, the concept of social support remains

fuzzy, and Lieberman stresses that "to generalize that all self-help groups work because of social support would be utter nonsense." In a study of widows and widowers Lieberman found that those who had established give-and-take personal relationships with other members benefited from their self-help group far more than those who hadn't; yet a similar study of bereaved parents found no added benefits with such relationships. Lieberman has also studied groups in which no members showed any psychological improvement whatsoever. "By no means are all self-help groups successful," he says. "We do have studies that are encouraging, but as to how they work in general and why they work and for whom, we just don't know."

Until more is known about self-help groups in general and AA in particular, some psychologists worry about the increasingly popular view that AA is the only way for alcoholics to achieve long-term sobriety. "AA is obviously very popular and still growing, but there are no data showing it's the best approach," says psychologist William R. Miller of the University of New Mexico. The only two experimental studies that exist compared people who were ordered by the courts to attend AA with others who were not; the studies found no significant impact for AA, Miller says.

With the courts routinely requiring convicted drunk drivers to attend AA, and most treatment centers doing the same, "AA is no longer real self-help," says Peele. "It's been medicalized. Self-help is a great tradition, but it can't be forced upon people. We're being held hostage by the groups now."

The tension between academics and self-helpers is

acknowledged by Riessman, the national clearinghouse director who has written three books on self-help and served on President Carter's Mental Health Commission. When speaking to self-help groups, he says he has to emphasize his own involvement in groups or else his audience will reject him as "just an observer." Even so, Riessman admits that an important factor in the current growth of self-help groups is the increasing number of referrals by psychologists, physicians and social agencies.

Psychologists such as Fawcett, however, offer self-help groups more than referrals. Fawcett hopes to translate his research on what makes groups tick into training materials for group leaders. And the California Self-Help Center has recently created a taped instruction program called Common Concern that leads groups through basic lessons in communication, running a group effectively and troubleshooting typical problems, such as giving premature advice and dealing with people who monopolize sessions.

UCLA's Jacobs believes that prominent professionals, such as Surgeon General Koop, can raise self-help from a provincial and spontaneous phenomenon to an effective movement. And the role of psychologists, she suggests, should be to give "tools and consultations" to help groups get started and maintain themselves when they get bogged down or have other problems. Sweeping her hand toward a window overlooking downtown Brooklyn, where she recently visited, Jacobs says, "I promise you, there are self-help groups all around this neighborhood. But right now they blend into the local scenery, like the PTA and the Elks. In coming years they may stand out as a legitimate way to deliver mental-health services."

Psychological Disorders

The history of mental and emotional disorders is sharply punctuated by changes in perspective. At various times, those who suffered from these disorders were persecuted as witches, tortured to drive out possessing spirits, punished as sinners, jailed as dangerous to society, confined to asylums as insane, and hospitalized as suffering from an illness. Today, psychologists propose that the view of disorders as "illnesses" has outlived its usefulness. We should think of them as either biochemical disturbances or disorders of learning, in which the person develops a maladaptive pattern of behavior which is then maintained by an inappropriate environment. At the same time, we need to recognize that these reactions to stressors in the environment, or to inappropriate learning situations, may be genetically predisposed, which is to say that some people may more easily develop the disorders than others.

Nonetheless, serious disorders are serious problems, and not just for the individual who is the patient or client. The impact of mental illness on the family and friends of the afflicted has often been overlooked, but deserves our full attention. The search for answers and the placing of blame are just two of the problems therapists must be alert to in dealing with families.

Dementia has always been a problem of grave concern. Difficulty in diagnosis, particularly early in its course, often confined the victim to a state of hopelessness. Better diagnostic procedures have made Alzheimer's disease a household term, yet many questions about its course and cause remain unanswered.

The most common diagnostic term applied to outpatients today is depression. This category undoubtedly covers a wide range of patterns of response. Recently, scientists and clinicians have become aware of a specific low-grade form of depression which is now called dysthymic disorder. Once discovered, it's very easy to get rid of!

While diagnostic labels have changed in the past decade, the underlying element of most maladaptive patterns of behavior continues to be anxiety. In "Anxiety and Panic: Their Cause and Treatment," we learn that a biochemical as well as a learning approach can best serve the diagnostician who deals with people beset by this most troubling condition.

Looking Ahead: Challenge Questions

What support systems do we need to provide to families of those who suffer from emotional problems and particularly from severe forms of mental disorders?

Considering our current knowledge about Alzheimer's disease, what seem to be the next logical steps in the search for the specific cause and the development of a reasonable treatment?

If a friend of yours appears to have a dysthymic disorder, how would you explain or describe it to her or him, and what would you encourage him or her to do about it?

How can we determine the specific cause of a given anxiety or panic attack? Based on whether the cause is chemical or learned, what can be done to eliminate these uncomfortable experiences?

WHEN MENTAL ILLNESS HITS HOME

Sometimes after months of silence the telephone would ring in the darkness, startling Mary Alexander from sleep. "Do you have a daughter . . . ?" The voice blandly official, the caller in some other town or state, in Minneapolis this time, or Pittsburgh, "Mrs. Alexander, do you have a daughter . . . ?" She would close her eyes, waiting for the next words, bracing for them. "Mrs. Alexander, do you have a daughter who is living on the golf course and disturbing neighbors?" Who is walking down the street in mid-December with no clothes on. . . . Who tried to throw herself in front of a bus. . . . "Mrs. Alexander, we have your daughter here in the hospital. . . ." In her mind are images of Janet years ago, building a fort with her three younger sisters, her blond hair in long straight locks. Janet on the chairlift with her father in Aspen, or reading, curled in the window seat of the big New England farmhouse, white chenille bedspreads, a framed picture of blue mountains and open fields. "I swear to God, I would rather my child had cancer than this agony of a disease. . . ."

"Deinstitutionalization has failed." It is the mental-health mantra of the '80s, a popular slogan, borrowed by politicians and pundits. On our streets, severely disturbed people are among the homeless, living without treatment or community resources, eating out of garbage cans, filing through revolving doors to hospitals and jail cells. Yet those who are homeless are only the most visible subplot of a larger story. In fact, 60 percent of the 2 million Americans with disabling mental illness live with their families at least part of the time, and hundreds of thousands more reside in nursing homes and privately run "board and cares." In quiet suburban neighborhoods and in Park Avenue apartments, parents take out second mortgages to pay for the care of mentally ill sons and daughters. Husbands, aunts, brothers offer prayers for a cure. Over the years, families shepherd those they love through a torturous labyrinth of mental-health services, often to no obvious benefit.

"More money" is the familiar cry of those who work within an overburdened system. But it is not just a problem of money. "There is a kind of Russian distribution system, where the food never reaches the shelves. It rots in the countryside," says Dr. John Talbott, chairman of psychiatry at the University of Maryland, who has long pondered these problems. There is a constant shortage of hospital beds, but no long-term plan for building the community services that could keep patients out of hospitals to begin with. There are outpatient clinics, but no one to make sure patients arrive there to be treated. There are model programs, but they reach only a fraction of those who are in need. There is a two-tiered network of care, public and private, rich and poor. But even wealth does not ensure good treatment.

In this fragmented and sublimely ineffective system, cities, states and the federal government play "chicken" to see which will shoulder the financial burden of the mentally ill. Mental-health workers squabble over priorities and semantics. Everyone is affected by the deeply cynical decision society seems to have made collectively, if unconsciously: We will do nothing.

In the face of this national tragedy, it is the families of the mentally disturbed who are finally forcing change. A coalition of families, the National Alliance for the Mentally Ill, almost singlehandedly persuaded the National Institute of Mental Health to shift its $345 million research program away from more sociological studies, toward research on the cause and treatment of schizophrenia and other serious disorders. In Chicago, St. Louis and New Orleans, when parents found rehabilitation centers or housing projects for the mentally ill nonexistent, they went out and created them. In Massachusetts, a state that has inspired its share of mental-hospital exposés, the Department of Mental Health two years ago decided to bring both families and former patients into the equation: In a unique collaborative arrangement, citizen monitors conduct unannounced inspections of all public psychiatric institutions. The involvement of families, says Dr. Herbert Pardes, president-elect of the American Psychiatric Association and a former NIMH director, "is one of the most important things to happen in the history of mental health."

Families, and patients themselves, want to change more than just programs and services; they are struggling to eliminate the entrenched stereotypes and age-old misconceptions still governing society's attitudes toward mental illness. It was not that long ago that insanity was a family secret, that a schizophrenic aunt or daughter was chained in the attic. And still, today, a qualified engineer is denied a job because three years ago he was treated for depression, a psychiatrist is disqualified as an expert witness because while in training she received psychotherapy, and a presidential candidate must act quickly to squelch rumors that he might have sought counseling after his brother's death.

The myths have to be debunked through constant repetition: Schizophrenia is not the same as "split personality"; mental illness is not the result of weak character or moral failure; most mental patients are not violent; serious mental disorders are not "hopeless," and patients can get better, with the right treatment.

"Progress is more often illusion than reality," says Dr. John Nemiah, editor of the *American Journal of Psychiatry,* writing about society's management of chronic mental illness. "We are perhaps no further along than we were 200 years ago—indeed, we may have been traveling in circles."

Mental illness has always baffled and disturbed. Anyone who has seen up close the disintegration of a mind by schizophrenia, the laceration of consciousness, the shredding of thought that is paired with deep apathy and withdrawal, must wonder how such a thing occurs. No less puzzling are the violently distorted moods of manic-depression, highs that send the sufferer into an unstoppable frenzy of words and wild ideas, lows that plunge him into such a state of despair that "one's only wish is for silence and solitude and the oblivion of sleep," as composer Hector Berlioz described it. "For anyone possessed by this," wrote Berlioz, who during his youth fell victim to crippling emotional swings, "nothing has meaning, the destruction of a world would hardly move him."

The musician's eloquence conveys the texture of psychic torment but not its prevalence. At any moment, 25 percent of hospital beds in the U.S. are filled by mental patients, more than the total for cancer, heart disease and respiratory illness patients combined. Insanity appears to have been common in past centuries as well; it is only society's response to it that has changed.

The Puritans believed "distraction," as they called it, was possession by the Devil, or else punishment for sins. Yet the strange behavior of those afflicted was looked upon with tolerance. The Puritans were certain of the moral order and could view departure from the rational without themselves becoming unsettled by it.

Through much of the 1700s, family or friends were expected to take care of the mentally ill. Thus James Otis, Jr., a prominent politician in prerevolutionary Massachusetts, was remanded to his father's house or taken to the country by colleagues when he periodically went mad, once smashing all the windows in Boston's town hall. When no family was present, community leaders took over, sometimes "auctioning out" the person to a foster family.

By the 19th century, this early version of a community mental-health system was breaking down. "What worked in small villages didn't work with urbanization," says Gerald Grob, professor of history at Rutgers University. Immigrants poured into American cities, and persons suffering from schizophrenia or other mental disorders wandered the streets or were sent to almshouses or jail cells. Dorothea Dix, the crusading schoolteacher who took up the cause of the mentally ill in the mid-1800s, found disturbed individuals living in sordid conditions, "confined in cages, closets, cellars, stalls, pens: Chained, naked, beaten with rods and lashed into obedience."

Humane treatment in mental hospitals, Dix felt, was the solution, and by the time of her death in 1887 every state had at least one public mental hospital. There, doctors practiced a treatment called "moral therapy," because insanity was, they believed, caused by a childhood spent in an improper environment. The hospitals were proud of their "cures" for mental illness, often discharging patients within a year. They kept meticulous—if peculiar—statistics. From the 1843 annual report of Utica State Asylum:

"Total weight on admission of
276 patients 34,856 lb.
Total weight of those
discharged and remaining,
December 1st 35,825 lb.
Increase in weight of all
received 1,029 lb."

Towns and cities initially paid for the care of their residents at the state hospital. But by the 1890s, in an effort to discourage communities from cutting costs by keeping the afflicted in local almshouses, mental patients were declared wards of the state. So began the warehousing that in this century was the function of state hospitals. Seizing the opportunity to shift the economic burden onto the state, local officials began to redefine senility as "psychiatric illness," sending thousands of elderly men and women, demented and physically fragile, to state institutions. Between 1900 and World War II, more than half of patients admitted to state hospitals were over 65 years of age.

From there, the story is all too familiar. There were exposés, *The Snake Pit, The Shame of the States.* New studies showed that patients could be treated effectively, humanely and less expensively, in the community, and the serendipitous development of antipsychotic drugs in the 1950s made this a viable alternative. Then, in the 1960s, the Great Society initiated a wholesale policy of deinstitutionalization. State hospitals emptied their wards, from 558,000 patients in 1955 to fewer than 130,000,

mostly short-term patients, today. At the same time, the Community Mental Health Centers Act of 1963 called for the opening of 2,000 community treatment centers around the nation, and the federal government poured millions of mental-health dollars into counties and cities. But the dream was never realized. Fewer than half the projected centers actually came into being. The bulk of federal funds was spent on mental-health "prevention," on therapy for divorced mothers and low-income families, not on care for the chronically ill.

Toward the end of his life, the painter Vincent van Gogh wrote to his brother, Theodore, "What consoles me is that I am beginning to consider madness as an illness like any other, and I accept it as such." Were there a credo for the family movement, it might well be van Gogh's words. "The evidence that serious mental illnesses are diseases is now overwhelming," says Dr. E. Fuller Torrey, a psychiatrist whose sister is schizophrenic and who recently published *Nowhere to Go: The Tragic Odyssey of the Homeless Mentally Ill.* "Why should we treat them any differently than Parkinson's or Alzheimer's or multiple sclerosis?"

But old attitudes die hard. With the rise of psychoanalysis in the United States in the mid-20th century came a view of mental illness that held mothers and fathers responsible. Freud himself doubted that schizophrenia and other psychotic disorders could be ameliorated through his "talking cure." But he talked of conflicts and drives and the role of early-childhood experiences, and others picked up the theme, adding the term "schizophrenogenic mother."

The family movement prefers to call mental illnesses "brain diseases" and speaks of Freud with disdain. It is more than a quibble over words. The notion that the patient or his family is somehow to blame has persisted in the public mind, affecting in a very real way the fate of those afflicted. Most private insurers require larger co-payments and set lower reimbursement ceilings for psychiatric disorders. To many families, this seems just another bitter legacy of an emphasis on mental "health" instead of mental illness, a focus that blurred distinctions between the "worried well" and the "walking wounded." And some argue that the former—those suffering from life dissatisfaction or other mild ills—should pay more for counseling out of pocket. The latter, those with more-serious disorders that require extended hospitalization or drug therapy, ought to be fully covered.

Deinstitutionalization has created other agonizing dilemmas, among them those of people who are desperately ill but don't want treatment. Family advocates are attempting to reshape policy

EXPLAINING THE INEXPLICABLE

Scientists are finding that a genetic predisposition may be triggered by stress

Over the centuries, everything from "an excess of passions" to the malevolent influence of the moon has been proposed as a scientific explanation for mental illness. But modern psychiatry, trading on technological advances in neuroscience and molecular genetics, is beginning to confirm what many suspected. The extreme changes in perception, behavior and mood that occur in serious mental disorders are, at least in part, biological.

Psychiatrists have always recognized that schizophrenia and manic-depression differ markedly from less severe complaints. Unlike "the blues," or mild anxiety, these illnesses can make it impossible for those afflicted to hold jobs or negotiate daily routines. While the emotional swings of manic-depression begin in adulthood, schizophrenia most often develops in adolescence or early adulthood. Many experts believe it will prove to be a family of illnesses rather than a single disorder, but there are common characteristics: Thought patterns become peculiar and convoluted. Hallucinations and delusions often mix with withdrawal and apathy.

Early evidence that changes in brain chemistry might be involved in schizophrenia and manic-depression came from the development of drugs to treat them. Researchers discovered that antipsychotic drugs, which help about 60 percent of schizophrenics, change the levels of a substance called dopamine, one of many chemicals that transmit nerve impulses in the brain. Antidepressants and drugs like lithium carbonate, used to treat mania, alter the balance of other neurotransmitters and bring relief to the vast majority of sufferers. But though scientists reason that these chemicals are involved in mental illnesses, their role is still unproved.

Window to the brain. The case for brain irregularities has been strengthened with the development of imaging devices that can take readings of brain structure and function. In schizophrenic patients, brain scans indicate that the frontal lobe—intimately tied up with high-order abilities such as future planning—shows lower-than-normal levels of blood flow during the performance of a simple cognitive task. Other studies have found that some schizophrenics have enlarged brain ventricles—the fluid-filled spaces within the brain—indicating that brain tissue has shrunk or developed abnormally.

At the same time, psychiatrists are building evidence for heredity's contribution to mental illness. Researchers have known for years that schizophrenia and manic-depressive illness tend to run in families. But only recently have they been able to start tracking down the specific gene or genes that may predispose someone to fall ill. Last fall, an international team of scientists reported finding an abnormality on chromosome 5 in 39 schizophrenic members of five families. An earlier, 11-year study of a Pennsylvania Amish family with a history of manic-depression found that afflicted individuals shared an abnormal gene on another chromosome, No. 11.

Yet this work is only the barest blush of a beginning. No one so far has succeeded in replicating the studies. And because all mental illnesses involve complex human behaviors, most experts believe genetic predisposition will not turn out to be as simple as a single abnormal gene.

The nature of nurture. Even without the specifics of inheritance, however, scientists have been able to estimate an individual's risk of developing severe mental illness. In schizophrenia, for example, a child with one schizophrenic parent runs an 8-to-18-percent likelihood of being afflicted. If both parents are schizophrenic, that figure jumps to between 15 and 50 percent. But unlike diseases such as Down syndrome, mental disorders are only in part genetic, as studies of identical twins have shown. Even when one twin is schizophrenic, the other has only a 50-to-60-percent chance of developing the disease.

However strong the influence of heredity, researchers believe that severe mental illness has a substantial nurture component as well. "The question is not nature vs. nurture, but the nature of nurture," says Dr. Jack Grebb, of New York University Medical Center. One theory suggests schizophrenia may result from prenatal events—infection by a virus, perhaps—that affect a fetus genetically susceptible to the illness. Another theory proposes stress as the triggering factor. There is some evidence that a high degree of emotional tumult in a family, good or bad, may make schizophrenic patients more prone to relapse. "But this doesn't suggest that the families of schizophrenics are any different from other families," says Dr. William Carpenter, director of the Maryland Psychiatric Institute. "It suggests that within family life there are things that patients may have a hard time dealing with." In a field filled with many more questions than answers, the fact that bad parenting is not likely to cause schizophrenia may be the one thing scientists are increasingly sure of.

here as well. The problem was dramatized last year in the courtroom battle of Joyce Brown, a k a Billie Boggs. Living on the streets of Manhattan, Brown was hospitalized against her will as part of an attempt by New York Mayor Ed Koch to widen the scope of his state's commitment law. When a trial judge concluded that Brown—who shouted at passers-by, ripped dollar bills into shreds and used the sidewalk as a commode—was sane, it triggered a storm of editorials. "We have condemned the homeless mentally ill to die with their rights on," protested columnist Charles Krauthammer.

Many families now are pressing for lawmakers to make it easier to force very ill patients into treatment, even if they do not pose a danger to themselves or others. As it now stands, lawyers, not doctors, decide when someone should be hospitalized, families say. In some urban areas, a patient must literally be slashing his wrists or brandishing a weapon before he can be held in a hospital. At least 15 states have rewritten their commitment laws to reflect this view. Yet civil libertarians and most former patients deeply oppose such legal reforms. A person who has committed no crime and who is not dangerous should not be incarcerated against his will, they say. At least one study suggests that changing laws only makes things worse, that it leads to even greater overcrowding in crisis clinics and amplifies the already dire shortage of hospital beds.

These are signs of a deeply ailing system, one that no simple wave of a legislator's pen will heal. "No matter where you look, something is broken and needs to be fixed," says Laurie Flynn, NAMI's executive director. Of the $17 billion plus spent annually in the U.S. on mental-health care, more must be funneled toward those who most need it, in the form of coordinated community services, networks of halfway and three-quarterway houses, crisis centers, outreach teams, housing, job training programs.

Innovative programs, programs that *work*, already exist in small pockets across the country, in Madison, Wis., in Tucson, Ariz., in Toledo, Ohio. The Robert Wood Johnson Foundation has awarded a total of $29 million to nine cities to redesign their mental-health systems. Even in New York City, where thousands are homeless or on the brink of homelessness and the bleak interior of the Bellevue Hospital crisis clinic is almost always crowded, there are islands of sanity. The solution is not, as Koch recently concluded, to take patients out of hospitals and place them in homeless shelters, even if the shelters offer mental-health services. Rather, there are places where mental patients live with dignity: The St. Francis residences, a program run by three Franciscan friars; Fountain House, where 4,000 mentally disable club members learn skills and function as capable members of a community, many living on their own in subsidized apartments.

The reign of the state hospitals ended in a flurry of exposés, accounts of patients chained to beds, lying in their own feces. A return to warehousing mental patients in large state institutions is not the answer. "It's not economically, legally, morally, ethically or clinically feasible," says Steven Schnee, superintendent of San Antonio State Hospital. "It's not necessary. It's not appropriate. Mentally ill people deserve the opportunity to make a contribution."

Until there is a cure for schizophrenia, there will be a need for long-term care for the small group of patients who cannot function even with medication, or who are continuously violent or suicidal. "Some patients require intensive treatment," says Leona Bachrach, of the University of Maryland. "It can be done in the community. We know that

because in a few places it has been done. But there is a lag between knowing and doing it, and into this gap many disabled people fall." In the meantime, state hospitals, most of which are themselves overcrowded, try to fill this role.

Yet the most basic obstacle to treating mental illness is neither lack of knowledge nor lack of money. It is a question of values. The values of a psychiatric profession that rewards private practice and economically penalizes those who choose to work with the severely ill in the public sector; a society that takes cancer and heart disease seriously but largely ignores mental illness; the values of citizens who don't want halfway houses in *their* neighborhoods and often forget that the homeless man they see on the television screen is also someone's son, someone's brother.

PATIENTS FOR SALE: SUPPLY IS UP, DEMAND DOWN

In overcrowded psychiatric emergency rooms, healers become auctioneers

In a strained mental-health system, beds are scarce and indigent patients unpopular, a reality captured by the title of a recent journal article: "The Hospitalizable Patient as Commodity: Selling in a Bear Market." Inner-city psychiatric emergency rooms from New York to San Francisco are battlegrounds in a war between the private and public sectors as workers struggle to secure beds for their patients. These crisis clinics are a microcosm of the larger system, a showcase for forces that crush idealism and make good care all but impossible.

Police bring in a flood of patients, the psychic casualties of downtown streets and welfare hotels. Overwhelmed emergency rooms try to stem the tide. Public hospitals must treat anyone who comes in, so their emergency rooms devise subtle ways to discourage customers. In one Manhattan crisis clinic, administrators require police to stay until a disposition is reached for any patient they bring in. The process can take hours.

Psychiatric emergency rooms are supposed to provide brief treatment and, if necessary, find patients beds in hospitals

or halfway houses. But this task is more difficult to do for some patients than for others, forcing even the most dedicated care provider into the role of salesman. Emergency-room workers must coax and cajole, cutting through the skepticism of an admissions nurse at the other end of a telephone line. Private hospitals and nursing homes are picky about whom they will take. State hospitals often have quotas for how many patients they accept from a given city or county.

Creative excuses. For hospitals on the receiving end, the cardinal rule is to find an excuse for keeping out undesirable patients. "We only admit medicaid patients one day a week" was one creative explanation given doctors at a Bronx emergency room by a hospital that would not take a 16-year-old suicidal patient. It took 13 days and negotiations with 10 hospitals before the girl was finally placed in a locked psychiatric ward.

The sellers have their techniques, too. "If you make a patient sound too bad, hospitals won't take him," says Joe Larson, a psychiatric nurse at San Francisco General Hospital's psychiatric emergency room. "If he doesn't sound bad enough, they're afraid his medicaid will be cut off and they'll be stuck with the bill."

The hardest patients to sell are the repeaters with bad reputations, the fire set-

ters and those who are potentially violent. Drug abuse is a negative selling point. So is no health insurance, AIDS, incontinence or a need for long-term care or constant observation.

More often than not, the emergency-room workers fail, and their unfortunate charges spend as long as a week sleeping on foldout armchairs, watching television and pacing in cramped quarters beneath blue-white fluorescent lights. In Northern California, four psychiatric emergency rooms were recently issued citations by state officials for keeping patients longer than the mandated 24-hour limit. But they have no choice. If a patient is dangerous to himself or others, the hospital cannot let him go.

Ultimately, difficult patients often end their emergency-room stay by being sent to the overcrowded wards of the same city hospitals—dumping grounds for the poor and the uninsured, for patients no one else will take. "We enter the field with the best of intentions, to comfort, aid and assist," writes Stephen Goldfinger, M.D., of Harvard University Medical School. "And yet how easy it becomes to lose these lofty motivations when confronted with the daily realities. . . . We are all—patients, planners and practitioners—diminished by this process."

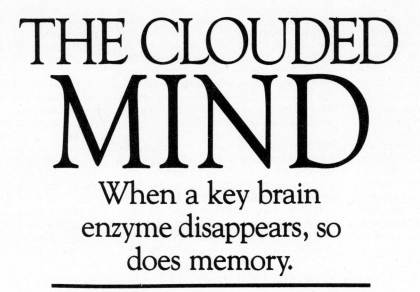

THE CLOUDED MIND

When a key brain enzyme disappears, so does memory.

Michael Shodell

Michael Shodell is a contributing editor of Science 84.

Old age, even in cultures where it is venerated, is often viewed with ambivalence. And as living standards and medicine continue to improve, more and more of us will be the butts of Fan Ch'eng-ta's fine joke. For with an increased life-span, afflictions that once were rare have become common. Among the gravest of these is Alzheimer's disease, an illness that destroys the mind, leaving the body behind as a grim reminder of the person who once was there. As cancer, another all-too-familiar companion of the later decades, has become a relentless reminder of the urgency in seeking the secrets of the cell, so Alzheimer's disease has left us with another pressing challenge—uncovering the mysteries of the mind.

Alzheimer's disease is one of the most fearsome and devastating aspects of aging: It has no known cause, no prevention, no cure. It afflicts about a million people, roughly five percent of the population over 65. By the year 2000 an estimated three to four million Americans, or one of every 10 adults over 65, will be a victim. Hundreds of scientists around the world are dedicated to understanding this affliction. Some are isolating Alzheimer's biochemical defects in the brains of victims, others are comparing these to similar ones in other dementias, while still others are looking at rare dementia-causing diseases from distant parts of the globe.

In this way, they hope to pin down Alzheimer's cause, which is as elusive today as it was in 1906 when the German neurologist Alois Alzheimer first described the disease in a report entitled "Concerning a unique illness of the brain cortex." Alzheimer was the first to show that senile dementia was not just a natural wearing out of the mind, a belief common then as it had been through the centuries. Shakespeare reflected that conviction when he described the last age of man as "second childishness and mere oblivion." While severe dementia may be caused by a number of illnesses, such as brain tumors, alcoholism, or arteriosclerosis of brain blood vessels, Alzheimer's disease is by far the single most prevalent cause of mental deterioration in the elderly.

Victims initially have trouble remembering recent events. Gradually, as their minds deteriorate, they become more confused and forgetful, repeating questions asked moments before, for example, or getting hopelessly lost while traveling to previously familiar places. Disorientation grows, and memories of the past disappear, sometimes accompanied by paranoia, hallucinations, and violent mood swings. Patients can no longer cook, drive, or use tools. Later, they lose their ability to read, write, eat, walk, or talk. Finally the disease culminates in a full dementia, the undoing of the mind.

In his seminal paper Alzheimer first described one of the two physical characteristics of the disease: the clumping of fibers within nerve cells, called neurofibrillary tangles. The other—the so-called senile plaques—are filled with knobby, abnormal nerve axons and terminals wreathed around amyloid, a waxy, translucent protein that looks like rippled pasta. These structures nest among the mass of normal brain cells and fibers in the cerebral cortex, the outer layer of the brain in which higher thought processes and abilities originate, and the hippocampus, which seems to play a special role in learning and memory. The plaques and tangles can easily be seen with a low-power microscope.

In examining his deceased patient's brain, Alzheimer was following a medical tradition begun in the mid-18th century by the Italian anatomist Giovanni Battista Morgagni, whose studies of more than 700 autopsies demonstrated for the first time, among other things, that hemorrhaging of the brain produced paralysis on the opposite side of the body, perhaps the first time anyone connected stroke with the rupturing of brain vessels.

Today, autopsy is still a major source of medical information that can be obtained in no other way. In Alzheimer's victims, for instance, autopsy reveals the presence of the plaques and tangles essential for a final diagnosis of the disease. Diagnosis while the patient is alive can only be made provisionally, based on psychological and performance tests and the patient's family and case histories. Moreover, since old animals do not get Alzheimer's, autopsies provide the only way to perform research on actual brains.

The first autopsies of Alzheimer's patients clearly revealed that plaques and tangles were the disease's signature upon the brain. The structures correlated well with the disease; the sicker the person, the more he had. But the plaques and tangles also appeared in the brains of apparently healthy older people, although to a considerably lesser extent, perhaps because of their age or because of some environmental injury. In the mid-1970s, researchers found to their surprise that the signature of Alzheimer's was indeed writ upon the cortex, but the hand that did the writing was located in another region of the brain altogether.

One of the first indications of what was actually going on came from Peter Davies, then at the Institute of Neurology in London and now at Albert Einstein College of Medicine in New York City. He showed that the cortices and hippocampi of Alzheimer's sufferers had a tremendously reduced level—from 60 to 90 percent compared to age-matched controls—of an enzyme called choline acetyltransferase, or CAT, needed for making the chemical acetylcholine.

Acetylcholine is one of the essential brain substances known as neurotransmitters, specialized chemicals that carry messages between neurons. Within the brain's three-pound gelatinous mass are more than one trillion neuron cells, each having on average about 50,000 different connections to other neurons. Just one cubic centimeter of cerebral cortex contains approximately one trillion such neuron-to-neuron connections. And it is within this extraordinary labyrinthine network that the mind and memory are located, as well as the terrible defects that are the cause of degenerative illnesses like Alzheimer's disease.

Neurotransmitters such as acetylcholine are at the heart of the functioning of that network. Without them the neuronal wires of communication would still be in place, but the lines would be dead. Although dozens of neurotransmitters are now known, and more are discovered every year, any particular neuron usually stores enzymes that make predominantly just one neurotransmitter. Moreover, groups of neurons that generally make the same transmitter are often found clustered together in defined areas of the brain known as nuclei. The neurons themselves may have very long projections, or axons, for carrying their chemicals to distant regions of the brain. Thus, a deficiency of acetylcholine in one part of the brain could be caused by the lack of enzymes in some distant nucleus of the brain.

In the late 1970s and early 1980s, Joseph T. Coyle, Donald Price, and Mahlon DeLong at the Johns Hopkins University School of Medicine demonstrated that this scenario exactly captures Alzheimer's fatal process: The deficit of the enzyme and its neurotransmitter appears in the cortex, but the actual source of the problem lies some distance away in a small region known as the nucleus

basalis, lying just above the site where the optic nerves meet and cross. Moreover, autopsies revealed shrunken and abnormal cells or an unmistakable and dramatic loss of neurons from the nucleus basalis in Alzheimer's sufferers—up to 75 percent in some cases—but not in most age-matched controls, which explained why there was so little enzyme being manufactured.

Alzheimer's disease began to look, at least to some researchers, like a neurotransmitter-specific disease. The classic example of this sort of ailment is Parkinson's disease, typically appearing in the middle years of life. Its symptoms include tremors and severe problems of muscular control, sometimes complicated by dementia. The disease is caused by a loss of neurons in the base of the brain, which actually depletes dopamine in the cortex. Drugs can increase the levels of dopamine in the brain, at least for awhile, and temporarily bring the Parkinson symptoms under control, but the progressive brain cell loss continues, compounding the disease effects and making the drugs less and less effective as the illness progresses. Similar approaches to Alzheimer's disease, using drugs that should increase or otherwise enhance brain acetylcholine activity, have not proven equally effective even in the short term, perhaps because other neurotransmitters are involved in Alzheimer's or because the drugs available now don't increase acetylcholine activity enough.

One still highly experimental approach that might accomplish this sort of goal has recently been attempted in Parkinson's disease. Functioning cells from the adrenal glands, which produce a chemical closely related to dopamine, have been transplanted to the deteriorating brains of two Parkinson's disease patients at the Karolinska Institute in Stockholm, but it is still too soon to tell if the technique will have any value in the long run for Parkinson's—or Alzheimer's.

Other researchers are trying a different tack by relating a lack of acetylcholine to memory loss. Folklorists wrote about how jimson or devil weed could erase memories for as much as a week or more. Scopolamine, the active ingredient, produces the same effect but for short intervals when given in small doses. It was once used regularly, for example, to reduce the perceived pain of labor, by erasing the mother's recollections of the birth of her child. Experiments with young adult volunteers have shown that scopolamine, by blocking acetylcholine receptors, affects memory. Intrigued with the ability of this drug to interfere with the normal functioning of a specific neurotransmitter, researchers attempted to examine its exact relation to memory and other cognitive functions. When David Drachman of the University of Massachusetts Medical Center administered scopolamine to healthy young volunteers, a temporary state of memory loss and confusion resulted that was, at least under the restricted testing procedures used, virtually indistinguishable from the responses of old people and similar to those of Alzheimer's patients.

The best approach to Alzheimer's, of course, would be to learn how to prevent the terrible symptoms from arising in the first place. And that means finding the cause. One possibility is that Alzheimer's disease lies in the genes. One such disease in which the faulty genes are clearly hereditary—all children with the fatal illness have an affected parent—is Huntington's disease or Huntington's chorea, from the same Greek root as choreography, referring to the jerky spasmodic movements of the head, limbs, and body. Researchers have recently isolated a marker for the disease on a particular region of chromosome number four.

Similar hereditary connections have been found in Alzheimer's disease, although they are much less conclusive than in Huntington's disease. Several family trees have been described in which the incidence of Alzheimer's disease can be traced back for up to seven and even eight generations, but the more common pattern appears not to be hereditary at all. These differing patterns could suggest instead that there are nongenetic varieties of the disease and types that are hereditary as well. There might even be a genetic component in all forms of Alzheimer's disease, but the hereditary trait shows up clearly only when there is reliable medical data going back several generations or a sufficient number of older people represented on the receding branches of any given family tree. There might be still another type of Alzheimer's in which genes control the susceptibility to the disease, but the environment triggers the ailment.

The distinction between hereditary and nonhereditary diseases began to break down in the 1960s, largely because of the demonstration of what are known as slow virus diseases. These sorts of infections originally came to light through study of a strange illness at first apparently of interest only to the isolated Fore tribe of the forested highlands of New Guinea—the only people in the world known to get the disease of kuru, which means fear or trembling. Through a combination of anthropological, medical, and epidemiological creativity and tenacity, D. Carleton Gajdusek of the U.S. National Institutes of Health was able to show that this illness, which appeared to be a classic chronic degenerative disorder, was actually caused by an infectious agent. The kuru agent was not passed from person to person, but rather from the dead to the living as the mothers and children handled the infected brains of the deceased as part of their mourning ritual. The disease progressively attacks the brain and nervous system of its victims, who first shiver, stagger, slur their speech, eventually can neither walk nor sit up without assistance, and, finally unable to chew or swallow, die.

The discovery of this agent, and the establishment of its ability to have infected years or even decades before its devasting effects have become unleashed upon the brains of its victims—effects that include dementia and probably the senile plaques in the victims' brains as well—brought a new perspective to the consideration of degenerative neurological disease. Such kurulike agents are now known to occur in a variety of species, including the widespread scrapie disease of sheep, and another human affliction known as Creutzfeldt-Jakob syndrome that occurs virtually worldwide. Named after the German scientists who discovered it in 1920, Creutzfeldt-Jakob syndrome causes a severe form of senility that strikes people in their middle to later decades and progresses far more rapidly than Alzheimer's. It is also a disease, although far rarer than Alzheimer's, for which family inheritance patterns have been demonstrated in some instances. But even in these cases, infectious slow viruses—similar to the kuru and sheep scrapie viruses—are the actual cause.

Another seemingly isolated incidence of disease on a remote Pacific island offers yet another possible candidate as the cause of Alzheimer's—the environment. A tribe known as the Chamorros, living in a relatively underdeveloped region on Guam, develop extremely high incidences of Lou Gehrig's disease (amyotrophic lateral sclerosis or ALS)—the progressive wasting of muscles that killed baseball's "iron man"—as well as Parkinsonlike ailments and dementia accompanied by Alzheimerlike neurofibrillary tangles. It turns out that the region of Guam where the tribe lives is almost entirely devoid of such essential minerals as calcium and magnesium. Neuropathologist Daniel Perl of the University of Vermont believes that these deficits combined with and possibly leading to unusually high accumulations of heavy metals, especially aluminum, seem to play a role in the genesis of the illnesses of the Chamorros. In addition, Perl has shown that the tangles in the brains of victims of Alzheimer's disease also contain aluminum and that this metal, when injected into the brains of experimental animals, can also lead to the formation of similar, although not identical, tangles.

This discovery has caused people to worry about using aluminum pots, pans, foil, deodorants, and Rolaids for fear the metal will accumulate in the brain. Perl says that the evidence available is not sufficient to warrant these concerns. Aluminum is the most ubiquitous metal on Earth, and it is impossible to avoid it. Although it is definitely toxic to the nervous system, most people luckily have efficient barriers to prevent aluminum from getting into the brain. Perl says he is now trying to find out what the barrier mechanisms are that keep aluminum out. He is also studying the potential effects of advancing age, slow viruses, and other factors on the integrity of the barrier system.

The list of suspects implicated in Alzheimer's disease, then, is distressingly broad: genetics, infectious agents, and environment—either acting alone or in concert. Should the cause be infectious or environmental, researchers might be able to eliminate or inactivate it. But what if it should be something more fundamental and far-reaching—a genetic program for senility that is part of the aging process—one of the seven stages of man? Were that so, Alzheimer's would not be a disease at all. There would be no cure. Doctors could only make the affliction more bearable.

By comparing Alzheimer's to known diseases such as Parkinson's, kuru, and Creutzfeldt-Jakob, however, it seems likely that Alzheimer's is a true disease. As such there is hope for seeking its causes and its possible cures. Then aging need not portend Shakespeare's "mere oblivion" after all, but rather a stage of life to be appreciated for its own strengths as well as for its weaknesses—a stage as legitimate and no more pathological than any other.

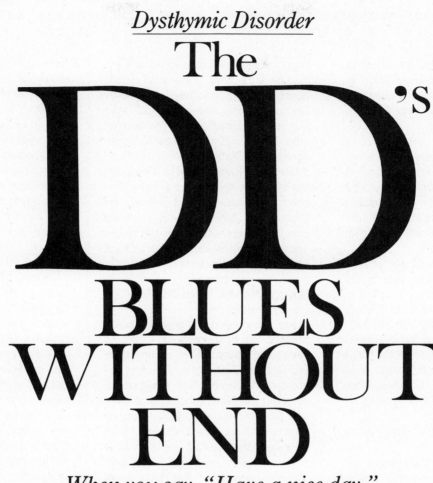

Dysthymic Disorder

The DD's

BLUES WITHOUT END

*When you say, "Have a nice day,"
five million Americans don't know what
you're talking about.*

Winifred Gallagher

Winifred Gallagher *is a Senior
Editor at* American Health.

The psychiatrist asked his patient how long she'd been in poor spirits. "Since the sperm hit the egg," she said. "I can tell by the way other people act that they're happy, but I don't know what that's like. I never have a happy day."

Research now shows that her melancholy description may not be just a colorful exaggeration. About five million Americans—twice as many women as men—suffer from a chronic, sometimes lifelong, low-grade depression called "dysthymic disorder" (DD). The typical DD victim is in her late 30s to 40s, but epidemiologists are alarmed by DD's increasing prevalence in younger people, particularly children.

Considering the long, grey shadow DD casts, it's unfortunate that the af-flicted—and their families and friends—often have no idea that this unhappiness is caused by a very treatable disease. Often, the sufferer has repeatedly sought help from physicians and psychotherapists for secondary symptoms such as fatigue, or personality problems like low self-esteem. In fact, until recently, a DD victim was said to be suffering from a

Sadness gradually seems normal—"the way life is."

DD rates are twice as high for women as for men . . . High-risk ages: 30s and 40s . . .

"depressive personality." Now health professionals are learning that until the patient's depression itself is identified and treated, she's not very likely to get better.

Psychologists used to focus on a more obvious form of the blues known as a "major depressive episode." A major depression profoundly upsets a person's mental and physical equilibrium, but its symptoms generally subside in six to nine months—or, with treatment, within weeks.

In contrast, the symptoms of DD, which persist for at least two years, are mild enough to permit a victim to go through the motions of life at home and work. As the months go by, sadness gradually seems normal, at least for her—"the way life is" or "the way I am." She and her circle forget what she was like before the blues descended. This confusion of illness with personality or the circumstances of life often keeps DD sufferers from finding the right help.

Once DD is diagnosed, treatment can bring prompt, dramatic relief. Many patients are helped by newer, short-term psychotherapies that teach practical ways to correct the intellectual and emotional distortions caused by the blues. A growing body of research is prompting more doctors to prescribe aerobic exercise for both depressed and anxious patients. But the latest advance is the use of an old remedy in a new way.

Antidepressant medicines were previously prescribed only for shorter, severe "biological" depressions. Recently James Kocsis and Allen Frances, professors of psychiatry at New York Hospital-Cornell Medical Center, have shown that antidepressants can often relieve mild chronic melancholy. One patient summed up the results of drug treatment this way: "For the first time in my life, I feel like I'm not walking waist-deep in mud."

"DD is a very substantial public health problem that has been vastly overlooked and unrecognized," says Dr. Robert Hirschfeld, a psychiatrist who directs off-site research sponsored by the National Institute of Mental Health in Rockville, MD. This year, the NIMH is sponsoring a major outreach program—Project D/ART, for Depression Awareness, Recognition and Treatment—to teach the public and health professionals about DD and other forms of depression.

Whiny, Moody, Guilt-Ridden

Just about everyone gets mildly depressed on occasion—you'd almost have to be crazy not to, according to Dr. Gerald L. Klerman, a leading depression researcher and professor of psychiatry at New York Hospital-Cornell. On any given day, 10% of Americans say they're melancholy. About 40% claim they've had five to 10 blue days in a year. "A friend might say, 'What's the matter? You don't seem like yourself lately,' " says Klerman. "This type of brief, mild depression is the psychological equivalent of the common cold, and there's a lot of it going around."

Like these "normal" depressions, DD often starts out as an understandable reaction to a dispiriting event. But in DD, the symptoms, though mild, drag on and on. "It's normal to be upset about a friend's death or getting fired, but not to say 'I'll never have another friend' or 'I'm worthless,' " says Dr. Kocsis. "When the person's ideas about what's going on are unrealistic, and melancholic symptoms persist, he or she is heading toward a psychiatric disorder."

Like other sick people, victims of DD feel poorly. Their physical symptoms—often fatigue or aches and pains—are troublesome. Their psychological ones are worse: dysphoria (unhappiness) and anhedonia (the inability to feel pleasure). Dysthymics tend to be pessimistic, whiny, moody and guilt-ridden, as well as sad. They're bored, and sometimes boring. They feel helpless and hopeless. If something good happens, they think it's a fluke; if something bad happens, they know it's their fault. "You can recognize dysthymics by their unhappy yet functional lives," says Dr. Frances. "They suffer."

Dysthymics suffer most in those aspects of life that call for spontaneity, fun, intimacy and sensitivity toward others. They usually do better at work than at love or play—Abraham Lincoln was a depressed superachiever. Often, pessimism and poor self-esteem prevent a victim from developing either her public or private potential. "Dysthymics tend to have a job, but not a great job, and a marriage, but not a great marriage," says Kocsis. "Just as they're chronically depressed, they can end up 'chronically wed'—stuck in a bad relationship they can't get themselves out of."

A bout of DD, like a struggle with major depression, can be almost as grueling for close associates as for the victim. The toll it takes on relationships is one reason that prompt treatment is important, says Klerman: "Studies show that most people first respond to a depressed person with sympathy and support. But if the sadness and complaints persist, that sympathy gives way to irritability and avoidance. This is a normal reaction that ends up isolating the patient even more. She feels that nobody likes her—and sometimes she's right."

"To me, the question is not why people get depressed. After all, human life is stressful," says Klerman. "The question is why some people

For many people, depression seems to run in the family.

Increasing risk in kids . . . Symptoms last at least two years . . . Often goes untreated . . .

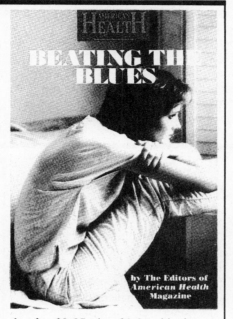
stay depressed. Most people can turn it off after five or 10 days and cope, while others get hung up for years on end, and make everyone miserable."

Biochemistry of the Blues

Today, biological psychiatrists think that DD is often caused by the same unfortunate conjunction of external stress and biological predisposition that triggers more severe depressions. Along with his genes, a victim inherits a tendency to have unbalanced levels of neurotransmitters, the chemicals that govern the electrical transmission of information throughout the brain. When this communication sys-

tem malfunctions, so does the ability to think and feel appropriately.

Studies show that lots of DD patients and their relatives have had—or will have—episodes of major depression as well. Klerman suspects that many dysthymics—with the exception of those who've had DD since they were kids—had an acute episode of major depression that they never really recovered from. He points out that while most of those who suffer a major depressive episode are over it in a year, 15% aren't; three years later, about 5% of them still feel blue. These people may be "left with a residual anhedonia, pessimism and fatigue," says Klerman.

Researchers are more puzzled by cases of DD that begin early in life. (Until quite recently, it was believed that children didn't suffer from true depression.) Many juvenile depressions—usually responses to traumas like divorce or the death of a parent—do seem to disappear on their own in time. But a substantial number of DD patients have been depressed for no discernible reason since an undetermined point in childhood. Interviews with their families back up their accounts—they were indeed sad kids. They often have depressed relatives, suggesting that depression may be a family trait.

Determining DD's cause—whether biological or psychological—is not a prerequisite for effective treatment. "Everything in life is biological as well as psychological—look at the biological way the brain responds to hope in placebo experiments!" says Frances. "The brain is constantly influenced both by one's experiences and its own chemistry. So it's not surprising that there are biological and psychological ways to break up the cycle of depressed neurochemistry, thoughts and experiences. The right intervention in any one of these areas—with drugs, psychotherapy, behavioral changes—could turn the vicious cycle into a benign one."

Drugs: An Old Innovation

Just as many factors can contribute to a headache, many influences combine to produce an individual's depression. Once DD has been diagnosed, the victim's treatment has to be tailored to his psyche, chemistry or both—a painstaking process that can take some time. "Patients get demoralized if one approach doesn't work. But not to despair! Almost everyone

Drug therapy helped a depressed lawyer finally begin her practice.

On any day, 10% of Americans are blue . . . 40% have 5 to 10 blue days a year . . .

will benefit from one of a combination of treatments," says Frances. "You can be a nonresponder to one, and do very well on another."

Frances' point was made plain in the controlled drug study of dysthymics Kocsis and he completed in 1986. Most of their 53 patients, who had been depressed for an average of 19 years, had previously tried psychotherapy without success. 28 of these patients were then given the antidepressant Tofranil, without accompanying talk therapy. Six weeks after they started to take the drug, about 60% of the subjects who stuck with the treatment had recovered. Even the researchers were somewhat surprised by how well the antidepressant worked.

The major hitch in antidepressant treatment is that the drugs don't start working until three weeks after they're first prescribed. The patient usually takes several capsules daily for six to 12 months; when they're no longer needed, the dosage is tapered off under careful medical supervision. Side effects are usually mild—for example, dry mouth, constipation and brief memory lapses. While psychiatrists often supervise antidepressant treatment, the drugs can be prescribed and successfully monitored by general practitioners—the doctors that most victims of DD consult first.

Unfortunately, a longstanding bias against psychiatric drugs can lead doctors and patients to regard medication as a "defeat," instead of as part of a systematic approach to finding the right treatment. "Until recently, no one would have thought of giving medication to a mildly depressed patient, because his was considered a 'psychological' disorder that needed psychotherapy," says Kocsis. He and Frances suggest that a patient try psychotherapy first; if symptoms persist

after six months, an antidepressant should be considered, or even a combination of drugs and talk.

"The patients in our study really got better," says Frances. "We're not just talking about taking the edge off the latest blip in their depression, but about feeling better than they'd ever felt before." One subject, in her mid-30s, had been so demoralized by the

blues that she'd been working as a secretary even though she had a law degree. Shortly after starting on the antidepressant, she began a successful career as a lawyer.

Traditional psychodynamic therapists believe that depression is caused by guilt, anger, dependency and excessive need for approval. They try to help the patient gain control over the

---

DOES SOMEONE YOU KNOW HAVE DD?

"We don't have a blood test to determine whether someone is a latent dysthymic," says Dr. Gerald Klerman of New York Hospital-Cornell. "The diagnosis must be based on the individual's report of his symptoms and functioning." How does a doctor or friend tell if someone is depressed? "He should ask," says Klerman, "and he often doesn't."

Three or four "Yes" answers to the following questions could mean that someone you know is suffering from DD. Has the person been:

■ In a blue mood for most of the day, more days than not, for at least two years? (Children and teens may seem irritable rather than depressed; they need to have symptoms for only a year to fit the DD criteria.)

■ Free of the blues only for periods of less than two months at a time during the past two years?

■ Eating too much or not enough?

■ Sleeping too much or not enough?

■ Complaining of low energy?

■ Demonstrating poor self-esteem?

■ Having difficulty concentrating or making decisions?

■ Showing signs of desperation or hopelessness?

In addition, these symptoms must

not be the result of psychosis, depressive disorders besides DD, or physical influences on mood, such as antihypertension drugs.

Many victims of DD bear other emotional burdens as well—often anxiety and alcohol or drug abuse. Some of their symptoms overlap with those of other psychiatric disorders.

For information on how to find a health professional qualified to diagnose and treat DD, contact:

■ National Depressive and Manic-Depressive Association (NDMDA), Merchandise Mart, PO Box 3395, Chicago, IL 60654. Patient-run educational support and a referral network for patients and their families. Send an SASE with 56¢ postage on it.

■ National Alliance for the Mentally Ill (NAMI), 1901 N. Fort Myer Drive, Suite 500, Arlington, VA 22209. Support and education for patients and families; 800 affiliates nationwide.

■ The National Mental Health Association (NMHA), 1021 Prince St., Alexandria, VA 22314-2971; 703-684-7722. The nation's oldest organization concerned with all aspects of mental health; 600 affiliates nationwide.

■ Depression Awareness, Recognition and Treatment Program (D/ART), National Institute of Mental Health, 5600 Fishers Lane, Rockville, MD 20857; Attn: D/ART Public Inquiries. Health care providers and the public can request information.

People with DD need short-term therapy—not endless analysis.

5% of those with major depression still suffer after 3 years ... Drug therapy brings relief to 60% ...

unconscious conflicts that underlie those emotions. Some are undoubtedly helped, but the results are unpredictable and the treatment is lengthy and expensive.

Today, a second generation of eclectic psychotherapists is attacking depression with "psychoeducation," rather than introspection and reflection on the past. As far as they're concerned, the blues come from "depressed" patterns of thinking, feeling, acting, and dealing with others. But if that's true, learning new, positive patterns can be the cure.

Talk Therapy vs. Drugs

Studies have shown these new talk therapies work: Their overall results are comparable to those of antidepressants. *Cognitive therapy* corrects the depressed person's typically negative, distorted thoughts, which inspire the self-destructive behavior that worsens their depression. *Interpersonal psychotherapy* (IPT) uses the patient's ability to function in relationships as a gauge of his emotional health; by strengthening his coping and communication skills, social bonds also become the means of relieving his depression. *Behavioral therapy* combines aspects of these two approaches and adds a third focus: learning to balance life's pluses and minuses.

According to behaviorist Robert Becker, associate professor of psychiatry at the Medical College of Pennsylvania in Philadelphia, each person has a "set point" beyond which he can't neutralize stresses with rewards. When a negative event—say, divorce—pushes him beyond that point,

he feels upset. If his life has revolved around his wife for a decade, his skills at forming new relationships are rusty, or nonexistent. Feeling isolated and out of synch, he may become seriously depressed.

Along with negative thinking, poor social interactions and diminished capacity for pleasure, the depressed often have difficulty managing their time, says Peter Lewinsohn, a behavioral psychologist at the University of Oregon and the Oregon Research Institute. "Because they have trouble balancing the positive and negative—say, work and play—they often need to learn how to structure the kind of productive day that will decrease their depression," he says. "They need to learn to work for four hours, *then* fool around with the dog."

In a course of 15 weekly sessions of behavioral therapy ($60 to $90 each), the patient/student and his therapist/teacher attack depression with carefully planned lessons, demonstrations and homework assignments that increase social skills and maximize life's pleasures. Soon, changes in behavior lead to changes in thoughts and feelings—a process that eventually vanquishes depression in about 70% of patients, according to Dr. Becker. He recalls one depressed subject, a young woman who longed to marry:

"Her method of bringing about her goal was to fantasize about a particular man, then, one day, blurt out that she loved him. When the guy withdrew in shock, she decided that men always rejected her and she'd better give up. During therapy, she learned that relationships happen in stages—something she really hadn't understood before. Her first assignment was to

say hello and introduce herself to a man. The next week, she had to have a chat with him.

"Slowly, she learned that there are gradual stages to intimacy—that she needed to be friends with a man before marrying him. Before long, her social activity increased and she began dating. Her depressed mood disappeared. And the therapy also transferred over into other areas, so her relationships with her parents and co-workers became better as well."

Science is progressing in its search for the causes and cures of DD's unremitting sadness—happily, a state that most people can't even imagine. "A healthy person will say to a dysthymic, 'Pull yourself together! This trouble is all in your mind!' " says Klerman. "Remember that just as the healthy person can't grasp chronic blues, the dysthymic can't understand—or has forgotten—what it is to be spontaneous or joyful."

Now, several effective treatments mean that the good spirits of most victims of DD can be restored. "In the process of rethinking depression, we've begun to treat many more 'normal people,' " says Klerman. "In an earlier era, dysthymics would have said their suffering was God's will and resigned themselves to it. These days, they can say it's caused by catecholamines or stress!"

Opinions may differ about the causes and cures of DD, but on one point, all the experts agree. "People who come in for treatment do well," says Dr. Lewinsohn. "Our problem now is getting the majority of the depressed to take advantage of the help that's available."

Anxiety and Panic: Their Cause and Treatment

UNCOVERING THE BIOLOGICAL ROOTS OF THE TERRIFYING ANXIETY THAT STRIKES MILLIONS WITHOUT WARNING.

Scott M. Fishman and David V. Sheehan

Scott M. Fishman is a research associate with the endocrine unit at Massachusetts General Hospital. David V. Sheehan is professor of psychiatry and director of clinical research, University of South Florida School of Medicine.

Susan, a 25-year-old legal secretary, was about to leave her office one night when she was suddenly overwhelmed by anxiety she had never experienced before—an intense panicky sensation that something dreadful and frightening was going to happen to her. She became flushed and found breathing difficult, almost as though she were choking.

She struggled to maintain her composure, but within seconds she felt dizzy and lightheaded. Waves of fear coursed through Susan. The sound of her heart beating fast and strong and the sensation of blood rushing through her body at great pressure made her think that she might be dying. Her legs were rubbery, but she managed to make it outside for some fresh air. Gradually the

feeling subsided. Relieved but still shaky, she made her way home.

Susan had suffered a panic attack. For many people around the world—4 million to 10 million in the United States alone—such attacks strike with little warning and for no apparent reason. Most of the victims are women, usually in their childbearing years. What they experience is unlike ordinary anxiety, the nervousness most people experience before giving a speech or being interviewed for a job. As Susan described the terror of her attack, "It could not be worse if I were hanging by my fingertips from the wing of a plane in flight. The feeling of impending doom was just as real and frightening."

In the months that followed, the attacks grew more frequent. Occasionally there would be only a few symptoms. Other times the fierce anxiety would strike with multiple symptoms and terrifying force. Lightheadedness; dizziness; rubbery legs; difficulty breathing; a racing, palpitating heart; choking and tingling sensations; changes in mental perception—any or all might be involved.

As the attacks continued, Susan

feared that one might occur while she was driving her car, so she gave up driving. She began to avoid situations and places in which attacks occurred. Gradually the phobias grew so numerous that she could no longer work at her job and was terrified even to spend time with others. Finally, the paralyzing fear confined her to her home.

The array of symptoms that characterize panic disorder can be so confusing and numerous that accurate diagnosis is difficult. In Susan's case, she saw firsthand how the disorder can disguise itself as many other conditions. In several months, Susan saw a cardiologist, a neurologist, an ear, nose and throat specialist, a gastroenterologist and an endocrinologist, none of whom uncovered any physical disorder. Finally, she saw a psychiatrist who specialized in anxiety disorders, and she started on an effective treatment plan. After the attacks were blocked with an anti-panic drug, Susan worked with a psychologist to overcome the debilitating phobias that she had learned in reaction to the attacks.

The fact that certain drugs block or relieve panic attacks suggests that the

THE FACT THAT CERTAIN DRUGS BLOCK OR RELIEVE PANIC SUGGESTS THAT THE DISORDER HAS A BIOCHEMICAL BASIS. BUT AT THE MOMENT WE KNOW MORE ABOUT WHAT DRUGS WORK THAN WHY THEY WORK.

disorder has a biochemical basis. But at the moment we know more about what drugs work than why they work.

Before researchers could study panic disorder in an organized way, they needed a technique—what scientists call a research model—to cause panic attacks in the laboratory so that biochemical changes could be studied as they occurred. Without this, researchers and patients would have to wait together for a spontaneous attack, a method that is clearly impractical. A look back into research provided a better answer.

During the 1940s, several researchers had observed that strenuous exercise intensified the symptoms of people with chronic anxiety. These patients also had higher levels of lactic acid in their blood when they worked out than did normal individuals who did the same amount of exercise. The anxiety of the former group increased as the levels of lactic acid rose in their blood, while people in the normal group experienced no such anxiety.

Psychiatrist Ferris Pitts of the University of Southern California School of Medicine used these findings as the basis for research in which he injected chronic-anxiety patients with sodium lactate. The injections produced panic similar to their usual attacks, while normal people had no such responses to the lactate. When he gave lactate to anxiety sufferers in the form of an infusion (a constant flow of sodium lactate), he found he could stop their panic simply by turning off the flow. This discovery gave researchers the tool they needed for monitoring panic attacks and comparing the biochemical reactions of patients with those of others.

Whatever its cause, a panic attack ultimately must involve the brain. To explain this involvement, Daniel Carr, an endocrinologist at Massachusetts General Hospital, has developed a theory that integrates information from a number of studies in which panic attacks were provoked. He notes that inhaling modest amounts of carbon dioxide has the same effect as lactate infusion: It produces attacks in nearly all predisposed patients but rarely in normal men and women. This explains a phenomenon doctors in the armed forces have observed: People with chronic anxiety cannot tolerate wearing gas masks, apparently because the masks make them breathe in some of their own exhaled carbon dioxide.

Carr states that lactate and carbon dioxide act on sensors, called chemoceptors, that work like smoke

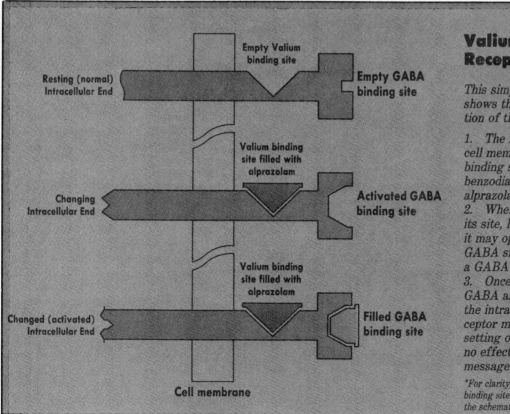

Resting (normal) Intracellular End

Empty Valium binding site

Empty GABA binding site

Changing Intracellular End

Valium binding site filled with alprazolam

Activated GABA binding site

Changed (activated) Intracellular End

Valium binding site filled with alprazolam

Filled GABA binding site

Cell membrane

Valium/GABA Receptor

This simplified schematic* shows three stages in activation of the receptor complex:

1. The receptor, lodged in a cell membrane, has unfilled binding sites for GABA and a benzodiazepine (Valium, alprazolam, etc.) molecule.
2. When alprazolam binds to its site, like a key into a lock, it may open (activate) the GABA site, allowing it to bind a GABA molecule.
3. Once both alprazolam and GABA are bound and active, the intracellular end of the receptor may change its shape, setting off a "chemical domino effect" that can transmit a message inside the cell.

*For clarity, ion channels and alternative binding sites have been eliminated from the schematic.

alarms to monitor the acidity in blood. In normal individuals, the alarm signals that serious changes have occurred, such as a buildup of carbon dioxide, which may indicate that oxygen is not reaching the body's organs. When this happens, panic may be a useful reaction, pushing people to take appropriate action before they suffocate. But in someone who suffers from panic disorder, Carr suspects that faulty or oversensitive chemoceptors create terror when there is no reason for it.

One test of Carr's theory is to see if drugs known to enhance the sensitivity of chemoceptors worsen panic symptoms. Caffeine and progesterone, both of which stimulate chemoceptors, have yet to be tested in panic patients. But since we know that progesterone is secreted during the luteal phase of the menstrual cycle, this may be one reason that more women than men have panic attacks and why some women suffer most from anxiety prior to menstruation. The same factors may help explain premenstrual syndrome, a condition characterized by many of the symptoms exhibited during panic attacks: anxiety, irritability, nausea, headache, lightheadedness.

IN SOMEONE WHO SUFFERS FROM PANIC DISORDER, FAULTY OR OVERSENSITIVE CHEMOCEPTORS MAY CREATE TERROR WHEN THERE IS NO REASON FOR IT.

Neuroscientist Eugene Redmond of Yale University studied the relationship between brain activity and anxiety attacks by implanting electrodes in the brains of stumptailed monkeys. When he electrically stimulated the locus ceruleus, a region that has a diminished blood-brain barrier, the monkeys behaved as if they were panicked, anxious or fearful. When Redmond damaged the area surgically, the monkeys were unresponsive to

PHOBIA THERAPY: LEARNING HOW TO

Everyone experiences anxiety at times—a troubled uneasiness of mind mixed with uncertainty and doubt. But when the feeling is persistent, with an intensity out of proportion to the object or situation that caused it, therapists call the condition phobia.

Phobias can develop in several ways. They can result from anxiety attacks, as people associate their feelings of panic with the places and situations in which they occur. They can grow out of specific experiences—a dog bite received in childhood, for example. Or they can be learned from others, such as by observing parents who fear lightning or bugs. In some cases the fear is displaced from its original source to a different place or situation.

The *Diagnostic and Statistical Manual of Mental Disorders* of the American Psychiatric Association divides phobias into three broad categories: simple phobias, social phobias and agoraphobia. Simple, monosymptomatic phobias are most commonly triggered by specific objects, animals or situations—irrational, consuming fear of heights, cats or enclosed spaces, for example. Social phobias are brought on by the presence of other people. They may prevent sufferers from speaking before an audience, eating in restaurants or writing their names when someone else is around.

Agoraphobia (fear of open spaces) is more complex and harder to treat. Psychologist Alan Goldstein of Temple University, who runs a phobia program in Bala Cynwyd, Pennsylvania, calls it "a fear of fear." Agoraphobia can completely incapacitate otherwise normal individuals, eventually making them afraid even to leave their houses.

Phobias are treated today with psychotherapy, behavioral therapy, cognitive therapy, drug therapy or a combination of these. In psychotherapy, the objective is to help patients understand the roots of their disorder. Today, most psychologists believe that psychotherapy is not very effective by itself in helping the phobic patient. Simple phobias and social phobias are most commonly treated today with behavior therapy—getting patients to learn new, more appropriate responses to whatever it is they fear. "The key to behavioral treatment is exposure to the stimulus," says Stephen Garber, a psychologist from Atlanta who specializes in treating phobia and anxiety. There are at least three behavioral techniques to accomplish this.

Systematic desensitization, developed in the 1950s, is still widely used. The therapist discusses the phobia with the patient and constructs a hierarchy of fears. For someone who fears driving, for example, the hierarchy might consist of opening the car door, sitting inside, placing the key in the ignition, turning the key and, finally, stepping on the accelerator pedal. As the therapy proceeds, patients imagine doing each of the feared actions and progress to the point where they can actually do them. The therapist teaches them how to relax during each step, using meditation, deep breathing or other techniques.

In "implosive" or "flooding" therapy, the therapist guides the patient through the entire feared situation all at once, either by imagining it ("implosive") or actually experiencing it ("flooding"). The idea is to have patients experience the fear for as long as possible, so that they emerge tired and mentally fatigued but no longer fearful.

A third behavioral approach, modeling, was spearheaded by psychologist Albert Bandura of Stanford University. He suggests that one possible cause of phobias is inappropriate responses that are learned in early life from parents, relatives and friends. A child who sees his mother recoil from a harmless snake, for example, may develop a persistent fear of all snakes in later life. Bandura adds that the media can often heighten various fears—of sharks, for in-

DEAL WITH FEAR AND THE FEAR OF FEAR

JOHN GOODMAN

*AGORAPHOBIA
CAN COMPLETELY
INCAPACITATE OTHERWISE
NORMAL INDIVIDUALS,
EVENTUALLY MAKING THEM
AFRAID EVEN TO LEAVE
THEIR HOUSES.*

stance. Modeling consists of watching someone else (usually the therapist) go through the feared situation and react appropriately. An ophidiophobe (one who fears snakes) might watch the therapist calmly handle a harmless snake.

Cognitive therapy, typified by Albert Ellis's Rational-Emotive Therapy, focuses on altering patients' self-perceptions, teaching them to deal with situations rather than avoid them. Patients learn to monitor their fearful thoughts during an attack and substitute more rational responses to the situation.

Whatever approach therapists use,

they must help their patients deal with immediate anxiety each time the feared situation arises. Until recently, minor tranquilizers such as Valium and Librium were often prescribed to make patients comfortable enough to continue therapy. Now, Goldstein says, "Most psychologists stay away from drug therapy for monosymptomatic phobias, because while there is some evidence that tranquilizers ease anxiety, they may block the recovery process as a whole." It is important for phobia sufferers to experience and control the fear, not to avoid it. Instead of prescribing drugs, psychologists teach their patients relaxation, deep breathing and, less often, self-hypnosis and biofeedback techniques to deal with anxiety.

Panic attacks create especially difficult problems. People who suffer such attacks suddenly become frightened, experience heart palpitations, chest pains, trembling, nausea, feelings of suffocation and a variety of other unpleasant sensations—all with no apparent cause. The fear remains even after the attack itself is over, and the victims start to feel panicky everywhere. When the fear becomes so pervasive that they feel safe only at home, the victims are suffering from agoraphobia.

"A person who had her first panic attack in a French restaurant might initially avoid the restaurant," Garber says, but the trail of illogic can spread like wildfire. "A series of attacks can lead to a more generalized fear. In a period of months, she might avoid all French restaurants, then avoid eating out at all, then avoid driving near a restaurant and finally avoid driving altogether."

Many of the same approaches used for treating the simpler phobias have been used for agoraphobia, with less success. The TERRAP program, developed by psychiatrist Arthur Hardy in Menlo Park, California, has treated thousands of agoraphobic patients since 1975 with a combination of behavioral, cognitive and experi-

ential techniques. At Temple University, Goldstein runs several treatment programs with a four-point attack. "We teach agoraphobic patients to relax, to use breath control and to stop their panicking thoughts and focus on the 'here and now' to help them deal with panic attacks," he says. "To deal with the avoidant behavior, we use behavioral therapy and exposure techniques to build coping skills. We help them to identify their feelings and get in touch with them. We determine whether there are unresolved grief issues and help them come to grips with them if there are." Finally, Goldstein examines the family environment for clues as to what at home might be reinforcing the disorder.

Some therapists argue that drug therapy is no more useful for agoraphobics than for those with simple phobias. But there are others who see drugs as useful for treating the panic aspect of the disorder. "We are coming to realize that some people respond well to the drugs while others do not," says psychiatrist Robert DuPont, founding president of the Phobia Society of America. "Still others respond to behavioral or cognitive treatment but don't respond to the drugs, and some respond to both."

DuPont calls phobias "the most treatable of psychiatric disorders." Some 70 or 80 percent of all patients with simple or social phobias can be cured. And with recent advances in understanding the biological bases of panic attacks, even agoraphobia and panic disorder soon may be reliably treated.

To receive a free fact sheet on phobia treatments and advice on how to find effective treatment in your area, send a stamped, self-addressed envelope to: The Phobia Society of America, Department PT, 5820 Hubbard Drive, Rockville, Maryland 20852. For $2.50, the center will send a list of more than 250 treatment centers around the country.

—Jeff Meer

threats and didn't show normal fear when approached by humans or dominant monkeys. Since the locus ceruleus is rich in cells that contain the neurotransmitter norepinephrine, Redmond concluded that panic, anxiety and fear may be controlled by changes in norepinephrine metabolism in this brain region. Finding an isolated area such as this—one vulnerable to the influence of substances in the blood due to its lack of a protective blood-brain barrier—gives us valuable information about the physiological roots of panic attacks.

Three distinct classes of drugs are known to relieve panic attacks: the monoamine oxidase (MAO) inhibitors and the tricyclics (both antidepressants) and a newly available drug, alprazolam (a benzodiazepine). Researchers also know that patients who suffer from panic attacks experience less fear if they receive these drugs before they receive lactate infusions. It seems that the drugs change the patients' metabolism, eliminating their abnormal sensitivity to lactate.

While the anti-panic drugs relieve anxiety symptoms, they can have undesirable side effects, including drowsiness or high blood pressure. To find other useful drugs that don't have these effects, researchers must understand precisely how and in what parts of the body the anti-panic drugs work. Since the MAO inhibitors and the tricyclics act on norepinephrine, it may be that norepinephrine affects anxiety by transmitting a nerve signal through the locus ceruleus. But we don't know how the antidepressant properties of these drugs relate to their anti-panic effects.

Alprazolam has fewer side effects than do the other anti-panic drugs and provides faster relief, but researchers are even less certain how it works, except that it seems to operate differently from the antidepressants. We know that alprazolam binds to the same receptor molecules in the brain that bind Valium, a benzodiazepine drug that has a chemical structure in common with alprazolam. (A drug or neurotransmitter "binds" to chemical receptors that are shaped to receive and use it rather than other chemicals.)

We know that when taken in therapeutic doses, both Valium, which is ineffective in treating panic attacks, and alprazolam change the shape of the re-

THE ANXIOUS BRAIN

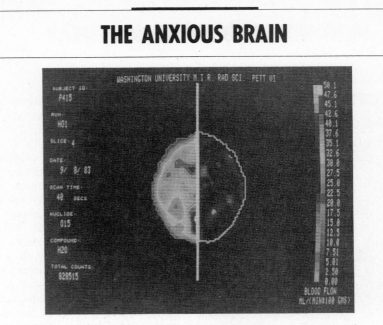

PET scan shows blood flow in the parahippocampal gyrus of a person susceptible to panic attacks. The lighter area at right indicates higher blood flow in that hemisphere.

A research team at the Washington University School of Medicine in St. Louis has discovered an interesting difference in blood flow in the brains of people who suffer panic attacks and of those who don't. They examined seven individuals who had such attacks in response to injections of lactate, three who were not lactate sensitive and six with no history of the disorder. Using positron emission tomography (PET scans), the researchers measured blood flow in seven areas of the brain that are thought to control panic and anxiety reactions. In one of these areas, the parahippocampal gyrus, the researchers observed a startling difference between the lactate-sensitive patients and the others.

In every lactate-sensitive patient, the blood flow on the right side of the gyrus was much higher than on the left side (see illustration). This difference was not seen in the other two groups. "There is usually a great degree of symmetry in the brain," explains neurologist Marcus Raichle, a member of the research team, "but this difference went well beyond the normal range of that symmetry. In every instance the pattern of blood flow was different than normal, and the flow on the right side was higher than the left."

Neither the high flow on the right side nor the low flow on the left was outside the normal range for those regions. It was the large difference between the two that was significant. To confirm their finding, the researchers gave PET scans to 20 additional volunteers, and they found this distinctive pattern in only one, a 34-year-old woman. Her psychiatric history showed symptoms of panic attacks, and when the researchers gave her a lactate injection, she had an attack. None of the other 19 volunteers reported any history of psychiatric illness.

It appears that this brain abnormality consistently distinguishes lactate-sensitive panic sufferers from other people. The researchers say it may reflect an exaggeration of the normal hemispheric specialization in part of the brain important to the expression of anxiety. "The difference in blood flow between hemispheres probably is connected with difference in metabolic rate," Raichle explains. "Any changes in blood flow reflect differences in the activity of nerve cells on the two sides."

—Joshua Fischman

THE DISCOVERY OF RECEPTORS IN THE BRAIN FOR VALIUM, A MANMADE SUBSTANCE, HAS STIMULATED A SEARCH FOR A NATURALLY OCCURRING HORMONE THAT REGULATES ANXIETY THROUGH THE SAME RECEPTORS.

ceptor molecule they share. Further changes may then occur at the receptor molecule for a neurotransmitter known as gamma-amino butyric acid (GABA). The GABA receptor is closely associated with the Valium receptor, as shown in the diagram on a previous page. Perhaps the chemical interaction between alprazolam and the Valium receptor changes the metabolism of GABA, which in turn produces a series of changes in the biochemistry of the cell and thus lessens anxiety.

The fact that there are receptors in the brain for Valium, a manmade substance, has stimulated a search for a naturally occurring hormone that regulates anxiety through the same receptors. The body might not have a receptor for Valium if it did not naturally produce a substance that binds with it.

The body's natural opiates were discovered through this same reasoning. Researchers found receptors for narcotics such as morphine and heroin before they knew that the body produces its own opiate hormones and neurotransmitter inhibitors (beta endorphin and the enkephalins) that bind to the same receptors. It may be that panic disorder is a deficiency disease much like diabetes. Diabetes occurs when the body does not produce enough insulin. Perhaps panic disorder results when a hormone or neurotransmitter that normally regulates anxiety is missing or deficient in some way.

Studies of panic disorder in families and among twins suggest that it has a genetic basis. Individuals who have relatives with panic anxiety are more likely to suffer similar attacks than are those with no family history of such attacks. Furthermore, identical twins, who have exactly the same genetic makeup, are more likely to both suffer from panic attacks than are fraternal twins, who share the same environment but only half the genes.

As in many scientific pursuits, new answers lead to new questions. Although we have much more to learn about panic disorder, its biological basis seems clear. As our understanding increases, we hope to develop accurate diagnostic tests to identify people who are susceptible to panic disorder, give them proper treatment earlier and prevent or lessen the development of the phobias and other problems that result from such attacks.

Psychological Treatments

A major problem long confronting psychology has been the definition of therapeutic interventions—psychotherapy. As new theories and models have emerged from research on a variety of fronts, new applications in therapy have followed. The result has been an increasingly complex, and increasingly confusing, array of helping efforts. In this section we will read several articles in which more than one method is applied. Perhaps what we really need is not new methods, or even comparisons among methods. Perhaps a new way of focusing on the therapeutic paradigm will reduce our focus or emphasis on methods, procedures, and underlying theories. In the meantime, the plethora of procedures continues to grow.

Most of the recent developments have involved attempts to ensure that psychotherapy provides the help it promises, and the first two articles in this section deal with that issue. The first article, by Daniel Goleman, focuses on the responsibility of the client, while the second, by Paul Quinnett, emphasizes both the essential features of successful therapeutic methods and the shared responsibility for making the therapeutic relationship work well.

In recent years, the most common diagnostic label used in outpatient settings is depression, yet the causes and cures of this condition remain undiscovered. In "The Good News About Depression," Laurence Cherry sug-

gests that depression is not a single disorder, but a family or class of disorders for which there must be an array of appropriate treatments.

When we think of psychotherapy, we generally envision adults as clients, or perhaps school-aged children. But as we become more alert to the development of emotional problems, we find the roots extending into very early infancy. It seems only natural, then, to read an article describing infant psychotherapy and the early signs and symptoms that prompt parents to bring their infants to the clinician.

Not all people who suffer from emotional distress receive or benefit from professional intervention. Rapidly growing in popularity and availability, self-help groups are the major (or only) source of support and encouragement many people get as they shed maladaptive habits and develop new strengths and skills. As Franklin points out, these groups deal with a wide range of problems, but share certain characteristics and strategies.

Throughout this section, we see the direct application of principles derived from psychological research to the understanding and treatment of disordered and inappropriate behavior. This is the ultimate goal of psychology: to improve the human condition. It is a goal well worth seeking, both personally and professionally.

Looking Ahead: Challenge Questions

One of the most serious challenges facing psychologists today is the need to demonstrate that psychotherapy is effective. How can both client and therapist assume or share responsibility for monitoring the progress of therapy?

How can we have more than one theory and more than one effective treatment for depression? Is depression not one disorder? If you were conducting research into the causes of depression, what type of study would you design next?

Is it fair to compare different treatments, when people who really need help are assigned at random to control conditions? Is it reasonable to believe that we will find a single best treatment for depression? According to current research knowledge, what treatment method works best?

How could a parent or other concerned adult know that an infant needed psychotherapy? What types of therapy work with infants? How could we tell if the therapy was working?

Under what conditions should a person seek support from a self-help group? Are such groups likely to produce as much benefit as working with a professional therapist?

When to Challenge The Therapist—and Why

Daniel Goleman

Daniel Goleman writes about psychology for
The New York Times.

How patients should evaluate their own treatment—and what they should do about it.

OR ANYONE UNDERGOING PSY-
chotherapy, the question is inevitable. Is it
working? When symptoms linger, or problems
that seemed gone reappear, or doubts arise
about the therapist, it's natural to wonder. Is it
time to switch therapists? Or is the treatment,
in fact, working to the extent it can? And is the
pain that persists essentially what everyone
must suffer from time to time?

Until recently, there have been no sure standards by which patients could assess the effectiveness of therapy. But new research has shed
light on what actually happens in the course of
treatment and has spelled out what progress patients can expect.

Moreover, psychotherapy researchers are
now encouraging patients who have doubts
about their treatment or their progress to take
up those doubts forthrightly with their therapists. According to the orthodox Freudian view,
patient complaints indicate a problem not with
the therapy, but with the patient, a result of
negative transference, in which childhood conflicts with parents are projected onto the therapist. But most experts now agree that such
doubts can signify real problems with the therapy and need to be carefully examined.

Research by Lester Luborsky, a clinical psychologist at the University of Pennsylvania and
author of "Who Will Benefit from Psychotherapy?" published this fall, provides more reason
to treat the matter with some urgency. He has
found that up to a tenth of all patients may actually be harmed by therapy — their problems get
worse or they end up frustrated or unhappy with
the course of treatment.

IN THE PAST, THE LACK OF OBJECTIVE guidelines made it difficult for patients to know what should happen at what point in therapy. While there can be no universal timetable, recent studies have shown that the most noticeable improvements tend to occur toward the beginning of treatment. As therapy continues, it takes longer for changes to occur, because the problems being dealt with are more deep-seated. The most profound changes, which affect longstanding personality characteristics, are the slowest.

These conclusions are based on studies involving 2,431 patients done by a research team led by Kenneth I. Howard, head of clinical psychology at Northwestern University. Howard found that for people in once-a-week therapy (the frequency of visits for 90 percent of patients), there is a striking pattern of improvement: a negatively accelerating curve.

Using statistical methods to describe the overall improvement of patients (rather than improvements in any one symptom), the researchers developed a way to predict their recovery: 10 percent of patients improve before the 1st session; 20 percent have improved after the 1st session; 30 percent after the 2d session; 40 percent after the 4th session; 50 percent after the 8th session; 60 percent after the 13th session; 70 percent after the 26th session; 80 percent after the 52d session, and 90 percent after the 104th session.

That final 90 percent figure is considered a "ceiling effect" beyond which little additional improvement can be expected. The reason: psychotherapy does not help everyone, and those who are going to improve will almost certainly have shown at least some progress within two years.

The study found that 10 percent of patients show improvement after making an appointment, even before seeing a therapist. This may simply be relief at having done something concrete about getting help. Or it may reflect a spontaneous remission, the clearing up of problems without outside help.

Another recent study, by Howard and Marc A. Zola, a psychologist at the Institute of Living in Hartford, examined which of 90 common patient complaints clear up, on average, at what point in treatment. Their findings, reported at a meeting of the Society for Psychotherapy Research, are based on checklists filled out by 351 patients, in which they noted their symptoms before starting treatment and at various stages in therapy.

The first eight sessions of therapy mark a "remoralization phase," in which acute symptoms of distress tend to dissipate rapidly and the patient regains at least a guarded sense of optimism. Many symptoms clear up in these first sessions, changing little more, if at all, throughout the rest of treatment. These problems include difficulty controlling impulses, such as the urge to smash things or getting into frequent arguments; trouble thinking straight, concentrating or making decisions, or feeling "blocked" in finishing things; being demoralized, feeling inferior or being lonely, even when with friends.

During this phase, the therapist "helps the patient settle down and establish a working relationship," says Howard. "The patient should get the message that he's not alone with his troubles, that there is some hope, that he's found someone to help."

In the next phase, which lasts roughly from the second month of treatment to the sixth, there is a "remobilization" of the patient's ability to handle life. At this point many symptoms of anxiety and depression tend to abate, such as lack of energy, hope or interest in life and feelings of fearfulness or nervousness.

The last phase, from six months onward, is largely "preventive," according to Howard. In this stage therapy focuses on habitual personality patterns that cause self-defeating reactions to life, such as feelings of worthlessness, mistrust and self-blame. Therapy during this phase is intended to help the patient find ways to prevent a recurrence of his or her symptoms.

"This is the phase in therapy where patients are trying to understand themselves better, not just looking for the relief of some troubling problems," says Howard. "The focus shifts to the recurrent patterns in a person's life — the failed relationships, for example."

ALTHOUGH THESE FINDings are not meant as a standard for measuring progress in any specific case, they may reassure some people who are impatient with the pace of therapy, and may raise doubts in others. Doubts — about the therapist or the therapy itself — can arise at any time in the course of treatment. Even though such feelings are common, patients are often reluctant to discuss them for fear of sabotaging the experience, especially in short-term therapy, which can be fewer than 12 sessions. "There's a wish to keep things happy, because if it got too negative, therapy might end before the negativity is resolved," Lester Luborsky says of shorter therapy.

"Patient misgivings represent one of the most thorny problems for patient and therapist alike," says Dr. Robert S. Wallerstein, a psychiatrist at the University of California, San Francisco School of Medicine and president of the International Psychoanalytical Association. "Sometimes it means that these two people just don't work well together," he says.

If doubts occur at the first meeting of patient and therapist, experts say that it's wise to shop

The key to productive therapy is the formation of a good working alliance. Candor and respect between patient and therapist increases the likelihood that treatment will be successful.

around, and advise consulting two or three therapists before settling on one. Howard has found that a patient's first impression of a therapist is usually accurate. If at the first session the patient feels that the therapist is apprehensive, unsure of himself or inattentive, it is a good indication that the treatment won't be productive. "If the therapist strikes you from the start as not connected to you, it's a warning you'll have to spend lots of time and energy forming a good working relationship, as opposed to finding a therapist where you click," Howard says.

That is not to say that for therapy to work patient and therapist must immediately feel perfectly attuned to each other. Sometimes when a first session seems "virtually perfect," Kenneth Howard notes, the following sessions are a letdown by comparison.

In a study by Howard in which patients evaluated their therapy after each session, in those cases where a therapist struck a patient as "off" from the beginning and where that perception stuck, the results of the treatment were generally poor. When patient and therapist became more attuned to each other as time went on, the outcome tended to be positive, even if the patient's first impression was not favorable.

The key to productive therapy, according to Lester Luborsky, is the formation of a good working alliance. If the patient feels understood by the therapist, has confidence that the therapist can help and feels that they have similar ideas about how treatment should proceed, the relationship has a good chance of yielding positive results.

Even in successful therapy, however, patients sometimes have misgivings. In such cases, Dr.

Wallerstein says, "the feelings may be a symptom of precisely what the patient is in therapy to resolve." These feelings frequently emerge after six months or so, once the problem that brought the patient to treatment has receded. In the foreground at this time are issues between patient and therapist that represent patterns of conflict that sometimes go back to the patient's childhood.

"The issues are the same ones that have to be negotiated in any intimate relationship: hostility, trust, dependency and sexuality," says Howard. "When they emerge, they are expressed as a conflict with the therapist. Whether therapy ends at this point depends on the willingness of client and therapist to confront what's going on. Some patients suddenly see their therapist as a malevolent force trying to keep them dependent, or as being angry or disappointed with them."

Candor between patient and therapist increases the likelihood that treatment will be successful. It's crucial that the patient discuss negative feelings with the therapist, and work toward a resolution. If that doesn't happen, the therapy can founder. Dr. Wallerstein says that "many abrupt endings the therapist can't account for are due to the patient having deep misgivings he could not bring himself to mention."

What happens after doubts are raised is a telling sign of whether the working relationship is a sound one. While some therapists welcome a patient's expression of doubts, others feel threatened, which is likely to inhibit future communication. "If a therapist gets defensive about a patient's misgivings, that puts a sharp limit on the treatment," says Dr. Wallerstein. "You want to be free to say whatever is on your mind to your therapist."

If things don't improve once doubts are aired, it's probably better for the patient to find another therapist. Researchers at Payne Whitney Clinic in New York found that dissatisfied patients made more progress when they switched therapists rather than staying with one with whom they felt unhappy. "Too many patients feel that if they don't do well, they're failures as patients, rather than

seeing that the particular match just did not work out," says Luborsky. Few patients realize that they are free to consult with another therapist if they have serious doubts about their treatment.

Most consulting therapists insist that the patient first discuss his doubts with the current therapist. Then the consulting therapist will meet separately with the patient and the therapist, and recommend either that therapy continue or that it be stopped.

When to terminate therapy can be a point of disagreement between patient and therapist. Early in treatment most patients feel better before they seem better to their therapists, according to Howard's research. He found that, in general, patients rated themselves as more improved than their therapists did. It was not until after six months of treatment that patients' and therapists' ratings of progress dove-tailed more often than not.

How, then, can a patient know when therapy is completed? Luborsky advises that if the patient feels that the problems that brought him to treatment are under control, and if he believes that the gains can be maintained without the therapist, then it's time to discuss terminating the treatment. The patient should review his original goals with the therapist and decide if they have been met.

Often, however, the prospect of ending therapy raises insecurities about being on one's own. Therapists say that it is quite common for symptoms to recur as a patient faces the end of treatment. If they do, the patient and therapist should discuss why the problems have reappeared, and usually they will wane.

Therapy is as much an art as a science. Unlike surgery, where success is clearly defined, the results of psychotherapy are highly subjective. Although studies have yielded general guidelines with which to gauge the progress of treatment, therapy is still an individual experience with periods of both rapid and barely discernible change, and with times of confidence in the process and of doubts.

"Patients need to be reminded over and over that when therapy is working, there will be times they don't feel it is helping them at all," says Luborsky. "It is those times that can be very fruitful, if you talk them over with your therapist. What may seem like the low point in therapy may actually turn out to be the most productive."

The Key to Successful Therapy

PAUL G. QUINNETT

Paul G. Quinnett, Ph.D., is director of adult services at the Spokane Community Mental Health Center and has a private practice. He is the author of two books, The Troubled People Book *and* Suicide: The Forever Decision, *both published by Continuum.*

nxiety, depression, headaches, panic attacks, anger, loneliness — these and other signs of distress are what prompt most people to seek out therapy. And while they're usually unsure about what's causing the problem, they hope the therapist will relieve it directly — or at least help them find relief for themselves.

This pain is the first thing I see when someone comes into my office, and it becomes the first order of business: Relieve the person's distress as quickly as possible. But although symptoms usually bring people to therapy, simply relieving distress won't produce lasting benefits. This requires goal-setting, a task I consider the heart of successful therapy. This usually happens in two stages: early, short-term objectives followed by later, long-term goals.

To get the most out of therapy, it's important to understand how the process operates. Therapists generally start with what we call our working hypothesis — a best-guess answer to the age-old therapy question: Why now? What, we ask ourselves, tipped the scales? What happened that brought this man or woman to this particular office at this particular time?

We try to come up with some sort of answer by the end of the first interview. Doing so helps us make a better diagnosis of what's wrong, which in turn often suggests a specific treatment. Moreover, as we accumulate more and more research, better diagnoses should lead to more effective therapies. The answer to "why now" also makes it more apparent exactly what the client needs and expects from us.

If the answer is simple, the goals we set later can usually be simple. If the client says, "I want you to teach me to be strong enough to ask my boss for a raise," the therapist can say yes he can or no he can't. "I want to lose 30 pounds" or "I'm afraid of heights and I'd like to fly to Chicago to see my mother" are equally clear.

It is the rare client, however, who comes to a first appointment with such specific, measurable goals. Most are much less sure what it is they hope therapy will accomplish, beyond giving them some immediate relief. But unless goals are set as soon as possible, clients may waste time and money looking for help that doesn't exist, and therapists may waste the clients' time working on problems the clients don't consider problems.

Stage One: Setting Early Goals

Here's how to start deciding what you want your therapy to accomplish:

1. As best you can, jot down what you think is causing you distress. This list of events, relationships or stresses can be long or short, but simply writing them down can help you understand better what has been going on, and going wrong.

Bringing this information to your first session will help the therapist understand you better from the start, and the process of preparing it may help you collect your thoughts for the first appointment. Your insight reveals a lot about how you think and how you understand the way life works. Left to their own devices and theories, therapists may come up with all sorts of reasons their clients are suffering. They can be dead wrong and start therapy off on the wrong track, heading in the wrong direction.

2. After the first visit, consider carefully how comfortable you felt. Will you and the therapist be able to work together week after week? Since a good relationship is so important in successful therapy, you should feel a satisfying level of trust and understanding early on.

If you didn't like her, or felt he talked down to you, or found yourself drawing away and losing hope, look for another therapist. Research suggests that patient-therapist compatibility is the best predictor of how well therapy will go. It's important, however, not to give up on therapy itself just because you don't click with the first person you see.

3. As you work with your chosen therapist in setting early goals, try to make them measurable in some way. This isn't always easy, but when the changes you want can be measured, it's a lot easier to tell, down the road, how well the therapy is working.

For example, if you and your mother have a disastrous relationship, one goal might be to carry on a telephone conversation with her without losing your temper. After you've done this three or four times, you'll know you've made progress.

Sleeping through the night without nightmares, raising your grade-point average, gaining or losing weight, giving a speech without your knees knocking together — all are measurable goals that will let you know how the therapy is going. Goals that are broad, vague or built on psychobabble ("I want to get my head together," or "I want to be a fully realized human being") are neither helpful to you or your therapist nor are they easily achievable.

It's best to help set your own goals. But if you like leaving difficult questions to the experts or find this goal-setting business confusing, don't worry about it. A big part of any therapist's job is to help you clarify exactly what it is you want to change and to help you agree on what the two of you will do together to achieve it.

Long-Term Goals: The Important Next Step

While agreeing on early, measurable goals is vital, I often spend much of my time helping a client clarify longer-term goals for change that are really goals for life: success, rewarding relationships, creative expression, a sense of competence and confidence in handling conflict — the ability, in Freud's words, "to love and work."

Because determining what you'd like to do with the rest of your life involves your personality, beliefs, values, dreams, ambitions and imagination, there is no easy way to go about it. But successful therapy demands precisely this sort of self-exploration: looking into your future after carefully examining your past and, in the process, preparing you to set a fresh course for the life you want.

One recent client — I'll call her Sandra — is a good example of how the process works. She had come through her divorce successfully, moved to a new apartment and was thinking of changing her job. After 20-some sessions, we were sorting out the kind of future she wanted. It was the first time in her life, Sandra told me, that she felt truly responsible for her own future. The experience was both heady and frightening.

"Ted always made the big decisions," she explained. "I guess I just came to rely on him. In a way, I can feel myself wanting you to tell me what to do next."

But Sandra had learned the therapist's Prime Directive: We help people grow; we don't tell them where and how. She had also learned that excessive dependency could be destructive. As we entered the final stages of therapy, Sandra was doing the hard work, setting goals for herself, her future.

"It's scary," she admitted, "this taking charge of my life. But then again, it feels pretty good."

Three Issues to Settle Before You Choose a Therapist

✳ **Do you agree on methods?** Even after you and your therapist see eye-to-eye on the goals of therapy, you may not agree on just how to achieve them. Therapists use particular methods because they believe in them. But it's your mind and your body. If you believe, based on what you've heard, that hypnosis will work better than biofeedback for your tension headaches, then you'd best start with someone who practices hypnosis.

✳ **Does your therapist believe in partnership?** Most therapists now feel clients have every right to be closely involved in all phases of their therapy, from the setting of goals to agreeing on the type and length of therapy. If the first therapist objects to such a shared approach, consider taking your business elsewhere.

✳ **Are you looking for an evaluation or therapy?** If you want a professional opinion in a dispute over child custody, say, or would like to know whether Uncle Harry is competent to manage his millions, what you are asking for is an evaluation. If your aim is treatment for a personal problem, or for someone else's problem, it's therapy you're after.

An evaluation generally implies that the therapist's findings or opinions will be used later for some purpose other than therapy. Beware of a therapist who is willing to give his professional opinion but isn't really competent in that area.

To avoid such problems, try to talk to a therapist by phone before you set up a formal interview. That way, you both understand just what you are meeting about, what you want done and whether this person is the one to do it.   —P.G.Q.

The Good News About Depression

Laurence Cherry

There are so many resources available (including light therapy, new antidepressants, and short-term counseling) that, a noted psychiatrist promises, "80 percent of the depressed can be significantly helped."

THE ELEGANT YOUNG WOMAN, TOO depressed to deal with the demands of her fast-paced job, has not been to work in three days; the deep-voiced man in his fifties, still troubled by a recent divorce, has not had the energy to open his mail in weeks. "I just watch it piling up, bills and all," he says indifferently. "I suppose I'll mind when Con Ed shuts off my electricity, but right now I don't give a damn."

An evening storm splatters the city but draws no comment from the people in the cozy auditorium on East 62nd Street. At this weekly meeting of Depressives Anonymous, one of several groups formed in recent years to help people cope with the blues, conversation centers on more pressing problems: how to make it through the night, how to summon the energy to arrive at work the next morning.

Depression has been with us for centuries, of course. Its celebrated victims have included the Bible's King Saul, England's first Queen Elizabeth, Abraham Lincoln, and, more recently, Ernest Hemingway, the poets Anne Sexton and Robert Lowell, and First Lady Betty Ford. Depression was the "black dog" that shadowed much of Winston Churchill's adult life.

What's more, the number of sufferers is growing. This past year, scientists at the National Institute of Mental Health reported that the incidence of depression of all kinds has "shockingly" increased. "This is particularly true among people born since 1940," says Dr. Elliot S. Gershon of the Clinical Neurogenetics Branch of NIMH. "More people are becoming depressed, and at much younger ages." The ailment is so prevalent, in fact, that some NIMH scientists privately speculate that an unknown "Agent Blue" may be spurring its spread.

Today, some 14 million Americans suffer from prolonged depression; one in four women and one in ten men can expect to suffer a serious bout at some point in their lives. The average age at the onset of the disease has dropped from about 40 a generation ago to the mid-twenties today, and some experts now estimate that depression affects 10 percent of those under 12. Between 1980 and 1984, adolescent admissions to private psychiatric hospitals increased more than 350 percent, with depression often cited as one of the main reasons for the rise.

But there's some cheering news. New antidepressants, as well as older drugs being used in novel ways, are producing dramatic relief. Research into light therapy and sleep cycles is showing great promise. And new psychiatric services at medical centers—as well as local support groups—have proliferated, helping the depressed deal better with their condition. "Well over 80 percent of people can be significantly helped," says Dr. David J. Kupfer, chief of the Department of Psychiatry at the University of Pittsburgh School of Medicine at the Western Psychiatric Institute and Clinic, who was chairman of a special 1984 consensus conference on mood disorders sponsored by the National Institutes of Health. "We've accomplished a lot."

To publicize psychiatry's increasing ability to relieve depression, NIMH is organizing a national Depression Awareness, Recognition and Treatment campaign (D/ART), which it hopes will be under way by the fall. Brochures for the public and special seminars for general practitioners and mental-health professionals—"often abysmally ignorant about effective treatment," says one top NIMH official—will emphasize that today, depression *can* be controlled. Astonishingly, "fewer than 20 percent of seriously depressed people in this country are being properly treated," says Dr. Robert M. A. Hirschfeld, chief of the Affective and Anxiety Disorders Research Branch at NIMH and the D/ART campaign's clinical director. "But there's no reason why. No depressed person nowadays should have to listen to someone—a relative or a professional—say, 'Come on now, just pull yourself together.' We've gone way past that in what we know and what we can offer, and we have to get the word about that out."

TREATING CHRONIC MILD DEPRESSION

DEPRESSION COMES IN MANY GUISES. According to psychiatry's bible, the *Diagnostic and Statistical Manual of Mental Disorders III,* issued in 1980 and currently being revised, there are at least a half-dozen subtypes, from major *unipolar* depression—depression that usually lingers for months before lifting—to the seesaw ups and downs of manic-depressive (*bipolar*) illness. "We've acquired a welter of labels," concedes Dr. Frederic Quitkin, head of the Depression Evaluation Service at the New York State Psychiatric Institute. "Probably the most important thing to remember is that depression occurs on a *spectrum,* from the ordinary down moods that everyone experiences to the major, crippling kinds of depression that may require hospitalization."

Scientific attention once focused almost exclusively on one end of the spectrum—depression that is almost totally incapacitating. But now scientists are finally paying attention to a long-ignored, less flamboyant form of the illness—chronic mild depression. Some 3 to 6 percent of people in the U.S. experience this kind of depression, according to NIMH's current Epidemiology Catchment Area Study, which involved 20,000 people in five cities (Baltimore, Los Angeles, St. Louis, New Haven, and Durham, North Carolina). These are not the people rushed to hospital emergency rooms with stomachs needing to be pumped, or slashed wrists. "Chronic mild depressives go to work and maintain relationships, but they never seem to get out from under the black cloud hanging over them," says Dr. James Kocsis, director of the Clinical Inpatient Research Unit at the Payne Whitney Clinic of New York Hospital—Cornell Medical Center. "Often they tell us they don't answer their phones because they're too down." This depressed mood almost never abates; instead, chronic mild depressives consider their gloominess to be the normal way of experiencing life and can't quite fathom why other people seem so energetic or buoyant.

In a certain subgroup of these mild depressives—"atypical" depressives—the bleak mood can sometimes briefly improve, doctors at the New York State Psychiatric Institute have noted. "A compliment, a success, an unexpected phone call from an acquaintance can cheer them up immensely," says Quitkin. "But their good mood doesn't last long. A few hours later, they're back in the dumps." These atypical victims reverse some of the symptoms of major depression: Instead of suffering from insomnia, for example, they oversleep (they may occasionally sleep as much as twelve to fifteen hours a day); rather than avoiding food, they overeat; and they feel

Chronic mild depressives believe that constant gloominess is normal; they can't fathom why others are so buoyant.

worst in the evening, rather than in the morning. "There's another marked trait—hypersensitivity to rejection," says Quitkin. "Trivial slights can devastate victims of atypical depression."

Only a few years ago, chronic mild depressives would not have been considered suitable candidates for antidepressants; their persistently low mood and social ineptitude would have been regarded as personality flaws that only long-term psychotherapy could, possibly, cure. But at the New York Psychiatric Institute, a recent twelve-week study of 120 atypical depressives revealed that over 75 percent responded to the antidepressant Nardil (phenelzine); a mere 24 percent improved on a placebo. "And within a few months, if you give these people standard psychological tests, including social-adjustment scales, you see striking changes," says Quitkin. "They're making friends, getting along better at work. That's amazing, since improving patients' social skills is one of the hardest things to achieve. But this happens so quickly—usually within six weeks—that we now believe these people have a flaw in their neurochemistry that kept their mood down and made them so clumsy around others."

Celia Burke (not her real name), 47, a former copy editor at a Manhattan publishing house, has worked on and off (mostly off) as an office temp for the past five years. For most of her life, she's lived with her mother. She'd already been in therapy for years, Celia told researchers at the New York State Psychiatric Institute last fall, but had not been helped. She was enrolled in a six-month study at PI and was informed she would be given Nardil or a placebo. For weeks, Celia felt nothing. "But then in the fifth week, I suddenly felt a *surge* of energy," she recalls. "I bounded up subway steps. And my life's turned around. I'm dating again for the first time in years, I'm going on job interviews, I'm full of goals."

Other kinds of antidepressants seem able to help victims of both chronic mild depression and major episodic depression—if doctors can only be motivated to write the prescription. (At Payne Whitney, researcher Kocsis found that despite the fact that three quarters of patients studied had been in psychotherapy, only 15 percent had ever received a trial course of antidepressants. Well over half responded "beautifully" when the Payne Whitney team prescribed them.) Unfortunately, the old split between the drugs-only or psychotherapy-only camps persists in depression treatment, although the gap is narrowing. "Part of the message we're trying to get out to practitioners around the country is that flexibility's the key," says psychologist Harold Goldstein, coordinator of training of NIMH's D/ART campaign. "If a month or two has gone by and talk therapy isn't helping your patient's depression, it may be time to try drugs, just as psychotherapy can often help people taking antidepressants recover even more quickly."

Indeed, the impressive ability of two new types of brief psychotherapy to help the depressed was underscored only a few weeks ago, when scientists announced the results of a long-awaited major NIMH-supported study. It turns out that both cognitive behavior therapy (which teaches patients to identify and change unrealistic, negative, or pessimistic views of the world and themselves) and IPT, interpersonal psychotherapy (which focuses on helping the depressed improve their dealings with others), ease depression as effectively as the standard antidepressant drug Tofranil. All three approaches dramatically improved the mood of depressed subjects within the startlingly short span of sixteen weeks.

Along with more rapidly effective forms of psychotherapy, psychiatrists can now offer the depressed an array of new drugs (pgs. 223-224) as well as better strategies for using some older ones. The new drugs have fewer side effects (such as the all-too-common blurry vision, constipation, or dizziness) than the older drugs. And some begin to work more quickly—often within days, rather than weeks—thereby shortening the "suicide watch" period, when doctors must anxiously watch very depressed patients to be sure they don't harm themselves. "Today, up to three quarters of the depressed can be helped with the right medication," says Dr. Leslie L. Powers, former director of Group Psychotherapy at St. Luke's-Roosevelt Hospital Center. "We can tell patients who may have tried and failed before, 'Look, there are new drugs, new combinations, that can help you now. We know a lot more about dosages that work, and which drugs may succeed when others have not. It's a different ball game.'"

IMPROVING MOOD WITH LIGHT

'IT'S THIS DREARY WINTER—THAT'S WHY I'm depressed," people have been complaining for years. And for years experts have dismissed the idea as an old wives' tale. But it seems dreary winters *can* cause prolonged depression—at least for victims of a newly discovered kind of depression called Seasonal Affective Disorder (SAD). No one yet knows how many people suffer from the syndrome. "My guess is that there are many thousands in the New York metropolitan area alone," says Dr. Michael Terman, research psychologist at the New York State Psychiatric Institute and head of its Light Therapy Program. These are the people who grow depressed as the long hours of summer light begin to give way to the shortened days of fall and winter. They become lethargic, sleepy, and begin to gorge themselves on carbohydrates. Their ability to concentrate, work, and enjoy sex begins to fade as well.

Dr. Norman Rosenthal, chief of outpatient services at the Clinical Psychobiology Branch at NIMH, was the man chiefly responsible for identifying the disorder in the late seventies. In 1980, basing his work on other research at the institute, he and his team came up with a tentative explanation of how the disorder might be triggered. Although biologists have long known that light affects animal behavior (as in determining reproductive cycles), only recently were they able to prove that the pineal gland, a tiny protuberance at the base of the brain, is not a vestigial organ (like the appendix) but the body's "Dracula" gland. Coming to life each night, it

secretes melatonin, a hormone that seems to play a key role in maintaining the biological clock that keeps our body rhythms running smoothly on their daily cycles. Taken orally, the hormone makes subjects drowsy, lethargic, drained. NIMH researchers proved that light suppresses melatonin production.

Based on hundreds of cases, says Rosenthal, the profile of a typical SAD victim has gradually emerged. She (female SAD victims far outnumber male victims) is a woman in her early thirties who has suffered from the syndrome, often without understanding what was wrong, for years.

Treatment for SAD is remarkably simple: exposure to a two-by-four-foot rectangular fixture studded with Vita-Lites—special fluorescent lights devised in the mid-seventies that include all the colors found in natural daylight, from far red to ultraviolet. Vita-Lites are manufactured by the Duro-Test Corporation of North Bergen, New Jersey; the fixture it designed produces 2,500 lux—slightly less than the light outside just when the sun is over the horizon on a clear day. (To compare: The standard fluorescent lighting in an office is 500 lux; the light outdoors at noon on a sunny June 21 is about 113,000 lux.)

Those who respond to treatment do so remarkably quickly—usually within four days, report Rosenthal and Terman. The turnaround can be dramatic. Last November, RoseAnne Tockstein, 42, of Franklin Lakes, New Jersey, happened to hear a friend mention the research on winter depression being conducted at the New York State Psychiatric Institute. Raised in Wisconsin, where winters are long and cloudy, she remembers her strange seasonal slumps. Her husband's career required the couple to relocate to New York. "It's a little better than Wisconsin, but come October, just about the time we go off daylight saving time, the same old depression begins," she says. "In spring, summer, I'm a go-getter—a hospice volunteer, industrial photographer, floral designer. But in winter, during those inevitable stretches of overcast weather, I'll just get up, stare out the window, and spend the rest of the day in bed. I don't function." Tockstein saw various doctors and described her symptoms; most were skeptical, and none could offer her any help.

After interviews and tests by the light-therapy staff at the New York State Psychiatric Institute, Tockstein began her first light treatment last December 6, sitting in front of a light fixture that resembles a large, glowing mirror. (The lights hurt her eyes, but now she does office work in front of them without any discomfort.)

At first, she was disappointed; she saw no change in her mood. But after three days of treatment, Tockstein's depression began to lift. The institute lent her a Vita-Lite unit, which she installed in her family room. She sat in front of it every day from 6 to 8 A.M. and 6 to 7 P.M.

The log Tockstein has kept shows her steady improvement. Last December 11, she wrote: "Today is gray, foggy, overall dreary, the kind that always put me into a depression.... But I don't have to head for bed." On December 29: "I woke up tired, but felt emotionally well. Wonderful day. I'm much better—near my old summer energy levels."

'In my fifth week on the antidepressant, I felt a *surge* of energy," one patient recalls. "I bounded up the steps. I'm dating again for the first time in years. My life's turned around."

Children, too, seem to suffer from SAD. "This is an area we're just beginning to explore," says Rosenthal. His team has treated four boys and two girls, ages six to fourteen, who began to complain of being tired and unhappy in school in the late fall; they slept later as the weeks passed, had difficulty waking up, cried, and complained of headaches; January and February were their worst months. When Rosenthal put the children on a light-therapy regimen, almost all of them rapidly improved: One, a champion swimmer whose times had always mysteriously dropped in the winter, broke his previous records; another, a thirteen-year-old boy, made the honor roll at school for his first winter ever.

Some depression researchers even suggest now that millions of adults who don't have a full-blown case of SAD may nevertheless be suffering from a wintertime loss of emotional equilibrium. "They still function, but without the ease or efficiency that they have in other seasons," says Michael Terman. (Those wishing to take part in light-therapy studies at the New York State Psychiatric Institute are welcome to call 212-960-5714.) Other investigators theorize that "for one reason or another, a large number of depressed people are light-starved *throughout* the year," says Dr. Jack D. Blaine, a psychiatrist at NIMH.

Not surprisingly, as news about SAD has spread, Duro-Test reports soaring sales of its light units, available for $477. But most experts caution against self-treatment. "People may wrongly diagnose themselves as being SAD sufferers when in fact they're suffering from another kind of depression," says Dr. Boghos Yerevanian, head of the Affective Disorders Program at the University of Rochester Medical Center, where light therapy for depression is also being studied. "No eye damage has yet been reported, for example, but obviously we can't yet predict long-term consequences; this is still too new." For SAD victims with manic-depressive illness as well, says Yerevanian, "the lights may push them into a manic episode; they may become agitated and grandiose. We've heard of cases where secretaries who used the units went out and bought $25,000 cars they couldn't possibly afford. Light therapy appears to be generally safe, but it isn't something you should trifle with."

RESETTING THE BIOLOGICAL CLOCK

LIGHT THERAPY FOR DEPRESSION HAS helped to illustrate the important role of the body's daily rhythms: Light treatments in the morning, for example, are generally more effective than those given at night. Moreover, victims of unipolar depression generally feel worse in the morning; manic-depressives are more gloomy as the day wears on; most atypical depressives are at their lowest in the evening.

Depression plays havoc with sleep. "The sleep cycles of depressed people are disordered in all kinds of ways," says Dr. Neil Kavey, head of the Sleep Disorders Center at Columbia-Presbyteri-an Medical Center. Most depressed people take a long time to fall asleep and wake hours earlier than others. In the non-depressed, the first REM period of the night—when dreaming usually occurs—generally begins 90 minutes after falling asleep, but in the severely depressed, it may begin a mere 20 minutes after falling asleep. Moreover, the REM activity of the severely depressed is abnormal, with unusually intense bursts of eye movement. The pattern of healthy sleep is altered: The depressed generally have the most REM activity during the first third of the night; the healthy usually experience the most REM periods during the last third of the night.

In many sleep labs, such as those at Columbia-Presbyterian and Montefiore Medical Center, doctors can now routinely use these striking differences to decide whether a person is clinically depressed or suffering from an illness—such as Alzheimer's disease—that can mimic true depression. "Testing to see if REM periods occur abnormally early in the night is usually a neat, easy way of confirming depression," says Kavey.

As useful is a sleep-monitoring technique that can predict whether a particular antidepressant will work. If it is successful, it will usually move REM patterns closer to normal within two nights. "This can save you precious time—weeks, in fact—by preventing you from keeping the patient on a medication that isn't going to help him," says one expert. "You can then turn to another antidepressant that *will* work."

It was not a very long step from using sleep patterns to diagnose depression and predict a drug's potency to actually modifying sleep to improve mood. At the Sleep-Wake Disorders Center at Montefiore, researchers are doing just that with patients whose body clocks have gone awry. The human organism seems naturally set to a 25-hour cycle; most of us use time cues from light and clocks to adapt to a 24-hour day. "But in some patients—mostly adolescents—the ordinary cues just aren't enough," says psychologist Paul Glovinsky, a Montefiore sleep expert. "The result is someone who can't function in sync with a normal day, and as a result may become progressively more depressed."

Christopher (not his real name), a sixteen-year-old student at a New England prep school, came to Montefiore last August, referred by a psychiatrist whom his parents in Westchester had consulted about his worsening depression. Once an honor student and star athlete, he fell asleep in class five times last year, annoying himself and angering his teachers. "He was on academic probation, had lost his enthusiasm for sports, and talked openly about suicide," says Glovinsky. His sleep habits had changed drastically during the past year. Where once he had gone to sleep at 11 P.M., he was now unable to fall asleep until 3 A.M.

Monitoring confirmed his disordered sleep patterns. "We put him on a 27-hour day for a week, in effect resetting his body clock," says Glovinsky. The first night of treatment, Christopher went to bed at 3 A.M. and was awakened at 10:30 in the morning; the following day he went to bed at 6 A.M. and was roused at 12:30 in the afternoon. Within a week, he had been moved

In fall and winter, many people become lethargic and lose their ability to concentrate, work, and enjoy sex. A new therapy—exposure to special lights—may improve their mood within three days.

back to a falling-asleep time of 11 P.M.—and was able to maintain it at that hour. His fatigue and depression soon vanished. Back at school, the eleventh-grader is doing well; his mother recently phoned the sleep center to thank the staff for performing "a miracle." The Montefiore team has treated almost two dozen other depressed young victims of this delayed-sleep-phase syndrome; although the specialists are still unsure exactly why their chronotherapy is so successful, many of their patients report improvement in mood.

The striking connection between sleep and depression has been demonstrated even more graphically by another discovery: Depriving depressed patients of sleep, even for one night, can often immediately buoy their spirits. The key seems to be not lack of sleep but elimination of REM periods. Unfortunately, the effect lasts only a few days—but frequently that's all that's required before an antidepressant can take effect. "We use this to tide some patients over until their drugs begin to act," says Glovinsky. "It usually works very well indeed."

> **D**epriving depressed patients of sleep, even for one night, can often immediately buoy their spirits.

SHOCK THERAPY: ENLIGHTENED USES

A MIDDLE-AGED WOMAN LIES IN AN anesthesia-induced sleep in a narrow, brightly painted room in the New York State Psychiatric Institute. Her scalp is wreathed with tiny electrodes that look like a tangle of hair curlers; the only sound is the low, persistent thump of monitors tracking her vital functions. As a psychiatrist applies electric current to her temples, her legs and arms jerk almost imperceptibly; five minutes later, wheeled into a makeshift recovery cubicle in an adjoining room, she is awake, still a bit groggy, eager to know about her breakfast. The entire procedure has taken no longer, and has been barely more dramatic, than a session in a dentist's chair.

ECT—electroconvulsive (electroshock) therapy, the oldest of the treatments in use for depression—has never quite lived down its spooky reputation as a psychiatric torture callously practiced on the poor and helpless, an indelible image left behind by popular movies like *One Flew Over the Cuckoo's Nest*. Groups of former mental patients in California and Vermont have recently tried to have the treatment banned altogether. "But ECT bears little similarity to the old caricature," says Dr. Arnold J. Friedhoff, professor of psychiatry at NYU School of Medicine and a member of a panel of experts who participated in a special NIMH conference on electroconvulsive therapy held last July. "The procedure's become both acceptable *and* respectable again in depression treatment." Between 10 and 20 percent of depressed patients do not respond to drugs or cannot be given them because of medical conditions (such as certain serious heart problems). Moreover, in cases where patients are

> **S**hock therapy has become both acceptable and respectable again in treating depression.

violently suicidal, ECT can often offer prompt relief.

Many experts admit that in the past, ECT was indeed wrongly administered to patients who could not benefit from it, such as those with vague anxiety disorders. Today, only about 60,000 to 100,000 people a year receive ECT treatments, about half the number getting them twenty years ago. Contrary to the stereotype, the typical ECT patient is well-to-do and receiving treatment for major depression in a university teaching hospital after drug therapy has failed. Public hospitals avoid giving ECT; it's too expensive.

Memory loss is one of the main complaints of patients who've undergone ECT, and the recent NIMH conference agreed that the loss is real, generally involving poor recall of events that occurred six months before and two months after treatment. Partly to lessen the impact on memory, low-dose ECT—about one third as strong as the standard dose—is becoming more popular. A five-hospital study in the New York area is evaluating its effectiveness.

But Dr. Harold Sackeim of the New York State Psychiatric Institute admits that even in its improved version, ECT is most often used only with the small percentage of the depressed for whom other treatments haven't worked, or probably won't. As researchers unravel the biochemical and other mysteries of depression, acquiring an ever-sharper skill in dealing with the complexities of this most common of mental ailments, the role of ECT is likely to shrink even more. "Only three decades ago, this was about all we could offer the depressed," Sackeim says. "It's a good measure of the astonishing progress we've made in recent years that it's now just one option out of several. And we're delighted that's so."

DEPRESSION CLINICS

O BVIOUSLY, NO PLACE SEEMS LIKE A very lucky place in which to be depressed. But New Yorkers *are* lucky in that this city offers a diversity of specialized services and support groups—many of them newly formed—to help the troubled. "Outpatient mood-disorder programs" have become so trendy, in fact, that it would make sense to check with your local hospital to see if it has already established one. Here's a sampling of the many programs for the depressed available in the metropolitan area. Unless otherwise noted, all are open Monday through Friday between 9 A.M. and 5 P.M.

The **Depression Evaluation Service, New York State Psychiatric Institute,** 722 West 168th Street (960-5734). Few in the field would deny that PI, with its host of ongoing depression studies, is the leading research and treatment center for depression in the metropolitan area. Its Depression Evaluation Service, an outpatient clinic, offers free diagnosis and treatment to all those accepted into its research projects. "Subjects really get about $3,000 worth of treatment free, and the only risk they face is possibly being exposed to a harmless placebo for six weeks," says director Frederic Quitkin. "If a patient doesn't respond to the drug we're investigating, he or she doesn't continue in the study, but we offer access to all other possible forms of treatment [at no cost]." Quitkin notes that PI is now studying and treating people with alcohol problems and a history of depression, anxiety, or panic. Along with the main facility at 168th Street, the institute maintains a satellite depression clinic at 79th Street and Third Avenue. A few sessions are scheduled until 8 P.M. on Mondays.

Child and Adolescent Depression and Suicidal Disorders Clinic, Columbia-Presbyterian Medical Center, 622 West 168th Street (305-3093). In 1984, Presbyterian Hospital established this adolescent clinic to deal with the growing numbers of depressed youngsters. A staff of child psychiatrists, psychologists, and nurse clinicians diagnoses and treats about 200 children and adolescents a year—some as young as six years old. "We evaluate them and then decide which treatment would be most effective," says the director, Dr. Paul Trautman. "Medication, family therapy, and group therapy are all options." Each session is $50; some patients may pay on a sliding scale.

Depression Clinic and **Post-Schizophrenia Depression Program, Mount Sinai Medical Center,** 1450 Madison Avenue, at 99th Street. These clinics treat about 50 patients a year and evaluate many more, says Dr. Samuel Siris, director of outpatient psychiatry at Mount Sinai. Therapy ranges from drugs to group therapy, individual counseling, or a combination of techniques. Associated with the clinic is a special program—reportedly unique in the country—for the treatment of depression in schizophrenics whose illness has stabilized, usually thanks to medication. "Although these patients aren't hearing voices anymore, they're often very, very down," says Siris. "Sometimes this is a result of the antipsychotic drugs they have to take, but in other cases it seems to be quite a separate problem. But no matter what the cause, we've had good success in treating their depression in many cases." Fees are based on the patient's ability to pay. For more information, call the Depression Clinic (650-7191) or the Post-Schizophrenia Depression Program (650-7192).

The **Adolescent Health Center at Mount Sinai Medical Center,** 19 East 101st Street (650-6016), deals with the gamut of adolescent medical problems. "But frequently you find that teenagers who come with headaches, stomach pain, or chronic fatigue are really suffering from depression," says Dr. Richard Wortman, a psychiatrist and director of the center's Mental Health Unit. After diagnosis, the hundreds of depressed adolescents who come to the center each month

> New York City offers a diversity of services and support groups to help the troubled.

YOUTH SUICIDE

PSYCHIATRIC DOGMA ONCE HELD THAT ONLY adults, never children or adolescents, could be "truly" depressed. "We've learned that was nonsense," says Charlotte Ross, director of the newly established Youth Suicide National Center in Washington, D.C. Within the past two decades, the suicide rate among children and adolescents has increased threefold; suicide is now the third leading cause of death for those between 15 and 24, with 5,000 such deaths verified in 1984 and an estimated 120 attempts for each death.

Very few studies on youth suicide have been conducted; all have presented only rudimentary findings. One study, begun in 1984 and headed by Dr. David Shaffer, director of child psychiatry at Columbia University, is examining all suicides under nineteen in the New York metropolitan area. Almost two thirds of the teens studied had seen a mental-health professional, but only one fifth had shown clear-cut signs of suffering major depression. Two thirds had a history of antisocial behavior or drug or alcohol abuse; 14 percent were homosexual, and often under severe social stress. "But the most striking characteristic we've seen in young suicides and suicide attempters is that they tend to be both impulsive and poor problem solvers," says Paul Trautman, head of the adolescent clinic at the Columbia-Presbyterian Medical Center. "Suicide isn't something they plan, it's just something they do—usually on the spur of the moment." One sixteen-year-old boy Trautman treated had a fight with a friend over a radio, went home, and swallowed 60 sleeping pills; his parents found him unconscious a few hours later when they returned home, and rushed him to the hospital, where his stomach was pumped. "This wasn't the result of premeditation, or even prolonged depres-

sion," says Trautman. "The boy was angry, happened to see the pills in his parents' bedroom, and thought, 'Why not?'"

Other experts don't feel that the Columbia study reflects the truth about adolescent suicide. "Yes, some attempters are impulsive, antisocial types," says Ross. "But that's only one subgroup. Just as often, these are cream-of-the-crop kids—class presidents, top honor students—who are simply very unhappy behind their façade of unruffled success."

Treatment for suicide attempters usually involves psychotherapy and family therapy. Most medical centers reserve ECT only for those over eighteen because of the memory losses it can cause; until recently, even giving antidepressants to adolescents was unusual. "But that's become much more common within the past five years," says Trautman; some pilot studies have even reported success at treating very depressed or suicidal children under age twelve with drugs.

Prevention obviously is the main goal in coping with teen suicide. But Ross doubts if conventional psychiatric treatment is an effective preventive measure, because "most kids hate therapy—there's too much stigma attached to it." One of the aims of the Youth Suicide National Center is to bring suicide prevention into the classroom, where until recently it was usually a taboo subject. "Suicidal kids don't turn to counselors, or their parents—over 90 percent look to their friends for help," she says. "We're promoting efforts in which people go into schools and teach kids the warning signs of depression and suicide that they can spot in their classmates." This has already worked in California, which has one of the most active state teen-suicide-prevention programs, says Ross. Governor Mario Cuomo's task force on teen suicide is studying a similar approach for dealing with the problem in New York.   —L.C.

typically undergo a one-month trial of psychotherapy before drug treatment (if any) is attempted. Self-referral by teenagers is welcomed; parents need not be informed, although the staff usually encourages family involvement. A few patients pay nothing, if their financial circumstances warrant that; others pay from $5 to $30 per session. The center is open Monday through Friday from 8:30 A.M. to 5:30 P.M.

Anxiety and Depression Clinic, New York Hospital–Cornell Medical Center, Westchester Division, 21 Bloomingdale Road, White Plains, New York (914-997-5967). Established only this past March, the clinic emphasizes a multidisciplinary approach to anxiety, phobia, and depression treatment, says its chief, Dr. Joseph Deltito. That includes drug therapy, psychotherapy, stress management, hypnosis, and behavior therapy. "We think our strength is that we don't favor one therapeutic approach over another," Deltito says. The clinic draws most of its patients (who must be eighteen or older) from the Bronx, and Westchester, Fairfield, and Rockland counties, but a few come from as far away as Brooklyn and New Jersey. Fees range from $5 to $100 per session, based on the patient's ability to pay.

At the **Mood Disorder Clinic at Hillside Hospital,** a division of Long Island Jewish Medical Center at 76th Avenue and 266th Street, Glen Oaks, Queens (718-470-8151), the depressed are offered both drug treatment and psychological support. Current research projects include the use of the new but not yet marketed antidepressant Wellbutrin; low-dose lithium for manic-depressives; Pramircetam, a new drug that *may* help reduce memory loss after ECT; and other drugs. Fees are based on the patient's ability to pay.

Affective Disorders Clinic, Montefiore Medical Center, 111 East 210th Street, the Bronx, New York (920-4596). Although all kinds of depression are treated at Montefiore, the main activity is investigating the biology of depressive illness and how patients respond to one tricyclic antidepressant, desipramine (Norpramin, Pertofrane). Those enrolled in the research project are treated with the drug or a placebo for six weeks; subjects who benefit from the drug are continued on it for six months, while others are referred for different kinds of treatment. Fees are levied on a sliding scale. "Self-referrals are very welcome," says the director, Dr. Gregory Asnis. The clinic is open Monday through Friday from 9 A.M. to 7 P.M.

The **Affective Disorders Clinic at Beth Israel Medical Center,** First Avenue near 15th Street (420-4135), opened last month. The clinic mostly treats depressed patients ranging from pre-teenagers to people in their late seventies. "We offer the full range of antidepressant drugs but especially emphasize short-term interpersonal psychotherapy, lasting no longer than ten to fifteen weeks," says psychologist Steven Klee, the program director. Each session costs $50, but there's a sliding-scale fee applied in some cases.

Depression Studies Program, New York University Medical Center, 560 First Avenue, at 32nd Street (340-5705). "Our emphasis here is on a sadly neglected problem—depression in the elderly," says staff psychiatrist Dr. Robert McCue, clinical instructor of psychiatry at the NYU School of Medicine. "Although geriatric depression is the most common psychiatric illness among the aged, we still know little about it." What *is* known is that older patients often take longer than younger patients to respond to antidepressants—sometimes several weeks longer. "The elderly are often misdiagnosed as hopeless, when in fact they would respond in time if their doctors were more patient," says McCue. "We've seen tragic mistakes. In our experience, most older people *do* eventually respond well to antidepressants." Those who improve are followed for up to three years. "We try not to give up on anyone," says McCue. Diagnosis and treatment are free to those 55 and older.

SUPPORT GROUPS

IN ADDITION TO THESE PROFESSIONAL services, a wide variety of nonprofit support groups for the depressed—and their relatives—have also sprung up in New York. Self-help is the theme, and in many cases these groups can indeed be helpful.

Depressives Anonymous. Founded in 1977 by psychiatrist and author Dr. Helen DeRosis (*The Book of Hope*), Depressives Anonymous meets most Wednesday evenings in the auditorium of the Karen Horney Clinic, 329 East 62nd Street. "This is a self-help group where the focus is strictly on the depression, the stress associated with it, and what concrete steps the person can take to get out of it," says DeRosis, a motherly-looking woman who occasionally serves as moderator. At a recent meeting, for example, a woman depressed about her unfinished graduate thesis agreed she could probably manage to write a page a day; an older woman distraught over the end of a romantic relationship agreed that she could get in touch with several acquaintances she hadn't seen in some time. "These small steps can help you out of your depression," urged DeRosis. For information, send a stamped envelope to Depressives Anonymous, 329 East 62nd Street, New York, New York 10021.

The **Manic and Depressive Support Group** (924-4979) was founded in 1981 by depressives, manic-depressives, and some of their family members. There are chapters in Manhattan, Long Island, and New Jersey; groups are also forming in the Bronx and Westchester. Separate lecture-meetings for depressives and manic-depressives are held once a month at Beth Israel Medical Center; the meetings, involving a talk and question-and-answer session, are open to patients and their families and friends. These are large gatherings; as many as 250 people turn out. At other monthly meetings, members form into small groups of a half-dozen or so and share advice, complaints, and encouragement about the difficulties—often medication-related—of understanding their ailment. Membership is $25 per year (individual) or $40 (family). Non-members pay $3 per session. For information, write the Manic and Depressive Support Group, 15 Charles Street, 11H, New York, New York 10014.

> **"F**requently," says the director of Mount Sinai's Mental Health Unit, "teenagers who come in with headaches, stomach pain, or chronic fatigue are really suffering from depression."

At **Recovery, Inc.,** participants are gently taught not to use the word "depressed"; the less dramatic term "lowered feelings" is preferred. "But obviously, depression is one of the problems we see most often," says spokeswoman Marion Zukoff. Recovery is an international nonprofit support network that subscribes to the tenets of Dr. Abraham A. Low, the late Chicago psychiatrist. In the 1930s and 1940s, Low was a pioneer in advocating and organizing self-help groups for those with nervous problems, including former mental patients. At the amiable Friday-evening Recovery meeting I attended at St. Vincent's Hospital, Dr. Low's writing and common-sense dictums served as the focus for a discussion of problems; afterward, most of the dozen participants adjourned to a coffee shop on Sixth Avenue for more informal group support. (Low believed that after-meeting socializing is often crucial for troubled people, who frequently isolate themselves.) Recovery meetings are held nightly somewhere in the metropolitan area—in churches, synagogues, Ys, mental-health clinics, and other public spaces. Contributions are requested. For more information, call 718-266-4715; in Westchester, 914-968-6021; in Nassau, 516-333-6500; in Suffolk, 516-289-3071.

New Images for Widows (972-2084) was formed in 1983 by author Lynn Caine (*Widow*) and social worker Pat Bertrand. Its aim is to help widows and widowers in the metropolitan area through the trying initial weeks of bereavement and then through the slow process of readjustment to the social world. "The standard rule of thumb among psychiatrists has been that widows experience depression in some form for at least a year following the death of a spouse," says Dr. Ronee I. Herrmann, medical adviser to the group. "In fact, in many cases the depression continues for three to five years." The subgroup Social Networks for the Widowed, which has 85 members ranging from women (and some men) in their twenties to those in their seventies, holds monthly meetings and regular outings. Membership is $15; meetings are $5.

Families of Depressives. "I started the group in 1983 because there was nowhere I could turn," Myrna explained to me over the phone. When her husband was being treated for depression, she found herself in a quandary familiar to relatives of the depressed: how to cope with the new situation and how to deal with a painful lack of understanding from relatives and friends. "I did my crying and said, 'Enough of that,'" she says. "I was sure that there must be others in the same boat." There were. She got in touch with the New York City Self-Help Clearinghouse and soon had formed a group. Now composed of about a dozen members—its numbers constantly fluctuate as relatives improve—it meets every other Wednesday evening at the Brotherhood Synagogue at 28 Gramercy Park South.

The depressed relative is deliberately *not* invited to attend; this is the time when spouses, parents, children, or siblings can air all their accumulated grievances and complaints. "You walk a thin line between love and resentment," one woman admitted in their free-ranging discussion. The resentment is directed at doctors who prescribe medications that may not work as quickly as hoped or cause troublesome side effects; at uncooperative friends and relatives; at the demands of the depressed person himself (most of the Families of Depressives participants are women). But the deep ties of affection were as obvious as the understandable irritation. "Thank God for Wednesday evenings; we laugh and cry and go back to our posts in a decent mood," said a woman whose aged mother has been intermittently depressed for the past two years. "This is what keeps *us* from going down the tubes ourselves." Information about doctors and new treatments is exchanged; in between the weekly meetings, many members participate in a telephone support network. Contributions ($2) for rental of the room are required. For more information, get in touch with the New York City Self-Help Clearinghouse, 186 Joralemon Street, Suite 1100, Brooklyn, New York 11201, or call 718-352-4290.

NEW, FAST-ACTING ANTIDEPRESSANTS

TRADITIONAL TRICYCLIC DRUGS (THE name derives from their three-ring chemical structure), such as Tofranil and Elavil, have been on the market since the early sixties. They continue to be prescribed, along with lithium, for manic-depressive illness. But doctors can now choose among several newer drugs as well as older ones being used in new ways. Here are several, most of which have come on the market in the last six years:

Asendin (amoxapine). Introduced in 1980, Asendin has a mild sedative effect along with its antidepressant properties; its mechanism of action is still not well understood.

Advantages: "Asendin's biggest asset is that it works quickly," says Dr. Arnold Friedhoff, professor of psychiatry at NYU's School of Medicine and director of its Millhauser Laboratories, who participated in researching the drug. "According to our studies, it was effective within four days—or earlier."

Drawbacks: It may be harmful to patients with cardiovascular problems. It causes drowsiness in 14 percent of those taking it, constipation in 12 percent, blurred vision in 7 percent.

Desyrel (trazodone). Introduced in 1982, it is unrelated to tricyclics or other antidepressants.

Advantages: Rarely causes the dry mouth, constipation, urinary retention, or cardiac problems common with older drugs.

Drawbacks: In some male patients, Desyrel has caused priapism—a disorder that involves prolonged erection of the penis; this sometimes requires surgery and has led to permanent impotence. Mead Johnson (the manufacturer of the drug), while stating that such cases are "extremely rare," strongly advises male patients with "prolonged or inappropriate erection" to immediately discontinue use and consult their physician.

> **P**articipants adjourn to a nearby coffee shop after the amiable Recovery meetings; socializing is crucial for troubled people, who often isolate themselves.

The depressed relative is *not* invited to attend meetings of the support group Families of Depressives; this is the time when spouses, parents, and children can air their grievances. "You walk a thin line between love and resentment," one woman admits.

Ludiomil (maprotiline). *Advantages:* Fewer cardiovascular side effects are reported with Ludiomil than with older antidepressants.

Drawbacks: The drug causes dry mouth in 22 percent of patients, drowsiness in 16 percent.

Tegretol (carbamazepine). *Advantages:* It has been used as an anti-convulsant drug for epileptics; researchers at NIMH have found that some 60 percent of manic-depressives who do not do well on lithium do, in fact, do well on Tegretol. Patients who have many seesaw mood swings during a year appear to do better on Tegretol.

Drawbacks: The drug may impair bone-marrow function and cause blood abnormalities.

Xanax (alprazolam). *Advantages:* Used primarily for victims of anxiety disorders—especially for those who suffer panic attacks—Xanax is now also being employed as an antidepressant, particularly for those who suffer from depression combined with agitation. It is especially helpful in mild to moderate depressions.

Drawbacks: Chemically related to Valium, Xanax poses similar problems of dependence with prolonged use.

Nardil (phenelzine). "Nardil is two decades young," says Dr. Frederic Quitkin of the Depression Evaluation Service of the New York State Psychiatric Institute. A member of the monoamine oxidase inhibitor (MAOI) family (which also includes Parnate and Marplan), it was largely discarded in the 1970s because of the strict diet that patients taking it must follow. Within the past two years, the drug has been increasingly prescribed.

Advantages: According to studies at PI, Nardil is the most effective drug yet tested for atypical depression.

Drawbacks: When combined with the substance tyramine, found in some food, beverages, and drugs, Nardil can cause blood pressure to soar. Patients must therefore follow a careful regimen. Prohibited items include processed meats, aged cheeses, pickled foods, beer, red wines, sherry, amphetamines, barbiturates, some cough medicines, and nasal decongestants. Research continues into MAOI drugs that will be as effective as Nardil without its potential dangers; one, deprenyl, is currently being tested in New Jersey and at the New York State Psychiatric Institute and, according to experts, may be marketed within the next two to three years.

Infants in Need of Psychotherapy? A Fledgling Field Is Growing Fast

DANIEL GOLEMAN

> 'Therapy for minor problems in infancy can prevent major problems later in life.'

Baby blocks are the latest accessories in some psychiatrists' offices, as a new idea is gaining popularity: psychotherapy for infants.

The fledgling field, virtually nonexistent a dozen years ago, is growing rapidly. No one knows how many children have been treated or need treatment because the Government does not keep statistics on it, but as many as 10,000 professionals are now offering such therapy. In addition to psychiatrists and psychologists, the practitioners include pediatricians, social workers and nurses.

For parents, this means that there is somewhere to turn for expert advice on the emotional ups and downs of babies, and to lay to rest fears, often ungrounded, that something is awry. And, if a baby is found to have an emotional problem, a psychotherapist stands ready to help.

'Window of Opportunity'

The field's fundamental assumption is, in essence, that an ounce of prevention is worth a pound of cure.

"Therapy for minor problems in infancy can prevent major problems later in life," said Dr. Robert Emde, a psychiatrist at the University of Colorado Medical School. "This is a prime window of opportunity." Dr. Emde is also president of the World Association for Infant Psychiatry, the main professional group in the field.

In extreme cases, when the parent is inadequate or absent, therapy involves a team of caretakers who substitute for the parents. For children who are less disturbed, therapy focuses on evaluating what is wrong in the relationship between the parent and child and then coaching the parent to better respond to the child's needs.

In part, the rise of infant psychiatry is traced to recent research into emotional development in infants. While the benchmarks of biological growth have long been known, those of emotional growth have only recently been charted, allowing clear guidelines for spotting troubled infants for the first time.

"We now know much more than ever before about the emotional, social and behavioral development of normal infants," said Dr. Justin D. Call, chief of Child and Adolescent Psychiatry at the University of California at Irvine, a founder of the field. "It makes the recognition of problems clearer much earlier in life than had been possible.

Putting Infancy on the Map

"It put infancy on the psychiatric map," he said. "We saw that we should be intervening before the age of 3." Infancy is reckoned to end at that age.

Dr. Eleanor Szanton, director of the National Center for Clinical Infant Programs in Washington, said 20 times more infants were being seen for emotional difficulties and related problems than were seen 10 years ago because professionals now knew what to look for. Most parents, though, do not yet know to ask for help, she said.

A separate trend has also contributed to the interest in infant psychotherapy. In the last two decades, Dr. Call noted, there has been a steady increase in the number of infants born to mothers who take drugs or mothers in their early teens. Rates of infant abuse and neglect have also gone up. All these factors are tied to the likelihood of serious emotional problems in infants.

For some parents, the mere list of troubles the field treats is likely to stir concern. Much of it is unwarranted, therapists say, noting that parents

have muddled through for ages without the help of infant psychiatry.

Still, various studies are showing there is a genuine need for infant psychiatry. Surveys of infants brought to pediatricians' offices in various cities have found that from 10 percent to 15 percent have a severe emotional problem, such as depression or an inability to respond to people, Dr. Call said.

Ten to 15 percent more have mild problems, like being withdrawn, that would benefit from short-term treatment, said Dr. Call.

Dr. Szanton said, "Perhaps the saddest problem of all in infants is failure to thrive, where a baby gains no weight, becomes indifferent to the world, and withers."

For practioners of infant psychotherapy, there are only a few formal training programs in departments of psychiatry or pediatrics. Some social work and nursing programs also offer courses.

The majority of those now working in the field have attended short-term training programs. The first of these postgraduate training institutes was held in 1978 with 400 participants; the most recent was held two years ago and attendance jumped to 1,200.

For a child needing psychotherapy, insurance policies that pay for psychiatric care will usually cover the costs of treating an infant. But therapists say the policies often require formal diagnosis of a specific psychological problem, which can alarm parents when expressed clinically.

The most serious psychological dis-

Benchmarks of emotional growth have only recently been charted.

Infant Behavior: When to Be Concerned

Many things that distress parents of babies are not signs of serious problems, but certain behaviors and traits may indicate an underlying problem and should be brought to the attention of a pediatrician.

	Usually Not Problems	Possibly Signs of Psychological Disturbance
BIRTH TO ONE MONTH		
	Preference for eating every two hours. Prickly heat rash. "Not satisfied" with feeding. Wanting to be held "all the time." Grunting and red face with bowel movements. Sucking finger or thumb.	Failure to gain weight. Excessive spitting up. Absence of eye contact. Failure to hold head up. Failure to show anticipatory behavior at feeding. Failure to hold on with hands. Ticlike movements of face and head.
2 TO 3 MONTHS		
	Irritable crying. Colic. Constipation. Not sleeping through the night.	Failure to thrive. Indifference to human face, voice and play overtures. Persistent hyperactivity. Persistent sleep disturbance. Vomiting and diarrhea without physical illness. Hyperresponsiveness or hyporesponsiveness.
4 TO 6 MONTHS		
	Demands for attention. Preference for being propped up. "Spoiled." Teething or biting problems.	Wheezing without infection. Failure to enjoy upright position. Indifference toward feeding. Excessive rocking, except at night or when alone. Rumination (swallowing regurgitated food).
7 TO 9 MONTHS		
	Dropping things. Messy feeding. Disrupted sleep associated with teething, move to new home or illness. "Temper."	Unpatterned sleeping and eating. Eating problems like refusing to use hands or to hold glass or a very limited diet. Failure to imitate simple sounds and gestures. Lack of distress with strangers. Failure to show and respond to recognizable signals, like joy, surprise or fear. Self-destructive behavior. Withholding of bowel movements. Apathy
10 TO 16 MONTHS		
	Getting into things; climbing. Declining appetite. Problems with self-feeding and being fed. Screaming. Mild tantrums. Attachment to "security blanket."	Absence of words. Withdrawn behavior. Excessive rocking and posturing. Absence of distress at separation. Night wandering. Excessive distractibility.

Source: adapted from J. D. Call in "Practice of Pediatrics." Harper & Row

The New York Times/March 23, 1989; illustrations by Giora Carmi

turbances in infants are usually attributed to parental abuse or neglect of a baby's basic needs, like warmth or regular meals. Doctors say neglect, including of an infant's emotional needs, can slow intellectual growth.

Variety of Symptoms

Doctors who treat infants with severe problems say they display a variety of symptoms, including continuous inconsolable crying and frantic shaking, a tendency to shrink from touch, extreme sadness, lethargy, and indiscriminate rage.

Much of the work in infant psychiatry is with milder problems. Among the more common varieties are "attachment disorders," in which infants have difficulty forming a trusting bond with parents. The child, for instance, may shrink from parents or not respond. While the attachment problems can sometimes be severe, they are often mild, reflecting minor idiosyncracies in how parents treat an infant.

One such baby was treated by Dr. Stanley Greenspan, a professor of child health and development at George Washington University medical center.

"He was just 9 months," Dr. Greenspan said. "He was highly irritable and would cry for an hour at the slightest irritant. Whenever his mother would leave the room, he'd throw a tantrum. But while she was with him, he's just lie there passively."

In evaluating the infant, Dr. Greenspan discovered he was hypersensitive to touch, so that a normally enjoyable cuddle would irritate him. His mother had responded to his extreme irritability by becoming overprotective. If he began to reach for something, she would get it for him before he could complete the motion.

"She was making him passive by hovering and anticipating his every move," Dr. Greenspan said. In a few sessions, Dr. Greenspan got her to delay her impulse to intervene. At the same time, he encouraged the parents to handle their baby more gingerly, so as not to irritate his skin.

"A new focus of therapy in infant psychiatry is on treating disturbances in relations between parents and infant," Dr. Call said.

Typical of these problems are lonely parents who become excessively dependent on their infants, and who keep the infant from developing the normal independence of a 2-year-old. Another common pattern is seen when parents discipline an infant with stiff corporal punishment.

"Corporal punishment, especially when the child is too young to understand it, can lead the child to become defiant, even start provoking punishment, and, finally, estranged from his parents," Dr. Call said.

Then there are the problems that worry parents, but are only part of the normal travails of infancy.

"There are a fair number of kids who by temperament are hypersensitive to stimulation, irritable and sleep poorly," said Dr. Emde. "It's one of the most common complaints from parents. When we evaluate the child, we let the parents know it's common and doesn't go on forever."

He added: "There are some practical steps parents can take, such as keeping things quiet and calm around the infant. But when parents are far more anxious than they need to be, it just makes matters worse."

Help yourself: self-care for emotional problems

NESHAMA FRANKLIN

I had no choice," Kirsten Nielsen says. "I just had to gut it out." That's how this 42-year-old mother of two sons describes her successful two-year effort to manage her manic-depression without lithium. Nielsen, of Santa Cruz, California, elimi-

> **Support groups are comforting, non-judgmental, and inexpensive.**

What's wrong with therapy?

It is estimated that almost one-third of the population receives professional therapy sometime in their lives. At an average cost of about $65 an hour, psychotherapy is a big business. Although there is no doubt that it is beneficial to many, there is a great deal wrong with it—both the way it is presented to the public and the way it is practiced.

The abuses can be grouped into four categories: misleading promises about its scope and effects; use of one kind of therapy when another is more effective; use of psychotherapy when alternative treatments are superior in results or cost; and too-lengthy terms of treatment.

Promises, promises

Psychotherapy is promoted as useful for all the traditional psychological problems, as well as new problems discovered almost daily: midlife crisis, computer phobia, and conversion to unpopular religious beliefs. Of 500 people who came to one large New York psychiatric clinic for evaluation, therapy was recommended for all but four. Imagine the outcry if surgery were recommended for 99 percent of patients coming to a medical clinic. Whenever a method is universally prescribed, one of two things must be true: The Millennium has arrived or something is seriously wrong.

Another promise of therapy is overwhelming change of personality. Fringe therapies such as primal scream and est are not alone in claiming dramatic change. Psychoanalysis, the oldest and in many people's eyes the most respectable therapy, produces, in the words of Anna Freud, "thoroughgoing personality changes," and some therapists talk about reorganizing or remaking personalities. But as New York psychologist Albert Ellis notes, ther-

apists talk and write about their most spectacular successes; "the poor, partial, or later-relapsing 'successful' cases are much less often published." Only a small percentage of clients are changed to a degree that justifies using terms like "recovery" or "cure."

Which therapy?

The second abuse of therapy is in using a form that is less effective or efficient than another. We now know that certain methods work better for certain problems. Brief sex therapy has demonstrated its superiority for problems like lack of orgasm, premature ejaculation, and erection complaints. Behavioral methods have proven best for phobias, obsessive-compulsive problems, and some social skill deficiencies. Depression can be successfully attacked using specialized short-term therapies. Finally, hypnosis, relaxation training, and cognitive therapy have shown promise in the control of pain.

Since the majority of therapists do not practice behavioral or sex therapy, many problems undoubtedly are being treated with inferior methods. And worse, the patients are not informed of choices.

Alternatives

The third category of abuse is using psychotherapy when alternative treatments are more effective or less costly. Many people who find their way into a therapist's office would benefit from drugs they are not offered. If the therapist is a psychologist, clinical social worker, psychiatric nurse, or marriage counselor, he or she cannot prescribe drugs.

Medication is not the only alternative to psychological therapy. There is considerable evidence that professional therapy is no more beneficial for a number of problems than attending self-help groups (many of which are free or relatively inexpensive), or just talking to

Reprinted from *Utne Reader,* March/April 1987, pp. 33–39. Excerpt from *Medical Self-Care,* Winter 1984. Reprinted by permission of Medical Self-Care Magazine, Point Reyes, CA. One year subscription $15.00.

nated lithium using a unique self-management regimen she developed in partnership with San Francisco psychiatrist Dr. Jeffry Ordover. Ordover warned her that living without lithium would be "the hardest thing she would ever do." Nielsen learned that he was right. Since its introduction in the early 1970s, lithium carbonate has become much more than simply the "drug of choice" to control the debilitating mood swings of manic-depression. Many psychiatrists consider it a "miracle drug."

Nielsen and Ordover are quiet pioneers on the frontiers of the mental health system. They are breaking new ground beyond traditional psychotherapy and drug treatments. The trail is rocky, but they are not alone. Growing numbers of ex-mental patients and people troubled by serious emotional problems are coping successfully with their conditions using alternative therapies based on support groups and other self-care practices.

Numerous self-help and support groups around North America help participants deal with a whole range of personal problems, often as adjuncts to professional therapy and/or medical treatment. Many focus on mental health problems—phobias, compulsions, coping with traumatic events or chronic problems, or just dealing with emotional stress in general. Some ex-mental patients have formed groups that an interested but untrained person.

Psychologists at Vanderbilt University assigned young men with garden variety neuroses to one of two groups of therapists. The first consisted of the best professional psychotherapists in the area, with an average 23 years of experience; the second group was made up of college professors with reputations of being good people to talk to but with no training in psychotherapy. Therapists and professors saw their clients for no more than 25 hours. The results: "Patients undergoing psychotherapy with college professors showed . . . quantitatively as much improvement as patients treated by experienced professional psychotherapists."

Research indicates that Alcoholics Anonymous is as useful as professional therapy for treating alcoholics. The cure rate isn't high—addictions being resistant to change—but therapy doesn't work any better. Likewise, when it comes to weight problems and drug abuse, no data support the contention that professional therapy is more effective than groups like Weight Watchers. Why induct drinkers, smokers, overweight people, and drug abusers into lengthy, often expensive, and usually fruitless therapy?

How long has this been going on?

The fourth abuse of psychotherapy is carrying it on interminably. Although a good deal of therapy consists of fewer than 20 sessions, much of the brief work is done in clinics and agencies where time limits are enforced. In private practice, where therapists are free to do as they choose, lengthy therapy is often the rule.

What's wrong with therapy taking two, four, or more years? Only one thing: Although for decades the bias among therapists has been that lengthy therapy is best, there is no evidence that longer is better. The few therapies

At an average cost of $65 an hour, psychotherapy is big business. And as is often the case with big business, consumers must be wary.

that have demonstrated effectiveness—behavioral therapy, cognitive therapy, and sex therapy—are all typically brief. Not one of the longer psychotherapies has demonstrated its superiority to briefer treatment for any problem. In the last two decades a small but vocal group of psychoanalysts have called lengthy therapy unnecessary and have offered evidence that changes can be brought about in fewer than 25 sessions.

—Bernie Zilbergeld
Science 86

Excerpted with permission from Science 86 *(June 1986). Time, Inc. has since acquired Science 86 and merged it with* Discover *magazine. Subscriptions: $24/yr. (12 issues) from Discover, Time-Life Bldg., 541 N. Franklin Court, Chicago, IL 60611.*

Got a problem? See a friend.

For far too long people have been led to believe that the person suffering from an excess of life's problems needs "expert" medical and psychotherapeutic intervention (thus allowing the "patient" to qualify for "illness") to the ultimate detriment of his mental equilibrium and often at considerable financial cost. Such a view is dangerous nonsense. Clearly there are differences between real psychiatric disease such as schizophrenia and manic-depressive illness and those normal but unpleasant mental states that are an inescapable and often valuable part of everyday living.

I believe we need a redefinition of the proper boundaries of psychological illness. We need a tougher, more rigorous and uncompromising attitude toward what does and what does not constitute disease. Therapists have mistakenly categorized millions of people mentally ill when their chief deficiency is an inadequate approach to problems and unrealistic expectations of what life should give them. A huge therapy industry has created itself to minister to, and profit from, the plight of these "neurotics."

For the therapists to take money for mere talk is, I would argue, in many cases both negligent and, despite the purest of motives, irresponsible. They harm the individual in his pursuit of mental health and encourage dependency and sterile introversion. Above all, they delay interminably that brave confrontation of life's problems in which alone salvation lies. The widespread popularity of such an approach comes on the fact that talking about ourselves is strongly pleasurable, that we all like to be the center of attention. In pandering to this mildly unworthy desire, these people do us more than a disservice. For, to the extent that such talk-therapy is pleasant, and its withdrawal difficult and traumatic, I would argue that, like Valium and cocaine, it is psychologically addictive. In the short term it may make us feel better—a quick fix of confidence—but over the years we will pay a considerable price in terms of dependency and lowered self-esteem.

Ostensibly opposed to talk-therapists, but in fact sharing their expert/patient approach, are the medico-biologists. Instead of intellectual insights and exotic theories, their stock-in-trade is chemical panaceas that they dish out like candy to individuals who are not ill. In both cases the end result is the same: a passive "patient" prostrate at the feet of the "healer," suffering the psychological pain of guilt as he learns to like himself less.

Talk therapy and Valium offer no solutions in the absence of real illness. They must be replaced by something of value. I offer Moral Therapy, a philosophy based not on fantasies, pseudo-intellectual gymnastics, or chemistry, but on common sense, on what we know in our hearts. Nobody gets paid for prac-

combine mutual support with political advocacy.

At a time when U.S. government agencies have cut back on mental health programs, and when traditional networks such as extended families and neighborhood and religious groups may be unavailable, mutual aid groups can provide crucial support for people who feel stigmatized, ignored, or isolated. They offer welcome relief from the waiting lists and bureaucracies that typify what Ralph Nader's Health Research Group called "the mental health maze." Support

The self-help approach and professional services need not be mutually exclusive nor antagonistic.

groups are comforting, non-judgmental, and inexpensive. Sharing insights and down-to-earth techniques for surmounting serious problems inspire those in the group to "keep on keeping on."

Unfortunately, there has been considerable resistance to—and ignorance about—the self-help/support-group movement from the professional community. Physicians and psychotherapists sometimes have difficulty reconciling them with their own clinical, analytical, illness-oriented model. Some professionals criticize support groups for operating with limited knowledge apart from professional guidance, or for basing their approach on "emotion" rather than "science."

The self-help/support-group approach and professional services need not be mutually exclusive nor antagonistic. In fact, if more mental health workers got involved in support-group work, they might find welcome relief from the burn-out that plagues their profession.

ticing Moral Therapy. Nobody profits from solving the problems of others except in feeling that natural satisfaction we all experience when we have been of service. There are no experts, no training institutes, no degrees or examinations, no gurus. There is nothing but us, our experience of life, our warmth and empathy, the voice of our conscience.

In the absence of psychological illness, we can practice the principles of Moral Therapy on ourselves and on others. Contentedness can exist only if self-respect is high. Only if we like ourselves can we be happy. At all times and in all situations we must obey our own moral codes. Only by doing what we ourselves consider to be right and good can we travel the road to self-respect. Insofar as we disregard our moral imperatives we must suffer the psychological pain of guilt. If we use the guilt mechanism properly and recoil from those actions that cause it to operate, it will serve us well. In the absence of disease, then, guilt is good for us.

With the right help from friends and loved ones, we can all learn to like ourselves more. As concerned and forceful friends, we can become the practitioners of a new Moral Therapy. Into the vacuum created by the disappearance of the paid "expert" will step family, friends, priests, neighbors, husbands, wives, and children. For too long their rightful role has been wrongfully usurped by impostors. The time has come for them to reclaim it.

In particular we should realize and encourage others to realize that self-respect is increased by searching out and achieving more difficult rather than easier objectives. By seeking difficulty and avoiding the easy way in pursuit of what we consider to be worthy ambitions, we will like ourselves more.

—Garth Wood

Excerpted with permission from the book The Myth of Neurosis *(1986, $15.96, $7.95 paperback, Harper & Row, 10 E. 53rd St., New York, NY 10022). ©1983, 1986 by Dr. Garth Wood.*

Many support groups deal with serious mental health problems. Two of the largest are Recovery, Inc., and Emotions Anonymous, which sponsor groups throughout North America. Recovery, Inc., was founded in 1937 by Abraham Low, M.D., a Vienna-trained non-Freudian psychiatrist, to supplement after-care services for ex-mental patients. The organization is now open to anyone. Today Recovery, Inc., sponsors about 1,000 support groups that meet weekly throughout North America and abroad.

The groups are led by members who have attended consistently for at least six months, and who have used the techniques successfully themselves. The organization sees itself as a supplement to—not a replacement for—professional therapy and enjoys broad support among psychiatrists and other therapists. Many participants are referred by a therapist.

The presentations at a typical Recovery meeting follow a strict formula: first a brief de-

scription of the traumatic incident, then the symptom(s) it provoked. Recovery calls this "spotting," recognizing problems and the reactions they cause. Next comes "coping," a brief rundown of how the person dealt with the incident using either will power or muscle control. Participants also describe the way they would have reacted before their Recovery training. Finally, they "endorse" themselves, pat themselves on the back for their insights and coping actions. Endorsement is often difficult because most people with emotional problems—for that matter, most people in general—tend to negate their accomplishments.

A young man, who seemed markedly nervous and withdrawn, said he'd been to a party where he felt everyone acted cold toward him. He "spotted" this as "fearful temper." ("Fearful temper" and "angry temper" are two sides of the same coin. The former is self-blame, which leads to depression; the latter is blaming others, which leads to acting out.) He started to shake and in

Most people with emotional problems tend to negate their accomplishments.

pre-Recovery days would have screamed and made a scene, but he was able to control the impulse. The group endorsed him for going to the party in the first place. "It's strengthening to do the things you fear." "It's good that you were 'self-led' and not 'symptom-led'." "It's average to feel uncomfortable when you don't know people." (The concept of "being average" comes up frequently in Recovery groups. It's the recognition that one's symptoms are normal, not pathological.) The phrases in quotes came up frequently. At first they sounded like jargon, but I gradually came to appreciate their value as code words that helped the members recognize their hard-won victories over fears and former habits.

Founded in 1971, Emotions Anonymous (EA) is patterned after the original self-help group, Alcoholics Anonymous (AA). EA adapted the AA program of confession, mutual aid, and 24-hour-a-day telephone support among members.

All the "Anonymous" organizations share a simple, homespun, non-religious spirituality. Weekly meetings open with a prayer: "God grant me the serenity to accept the things I cannot change, the courage to change the things I can, and the wisdom to know the difference." Speakers at EA meetings first admit that by themselves they are powerless over their emotions, then say they could be restored to sanity by a power greater than themselves. This power is open to individual interpretation. For some, it's "The Man Upstairs"; for others it's "Life Itself." The focus is on coping, on learning to live in relative peace despite unsolved problems, and on living life "one day at a time."

Although Recovery, Inc., and Emotions Anonymous deal with a broad range of emotional problems, there are also a host of problem-specific groups and support networks. To find one that meets your individual needs, contact your local community mental health center, or the National Self-Help Clearinghouse (33 W. 42nd St., Room 1227, New York, NY 10036).

Co-Counseling is an approach that trains people to give and accept reciprocal emotional support. Co-Counseling classes themselves serve as support groups, and after the training period, each member gets a list of local members available for counseling sessions.

The National Alliance for the Mentally Ill (NAMI) is a grassroots coalition of friends and relatives of those with serious mental health problems. The organization advocates for the mentally ill by promoting improved services.

The American Schizophrenia Association sponsors support groups for the families of schizophrenics, and explores such issues as residential treatment, relaxation training to reduce the side effects of medications, and orthomolecular therapy with vitamin and mineral supplements.

Studies have shown that success of therapy has less to do with methodology than the mere fact of recognizing a problem and deciding to do something about it. If the process of trying to cope with "the slings and arrows of outrageous fortune" seems beyond your strength, take heart. Whatever your situation, others who face similar challenges are eager to help.

Excerpted with permission from Medical Self-Care *(Winter 1984). Subscriptions: $15/yr. (6 issues) from Medical Self-Care, Box 1000, Point Reyes, CA 94956. Back issues: $2.50 from same address.*

The concept of "being average" comes up frequently in recovery groups.

Selected Contributors

Altemeyer, Bob is a professor of psychology at the University of Manitoba, Winnipeg. He has done extensive work in authoritarianism, written numerous books in the field, and received awards for his research.

Bettelheim, Bruno is a child psychologist who originated the psychoanalytic theory of infantile autism. He was professor of education (1950–1973) and founder of the Orthogenic School at the University of Chicago.

Blackmore, Susan has done extensive research in the Brain and Perception Laboratory at the University of Bristol.

Eysenck, Hans J. is a professor at the Institute of Psychiatry of the University of London, where he started the discipline of clinical psychology in Great Britain. He has pioneered the use of behavior therapy as well as research in personality theory and measurements.

Fishman, Scott M. is a research associate with the endocrine unit at Massachusetts General Hospital.

Goldstein, Allan L. is professor and chairman of the department of biochemistry at the George Washington University School of Medicine.

Goleman, Daniel is a practicing psychologist and frequently writes about behavioral sciences for *The New York Times*.

Hall, Nicholas R. is associate professor of neuroendocrinology and immunology in the department of biochemistry at the George Washington University School of Medicine in Washington, D.C.

Herrnstein, Richard J. is a professor of psychology at Harvard, known for his research in intelligence.

Knight, Charles is a senior fellow at the Commonwealth Institute, where he is working on alternatives for U.S. defense policy.

Kriegman, Daniel is a clinical psychologist and president of Human Services Cooperative, an agency structured around the principles of worker ownership.

Levy, Jerre is a biopsychologist at the University of Chicago.

Quinnett, Paul G. is director of adult services at the Spokane Community Mental Health Center and is the author of a number of books on personal problems.

Sheehan, David V. is professor of psychiatry and director of clinical research, University of South Florida School of Medicine.

Skinner, B. F. (Burrhus Frederic) is a professor emeritus of psychology at Harvard University. He developed methods for studying behavior within the framework of operant conditioning.

Spiegel, David is an associate professor of psychiatry and director of the adult psychiatric outpatient clinic at the Stanford University Medical Center.

Thayer, Stephen is a professor of psychology at City College and the Graduate Center of the City University of New York.

Treffert, Darold, a psychiatrist, has been director of several psychiatric hospitals, and has studied savants for the last twenty-six years.

Wilson, James Q. is a professor of government at Harvard who has done significant research and writing on the nature of crime. He has also written important articles about American politics.

Glossary

This Glossary of 468 psychology terms is included to provide you with a convenient and ready reference as you encounter general terms in your study of psychology which are unfamiliar or require a review. It is not intended to be comprehensive but taken together with the many definitions included in the articles themselves it should prove to be quite useful.

Abnormal Irregular, deviating from the norm or average. Abnormal implies the presence of a mental disorder that leads to behavior that society labels as deviant. There is a continuum between normal and abnormal. These are relative terms in that they imply a social judgment. *See* Normal.

Accommodation Process in cognitive development; involves altering or reorganizing the mental picture to make room for a new experience or idea.

Acetylcholine A neurotransmitter involved in memory.

Achievement Drive The need to attain self-esteem, success, or status. Society's expectations strongly influence the achievement motive.

ACTH (Adrenocorticotropic Hormone) The part of the brain called the hypothalamus activates the release of the hormone ACTH from the pituitary gland when a stressful condition exists. ACTH in turn activates the release of adrenal corticoids from the cortex of the adrenal gland.

Action Therapy A general classification of therapy (as opposed to insight therapy) in which the therapist focuses on symptoms rather than on underlying emotional states. Treatment aims at teaching new behavioral patterns rather than at self-understanding. *See* Insight Therapy.

Actor-Observer Attribution The tendency to attribute the behavior of other people to internal causes and the behavior of yourself to external causes.

Acupuncture The technique for curing certain diseases and anesthetizing by inserting needles at certain points of the body, developed in China and now being studied and applied in the West.

Adaptation The process of responding to changes in the environment by altering one's responses to keep one's behavior appropriate to environmental demands.

Addiction Physical dependence on a drug. When a drug causes biochemical changes that are uncomfortable when the drug is discontinued, when one must take ever larger doses to maintain the intensity of the drug's effects, and when desire to continue the drug is strong, one is said to be addicted.

Adjustment How we react to stress; some change that we make in response to the demands placed upon us.

Adrenal Glands Endocrine glands involved in stress and energy regulation.

Affective Disorder Affect means feeling or emotion. An affective disorder is mental illness marked by a disturbance of mood (e.g. manic depression.)

Afferent Neuron (Sensory) A neuron that carries messages from the sense organs toward the central nervous system.

Aggression Any act that causes pain or suffering to another. Some psychologists believe that aggressive behavior is instinctual to all species, including man, while others believe that it is learned through the processes of observation and imitation.

Alienation Indifference to or loss of personal relationships. An individual may feel estranged from family members, or, on a broader scale, from society.

All-or-None Law The principle that states that a neuron only fires when a stimulus is above a certain minimum strength (threshold), and when it fires, it does so at full strength.

Altered State of Consciousness (ASC) A mental state qualitatively different from a person's normal, alert, waking consciousness.

Altruism Behavior motivated by a desire to benefit another person. Altruistic behavior is aided by empathy and is usually motivated internally, not by observable threats or rewards.

Amphetamine A psychoactive drug that is a stimulant. Although used in treating mild depressions or, in children, hyperactivity, its medical uses are doubtful, and amphetamines are often abused. *See* Psychoactive Drug.

Anal Stage Psychosexual stage, during which, according to Freud, the child experiences the first restrictions on his impulses.

Animism The quality of believing life exists in inanimate objects. According to Piaget, animism is characteristic of children's thinking until about age two.

Antisocial Personality Disorder Personality disorder in which individuals who engage in antisocial behavior experience no guilt or anxiety about their actions; sometimes called sociopathy or psychopathy.

Anxiety An important term that has different meanings for different theories (psychoanalysis, behavior theory); a feeling state of apprehension, dread, or uneasiness. The state may be aroused by an objectively dangerous situation or by a situation that is not objectively dangerous. It may be mild or severe.

Anxiety Disorder Fairly long-lasting disruptions of the person's ability to deal with stress; often accompanied by feelings of fear and apprehension.

Applied Psychology The area of psychology that is most immediately concerned with helping to solve practical problems; includes clinical and counseling psychology, and industrial, environmental, and legal psychology.

Aptitude Tests Tests which are designed to predict what can be accomplished by a person in the future with the proper training.

Arousal A measure of responsiveness or activity; a state of excitement or wakefulness ranging from deepest coma to intense excitement.

Aspiration Level The level of achievement a person strives for. Studies suggest that people can use internal or external standards of performance.

Assertiveness Training Training which helps individuals stand up for their rights while not denying rights of other people.

Assimilation Process in cognitive development; occurs when something new is taken into the child's mental picture of the world.

Association Has separate meanings for different branches of psychology. Theory in cognitive psychology suggests that we organize information so that we can find our memories systematically, that one idea will bring another to mind. In psychoanalysis, the patient is asked to free associate (speak aloud all consecutive thoughts until random associations tend of themselves to form a meaningful whole). *See* Cognitive Psychology, Psychoanalysis.

Associationism A theory of learning suggesting that once two stimuli are presented together, one of them will remind a person of the other.

Ideas are learned by association with sensory experiences and are not innate. Among the principles of associationism are contiguity (stimuli that occur close together are more likely to be associated than stimuli far apart), and repetition (the more frequently stimuli occur together, the more strongly they become associated.)

Association Neurons Neurons that connect with other neurons.

Attachment Process in which the individual shows behaviors that promote the proximity or contact with a specific object or person.

Attention The tendency to focus activity in a particular direction and to select certain stimuli for further analysis while ignoring or possibly storing for further analysis all other inputs.

Attitude An overall tendency to respond positively or negatively to particular people or objects in a way that is learned through experience and that is made up of feelings (affects,) thoughts (evaluations,) and actions (conation.)

Attribution The process of determining the causes of behavior in a given individual.

Autism A personality disorder in which ae child does not respond socially to people.

Autonomic Nervous System The part of the nervous system (The other part is the central nervous system.) that is for emergency functions and release of large amounts of energy (sympathetic division) and regulating functions such as digestion and sleep (parasympathetic division.) *See* Biofeedback.

Aversion Therapy A counterconditioning therapy in which unwanted responses are paired with unpleasant consequences.

Avoidance Conditioning Situation in which a subject learns to avoid an aversive stimulus by responding appropriately before it begins.

Barbiturates Sedative-hypnotic, psychoactive drugs widely used to induce sleep and to reduce tension. Overuse can lead to addiction. *See* Addiction.

Behavior Any observable activity of an organism, including mental processes.

Behaviorism A school of psychology stressing an objective approach to psychological questions, proposing that psychology be limited to observable behavior and that the subjectiveness of consciousness places it beyond the limits of scientific psychology.

Behavior Therapy The use of conditioning processes to treat mental disorders. Various techniques may be used, including positive reinforcement in which rewards (verbal or tangible) are given to the patient for appropriate behavior, modeling in which patients unlearn fears by watching models exhibit fearlessness, and systematic desensitization in which the patient is taught to relax and visualize anxiety-producing items at the same time. *See* Insight Therapy, Systematic Desensitization.

Biofeedback The voluntary control of physiological processes by receiving information about those processes as they occur, through instruments that pick up these changes and display them to the subject in the form of a signal. Blood pressure, skin temperature, etc. can be controlled.

Biological (Primary) Motives Motives which have a physiological basis; include hunger, thirst, body temperature regulation, avoidance of pain, and sex.

Biological Response System System of the body that is particularly important in behavioral responding; includes the senses, endocrines, muscles, and the nervous system.

Biological Therapy Treatment of behavior problems through biological techniques; major biological therapies include drug therapy, psychosurgery, and electroconvulsive therapy.

Bipolar Disorder Affective disorder which is characterized by extreme mood swings from sad depression to joyful mania; sometimes called manic-depression.

Body Language Communication through position and movement of the body.

Brain Mapping A procedure for identifying the function of various areas of the brain; the surgeon gives tiny electrical stimulation to a specific area and notes patient's reaction.

Brain Stimulation The introduction of chemical or electrical stimuli directly into the brain.

Brain Waves Electrical responses produced by brain activity that can be recorded directly from any portion of the brain or from the scalp with special electrodes. Brain waves are measured by an electroencephalograph (EEG). Alpha waves occur during relaxed wakefulness and beta waves during active behavior. Theta waves are associated with drowsiness and vivid visual imagery, delta waves with deep sleep.

Bystander Effect Phenomenon in which a single person is more likely to help in an emergency situation than a group of people.

Cannon-Bard Theory of Emotion Theory of emotion which states that the emotional feeling and the physiological arousal occur at the same time.

Catatonic Schizophrenia A type of schizophrenia which is characterized by periods of complete immobility and the apparent absence of will to move or speak.

Causal Attribution Process of determining whether a person's behavior is due to internal or external motives.

Cautious Shift Research suggests that the decisions of a group will be more conservative than that of the average individual member when dealing with areas for which there are widely held values favoring caution (e.g. physical danger or family responsibility). *See* Risky Shift.

Central Nervous System The part of the human nervous system which interprets and stores messages from the sense organs, decides what behavior to exhibit, and sends appropriate messages to the muscles and glands; includes the brain and spinal cord.

Central Tendency In statistics, measures of central tendency give a number that represents the entire group or sample.

Cerebellum The part of the brain responsible for muscle and movement control and coordination of eye-body movement.

Cerebral Cortex The part of the brain consisting of the outer layer of cerebral cells. The cortex can be divided into specific regions: sensory, motor, and associative.

Chaining Behavior theory suggests that behavior patterns are built up of component parts by stringing together a number of simpler responses.

Character Disorder (or Personality Disorder) A classification of psychological disorders (as distinguished from neurosis or psychosis). The disorder has become part of the individual's personality and does not cause him discomfort, making that disorder more difficult to treat psychotherapeutically.

Chromosome *See* Gene.

Chunking The tendency to code memories so that there are fewer bits to store.

Classical Conditioning See Pavlovian Conditioning.

Client-Centered Therapy A nondirective form of psychotherapy developed by Carl Rogers in which the counselor attempts to create an atmosphere in which the client can freely explore himself and his problems. The client-centered therapist reflects what the client says back to him, usually without interpreting it.

Clinical Psychology The branch of psychology concerned with testing, diagnosing, interviewing, conducting research and treating (often by psychotherapy) mental disorders and personality problems.

Cognitive Appraisal Intellectual evaluation of situations or stimuli. Experiments suggest that emotional arousal is produced not simply by a stimulus but by how one evaluates and interprets the arousal. The appropriate physical response follows this cognitive appraisal.

Cognitive Behavior Therapy A form of behavior therapy which identifies self-defeating attitudes and thoughts in a subject, and then helps the subject to replace these with positive, supportive thoughts.

Cognitive Dissonance People are very uncomfortable if they perceive that their beliefs, feelings, or acts are not consistent with one another, and they will try to reduce the discomfort of this dissonance.

Cognitive Psychology The study of how individuals gain knowledge of their environments. Cognitive psychologists believe that the organism actively participates in constructing the meaningful stimuli that it selectively organizes and to which it selectively responds.

Comparative Psychology The study of similarities and differences in the behavior of different species.

Compulsive Personality Personality disorder in which an individual is preoccupied with details and rules.

Concept Learning The acquisition of the ability to identify and use the qualities that objects or situations have in common. A class concept refers to any quality that breaks objects or situations into separate groupings.

Concrete-Operational Stage A stage in intellectual development according to Piaget. The child at approximately seven years begins to apply logic. His thinking is less egocentric, reversible, and the child develops conservation abilities and the ability to classify. *See* Conservation.

Conditioned Reinforcer Reinforcement that is effective because it has been associated with other reinforcers. Conditioned reinforcers are involved in higher order conditioning.

Conditioned Response (CR) The response or behavior that occurs when the conditioned stimulus is presented (after the CS has been associated with the US).

Conditioned Stimulus (CS) An originally neutral stimulus that is associated with an unconditioned stimulus and takes on its capability of eliciting a particular reaction.

Conditioned Taste Aversion (CTA) Learning an aversion to particular tastes by associating them with stomach distress; usually considered a unique form of classical conditioning because of the extremely long interstimulus intervals involved.

Conduction The ability of a neuron to carry a message (an electrical stimulus) along its length.

Conflict Situation which occurs when we experience incompatible demands or desires.

Conformity The tendency of an individual to act like others regardless of personal belief.

Conscience A person's sense of the moral rightness or wrongness of behavior.

Consciousness Awareness of experienced sensations, thoughts, and feelings at any given point in time.

Consensus In causal attribution, the extent to which other people react the same way the subject does in a particular situation.

Conservation Refers to the child's ability to understand laws of length, mass, and volume. Before the development of this ability, a child will not understand that a particular property of an object (e.g. the quantity of water in a glass) does not change even though other perceivable features change.

Consistency In causal attribution, the extent to which the subject always behaves in the same way in a particular situation.

Consolidation The biological neural process of making memories permanent; possibly short-term memory is electrically coded and long-term memory is chemically coded.

Continuum of Preparedness Seligman's proposal that animals are biologically prepared to learn certain responses more readily than others.

Control Group A group used for comparison with an experimental group. All conditions must be identical for each group with the exception of the one variable (independent) that is manipulated. *See* Experimental Group.

Convergence Binocular depth cue in which we detect distance by interpreting the kinesthetic sensations produced by the muscles of the eyeballs.

Convergent Thinking The kind of thinking that is used to solve problems having only one correct answer. *See* Divergent Thinking.

Conversion Disorder Somatoform disorder in which a person displays obvious disturbance in the nervous system, however, a medical examination reveals no physical basis for the problem; often includes paralysis, loss of sensation, or blindness.

Corpus Callosum Nerve fibers that connect the two halves of the brain in humans. If cut, the halves continue to function although some functions are affected.

Correlation A measurement in which two or more sets of variables are compared and the extent to which they are related is calculated.

Correlation Coefficient The measure, in number form, of how two variables vary together. They extend from −1 (perfect negative correlation) to +1 (perfect positive correlation).

Counterconditioning A behavior therapy in which an unwanted response is replaced by conditioning a new response that is incompatible with it.

Creativity The ability to discover or produce new solutions to problems, new inventions, or new works of art. Creativity is an ability independent of IQ and is open-ended in that solutions are not predefined in their scope or appropriateness. *See* Problem-Solving.

Critical Period A specific stage in an organism's development during which the acquisition of a particular type of behavior depends on exposure to a particular type of stimulation.

Cross-Sectional Study A research technique that focuses on a factor in a group of subjects as they are at one time, as in a study of fantasy play in subjects of three different age groups. *See* Longitudinal Study.

Culture-Bound The idea that a test's usefulness is limited to the culture in which it was written and utilized.

Curiosity Motive Motive which causes the individual to seek out a certain amount of novelty.

Cutaneous Sensitivity The skin senses: touch, pain, pressure and temperature. Skin receptors respond in different ways and with varying degrees of sensitivity.

Decay Theory of forgetting in which sensory impressions leave memory traces that fade away with time.

Defense Mechanism A way of reducing anxiety that does not directly cope with the threat. There are many types, denial, repression, etc., all of which are used in normal function. Only when use is habitual or they impede effective solutions are they considered pathological.

Delusion A false belief that persists despite evidence showing it to be irrational. Delusions are often symptoms of mental illness.

Dependent Variable Those conditions that an experimenter observes and measures. Called "dependent" because they depend on the experimental manipulations.

Depersonalization Disorder Dissociative disorder in which individuals escape from their own personalities by believing that they don't exist or that their environment is not real.

Depression A temporary emotional state that normal individuals experience or a persistent state that may be considered a psychological disorder. Characterized by sadness and low self-esteem. See Self-Esteem.

Descriptive Statistics Techniques that help summarize large amounts of data information.

Developmental Norms The average time at which developmental changes occur in the normal individual.

Developmental Psychology The study of changes in behavior and thinking as the organism grows from the prenatal stage to death.

Deviation, Standard and Average Average deviation is determined by measuring the deviation of each score in a distribution from the mean and calculating the average of the deviations. The standard deviation is used to determine how representative the mean of a distribution is. See Mean.

Diagnostic and Statistical Manual of Mental Disorders (DSM) DSM-III was published in 1980 by the American Psychiatric Association.

Diffusion of Responsibility As the number of witnesses to a help-requiring situation—and thus the degree of anonymity—increases, the amount of helping decreases and the amount of time before help is offered increases. See Anonymity.

Discrimination The ability to tell whether stimuli are different when presented together or that one situation is different from a past one.

Disorganized Schizophrenia A type of schizophrenia which is characterized by a severe personality disintegration; the individual often displays bizarre behavior.

Displacement The process by which an emotion originally attached to a particular person, object, or situation is transferred to something else.

Dissociative Disorders Disorders in which individuals forget who they are.

Distal Stimuli Physical events in the environment that affect perception. See also Proximal Stimuli.

Distinctiveness In causal attribution, the extent to which the subject reacts the same way in other situations.

Divergent Thinking The kind of thinking that characterizes creativity (as contrasted with convergent thinking) and involves the development of novel resolutions of a task or the generation of totally new ideas. See Convergent Thinking.

DNA See Gene.

Double Bind A situation in which a person is subjected to two conflicting, contradictory demands at the same time.

Down's Syndrome Form of mental retardation caused by having three number 21 chromosomes (trisomy 21).

Dreams The thoughts, images, and emotions that occur during sleep. Dreams occur periodically during the sleep cycle and are usually marked by rapid movements of the eyes (REM sleep). The content of dreams tends to reflect emotions (sexual feelings, according to Freud) and experiences of the previous day. Nightmares are qualitatively different from other dreams, often occuring during deep or Stage 4 sleep.

Drive A need or urge that motivates behavior. Some drives may be explained as responses to bodily needs, such as hunger or sex. Others derive from social pressures and complex forms of learning, for example, competition, curiosity, achievement. See Motivation.

Drive Reduction Theory Theory of motivation that states that the individual is pushed by inner forces toward reducing the drive and restoring homeostasis.

Drug Dependence A state of mental or physical dependence on a drug, or both. Psychoactive drugs are capable of creating psychological dependence (anxiety when the drug is unavailable,) although the relationship of some, such as marijuana and LSD, to physical dependence or addiction is still under study. See Psychoactive Drugs, Addiction.

Drug Tolerance A state produced by certain psychoactive drugs in which increasing amounts of the substance are required to produce the desired effect. Some drugs produce tolerance but not withdrawal symptoms, and these drugs are not regarded as physically addicting.

Effectance Motive The striving for effectiveness in dealing with the environment. The effectance motive differs from the need for achievement in that effectance depends on internal feelings of satisfaction while the need for achievement is geared more to meeting others' standards.

Efferent Neuron (Motor) A neuron that carries messages from the central nervous system to the muscles and glands.

Ego A construct to account for the organization in a person's life and for making the person's behavior correspond to physical and social realities. According to Freud, the ego is the "reality principle" that is responsible for holding the id or "pleasure principle" in check. See Id.

Egocentrism Seeing things from only one's own point of view; also, the quality of a child's thought that prevents him from understanding that different people perceive the world differently. Egocentrism is characteristic of a stage that all children go through.

Electroshock Therapy A form of therapy used to relieve severe depression. The patient receives electric current across the forehead, loses consciousness, and undergoes a short convulsion. When the patient regains consciousness, his mood is lifted.

Emotion A complex feeling-state that involves physiological arousal; a subjective feeling which might involve a cognitive appraisal of the situation and overt behavior in response to a stimulus.

Empathy The ability to appreciate how someone else feels by putting yourself in his position and experiencing his feelings. Empathy is acquired normally by children during intellectual growth.

Empiricism The view that behavior is learned through experience.

Encounter Groups Groups of individuals who meet to change their personal lives by confronting each other, discussing personal problems, and talking more honestly and openly than in everyday life.

Endocrine Glands Ductless glands that secrete chemicals called hormones into the blood stream.

Equilibration According to Piaget, the child constructs his understanding of the world through equilibration. Equilibration consists of the interaction of two complementary processes, assimilation (taking in input within the existing structures of the mind, e.g. putting it into mental categories that already exist) with accommodation (the changing of mental categories to fit new input that cannot be taken into existing categories) and is the process by which knowing occurs. One's developmental stage affects how one equilibrates.

Ethnocentrism The belief that one's own ethnic or racial group is superior to others.

Experiment Procedures executed under a controlled situation in order to test a hypothesis and discover relationships between independent and dependent variables.

Experimental Control The predetermined conditions, procedures, and checks built into the design of an experiment to ensure scientific control; as opposed to "control" in common usage, which implies manipulation.

Experimental Group In a scientific experiment, the group of subjects that is usually treated specially, as opposed to the control group, in order to isolate just the variable under investigation. See Control Group.

Experimental Psychology The branch of psychology concerned with the laboratory study of basic psychological laws and principles as demonstrated in the behavior of animals.

Experimenter Bias How the expectations of the person running an experiment can influence what comes out of the experiment. Experimenter bias can affect the way the experimenter sees the subjects' behavior, causing distortions of fact, and can also affect the way the experimenter reads data, also leading to distortions.

Extinction The elimination of behavior by, in classical conditioning, the withholding of the US, and in operant conditioning, the withholding of the reinforcement.

Extrasensory Perception (ESP) The range of perceptions that are "paranormal," (such as the ability to predict events, reproduce drawings sealed in envelopes, etc.).

Fixed-Action Pattern Movement that is characteristic of a species and does not have to be learned.

Fixed Interval (FI) Schedule Schedule of reinforcement in which the subject receives reinforcement for the first correct response given after a specified time interval.

Fixed Ratio (FR) Schedule Schedule of reinforcement in which the subject is reinforced after a certain number of responses.

Forgetting The process by which material that once was available is no longer available. Theory exists that forgetting occurs because memories interfere with one another, either retroactively (new memories block old) or proactively (old memories block new); that forgetting occurs when the cues necessary to recall the information are not supplied, or when memories are too unpleasant to remain in consciousness. *See* Repression.

Formal Operational Stage   According to Piaget, the stage at which the child develops adult powers of reasoning, abstraction, and symbolizing. The child can grasp scientific, religious, and political concepts and deduce their consequences as well as reason hypothetically ("what if. . . .").

Frequency Theory of Hearing   Theory of hearing that states that the frequency of vibrations at the basilar membrane determines the frequency of firing of neurons that carry impulses to the brain.

Frustration   A feeling of discomfort or insecurity aroused by a blocking of gratification or by unresolved problems. Several theories hold that frustration arouses aggression. *See* Aggression.

Functionalism   An early school of psychology stressing the ways behavior helps one adapt to the environment and the role that learning plays in this adaptive process.

Gene   The unit of heredity that determines particular characteristics; a part of a molecule of DNA. DNA (dioxyribonucleic acid) is found mainly in the nucleus of living cells where it occurs in threadlike structures called chromosomes. Within the chromosomes each DNA molecule is organized into specific units that carry the genetic information necessary for the development of a particular trait. These units are the genes. A gene can reproduce itself exactly, and this is how traits are carried between generations. The genotype is the entire structure of genes that are inherited by an organism from its parents. The environment interacts with this genotype to determine how the genetic potential will develop.

General Adaptation Syndrome (GAS)   The way the body responds to stress, as described by Hans Selye. In the first stage, an alarm reaction, a person responds by efforts at self-control and shows signs of nervous depression (defense mechanisms, fear, anger, etc.) followed by a release of ACTH. In stage 2, the subject shows increased resistance to the specific source of stress and less resistance to other sources. Defense mechanisms may become neurotic. With stage 3 come exhaustion, stupor, even death.

Generalization   The process by which learning in one situation is transferred to another, similar situation. It is a key term in behavioral modification and classical conditioning. *See* Classical Conditioning.

Generalized Anxiety Disorder   Disorder in which the individual lives in a state of constant severe tension; continuous fear and apprehension experienced by an individual.

Genetics   The study of the transfer of the inheritance of characteristics from one generation to another.

Genotype   The underlying genetic structure that an individual has inherited and will send on to descendants. The actual appearance of a trait (phenotype) is due to the interaction of the genotype and the environment.

Gestalt Psychology   A movement in psychology begun in the 1920s, stressing the wholeness of a person's experience and proposing that perceiving is an active, dynamic process that takes into account the entire pattern ("gestalt") of the perceptual field. *See* Behaviorism, Associationism.

Glia   Cells in the central nervous system that regulate the chemical environment of the nerve cells. RNA is stored in glial cells.

Grammar   The set of rules for combining units of a language.

Group Therapy   A form of psychotherapy aimed at treating mental disorders in which interaction among group members is the main therapeutic mode. Group therapy takes many forms but essentially requires a sense of community, support, increased personal responsibility, and a professionally trained leader.

Growth   The normal quantitative changes that occur in the physical and psychological aspects of a healthy child with the passage of time.

Gustation   The sense of taste. Theory suggests that the transmission of sense information from tongue to brain occurs through patterns of cell activity and not just the firing of single nerve fibers. Also, it is believed that specific spatial patterns or places on the tongue correspond to taste qualities.

Habit Formation   The tendency to make a response to a stimulus less variable, especially if it produced successful adaptation.

Hallucination   A sensory impression reported by a person when no external stimulus exists to justify the report. Hallucinations are serious symptoms and may be produced by psychoses. *See* Psychoses.

Hallucinogen   A substance that produces hallucinations, such as LSD, mescaline, etc.

Hierarchy of Needs   Maslow's list of motives in humans, arranged from the biological to the uniquely human.

Higher Order Conditioning   Learning to make associations with stimuli that have been previously learned (CSs).

Hippocampus   Part of the cortex of the brain governing memory storage, smell, and visceral functions.

Homeostasis   A set of processes maintaining the constancy of the body's internal state, a series of dynamic compensations of the nervous system. Many processes such as appetite, body temperature, water balance, heart rate are controlled by homeostasis.

Hormones   Chemical secretions of the endocrine glands that regulate various body processes (e.g. growth, sexual traits, reproductive processes, etc.)

Humanism   Branch of psychology dealing with those qualities distinguishing humans from other animals.

Hypnosis   A trancelike state marked by heightened suggestibility and a narrowing of attention which can be induced in a number of ways. Debate exists over whether hypnosis is a true altered state of consciousness and over to what extent strong motivating instructions can duplicate so-called hypnosis.

Hypothalamus   A part of the brain that acts as a channel that carries information from the cortex and the thalamus to the spinal cord and ultimately to the motor nerves or to the autonomic nervous system, where it is transmitted to specific target organs. These target organs release into the bloodstream specific hormones that alter bodily functions. *See* Autonomic Nervous System.

Hypothesis   A hypothesis can be called an educated guess, similar to a hunch. When a hunch is stated in a way that allows for further testing, it becomes a hypothesis.

Iconic Memory   A visual memory. Experiments suggest that in order to be remembered and included in long-term memory, information must pass through a brief sensory stage.

Theory further suggests that verbal information is subject to forgetting but that memorized sensory images are relatively permanent.

Id   According to Freud, a component of the psyche present at birth that is the storehouse of psychosexual energy called *libido*, and also of primitive urges to fight, dominate, destroy.

Identification   The taking on of attributes that one sees in another person. Children tend to identify with their parents or other important adults and thereby take on certain traits that are important to their development.

Illusion   A mistaken perception of an actual stimulus.

Imitation   The copying of another's behavior; learned through the process of observation. *See* Modeling.

Impression Formation   The process of developing an evaluation of another person from your perceptions; first, or initial impressions are often very important.

Imprinting   The rapid, permanent acquisition by an organism of a strong attachment to an object (usually the parent). Imprinting occurs shortly after birth.

Independent Variable   The condition in an experiment which is controlled and manipulated by the experimenter; it is a stimulus that will cause a response.

Inferential Statistics   Techniques that help researchers make generalizations about a finding based on a limited number of subjects.

Inhibition   Restraint of an impulse, desire, activity, or drive. People are taught to inhibit full expression of many drives (for example, aggression or sexuality) and to apply checks either consciously or unconsciously. In Freudian terminology, an inhibition is an unconsciously motivated blocking of sexual energy. In Pavlovian conditioning, inhibition is the theoretical process that operates during extinction, acting to block a conditioned response. *See* Pavlovian Conditioning.

Insight   A sudden perception of useful or proper relations among objects necessary to solve the problem.

Insight Therapy   A general classification of therapy in which the therapist focuses on the patient's underlying feelings and motivations and devotes most effort to increasing the patient's self-awareness or insight into his behavior. The other major class of therapy is action therapy. *See* Action Therapy.

Instinct   An inborn pattern of behavior, relatively independent of environmental influence. An instinct may need to be triggered by a particular stimulus in the environment, but then it proceeds in a fixed pattern. The combination of taxis (orienting movement in response to a particular stimulus) and fixed-action pattern (inherited coordination) is the basis for instinctual activity. *See* Fixed-Action Pattern.

Instrumental Learning   *See* Operant Conditioning.

Intelligence   A capacity for knowledge about the world. This is an enormous and controversial field of study, and there is not agreement on a precise definition. However, intelligence has come to refer to higher-level abstract processes and may be said to comprise the ability to deal effectively with abstract concepts, the ability to learn, and the ability to adapt and deal with new situations. Piaget defines intelligence as the construction of an understanding. Both biological inheritance and environmental factors contribute to general intelligence. Children proceed through a sequence of identifiable stages in the development of conceptual thinking (Piaget). The degree to which factors such as race, sex, and social class affect intelligence is not known.

Intelligence Quotient (IQ)   A measurement of intelligence originally based on tests devised by Binet and now widely applied. Genetic inheritance and environment affect IQ, although their relative contributions are not known. IQ can be defined in different ways; classically it is defined as a relation between chronological and mental ages.

Interference   Theory of forgetting in which information that was learned before (proactive interference) or after (retroactive interference) the material of interest causes the learner to be unable to remember the material.

Interstimulus Interval   The time between the start of the conditioned stimulus and the start of the unconditioned stimulus in Pavlovian conditioning. *See* Pavlovian Conditioning.

Intra-Uterine Environment   The environment in the uterus during pregnancy can affect the physical development of the organism and its behavior after birth. Factors such as the mother's nutrition, emotional and physical state significantly influence offspring. The mother's diseases, medications, hormones, stress level all effect the pre- and post-natal development of her young.

Intrinsic Motivation   Motivation inside of the individual; we do something because we receive satisfaction from it.

Introspection   Reporting one's internal, subjective mental contents for the purpose of further study and analysis. *See* Structuralism.

James-Lange Theory of Emotion   Theory of emotion which states that the physiological arousal and behavior come before the subjective experience of an emotion.

Labeling-of-Arousal   Experiments suggest that an individual experiencing physical arousal that he cannot explain will interpret his feelings in terms of the situation he is in and will use environmental and contextual cues.

Language   A set of abstract symbols used to communicate meaning. Language includes vocalized sounds or semantic units (words, usually) and rules for combining the units (grammar). There is some inborn basis for language acquisition, and there are identifiable stages in its development that are universal.

Language Acquisition   Linguists debate how children acquire language. Some believe in environmental shaping, a gradual system of reward and punishment. Others emphasize the unfolding of capacities inborn in the brain that are relatively independent of the environment and its rewards.

Latency Period   According to Freud, the psychosexual stage of development during which sexual interest has been repressed and thus is low or "latent" (dormant).

Law of Effect   Thorndike's proposal that when a response produces satisfaction, it will be repeated; reinforcement.

Leadership   The quality of exerting more influence than other group members. Research suggests that certain characteristics are generally considered essential to leadership: consideration, sensitivity, ability to initiate and structure, and emphasis on production. However, environmental factors may thrust authority on a person without regard to personal characteristics.

Learned Helplessness   Theory suggests that living in an environment of uncontrolled stress reduces the ability to cope with future stress that *is* controllable.

Learned Social Motives   Motives in the human which are learned; include achievement, affiliation, and autonomy.

Learning   The establishment of connections between stimulus and response, resulting from observation, special training, or previous activity. Learning is relatively permanent.

Lifespan   Span of time from conception to death; in developmental psychology, a lifespan approach looks at development throughout an individual's life.

Linguistic Relativity Hypothesis   Proposal by Whorf that the perception of reality differs according to the language of the observer.

Linguistics   The study of language, its nature, structure, and components.

Locus of Control   The perceived place from which come determining forces in one's life. A person who feels that he has some control over his fate and tends to feel more likely to succeed has an internal locus of control. A person with an external locus of control feels that it is outside himself and therefore that his attempts to control his fate are less assured.

Longitudinal Study   A research method that involves following subjects over a considerable period of time (as compared with a cross-sectional approach); as in a study of fantasy play in children observed several times at intervals of two years. *See* Cross-Sectional Study.

Love   Affectionate behavior between people, often in combination with interpersonal attraction. The mother-infant love relationship strongly influences the later capacity for developing satisfying love relationships.

Manic-Depressive Reaction   A form of mental illness marked by alternations of extreme phases of elation (manic phase) and depression.

Maternalism   Refers to the mother's reaction to her young. It is believed that the female is biologically determined to exhibit behavior more favorable to the care and feeding of the young than the male, although in humans maternalism is probably determined as much by cultural factors as by biological predisposition.

Maturation   The genetically-controlled process of physical and physiological growth.

Mean   The measure of central tendency, or mathematical average, computed by adding all scores in a set and dividing by the number of scores.

Meaning   The concept or idea conveyed to the mind, by any method. In reference to memory, meaningful terms are easier to learn than less meaningful, unconnected, or nonsense terms. Meaningfulness is not the same as the word's meaning.

Median   In a set of scores, the median is that middle score that divides the set into equal halves.

Memory   Involves the encoding, storing of information in the brain, and its retrieval. Several theories exist to explain memory. One proposes that we have both a short-term (STM) and a long-term memory (LTM) and that information must pass briefly through the STM to be stored in the LTM. Also suggested is that verbal information is subject to forgetting, while memorized sensory images are relatively permanent. Others see memory as a function of association—information processed systematically and the meaningfulness of the items. Debate exists over whether memory retrieval is actually a process of reappearance or reconstruction.

Mental Disorder   A mental condition that deviates from what society considers to be normal.

Minnesota Multiphasic Personality Inventory (MMPI)   An objective personality test which was originally devised to identify personality disorders.

Mode   In a set of scores, the measurement at which the largest number of subjects fall.

Modeling   The imitation or copying of another's behavior. As an important process in personality development, modeling may be based on parents. In therapy, the therapist may serve as a model for the patient.

Morality   The standards of right and wrong of a society and their adoption by members of that society. Some researchers believe that morality develops in successive stages, with each stage representing a specific level of moral thinking (Kohlberg). Others see morality as the result of experiences in which the child learns through punishment and reward from models such as parents and teachers.

Motivation   All factors that cause and regulate behavior that is directed toward achieving goals and satisfying needs. Motivation is what moves an organism to action.

Motor Unit   One spinal motoneuron (motor nerve cell) and the muscle fibers it activates. The contraction of a muscle involves the activity of many motoneurons and muscle fibers. Normally we are aware only of our muscles contracting and not of the process producing the contraction, although biofeedback can train people to control individual motor units. *See* Biofeedback.

Narcotic   A drug that relieves pain. Heroin, morphine, and opium are narcotics. Narcotics are often addicting.

Naturalistic Observation   Research method in which behavior of people or animals in the normal environment is accurately recorded.

Negative Reinforcement   Any event that upon termination, strengthens the preceding behavior; taking from subject something bad will increase the probability that the preceding behavior will be repeated. Involves aversive stimulus.

Neuron   A nerve cell. There are billions of neurons in the brain and spinal cord. Neurons interact at synapses or points of contact. Information passage between neurons is electrical and biochemical. It takes the activity of many neurons to produce a behavior.

Neurosis   Any one of a wide range of psychological difficulties, accompanied by excessive anxiety (as contrasted with psychosis). Psychoanalytic theory states that neurosis is an expression of unresolved conflicts in the form of tension and impaired functioning. Most neurotics are in much closer contact with reality than most psychotics. Term has been largely eliminated from DSM-III.

Nonverbal Behaviors   Gestures, facial expressions, and other body movements. They are important because they tend to convey emotion. Debate exists over whether they are inborn or learned.

Norm   An empirically set pattern of belief or behavior. Social norm refers to widely accepted social or cultural behavior to which a person tends to or is expected to conform.

Normal   Sane, or free from mental disorder. Normal behavior is the behavior typical of most people in a given group, and "normality" implies a social judgment.

Normal Curve   When scores of a large number of random cases are plotted on a graph, they often fall into a bell-shaped curve; there are as many cases above the mean as below on the curve.

Object Permanence According to Piaget, the stage in cognitive development when a child begins to conceive of objects as having an existence even when out of sight or touch and to conceive of space as extending beyond his own perception.

Oedipus Complex The conflicts of a child in triangular relationship with his mother and father. According to Freud, a boy must resolve his unconscious sexual desire for his mother and the accompanying wish to kill his father and fear of his father's revenge in order that he proceed in his moral development. The analogous problem for girls is called the Electra complex.

Olfaction The sense of smell. No general agreement exists on how olfaction works though theories exist to explain it. One suggests that the size and shape of molecules of what is smelled is a crucial cue. The brain processes involved in smell are located in a different and evolutionally older part of the brain than the other senses.

Operant Conditioning The process of changing, maintaining, or eliminating voluntary behavior through the consequences of that behavior. Operant conditioning uses many of the techniques of Pavlovian conditioning but differs in that it deals with voluntary rather than reflex behaviors. The frequency with which a behavior is emitted can be increased if it is rewarded (reinforced) and decreased if it is not reinforced, or punished. Some psychologists believe that all behavior is learned through conditioning while others believe that intellectual and motivational processes play a crucial role. *See* Pavlovian Conditioning.

Operational Definitions If an event is not directly observable, then the variables must be defined by the operations by which they will be measured. These definitions are called operational definitions.

Organism Any living animal, human or subhuman.

Orienting Response A relatively automatic, "what's that?" response that puts the organism in a better position to attend to and deal with a new stimulus. When a stimulus attracts our attention, our body responds with movements of head and body toward the stimulus, changes in muscle tone, heart rate, blood flow, breathing, and changes in the brain's electrical activity.

Pavlovian Conditioning Also called classical conditioning, Pavlovian conditioning can be demonstrated as follows: In the first step, an *unconditioned stimulus* (UCS) such as food, loud sounds, or pain is paired with a neutral *conditioned stimulus* (CS) that causes no direct effect, such as a click, tone, or a dim light. The response elicited by the UCS is called the *unconditioned response* (UCR) and is a biological reflex of the nervous system (for example, eyeblinks or salivation). The combination of the neutral CS, the response-causing UCS, and the unlearned UCR is usually presented to the subject several times during conditioning. Eventually, the UCS is dropped from the sequence in the second step of the process, and the previously neutral CS comes to elicit a response. When conditioning is complete, presentation of the CS alone will result in a *conditioned response* (CR) similar but not always the same as the UCR.

Perception The field of psychology studying ways in which the experience of objects in the world is based upon stimulation of the sense organs. In psychology, the field of perception studies what determines sensory impressions, such as size, shape, distance, direction, etc. Physical events in the environment are called distal stimuli while the activity at the sense organ itself is called a proximal stimulus. The study of perceiving tries to determine how an organism knows what distal stimuli are like since proximal stimuli are its only source of information. Perception of objects remains more or less constant despite changes in distal stimuli and is therefore believed to depend on relationships within stimuli (size *and* distance, for example). Perceptual processes are able to adjust and adapt to changes in the perceptual field.

Performance The actual behavior of an individual that is observed. We often infer learning from observing performance.

Peripheral Nervous System The part of the human nervous system which receives messages from the sense organs and carries messages to the muscles and glands; everything outside of the brain and spinal cord.

Persuasion The process of changing a person's attitudes, beliefs, or actions. A person's susceptibility to persuasion depends on the persuader's credibility, subtlety and whether both sides of an argument are presented.

Phenotype The physical features or behavior patterns by which we recognize an organism. Phenotype is the result of interaction between genotype (total of inherited genes) and environment. *See* Genotype.

Phobia A neurosis consisting of an irrationally intense fear of specific persons, objects, or situations and a wish to avoid them. A phobic person feels intense and incapacitating anxiety. The person may be aware that his fear is irrational, but this knowledge does not help.

Pituitary Gland Is located at the base of the brain and controls secretion of several hormones: the antidiuretic hormone that maintains water balance, oxytocin which controls blood pressure and milk production and ACTH which is produced in response to stress, etc. *See* ACTH.

Placebo A substance which in and of itself has no real effect but which may produce an effect in a subject because the subject expects or believes that it will.

Positive Reinforcement Any event, that upon presentation, strengthens the preceding behavior; giving a subject something good will increase the probability that the preceding behavior will be repeated.

Prejudice An attitude in which one holds a negative belief about members of a group to which he does not belong. Prejudice is often directed at minority ethnic or racial groups and may be reduced by contact with these perceived "others."

Premack Principle Principle that states that of any two responses, the one that is more likely to occur can be used to reinforce the response that is less likely to occur.

Prenatal Development Development from conception to birth. It includes the physical development of the fetus as well as certain of its intellectual and emotional processes.

Preoperational Stage The development stage at which, according to Piaget, come the start of language, the ability to imitate actions, to symbolize, and to play make-believe games. Thinking is egocentric in that a child cannot understand that others perceive things differently.

Primary Reinforcement Reinforcement that is effective without having been associated with other reinforcers; sometimes called unconditioned reinforcement.

Probability (p) In inferential statistics, the likelihood that the difference between the experimental and control groups is due to the independent variable.

Problem Solving A self-directed activity in which an individual uses information to develop answers to problems, to generate new problems, and sometimes to transform the process by creating a unique, new system. Problem solving involves learning, insight and creativity.

Projective Test A type of test in which people respond to ambiguous, loosely structured stimuli. It is assumed that people will reveal themselves by putting themselves into the stimuli they see. The validity of these tests for diagnosis and personality assessment is still at issue.

Propaganda Information deliberately spread to aid a cause. Propaganda's main function is persuasion.

Prosocial Behavior Behavior which is directed toward helping others.

Proximal Stimulus Activity at the sense organ.

Psychoactive Drug A substance that affects mental activities, perceptions, consciousness, or mood. This group of drugs has its effects through strictly physical effects and through expectations.

Psychoanalysis There are two meanings to this word: it is a theory of personality development based on Freud and a method of treatment also based on Freud. Psychoanalytic therapy uses techniques of free association, dream analysis, and analysis of the patient's relationship (the "transference") to the analyst. Psychoanalytic theory maintains that the personality develops through a series of psychosexual stages and that the personality consists of specific components energized by the life and death instincts.

Psychogenic Pain Disorder Somatoform disorder in which the person complains of severe, long-lasting pain for which there is no organic cause.

Psycholinguistics The study of the process of language acquisition as part of psychological development and of language as an aspect of behavior. Thinking may obviously depend on language, but their precise relationship still puzzles psycholinguists, and several different views exist.

Psychological Dependence Situation when a person craves a drug even though it is not biologically necessary for his body.

Psychophysiological Disorders Real medical problems (such as ulcers, migraine headaches, and high blood pressure) which are caused or aggravated by psychological stress.

Psychosexual Stages According to Freud, an individual's personality develops through several stages. Each stage is associated with a particular bodily source of gratification (pleasure). First comes the oral stage when most pleasures come from the mouth. Then comes the anal stage when the infant derives pleasure from holding and releasing while learning bowel control. The phallic stage brings pleasure from the genitals, and a crisis (Oedipal) occurs in which the child gradually suppresses sexual desire for the opposite-sex parent, identifies with the same-sex parent and begins to be interested in the outside world. This latency period lasts until puberty, after which the genital stage begins and mature sexual relationships develop. There is no strict timetable, but according to Freudians, the stages do come in a definite order. Conflicts experienced and not adequately dealt with remain with the individual.

Psychosis The most severe of mental disorders, distinguished by a person being seriously out of touch with objective reality. Psychoses may result from physical factors (organic) or may have no known physical cause (functional). Psychoses take many forms of which the most common are schizophrenia and psychotic depressive reactions, but all are marked by personality disorganization and a severely reduced ability to perceive reality. Both biological and environmental factors are believed to influence the development of psychosis, although the precise effect of each is not presently known. *See* Neurosis.

Psychosomatic Disorders A variety of body reactions that are closely related to psychological events. Stress, for example, brings on many physical changes and can result in illness or even death if prolonged and severe. Psychosomatic disorders can affect any part of the body.

Psychotherapy Treatment involving interpersonal contacts between a trained therapist and a patient in which the therapist tries to produce beneficial changes in the patient's emotional state, attitudes, and behavior.

Punishment Any event that decreases the probability of the preceding behavior being repeated. You can give something bad (positive punishment) to decrease the preceding behavior.

Rational-Emotive Therapy A cognitive behavior modification technique in which a person is taught to identify irrational, self-defeating beliefs and then to overcome them.

Rationalization Defense mechanism in which individuals make up logical excuses to justify their behavior rather than exposing their true motives.

Reaction Formation Defense mechanism in which a person masks an unconsciously distressing or unacceptable trait by assuming an opposite attitude or behavior pattern.

Reactive Schizophrenia A type of schizophrenia in which the disorder appears as a reaction to some major trauma or terribly stressful encounter; sometimes called acute schizophrenia.

Reality Therapy A form of treatment of mental disorders pioneered by William Glasser in which the origins of the patient's problems are considered irrelevant and emphasis is on a close, judgmental bond between patient and therapist aimed to improve the patient's present and future life.

Reflex An automatic movement that occurs in direct response to a stimulus.

Rehearsal The repeating of an item to oneself and the means by which information is stored in the short-term memory (STM). Theory suggests that rehearsal is necessary for remembering and storage in the long-term memory (LTM).

Reinforcement The process of affecting the frequency with which a behavior is emitted. A reinforcer can reward and thus increase the behavior or punish and thus decrease its frequency. Reinforcers can also be primary, satisfying basic needs such as hunger or thirst, or secondary, satisfying learned and indirect values, such as money.

Reliability Consistency of measurement. A test is reliable if it repeatedly gives the same results. A person should get nearly the same score if the test is taken on two different occasions.

REM (Rapid-Eye Movement) Type of sleep in which the eyes are rapidly moving around; dreaming occurs in REM sleep.

Repression A defense mechanism in which a person forgets or pushes into the unconscious something that arouses anxiety. *See* Defense Mechanism, Anxiety.

Reticular Formation A system of nerve fibers leading from the spinal column to the cerebral cortex that functions to arouse, alert, and make an organism sensitive to changes in the environment. *See* Cerebral Cortex.

Retina The inside coating of the eye, containing two kinds of cells that react to light: the rods which are sensitive only to dim light and the cones which are sensitive to color and form in brighter light. There are three kinds of cones, each responsive to particular colors in the visible spectrum (range of colors).

Risky Shift Research suggests that decisions made by groups will involve considerably more risk than individuals in the group would be willing to take. This shift in group decision depends heavily on cultural values. *See* Cautious Shift.

Rod Part of the retina involved in seeing in dim light. *See* Retina.

RNA (Ribonucleic Acid) A chemical substance that occurs in chromosomes and that functions in genetic coding. During task-learning, RNA changes occur in the brain.

Role Playing Adopting the role of another person and experiencing the world in a way one is not accustomed to.

Role Taking The ability to imagine oneself in another's place or to understand the consequences of one's actions for another person.

Schachter-Singer Theory of Emotion Theory of emotion which states that we interpret our arousal according to our environment and label our emotions accordingly.

Schizoid Personality Personality disorder characterized by having great trouble developing social relationships.

Schizophrenia The most common and serious form of psychosis in which there exists an imbalance between emotional reactions and the thoughts associated with these feelings. It may be a disorder of the process of thinking. *See* Psychosis.

Scientific Method The process used by psychologists to determine principles of behavior that exist independently of individual experience and that are untouched by unconscious bias. It is based on a prearranged agreement that criteria, external to the individual and communicable to others, must be established for each set of observations referred to as fact.

Secondary Reinforcement Reinforcement that is only effective after it has been associated with a primary reinforcer.

Self-Actualization A term used by humanistic psychologists to describe what they see as a basic human motivation: the development of all aspects of an individual into productive harmony.

Self-Esteem A person's evaluation of himself. If a person "likes himself," feels he can control his actions, that his acts and work are worthy and competent, his self-esteem is high.

Self-Fulfilling Prophecy A preconceived expectation or belief about a situation that evokes behavior resulting in a situation consistent with the preconception.

Senses An organism's physical means of receiving and detecting physical changes in the environment. Sensing is analyzed in terms of reception of the physical stimulus by specialized nerve cells in the sense organs, transduction or converting the stimulus' energy into nerve impulses that the brain can interpret, and transmission of those nerve impulses from the sense organ to the part of the brain that can interpret the information they convey.

Sensitivity Training Aims at helping people to function more effectively in their jobs by increasing their awareness of their own and others' feelings and exchanging "feedback" about styles of interacting. Sensitivity groups are unlike therapy groups in that they are meant to enrich the participants' lives. Participants are not considered patients or ill. Also called T-groups.

Sensorimotor Stage According to Piaget, the stage of development beginning at birth during which perceptions are tied to objects which the child manipulates. Gradually the child learns that objects have permanence even if they are out of sight or touch.

Sensory Adaptation Tendency of the sense organs to adjust to continuous, unchanging stimulation by reducing their functioning; a stimulus that once caused sensation no longer does.

Sensory Deprivation The blocking out of all outside stimulation for a period of time. As studied experimentally, it can produce hallucinations, psychological disturbances, and temporary disorders of the nervous system of the subject.

Sex Role The attitudes, activities, and expectations considered specific to being male or female, determined by both biological and cultural factors.

Shaping A technique of behavior shaping in which behavior is acquired through the reinforcement of successive approximations of the desired behavior. *See* Successive Approximations.

Sleep A periodic state of consciousness marked by four brain-wave patterns. Dreams occur during relatively light Stage 1 sleep. Sleep is a basic need without which one may suffer physical or psychological distress. *See* Brain Waves, Dreams.

Sleeper Effect The delayed impact of persuasive information. People tend to forget the context in which they first heard the information, but they eventually remember the content of the message sufficiently to feel its impact.

Social Comparison Theory proposed by Festinger which states that we have a tendency to compare our behavior to others to ensure that we are conforming.

Social Facilitation Phenomenon in which the presence of others increases dominant behavior patterns in an individual; Zajonc's theory of social facilitation states that the presence of others enhances the emission of the dominant response of the individual.

Social Influence The process by which people form and change the attitudes, opinions, and behavior of others.

Socialization A process by which a child learns the various patterns of behavior expected and accepted by society. Parents are the chief agents of a child's socialization. Many factors have a bearing on the socialization process, such as the child's sex, religion, social class, and parental attitudes.

Social Learning Learning acquired through observation and imitation of others.

Social Psychology The study of individuals as affected by others and of the interaction of individuals in groups.

Sociobiology The study of the genetic basis of social behavior.

Sociophobias Excessive irrational fears and embarrassment when interacting with other people.

Somatic Nervous System The part of the peripheral nervous system that carries messages from the sense organs and relays information that directs the voluntary movements of the skeletal muscles.

Somatoform Disorders Disorders characterized by physical symptoms for which there are no obvious physical causes.

Somesthetic Senses Skin senses; includes pressure, pain, cold, and warmth.

Species-Typical Behavior Behavior patterns common to members of a species. Ethologists state that each species inherits some patterns of behavior (e.g. birdsongs).

Stanford-Binet Intelligence Scale Tests that measure intelligence from two years through adult level. The tests determine one's intelligence quotient by establishing one's chronological and mental ages. *See* Intelligence Quotient.

State-Dependent Learning Situation in which what is learned in one state can only be remembered when the person is in that state.

Statistically Significant In inferential statistics, a finding that the independent variable did influence greatly the outcome of the experimental and control group.

Stereotype The assignment of characteristics to a person mainly on the basis of the group, class, or category to which he belongs. The tendency to categorize and generalize is a basic human way of organizing information. Stereotyping, however, can reinforce misinformation and prejudice. *See* Prejudice.

Stimulus A unit of the environment which causes a response in an individual; more specifically, a physical or chemical agent acting on an appropriate sense receptor.

Stimulus Discrimination Limiting responses to relevant stimuli.

Stimulus Generalization Responses to stimuli similar to the stimulus that had caused the response.

Stress Pressure that puts unusual demands on an organism. Stress may be caused by physical conditions but eventually will involve both. Stimuli that cause stress are called stressors, and an organism's response is the stress reaction. A three-stage general adaptation syndrome is hypothesized involving both emotional and physical changes. *See* General Adaptation System.

Structuralism An early school of psychology that stressed the importance of conscious experience as the subject matter of psychology and maintained that experience should be analyzed into its component parts by use of introspection. *See* Introspection.

Sublimation Defense mechanism in which a person redirects his socially undesirable urges into socially acceptable behavior.

Subliminal Stimuli Stimuli that do not receive conscious attention because they are below sensory thresholds. They may influence behavior, but research is not conclusive on this matter.

Substance-Induced Organic Mental Disorders Organic mental disorders caused by exposure to harmful environmental substances.

Suggestibility The extent to which a person responds to persuasion. Hypnotic susceptibility refers to the degree of suggestibility observed after an attempt to induce hypnosis has been made. *See* Persuasion, Hypnosis.

Superego According to Freud, the superego corresponds roughly to conscience. The superego places restrictions on both ego and id and represents the internalized restrictions and ideals that the child learns from parents and culture. *See* Conscience, Ego, Id.

Sympathetic Nervous System The branch of the autonomic nervous system that is more active in emergencies; it causes a general arousal, increasing breathing, heart rate and blood pressure.

Synapse A "gap" where individual nerve cells (neurons) come together and across which chemical information is passed.

Syndrome A group of symptoms that occur together and mark a particular abnormal pattern.

Systematic Desensitization A technique used in behavior therapy to eliminate a phobia. The symptoms of the phobia are seen as conditioned responses of fear, and the procedure attempts to decondition the fearful response until the patient gradually is able to face the feared situation. *See* Phobia.

TAT (Thematic Apperception Test) Personality and motivation test which requires the subject to devise stories about pictures.

Taxis An orienting movement in response to particular stimuli in the environment. A frog, for example, always turns so its snout points directly at its prey before it flicks its tongue. *See* Orienting Response.

Theory A very general statement that is more useful in generating hypotheses than in generating research. *See* Hypotheses.

Therapeutic Community The organization of a hospital setting so that patients have to take responsibility for helping one another in an attempt to prevent patients from getting worse by being in the hospital.

Token Economy A system for organizing a treatment setting according to behavioristic principles. Patients are encouraged to take greater responsibility for their adjustment by receiving tokens for acceptable behavior and fines for unacceptable behavior. The theory of token economy grew out of operant conditioning techniques. *See* Operant Conditioning.

Traits Distinctive and stable attributes that can be found in all people.

Tranquilizers Psychoactive drugs which reduce anxiety. *See* Psychoactive Drugs.

Trial and Error Learning Trying various behaviors in a situation until the solution is hit upon; past experiences lead us to try different responses until we are successful.

Unconditioned Response (UR) An automatic reaction elicited by a stimulus.

Unconditioned Stimulus (US) Any stimulus that elicits an automatic or reflexive reaction in an individual; it does not have to be learned in the present situation.

Unconscious In Freudian terminology, a concept (not a place) of the mind. The unconscious encompasses certain inborn impulses that never rise into consciousness (awareness) as well as memories and wishes that have been repressed. The chief aim of psychoanalytic therapy is to free repressed material from the unconscious in order to make it susceptible to conscious thought and direction. Behaviorists describe the unconscious as an inability to verbalize. *See* Repression.

Undifferentiated Schizophrenia Type of schizophrenia which does not fit into any particular category, or fits into more than one category.

Validity The extent to which a test actually measures what it is designed to measure.

Variability In statistics, measures of variability communicate how spread out the scores are; the tendency to vary the response to a stimulus, particularly if the response fails to help in adaptation.

Variable Any property of a person, object, or event that can change or take on more than one mathematical value.

Weber's Law States that the difference threshold depends on the ratio of the intensity of one stimulus to another rather than an absolute difference.

Wechsler Adult Intelligence Scale (WAIS) An individually administered test designed to measure adults' intelligence, devised by David Wechsler. The WAIS consists of eleven subtests, of which six measure verbal and five measure performance aspects of intelligence. *See* Wechsler Intelligence Scale for Children.

Wechsler Intelligence Scale for Children (WISC) Similar to the Wechsler Adult Intelligence Scale, except that it is designed for people under fifteen. Wechsler tests can determine strong and weak areas of overall intelligence. *See* Wechsler Adult Intelligence Scale (WAIS).

Whorfian Hypothesis The linguistic relativity hypothesis of Benjamin Whorf; states that language influences thought.

Withdrawal Social or emotional detachment; the removal of oneself from a painful or frustrating situation.

Yerkes-Dodson Law Prediction that the optimum motivation level decreases as the difficulty level of a task increases.

Source for the Glossary:
The majority of terms in this glossary are reprinted from *The Study of Psychology*, Joseph Rubinstein. ©The Dushkin Publishing Group, Inc., Guilford, CT 06437.
The remaining terms were developed by the Annual Editions staff.

Index

Credits/ Acknowledgments

Cover design by Charles Vitelli

1. The Science of Psychology
Facing overview—United Nations photo by Christina D. Sagona.

2. Biological Bases of Behavior
Facing overview—Medical World News

3. Perceptual Processes
Facing overview—EPA-Documerica.

4. Learning and Memory
Facing overview—United Nations photo by D. Mangurian.
68—United Nations photo by John Isaac.

5. Cognitive Processes
Facing overview—United Nations photo by Milton Grant.

6. Motivation and Emotion
Facing overview—WHO photo by J. Mohr.

7. Development
Facing overview—United Nations photo by John Isaac.

8. Personality Processes
Facing overview—United Nations photo.

9. Social Processes
Facing overview—United Nations photo by E. Nielsen.
181—Chart: Earth Surface Graphics.

10. Psychological Disorders
Facing overview—The Dushkin Publishing Group, Inc., photo by Cheryl Kinne.

11. Psychological Treatments
Facing overview—The Dushkin Publishing Group, Inc.

ANNUAL EDITIONS: PSYCHOLOGY 90/91
Article Rating Form

Here is an opportunity for you to have direct input into the next revision of this volume. We would like you to rate each of the 45 articles listed below, using the following scale:

1. Excellent: should definitely be retained
2. Above average: should probably be retained
3. Below average: should probably be deleted
4. Poor: should definitely be deleted

Your ratings will play a vital part in the next revision. So please mail this prepaid form to us just as soon as you complete it.
Thanks for your help!

Annual Editions revisions depend on two major opinion sources: one is our Advisory Board, listed in the front of this volume, which works with us in scanning the thousands of articles published in the public press each year; the other is you—the person actually using the book. Please help us and the users of the next edition by completing the prepaid article rating form on this page and returning it to us. Thank you.

Rating	Article	Rating	Article
	1. Consciousness: Science Tackles the Self		24. Crack in the Cradle
	2. Social Evolution, Psychoanalysis, and Human Nature		25. Shattered Innocence
	3. Right Brain, Left Brain: Fact and Fiction		26. Punishment versus Discipline
	4. How the Brain Really Works Its Wonders		27. The Myth About Teen-Agers
	5. Is It One Clock, or Several, That Cycle Us Through Life?		28. The Vintage Years
	6. The Gene Hunt		29. Biology, Destiny, and All That
	7. A Pleasurable Chemistry		30. Do Optimists Live Longer?
	8. Are We Led by the Nose?		31. Health's Character
	9. No Simple Slumber		32. Erikson, in His Own Old Age, Expands His View of Life
	10. New Light on the Chemistry of Dreams		33. Are Criminals Made or Born?
	11. The Healing Trance		34. Marching in Step
	12. How to Discover What You Have to Say—A Talk to Students		35. Close Encounters
	13. How Kids Learn		36. Getting Help From Helping
	14. Our Dual Memory		37. When Mental Illness Hits Home
	15. Extraordinary People		38. The Clouded Mind
	16. Intelligence: New Ways to Measure the Wisdom of Man		39. Dysthymic Disorder: The DD's Blues Without End
	17. Getting Smart About IQ		40. Anxiety and Panic: Their Cause and Treatment
	18. New Scales of Intelligence Rank Talent for Living		41. When to Challenge the Therapist—and Why
	19. Capturing Your Creativity		42. The Key to Successful Therapy
	20. Abraham Maslow and the New Self		43. The Good News About Depression
	21. Emotions: How They Affect Your Body		44. Infants in Need of Psychotherapy? A Fledgling Field Is Growing Fast
	22. Thinking Well: The Chemical Links Between Emotions and Health		45. Help Yourself: Self-Care for Emotional Problems
	23. Dangerous Thoughts		

(Continued on next page)

ABOUT YOU

Name_____ Date_____

Are you a teacher? ☐ Or student? ☐

Your School Name _____

Department _____

Address _____

City _____ State _____ Zip _____

School Telephone # _____

YOUR COMMENTS ARE IMPORTANT TO US!

Please fill in the following information:

For which course did you use this book? _____

Did you use a text with this Annual Edition? ☐ yes ☐ no

The title of the text? _____

What are your general reactions to the Annual Editions concept?

Have you read any particular articles recently that you think should be included in the next edition?

Are there any articles you feel should be replaced in the next edition? Why?

Are there other areas that you feel would utilize an Annual Edition?

May we contact you for editorial input?

May we quote you from above?

ANNUAL EDITIONS: PSYCHOLOGY 90/91